AMERICAN URBAN HISTORY

An Interpretive Reader with Commentaries
THIRD EDITION

EDITED BY

ALEXANDER B. CALLOW, JR.

UNIVERSITY OF CALIFORNIA, SANTA BARBARA

New York   Oxford
OXFORD UNIVERSITY PRESS
1982

Library of Congress Cataloging in Publication Data
Main entry under title:

American urban history.

Includes bibliographical references.
1. Cities and towns—United States—History.
I. Callow, Alexander B.
HT123.A666   1982   307.7′6′0973   81–4465
ISBN 0–19–502981–X (pbk.)   AACR2

Printing (last digit): 9 8 7 6 5 4 3 2 1

Printed in the United States of America

To my sons: Scott and Sean Michael

This new edition is shorter and more compact than its predecessor. Nearly half of the essays of the second edition have been deleted, and over a fourth of the essays of the third edition constitute new selections. Two chapters were replaced with "The City in Social Conflict," and "The City in Post-Industrial Society." As in the previous editions, I have maintained an interdisciplinary approach and have tried to select essays that are interpretive, well-written, and, not the least, make a contribution to the study of American urban history. Once again I would like to acknowledge the editorial staff of Oxford University Press for their help and encouragement.

Santa Barbara, California   ALEXANDER B. CALLOW, JR.
August, 1981

Contents

Introduction

This is a book about what O. Henry called "a ragged purple dream, the wonderful, cruel, enchanting, bewildering, fatal, great city." It is an attempt to achieve a perspective on a phenomenon that in the past was a critical unifying force in our history and in the present has been described as our No. 1 problem—the American city.

American Urban History is neither a narrative textbook, a collection of primary documents, nor a combination of "conflicting" interpretations. It is an attempt to bring together, chronologically and topically, widely scattered interpretative essays that illuminate important themes and problems in American urban history and encourage an analytical approach to the study of the city. Some selections are broad in scope; others tackle specific topics; none are definitive, but most are provocative and well written. This is, then, largely a book of ideas, introducing what Daniel Boorstin calls "organizing ideas," concepts that fashion the bony, intellectual anatomy of American urban history and give shape to the countless "facts" about the American city.

Each of the nine chapters is preceded by a commentary that introduces the major ideas of the readings, correlates them with the central historical theme of the chapter, underscores notions of particular analytical interest, and raises further questions suggested (or ignored) by the selected essays, in the hope they will not only serve as guidelines but also that they and the selections will be the hors d'oeuvres to a larger feast if the student is excited to plunge deeper, through independent reading and research.

This book is predicated upon the proposition that urban history should have an interdisciplinary approach. Consequently, the selections include some of our best American urban historians as well as some of our ablest students of other phases of urban affairs.

This book is also based upon a few underlying principles that I feel should characterize the study of the American city. Broadly defined, there are two schools of thought concerning the best way to approach and to understand the history of the American city. One group sees the city as a reflection of national history—indeed, as one of the main currents in the mainstream of American history. Its members seek to reveal the impact of the city upon American history and the impact of history upon the city. The other group stresses the importance of the city as a singularly important phenomenon in itself. To this group the city has coherence, unity, muscles, and sinews of its own. They avoid stitching urban history into the conventional periodization of American history, such as the City and Jacksonian Democracy, the City and the Civil War, the City and the New Deal, insisting that such an approach is archaic and myopic for at least two reasons: the characteristics of urban developments do not always coincide with developments in national history, and such an approach obscures developments that we urgently need to know more about, namely, the various processes of urbanization. I occupy a middle position between these two approaches, not unmindful of both the smugness that moderation implies and the fact that one can get run over in the middle of the road. It seems to me that the two views are not necessarily contradictory and that a better perspective is achieved by trying to balance the two, and I have made my selections accordingly. In a day when we still do not have consensus on what the city is, as well as what we really mean by *urban*, the door should be open to all kinds of approaches. Our future depends upon it.

AMERICAN URBAN HISTORY

I THE CITY IN HISTORY

It has been said that the history of civilization "from Memphis, Egypt, to Memphis, Tennessee," is written in the rise and fall of cities. Perhaps, paradoxically, the city in history has been both inseparable from the course of human history yet a separate historical phenomenon of its own. It has mirrored some of the major tensions of the human condition—rich versus poor, greed versus compassion, change versus tradition, the individual versus the mass, ideology versus ideology. It has reflected the best and worst in humanity —the hospital and the tenement, the clearinghouse of ideas, music, and the arts, and the refuge of filth, disease, and misery. Indeed, few of humanity's other creations have been so bewilderingly complex, so infinitely diverse, so compounded by extremes and contradictions.

There is no better example of this than the American city, until recently the scene of unprecedented rapid urbanization. In comparison with the European urban heritage, which stretches back roughly 5500 years, the American transformation from village to city was achieved in a dazzlingly short space of time. From the eighteenth century on, Americans experienced the painful yet rewarding metamorphosis of an agrarian nation becoming an urban-industrial giant that left few of its political, economic, and social institutions untouched, be they the farm, the factory, or the family. In 1790, for example, only a little over 4 percent of the American population lived in cities; today 70 percent of Americans live in urban areas. Richard Hofstadter summed it up well: "The United States was born in the country and has moved to the city."

All of this, of course, begs several questions. How do we account for the rise of the city? What historical forces, what processes of urbanization played determining roles? What was the impact of the rise of the city upon American society? It is the purpose of this chapter to grapple with this questions by showing that behind the maze of complexities, were patterns—political, eco-

3

nomic, social, technological—in as well as outside the city, that shaped the rise of urban America and gave its history some coherence.

We begin with two essays, each broad in scope, each analytical and synthetical in nature, each bristling with organizing ideas that illuminate successively the rise of the city, major themes in American urban history, and the internal generating forces behind the city itself. We begin, then, with generalizations, hoping to sketch guidelines that from the very beginning may help one to steer a course through the sea of "facts" about American urban history.

Gideon Sjoberg sets the course by mapping, as it were, the embarkation port, the first urban creation—the preindustrial city. While this is not *American* urban history, it does provide an expansive historical background making American urban history more meaningful. After all, urbanization was a worldwide phenomenon. American cities were not popped out of a vacuum; hence, the more insights we can get about our antecedents the better comprehension we will have of our own experience. European scholars have chided American historians for their narrow provincialism which often neglects the critical fact that historically we are a part of Western civilization.

In a remarkably compact and well-organized essay, Sjoberg gallops through the centuries, pinning his discussion upon two major questions: what forces account for the origin of cities, and what stages did cities pass through before reaching modern times? Both answers depend upon the technological, economic, social, and political patterns of three levels of human development: the preurban or "folk" society, the preindustrial or "feudal" society, and the modern or "industrial" society. It was in the preindustrial period that the world's first cities emerged, mainly because of the interrelationship of several important factors: a surplus of food, the development of a class structure that provided leadership and harnessed labor power, the appearance of writing, which permitted a written tradition, and a technology that exploited new sources of energy. Contingent upon these elements were two other necessities of urbanization: (1) a social system of full-time specialists who could handle the food surplus and build the public buildings, city walls, and irrigation systems, and (2) a favorable environment that yielded an agricultural and water supply to sustain the urban dwellers.

Sjoberg traces the evolution of cities over time, from the Near East and the Orient to the Mesoamerican cities of the New World. He relates the rise and fall of empires to urbanization and concludes with a discussion of the emergence of the first modern cities of England. Implicit throughout Sjoberg's analysis is that each period of urbanization builds upon the other in a pattern of evolution. This thesis sets the stage for a major argument among urbanists regarding the development of the modern city—was the process evolution or revolution?

In the next selection, Oscar Handlin provides a historical background, without which the history of the American city is incomprehensible. For the American city was heir to a clutch of forces that generated one of the main turning points in world history: the conversion of the medieval preindustrial city into the sprawling, creative, and disruptive modern city. His thesis is that this transformation constituted not a simple process of evolution, but a drastic break from the past. The continuity of history was ruptured by the emergence of something singularly new, the modern city. Handlin sees the catalysts of this remarkable phenomenon as the rise of the centralized nation-state, technological innovations, the novel development in production and capital constituting the rise of modern industry, and the subsequent explosion in the urban population. If one major characteristic of the emerging modern city must be underscored, however, it is the change and disruption of the heart of the medieval preindustrial social system—the traditional, corporate, communal organization of households, at once a social and economic institution.[1] The American city, then, was born and grew into adolescence during the transitional stage between the preindustrial and modern industrial city.

1. For interesting, and conflicting, interpretations of the city in history, see Henri Pirenne, *Medieval Cities* (Princeton: Princeton University Press, 1925); Max Weber, *The City* (Glencoe, Ill.: The Free Press of Glencoe, 1958); Lewis Mumford, *The City in History* (New York: Harcourt, Brace and World, 1961); and especially, Gideon Sjoberg, *The Preindustrial City* (New York: The Free Press, 1960); and Jane Jacobs, *The Economy of Cities* (New York: Random House, 1969).

Other broad approaches to the American city include W. Stull Holt, "Some Consequences of the Urban Movement in American History," *Pacific Historical Review*, Vol. XXII (November 1953), pp. 337–51; Emrys Jones, *Towns and Cities* (London and New York: Oxford, 1966); Leo F. Schnore, "The City as a Social Organism," *Urban Affairs Quarterly*, Vol. I, No. 3 (March 1966), pp. 58–69. See also Philip M. Hauser and Leo F. Schnore (eds.), *The Study of Urbanization* (New York: John Wiley, 1965), for a series of valuable essays by a number of social scientists, discussing the methods and literature of their respective disciplines.

The Origin and Evolution of Cities

GIDEON SJOBERG

Men began to live in cities some 5,500 years ago . . . however, the proportion of the human population concentrated in cities did not begin to increase significantly until about 100 years ago. These facts raise two questions that this chapter proposes to answer. First, what factors brought about the origin of cities? Second, through what evolutionary stages did cities pass before the modern epoch of urbanization? The answers to these questions are intimately related to three major levels of human organization, each of which is characterized by its own technological, economic, social and political patterns. The least complex of the three—the "folk society"—is preurban and even preliterate; it consists typically of small numbers of people, gathered in self-sufficient homogeneous groups, with their energies wholly (or almost wholly) absorbed by the quest for food. Under such conditions there is little or no surplus of food; consequently the folk society permits little or no specialization of labor or distinction of class.

Although some folk societies still exist today, similar human groups began the slow process of evolving into more complex societies millenniums ago, through settlement in villages and through advances in technology and organizational structure. This gave rise to the second level of organization: civilized preindustrial, or "feudal," society. Here there is a surplus of food because of the selective cultivation of grains—high in yield, rich in biological energy and suited to long-term storage—and often also because of the practice of animal husbandry. The food surplus permits both the specialization of labor and the kind of class structure that can, for instance, provide the leadership and command the manpower to develop and maintain extensive irrigation systems (which in turn make possible further increases in the food supply). Most preindustrial societies possess metallurgy, the plow and the wheel—devices, or the means of creating devices, that multiply both the production and the distribution of agricultural surpluses.

Two other elements of prime importance characterize the civilized preindustrial stage of organization. One is writing: not only the simple keeping of accounts but also the recording of historical events, law, literature and religious beliefs. Literacy, however, is usually confined to a leisured elite. The other element is that this stage of organization has only a few sources of energy other than the muscles of men and livestock; the later preindustrial societies harnessed the force of the wind to sail the seas and grind grain and also made use of water power.

It was in the context of this second type of society that the world's first cities developed. Although preindustrial cities still survive, the modern industrial city is associated with a third level of complexity in human organization, a level characterized by mass literacy, a

Gideon Sjoberg, "The Origin and Evolution of Cities," *Scientific American*, Vol. 213, No. 3 (September 1965), 54–62. Reprinted with permission. Copyright © 1965 by Scientific American, Inc. All rights reserved.

fluid class system and, most important, the tremendous technological breakthrough to new sources of inanimate energy that produced and still sustains the industrial revolution. Viewed against the background of this three-tiered structure, the first emergence of cities at the level of civilized preindustrial society can be more easily understood.

Two factors in addition to technological advance beyond the folk-society level were needed for cities to emerge. One was a special type of social organization by means of which the agricultural surplus produced by technological advance could be collected, stored, and distributed. The same apparatus could also organize the labor force needed for large-scale construction, such as public buildings, city walls and irrigation systems. A social organization of this kind requires a variety of full-time specialists directed by a ruling elite. The latter, although few in number, must command sufficient political power—reinforced by an ideology, usually religious in character—to ensure that the peasantry periodically relinquishes a substantial part of the agricultural yield in order to support the city dwellers. The second factor required was a favorable environment, providing not only fertile soil for the peasants but also a water supply adequate for both agriculture and urban consumption. Such conditions exist in geologically mature and mid-latitude river valleys, and it was in such broad alluvial regions that the world's earliest cities arose.

What is a city? It is a community of substantial size and population density that shelters a variety of nonagricultural specialists, including a literate elite. I emphasize the role of literacy as an ingredient of urban life for good reasons. Even though writing systems took centuries to evolve, their presence or ab-

sence serves as a convenient means for distinguishing between genuinely urban communities and others that in spite of their large size and dense population must be considered quasi-urban or nonurban. This is because once a community achieves or otherwise acquires the technological advance we call writing, a major transformation in the social order occurs; with a written tradition rather than an oral one it is possible to create more complex administrative and legal systems and more rigorous systems of thought. Writing is indispensable to the development of mathematics, astronomy and the other sciences; its existence thus implies the emergence of a number of significant specializations within the social order.

As far as is known, the world's first cities took shape around 3500 B.C. in the Fertile Crescent, the eastern segment of which includes Mesopotamia: the valleys of the Tigris and the Euphrates. Not only were the soil and water supply there suitable; the region was a crossroads that facilitated repeated contacts among peoples of divergent cultures for thousands of years. The resulting mixture of alien and indigenous crafts and skills must have made its own contribution to the evolution of the first true cities out of the village settlements in lower Mesopotamia. These were primarily in Sumer but also to some extent in Akkad, a little to the north. Some—such as Eridu, Erech, Lagash and Kish—are more familiar to archaeologists than to others; Ur, a later city, is more widely known.

These early cities were much alike; for one thing, they had a similar technological base. Wheat and barley were the cereal crops, bronze was the metal, oxen pulled plows and there were wheeled vehicles. Moreover, the city's leader was both king and high priest;

the peasants' tribute to the city god was stored in the temple granaries. Luxury goods recovered from royal tombs and temples attest the existence of skilled artisans, and the importation of precious metals and gems from well beyond the borders of Mesopotamia bespeaks a class of merchant-traders. Population sizes can only be guessed in the face of such unknowns as the average number of residents per household and the extent of each city's zone of influence. The excavator of Ur, Sir Leonard Woolley, estimates that soon after 2000 B.C. the city proper housed 34,000 people; in my opinion, however, it seems unlikely that, at least in the earlier periods, even the larger of these cities contained more than 5,000 to 10,000 people, including part-time farmers on the cities' outskirts.

The valley of the Nile, not too far from Mesopotamia, was also a region of early urbanization. To judge from Egyptian writings of a later time, there may have been urban communities in the Nile delta by 3100 B.C. Whether the Egyptian concept of city living had "diffused" from Mesopotamia or was independently invented (and perhaps even earlier than in Mesopotamia) is a matter of scholarly debate; in any case the initial stages of Egyptian urban life may yet be discovered deep in the silt of the delta, where scientific excavation is only now being undertaken.

Urban communities—diffused or independently invented—spread widely during the third and second millenniums B.C. By about 2500 B.C. the cities of Mohenjo-Daro and Harappa were flourishing in the valley of the Indus River in what is now Pakistan. Within another 1,000 years at the most the middle reaches of the Yellow River in China supported urban settlements. A capital city of the Shang Dynasty (about 1500 B.C.) was uncovered near Anyang before World War II; current archaeological investigations by the Chinese may well prove that city life was actually established in ancient China several centuries earlier.

The probability that the first cities of Egypt were later than those of Sumer and the certainty that those of the Indus and Yellow rivers are later lends weight to the argument that the concept of urban living diffused to these areas from Mesopotamia. Be this as it may, none will deny that in each case the indigenous population contributed uniquely to the development of the cities in its own area.

In contrast to the situation in the Old World, it appears certain that diffusion played an insignificant role or none at all in the creation of the pre-Columbian cities of the New World. The peoples of Mesoamerica—notably the Maya, the Zapotecs, the Mixtecs and the Aztecs —evidently developed urban communities on a major scale, the exact extent of which is only now being revealed by current investigations. Until quite recently, for example, many New World archaeologists doubted that the Maya had ever possessed cities; it was the fashion to characterize their impressive ruins as ceremonial centers visited periodically by the members of a scattered rural population. It is now clear, however, that many such centers were genuine cities. At the Maya site of Tikal in Guatemala some 3,000 structures have been located in an area of 6.2 square miles; only 10 percent of them are major ceremonial buildings. Extrapolating on the basis of test excavations of more than 100 of these lesser structures, about two-thirds of them appear to have been dwellings.

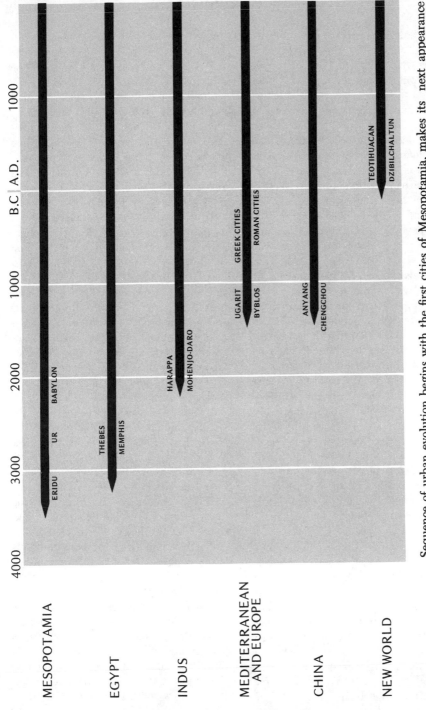

Sequence of urban evolution begins with the first cities of Mesopotamia, makes its next appearance in the Nile Valley, then extends to the Indus, to the eastern Mediterranean region and at last to China. In each area, the independently urbanized New World included, cities rose and fell but urban life, once established, never wholly disappeared.

If only half the present-day average household figure for the region (5.6 members) is applied to Tikal, its population would have been more than 5,000. At another major Maya site— Dzibilchaltun in Yucatán—a survey of less than half of the total area has revealed more than 8,500 structures. Teotihuacán, the largest urban site in the region of modern Mexico City, may have had a population of 100,000 during the first millennium A.D.

Although only a few examples of writing have been identified at Teotihuacán, it is reasonable to assume that writing was known; there were literate peoples elsewhere in Mesoamerica at the time. By the same token, the achievements of the Maya in such realms as mathematics and astronomy would have forced the conclusion that they were an urban people even in the absence of supporting archaeological evidence. Their invention of the concept of zero (evidently earlier than the Hindus' parallel feat) and their remarkably precise calculation of the length of the solar year would surely have been impossible if their literate elite had been scattered about the countryside in villages rather than concentrated in urban centers where a cross-fertilization of ideas could take place.

Mesoamerica was by no means the only area of large, dense communities in the New World; they also existed in the Andean region. A culture such as the Inca, however, cannot be classified as truly urban. In spite of—perhaps because of—their possession of a mnemonic means of keeping inventories (an assemblage of knotted cords called a quipu) the Incas lacked any conventionalized set of graphic symbols for representing speech or any concepts other than numbers and certain broad classes of items. As a result they were denied such key structural elements of an urban community as a literate elite and a written heritage of law, religion and history. Although the Incas could claim major military, architectural and engineering triumphs and apparently were on the verge of achieving a civilized order, they were still quasi-urban at the time of the European conquest, much like the Dahomey, Ashanti and Yoruba peoples of Africa.

The New World teaches us two lessons. In Mesoamerica cities were created without animal husbandry, the wheel and an extensive alluvial setting. One reason for this is maize, a superior grain crop that produced a substantial food surplus with relatively little effort and thus compensated for the limited tools and nonriverine environment. In the Andean region imposing feats of engineering and an extensive division of labor were not enough, in the absence of writing, to give rise to a truly urban society.

In spite of considerable cultural diversity among the inhabitants of the Near East, the Orient and the New World, the early cities in all these regions had a number of organizational forms in common. The dominant pattern was theocracy—the king and the high priest were one. The elite had their chief residences in the city; moreover, they and their retainers and servants congregated mainly in the city's center. This center was the prestige area, where the most imposing religious and government buildings were located. Such a concentration had dual value: in an era when communications and transport were rudimentary, propinquity enhanced interaction among the elite; at the same time it gave the ruling class maximum protection from external attack.

At a greater distance from this urban nucleus were the shops and dwellings of artisans—masons, carpenters, smiths, jewelers, potters—many of whom served the elite. The division of labor into crafts, apparent in the earliest cities, became more complex with the passage of time. Artisan groups, some of which even in early times may have belonged to specific ethnic minorities, tended to establish themselves in special quarters or streets. Such has been characteristic of preindustrial cities in all cultural settings, from the earliest times to the present day. The poorest urbanites lived on the outskirts of the city, as did part-time or full-time farmers; their scattered dwellings finally blended into open countryside.

From its inception the city, as a residence of specialists, has been a continuing source of innovation. Indeed, the very emergence of cities greatly accelerated social and cultural change; to borrow a term from the late British archaeologist V. Gordon Childe, we can properly regard the "urban revolution" as being equal in significance to the agricultural revolution that preceded it and the industrial revolution that followed it. The city acted as a promoter of change in several ways. Many of the early cities arose on major transportation routes; new ideas and inventions flowed into them quite naturally. The mere fact that a large number of specialists were concentrated in a small area encouraged innovation, not only in technology but also in religious, philosophical and scientific thought. At the same time cities could be strong bulwarks of tradition. Some—for example Jerusalem and Benares—have become sacred in the eyes of the populace; in spite of repeated destruction Jerusalem has retained this status for more than two millenniums.

The course of urban evolution can be correctly interpreted only in relation to the parallel evolution of technology and social organization (especially political organization); these are not just prerequisites to urban life but the basis for its development. As centers of innovation cities provided a fertile setting for continued technological advances; these gains made possible the further expansion of cities. Advanced technology in turn depended on the increasingly complex division of labor, particularly in the political sphere. As an example, the early urban communities of Sumer were mere city-states with restricted hinterlands, but eventually trade and commerce extended over a much broader area, enabling these cities to draw on the human and material resources of a far wider and more diverse region and even bringing about the birth of new cities. The early empires of the Iron Age—for instance the Achaemenid Empire of Persia, established early in the sixth century B.C., and the Han Empire of China, established in the third century B.C.—far surpassed in scope any of the Bronze Age. And as empires became larger the size and grandeur of their cities increased. In fact, as Childe has observed, urbanization spread more rapidly during the first five centuries of the Iron Age than it had in all 15 centuries of the Bronze Age.

In the sixth and fifth centuries B.C. the Persians expanded their empire into western Turkestan and created a number of cities, often by building on existing villages. In this expansion Toprakkala, Merv and Marakanda (part of which was later the site of Samarkand) moved toward urban status. So too in India, at the close of the fourth century B.C., the Mauryas in the north spread their empire to the previously nonurban south and into Ceylon, giving impetus to the birth of cities such as Ajanta and Kanchi. Under the Ch'in and Han dynasties, between the third century B.C. and the third century A.D., city life took hold in most of what was then China and beyond, particularly to the south and west. The "Great Silk Road" extending from China to Turkestan became studded with such oasis cities as Suchow, Khotan and Kashgar; Nanking and Canton seem to have attained urban status at this time, as did the settlement that was eventually to become Peking.

At the other end of the Eurasian land mass the Phoenicians began toward the end of the second millennium B.C. to spread westward and to revive or establish urban life along the northern coast of Africa and in Spain. These coastal traders had by then developed a considerable knowledge of shipbuilding; this, combined with their far-reaching commercial ties and power of arms, made the Phoenicians lords of the Mediterranean for a time. Some centuries later the Greeks followed a rather similar course. Their city-states—actually in a sense small empires—created or rebuilt numerous urban outposts along the Mediterranean shore from Asia Minor to Spain and France, and eastward to the most distant coast of the Black Sea. The empire that did the most to diffuse city life into the previously nonurban regions of the West— France, Britain, the Low Countries, Germany west of the Rhine, central and even eastern Europe—was of course Rome.

Empires are effective disseminators of urban forms because they have to build cities with which to maintain military supremacy in conquered regions. The city strongholds, in turn, require an administrative apparatus in order to tap the resources of the conquered area and encourage the commerce needed both to support the military garrison and to enhance the wealth of the homeland. Even when a new city began as a purely commercial outpost, as was the case under the Phoenicians, some military and administrative support was necessary if it was to survive and function effectively in alien territory.

There is a significant relation between the rise and fall of empires and the rise and fall of cities; in a real sense history is the study of urban graveyards. The capitals of many former empires are today little more than ghostly outlines that only hint at a glorious past. Such was the fate of Babylon and Nineveh, Susa in Persia, Seleucia in Mesopotamia and Vijayanagar in India. Yet there are exceptions. Some cities have managed to survive over long periods of time by attaching themselves first to one empire and then to another. Athens, for example, did not decline after the collapse of Greek power; it was able to attach itself to the Roman Empire, which subsidized Athens as a center of learning. Once Rome fell, however, both the population and the prestige of Athens dwindled steadily; it was little more than a town until the rise of modern Greece in the 19th century. On the other hand, nearby Byzantium, a city-state of minor importance under Roman rule, not only became the capital of the Eastern Roman Empire and its successor, the Ottoman Empire, but as Istanbul remains a major city to this day.

In the light of the recurrent rise and decline of cities in so many areas of the world, one may ask just how urban life has been able to persist and why the skills of technology and social organization required for city-building were not lost. The answer is that the knowledge was maintained within the framework of empires—by means of written records and oral transmission by various specialists. Moreover, all empires have added to their store of skills relating to urban development as a result of diffusion—including the migration of specialists—from other civilized areas. At the same time various civilized or uncivilized subjects within empires have either been purposely educated by their conquerors or have otherwise gained access to the body of urban lore. The result on occasion is that the subjects challenge the power of the dominant ruling group.

The rise and fall of the Roman Empire provides a highly instructive case study that illuminates several relations between the life-span of cities and the formation and decline of empires. The Romans themselves took many elements of their civilization from the Etruscans, the Greeks and other civilized peoples who came under their sway. After Rome's northward expansion in western Europe and the proliferation of Roman cities in regions inhabited by so-called "barbarians"—in this instance preliterate, or "noncivilized," peoples—the Roman leaders were simply unable to staff all the bureaucratic posts with their own citizens. Some of the preliterates had to be trained to occupy such posts both in their own homelands and in the cities on the frontier. This process made it possible for the Romans to exploit the wealth of conquered regions and may have pacified the subjugated groups for a time, but in the long run it engendered serious conflicts. Eventually the Ostrogoths, Vandals, Burgundians and others—having been partially urbanized, having developed a literate elite of their own and having acquired many Roman technological and administrative skills—turned against the imperial power structure and engineered the collapse of Rome and its empire. Nor is this a unique case in history; analogies can be perceived in the modern independence movements of such European colonies as those in Africa.

With the breakup of the Roman Empire, not only did the city of Rome (which at its largest may have had more than 300,000 inhabitants) decline markedly but many borderland cities disappeared or shrank to small towns or villages. The decline was dramatic, but it is too often assumed that after the fall of Rome cities totally disappeared from western Europe. The historian E. Ewig has recently shown that many cities continued to function, particularly in Italy and southern France. Here, as in all civilized societies, the surviving cities were the chief residences and centers of activity for the political and religious elite who commanded the positions of power and privilege that persisted during the so-called Dark Ages.

In spite of Rome's decline many of the techniques and concepts associated with literate traditions in such fields as medicine and astronomy were kept alive; this was done both in the smaller surviving urban communities of Europe and in the eastern regions that had been ruled by the Romans—notably in the cities of the succeeding Eastern Roman Empire. Some of the technology and learning associated with Rome also became the basis for city life in the Arab empires that arose later in the Near East, North Africa, Spain and even central Asia. Indeed, the Byzantine and Arab empires—which had such major intellectual centers as Constantinople, Antioch, Damascus, Cairo and Baghdad—advanced beyond the knowledge inherited from antiquity. The Arabs, for example, took from the Hindus the concept of zero and the decimal system of numerals; by utilizing these concepts in both theory and practice they achieved significant advances over the knowledge that had evolved in the West. Eventually much of the new learning was passed on to Europe, where it helped to build the foundations for the industrial revolution.

In time Europe reestablished extensive commercial contact with the Byzantine and Arab empires; the interchange that followed played a significant role in the resurgence of urban life in southern Europe. The revitalization of trade was closely associated with the formation of several prosperous Italian city-states in the 10th and 11th centuries A.D. Venice and other cities eventually were transformed into small-scale empires whose colonies were scattered over the Mediterranean region—a hinterland from which the home cities were able to extract not only many of their necessities but also luxury items. By A.D. 1000 Venice had forged commercial links with Constantinople and other cities of the Eastern Roman Empire, partly as a result of the activities of the Greek colony in Venice. The Venetians were able to draw both on the knowledge of these resident Greeks and on the practical experience of sea captains and other specialists among them. Such examples make it clear that the Italian city-states were not merely local creations but rather products of a multiplicity of cultural forces.

Beginning at the turn of the 11th century A.D. many European cities managed to win a kind of independence from the rulers of the various principalities and petty kingdoms that surrounded them. Particularly in northern Italy urban communities came to enjoy considerable political autonomy. This provided an even more favorable atmosphere for commerce and encouraged the growth of such urban institutions as craft guilds. The European pattern is quite different from that in most of Asia (for instance in India and China), where the city was never able to attain a measure of autonomy within the broader political structure. At the same time the extent of self-rule enjoyed by the medieval European cities can be exaggerated and often is; by the close of the Middle Ages urban self-rule was already beginning to be lost. It is therefore evident that the political autonomy of medieval cities was only indirectly related to the eventual evolution of the industrial city.

It was the industrial revolution that brought about truly far-reaching changes in city life. In some nations today . . . the vast majority of the inhabitants are city dwellers; nearly 80 percent of the people in the United Kingdom live in cities, as do nearly 70 percent of the people of the U.S. Contrast this with the preindustrial civilized world, in which only a small, socially dominant minority lived in cities. The industrial revolution has also led to fundamental changes in the city's social geography and social organization; the industrial city is marked by a greater fluidity in the class system, the appearance of mass education and mass communications and the shift of some of the elite from the center of the city to its suburban outskirts.

Although there are still insufficient data on the rise of the industrial city— an event that took place sometime between 1750 and 1850—and although scholars disagree over certain steps in the process, the major forces at work in the two or three centuries before the industrial city emerged can be perceived clearly enough. Viewed in the light of Europe's preindustrial urban era, two factors are evident: the expansion of European power into other continents and the development of technology based on inanimate rather than animate sources of energy. The extension of European trade and exploration (which was to culminate in European colonialism) not only induced the growth of cities in Asia, in parts of nonurban Africa and in the Americas but also helped to raise the standard of living of Europeans themselves and made possible the support of more specialists. Notable among the last was a new occupational group—the scientists. The expansion abroad had helped to shatter the former world view of European scholars; they were now forced to cope with divergent ideas and customs. The discoveries reported by the far-ranging European explorers thus gave added impetus to the advance of science.

The knowledge gained through the application of the scientific method is the one factor above all others that made the modern city possible. This active experimental approach has enabled man to control the forces of nature to an extent undreamed of in the preindustrial era. It is true that in the course of several millenniums the literate elite of the preindustrial cities added significantly to man's store of knowledge in such fields as medicine, astronomy and mathematics, but these scholars generally scorned mundane activities and avoided contact with those whose work was on the practical level. This meant that the scholars' theories were rarely tested and applied in the everyday realm. Moreover, in accordance with prevailing religious thought, man was not to tamper with the natural order or to seek to control it, in either its physical or its social aspect. For example, medical scholars in Greek and Roman cities did not dissect human cadavers; not until the 16th century in Europe did a physician—Andreas Vesalius of Brussels—actually use findings obtained from dissection to revise ancient medical theories.

In the field of engineering, as late as the 17th century most advances were made by artisans who worked more or less on a trial-and-error basis. With the development of the experimental method, however, the learning of the elite became linked with the practical knowledge of the artisan, the barber-surgeon and the like; the result was a dramatic upsurge of knowledge and a fundamental revision of method that has been termed the scientific revolution. Such was the basis of the industrial revolution and the industrial city.

That the first industrial cities appeared in England is hardly fortuitous; England's social structure lacked the rigidity that characterized most of Europe and the rest of the civilized world. The Puritan tradition in England—an ethical system that supports utilitarianism and empiricism—did much to alter earlier views concerning man's place in nature. In England scholars could communicate with artisans more readily than elsewhere in Europe.

The advent of industrialism brought vast improvements in agricultural implements, farming techniques and food preservation, as well as in transportation and communication. Improved water supplies and more effective methods of sewage disposal allowed more people to congregate in cities. Perhaps the key invention was the steam engine, which provided a new and much more bountiful source of energy. Before that time, except for power from wind and water, man had no energy resources other than human and animal muscle. Now the factory system, with its mass production of goods and mechanization of activity, began to take hold. With it emerged a new kind of occupational structure: a structure that depends on highly specialized knowledge and that functions effectively only when the activities of the component occupations are synchronized. This process of industrialization has not only continued unabated to the present day but has actually accelerated with the rise of self-controlling machines.

The evolution of the industrial city was not an unmixed blessing. Historians have argued through many volumes the question of whether the new working class, including many migrants from the countryside, lost or gained economically and socially as the factory system destroyed older social patterns. Today, as industrialization moves inexorably across the globe, it continues to create social problems. Many surviving traditional cities evince in various ways the conflict between their preindustrial past and their industrial future. Nonetheless, the trend is clear: barring nuclear war, the industrial city will become the dominant urban form throughout the world, replacing forever the preindustrial city that was man's first urban creation.

The Modern City as a Field of Historical Study

OSCAR HANDLIN

Seen from above, the modern city edges imperceptibly out of its setting. There are no clear boundaries. Just now the white trace of the superhighway passed through cultivated fields; now it is lost in an asphalt maze of streets and buildings. As one drives in from the airport or looks out from the train window, clumps of suburban housing, industrial complexes, and occasional green spaces flash by; it is hard to tell where city begins and country ends. Our difficulties with nomenclature reflect the indeterminacy of these limits; we reach for some vague concept of metropolis to describe the release of urban potential from its recognized ambit.

Contrast this visual image with that of the ancient or medieval city. It is still possible, coming up the Rhone, to see Sion in the Valais much as it looked four hundred years ago. From a long way off, one can make out its twin castles jutting into the sky. But the vineyards and orchards, the open fields and clumps of woodland, reach along the roadside to the edge of town. There, we cross a boundary to enter another universe, one which is whole and entire to itself. The record of sieges that lasted for months on end confirms the impression of self-containment. It is much so that Paris must once have been, and Athens.

The cities of the past were, of course, vulnerable to external assault and to disruptive changes that emanated from without. Wars, shifts in patterns of production and trade, and cultural innovations gathered force outside their walls and yet decisively altered their history. But even when they held agricultural lands and even when some residents tilled the soil, those earlier communities possessed an individual life of their own in a sense that their modern successors do not. The ancient world had been a world of cities, but each had been a world unto itself. The towns of the Middle Ages and the Renaissance, even those of the eighteenth century, were self-contained entities walled off from their surroundings, with which they had only precisely defined contacts. They provided a marketplace for the products of rural craftsmen and husbandmen; but the main lines of their trade ran to distant, often overseas, places. They were centers of administration. But the governmental and ecclesiastical functionaries existed apart in detachment. The distance between London and Westminster, between Paris and Versailles, even between Milan and the castle of the Sforzas, was more than symbolic; it measured the genuine isolation of the life of the bourgeois.[1]

On the map today London and Paris and Milan occupy the same sites as did the places which bore those names three hundred years ago; and subtle institutional and cultural ties run across the centuries. But it would be a mistake to regard the later communities as merely, or even primarily, the descendants of the earlier ones. The modern city is essentially different from its predecessors, and the core of the difference lies in the fact that its life is not that "of an organism, but of an organ." It has become "the heart, the brain, perhaps only the digestive stem, of that great leviathan, the modern state." Its history cannot be understood apart from that of the more comprehensive communities of which it is a part.[2]

The distinctive feature of the great modern city is its unique pattern of relations to the world within which it is situated. Large enough to have a character of its own, the modern city is yet inextricably linked to, dependent upon, the society outside it; and growth in size has increased rather than diminished the force of that dependence. Out of that relationship spring the central problems of urban history—those of the organization of space within the city, of the creation of order among its people, and of the adjustment to its new conditions by the human personality.

It is, of course, perfectly possible to approach the history of these communities in a purely descriptive fashion—to prepare useful accounts of municipalities, markets and cultural centers on an empirical basis. But such efforts will certainly be more rewarding if they are related to large questions of a common and comparative nature. These introductory remarks aim to define some of those questions.

The forces that made the modern city what it is took form outside its own limits. Hence the increases were always unexpected and unanticipated. In the sixteenth and seventeenth centuries London, the first truly modern city, was repeatedly forbidden to grow; men who knew it as it was could not conceive what it would become. For the same reason, projections of future trends—whether prophetic or scientific—almost without fail fell far short of actuality, even in the most optimistic cultures. It was rare indeed that the facilities of a community anticipated its later needs, as those of Los Angeles did. The direction and rate of expansion were not foreseen because the generative impulses were not contained within the older urban society of merchants, artisans, and functionaries. They sprang from three profound and interrelated changes in the society external to them —the development of the centralized national state, the transformation of the economy from a traditional, household, to a rational, capital-using basis, and the technological destruction of distance.[3]

The political changes were first to show themselves; here the medieval cities were at their weakest. Few of them had ever disposed of substantial military force. Venice and Ragusa were unusual in this respect, perhaps because of their relation to the sea. Most other towns, at best, found protection from a stadtholder, or at worst, remained the victims of *condottieri* or feuding barons. Often they welcomed the security of monarchical authority, but they had no illusions about the extent to which that would increase their own power. In the face of any assertion of royal or national will, they could only acquiesce.[4]

That dependent situation has persisted to this day. Despite their wealth and their critical economic position, the great cities do not control themselves; indeed most of them remain underrepresented in their ability to influence state policy. Their subordination in the polity has decisively shaped many aspects of their development.

The economic metamorphosis from which the modern city emerged is conventionally referred to as industrialization—an inappropriate designation because factory production was only slowly, and late, incorporated into the urban economy and was, in any case, only one aspect of a more general development. The eye of the change occurred outside the city rather than within it. First in agriculture and then in industry, old household-oriented modes of production gave way to large-scale rationalized forms, ultimately mechanized, that immensely increased output. The need to distribute the products to territorially wide, rather than to local, markets directly implicated the city.

The influence of technological change upon communications needs little comment. The evidences are all about us; and the development that led from the early roads and canals to the railroad, the telephone, the wireless, and the airplane permitted the speedy concentration of goods, messages, and persons at the focal points of ever wider areas. The simultaneous acceleration in managerial skills that permitted the organized deployment of great numbers of men and materials was equally impressive. The pace of innovation was particularly rapid in the half century after 1875 when the character of the modern city was most precisely defined. Why there should have been so striking an outburst of creativity in those years is as elusive a question as why there should have been so striking a failure of creativity thereafter.

The centralized national state, the new productive system, and vastly improved communications created the modern city. Together they increased its population, they endowed it with novel economic functions, and they imposed upon its way of life a fresh conception of order.

The initial manifestation of the change was a rapid growth in urban population. The centralizing tendencies of the emerging states of the sixteenth and seventeenth centuries brought significant groups of newcomers to the capitals and to regional subcenters. Operations, formerly dispersed in particular units of administration, were now concentrated; and the steady growth of state power created many additional places. Numerous functionaries carried on the expanded volume of government business and brought with them their families and retainers. Moreover many noblemen found it necessary to live close to the focus of authority, either through choice to be near the source of favors as in Bourbon France, or through compulsion to be subject to control as in Tokugawa Japan. Ancillary educational and religious institutions gravitated in the same direction. All the people thus drawn to the city created a market for trade, crafts, and services which swelled the economy of their place of residence.[5]

These developments had subtle, long-term effects. Channels of communication with the rest of the country were established that deepened through use and that conditioned the routes of later railroad and telephone lines. In some places the extensive fiscal transactions of the central government laid a basis for subsequent banking developments. As important, the seat of power acquired a symbolic value that later acted as a magnet for other detached elements in the society; and national citizenship facilitated their free entry.

Urban population expanded preponderantly by immigration. Cataclysms of many types outside the city borders precipitously swelled the streams that flowed into it. A stroke of fortune such as the discovery of gold near San Francisco and Johannesburg, or population pressure in the hinterland, or a disaster such as the migrations into Bombay and Calcutta after partition quickly raised the number of residents. Colonial trade contributed to the same effect in London and Amsterdam. Most important of all, structural changes in agriculture and industry involved a total reorganization of the labor force and effectively displaced great numbers of human beings for whom the city was the only refuge.[6]

From these sources was derived the rapid increase in numbers characteristic of the metropolis. Through the nineteenth century the pace accelerated, with the very largest places growing more rapidly than the smaller ones. In 1800 the twenty-one European cities with a population of 100,000 or more held, in all, somewhat more than four and a half million souls, one thirty-fifth of the total. In 1900 there were 147 such places with a population of 40,000,000 or one-tenth of the total; and thirteen and one-fourth million lived within the narrowly defined political limits of the six largest cities. Were there means of estimating the true size of the urban districts involved, the number would be larger still. The same cities in 1960 had a population of about 24,000,000 —again a gross underestimation of their genuine numbers. Meanwhile places of comparable dimension had appeared in America and Asia. In 1961 well over

85,000,000 persons lived in the world's twenty largest cities, each of which contained 2,500,000 or more residents. And the process was not yet over.[7]

Mere accretions of population, however, changed the fundamental character of the city but slightly. New people came in, but their presence in itself called for few radical accommodations on the part of the old residents who generally prospered from the increased demand for their services. The city spread through the addition of new areas to its living space. But the organization of life for some time remained much what it had been earlier. Growth to great size was a necessary precondition, but did not in itself bring the modern city into being. Edo (Tokyo) in 1868 is said to have had a population of about a million, London in 1660 held more than one-half million people; yet these places were but extended towns which functioned according to patterns set long before. Their nobility, mercantile pursuits, and artisans' handicrafts formed larger aggregates than before, but they were aggregates of units that were essentially unchanged. Characteristically, in such places the building trades occupied a large part of the total labor force, and they altered but little with the passage of time. Other pursuits remained much as they had been earlier. The number of smiths and tailors, or drapers and merchants grew; but the mere multiplication of stalls and shops did not change the character of the bazaar, of the lane or of the exchange.[8]

Nor did the new needs thrust upon the city by the transformation of agriculture and industry after the eighteenth century alone give it its modern identity. Viewed simply on the economic plane, there was nothing inherently novel in the relationship of the city to these changes. It had long been accustomed to receiving the placeless men who sought its shelter and it had always provided a market for the products of the countryside. What was new was the desire, and the ability, to impose a rational order upon the relations created by the new productive system. The evolution of that order not only brought the city into intimate dependence upon the surrounding society; it also entailed a thoroughgoing transformation in the urban way of life.

Earlier markets had been dominated by the characteristics of the fair; buyers and sellers had approached in the expectation that they might meet one another, but the actual encounters had been shot through with chance. Monopolies and other political controls, various systems of correspondence and intelligence, and numerous other devices had aimed to impart some regularity to these transactions, particularly in the exchange of the great staples—wine, wool, and later, spices, tea, tobacco, and sugar. But distance and the vagaries of household production had limited the utility of these efforts. In effect, the movement of goods came to a halt, started and stopped, within the city, and that discontinuity gave the entrepôt a considerable degree of autonomy.

That situation ceased to be tolerable after the eighteenth century. The new techniques resulted in a large and growing capacity for production far beyond local need; they involved heavy capital investments and considerable risk; and they entailed difficult administrative problems. The success of any enterprise hinged upon the ability to anticipate with some precision a favorable relationship between cost of production and selling price. It could only survive by

planning, however primitive the means by later standards; and planning required dependability and predictability in access both to markets and to supplies.

The city supplied the essential mechanism: from it radiated the communications network—increasingly more extensive and more rapid—and within it were situated the facilities for transshipping, storing, and processing commodities on their way from producer to consumer. Here, too, was the apparatus of accounting and credit that made the movement of goods possible. The task of the city was that of speedy transmission. The more sensitive communications became, the more thoroughly the city was entangled in a mesh of relations that deprived it of autonomy and integrated it into a larger economic and social whole.[9]

The new role had profound consequences for the internal life of the city. Its effectiveness in the productive system of which it was a part depended upon its ability to create an appropriately functioning order within its own boundaries. The pressures toward doing so were critical in its development.

One can discover premature efforts to create such novel economic relationships in the role of Milan in Lombardy and in the experience of other Renaissance cities with their hinterlands. Such developments were abortive, not only because of their restricted territorial scope and because of technological limitations, but also because the corporate life inherited from the middle ages survived, indeed grew stronger; and that life significantly inhibited further changes. The seventeenth-century syndics who sat for Rembrandt's corporation portraits were custodians of communal organizations which resisted untoward changes. The destruction of their way of life was the necessary preliminary to the creation of a new urban order more in accord with the developing productive system.[10] Where that corporate life was weak or nonexistent to begin with, as in the United States, the process was all the faster.

Destruction of the older way of life was achieved through a convergence of political and economic forces. The national state eroded traditional elements of control and created new loci of power that dominated the city from outside it. The local aristocracy dwindled in importance; the old corporations were drained of influence; privileges were reshuffled; and new people rose to prominence. More generally, the national state undermined all traditional affiliations. It recognized only the indiscriminate relationship of citizenship. In its eyes there were only individuals, not members of clans, guilds, or even of households.

The changes in the productive system redistributed wealth to the advantage of men who could cast aside inherited modes of action to capitalize on fresh opportunities. The new economy encouraged the pursuit of individual profit rather than of status within a defined community; and the city housed a pack of people seeking after gain:

> Where every man is for himself
> And no man for all.[11]

The result was a new concept of orderly city life, one that no longer rested on a corporate organization of households, but instead depended upon a complex and impersonal arrangement of individuals. The process was already at work in the sixteenth century in England; it was immensely stimulated by the American and the French revolutions and was complete by the end of the nineteenth century.

We shall better be able to understand the character of the inner order of the modern city by regarding some of its specific manifestations.

An entirely new pattern for disposing of space appeared. The layout of the old city was altogether inappropriate. The population had already spread beyond the encircling walls and waters but it was inefficiently organized by a cumbersome and anachronistic plan. Churches, palaces, and other monumental structures occupied central places; squares and plazas pockmarked the limited area; and the streets ran but the short distances between nearby termini.

There was no reason why they should do more, for men had little need to travel since the household was both residence and place of work. Various districts were differentiated by occupational, class, or religious distinctions. But in each case, the basic unit was a self-contained familial entity that had a precisely defined place in the corporate life of the city. An increase in numbers was accommodated by multiplying the units, not by altering their character. In those unusual situations, as in the ghettoes, where space was constricted, the buildings rose upward and expansion was vertical. More frequently, where room was available, new clusters of settlement split off from the old and expansion was lateral. But until well into the nineteenth century growth in most places had simply multiplied the number of clusters; it had not altered their essential character.[12]

Reconstruction of the city plan depended upon the differentiation of living and working quarters. Such specialized use of space, reflecting the growing impersonality of business and its separation from the household, became prevalent everywhere except in professions like medicine, and in the service crafts where a personal relationship survived. Elsewhere, the dispersal of the population went hand in hand with the destruction of the household and was eased by the engulfment of suburb after suburb. The father and mother and children lived together but their life was detached from work. The categories of experience they shared in the home were unrelated to those of the job. Each individual left after breakfast to take up a separate task in the counting house or the shop or on the scaffold, to return in the evening to his residence some distance away, for each was an integer subject to a separate reckoning in the accounting of the productive system.[13]

The division of function was economical. Every productive or distributive operation became more efficient when it selected the individual employee according to his talents or cost apart from considerations of kin and clan, of family or ethnic grouping. Of course, no society fully realized the ideal of total fluidity that permitted its population to be sorted out in this manner; but the separation of work from residence encouraged an approach in that direction. The fact that single men and women always constituted a large proportion of the migrants into the city stimulated the trend as did related alterations in the behavior of settled families.

As a result space was released from all sorts of traditional expenses. The enterprise no longer had to bear the charge on land of high value, of wasteful drawing rooms and gardens. Precious urban acreage was withdrawn from farming. And the distribution of population by income levels permitted a rational valuation of space in terms of an abstract, calculated, rent. Speculation was the incidental by-product, rather than the cause, of this development.[14]

Specialization required and facilitated the construction of an entirely new urban plant, a good part of which was built with the aid of a remarkable burst of innovation that began shortly after 1820 and which reached its peak between 1875 and 1925. Space was reallocated with an eye toward its most profitable use; and buildings directed toward a single function—trade, industry, or residence—went up with ruthless efficiency. The process of differentiation created demands for services which theretofore had been unneeded or had been supplied within the household, for fresh foods, milk, water, waste disposal, light, transportation, and recreation. In the frenzy of construction, the city was entirely recast and its ties to the past obliterated. Even topography ceased to be an obstacle; hills were razed, marshes and lakes filled in, and shore lines extended to make way for the limitless grid. Goethe could still make out medieval Frankfurt in place names, markets, buildings, fairs, and topography. By 1870, hardly more than a few of these monuments and ceremonies survived.[15]

Now begins the time of travel, at first on foot. Dickens' characters still walk across London, and at about the same time a resident of Tokyo thinks nothing of tramping five miles to and five miles from his destination every day. Even in twentieth century Rio or Tokyo an inefficient transport system compels workers to spend six hours a day between home and job.[16] But in cost-conscious societies speed is an important consideration; in its interest new streets are driven through the city, straight and wide to carry an ever heavier stream of vehicles—at first horse drawn, later, motor propelled. The wheels roll above and below as well as on the ground and inconvenient rivers are bridged over and tunneled under. The critical breakthrough comes with the appearance of the common carrier. At the beginning of the nineteenth century, every conveyance still bears the appearance of the personal or family carriage or litter —even the long distance stages that take fare-paying passengers. It is not at all clear, when the first railroads are built, that they will follow a different line of development. But the carriages are thrown open for all to enter; mass travel becomes possible; and the meanest laborer moves on wheels.

The pace and ingenuity of this work were impressive by any standard. That the subways of London, Paris, New York, and Boston were built faster than those of Moscow, Stockholm, or Rome fifty years later must mean something, although it would be hazardous to try to make the meaning precise. Any such comparison is to some degree arbitrary and perhaps far-fetched. Yet the standard of achievement certainly was not lower a half century ago than now, if we take into account the presumed improvement in technology since then. Travelers to New York today are aware that it will take seven years (1957-1964) to reconstruct La Guardia Airport and that Idlewild has been more than a decade in the building. Their predecessors fifty years ago were likely to reach the city through one of the largest buildings ever theretofore constructed at one time, one covering eight acres of ground, with exterior walls of one half a mile. They could enter through two tunnels under the Hudson River and

four under the East River extending more than eighteen miles from Harrison, New Jersey, to Jamaica, Long Island. Work on this project began in June 1903; the Hudson tunnels were finished in three years, the East River tunnels in less than five and the Pennsylvania station in less than six. In September, 1910, the whole complex was in operation.[17]

The modern city demanded an immense number and variety of new buildings. Already in the eighteenth century architects like Claude-Nicholas Ledoux were compelled to devise new shapes for warehouses, for banks, for other commercial structures, and for dwellings appropriate to various classes of residents. Considerations of cost compelled them to adhere to the rule of geometry, and to stress functionalism and the rational organization of materials and space. In doing so they struggled against counterpressures toward tradition and individualism, against counterpulls toward exoticism and a romanticized view of nature. By the second half of the nineteenth century, they had begun to work out the styles that accommodated the life of the modern city.[18]

Certainly the New York tenement block of 1900 was an unlovely object. Having dispensed with the old central court, it could pile its residents up in suffocating density. The reformers of the period were altogether right to attack overcrowding there and elsewhere and to complain that the cities had not adequately met their housing needs. Only, one must remember that overcrowding and need are relative concepts; and few later efforts have been notably more successful.[19] Comparison with the experience of Moscow in the 1930's, to say nothing of Calcutta in the

1950's, puts the achievements of a half-century ago in better perspective.[20]

The altered situation of the city called also for a new conception of time. In the rural past, years, months, days, and hours had been less meaningful than seasons, than the related succession of religious occasions, than the rising and setting of the sun. Small communities had their own flexible conceptions of chronology. Such habits had extended to the city as well. Each household had a large margin within which to set its own pace, for the tempo of all activities was leisurely. An analysis of the course of an eighteenth-century merchant's day, for instance, revealed long disposable intervals so that even when he was busy, it was upon terms he could shape for himself.[21]

The complex interrelationships of life in the modern city, however, called for unprecedented precision. The arrival of all those integers who worked together, from whatever part of the city they inhabited, had to be coordinated to the moment. There was no natural span for such labor; arbitrary beginnings and ends had to be set, made uniform and adhered to. The dictatorship of the clock and the schedule became absolute.[22]

No earlier human experience had made such demands. The army camp, plantation labor, and the ship's crew which came closest to it were coherent, closed societies, the members of which lived close together and in isolation from outsiders; the tasks involved had a rhythm of their own that regulated their budgets of time. But the modern city could not function except under the rule of a precise and arbitrary chronological order which alone could coordinate the activities of thousands of individuals whose necessary encounters with one another were totally impersonal. By the same token, literacy or some alternative code of signals was essential to the coexistence of people who did not know one another.

The new uses of space and time were indicative of what order meant in the modern city. Its complex life demanded myriad daily contacts of such sensitivity that it could not depend, as earlier, upon well-established and static connections among the stable households and the fixed corporate groups in which its population had been distributed. Instead it required its residents to behave individually and impersonally in terms of their function, and it assured regularity of contacts by rigid allocations of space and time.

That order made it possible to bring manufacturing, like other large-scale activities, into the cities. The planners of the early great factories thought of the only models of disciplined activity familiar to them, the barrack and the army camp; their sites—visionary or actual—were therefore invariably in the countryside, where the tolling bell from the clock tower of the mill replaced that of the village church. The similarity in design of factories and prisons was by no means coincidental.[23]

The urban factory was conceivable only well in the nineteenth century when it was possible to imagine that a labor force would come to work regularly and dependably. The process of transition in actuality took a number of forms. Some factory centers, like Manchester, grew into cities. In other cases, as in Pittsburgh or Zurich, a commercial center expanded to engulf nearby industrial communities. Elsewhere industry was drawn in by the attractions of superior transportation facilities, or by the presence of an abundant labor supply, as in Berlin, or Chicago; or the shift was a product of conscious government decisions as in Moscow after 1928. But whatever the immediate impulse, the necessary condition was the order that permitted the factory to function.[24]

The way of life of the modern city created grave social and personal problems. Any increase of size had always complicated the police of the community. But so long as the family, the clan, or the guild remained accountable for the behavior of its members, so long as the normal ambit of activities was restricted to a familiar quarter, the primary danger of deviant behavior came from strangers. When the decay of the household weakened the sense of collective security, the initial response was to control or exclude outsiders, to arrive at some accommodation with violent elements, and to maintain the isolation of the district within which its residents felt safe. At the end of the eighteenth century, as large a place as London had not moved beyond this point.

But these expedients were not long useful. The modern city was no *colluvies gentium*—a fortuitous accumulation of unfused populaces—as were ancient Rome, or Alexandria. Extended travel and promiscuous contacts were essential to it; and the frequent mingling of men unknown to each other generated the need for holding each individual responsible for his behavior. The ultimate goal was some sort of total index that would precisely identify and infallibly locate each person so that he could be called to account for his obligations and punished for his delinquencies. The steady development of governmental power, the contrivance of numerous devices for registration, and the appearance of a professional corps

of administrators were steps toward an approximation of that goal.

More was involved than the containment of criminality. The urban resident had positive as well as negative responsibilities. He had not merely to refrain from such actions as were injurious to others; he was expected, in ways that were difficult to define explicitly, also to contribute to the total well-being of the community by civic actions. The collective tasks of the old household and guild could not be left in abeyance. Someone had to provide care for dependent persons, education for children, facilities for worship, media for cultural and sociable expression, and commemorative monuments and objects of awe and beauty. The police of a city thus included a wide range of functions connected with its health and security. The state assumed some of these obligations, but the scope of its activity varied widely from country to country. Although we cannot yet explain convincingly the differences in the depth of its involvement, it is clear that it nowhere preempted the field entirely. Much remained to be done through other forms.[25]

It was not possible, although men often longed to do so, to revive the old corporate institutions or the solidary rural communities from which so many residents had migrated. The modern city contained too many disparate elements, too often thrown together, and in too fluid a pattern of relations to permit such regressions. Instead, where abstinence by the state left a vacuum, the characteristic device of a voluntary association, directed toward the specific function, met the need. The rapid proliferation of such organizations drew together memberships united by common interests, common antecedents, or common point of view. The wide expanse of the city and the continuing migration which peopled it, shaped such groupings. In some places the effective modes of organization fell within territorial, neighborhood lines; the *quartier,* ward, *ku,* or *favela* was the matrix within which associations formed. Elsewhere cultural or ethnic affiliations supplied the determining limits of cooperative action.[26]

For a long time, the cost of this adjustment was recurrent, overt conflict. Leadership was effective only within limited circles, and there were few means of resolving the frequent crises that led easily into outbreaks of violence. Bread riots in the West and rice riots in the East expressed the desperation of the uncared-for elements in the community; and racial or social antipathies, smoldering beneath the surface, erupted at the least disturbance.[27]

By the end of the nineteenth century, the instruments for controlling such dangerous disorders were at least available, if not always effectively used. The reconstruction of the great cities permitted a strategic disposition of power to contain the mob. The maintenance of an armed police force deterred overt lawbreakers. Moreover, by then a complex of philanthropic, religious, educational, and cultural institutions had begun to elicit the acquiescence of the urban masses through persuasion. Thereafter conflicts took more negotiable forms, in the bargaining of labor unions and employers, and in politics which was less a partisan contest for power than an instrument of group accommodation. Disputes were increasingly subject to conciliable resolution through the mediating efforts of recog-

nized leaders. However, the issues which could be confronted on the municipal level were limited and concrete; and the deeper economic and emotional grievances of the population were likely to be displaced into other channels.[28]

The life of the modern city created subtle personal problems. Here were distilled many of the general effects of change in the past two centuries: the break with tradition and the dissolution of inherited beliefs, the impact of science and technology, and the transformation of the family and of the productive system. In the city, as elsewhere, such decisive innovations were a source of both release and tension in the human spirit. Only, concentrated as they were in their urban form, these new impulses were far more volatile than elsewhere. Furthermore, the man of the city passed through experiences unique to his setting. The number and variety and speed of his contacts, the products of an original conception of space and time, the separation from nature, the impersonality and individuality of work all were novel to the human situation.

Evidence of the negative consequences was painfully abundant. On the Bowery or in Brigittenau drifted the uprooted masses who had lost personality, identity, and norms and who now were trapped in every form of disorder. The deterioration of man to bum was all too familiar in every modern city. Even the less desperate were heedless of the restraints of church and family; in London, Berlin, and New York of the third quarter of the nineteenth century, a majority of marriages and burials were unsolemnized by the clergy. The most prosperous tore at each other in vicious competition except when they indulged in fierce and expensive debauchery. High rates of mortality, suicide, alcoholism, insanity, and other forms of delinquency showed that men reared in one environment could not simply shift to another without substantial damage to themselves.[29]

At the high point of change, in the half century after 1875, there were two distinct, although not contradictory, interpretations of the effects of the modern city upon the human personality. Those who focused their attention upon institutional developments, like Georg Simmel, Emile Durkheim, and, to some extent, Max Weber, took particular note of the decay of old forms which left the individual unsheltered, unprotected, and isolated, and therefore prone to deterioration. The later exaggerations of Spengler and Mumford distend these insights into a vision of imminent catastrophe.[30]

Exaggeration was easy because personal disorders were more visible in the city than in the country. But these observers were also limited by a fixed preference for what the city had been, a total systematic unit comprehending a defined order of institutions that no longer existed. It is significant that their views mirrored somber predictions, made long before. Rousseau and others had already warned of the inevitable results of urban detachment from nature before the process had even taken form. "Of all animals man is least capable of living in flocks. Penned up like sheep, men soon lose all. The breath of man is fatal to his fellows. . . . Cities are the burial pit of the human species."[31]

The personal hardships of adjustment to city life were genuine but they were distorted when examined in the perspective of the corporate, rural past. Other observers, whose gaze was fastened on the residents as human beings, made out a somewhat different pattern. "What can ever be more stately and admirable to me," asked Whitman, "than mast-hemm'd Manhattan?" Observing the curious procession of the ferry riders leaving work behind for their thousands of homes, he felt and expressed the wonder of their each being a person.[32] This was often the response of compassionate onlookers. At first regard, the city was totally inhuman; jungle, wilderness, hive, machine—these were the terms of the metaphors that sprang spontaneously to mind. But those sensitive enough to look more deeply found marvelous assertions of the human spirit even under these unpropitious circumstances. Here life was real and hard, and tested the human heart and mind so that emotions were deeper and reason more acute than elsewhere. Social scientists influenced by the Darwinian conception of the survival of the fittest readily assumed that the city was the new environment within which a new, superior man would develop. And some who began half to understand the character of that life were tempted to idealize and romanticize even its least lovely aspects, the slums, the ruthless competition, and the grinding order.[33]

The two responses were not irreconcilable; indeed, in retrospect, they seem almost complementary, or perhaps, they were but different ways of describing the identical process. The decay of familiar institutions was another way of saying the release from traditional restraints; the unsheltered individual was also the liberated individual. The breakdown of the household and the attenuation of all the relationships formerly centered in it were the conditions of the liberation of modern man to all his painful tensions, all his creative opportunities. The hard stone of the city streets provided the stage for this drama; and it is the task of historical scholarship to explain its triumphs, its defeats, and its conflicts.

The modern city provided the scene for great outbursts of cultural creativity. Georgian London, Paris in the first decades of the Third Republic, Vienna toward the end of the reign of Franz Joseph, and Berlin of the 1920's were the settings of great achievements of the human spirit, in literature, in art, in music, and in science. Yet these were also, and at the same time, the scenes of bitter struggles for existence, of acute hardships suffered by hundreds of thousands of ill-prepared newcomers beaten down by insoluble problems. John Gay and William Hogarth, Anatole France and Honoré Daumier, Robert Musil and Berthold Brecht, and Charlie Chaplin and René Clair compiled a record of personal disasters, of moral disintegration, of human costs so high it could only be contemplated under the palliative gloss of humor. The laughter of their audiences did not conceal, it recognized the harsh truth. Yet the withering away of traditional guides to life, so debilitating in many ways, also set the individual free, left room for spontaneity and discovery, brought together selective new combinations of people, ideas, and forms, that permitted man to catch unsuspected glimpses of an unknown universe and an unfamiliar self.

Every aspect of the development of the modern city generated conflicts not resolvable within its own boundaries; that was a condition of its intimate relations with the society beyond its borders. The urban residents were divided among themselves, and they had to reckon with outsiders in their midst and beyond the walls, whose interests were intimately bound up with their own. Disputes of great importance were the result.

The city plan was therefore never simply the realization of an abstract design. Even in places created entirely afresh, as in Washington or St. Petersburg, it was the product of inescapable compromises. Within the city, the primary interest of the entrepreneurial groups and of the laboring population was to economize on the use of space. They wanted low rents, an efficient, functional allocation of the resources, and speedy interior transportation.

Such people met the determined, and sometimes effective, resistance of other elements, whose conceptions were still dominated by the static images of the rural landscape. The aristocracy—genuine and putative—wished to bring with them the commodious features of their landed estates. They expected the city to provide them with elegant squares to set off their homes, with picturesque monuments, and with parks and boulevards that would supply a back drop for the May Corso, for the Spring Parade, for the *ausflug* or Sunday excursion, for the gentleman on horseback and the lady in her carriage. Public transportation concerned them not at all.[34]

Immigrants who prospered to a lesser degree clung to the rural village as the model of home; they built wasteful villas in the sprawling suburbs and sought a restricted transport system that would take them conveniently to their desks and counters, yet prevent the city from engulfing them. Often their dogged struggles for autonomy hopelessly complicated any effort at urban reorganization, a problem as troublesome in Vienna, Leipzig, Manchester, and Liverpool in 1890 as in Boston and Nashville in 1960.[35]

The persistence of the rural model prevented these people from thinking of the city as a whole and as it was. From Robert Owen, Fourier, and the utopian socialists, to Ebenezer Howard, Frank Lloyd Wright, and Lewis Mumford, a good-hearted but illusory plea went forth for the rebuilding of urban life in garden cities or multiplied suburbs, where adults would not be tempted to squander their resources in the pub or music hall, nor children theirs in the sweetshop; and all would have access to the salubrious and moral air of the countryside.[36]

To such pressures were added those of agriculturists and industrialists in the hinterland concerned only with lowering the cost of transshipment, and of the state, increasingly preoccupied with security against insurrection or lesser threats to order. The great planners, like Baron Haussmann in Paris, found room for maneuver in the play of these forces against one another. But rarely did they find the city material they could mold into a unified and coherent whole.[37]

Urban elements were at a disadvantage in the determination of both municipal and national policies. The level of tariffs in the 1880's and 1890's, the routes of canals and railroads, and the character of the banking system vitally affected all cities. Yet their influence was perilously weak, underrepresented in the councils of state and divided, while the rural interests were monolithic and well entrenched. Paris, Rio, Rome did not govern themselves; and voices from the Platteland or Upstate were more likely to command than those from Johannesburg or New York. The political power of the country generally outweighed the economic power of the city.[38]

The clash of interests took its most subtle and most significant form in the contact of the diverse cultures that converged on the modern city. The folk traditions of the old bourgeois did not survive the disintegration of the corporate bodies in which it had been embedded; it was totally disrupted by the pressure from both above and below of alien elements.

The aristocracy surrendered its isolation and shifted some of its activities to the city. Still stabilized by its landed estates, it also drew support from new wealth and, in the nineteenth century, began the quest for a uniform, hierarchical culture at the peak of which it could stand. It wished more than indulgence in a lavish style of life; it wished also general acquiescence in its position. Indeed, to some extent it flouted the conventions of inferiors precisely in order to demonstrate its superiority. Legally recognized rank as in England and Prussia, the pretense of ancient lineage as in Austria and France, or arbitrary registers of inclusion as in the United States, asserted its claims to pre-eminence. In addition, it transformed the theater, the opera and the museum into institutions to display its dominance. The aristocracy turned music into classics, art into old masters, and literature into rare books, possessions symbolic of its status.[39]

The problems of other migrants into the city were of quite another order. The mass of displaced peasants were eager to transplant their inherited culture but the soil was inhospitable. Folk wisdom, inappropriate to the new conditions, took on the appearance of superstition; and folk art, detached from its communal setting, lost much of its authenticity. However these people fared, they were driven by anxiety—to retain the rewards of success, to avoid the penalties of failure. Some escaped through alcohol; others found moments of relief in the excitement of the yellow press, the music hall, and the popular theater.[40]

Above all, they needed to interpret their lives by seeing themselves as actors in a meaningful drama, and since it was inconceivable that they should be conquering heroes, they most readily visualized themselves as victims.

Of whom? Rarely of the aristocrat. Peasant and gentleman had a long history of accommodation; and their roles in city life engendered few direct conflicts. The lowly felt no compulsion to ape the high born, and gaped at the splendor of the carriages on the way to the opera without envy.

More often the villains were the capitalists, big business, whose wealth was abstract, was located in no communal context, and was attached to no responsibilities of position. Or sometimes, the enemy was the stranger—the Slav or the Jew or the Catholic or the Protestant Masons or the barbaric foreigner—who could be blamed for the ills of the city. Inhuman materialism, disregard of traditional faith, sensuality and obscenity were crimes against man; and for crimes, criminals were responsible; and they who came were guilty so that we who left home were but the innocent victims.[41]

The factory workers and craftsmen who held places in disciplined organizations found belief in socialism; the class struggle explained their present situation and offered them the hope of an acceptable future. But millions of place-less men could not so readily tear themselves away from the past. The shopkeepers and clerks, the casual laborers, the chaotic mass of men without function did not want the future; they wanted the security of the homes and families and blood communities they had never had or had lost in migration. That is, they wanted a miracle; and in their eagerness they became the gullible victims of nationalistic, racist, religious and quasi-religious fantasies of every sort. There is a particular interest, in Europe, in the ease with which these people allied themselves with some sectors of the aristocracy under the banner of a universal faith—Ultramontane Catholicism, pan-Germanism, pan-Slavism. Drumont and the royalist officer corps in France, Luëger and Prince Alois Liechtenstein in Austria, illustrated the attractiveness of tradition and authority for the demagogue and his mob. Perhaps analogous elements were involved in the revival of Shinto in Japan after 1868; they were certainly present in the history of fascism.[42]

The true miracle, however, was the emergence of a sense of civic consciousness connected with the old burgher traditions but responsive to the new character of the modern city. Its characteristics were tolerance to the point of latitudinarianism, rationalism, cosmopolitanism, pragmatism, and receptivity to change. It attracted the settled middle-class elements of the city, the leaders of organized labor and even demagogues suddenly charged with responsibility, as Luëger was in Vienna and La Guardia in New York; its essence was a creative reaction to the problems of the place; its achievement was the monumental building of the city to which I earlier referred.

Some decades ago—and I am deliberately vague about the date—a significant change appeared. The immediate local causes seemed to be the two wars, the depression, and new shifts in technology and population. However, these may be but manifestations of some larger turning in the history of the society of which the modern city is a part.

The differences between city and country have been attenuated almost to the vanishing point. The movement of people, goods, and messages has become so rapid and has extended over such a long period as to create a new situation. To put it bluntly, the urbanization of the whole society may be in process of destroying the distinctive role of the modern city. It is symptomatic of this change that, in western societies, most migrations now originate, as well as terminate, in the modern metropolis.

This change may be related to a general slackening of urban spirit. The worldwide movement to the suburbs is not in itself new; this was always one of the ways in which the city expanded. What is new is the effective motivation—the insistence upon constructing small, uniform, coherent communities, and the surrender of the adventure of life in the larger units with all the hazards and opportunities of unpredictable contacts. Increasingly the men who now people the metropolis long for the security of isolation from the life about them. They strive to locate their families in space, with a minimum of connections to the hazards of the external world.[43]

Finally, there has been a perceptible decline in urban creativity. The regression to private transportation is indicative of what has been happening in other spheres as well. Despite other advances in technology and despite refinements in methods, the last thirty or forty years have witnessed no innovations to match those of the thirty or forty years earlier. We have done little more than elaborate upon the inherited plant; nowhere has there been an adequate response to the challenge of new conditions.

We console ourselves with the calculation that if the modern city has ceased to grow, the metropolitan region continues to expand. What difference that will make remains to be seen. In any case, it seems likely that we stand at the beginnings of a transformation as consequential as that which, two hundred years ago, brought the modern city into being.

Therein lies the historian's opportunity to throw light on the problems of those involved with today's city, either as practitioners or as participants. His task is not to predict, but to order the past from which the present grows in a comprehensible manner. He can illuminate the growth of the modern city from the eighteenth to the twentieth centuries to make clear what was permanent and what transient, what essential and what incidental, in its development.

Such an account as this essay has presented has perforce touched upon a few themes abstracted from a large number of cases. Yet the historian must deal with particulars, not with generalities. Certainly the stress, laid here upon the connections between the modern city and the surrounding society points to the decisive role of political, cultural, and economic variants, widely different from place to place.

Comparisons crowd immediately to mind. Did the differences between

Washington and St. Petersburg in 1900, new capitals of expanding nations, emanate from the hundred-year disparity in their ages or from discernible differences between the United States and Russia? Did Shanghai and Singapore become what they did because they were perched on the edge of Oriental societies or because they were colonial enclaves? Did a tropical situation set the experiences of Rio and Havana apart from those of cities in the temperate zone; did their European population distinguish them from other tropical cities? Why did some cities fail to grow as others did, why were some more successful than others in resolving their problems?

No amount of theorizing about the nature of the city will answer questions such as these. We need fewer studies of the city in history than of the history of cities. However useful a general theory of the city may be, only the detailed tracing of an immense range of variables, in context, will illuminate the dynamics of the processes here outlined.[44] We can readily enough associate such gross phenomena as the growth of population and the rise of the centralized state, as technological change and the development of modern industry, as the disruption of the traditional household and the decline of corporate life. But how these developments unfolded, what was the causal nexus among them, we shall only learn when we make out the interplay among them by focusing upon a city specifically in all its uniqueness.

In the modern city, the contest between the human will and nature assumed a special form. Here man, crowded in upon himself and yet alone, discovered his potentialities for good and evil, for weakness and strength.

Compelled to act within a framework of impersonal institutions, he was forced to probe the meaning of his own personality.

In the balance for two centuries now has lain the issue of whether he will master, or be mastered by, the awesome instruments he has created. The record of that issue deserves the best energies of the historian.

NOTES

1. Max Weber, *The City* (Translated and edited by Don Martindale and Gertrud Neuwirth; Glencoe, [1958]), 70 ff.; Raffaele d'Ambrosio, *Alle Origini della città le prime esperienze urbane* (Napoli, 1956); A. Temple Patterson, *Radical Leicester* (Leicester, 1954), 3, 165.
2. George Unwin, *Studies in Economic History* (London, 1927), 49.
3. Norman G. Brett-James, *Growth of Stuart London* (London, [1935]), 67 ff., 105 ff., 296 ff.; Walter Besant, *London in the Time of the Tudors* (London, 1904), 83; Boyle Workman, *The City that Grew* (Caroline Walker, ed., Los Angeles, 1935), 266 ff.
4. William A. Robson, *Great Cities of the World: Their Government, Politics and Planning* (New York, [1955]), 78 ff.; Société Jean Bodin, *Recueils*, VI (1954), 265 ff., 367 ff., 434 ff., 541 ff., 612.
5. See, e.g., Franklin L. Ford, *Strasbourg in Transition 1648-1789* (Cambridge, 1958), 159 ff.; Lewis Mumford, *The City in History. Its Origins, Its Transformations, and Its Prospects* (New York, [1961]), 386 ff.; *Golden Ages of the Great Cities* (London, 1952), 192.
6. Adna F. Weber, *The Growth of Cities in the Nineteenth Century* (New York, 1899), 230 ff.; Besant, *London in the Time of the Tudors*, 226 ff.; Walter Besant, *London in the Eighteenth Century* (London, 1903), 213 ff.; Percy E. Schramm, ed., *Kaufleute zu Haus und über See Hamburgische Zeugnisse des 17., 18., und 19. Jahrhunderts* (Hamburg, 1949), pt. II; Emile Vandervelde, *L'Exode rural et le retour aux champs* (Paris, 1903), 39 ff.; Robson, *Great Cities*, 112 ff., 141, 683.
7. *Information Please Almanac, 1961*, 658; Edmund J. James, "The Growth of Great Cities," *Annals of the American Academy of Political and Social Science*, XIII (1899), 1 ff.; Weber, *Growth of Cities*, 20 ff., gives extensive nineteenth-century statistics. See also for more recent data, International Urban Research, *The World's Metropolitan Areas* (Berkeley, 1959); Kingsley Davis, "The Origin and Growth of Urbanization in the World," *American Journal of Sociology*, LX

(1955), 429 ff.; Norton S. Ginsburg, "The Great City in Southeast Asia," *ibid.*, LX, 455 ff.; Robert I. Crane, "Urbanism in India," *ibid.*, LX, 463 ff.; Donald J. Bogue, "Urbanism in the United States, 1950," *ibid.*, LX, 471 ff.; Irene B. Taeuber, *Population of Japan* (Princeton, 1958), 25 ff., 45 ff., 96 ff., 126 ff., 148 ff.; Kingsley Davis, *Population of India and Pakistan* (Princeton, 1951), 127 ff.; Vandervelde, *L'Exode rural*, 16 ff.; Edmond Nicolaï, *La Dépopulation des campagnes et l'accroissement de la population des villes* (Bruxelles, 1903); R. Price-Williams, "The Population of London, 1801-81," *Journal of the Statistical Society*, XLVIII (1885), 349 ff.
8. For the population of earlier European cities, see Roger Mols, *Introduction à la démographie historique des villes d'Europe* (Louvain, 1955), II, 502 ff. See also M. Dorothy George, *London Life in the XVIIIth Century* (London, 1925), 155 ff.
9. Robert M. Fisher, ed., *The Metropolis in Modern Life* (Garden City, 1955), 85 ff.; Weber, *Growth of Cities*, 170 ff. For earlier market relations see, "La Foire," Société Jean Bodin, *Receuils*, V (1953), *passim*.
10. See Douglas F. Dowd, "Economic Expansion of Lombardy," *Journal of Economic History*, XXI (1961), 143 ff.; *Storia di Milano* (Milan, 1957-1960), VIII, 337 ff., XIV, 835 ff.; Jakob Rosenberg, *Rembrandt* (Cambridge, 1948), I, 70 ff.; Weber, *The City*, 91 ff.; Mumford, *City in History*, 269 ff., 281 ff.; Société Jean Bodin, *Receuils*, VII (1955), 567 ff.; Schramm, *Kaufleute*, 185 ff.
11. Robert Crowley, quoted in Mumford, *City in History*, 343.
12. Gideon Sjoberg, *The Preindustrial City Past and Present* (Glencoe, [1960]), 100 ff.; Martin S. Briggs, "Town-Planning," Charles Singer, *et al.*, eds., *History of Technology* (New York, 1957), III, 269 ff.; *Golden Ages*, 31-34, 67, 230; Mumford, *City in History*, 299 ff.
13. See Otis D. and Beverly Duncan, "Residential Distribution and Occupational Stratification," *American Journal of Sociology*, LX (1955), 493 ff.; R. P. Dore, *City Life in Japan. A Study of a Tokyo Ward* (Berkeley, 1958), 91 ff.
14. Mumford, *City in History*, 421 ff.; Fisher, *Metropolis in Modern Life*, 125 ff.; Weber, *Growth of Cities*, 322 ff.
15. *The Auto-Biography of Goethe. Truth and Poetry: From My Own Life* (John Oxenford, transl., London, 1948), 3, 4, 7-10, 12 ff.
16. Fukuzawa Yukichi, *Autobiography* (transl. by Eiichi Kiyooka, Tokyo, [1948]); Robson, *Great Cities*, 510; Brett-James, *Stuart London*, 420 ff.
17. Pennsylvania Railroad Company, *The New York Improvement and Tunnel Extension of the Pennsylvania Railroad* (Philadelphia, 1910).
18. Emil Kaufmann, "Three Revolutionary Architects," *Transactions of the American Philosophical Society*, XLII (1952), 494 ff.; Helen Rosenau, *The Ideal City in Its Architectural Evolution* (London, [1959]), 79 ff.
19. Mumford, *City in History*, 465 ff.; Dore, *City Life in Japan*, 40 ff.; Reinhard E. Petermann,

Wien im Zeitalter Kaiser Franz Joseph I (Vienna, 1908), 128 ff.
20. Alec Nove, ed., *The Soviet Seven Year Plan* (London, [1960]), 75 ff.; Harry Schwartz, *Russia's Soviet Economy* (2 ed., New York, 1954), 453 ff.; Robson, *Great Cities*, 384 ff.
21. Arthur H. Cole, "The Tempo of Mercantile Life in Colonial America," *Business History Review*, XXXIII (1959), 277 ff.; *Golden Ages*, 44, 45.
22. On the problem of time, see Pitirim A. Sorokin and Robert K. Merton, "Social Time: A Methodological and Functional Analysis," *American Journal of Sociology*, XLII (1937), 615 ff.
23. Kaufmann, "Three Revolutionary Architects," 509 ff.; Rosenau, *Ideal City*, 121, 133.
24. See, e.g., Catherine E. Reiser, *Pittsburgh's Commercial Development 1800-1850* (Harrisburg, 1951), 28, 191 ff.
25. Louis Wirth, "Urbanism as a Way of Life," *American Journal of Sociology*, XLIV (1938), 20 ff.; Patterson, *Radical Leicester*, 222 ff.; Dore, *City Life in Japan*, 71 ff.
26. See, in general, Lloyd Rodwin, ed., *The Future Metropolis* (New York, 1961), 23 ff. For specific illustrations see Louis Chevalier, "La Formation de la population parisienne au XIXe Siècle," Institut National d'Etudes Démographiques, *Travaux et Documents*, X (1950); Alphonse Daudet, *Numa Roumestan—Moeurs parisiennes* (Paris, 1881), ch. iii; Dore, *City Life in Japan*, 255 ff.; Alexander Campbell, *The Heart of Japan* (New York, 1961), 3 ff.; William A. Jenks, *Vienna and the Young Hitler* (New York, 1960), 4.
27. Société Jean Bodin, *Receuils*, VII (1955), 398 ff.; J. B. Sansom, *The Western World and Japan* (New York, 1958), 242; J. D. Chambers, *Nottinghamshire in the Eighteenth Century* (London, 1932), 40 ff.; Besant, *London in the Eighteenth Century*, 475 ff.; George Rudé, *The Crowd in the French Revolution* (Oxford, 1959), 232 ff.
28. Robson, *Great Cities*, 210 ff.
29. See Petermann, *Wien*, 331 ff.; Jenks, *Vienna and the Young Hitler*, 11; George, *London Life*, 21 ff.; Besant, *London in the Eighteenth Century*, 140 ff., 263 ff.; Fisher, *Metropolis in Modern Life*, 18 ff.
30. Georg Simmel, "Die Grosstädte und das Geistesleben," *Jahrbuch der Gehe-Stiftung zu Dresden*, IX (1903), 187 ff.; Kurt H. Wolff, ed., *Georg Simmel, 1858-1918*, (Columbus, Ohio, [1959]), 100 ff., 221 ff.; Emile Durkheim, *De la Division du travail social* (5 ed., Paris, 1926), *passim*, but especially the preface to the second edition; Oswald Spengler, *The Decline of the West* (New York, 1950), II, 92 ff.; Mumford, *City in History*, *passim*. See also Wirth, "Urbanism as a Way of Life," *loc. cit.*, 20 ff.
31. J[ean]. J[acques]. Rousseau, *Emile ou de l'éducation* (Paris, 1854), Book I, p. 36; Robert A. Kann, *A Study in Austrian Intellectual History* (New York, 1960), 63; see also the point of view

implicit in such novels as E. M. Forster, *Howard's End* (London, 1910).

32. Walt Whitman, *Complete Writings* (New York, 1902), I, 196.

33. See also Weber, *Growth of Cities*, 368 ff., 441 ff.

34. See Percy E. Schramm, *Hamburg, Deutschland und die Welt* (Hamburg, [1952]), 350 ff.; Mumford, *City in History*, 395 ff.

35. Robson, *Great Cities*, 30 ff., 60 ff., 75 ff.; Sam B. Warner, *Street Car Suburbs* (Cambridge, 1962); Weber, *Growth of Cities*, 469 ff.; H. J. Dyos, *Victorian Suburbs* (Leicester, 1961).

36. Rosenau, *Ideal City*, 130 ff.; Robert Owen, *Book of the New Moral World* (London, 1842), II, 16; Ralph Neville, *Garden Cities* (Manchester, 1904); G. Montague Harris, *The Garden City Movement* (London, 1906); Mumford, *City in History*, 514 ff.

37. David H. Pinkney, *Napoleon III and the Rebuilding of Paris* (Princeton, 1958), 25 ff.

38. Robson, *Great Cities*, 685; Schramm, *Hamburg*, 187 ff.

39. Oscar Handlin, *John Dewey's Challenge to Education* (New York, [1959]), 33 ff., George D. Painter, *Proust; the Early Years* (Boston, 1959), Robert Musil, *The Man Without Qualities* (London, 1953); Hans Rosenberg, *Bureaucracy, Aristocracy and Autocracy* (Cambridge, 1958), 182 ff.; Hannah Arendt, *The Origins of Totalitarianism* (New York, [1951]), 54 ff.; Norman Jacobs, ed., *Culture for the Millions?* (Princeton, 1961), 43 ff.; Kann, *Austrian Intellectual History*, 146 ff.

40. Jacobs, *Culture for Millions?* 64 ff.

41. Oscar Handlin, *Adventure in Freedom* (New York, 1954), 174 ff.; Kann, *Austrian Intellectual History*, 50 ff., 109 ff.

42. Dore, *City Life in Japan*, 291 ff.; Arendt, *Origins of Totalitarianism*, 301 ff.; Jenks, *Vienna and the Young Hitler*, 40 ff., 74 ff., 126 ff.

43. Mumford, *City in History*, 511 ff.; Louis Wirth, *Community Life and Social Policy* (Chicago, [1956]), 206 ff.

44. Weber, *The City*, 11 ff.; Wirth, "Urbanism," 8 ff.; Sjoberg, *Preindustrial City*, 4 ff., 321 ff.

II THE CITY IN COLONIAL AMERICA

American urban history began with the small town—five villages hacked out of the wilderness. Each of these villages was geographically endowed to profit from seaborne commerce; each an "upstart" town with no past, an uncertain future, and a host of confounding and novel problems; each faced with surviving fire, disease, and war, and surviving the mightiest of problems that arise when humans gang together, trying to live and interact with tolerance and responsibility.

From their first rude beginnings in the 1600s to the American Revolution, five towns became five cities, five towns in the wilderness became five cities in revolt. The rise of New York, Boston, Newport, Philadelphia, and Charlestown underscored one major theme in the history of the American city: size is disproportionate to influence. In its first 150 years, this was a profoundly agrarian country with only a small portion of the population living in the five major cities, yet the influence, the power, the vitality of the cities transcended their size. By the end of the colonial period the cities imperially dominated their own immediate hinterland; each had grown economically mature as distributing, producing, marketing centers that helped pierce the backcountry with a transportation system that forged new towns and cities; each acted as a magnet luring the native farmer and the foreign immigrant alike by its opportunities and amenities. The cities had become the intellectual and cultural centers of a new nation, the frontiers of social change. Above all, they were symbols of one underlying cause of the American Revolution: the growth of an embryo nation into political, economic, and social maturity that demanded its own identity.

Today when we are so concerned about the idea and need for community, Darrett Rutman gives us an analysis of one of the first attempts at collective action in John Winthrop's search for community on the eve of the founding of Boston. With compassion, a touch of irony, and a sense of tragedy, Rutman explores the aspirations of the Puritan leader's search for an ideal community, "a Citty upon a hill."

Winthrop, an enormously complex man, was, like his ship the *Arbella*, on a voyage between two worlds, the old and the new, the premodern and the modern. As a man of the seventeenth century, he felt the need to reconcile the key concepts of his time: status, property, and God. As a leader of a blind thrust into the wilderness, a flank attack upon the corruptions of Christendom, he felt the need to go beyond his own time to create a secular heaven on earth. For with all the rhetoric about "a citty of God" he was a "Puritan" in only a limited way, and his mission, according to Rutman, was religious only in the simplest sense. His errand to the new world was a lay movement, founded on earthly social ideals. Its essence a "secular monestary" geared to the all-encompassing ideal of community—a sense of collective responsibility. Winthrop demanded a literal application of "love thy neighbor as thyself." Status, property, and God were seen in the light of brotherhood. Commerce was corrupt and must be balanced by charity and mercy. People must blend their aspirations and restrain their greed to the benefit of both the welfare of their fellow citizens and the good of the community.

Utopianism is fragile, for all its nobility. The opportunities of the new world broke the spine of the ideal community. They excited the acquisitive urges of the English; they nourished the seed of individualism, which shattered the notion of collective responsibility. The inherent contradictions of the seventeenth-century mind helped create the bickering that destroyed the unity Winthrop sought. Institutions slipped away from the communal ideal and shaped themselves instead to the nature of the New World. In one sense the failure of the "Citty upon a hill" was inevitable (hindsight being twenty-twenty). It was doomed by its own impracticalities. Can the idea of the "brotherhood of man" survive in an acquisitive community? Thus Winthrop's ideal can be seen as a casualty of modernity in America. As Professor Rutman makes clear, it can also be seen as a tragedy, the failure of a majestic idea.

The next selection is from *The Private City*, which won the Beveridge Prize in 1969. In this book Sam Bass Warner measures the present against the past and asks what went wrong. In the last fifty years, an era of extraordinary change, European countries initiated programs and devised institutions that have far outstripped American efforts to cope with urban problems. When confronted with problems of poverty, racial integration, decent housing, adequate medical care, effective schools, urban amenities such as recreational areas, Americans have staggered and failed. Why? Warner finds his answer not in some peculiar consequence of the urbanization process or in the breakdown of the political system, which are symptoms but not causes. He finds it in an attitude, a value system, an ideological commitment, which more than anything shaped the form, the character, and the flaws of the American city. He calls it privatism. And he finds its origins in colonial Philadelphia, which in his view is the prototype of the American city.

The essence of privatism

lay in its concentration upon the individual and the individual's search for wealth. Psychologically, privatism meant that the individual should seek happiness in personal independence and in the search for wealth; socially, privatism meant that the individual should see his first loyalty as his immediate family, and that a community should be a union of such money-making, accumulating families; politically, privatism meant that the community should keep the peace among individual money-makers, and, if possible, help to create an open and thriving setting where each citizen would have some substantial opportunity to prosper.

While he argues that privatism does not illuminate the whole of the American character and does in fact exist in other cultures, it is nonetheless "the most important element" for understanding how our cities have become what they are. The privatism of realtors, speculators, and investors shaped the physical contours of the city. Economic enterprise, not community action, accounts for the welfare of the people. Political decisions were made according to the aspirations of the business community.

Warner develops his thesis by examining three conditions of eighteenth-century Philadelphia that nourished the phenomenon of privatism: its individualized structure of work, its broad prosperity, and its open society and economy. He gives us vivid portraits of family life, working conditions, the bustle of the market place, the activity of (or lack of) municipal government, and a sense of that vital center of communications, the institution of the tavern.

Privatism is a most interesting thesis and will no doubt influence the thinking of many students of the American city. And for those, nervous about its all-encompassing application, it might raise many questions. Is it overstated? Are there other forces of urbanization equally important but neglected? Can one sense economic if not cultural determinism? Indeed, *is* Philadelphia representative historically of all other American cities?

Boston: "A Citty upon a Hill"

Darrett B. Rutman

The mind of any period or people of the past is an indescribable thing, for it is a conglomerate of the ever-changing desires, prejudices, and standards of the incoherent many as well as of the vociferous few. The writings of the leading figures will echo basic assumptions which, at the given moment, guide to a degree the conduct of the generality; but the compilation of assumptions does not constitute a description of the mind. What is written or said in one place at one time may not reflect another place or another time, although the difference be only a year or a score of miles. Certainly this is true with regard to the mind of the people called Puritans who sailed from England in 1630 intending to settle somewhere in the area of Massachusetts Bay. What the laymen and ministers who led them wrote before or after their migration will tell the present little about the total movement, for it was only the great who wrote, and even their thoughts were subject to change as their condition changed, first from old England to New, then as time progressed.

The mind of one man at one place and time is clear to us, however: that of John Winthrop, lawyer, manor lord of Groton in Suffolk, England, first governor of the Massachusetts Bay commonwealth, he whom the "Chiefe undertakers" of the migration would not do without, "the welfare of the Plantation" depending "upon his goeinge" with them to the New World.[1] En route across the Atlantic on the *Arbella,* the flagship of the 1630 migration—poised, as it were, between two worlds—Winthrop prepared a lay sermon, "A Modell of Christian Charity," which he delivered to his fellow passengers. In one phrase of the peroration he summed up his thought: "Wee shall be as a Citty upon a Hill."[2]

Winthrop's expression was much more than a literary conceit borrowed from the Gospel of Matthew. It reflected the core of his thinking about the society he and his fellows intended to establish. It would be a "city," first, in the literal, physical sense, for the leaders of the Winthrop fleet—eleven ships carrying some seven hundred passengers—anticipated settling in one centralized community.[3] Within the community each settler would have his house and garden; beyond it would be the fields which the generality would cultivate and on which they would graze their cattle, and the larger farms granted to the more wealthy and prominent as their due, or for services rendered the group, or in return for their investment in the enterprise—large enclaves in the wilderness worked by servants. But the community would be the center, the seat of the church, the place of government, a fortified refuge should the Indians prove hostile or foreign enemies make an appearance.

It would be a city, secondly, in the sense of a "city of God." Man would serve God here in all the ways that

From *Winthrop's Boston: Portrait of a Puritan Town, 1630–1649* by Darrett B. Rutman. Copyright © 1965 The University of North Carolina Press. Published for the Institute of Early American History and Culture. Reprinted by permission of the publisher.

God demanded He be served. A meetinghouse where God's word in all its purity could be heard would bulk large, and men would worship God as He would have them worship. But far more: Men would serve their fellow men in this city as God would have them serve; men would fit into a society of men in such a way that the society would redound to God's credit, add luster to His crown.

The idea of a godly society predominated in Winthrop's thoughts as he crossed the Atlantic, his *Arbella* discourse being devoted to it rather than to other aspects of the city. And this was natural. For while Winthrop and his fellows of 1630 were coming from a society where ideas of Christian brotherhood and right conduct were expounded from every pulpit, where "the whole society of man" was constantly being claimed for God,[4] it was nevertheless a crass, cruel society marked by fundamental social, political, and particularly economic changes in which emerging individualism, having disrupted the social unity of the past, was proceeding to extol and enrich the greater individual at the expense of the lesser. Some men during the century antedating Winthrop had already come to the conclusion that change at the expense of brotherhood was wrong. The commonweal movement had risen, eschewing the idea that a man could seek his profit without thought of others or limitations by church or state: "If the possessioners would consider themselves to be but stewards and not lords over their possessions," Robert Crowley had written in the mid-sixteenth century, "this oppression would soon be redressed. But so long as this persuasion sticketh in their minds: It is mine own, who should warn me to do with mine own as myself listeth? it shall not be

possible to have any redress at all."[5] During the years between Crowley and Winthrop the state had intervened with a succession of statutes regulating the economy and providing for the impotent poor; the church had preached of morals and conscience and the cause of the community above private gain. But the laws remained, to 1629, largely ineffectual; the pulpit was too often ignored. "Conscience," a contemporary wrote, "is a pretty thing to carry to church but he that useth it in a fair market or shop may die a beggar."[6]

To Winthrop, England in 1622 had been "this sinfull lande."[7] And the sin he wrote of was social in nature. Two years later, in a list of "common grevances groaninge for reformation" drawn up in consultation with others, he had listed some of the causes of his dissatisfaction. Among them were those referring to the condition of the church— "the daylye encrease of the multitudes of papistes," "scandalous and dombe ministers," the "suspension and silenceing of many painfull learned ministers for not conformitie in some poynts of ceremonies." But most of Winthrop's complaints referred to lay affairs: "the common scarcitie of woode and tymber," the necessity of reforming the system for "mendinge of hie wayes," "horse stealeinge," inequitable taxation, "the greate delayes in swetes of lawe" and "the undoeinge of many poor familyes" through the actions of "the multitude of Atturnies in the Courtes" and the "multitude and lewdnesse of Baylyfs," "the pittifull complainte of the orphanes fatherlesse and many poore creditors," the "intollerably burdened" farmer subjected to abuses by the "clerke of the market."[8]

Subsequently, as he prepared to leave England in 1629, he was more pointed. God, he wrote, had given "the sons of men" the whole earth that it might "be tilld and improved by them"; he had commanded them "to encrease and multiply and replenish the earth and subdue it . . . that man may enjoye the fruit of the earth, and God may have his due glory from the Creature." But pointing to the vagrants and beggars of England's countryside and cities, the malpractices of the market, the ponderous legal machinery with which he was so familiar, the extremes of rich and poor, he asked where "is the happiness we should rest in?" "In the civill state"? "What means then the bleating of so many oppressed with wronge, that drink wormwood, for righteousness? why doe so many seely sheep that seeke shelter at the judgment seates returne without their fleeces? why meet we so many wandering ghostes in shape of men, so many spectacles of misery in all our streetes, our houses full of victuals, and our entryes of hunger-starved Christians? our shoppes full of riche wares, and under our stalles lye our own fleshe in nakednesse." "Our people perish for want of sustenance and imployment," he went on; "many others live miserably and not to the honor of so bountifull a housekeeper as the lord of heaven and earth is . . .: all our townes complain of the burden of poore people and strive by all menes to ridde any such as they have, and to keepe of[f] such as would come to them." To him, commerce was corrupt. He could not cite a single case "wherein a man may looke for recompence sutable to his expence of tyme and industrye, except falsehood be admitted to equall the ballance." Agriculture in England was uneconomic: "If we should imploye our children in that waye now, their worke would soon eate up their stocks." Redress? It "might be had in these

thinges by the magistrate, [but it] dothe not conclude that it shalbe."[9]

Winthrop himself was not personally oppressed in this society. Indeed, he was a comparatively well-to-do member of the English gentry. But his sensibilities were moved by the England about him. He dreamed of a better society, and sought the New World to make it a reality. The "Modell of Christian Charity" was his exposition of the nature of the new society he wished to establish in New England.[10]

In common with Christianity from its inception, Winthrop had of necessity to reconcile status, property, and God. He was too much a part of the seventeenth century to abandon any one of the three. God was, to him, the supreme, omnipotent, and omnipresent Prince of Heaven, the creator of all for His own purposes; God it was who had sent His son to live among men, humbly and without riches, appealing more to the poor in possessions and heart than to the wealthy and vain and promising in effect that the lowest on earth should be the highest in heaven.

Yet society, as it existed, was distinguished by its divisions into rich and poor, high and low; property existed, and the divisions of society rested largely upon its possession or lack. The mental image of God the creator and Christ who preached of rich men and eyes of needles had to be reconciled to the very real picture of property and status. Hence Winthrop began his discourse by establishing the God-ordained nature of social stratification and the ownership of property: "God Almightie in his most holy and wise providence hath soe disposed of the Condition of mankinde, as in all times some must be rich some poore, some highe and eminent in power and dignitie; others meane and in subjeccion." He had done so for a number of reasons: because His glory is made manifest in the creation of variety; because He can display His power over the wicked rich by restraining them from eating up the poor, and over the wicked poor by preventing them from rising up against their superiors; because He would have a setting in which His saints could display themselves, the sainted rich by their love, mercy, gentleness, the sainted poor by their faith, patience, obedience; and finally, He had arranged mankind in orders so that all men might have need for one another. The conclusion Winthrop desired was easily and logically drawn from such a godly and purposeful arrangement: No man is made more honorable or rich out of respect of himself, but for the purposes of God; God therefore has a first call upon his property.

Yet all too obviously there was a misuse of property and position in Winthrop's England and in the world at large, for the rich regularly ate the sustenance of the poor and, on occasion, the poor rose up against the rich. In the lore of Christianity and the Protestant theology of the churches of England, Winthrop found the solution. Man, living in the light of God, would have that perfect love toward God and mankind which would result in a godly use of property. Adam, before the fall, had such love, but Adam had wrenched himself and his posterity from his creator. As a consequence, love for one's brother was corrupted: "Every man is borne with this principle in him, to love and seeke himselfe onely." In this condition he would remain "till Christ comes and takes possession of the soule," gathering together the scattered bones of "perfect old man Adam" and infusing

a new principle, "Love to God and our brother."

Looking out over the passengers aboard the *Arbella,* seeing in his mind's eye the men and women aboard the *Ambrose, Talbot, William and Francis,* and the other vessels of the fleet—men and women gathered together through the efforts of himself and his friends— Winthrop thought of the settlers as either actually or potentially infused with this regenerating principle. "Wee are a Company professing our selves fellow members of Christ," he wrote; before, in England, we were scattered, "absent from eache other many miles, and had our imploymentes as farre distant." But having embarked on this voyage "wee ought to account our selves knitt together by this bond of love, and live in the exercise of it." Status and property would then assume their proper position as godly gifts, given for God's purposes. Specifically, Winthrop asked charity of the settlers— the giving of one's abundance in ordinary times, and the giving even beyond one's means on extraordinary occasions. He would have them temper the spirit of commerce with mercy, giving where it was necessary, lending only where feasible in terms of the capability of the recipient to repay, forgiving a debt when the debtor could not pay.

Winthrop's vision of Christian "love" involved more than mere mercy and charity, however. It embodied his desire for form, unity, and stability in society. Without Christian love, he wrote, society could never be perfect. Men would strive after their own good without thought of the well-being either of their fellows in the society or of the society as a whole. The community resulting from such individuality would be no more than an association of independent objects "as disportionate and as much disordering as soe many contrary quallities or elements." On the other hand, Christian love pervading the society would serve as the "ligament" binding the individual members to the one body. Individuality would remain, but "all the partes of this body being thus united" would be "soe contiguous in a speciall relacion as they must needes partake of each others strength and infirmity, joy, and sorrowe, weale and woe." "This sensiblenes and Sympathy of each others Conditions will necessarily infuse into each parte a native desire and endeavour, to defend preserve and comfort the other." Implicitly, each member of the body would have its place and duty in the total structure, some to serve, others to be served, some to rule, others to be ruled, all happily accepting their place and work for the benefit of all. Winthrop's simile was man's mouth, which "is at all the paines to receive, and mince the foode which serves for the nourishment of all the other partes of the body, yet it hath noe cause to complaine; for . . . the other partes send backe by secret passages a due proporcion of the same nourishment in a better forme for the strengthening and comforteing the mouthe."

"Goe forth, every man that goeth, with a publick spirit, looking not on your owne things onely," John Cotton, the eminent minister of Boston, England, had exhorted the *Arbella's* passengers in his farewell sermon.[11] Winthrop, describing the individual's duty in the model society, echoed him: "The care of the publique must oversway all private respects." "Wee must love brotherly without dissimulation, wee must love one another with a pure heart fervently wee must beare one anothers burthens, wee must not looke onely on our owne things, but allsoe on the things of our brethren." Conscience tells us this, Winthrop preached, but so too does necessity, for recall that we are going to a strange, forbidding land where dangers and difficulties will constantly beset us. "Wee must be knitt together in this work as one man, wee must entertaine each other in brotherly affeccion, wee must be willing to abridge our selves of superfluities, for the supply of others necessities, wee must uphold a familiar Commerce together in all meekness, gentlenes, patience and liberallitie, we must delight in each other, make others Conditions our owne[,] rejoyce together, mourne together, labour, and suffer together." And, finally, the settlers were to do these things not by command of the magistrate (the law having proved futile in England when it sought to impose itself on the spirit) but by virtue of the godly nature of that love which joined them together. Whatever coercion Winthrop would invoke would not be man's, but God's. We have a covenant with Him, he said; we have accepted the obligation to live in such a way that ourselves and our posterity might be better preserved from the common corruptions of the world; if we should fail and embrace this present world, pursue carnal intentions, the Lord will break out in wrath against us.

In his discourse, Winthrop did not deal with the nature of government and church, though perhaps these subjects had been contemplated to some extent by the leaders while still in England.[12] Yet his view of the nature of government is implicit both in his discussion of men rich and poor, "highe and eminent in power and dignitie;

others meane and in subjection," and in his comment about the covenant binding the settlers with God. The first thought took cognizance of the natural disparity between men which Winthrop, as the master of Groton, could not help accepting and which the English pulpit constantly pronounced as God's will, minister William Perkins, for example, writing that "God hath appointed that in every societie one person should be above or under another; not making all equall, as though the bodie should be all head and nothing else."[13] Reacting against conditions in England, however, Winthrop could not allow natural disparities to go untempered: Power was not a right of the mighty but a godly duty to deal in "love, mercy, gentlenes, temperance" with those in subjection.

The second thought pertaining to government in the "Modell" reflected the pervasive contemporary view of the nature of the state which held that man in society selected the forms and personnel of government by way of a compact, and then bound himself to that government. In the western world, this idea of contract—or compact, or covenant—was ancient, but it was particularly relevant for the religious polemicists of the sixteenth and seventeenth centuries. The French *Vindiciae Contra Tyrannos*, establishing a philosophic basis for Protestants to rebel against a Catholic king, argued for the sovereignty of the people and the contracts which a people, as a people of God, made with God that "it will remain the people of God" and with its ruler "to obey the king truly while he rules truly."[14] Protestant England wrote of the "covenant and bargaine" inherent in the coronation of the king by which "the people is bound and sworne to

doe their allegance to their Kings, so the Kings are also solemnly sworne to maintaine and defend true Religion, the estate of Justice, the peace and tranquility of their subjects, and the right and priviledges (which are nothing but the Lawes) of the Realme."[15] Richard Hooker, in his *Ecclesiastical Polity*, would have kings hold "their right to the power of dominion, with dependency upon the whole entire body politic over which they rule as kings," though he attempted to avoid the tendency toward revolutionary doctrine by confirming the divine nature of kings once established. "God creating mankind did endue it naturally with full power to guide itselv, in what kind of societies soever it should choose to live," yet those on whom power "is bestowed even at men's discretion, they likewise do hold it by divine right," for "albeit God do neither appoint the thing nor assign the person; nevertheless when men have established both, who doth doubt but that sundry duties and offices depending thereupon are prescribed in the world of God." Therefore, Hooker concluded, "we by the law of God stand bound meekly to acknowledge them for God's lieutenants."[16]

From the aura of his times and from the Gospel—for he cited only the Gospels as his authority—Winthrop derived his own idea of the covenant. He spoke of the settlers having "entered into Covenant" with the Lord by virtue of their having committed themselves to His protection on the voyage and in the land where they were going. The covenant, though, was in the simplest of terms: their agreement to be God's people, to live in a godly fashion— that fashion which Winthrop had already outlined in terms of Christian love—in return for which "the Lord will be our God and delight to dwell among us." Having said this, he needed to say nothing more about government, for the divisions of rich and poor, rulers and ruled, were ordained by God. Consequently, in his city, the natural leaders —the wealthy, the gentlemen—would rule in the interest of the people, seeking "their welfare in all things,"[17] and the people would accept the government of these natural leaders out of their own God-ordained duty to "faithe, patience, obedience."

Only subsequently would Winthrop elaborate on the covenant between the rulers and ruled. Fifteen years later, to the Massachusetts General Court and through it to the populace, he was to define the covenant in terms of "the oath you have taken of us"—the oath of fidelity required of all inhabitants by that time—"which is to this purpose, that we shall govern you and judge your causes by the rules of God's laws and our own, according to our best skill." But the governors were not self-appointed; they were, rather, God-appointed through the people. "It is yourselves," he said, "who have called us to this office, and being called by you, we have our authority from God, in a way of ordinance, such as hath the image of God eminently stamped upon it, the contempt and violation whereof hath been vindicated with examples of divine vengeance."[18]

In contemplating the nature of the church, Winthrop also undoubtedly derived his ideas from the aura of his times, most notably from the assumptions of the churches of England. His terminology in the "Modell of Christian Charity" was that of English Calvinism. He saw the effects of the difficult economic and social adjustment in England

in terms of the depravity of man. His own social attitudes and those he would have the settlers adopt were phrased in terms of the regeneration of man. He reflected faithfully the utter dependence of man upon God in effecting this regeneration, quoting the Apostle John in describing his Christian love, the ligament of the new society. "Love cometh of god and every one that loveth is borne of god, soe that this love is the fruite of the new birthe, and none can have it but the new Creature."

Yet Winthrop expressed social ideas in theological terms only because there were no other terms available to him, not because they formed the basis of his thought. He was not bound by the logic of the theology he expressed; indeed, he regularly violated that logic. His equating of Christian love with "new birthe," for example, echoed basic Calvinism and its relegation of man to the status of "an empty vessel" awaiting God's pleasure in filling it, a mute, inactive recipient of God's free grace. But there is no indication that Winthrop in his *Arbella* discourse was directing his words to a particular body of love-infused saints within the total number of settlers, nor was there a thought in the "Modell" or elsewhere in Winthrop's writings of the impossibility of creating a society bound by Christian love when the persons embarked on the attempt included (as they must have included) regenerates and reprobates, saints and sinners. There is, then, the paradox in the "Modell" of anticipating a society of saints and sinners held together by a quality available only to the saints.

The paradox, though it does not disappear, becomes at least explicable on realizing the confused, chaotic, and contradictory thought of the English churches from which Winthrop was emerging. There was the England of the Thirty-Nine Articles of Faith, a reiteration of basic Calvinism, but there was also the England which had drifted away from Calvin to pronounce that "despite the fact that man cannot will himself into salvation [or into Winthrop's Christian love], nonetheless he does possess the capacity to cooperate with and consent to God's will to save him."[19] There was the England, too, which had gone even further, exceeding the limitations on ministerial activity inherent in Calvinism by actively soliciting conversion, as when Hugh Peter prayed for the Queen that "the light of Goshen might shine into her soul, and that she might not perish in the day of Christ" or reported his activity at St. Sepulchre in London: "There was six or seven thousand Hearers, and the circumstances fit for such good work" that "above an hundred every week were persuaded from sin to Christ."[20] As one modern study expresses it, "the very activities of an intensely proselytizing and evangelical church, as early [English] Protestantism was, are directly contradictory, in terms of simple logic, to strict predestinarian doctrine. Indeed, the whole literature of English Protestantism is a product of ministerial enthusiasm which seems constantly to be overstepping the limits which logically it has set for itself."[21] In this climate, is it too much to expect that Winthrop should pay homage to God's free grace and proceed illogically to the optimistic view of man's ability to rise above his depraved nature by himself and form a godly society on earth? For in the last analysis, the "Modell of Christian Charity" is an optimistic document. All the men and women of the migration were considered to be capable of that Christian love for brothers and for the community necessary to the creation of a godly city. Christians all, the settlers were "to worke upon their heartes, by prayer meditacion continuall exercise . . . till Christ be formed in them and they in him all in eache other knitt together by this bond of love."

In still another area—that of church polity—English thought was confused. On the one hand, the religious establishment constituted a national church embracing the total population of England; it was, too, an authoritarian church, pyramidally organized from the peak of earthly authority (the king) downward through archbishops, bishops, and priests to the lowly communicant. On the other hand, however, theory held that original authority rested in the individual congregations within the church and was merely delegated upward. Richard Hooker, in constructing a philosophic basis for the episcopal hierarchy, had written of "the whole body of the Church being the first original subject of all mandatory and coercive power within itself." That the churches in England had granted power to a higher body and even a single man (as had the people of England with regard to the state) did not diminish the validity of the concept of original power residing at the bottom, and Hooker could even envision the congregations drawing power back to themselves in extreme cases. Theory also held that there were in reality two churches, one visible, one invisible. Hooker, concerned as he was with the visible institutional church of all Englishmen, nevertheless recognized the true saints of the invisible church as well, "that Church of Christ, which we

properly term his body mystical" and
which resides within the body of the
institutional church but cannot be "sen-
sibly discerned by any man," only by
God. William Perkins, too, spoke of the
church as a "mixt . . . companie of
men . . . true beleevers and hypocrites
mingled together," the believers being
the invisible church known to God, the
totality being the visible church of man.
James Ussher, on the other side of
many doctrinal fences from Perkins,
similarly acknowledged the outer church
but stressed that true membership was
confined to those who "are by the Spirit
and Faith secretly and inseparably con-
joyned unto Christ their head." And
along with some other English Protestants, he strained the logical barrier—
that God, not man, identifies His saints
—to advise the godly to shun the ungodly, "to renounce all fellowship with
sin and sinners" and keep company
with "one another in faith and love . . .
in the society of the Saints."22 The
espousal of the communion of the elect
was the antithesis of the principle of
a national church.

As Winthrop and his companions
sailed, English religious thought was—
as it had been for long, and would be
for longer yet—in the throes of a reconciliation of its innate contradictions.
Orthodox Anglicanism was being ham-
mered out, and with it dissent. The
process was agonizing, the intellectual
air electric with clashing doctrines, the
disputations of the clerics in print and
pulpit a thunderous discord. The forms
and practices of worship were in constant dispute as many, frequently the
most ardent and zealous of the church-
men, called for a wiping away of the
last vestiges of Catholicism and a return
to the verities of the primitive church of
the first centuries after Christ. The
mingling of godly and ungodly within

the church, at times under the spiritual care of ministers who were themselves ungodly, was for some church-
men a most heinous error. Such clerics
stressed the communion of the elect at
the expense of the national church and
sought, by excluding the palpably ungodly, to form a rough correlation between the visible and invisible churches.
They tended, moreover, to accent the
congregational nature of the churches.
Finding in their studies of the New
Testament and the "fathers" of the
church that the primitive church had
been congregationally organized, they
considered the hierarchy of prelates
found in England an aberration from
Christ's pure structure and, going
beyond Hooker's theoretic congregationalism, they argued for a return of
actual authority to the English congregations. Here and there extremists renounced the English churches entirely,
declared them "false and counterfeit,"
and set about establishing separatist
congregations, voluntarily covenanting
together to live as a people of God
under ministers of their own choosing
(rather than ministers set over them
by a bishop), free to discipline their
own membership, and admitting to
communion and to the baptism of
their children only those who, "so far
as men in charity could judge," were
"justified, sanctified, and entitled to
the promises of salvation, and life
eternal."23 Their course was a dangerous one, for separation was anathema to the English mind and such
"schismatics" were subject to persecution. But their number was small.
More normally the dissenting ministers
remained within the national church
as nonconformists, accepting the establishment with all its errors in the hopes
of an ultimate reformation, all the
while using casuistry and taking advan-

tage of the relative laxness of the hierarchy prior to the late 1620's and early 1630's to purify their services and, in some cases, profess in varying degrees and ways a vague and ill-defined congregationalism devoid of separatist connotations.

Winthrop and the leaders of the 1630 migration emerged from that area of England most affected by the dissenting zeal—London and the eastern counties from Kent to Lincoln; they were themselves zealous in their desire to cleave to God and undoubtedly familiar to an extent with the various arguments put forth by their ardent ministers. But as a group they do not appear as advocates of any precise synthesis.[24] They sailed as English Protestants and went out of their way to say so in *The Humble Request* to the congregations of England written and published as they departed. Belief was not leading them to separate from the English church, they wrote; the church was, rather, "our deare Mother," and they drew a parallel between themselves sailing to the New World to establish another church and the primitive church of Philippi "which was a colonie from Rome."[25] Winthrop's own writings reflect not that he had chosen between the contradictions in English religious thought, but the contradictions themselves. The very act of leaving sinful England to found a godly city was an expression of the idea of the communion of the elect; but the joining together of the godly and ungodly in the attempt (even with undertones of the ungodly being capable of conversion from sin to the good life) implied the idea of a universal church. The contradiction between the two went unresolved.

In the New World, however, resolution would be forced upon Win-throp and his followers. There they would be faced with the necessity of forming churches as centers for new communities without an existing prelacy to which the congregations could delegate power; they would find churches at Plymouth and Salem composed of the professedly godly and organized on a congregational basis. There, too, the newcomers would drift into the same practices, drawing upon the knowledge of congregational theory which they brought from England and using Salem and Plymouth as models. Yet the drift was not without difficulties, indicating that the practices they were to adopt were not implicit in Winthrop's "Citty upon a Hill." Indeed, Winthrop's initial contact with the congregational practices of Salem was seemingly something of a surprise. On first landing, he and some of his companions appeared at the Salem church seeking communion for themselves and the baptism of a child born at sea. They came, as they would to any church in England, to take advantage of the facilities held out to all. But Salem refused to accept them inasmuch as the church there had come to hold that the seals of the church (baptism and communion) should be offered only to covenanted members and those recommended by a similarly organized congregation. One or more of the Winthrop group was disturbed enough by the incident to report it to the Reverend John Cotton in England, prompting that worthy divine to write a critical letter to the Salem minister about the church's practices.[26]

Subsequently the leaders and ministers among the settlers found themselves divided over church polity. Samuel Fuller, who, together with others from Plymouth and Salem, was free with his advice as to the form of church organization which the newcomers should adopt, wrote of holding long wearisome conferences with the ministers and lay leaders of the Bay. "Opposers" of the Plymouth-Salem way "there is not wanting, and satan is busy," he reported to Governor William Bradford at Plymouth. The Reverend John Warham argued for a church organization in line with contemporary English practice, a universal church consisting "of a mixed people,—godly, and openly ungodly." Some of the leaders of the Winthrop fleet apparently insisted that the Reverend George Phillips should minister to them by virtue of his English ordination rather than a congregational call, for Phillips told Fuller during a private conference "that if they will have him stand minister, by that calling which he received from the prelates in England, he will leave them." (Years later Cotton Mather was to write that Phillips was, from the standpoint of what would become New England orthodoxy, "better acquainted with the true *church-discipline* than most of the ministers that came with him into the country.") The Reverend John Wilson, on the other hand, seemed more amenable in this regard, for he was to accept the call of the church gathered at Charlestown "with this protestation by all, that it was only as a sign of election and confirmation, not of any intent that [he] should renounce his ministery he received in England."[27]

That Winthrop and his compatriots sailed without a precise idea of the nature of the church they were to erect should not be surprising. The Winthrop migration was a lay movement, not clerical. "Able and sufficient Ministers" were sought after to journey with the settlers, for religion was an integral part of life.[28] But notably few ministers were willing to hazard themselves in the venture in 1629 and 1630. Only later would they come, and then eagerly, seeking sanctuary from Archbishop William Laud's attempt to create a Church of England out of the diverse churches of England.

As a lay movement, the ideals of 1630 were lay ideals, social, rather than religious, though to the extent that the church was a part of the social organization, it too would be reformed. Winthrop quite obviously did not subscribe to all the practices of the English church. His 1964 catalogue of "common grevances groaninge for reformation" included criticisms of the establishment, particularly the conduct of that part of the ministry which was corrupted by impoverishment and intent upon the pursuit of security in this world rather than the next; he preferred a simplicity of religious service, yet he conformed to the forms and practices of England, considering that "ceremonyes ar by our ch[urch] of England holden to be put thinges indifferent."[29] His great peculiarity, however, was his intensity, his literal application to society of the Biblical injunction to "love thy neighbor as thyself." Time after time this intensity— and its origin in the pulpit pronouncements and polemic literature of Protestant England—appears in his writings. As to "the estate of our Churche and Com[mon]w[ealth]," he wrote just prior to the migration, "let the grones and fears of Godes people give a silent answer: If our condition be good, why doe his Embassadours [the ministers] turne their messages into complaintes and threateninges? why doe they so constantly denounce wrathe and judgment against us? why doe they pray so muche for healinge if we be not sicke?"[30] And on the *Arbella*, summing up the duties of the citizen in the godly society, he preached, "Whatsoever wee did or ought to have done when wee lived in England, the same must wee doe and more allsoe where wee goe: That which the most in theire Churches maineteine as a truthe in profession onely, wee must bring into familiar and constant practise."

One can call Winthrop a "Puritan," but not in the sense of his holding to a logical edifice of theology and polity. He was a Puritan only in the most limited of senses—that of Perry Miller when he writes of "the Augustinian strain of piety" which leads men to that futile search for a road to bring them face to face with truth, God; of Alan Simpson and James F. Maclear when they write of Puritanism as a "blind thrust," an "unbelievable intensity" of feeling toward God and fellow man, "deep emotional longings for personal encounter and direct communion with God"; and of William Perkins when he described "Puritans and Presitions" as "those that most indeavour to get and keepe the puritie of heart in a good conscience."[31] Similarly, one can term Winthrop's errand to the New World "religious" in but the simplest sense of the word. His was a blind thrust into the wilderness, undertaken precipitously—there is no evidence of his preparing to remove prior to 1629—and without elaborate planning. Fear lay behind the movement to America, fear of the successes of Catholicism in the Counter Reformation then in progress. But more important as a motivating factor was what can be termed Winthrop's "social conscience"—his concern for the generality of an England which to him was growing "wearye of her Inhabitantes, so as man which is the most

pretious of all Creatures, is heere more vile and base, then the earthe they treade upon"—and his vision of a new society, perhaps one which in God's good time the rest of the world would emulate, a setting in which salvation would be more readily obtainable for himself and all who desired to live in Christ's shadow.[32] In the broadest sense of the word, too, one can call Winthrop a "utopian" as he crossed the Atlantic aboard the *Arbella*, a dreamer of heaven on earth; he would have Christian love pervade the new society, while holding that "to love and live beloved is the soules paradice, both heare and in heaven."

Ironically, however, Winthrop was doomed to failure, in large measure by the very land he chose for his venture. Reacting to the contemporary English scene, he envisioned a society in which men would subordinate themselves to their brothers' and the community's good, but he sought to erect that society in a land where opportunity for individual profit lay ready to every hand. And Winthrop's optimism that man could overcome his own nature—so illogical in view of his apparent Calvinism—was to prove sadly misplaced. Speaking aboard the *Arbella*, his was but one small voice, one mind, among hundreds; his dream was not necessarily that of the whole number of settlers, nor of those who would arrive in the commonwealth in the years ahead. On the contrary, to judge by actions in the New World, his was the exceptional mind. In America, the acquisitive instincts of the contemporary Englishman would rush to the surface, overwhelming Winthrop's communal ideal; conflicting minds would fragment the society which Winthrop would have perfectly united in thought, speech, judgment, and, above all, God's holy love. Institutions—defined as the various postures the community assumes in undertaking specific functions—would initially display the marks of Winthrop's ideal, but their evolution would reflect other minds and the new land. The process of disruption would begin immediately upon landing. Within two months a stunned Winthrop would write of Satan bending "his forces against us . . . so that I thinke heere are some persons who never shewed so much wickednesse in England as they have doone heer." Within five years another would comment that in leaving England men of pure hearts had "made an ill change, even from the snare to the pitt."[33] Within twenty years, Winthrop—who had rejected the vision of modern man he had seen in England and sought the refuge of a secular monastery (for that is what this "Citty upon a Hill" sums up to)—would be dead, and his commonwealth would be distinctly modern.

NOTES

1. "Perticular Considerations in the case of J:W: [1629]," in Massachusetts Historical Society, *Winthrop Papers*, 5 vols. (Boston, 1929-47), II, 133, hereafter cited as *Winthrop Papers*.
2. Matt. 5:14; "A Modell of Christian Charity," *Winthrop Papers*, II, 282-95. Except where otherwise noted, all quotations in this chapter are from the "Modell."
3. In the absence of a direct statement, the intent of the leadership to settle a single community must be assumed from the evidence of what happened. For elaboration, see Appendix I.
4. Charles H. and Katherine George, *The Protestant Mind of the English Reformation, 1570-1640* (Princeton, 1961), 183.
5. Quoted in Stanley T. Bindoff, *Tudor England* (Harmondsworth, Eng., 1950), 131.
6. Quoted in Wallace Notestein, *The English People on the Eve of Colonization, 1603-1630* (New York, 1954), 22.
7. Winthrop to Thomas Fones, Jan. 29, 1621/22, *Winthrop Papers*, I, 268.
8. Winthrop, "Common Grevances Groaninge for Reformation," ca. Feb-Mar., 1623/24, *ibid.*, 295 ff.

9. Winthrop, "General Observations [For the Plantation of New England, 1629]," and Winthrop to [?], 1629, *ibid.*, II, 115, 122-23.
10. In the absence of a major modern work on Winthrop, his own writings constitute his best biography; hence, because it is so replete with quotations, Robert C. Winthrop's *Life and Letters of John Winthrop . . .* , 2 vols. (Boston, 1864-67), is the most adequate. Highly suggestive, however, is Edmund S. Morgan, *The Puritan Dilemma: The Story of John Winthrop* (Boston and Toronto, 1958). Winthrop's political and to a lesser extent social thought have been the subject of occasional commentary, most notably by Stanley Gray, "The Political Thought of John Winthrop," *New England Quarterly*, 3 (1930), 681-705, and George L. Mosse, *The Holy Pretence: A Study in Christianity and Reasons of State from William Perkins to John Winthrop* (Oxford, 1957), chap. 6.
11. John Cotton, *Gods Promise to His Plantation . . .* (London, 1630), 19.
12. Arthur Tyndal to Winthrop, Nov. 10, 1629, *Winthrop Papers*, II, 166.
13. Williams Perkins, *The Works of That Famous and Worthie Minister of Christ*, 3 vols. (London, 1612-13), I, 755.
14. Quoted in Sir Ernest Barker, *Church, State and Education* (Ann Arbor, 1957), 87-88. On the impact of the *Vindiciae* in England see J. H. Salmon, *The French Religious Wars in England Political Thought* (Oxford, 1959), *passim*.
15. Thomas Beard, *The Theatre of God's Judgements . . .* , 3rd ed. (London, 1648), 10.
16. Richard Hooker, *Of the Laws of Ecclesiastical Polity*, Bk. VIII [1648], chap. 2, par. 5-6, 9, as reprinted in *The Works of . . . Mr. Richard Hooker*, 7th ed. (Oxford, 1887).
17. Thomas Hutchinson, comp., *A Collection of Original Papers Relative to the History of the Colony of Massachusetts-Bay* (Boston, 1769), 100.
18. James Kendall Hosmer, ed., *[John] Winthrop's Journal "History of New England," 1630-1649*, 2 vols. (N.Y., 1908), II, 237-39; hereafter cited as *Winthrop's Journal*.
19. George and George, *Protestant Mind of the English Reformation*, 64-65, quoting Bishop Lancelot Andrewes.
20. Quoted in Raymond Phineas Stearns, *The Strenuous Puritan: Hugh Peter, 1598-1660* (Urbana, 1954), 36, 44.
21. George and George, *Protestant Mind of the English Reformation*, 58.
22. Hooker, *Ecclesiastical Polity*, Bk. VIII, chap. 6, par. 3; Bk. III [1594], chap. 1, par. 2; Perkins, *Works*, III, 16; James Ussher, *A Body of Divinitie or The Summe and Substance of Christian Religion . . .* , 5th ed. (London, 1658), 188, 191.
23. *A True Confession of the Faith, and Humble Acknowledgment of the Alegeance, Which Wee Hir Majesties Subjects, Falsely Called Brownists, Doo Hould [towards] God, and Yield to Hir Majestie* (n.p., 1596), as reprinted in Williston

Walker, ed., *The Creeds and Platforms of Congregationalism*, Pilgrim Press ed. (Boston, 1960), 51; John Robinson, quoted in Edmund S. Morgan, *Visible Saints: The History of a Puritan Idea* (N. Y., 1963), 57.

24. See below, chap. 3, pp. 47-48, and Appendix II.

25. *The Humble Request of His Majesties Loyall Subjects, the Governour and the Company Late Gone for New England; to the Rest of Their Brethren in and of the Church of England* (London, 1630), as reprinted in *Winthrop Papers*, II, 232.

26. The child was William Coddingtons. *A Sermon Preached by the Reverend, Mr. John Cotton, Teacher of the First Church in Boston in New England. Deliver'd at Salem, [June] 1636* . . . (Boston, 1713), 1-2; John Cotton to Samuel Skelton, Oct. 2, 1630, in Thaddeus Mason Harris, *Memorials of the First Church in Dorchester* (Boston, 1830), 53-57.

27. Samuel Fuller to William Bradford, June 28, 1630, Mass. Hist. Soc., *Collections*, 1st Ser., 3 (1794), 75; Cotton Mather, *Magnalia Christi Americana; or, the Ecclesiastical History of New-England* . . . , 2 vols. (Hartford, 1853), I, 377; *Winthrop's Journal*, I, 51.

28. John Winthrop and others to [?], Oct. 27, 1629, *Winthrop Papers*, II, 163-64.

29. "Common Grevances," *ibid.*, I, 295 ff. 305; Christopher Hill, *Economic Problems of the Church: From Archbishop Whitgift to the Long Parliament* (Oxford, 1956), chap. 9.

30. Winthrop to [?], 1629, *Winthrop Papers*, II, 121.

31. Perry Miller, *The New England Mind: The Seventeenth Century*, Beacon Press ed. (Boston, 1961), 3 ff.; Alan Simpson, *Puritanism in Old and New England* (Chicago, 1955), 21, and *passim*; James Fulton Maclear, " 'The Heart of New England Rent': The Mystical Element in Early Puritan History," *Mississippi Valley Historical Review*, 42 (1956), 623; Perkins, *Works*, III, 15.

32. "General Observations," *Winthrop Papers*, II, 114.

33. Winthrop to Margaret Winthrop, July 23, 1630, and Nathaniel Ward to John Winthrop, Jr., Dec. 24, [1635], *ibid.*, 303, III, 216.

Philadelphia: The Private City

SAM BASS WARNER

American cities have grown with the general culture of the nation, not apart from it. Late eighteenth-century Philadelphia was no exception. Its citizens, formerly the first wave of a Holy Experiment, had been swept up in the tide of secularization and borne on by steady prosperity to a modern view of the world. Like the Puritans of Massachusetts and Connecticut, the Quakers of Pennsylvania had proved unable to sustain the primacy of religion against the solvents of cheap land and private opportunity. Quaker, Anglican, Presbyterian, Methodist, Pietist—each label had its social and political implications—but all congregations shared in the general American secular culture of privatism.[1]

Already by the time of the Revolution privatism had become the American tradition. Its essence lay in its concentration upon the individual and the individual's search for wealth. Psychologically, privatism meant that the individual should seek happiness in personal independence and in the search for wealth; socially, privatism meant that the individual should see his first loyalty as his immediate family, and that a community should be a union of such money-making, accumulating families; politically, privatism meant that the community should keep the peace among individual money-makers, and, if possible, help to create an open and thriving setting where each citizen would have some substantial opportunity to prosper.

To describe the American tradition of privatism is not to summarize the entire American cultural tradition. Privatism lies at the core of many modern cultures; privatism alone will not distinguish the experience of America from that of other nations. The tradition of privatism is, however, the most important element of our culture for understanding the development of cities. The tradition of privatism has always meant that the cities of the United States depended for their wages, employment, and general prosperity upon the aggregate successes and failures of thousands of individual enterprises, not upon community action. It has also meant that the physical forms of American cities, their lots, houses, factories, and streets have been the outcome of a real estate market of profit-seeking builders, land speculators, and large investors. Finally, the tradition of privatism has meant that the local politics of American cities have depended for their actors, and for a good deal of their subject matter, on the changing focus of men's private economic activities.[2]

In the eighteenth century the tradition of privatism and the social and economic environment of colonial towns nicely complemented each other. Later as towns grew to big cities, and big cities grew to metropolises, the tradi-

From *The Private City: Philadelphia in Three Periods of Its Growth* (Philadelphia: University of Pennsylvania Press, 1968), pp. 3-11; 14-21. Reprinted by permission of the publisher.

tion became more and more ill-suited to the realities of urban life. The tradition assumed that there would be no major conflict between private interest, honestly and liberally viewed, and the public welfare. The modes of eighteenth-century town life encouraged this expectation that if each man would look to his own prosperity the entire town would prosper. And so it had.

Founded in 1682 under William Penn's liberal instructions, and settled first with Quaker artisans and a few Quaker merchants, the town had since prospered as the capital of a thriving colony.[3] By 1720 Philadelphia was said to have 10,000 inhabitants; by 1775 it had more than doubled to 23,700.[4] The townsite bordered the Delaware and Schuylkill rivers, both of which tapped rich forests and excellent farm lands. The line of north-south trade ran nearby, and Philadelphia also lay within reach of the Susquehanna and Potomac rivers openings to the west. Philadelphia, thus, soon excelled in most of the staples of colonial trade, exporting furs, lumber, staves, iron, wheat, and flour, and importing rum, sugar, wine, and English manufactures.

Conditions outside the colony encouraged a heavy immigration of new settlers. Because Pennsylvania had been founded late, by comparison to other Atlantic colonies, west-bound space abounded on ships sailing from Great Britain and the Low Countries. Quakers, of course, fleeing persecution in England came to the colony in large numbers, but by the early eighteenth century their group came to be rivaled by Scotch-Irish and German immigrants. The Act of Union joining Scotland to England opened up the entire British Empire to poor Scots, while

Irish wars and famines, and rack-renting landlords drove their fellow Presbyterians from Ulster. On the continent west German peasants fled the destruction of Louis XIV's repeated wars. Finally, in America the Indian control of upstate New York deflected the flow of westward settlers south to Pennsylvania. The result of all these outside events was a boom in the colony and the town; Pennsylvania and Philadelphia had everything, settlers, natural resources, capital, religious freedom, and comparatively little government.[5]

Within the town three conditions confirmed its privatism—its individualized structure of work, its general prosperity, and its open society and economy. When eighteenth-century Philadelphians spoke of the individual and his search for wealth as the goal of government they were simply basing their political arguments on the common place facts of town life. The core element of the town economy was the one-man shop. Most Philadelphians labored alone, some with a helper or two. A storekeeper tended his shop by himself or with the aid of his family or a servant. Craftsmen often worked with an apprentice, or more rarely with another skilled man.[6]

More than at later times, this Philadelphia was a town of entrepreneurs. Artisans sewed shoes, made wagons, boiled soap, or laid bricks for customers who had already placed an order. Workers did not labor under the close price and time disciplines of manufacture for large-scale inventories or big speculative wholesale markets. Most Philadelphians were either independent contractors hiring out on a job-by-job basis, or they were artisan shopkeepers retailing the products of their work. Even the establishment of a large merchant more resembled a small store than a modern wholesale house. Such a merchant frequently had a partner and the two partners carried on the business with the aid of a full-time clerk and an apprentice or servant to help with errands.[7] When a cargo arrived at the pier the partners would hire some laborers to unload the goods and move them to the storehouse. Thus, a very large proportion of the town's men—artisans, shopkeepers, and merchants—shared the common experience of the individual entrepreneur.

In later years the work groups of factories, offices, stores, and constructions crews would have enormous significance for the discipline, acculturation, and education of Philadelphia's residents. Such groups were almost entirely absent from the eighteenth-century town. Shipyard, ropewalk, and distillery workers labored in groups of five and even ten, but theirs were exceptionally large urban production units. In the colonial era the plantation, whether for agriculture or manufacture, was the characteristic place of large work gangs.[8] In 1775, associated with Philadelphia's general run of family enterprises were only about 900 indentured servants, 600 slaves, and perhaps 200 hired servants who lived with their employers.[9] These helpers shared the discipline of family life and work; they did not live by the modes of the work gang. Taken all together the eighteenth-century exceptions to the entrepreneurial role had but little significance for the functioning of the town's society.

A German visitor of 1750 wrote: "Pennsylvania is heaven for farmers, paradise for artisans, and hell for officials and preachers."[10] By the same token, Philadelphia on the eve of the Revolution was a town of freedom and abundance for the common man. For young persons there was a great demand for apprentices in all lines of work. An unskilled laborer without connections could find work with board and wages to begin accumulating a little money for tools. An artisan who wanted to carry a few shopkeeping goods in his shop, or a storekeeper with a good reputation, could get his stock from the merchant and settle for his advance a year later.

The ordinary artisan or shopkeeper, if his health was good, could be assured of a comfortable, if frugal, living. To be sure, houses were small and rents high, and furnishings were spare compared to later levels of living: no carpets, no upholstered furniture, a sand-scrubbed floor, and whitewashed walls. Stoves and fireplaces only partially heated drafty rooms, and in severe winters the cost of firewood or imported coal was a major item of family expense. Nevertheless, at the city's markets food was cheap and plentiful. The earnings of the ordinary artisan and shopkeeper could support a wife and children without their having to take outside employment. The rapid growth of the town and its trade meant regular work and good earnings for artisans and easy business, if not wealth, for shopkeepers.[11]

Although the customary hours of work were long, sunrise to sunset, the pace of work was often easy and varied with the season. Those who worked outside their homes, like men in the building trades, took an hour for breakfast, a break in the middle of the day, and an hour for dinner in the afternoon. Coopers, shoemakers, smiths, and men who practiced their craft in their own houses and yards must have stopped work as customers and friends came in, and a trip or two to the local tavern must also have been usual. Although there were no formal vacations, the traditional English holidays and frequent *ad hoc* town celebrations provided about twenty days off each year.

Franklin's *Autobiography* abounds with injunctions for regular habits, and the reputation for diligence he established by staying at his bench for the entire formal working day suggests that his was an extraordinary pace. For most workers rush seasons of hard work and long hours alternated with slack times. These variations meant days for fishing or spare moments for gossip on the streets and visits to the tavern.

Such a commonplace prosperity, generous at least by eighteenth-century standards, confirmed the privatism of the town and its age. As important a confirmation came from the openness of its economy and society. The failure of the craft guilds to control the trades of the town gave newcomers and resident artisans alike an occupational freedom unknown in Europe. Shopkeepers and artisans—and often one man was both—could take up any craft or open any line of business they wished. Although Philadelphia had inherited English regulations favoring the "freemen" of the town, established artisans could not maintain their control of the town's businesses against newcomers. The carpenters and cordwainers managed to form associations to set prices for their work, but failed when they attempted to close the membership of their trades. In Philadelphia men added trades and lines of goods as they thought demand justified. Although this freedom undoubtedly produced a great deal of incompetent craftsmanship, the importance to the

individual artisan or shopkeeper of open trades and plentiful work cannot be overestimated. It meant for the common man that there was always a chance for a fresh start. This chance for a new beginning was the urban equivalent of the contemporary farmer's chance to pick up and try again in the West.[12]

Already in these years the American pattern of social mobility by property obtained. No invidious distinction between land and trade favored some occupations over others. As eighteenth-century Philadelphians grew rich they kept their original occupations, whether they were carpenters, distillers, printers, or lawyers. Whatever a man's occupation, there were only a few channels for investment open to the rising man. Since there were no banks, private money lending was the most important investment opportunity in the town. Houses and land were also a favorite way of using savings both among the rich and those with a little capital. Only 19 percent of the families of Philadelphia owned their houses and therefore home rentals offered a safe investment. Other opportunities were shares in voyages, marine insurance, and, of course, land and farms outside the town.[13]

The prosperity and abundant opportunity of the town should not be confused with an even distribution of wealth. According to the published tax list for 1774 the upper tenth of the taxpaying households owned 89 percent of the taxable property. In this respect late eighteenth-century Philadelphia resembled the later Philadelphias—it was a pyramid of wealth in which about five hundred men guided the town's economic life. Its unique quality lay in the general prosperity of the common artisan and shopkeeper and the widely shared entrepreneurial experience and goals of the artisan, shopkeeper, and merchant.[14]

The wealthy presided over a municipal regime of little government. Both in form and function the town's government advertised the lack of concern for public management of the community. The municipal corporation of Philadelphia, copied from the forms of an old English borough, counted for little. Its only important functions in the late eighteenth-century were the management of the markets and the holding of the Recorder's Court. A closed corporation, choosing its members by co-option, it had become a club of wealthy merchants, without much purse, power, or popularity.

By modern standards the town was hardly governed at all. The constable in each ward and a few watchmen provided an ineffective police, the safety of the house and shop being secured by citizens' helping each other to drive away intruders or pursue thieves.[15] Most streets went unpaved, the public wharves little repaired. There were no public schools, no public water, and at best thin charity.

The enduring contribution of the colonial era to Philadelphia government lay in its inauguration of the committee system of municipal government. This system, if system it may be called in the eighteenth century, consisted of placing the administration of specific tasks in the hands of independent committees, or commissions. The Pennsylvania Provincial Assembly, lacking faith in the municipal corporation, created a number of commissions. First came the Board of Assessors established to raise money to pay the debts of the corporation and to require that wharves and streets be repaired and a workhouse erected. Then came separate street commissioners, next the City Wardens to manage the night watch and the lighting of the streets, and, still later, a Board of Overseers of the Poor. None of these commissions' performance would satisfy modern municipal standards. The commissioners were elected officials, chosen under the colonial fifty-pound, freehold qualification by the voters of Philadelphia. Like the town's fire companies, lending libraries, and tavern clubs these commissions helped train Philadelphians to the habits of committee government, a form of management they would have to call upon when creating a new independent government during the Revolution. Like many of the laws and forms of the colonial era which passed into the usage of the subsequent Commonwealth of Pennsylvania, the committee system of government was the legacy of colonial municipal life to later Philadelphias.[16]

The real secret of the peace and order of the eighteenth-century town lay not in its government but in the informal structure of its community. Unlike later and larger Philadelphias, the eighteenth-century town was a community. Graded by wealth and divided by distinctions of class though it was, it functioned as a single community. The community had been created out of a remarkably inclusive network of business and economic relationships and it was maintained by the daily interactions of trade and sociability. Because it was small and because every rank and occupation lived jumbled together in a narrow compass the town suffered none of the communications problems of later Philadelphias.

At most, 23,700 people lived in Philadelphia on the eve of the Revolution, 16,500 in the city proper, 7,000 in the adjacent districts of Northern Liberties and Southwark. The town crowded next to its shore. Its wharves and warehouses stretched a mile and a half along the Delaware river, but the built-up blocks of houses at their deepest point, along Market street, reached back from the river at most half a mile to about Seventh Street.[17]

The settlement pattern of the town combined two opposing social tendencies. The clustering of marine trades and merchants next to the Delaware suggested the beginnings of the specialized industrial quarters then characteristic of European cities. On the other hand, the rummage of classes and occupations found in many Philadelphia blocks continued the old tradition of mixed work and residence characteristic of American and English country towns.

*   *   *

One can get some idea of the quality of urban life imposed by this settlement pattern by looking at one ward in a little detail. The Constable in making his enumeration of the residents of the Middle Ward left notes on his list showing when he turned the corner of a street. This record, plus some material from tax ledgers make it possible to reconstruct the settlement pattern of this ward in 1774.

As its name suggests, the Middle Ward lay in the center of town bounded on the north by Market Street, then the highway connecting Philadelphia to Chester and the south and to Lancaster and the west. The ward also was next to the market traffic. The sheds of the farmers' market in these years stretched up Market Street from the Delaware River only as far

as Fourth Street. The Middle Ward was not a crowded dockside ward, but began just behind the dockside wards at Second Street. Its well-filled section covered five blocks to Seventh Street, Market to Chestnut. Beyond these blocks of houses the farms of the ward extended all the way west to the Schuylkill River.

Many famous Philadelphians lived within the ward. The old-fashioned Quaker radical, Anthony Benezet, the Proprietors John and Richard Penn, two opponents of the British who later turned Tory, Joseph Galloway, and James Allen, and the steadfast revolutionaries Benjamin Franklin and Daniel Clymer all lived in the center of the ward. The State House Yard (now Independence Square) stood across Chestnut Street between Fifth and Sixth streets. Such distinction, however, did not create the solid blocks of *haut bourgeois* fashion that they would today; rather it embroidered the commonplace fabric which was the revolutionary town. In 1774 the Middle Ward was the home of at least 1,401 men, women, and children of every degree and condition from Proprietor to slave (Table 1).

The physical arrangements of the ward reflected the high cost of eighteenth-century housing and the crowding of Philadelphians near their port. Each of the Middle Ward's five settled blocks contained slightly less than five acres of land. On the first block of the ward (between Second and Third streets, the area nearest the Delaware River) there stood 137 dwellings, on the next 65, on the next 67, on the next 29, and on westernmost 39. To accommodate so many families in so little space some of the blocks of the ward had been cut by alleys so that little houses might be crowded onto the back lots of the houses facing the main streets. Strawberry Alley and Elbow Lane cut through the first block, Petty's Alley divided the third block, and Benjamin Franklin had begun the alley process with his house lot off Market Street in the second block of the ward. He had built a row of three houses on Market Street, thereby turning his home yard into an interior lot. His son-in-law Richard Bache, a merchant, rented one of the new row houses, Eden Haydock, plumber, rented another, and Frederick Stonemetz, a cooper, took the third. In the early nineteenth century Franklin's home parcel became Franklin Court, an alley lot which opened up the interior of the block.[18]

Such density of housing and such methods of land division had by 1774 destroyed the hopes of Penn and his surveyor for a "Green Town."[19] The practice of subdividing blocks with alleys and jamming tiny houses on vacant rear yards continued strongly for the next ninety years. By 1860 the density of population in Philadelphia's inner wards reached its all-time peak.[20] Then, in the second half of the nineteenth century the street railway opened up vast tracts of cheap suburban land and thereby destroyed the market for new alley construction. The old alleys with their dark and cramped houses, however, did not disappear at once. Rather they remained standing for years, giving discomfort to Philadelphia's poor for many generations, and the history of some alleys is not yet closed.

Already in the 1770's the crowding of the land exceeded the sanitary capabilities of the town. The streets and alleys reeked of garbage, manure, and night soil, and some private and public wells must have been dangerously polluted. Every few years an epidemic swept through the town. In the 1790's the city would pay a terrible price in deaths from recurring yellow fever.[21]

Though dangerous to health the eighteenth-century pattern of settlement guaranteed every citizen a knowledge of town life. At such density and small scale no generation could be raised ignorant of the other side of town, of the ways of life of the work-

Table 1

The Middle Ward of Philadelphia, April 8, 1774

Free Adults (346 households x 2 for wives)	692
Children	469
Negro Slaves	78
Bound Servants in Residence	65
Hired Servants in Residence	17
Inmates (other free adults living in households)	80
Population	1,401
Homeowners	80
Houserenters	266
Taxpayers living with other families	102
Total Taxpayers	448

ing class, or of the manners of the *haut bourgeois*. Within the Middle Ward at least 346 families with 469 children, 17 hired servants, 65 indentured servants, 78 Negro slaves, and 80 tenants share the settled 25 acres (Table 1). Those who left a record carried on seventy different occupations.[22]

Although merchants and shopkeepers, hatters, innkeepers, and tavernkeepers concentrated more heavily in this ward than in most others, variety best characterizes the occupational structure of the ward as it did all the other wards of the first Philadelphia. The Proprietors, the merchants, and the doctors shared the narrow compass of the Middle Ward with such ungenteel occupations as laborer, porter, carter, skinner, watchman, crier, paver, grazier, and even goatkeeper. The outer three blocks of the ward also housed several breweries and a distillery, and every one of the five blocks contained one or more of those notorious enemies of sweet residential air—the stable.[23]

One cannot, at this late date, reconstruct in detail the communications patterns of eighteenth-century Philadelphia, but the crowded living of the age encouraged a street and tavern life which more resembled the social habits of the later nineteenth and early twentieth-century immigrant ghettos than the isolated private family life of today's working class and middle class.

The high cost of building kept houses small, cramped, and in short supply. The common artisan's or shopkeeper's house was a narrow structure, about seventeen feet wide and twenty-five feet deep. A story-and-a-half high, it offered about eight hundred square feet of floor space on its ground floor and attic. Most often the owner plied

his trade in the largest front room. The Middle Ward records show that although some families had five to seven children, most had few. The average number of children per household was 1.3, and counting servants and slaves the average household was four persons. The small houses, thus, were cramped but not severely crowded. If the artisan or shopkeeper prospered he would add a kitchen ell or more likely move to a house of similar proportion with a kitchen ell at the rear. The house of an ordinary merchant or even a craftsman who had grown rich, would be like the artisan's house with the ell, but would be two and one-half stories instead of one and one-half. Such houses of the prosperous also possessed deep lots for gardens, a shed for a cow and some chickens, and perhaps a horse.[24]

A town of small houses, where most houses also served as stores, offices and workshops, encouraged people to live out upon the streets. Moreover, the pace of work, most of it governed by the seasons or advance orders from customers, was irregular, what one would call today a rural pace. Both the physical structure of the town and the pace of its work thus encouraged a more public, gossipy style of life than could later be sustained when a steady pace of work, and larger interiors drove people into sharply defined spaces for work and residence.

The ordinary housewife shopped daily, going to the baker's for her bread, and taking her meat and pies to the baker's oven to be cooked. Street peddlers called her out for fish, eggs, and produce, and twice a week the farmers of Philadelphia County held a full market at the public stalls. As in the nineteenth century with its dark tenements and crowded row houses, sunlight must have been a great source of pleasure for women sewing and spinning and many must have worked at these and other household chores out on their doorsteps, as their tenement sisters did years later.

For the husband the eighteenth-century custom of men's gossip at the tavern provided the first Philadelphia's basic cells of community life. Every ward in the city had its inns and taverns. The 1774 tax list recorded 93 tavernkeepers and 72 innkeepers in the city of Philadelphia, Southwark, and the Northern Liberties, approximately one neighborhood drinking place for every 140 persons in the city (23,000/165). The Middle Ward, alone, held 18 inns and taverns. Some must have served purely a neighborhood custom; others, like the London Coffee House or the City Tavern served as central communications nodes for the entire city.

Then, as now, each one had its own crowd of regulars and thus each constituted an informal community cell of the city. Out of the meetings of the regulars at the neighborhood tavern or inn came much of the commonplace community development which preceded the Revolution and proved later to be essential to the governance of the city and the management of the ward. Regular meetings of friends, or men of common occupations, led to clubs of all kinds and of every degree of formality from regular billiard sessions to fire companies and political juntos. Benjamin Franklin and the many community innovations of his junto showed the potential of these informal tavern groups. They provided the underlying social fabric of the town and when the Revolution began

made it possible to quickly gather militia companies, to form effective committees of correspondence and of inspection, and to organize and to manage mass towns meetings.

At the center of the town's communications system stood the merchants' coffee houses. On the eve of the Revolution Philadelphia had two such major meeting places—the old London Coffee House (established 1754), run by William Bradford, the newspaper publisher, and the new City Tavern (established 1773), just founded by a syndicate of merchants. The London Coffee House, located at Front and Market streets, adjacent to the town's principal market stalls and overlooking the Delaware, had been for many years the place where merchants gathered every noon to read incoming newspapers, to discuss prices, and to arrange for cargoes and marine insurance. These noon meetings in time ripened into the specialized institutions of exchanges, banks, and insurance companies. As yet, Philadelphia had but one insurance company and its merchants' business depended on the variety of functions of these daily tavern gatherings. For many years ship captains and travelers first stopped at the London Coffee House when they arrived in town, messages were left, auction notices posted and auctions held. Frequently on market days, after a parade through the streets, horses were auctioned in front of the tavern doors. Slaves and indentured servants stood before the same block.

As the town grew the importing merchants no longer had a need to be near the market dealers. The merchant community split into at least two parts. The new City Tavern surpassed the old London Coffee House as a place of fashion with the importing merchants, though its function remained that of its competitor. On May 19, 1774, Paul Revere brought his news of the closing of the Port of Boston to the City Tavern, and here numerous Revolutionary committees gathered. The still extant Philadelphia Assemblies were held at this new tavern, as was the endless series of banquets and balls which served the town with high entertainment.[25]

Because the merchants' tavern was a public place in a small town it escaped the limitations of later Philadelphia merchant centers—the exchanges, the Chamber of Commerce, and the gentlemen's clubs. These later gatherings were either meeting places of specialists and thereby encouraged only the brokers' or downtown merchants' view of the city, or they were closed organizations which directed their members' attention inward toward the sociability of the group. The eighteenth-century tavern, however, opened out to all the life of the street and it did not shield the leaders of the town from contact with the life that surrounded them.[26]

It was the unity of everyday life, from tavern, to street, to workplace, to housing, which held the town and its leaders together in the eighteenth century. This unity made it possible for the minority of Revolutionary merchants, artisans, and shopkeepers to hold together, run the town, and manage a share of the war against England, even in the face of Quaker neutrality and Tory opposition.

NOTES

1. Quaker historians agree that the Holy Experiment died from materialism and secularization during the eighteenth century, Frederick B. Tolles, *Meeting House and Counting House* (Chapel Hill, 1948), 240-243; Sydney V. James, *A People among Peoples* (Cambridge, 1963), 37-43, 211-215; and see the charges against his contemporaries in John Woolman, *The Journal of John Woolman* (F. B. Holles, Introduction, New York, 1961).

2. Howard Mumford Jones, *O Strange New World* (New York, 1964), 194-272, treats with this tradition as a blend of Christian and classical ideas.

3. Tolles, *Meeting House*, 41.

4. Carl Bridenbaugh, *Cities in the Wilderness* (N.Y. 1938), 303; and see notes to Table I. Also, James T. Lemon, "Urbanization of the Development of Eighteenth Century Southeastern Pennsylvania," *William and Mary Quarterly*, XXIV (Oct., 1967), 502-542; Hannah B. Roach, "The Planning of Philadelphia," *Pennsylvania Magazine*, XCII (January and April, 1968).

5. Marcus L. Hansen, *Atlantic Migration* (Cambridge, 1940), Ch. II.

6. Comments suggesting an individualized or family work structure, Carl Bridenbaugh, *The Colonial Craftsman* (New York, 1950), 126-129, 136-139, 141-143.

7. Harry D. Berg, "The Organization of Business in Colonial Philadelphia," *Pennsylvania History*, X (July, 1943), 157-177; Arthur H. Cole, "The Tempo of Mercantile Life in Colonial America," *Business History Review*, XXXIII (Autumn, 1959), 277-299.

8. Richard B. Morris, *Government and Labor in Early America* (New York, 1946), 38-40.

9. . . . The reconstruction of the Middle Ward as of April 8, 1773 showed seventeen hired servants in residence there. On this basis two hundred servants were guessed for the city.

10. Gottlieb Mittelberger, *Journey to Pennsylvania* (Oscar Handlin and John Clive, eds., Cambridge, 1960), 48.

11. Jackson Turner Main, *The Social Structure of Revolutionary America* (Princeton, 1965), 74-83, 115-163; Chapter IV; Mittelberger, *Journey*, 48-51, 74-75.

12. Morris, *Government and Labor in Early America*, 2-3, 141-143; the American jack-of-all-trades tradition, Mittelberger, *Journey*, 42-43; artisans' associations, Bridenbaugh, *Colonial Craftsman*, 141-143.

13. Wilbur C. Plummer, "Consumer Credit in Colonial Philadelphia," *Pennsylvania Magazine*, LXVI (October, 1942), 385-409. The homeownership percentage was calculated from the number of homeowners and renters listed in the manuscript version of the Seventeenth Eighteenth Penny Provincial Tax of April 8, 1774 (in possession of the Pennsylvania Historical and Museum Commission, Harrisburg). A reconstruction of the Middle Ward as of April 8, 1774 shows holdings of land and houses in small lots,

and pairs of structures, not big tracts. Rich men, like Israel Pemeberton, and men of few investments, both participated in the housing market.

14. The published version of the Seventeenth Eighteen Penny Provincial Tax, *Pennsylvania Archives, 3rd Series,* XIV (Harrisburg, 1897), 223-445, was used for a quick calculation of the distribution of taxable wealth. The taxpayers on this published list were arranged in order of the size of their published "assessment." The top ten percent, or 498 names, accounted for 89 percent of the 86,100 pounds of assessment given for Philadelphia, the Northern Liberties, and Southwark. This published list is not a sufficient guide to the distribution of wealth since the tax was largely a real property tax to which a head tax and a few personalty items were added. The very important property of stock-in-trade and money-on-loan went untaxed and hence unlisted. Also, the compilers of the published list mixed in many cases the taxes-paid entries with the assessment entries thereby distorting even the assessment distribution.

15. There are charming accounts of private policing in Henry D. Biddle, ed., *Extracts from the Journal of Elizabeth Drinker* (Philadelphia, 1889), robbery in her alley, Dec. 15, 1777; insane soldier wanders into the house June 30, 1778; "saucy Ann" and her soldier, Nov. 25, 26, Dec. 2, 1777, Jan. 4, 1778. A call for more considerate treatment of the town watchmen, Advertisement, *Pennsylvania Gazette,* Jan. 20, 1779.

16. For a description of the colonial government of Philadelphia, Judith M. Diamondstone, "Philadelphia's Municipal Corporation, 1701-1776," *Pennsylvania Magazine,* XC (April, 1966), 183-201; Edward P. Allinson & Boise Penrose, "The City Government of Philadelphia," *Johns Hopkins Studies in Historical and Political Science,* V (Baltimore, 1887), 14-33.

17. The tax records and constables' returns of 1774 and 1775 show dense settlement to end and Seventh Street with but a few families living on scattered farms west from this point to the Schuylkill river. A map made by John Reed of the City and Liberties of Philadelphia, supposed to have been made in 1774 (now in the possession of the American Philosophical Society) was shaded to show dense settlement to Tenth street.

18. Edward M. Riley, "Franklin's Home," *Historic Philadelphia* (American Philosophical Society, *Transactions,* XLIII, 1953), 148-160.

19. Anthony N. B. Garvan, "Proprietary Philadelphia as Artifact," *The Historian and the City* (Oscar Handlin and John Burchard, eds., Cambridge, 1964), 177-201.

20. Philadelphia City Planning Commission Map,

"Year of Population Peak, Philadelphia, by Wards," dated August, 1949.

21. Bad conditions in alley "huts" of the poor, presumably one-story houses with a sleeping attic reached by a ladder as in the typical rural one-room cabin, Benjamin Rush, *Autobiography of Benjamin Rush* (American Philosophical Society, *Memoirs,* XXV, 1948), 83-84; cellar of a drunken, perhaps insane woman oyster seller, *Journal of Elizabeth Drinker,* Sept. 2, 1793; eighteenth century epidemics, small pox, yellow fever, dysentery or typhoid, John Duffy, *Epidemics in Colonial America* (Baton Rouge, 1953), 78-100, 142-161, 220-230, and Struthers Burt, *Philadelphia Holy Experiment* (New York, 1946), 159.

22. No authority tells to what extent eighteenth century artisans worked at home as opposed to working outside. With the exception of the building and marine trades most artisans are supposed to have worked at home. This supposition gets some indirect confirmation from the general agreement that most men labored alone and that most businesses in the city were family businesses. Neither Bridenbaugh in his *Colonial Craftsman* nor Morris in his *Government and Labor* tell of many urban establishments which might have employed many workers outside of their own homes.

23. A good sense of what the mixed settlement pattern of the city meant is given by Alexander Graydon, *Memoirs of a Life, Chiefly Passed in Pennsylvania* (Harrisburg, 1811), 34-35.

24. The tax records of 1774 give evidence of a colonial housing shortage, for the ratio of occupied to unoccupied dwellings did not exceed two percent that year. Artisans' houses, Grant M. Simon, "Houses and Early Life in Philadelphia," *Historic Philadelphia,* 282-3; typical house for the prosperous, Advertisement, *Pennsylvania Gazette,* March 17, 1779.

25. The name "coffee house," which had been imported from England, merely designated a genteel tavern. Coffee, tea, lemonade, and beer were served, but the customers favored wines and liquors, Robert E. Graham, "The Taverns of Colonial Philadelphia," *Historic Philadelphia,* 318-323.

26. Graydon tells an amusing story of the confrontation of Benjamin Chew, lawyer for the Penns and then Recorder of the town and an alderman with two drunken British officers, *Memoirs,* 43-44; an excellent review of travellers and visitor's accounts mentions the importance to the social structure of the town of immigrant societies life St. David's and St. Tammany, Whitfield J. Bell, Jr., "Some Aspects of the Social History of Pennsylvania, 1760-1790," *Pennsylvania Magazine,* LXII (July, 1938), 301.

III THE CITY IN THE ANTEBELLUM PERIOD

The nineteenth century was "the century of cities." From Australia to Europe, urbanization was a fast-spreading phenomenon, but no country surpassed the United States in the speed and size of its urban growth. The popular conception of urban expansion usually associates it with the rise of the industrial giants in the forty years after the Civil War. But the first sixty years of the century were as dynamic as (and in some ways more dramatic than) the post–Civil War period. Cornfields, trading stations, forts, lake and river ports, construction camps, and whistle stops, developed into towns, small and large, and sometimes sank into ghost towns. It was a period of unprecedented optimism and wild speculation, where the enthusiasm of "manifest destiny" to conquer a continent was also poured into town and city building.

Perhaps never in our history have so many Americans shown such unbridled faith and competitive rivalry about their cities: undoubtedly, Athens, Ohio, would outshine her ancient Greek namesake, Chicago would outgrow New York, St. Louis would dominate the American heartland—all would be bigger and better than their wicked and dirty European counterparts. Never in our history has the United States experienced such rapid urban growth as in the four decades preceding the Civil War. From 1820 to 1860 the total population of the country increased by 226 percent, while the urban population increased by almost 800 percent. Whereas roughly 6 percent of Americans lived in cities in 1800, by 1860 20 percent were urban dwellers. Philadelphia was bigger than Berlin, New York was the third largest city in the world, and Chicago was the most spectacular of them all. A scruffy little village of fifty people in 1830, Chicago survived a panic and depression and, with little more than mud and a prayer, seized upon canal and railroad building to explode by 1853 into a city of 60,000 people with 150 hotels. Old and new cities in the East and South continued to grow, with the South, significantly for the later Civil War period, lagging behind. But nowhere was there more hope, lusty vitality, and bigger dreams in the seventy years after the formation of the new nation than in the urban expansion in the new West.

Richard Wade, in the first selection—a major essay in the literature of American urban history—describes the cities of the trans-Appalachian West from 1790 to 1830 as the "spearheads of the frontier." To the familiar array of such western characters as the hunter and farmer, Wade adds the urbanite, many of whom moved west to settle good towns rather than to cultivate good land. His thesis of the urban frontier is another important revision of the frontier thesis of Frederick Jackson Turner, for Wade shows that the city dweller often preceded the farmer in the westward plunge of the early nineteenth century. Cities like Cincinnati, Lexington, Louisville, St. Louis, and Pittsburgh were not only spearheads of settlement, but spearheads of political, economic, and cultural leadership as well. Although they worked in mutual dependence with the farm, the cities were more aggressive, more dynamic, and more creative than the farm in giving a frontier wilderness diversity, direction, growth, opportunity, and, above all, maturity.

Arthur M. Schlesinger has written that without the story of the city, the saga of American civilization is only half told. David Goldfield, in the next selection, says the same thing about the role of the city in the antebellum South. If Wade amends the frontier thesis, Goldfield challenges deeply entrenched notions about the Old South. His argument is provocative: historians have either neglected the role of urbanization in the antebellum South or dismissed it as being ineffectual. It is unfair and inaccurate, he says, to compare the South (and the West, for that matter) with the Northeast, which led the nation in urbanization and industrialization, and conclude that cities and industrial enterprise were anemic in the South. And he shows why. Moreover, industrialization is not always synonymous with urbanization, and he provides excellent examples to buttress his argument. If the South lacked a New York or a Philadelphia, size is not always that important. Goldfield emphasizes a theme that runs through much of American urban history: the size of a city is often disproportionate to its political, economic, and cultural impact upon the surrounding hinterland.

Probably the most persistent view of the Old South concerns its "passionate love affair" with slavery and the land. It is an argument with a one-two punch. First, Southerners "captured by visions of moonlight and magnolias, invested heavily in slaves and land," which left their urban centers sleepy market towns. Goldfield, however, shows that Southerners invested in an astonishing variety of economic enterprises. Second, Southerners embraced the rural ideal with such vigor that urban progress languished. But all sections of antebellum America celebrated agrarian values and the virtues of the honest yeoman. "In fact," Goldfield says, "middle-century Americans *generally* [italics mine] possessed ambivalent attitudes toward both urban and rural living that enabled them to build great cities and to write romantic literature exalting country life without apparent self-contradiction." Furthermore, to overemphasize ruralness is to neglect the impact of the cities upon the institution of slavery as well as on sectionalism itself.

The heart of the argument is that the South also participated in the great age of city-building in pre–Civil War America. The South engaged in two aspects of the urban process: the quantitative, in the building of the so-called economic superstructure (transportation facilities, industry, and export trade), in the increase in population, space, and wealth, and in the differentiation and separation of urban areas and functions; and the qualitative, in the development of an urban elite and, perhaps, above all, urban consciousness, civic pride, and city boosterism. "It is time," Professor Goldfield has written, "to place the magnolias on Main Street and to develop an urban view of southern history."

Cities did not grow as a result of urban rivalry alone, or transportation, or a convenient location, or the impersonal forces of urbanization. They were also the creatures of the men and women who lived in them—their hopes, their energy, their community spirit, their initiative, their adaptability. A railroad could make a city, a fire could break a city, but ultimately whether a city prospered through good luck or survived bad luck depended upon the spirit of its citizens. Daniel Boorstin catches the flamboyant spirit of the human element in urban manifest destiny by examining the roles and impact of three men, William B. Ogden of Chicago, Dr. Daniel Drake of Cincinnati, and William Larimer of Denver, who were representative of countless others in cities everywhere.

They were a new breed of the promotor extraordinary—the entrepreneur as the city booster, the dreamer as the city builder. They were "upstart businessmen" who helped build upstart cities. They pinned their hopes and fortunes to cities without a past and with only a future. They constituted a perfect marriage of city booster and self-booster, fusing private interests to community interests. Their energies at first directed to promoting real estate and railroads, spread to building practically every aspect of city life, from municipal services, hospitals, colleges, parks, and, not the least, politics. They in turn reflected an attitude of the general community, the booster spirit— an ethos, a state of mind, often a mystique, the intensity of or lack of which sealed the success or failure of many a city in America.

Urban Life in Western America, 1790-1830

RICHARD C. WADE

The towns were the spearheads of the American frontier. Planted as forts or trading posts far in advance of the line of settlement, they held the West for the approaching population. Indeed, in 1763, when the British drew the Proclamation Line across the Appalachians to stop the flow of migrants, a French merchant company prepared to survey the streets of St. Louis, a thousand miles through the wilderness. Whether as part of French and Spanish activity from New Orleans or part of Anglo-American operations from the Atlantic seaboard, the establishment of towns preceded the breaking of soil in the transmontane West.

In 1764, the year of the founding of St. Louis, settlers made the first plat of Pittsburgh. Twelve years later and four hundred miles down the Ohio, Louisville sprang up at the Falls, and the following decade witnessed the beginnings of Cincinnati and Lexington. Before the century closed, Detroit, Buffalo, and Cleveland were laid out on the Great Lakes. In fact, by 1800 the sites of every major metropolis in the old Northwest except Chicago, Milwaukee, and Indianapolis had been cleared and surveyed.

Furthermore, these urban outposts grew rapidly even in their infant decades. By 1815 Pittsburgh, already a thriving industrial center, had 8,000 inhabitants, giving it a slight margin over Lexington. Cincinnati estimated its population at 4,000 at the end of the war with Great Britain, while farther west Louisville and St. Louis neared half that figure.

The speed and extent of this expansion startled contemporaries. Joseph Charless, the editor of the *Missouri Gazette,* who had made a trip through the new country in 1795, remembered the banks of the Ohio as "a dreary wilderness, the haunt of ruthless savages," yet twenty years later he found them "sprinkled with towns" boasting "spinning and weaving establishments, steam mills, manufactures in various metals, leather, wool, cotton and flax," and "seminaries of learning conducted by excellent teachers."[1] The great transformation moved a Cincinnati bard to a somewhat heroic couplet:

> Here where so late the appalling sound
> Of savage yells, the woods resound
> Now smiling Ceres waves her sheaf
> And cities rise in bold relief.[2]

Not all the towns founded in the trans-Allegheny region in this period fared as well, however. Many never developed much beyond a survey and a newspaper advertisement. Others after promising beginnings, slackened and settled down to slow and unspectacular development. Still others flourished briefly then faded, leaving behind a grim story of deserted mills, broken buildings, and aging people—the West's first harvest of ghost towns. Most of these were mere eddies in the westward flow of urbanism, but at flood tide it

From *American Historical Review* (October 1958), pp. 14-30. Reprinted by permission of the publisher.

was often hard to distinguish the eddies from the main stream. Indeed, at one time Wheeling, Virginia, St. Genevieve, Missouri, New Albany, Indiana, and Zanesville, Ohio, were considered serious challengers to the supremacy of their now more famous neighbors.

Other places, such as Rising Sun, Town of America, or New Athens, were almost wholly speculative ventures. Eastern investors scanned maps looking for likely spots to establish a city, usually at the junction of two rivers, or sometimes at the center of fertile farm districts. They bought up land, laid it out in lots, gave the place a name, and waited for the development of the region to appreciate its value. Looking back over this period one editor called it a "city-making mania," when everyone went about "anticipating flourishing cities in vision, at the mouth of every creek and bayou."[3] This speculation, though extensive, was not always profitable. "Of the vast number of towns which have been founded," James Hall declared, "but a small minority have prospered, nor do we think that, as a general rule, the founders of these have been greatly enriched by their prosperity."[4]

Despite many failures, these abortive attempts to plant towns were significant, for they reveal much about the motives of the people who came West in the early period. Many settlers moved across the mountains in search of promising towns rather than good land, their inducements being urban opportunities rather than fertile soil. Daniel Drake, who was among the earliest urbanites of the frontier, later commented on this process:

It is worthy of remark, that those who made these beginnings of settlement, projected towns, which they anticipated would grow into cities. . . . And we may see in their origins, one of the elements of the prevalent tendency to rear up towns in advance of the country which has ever since characterized Ohio. The followers of the first pioneers, like themselves had a taste for commerce and the mechanic arts which cannot be gratified without the construction of cities.[5]

Proprietors competed for these urban migrants, most of whom came from "those portions of the Union which cherish and build up cities."[6] In fact, the preference of some settlers for towns was so great that in 1787 Lexington petitioned the Virginia legislature for incorporation to be "an inducement to well disposed persons, artizens [sic] and mechanics who from motives and convenience do prefer Town life."[7]

The West's young cities owed their initial success to commerce. All sprang from it, and their growth in the early years of the century stemmed from its expansion. Since the Ohio River was the chief artery of trade and travel, the towns along its banks prospered most. Pittsburgh, where the Allegheny meets the Monongahela, commanded the entire valley; Cincinnati served the rich farm lands of Kentucky and Ohio; Louisville fattened on the transshipment of goods around the Falls; and St. Louis, astride the Mississippi, was the focus of far-flung enterprises, some of which reached to the Pacific Ocean. Even Lexington, landlocked in a country of water highways, grew up as the central mart of Kentucky and Tennessee.

Though these cities were firmly established by the first decade of the century, the coming of the steamboat greatly enhanced their size and influence.[8] By quickening transportation and cutting distances, steam navigation telescoped fifty years' urban development into a single generation. The flow of commerce down river was now supplemented by a northward and eastward movement, giving cities added opportunities for expansion and growth. "The steam engine in five years has enabled us to anticipate a state of things," a Pittsburgher declared enthusiastically, "which in the ordinary course of events, it would have required a century to have produced. The art of printing scarcely surpassed it in beneficial consequences."[9] The "enchanter's wand" not only touched the established towns but created new ones as well. A French observer noted that "in the brief interval of fifteen years, many cities were formed . . . where before there were hardly the dwellings of a small town. . . . A simple mechanical device has made life both possible and comfortable in regions which heretofore have been a wilderness."[10]

As these commercial centers grew, some inhabitants turned to manufacturing. Indeed, this new interest spread so rapidly in Pittsburgh that in 1810 a resident likened the place to "a large workshop," and already travelers complained of the smoke and soot.[11] Between 1803 and 1815 the value of manufactured goods jumped from $350,000 to over $2,600,000, and the city's iron and glass products became known throughout the new country.[12] Watching this remarkable development, the editor of *Niles' Register* exclaimed: "Pittsburgh, sometimes emphatically called the 'Birmingham of America,' will probably become the *greatest manufacturing town in the world*"[13] Lexington also turned increasingly to industry, her ropewalks and textile mills supplying the whole West. Beginnings were more modest in other places, but every city had at least a few ambitious enterprises.

Some of this urban expansion rested

on a speculative base, and the depression of 1819 brought a reckoning. Lexington, already suffering from its landlocked position, received fatal wounds, while Pittsburgh, the West's foremost city, was crippled for a decade. Elsewhere, however, the setback proved only momentary and the mid-twenties saw the old pace renewed. Population growth again provides a convenient index of development. Cincinnati quickly overtook its faltering rivals, the number of its residents leaping from 6,000 in 1815 to over 25,000 in 1830. By the latter date the census recorded Pittsburgh's recovery. Though the figure had dropped to 7,000 during the depression, it rose to 13,000 in 1830. Farther west Louisville and St. Louis enjoyed spectacular expansion, the former boasting over 10,000 inhabitants at the end of the period, while the Mississippi entrepôt passed the 6,000 mark. Lexington alone lagged, its population remaining stable for the next two decades.

Even these figures, however, do not convey the real growth. In most places municipal boundaries could no longer contain the new settlers, and many spilled over into the suburbs. For instance, Allegheny, Bayardstown, Birmingham, Lawrenceville, Hayti, and East Liberty added nearly 10,000 to Pittsburgh's population, bringing the total to 22,000.[14] The same was true of Cincinnati where 2,000 people lived in the Eastern and Northern Liberties.[15] In Louisville, Preston's and Campbell's "enlargements" and Shippingport and Portland swelled the city's total to 13,000.[16] Ultimately, the urban centers annexed these surrounding clusters, but in the meantime local authorities grappled with early manifestations of the suburban problem.

As the cities grew they staked out extensive commercial claims over the entire West.[17] Timothy Flint calculated that Cincinnati was the central market for over a million people, while a resident asserted that its trade was "co-extensive with steamboat navigation on the western waters."[18] Louisville's economic penetration was scarcely less impressive. As early as 1821, a local editor declared that "the people of the greater part of Indiana, all Kentucky, and portions of Tennessee, Alabama, Illinois, Missouri, now report to this place for dry goods, groceries, hardware and queensware."[19] St. Louis' empire touched Santa Fe on the south, Canada on the north, and the Pacific on the west. "It is doubtful if history affords the example of another city," wrote Hiram M. Chittenden, "which has been the exclusive mart for so vast an area as that which was tributary to St. Louis."[20]

In carving out these extensive dependencies, the young metropolises overwhelmed their smaller neighbors. The rise of St. Louis destroyed the ambitions of Edwardsville across the Mississippi, which once harbored modest hopes of importance. Pittsburgh's recovery in the late twenties condemned Wheeling and Steubenville to minor roles in the upper Ohio region. And Louisville's development swallowed two Kentucky neighbors while reducing Jeffersonville and New Albany on the Indiana side of the river to mere appendages.

Not satisfied with such considerable conquests, the cities reached out for more. Seeking wider opportunities, they built canals and turnpikes and, even before 1830, planned railroads to strengthen their position. Cincinnati, Pittsburgh, and St. Louis tried to tap the increasing trade on the Great Lakes by water links to the North. Pennsyl-

vania's Iron City also hoped to become a major station on the National Road, and for a decade its Washington representatives lobbied to win that commercial bond with the East. Lexington, suffocating in its inland position, frantically strove for better connections with the Ohio River. A turnpike to Maysville was dashed by Jackson's veto, technical difficulties made a canal to the Kentucky River impractical, but some belated hope rose with the possibility of a railroad to Louisville or Cincinnati.

The intensive search for new advantages brought rivalry and conflict. Though the commerce of the whole West lay untouched before them, the cities quarreled over its division. Thus Louisville and Cincinnati fought over a canal around the Falls of the Ohio. The Kentucky town, feeling that its strength depended upon maintaining the break in transportation, obstructed every attempt to circumvent the rapids. Only when Ohio interests threatened to dig on the Indiana side did Louisville move ahead with its own project. Likewise, harsh words flew between Wheeling and Pittsburgh as they contended for the Ohio River terminus of the National Road. Smaller towns, too, joined the struggle. Cleveland and Sandusky, for instance, clashed over the location of the Ohio Canal, the stake being nothing less than control of the mounting trade between the Valley and the lakes. And their instinct to fight was sound, for the outcome shaped the future of both places.

Urban rivalries were often bitter, and the contestants showed no quarter. In the late twenties when only the success of Transylvania University kept Lexington's economy from complete collapse, Louisville joined the attack which ultimately destroyed the school. In a similar vein Cincinnatians taunted their upriver competitor as it reeled under the impact of the depression of 1819. "Poor Pittsburgh," they exclaimed, "your day is over, the sceptre of influence and wealth is to travel to us; the Cumberland road has done the business."[21] But even the Queen City found her supremacy insecure. "I discovered two ruling passions in Cincinnati," a traveler remarked, "enmity against Pittsburgh, and jealousy of Louisville."[22] This drive for power and primacy, sustained especially by merchants and articulated by editors, was one of the most consistent and striking characteristics of the early history of Western cities.

As they pursued expansive policies, municipalities also ministered to their own growing pains. From the beginning, urban residents had to contend with the problems of living together, and one of their first acts was to petition the territory or state for governing authority to handle them. The legislatures, representing rural interests and generally suspicious of towns, responded with charters bestowing narrow grants of power which barely met current needs and failed to allow for expansion. As localities grew, however, they developed problems which could be met only with wider jurisdiction. Louisville's charter had to be amended twenty-two times before 1815 and Cincinnati's underwent five major changes between 1815 and 1827. Others, though altered less often, were adjusted and remade until finally scrapped for new ones. Reluctantly, and bit by bit, the states turned over to the cities the responsibility of managing their own affairs, though keeping them starved for revenue by strict tax and debt limitations.

Despite inadequate charters and modest incomes, urban governments played a decisive role in the growth of Western cities. Since these were commercial towns, local authorities paid special attention to mercantile requirements. They not only constructed market houses but also extended municipal regulation over a wide variety of trading activity. Ordinances protected the public against adulterated foods, false measurements, and rigged prices. Some municipalities went even farther and assumed responsibility for seeing that "justice is done between buyer and seller."[23] In search of this objective, officials fixed prices on some goods, excluded monopolies from the market, and tried to equalize opportunities for smaller purchasers. To facilitate access to the exchange center, they lavished time and money on the development of wharves and docks and the improvement of streets.

Municipalities also tackled a wide variety of other problems growing out of urban life. Fire protection, at first casually organized, was placed on a more formal basis. Volunteer companies still provided the manpower, but government participation increased markedly. Local councils legislated against many kinds of fire hazards, and public money furnished most of the equipment. Moreover, some places, haunted by the image of Detroit's disaster in 1805, forbade the construction of wooden buildings in the heart of the city, a measure which not only reduced fire risks but also changed the face of downtown areas. The development of adequate police was much slower. By 1830 only Lexington and Louisville had regular patrols, and these were established with the intent more of control of slaves than the general protection of life and property. In other towns law enforcement was lax by day and absent at night, though the introduction of gas lighting in Pittsburgh and Cincinnati in the late twenties made the after-dark hours there less dangerous than before.

Congested living created new health hazards and especially increased the likelihood of epidemics. Every place suffered, but none like Louisville, which earned a grim reputation as the "Graveyard of the West" because of the constant visitations of yellow fever and malaria.[24] Cities took preventive measures, such as draining stagnant ponds and clearing streets and lots, and also appointed boards of health to preside over the problem. Municipal water systems, introduced in Pittsburgh and Cincinnati before 1830, made life healthier and certainly more comfortable, while the discussion of installing underground sewers pointed to still more extensive reform in sanitation.

In meeting urban problems, Western officials drew heavily on Eastern experience. Lacking precedents of their own, and familiar with the techniques of older cities, they frankly patterned their practice on Eastern models. There was little innovation. When confronted by a new question, local authorities responded by adopting tested solutions. This emulation characterized nearly every aspect of development—from the width of streets to housing regulations. No major improvement was launched without a close study of established seaboard practices. St. Louis' council, for example, instructed its water committee to "procure from the cities of Philadelphia and New Orleans such information as can be obtained on the subject of conveying water and the best manner of clearing it."[25] When Cincinnati discussed introducing underground sewers, an official group was designated to "ascertain from the city authorities of New York, Philadelphia, Baltimore and Boston, how far the sinking of common sewers is approved in those cities."[26] Pittsburgh undertook gas lighting only after exhaustive research and "very full enquiries at New York and Baltimore."[27]

Though the young towns drew upon the experience of all the major Atlantic cities, the special source of municipal wisdom was Philadelphia. Many Western urbanites had lived or visited there; it provided the new country with most of its professional and cultural leadership; it was the model metropolis. "She is the great seat of American affluence, of individual riches, and distinguished philanthropy," a Pittsburgh editorial declared in 1818. "From her . . . we have everything to look for."[28] Newspapers often referred to it as "our mother city."[29]

From street plans to cultural activity, from the shape of market houses to the habits of people, the Philadelphia influence prevailed. Robert Peterson and John Filson, who had a hand in the founding of Louisville, Lexington, and Cincinnati, borrowed the basic grid pattern of the original plats from the Pennsylvania metropolis.[30] Market location and design came from the same source, as did techniques for fire fighting and police protection. Western towns also leaned on Philadelphia's leadership in street lighting, waterworks, and wharving. Even the naming of suburbs—Pittsburgh's Kensington and Cincinnati's Liberties—came from the mother city. The result was a physical likeness which struck many travelers and which Philadelphians themselves recognized. Gideon Burton, for instance, remembered his first impression of Cincinnati in the 1820's: "How beautiful this city is," he remarked, "how much like Philadelphia."[31]

The Quaker City spirit, moreover, went beyond streets, buildings, and improvements, reaching into a wide range of human activity. Businessmen, yearly visitors in the East, brought marketing and promotion techniques from there;[32] young labor movements lifted their platforms from trade union programs in the mother city; employment agencies were conducted "principally on the Philadelphia plan."[33] The same metropolis trained most of the physicians of the West and a large share of the teachers and ministers. Caspar Wistar's famed Sunday evening gatherings of the intelligentsia provided the idea for Daniel Drake's select meetings of Cincinnati's social and cultural elite. Moreover, Philadelphia furnished the model of the perfect urbanite, for the highest praise that Western town dwellers could bestow upon a fellow citizen was to refer to him as their own "Benjamin Franklin."[34] In short, Philadelphia represented the highest stage of urban development, and progress was measured against this ideal.

Such borrowing was a conscious policy. In 1825 Mayor William Carr Lane of St. Louis, the most able urban statesman of the period, provided the justification. "Experience is the best guide . . . ," he told his councilmen. "The records of other towns are a source from which we may expect to derive useful hints. . . . It is therefore incumbent upon us to examine carefully what other communities similarly situated have done."[35] The process, however, was selective, not slavish. Investigation usually revealed a wide variety of possibilities, allowing Western cities to choose the most appropriate technique. Nevertheless, young towns preferred to meet their urban problems by adopting the established ways of the East. The challenge of the new country, far from producing a bold and fresh response, led to greater dependence on the older sections of the Union.

As transmontane cities developed they created societies whose ways and habits contrasted sharply with those of the countryside. Not only was their physical environment distinct, but their interests, activities, and pace of life also differed greatly. In 1811 a farmer near Lexington expressed the conflict as contemporaries saw it in a dialogue between "Rusticus" and "Urbanus." The latter referred to the "rude, gross appearance" of his neighbor, adding: "How strong you smell of your ploughed ground and corn fields. How dismal, how gloomy your green woods. What a miserable clash your whistling woodland birds are continually making." "Rusticus" replied with the rural image of the town dweller. "What a fine smooth complexion you have Urbanus: you look like a weed that has grown up in the shade. Can you walk your streets without inhaling the noxious fumes with which your town is pregnant? . . . Can you engage in calm contemplation, when hammers are ringing in every direction—when there is as great a *rattling* as in a storm when the hail descends on our house tops?"[36]

One of the most conspicuous differences was in social structure. The stratification of urban societies was in marked contrast with the boisterous equality of the countryside. Social lines developed very quickly in the city. Though not as tightly drawn as in the East, they represented the meaningful distinctions in Western communities. The groupings were basically economic, though professional people were set apart by their interest and training, and Negroes by their color. No rigid boundaries divided the classes, and movement between them was constant. Yet differences did exist; people felt them and contemporaries thought them significant. It is suggestive in this regard that the first great literary product of the West, *Modern Chivalry*, satirized the notion of equality, and the author, Hugh Henry Brackenridge, was one of Pittsburgh's leading citizens.

These divisions deepened in the postwar years. As the cities grew the sense of neighborliness and intimacy diminished, giving way to the impersonality characteristic of urban living. To old-timers the changing social configuration bred a deep nostalgia and raised the image of happier, simpler days. "We cannot help looking back with sorrowful heart, in that time of unaffected content and gaiety," a Pennsylvanian lamented, "when the unambitious people . . . in the village of 'Fort Pitt' in the yet unchartered town of Pittsburgh, were ignorant and careless of all invidious distinctions, which distract and divide the inhabitants of overgrown cities. Then all was peaceful heartfelt felicity, undisturbed by the rankling thorns of envy; and equality . . . was a tie that united all ranks and conditions in our community."[37] Town life in the West had never been that idyllic, but the distortion of the vision was itself a measure of the rapid change. "We have our castes of society, graduated and divided with as much regard to rank and dignity as the most scrupulous Hindoos maintain in defense of their religious prejudices," the same source admitted in 1826. Moreover, social distances were great. "Between the . . . classes . . . there are lines of demarcation drawn wide, distinct and not to be violated with impunity."[38] Nor was this stratification surprising. Having come from

places where differences mattered, early city dwellers tried to re-create them in a new setting. The urge for status was stronger than the appeal of equality, and as the towns expanded cleavages deepened.

Urban ways were further distinguished from rural habits by the collective approach to many problems. City living created issues which could not always be solved by the highly individualistic methods of agrarian society. Local governments assumed an ever wider responsibility for the conduct of community affairs, and voluntary associations handled a large variety of other questions. Merchants formed chambers of commerce to facilitate cooperation on common problems; professional people organized societies to raise the standards of their colleagues and keep out the untrained. Working people, too, banded together in unions, seeking not only greater economic strength but also fraternity and self-improvement. Religious and philanthropic clubs managed most charity and relief work, while immigrants combined to help new arrivals. In addition, other associations grew up to promote literature and music, encourage debating, advocate social innovations, support public causes, and conduct the welter of amusements which larger cities required. Just as conditions in the countryside placed greatest emphasis on individual effort, so the urban situation made cooperative action seem more appropriate.

Rural and metropolitan West were also separated by distinctive social and cultural developments. The towns very quickly produced a surprisingly rich and diversified life, offering opportunities in many fields similar to those of Eastern cities but lacking on the farm or frontier.[39] They enjoyed a virtual monopoly of printing presses, newspapers, bookstores, and circulating libraries. Theaters sprang up to encourage local players and traveling troupes, while in larger places museums brought the curious and the scientific to the townfolks.[40] In addition, every week brought numerous lectures and debates on all kinds of topics, keeping urban residents abreast of the latest discoveries and developments in every field. By 1815 these amenities had already lost their novelty. Indeed, some thought the civilizing process was getting out of hand. "Twenty sermons a week–," a Cincinnatian wearily counted, "Sunday evening Discourses on Theology–Private assemblies–state Cotillon parties –Saturday Night Clubs, and chemical lectures– . . . like the fever and the ague, return every day with distressing regularity."[41]

Of course, the whole transmontane region matured culturally in this period, but the towns played a strategic role. "Cities have arisen in the very wilderness . . . ," a St. Louis editor noticed in 1821, "and form in their respective states the *foci* of art and science, of wealth and information."[42] A Cincinnatian made a similar observation. "This *city*, in its growth and cultural improvements has anticipated the western country in general."[43] The hinterland, already bound to urban communities by trade, readily admitted its dependence. The *Pittsburgh Gazette* merely stated the obvious when it remarked in 1819 that the surrounding region "looks up to Pittsburgh not only as a medium through which to receive the comforts and luxuries of foreign commodities, but also a channel from which it can most naturally expect a supply of intellectual wealth."[44] Thus while the cities' merchants staked out markets in the countryside, their civic leaders spread a cultural influence into the same area.

This leadership extended into almost every field. For example, the educational opportunities of town children greatly exceeded those of their rural neighbors. Every municipality developed a complex of private tuition schools topped by an academy and, in every place except Louisville, a college. Moreover, the cities organized the movement of public schooling. Ohio's experience is illustrative. The movement for state legislation started in Cincinnati, received its major impetus from the local press, and was carried in the Assembly through the efforts of representatives from Hamilton county. It is also significant that the first superintendent of common schools in Ohio was Samuel Lewis of Cincinnati. Nor was this urban leadership surprising. The cities, as the great population centers, felt the educational pressure first and most acutely. In addition, they alone had the wealth needed to launch ambitious projects for large numbers of children. Hence the towns were ready for comprehensive public programs long before the countryside.

The most striking illustration of the cultural supremacy of the cities, however, was Lexington's unique reign as the "Athens of the West."[45] The area's largest town until 1810, it was early celebrated for its polish and sophistication and was generally conceded to be the region's capital of arts and science. But the coming of the steamboat and the depression of 1819 combined to undermine its economic position. To offset this commercial and industrial decline, Lexington's civic leaders inaugurated a policy of vigorous cultural expansion.[46] They built schools, subsidized Transylvania University, and advertised the many opportunities for advancement in learning and letters in the metropolis. Throughout the twenties this campaign was a spectacular success. The town became the resort of the most talented men of the new country. Educators, scientists, painters, lawyers, architects, musicians, and their patrons all flocked there. Transylvania University attained national eminence, attracting most of its faculty from the East and drawing students from better than a dozen states. Like a renaissance city of old Italy, Lexington provided the creative atmosphere for a unique flowering that for a decade astonished travelers and stimulated the best minds of the West.

In its golden age the town boasted the most distinguished collection of intellectuals the new country had ever seen in a single city. The central figure in this awakening was Horace Holley, a Unitarian minister from Boston and the president of Transylvania. Though not an accomplished scholar himself, he recruited a remarkable faculty and raised the institution from a small denominational college to a university of the first rank. The medical department achieved a special distinction. Its dean was Charles Caldwell, one of Benjamin Rush's favorite pupils, who turned down important posts in New York, Philadelphia, and Baltimore to join the Kentucky experiment. Members of the staff included the botanist, Charles Wilkins Short, Daniel Drake, later the author of a pioneering study of diseases in the Mississippi Valley, and the surgeon, Benjamin Winslow Dudley. Among them, too, was the furtive and erratic, yet highly talented, Turkish-born naturalist, Constantine Rafinesque, whose most fruitful years were spent in Lexington.[47]

The graduating class of the medical school in 1826 demonstrated the extent of the university's reputation and influence. With sixty-seven degrees granted in that year, twenty-eight of the recipients came from Kentucky, ten from Tennessee, five each from Virginia, South Carolina, and Alabama, three from Ohio, two each from Mississippi, Illinois, and Louisiana, and one each from North Carolina and Georgia. During the twenties the college trained many of the West's most distinguished people. In politics alone it turned out at least seventeen congressmen, three governors, six United States senators, and the president of the Confederacy. In the same decade the school produced scores of lawyers, clergymen, and physicians, who did much to raise professional standards in the new country. Few universities have left such a clear mark on a generation; in its heyday Transylvania fully deserved its title of the "Harvard of the West."[48]

The college was the center of this wilderness renaissance, but around it moved other figures—artists, architects, musicians, and poets—who gave added luster to the movement. In Matthew Jouett the city had the West's most famous painter. A student of Gilbert Stuart and a portraitist of considerable gifts, he made his studio the exciting headquarters for a group of promising young artists. Gideon Shryock provided Lexington with an architect equal to its enlightenment. After studying with William Strickland in Philadelphia, he brought the Greek revival across the mountains. His work, especially the state capitol at Frankfort and Morrison College at Transylvania, brought him immediate fame and has led a modern critic to assert that he "was almost a decade ahead of his time even when judged by sophisticated eastern standards."[49] Music shared the upsurge, and in 1817 townsfolk heard Anthony Phillip Hennrich conduct the first performance of a Beethoven symphony in the United States.

The glitter of this city drew young people from all over the transmontane region, including many from the countryside. In doing so, it provoked a familiar lament from the rural areas whose children succumbed to the bewitchment of Lexington. "We want our sons to be practical men," wrote a Kentucky farmer, "whose minds will not be filled with those light notions of refinement and taste, which will induce them to believe that they are of a different order of beings, or that will elevate them above their equals."[50] Later, agrarian representatives in the legislature joined the attack on Transylvania by voting to cut off state financial assistance.

No less striking than cultural cleavages were the differences in rural and urban religious development. Progress in the cities was steadier and more substantial—though less spectacular—than in the back country. Traveling ministers might refer to Pittsburgh as "a young hell, a second Sodom,"[51] and Francis Asbury might complain in 1803 that he felt "the power of Satan in those little, wicked western trading towns,"[52] but both churches and membership multiplied rapidly in urban centers. Furthermore, the growth owed nothing to the sporadic revivals which burned across the countryside at the beginning of the century. These movements were essentially rural, having their roots in the isolation of agricultural living and the spiritual starvation of people unattended by regular services. The city situation, with its constant contacts and

settled church organizations, involved neither of these elements. Instead, religious societies proliferated, sects took on such additional functions as charity and missionary work, and congregations sent money back East to aid their seminaries. Far from being sinks of corruption, Western cities quickly became religious centers, supplying Bibles to the frontier, assisting foreign missions, and, in the twenties, building theological schools to provide priests and ministers for the whole region.

Political life also reflected the growing rural-urban division. Though the rhetoric of the period often obscured them, differences existed from the very beginning. Suspicion of the towns led states to avoid economic and cultural centers when locating their capitals. Nearly all these cities sought the prize, but none was successful. The *Missouri Gazette* candidly stated the issue in 1820. "It has been said that St. Louis is obnoxious to our Legislature—that its growth and influence . . . are looked on with a jealous eye, and its pretensions . . . ought to be discouraged."[53] The same clash had earlier occurred in Kentucky, where state leaders virtually invented Frankfort to keep the capital away from Louisville or Lexington.

As the region developed, however, the conflict became increasingly apparent, though it was still expressed cautiously. "We must be permitted to say," an editor asserted in 1829, "that in Cincinnati we have separate interests" from the countryside.[54] Likewise, a Pittsburgher prefaced a strong attack on the neighboring areas by declaring that "we think it wrong to stir up a jealousy between city and county."[55] Nevertheless, the split represented one of the fundamental facts of Western politics.

Of course, farm dwellers easily outnumbered urbanites, but the latter wielded disproportionate power. The case of Jefferson and Oldham counties in Kentucky was illustrative. In the mid-twenties the combined vote reached 3,200, Louisville residents casting roughly a quarter of them. Yet the state senator and both representatives came from the city. In 1829 when a third assemblyman was added, the rural interests pleaded with Louisville leaders to name someone from the surrounding area. "It may seem strange," wrote an observer, "that it would be necessary thus to ask for the liberality of 800 voters in favor of 2,400. . . . Nevertheless, the concentrated energies of 800 do entirely outweigh the scattered influence of the 2,400—that all past experience teaches."[56] The situation was the same elsewhere. At one time all of Missouri's representatives in Washington—two senators and one congressman—as well as its governor came from St. Louis.

The cities' political influence rested on their ability to produce leadership. As the economic and intellectual centers of transmontane life they attracted the talented and ambitious in all fields. Politics was no exception. Nearly all the great spokesmen of the West had important urban connections and their activity often reflected the demands of their town constituents. Henry Clay was one of Lexington's most prominent lawyers when he went to the United States Senate in 1806. Thomas Hart Benton held local offices in St. Louis before moving on to the national scene, and William Henry Harrison, though he lived in nearby North Bend, had deep roots in Cincinnati affairs through most of his long public life. Moreover, all were alive to the interests of their city. Benton's successful attack on govern-ment factories in the Indian territory culminated a long and intense campaign by St. Louis merchants to break federal trade control on the Missouri. Clay's enthusiasm for an ample tariff on hemp derived at least as much from the pressure of Lexington's manufactures as from that of the growers of the Blue Grass. And Harrison, as state senator, led the campaign for public schools in Ohio largely at the behest of his Cincinnati supporters. These were not isolated cases; an examination of the careers of these men demonstrates the importance of their urban connections.

By 1830, then, the West had produced two types of society—one rural and one urban. Each developed its own institutions, habits, and living patterns. The countryside claimed much the larger population and often gave to transmontane affairs an agrarian flavor. But broadcloth was catching up with buckskin. The census of 1830 revealed the disproportionate rate of city growth. While the state of Ohio had four times as many inhabitants as it counted in 1810, Cincinnati's increase was twelve-fold. The story was the same elsewhere. Louisville's figure showed a growth of 650 per cent compared with Kentucky's 50 per cent, and Pittsburgh tripled in size while Pennsylvania did not quite double its population. By 1830 the rise of these cities had driven a broad wedge of urbanism into Western life.

Though town and country developed along different paths, clashes were still infrequent. The West was large enough to contain both movements comfortably. Indeed, each supported the other. The rural regions supplied the cities with raw materials for their mills and packinghouses and offered an expanding market to their shops and factories. In turn, urban centers served the surrounding areas by providing both the necessities and comforts of life as well as new opportunity for ambitious farm youths. Yet the cities represented the more aggressive and dynamic force. By spreading their economic power over the entire section, by bringing the fruits of civilization across the mountains, and by insinuating their ways into the countryside, they speeded up the transformation of the West from a gloomy wilderness to a richly diversified region. Any historical view which omits this aspect of Western life tells but part of the story.

NOTES

1. *Missouri Gazette* (St. Louis), July 13, 1816.
2. *Liberty Hall* (Cincinnati), June 11, 1815.
3. *Missouri Republican* (St. Louis), Aug. 29, 1825.
4. Hall, *The West: Its Commerce and Navigation* (Cincinnati, 1848), p. 227.
5. Drake, "Dr. Drake's Memoir of the Miami County, 1779-1794," Beverley Bond, Jr., ed., Historical and Philosophical Society of Ohio, *Quarterly Publications*, XVIII (1923), 58.
6. *Ibid.*
7. James R. Robertson, ed., *Petitions of the Early Inhabitants of Kentucky to the General Assembly of Virginia, 1769-1792* (Louisville, Ky., 1914), p. 106.
8. Louis C. Hunter, *Steamboats on the Western Rivers, An Economic and Technological History* (Cambridge, Mass., 1949), pp. 27-32.
9. Morgan Neville, "The Last of the Boatman," *The Western Souvenir for 1829* (Cincinnati, Ohio, n.d.), p. 108.
10. [Jean Baptiste] Marestier, *Mémoire sur les Bateaux à vapeur des États-Unis d' Amérique* (Paris, 1824), pp. 9-10.
11. Zadock Cramer, *Pittsburgh Almanack for the Year of Our Lord 1810* (Pittsburgh, Pa., 1810), p. 52.
12. Pittsburgh's industrial foundations are discussed in Catherine Elizabeth Reiser, *Pittsburgh's Commercial Development, 1800-1850* (Harrisburg, Pa., 1951), pp. 12-21.
13. *Niles' Register*, May 28, 1814.
14. *Pittsburgh Gazette*, Nov. 16, 1830.
15. *Cincinnati Advertiser*, Aug. 18, 1830.
16. United States *Census*, 1830, pp. 114-15.
17. For an appreciation of the economic importance of the cities in the growth of the West, see Frederick Jackson Turner, *Rise of the New West, 1819-1829* in *The American Nation: A History*, A. B. Hart, ed., XIV (New York, 1906), 96-98.

18. Flint, "Thoughts Respecting the Establishment of a Porcelain Manufactory at Cincinnati," *Western Monthly Review*, III (1830), 512; Benjamin Drake and Edward W. Mansfield, *Cincinnati in 1826* (Cincinnati, Ohio, 1827), p. 71.
19. *Louisville Public Advertiser*, Oct. 17, 1829.
20. Chittenden, *The American Fur Trade of the Far West* (2 vols., New York, 1902), I, 99.
21. *Pittsburgh Gazette*, Dec. 18, 1818.
22. *Pittsburgh Gazette*, Feb. 5, 1819.
23. *Pittsburgh Gazette*, Mar. 9, 1810.
24. Benjamin Casseday, *The History of Louisville from Its Earliest Settlement till the Year 1852* (Louisville, Ky., 1852), p. 49.
25. St. Louis City Council, Minutes, Court House, St. Louis, June 12, 1829.
26. Cincinnati City Council, Minutes, City Hall, Cincinnati, Oct. 6, 1827.
27. Pittsburgh City Council, City Council Papers, City Hall, Pittsburgh, May 10, 1827. The extent of Western urban indebtedness to the East is perhaps best illustrated in the establishment of the high school in Louisville. The building was "mainly after the plan of the High School of New York, united with the Public School Rooms of Philadelphia." Most of the teachers came from the East, while the curriculum and even reading assignments derived from "the High School of New York and some of the Boston establishments." *An Account of the Louisville City School, Together With the Ordinances of the City Council, and the Regulations of the Board of Trustees for the Government of the Institution* (Louisville, Ky., 1830), pp. 5 ff.
28. *Pittsburgh Gazette*, Oct. 27, 1818.
29. For example, see *Pittsburgh Gazette*, June 23, 1818.
30. For example, see Rufus King, *Ohio First Fruits of the Ordinance of 1787* (Boston, 1888), p. 209.
31. Burton, *Reminiscences of Gideon Burton* (Cincinnati, Ohio, 1895). The strategic location of Western cities in the life of the new country reminded some visitors of the regional supremacy of Philadelphia. Lewis Condict, for example, referred to Lexington as "the Philadelphia of Kentucky." "Journal of a Trip to Kentucky in 1795," *Proceedings of the New Jersey Historical Society*, n.s., IV (1919), 120.
32. *Cincinnati Enquirer*, Apr. 22, 1923.
33. *Pittsburgh Mercury*, Aug. 7, 1827.
34. The phrase was constantly used in characterizing John Bradford of Lexington and Daniel Drake of Cincinnati, but it was applied to others as well.
35. St. Louis City Council, Minutes, Court House, St. Louis, Apr. 25, 1825.
36. *Kentucky Reporter* (Lexington), July 2, 1811.
37. Samuel Jones, *Pittsburgh in 1826* (Pittsburgh, Pa., 1826), p. 43.
38. *Ibid.*
39. For a day-to-day account of the cultural offerings of a Western city between 1820 and 1830 see the highly informative but unpublished diary of William Stanley Merrill in the library of the Historical and Philosophical Society of Ohio (Cincinnati).
40. The development of the theater in Western

cities is outlined in Ralph Leslie Rush, *The Literature of the Middle Western Frontier* (New York,
1925), I, 352-400. For a detailed study of a single
town see William G. B. Carson, *The Theatre on
the Frontier, The Early Years of the St. Louis
Stage* (Chicago, 1932), pp. 1-134.
41. *Liberty Hall* (Cincinnati), Dec. 9, 1816.
42. *Missouri Gazette* (St. Louis), Dec. 20, 1820.
43. *Liberty Hall* (Cincinnati), June 29, 1819.
44. *Pittsburgh Gazette,* Apr. 30, 1819.
45. For Lexington's growth and brief supremacy
see Bernard Mayo, "Lexington, Frontier Metropolis," in *Historiography and Urbanization,* Eric F.
Goldman, ed. (Baltimore, Md., 1941), pp. 21-42.
46. See, for example, *Kentucky Reporter,* Oct. 4,
1820.
47. Transylvania's "golden age" is treated in detail in Walter William Jennings, *Transylvania, Pioneer University of the West* (New York, 1955),
pp. 99-124, and Niels Henry Sonne, *Liberal Kentucky, 1780-1828* (New York, 1939), pp. 160-
242.

48. The reputation of Lexington in Cincinnati is
charmingly portrayed in the letters of young Ohio-
ans attending Transylvania University to their
friends back home. See especially the William
Lytle Collection in the library of the Historical
and Philosophical Society of Ohio (Cincinnati).
49. Talbot Hamlin, *Greek Revival Architecture in
America: Being an Account of Important Trends
in American Architecture and American Life prior
to the War between the States* (New York, 1944),
p. 244.
50. *Kentucky Reporter* (Lexington), Feb. 16,
1824.
51. *Pittsburgh Gazette,* Sept. 23, 1803.
52. Francis Asbury, *Journal of Rev. Francis Asbury, Bishop of Methodist Episcopal Church* (n.p.,
1821), III, 127.
53. *Missouri Gazette* (St. Louis), Dec. 6, 1820.
54. *Cincinnati Advertiser,* Sept. 16, 1829.
55. *Pittsburgh Statesman,* Aug. 26, 1823.
56. *Louisville Public Advertiser,* July 28, 1824.

Urban Growth in the South

DAVID GOLDFIELD

Over a generation ago, W. J. Cash quickly disabused his readers of the plantation ideal. Yet, Scarlett and Rhett continue to cavort through the pages of southern history, reinterpreted and scaled down perhaps, but essentially unchanged. Historian David L. Smiley remarked recently that writers still view the Old South as "planter, plantation, staple crop, and the Negro, all set in a rural scene." Southern ruralness and the region's antipathy to urbanization have been historical clichés. Eugene D. Genovese, for example, referred to southern antiurbanism as a "quasi-religious faith." The Old South, Genovese continued, was a "backward-looking society" dominated by slaveholders and their plantations. Raimondo Luraghi, in a provocative article comparing the southern Italian experience with the southern American experience, affirmed the Old South's "agrarian, backward status." Other historians have reasoned that southerners were self-evidently unsympathetic to urban growth because cities characterized the North. Northern cities, of course, harbored abolitionists, feminists, and other would-be traducers of southern civilization. To encourage urbanization in the South would be to create an environment conducive to the destruction of southern institutions.[1]

Some historians have begrudgingly admitted the existence of an urban South. They have, however, either dismissed the city's role in the region entirely or accorded it a subservient and ineffectual place. Actually, urban growth in all southern states, except for Louisiana and those states where figures were unavailable, outstripped the section's increase in general population between 1840 and 1860. More specifically, scholars have emphasized the paucity and anemia of inferior towns in the Old South as evidence of the superficiality of southern urbanization.[2] Precisely the opposite was true: the most rapid rate of urbanization in the Old South occurred beyond the Appalachian region between 1840 and 1860. Memphis, an interior city, exhibited the rate of growth of 155 percent: the fastest of any southern city during the period. The emergence of Atlanta and Chattanooga and the steady development of Louisville attested to the health of interior settlements. Much of the lower Mississippi Valley was frontier well into the 1830s. The high percentages of the growth of the urban population reflected, in part, the newness of the region. There were, of course, no serious interior rivals to New Orleans, Richmond, or Baltimore. On the other hand New York, Boston, and Philadelphia overshadowed Pittsburgh, Cincinnati, and Chicago in the North. The dominance of coastal cities in both sections reflected more the commercial nature of the antebellum economy than any philosophical or economic disabilities prohibiting interior urban development.[3]

Writers acknowledging southern ur-

Reprinted by permission of Louisiana State University Press from *Urban Growth in the Age of Sectionalism* by David Goldfield, copyright © 1977, pp. i–xxx.

banization have pointed out the stunted nature of that development. Inadequate industrialization, one argument ran, rendered the South's cities little more than sleepy market towns reflecting the ideals of the surrounding countryside.[4] While it was accurate to belittle southern industrialization compared to the Northeast, this comparison was unfair since the Northeast was one of the most rapidly industrializing areas of the world at the time. The West also lacked industrial centers to match those of the Northeast, and in some industries the South's facilities were clearly superior.[5] Richmond contained the largest flour mill in the nation in 1860 and manufactured more tobacco than any other city in the world. Augusta's textile complex earned that city the title Lowell of the South. Wheeling glass achieved a national reputation, and its iron industry, for a time, rivaled Pittsburgh's.[6] The ability of the South to mount a war effort of four years' duration was testimony to the fact that an industrial potential existed prior to the Civil War.

Industrialization and urbanization are not synonymous. Francis Cabot Lowell took great pains to maintain a pastoral atmosphere in his industrial villages. Similarly, South Carolina industrialist William Gregg and Alabama textile entrepreneur Daniel Pratt viewed cities as inappropriate environments for industry.[7] Much of the South's industry was, in fact, small-scale, rural, and often plantation based—a fact that tended to depress southern industrial statistics. It is unclear whether industry is even essential for urban growth. Cincinnati, for example, achieved hegemony in the West over its industrial rival, Pittsburgh, by developing its commerce, not its manufacturing.[8]

A final argument advanced by historians to minimize the effect of south-

ern urban civilization emphasizes the pervasiveness of a rural ideal that smothered urban progress.[9] This rural-mindedness, though, was not a distinctly southern phenomenon. Prominent northerners excoriated the evils of urban civilization and extolled the benefits of pastoral life just as passionately as their southern counterparts. If, as some have charged, southern city dwellers poured profits into country homes and farms, there is no evidence that northern merchants and bankers did not long equally hard for a country estate. Northern reverence for rural quietude seemed to have little impact upon urban growth in the region. In fact, mid-nineteenth-century Americans generally possessed ambivalent attitudes toward both urban and rural living that enabled them to build great cities and to write romantic literature exalting country life without apparent self-contradiction. To hold that love of nature and rural virtues were antagonistic to urbanization is to establish a dichotomy that was not always clear to contemporaries.[10]

Implied and often explicit in the discussion on southern ruralness is that southerners, captured by visions of moonlight and magnolias, invested heavily in slaves and land and left urban enterprises languishing.[11] Southern rural investors, however, evidently understood that growing cities ultimately redounded to the benefit of their farms. Their investments did not stop at the city line because neither did their economic interests. Inventories of planters' estates indicated that well-to-do scions of the soil placed their profits in a variety of schemes during the 1850s when both capital and investment opportunities were relatively abundant in the region. Internal improvements and industrial firms, bank stock, and city bonds as well as land and labor attracted planters' money.[12]

Between 1850 and 1860, southern railroad mileage, constructed primarily with local capital, quadrupled while northern mileage (including that of western states), often aided by foreign capital, tripled. Industrial investments in the South increased by 64 percent during this period, compared with an increase of 83 percent for the more heavily industrialized northern states. Southern bank capital also compared favorably with northern financial institutions. A survey of bank capital in twenty-eight cities just prior to the southern railroad boom in 1848 revealed that banks in twelve southern cities possessed capital amounting to $56,-000,000 while in sixteen northern cities bank capital totaled $80,000,000. New York and Boston alone, though, accounted for more than half of the northern total ($45,000,000). Since planters held the bulk of investment capital in the South, it was not surprising that such enterprises benefited from rural largesse.[13]

The competition for the rural investment dollar was all the more severe as southern agriculture revived during the 1850s. Financing additional land and labor promised a profitable return; indeed more profitable, some scholars have asserted, than comparable enterprises anywhere in the Union. The wonder is that, considering the return from agriculture, planter capital found its way into such a broad spectrum of economic activities.[14]

Patriotism as well as profits motivated agriculturists to enhance the urban economic base. Southern rhetoric during the period between the Mexican War and the firing on Fort Sumter demonstrated an increasing appreciation for the efficacy of urban growth as a response to northern economic and political power. J. D. B. DeBow, an indefatigable spokesman for the urban South, achieved his greatest fame, and his *Review* its greatest circulation, during the decade prior to the Civil War.[15] George Fitzhugh, a leading proponent of planter society, also encouraged urban development as a means to sectional strength:

Towns and villages . . . afford respectable occupations in the mechanic arts, commerce, manufactures, and the professions. . . . They sustain good schools, which a sparse country neighborhood never can. They furnish places and opportunities for association and rational enjoyment to the neighborhood around. They support good ministers and churches. . . . Rivers and roads without towns, are mere facilities offered to agriculture to carry off the crops, to exhaust the soil, and to remove the inhabitants.[16]

Neither DeBow nor Fitzhugh were voices in the southern wilderness. Their writings were read widely and their calls for urban growth drew sympathetic responses throughout the antebellum South. Within the past decade, urban biographies of Natchez, New Orleans, and Houston; monographs dealing with various aspects of southern urban life; and a spate of articles have attested to this fact and have begun to redress the imbalance in southern historiography.[17]

These scholarly efforts and the general surge in urban history have underscored the fact that nineteenth-century cities possessed influence far greater than their small number warranted. They were crucibles of change in a changing society. This is not surprising. Richard Hildreth, marveling at the rapid pace of urbanization in what still was a predominantly rural society, observed that America's cities "are the central points from which knowledge, enterprise, and civilization stream out upon the surrounding country."[18] From Hildreth's vantage point (mid-nineteenth-century America) the urban phenomenon must have been truly impressive. The years between 1820 and 1860 witnessed the most rapid rate of growth of cities in American history. The decade between 1840 and 1850 showed the largest increase in urban population.[19] The South participated in the unprecedented urban growth, but mere numbers do not reveal the influence of southern cities. While population is an index of urban growth, it is not the only barometer of urbanization. Nineteenth-century Tokyo possessed more than three million residents but could hardly be called a city in the modern sense of extensive commercial connections, internal organization, urban services, and civic pride. Historians have begun to address themselves to the question of urbanization since it was such a pervasive phenomenon in the nineteenth century. Although a satisfactory model of urban growth has yet to appear, writers have isolated several factors crucial to the process of urbanization.

Scholars have employed two general measures of urbanization: quantitative and qualitative.[20] The quantitative measure includes two indicators of urbanization. The first is the development of an economic superstructure consisting of transportation facilities, industry, and export trade. The second quantitative index measures the increase in population, area, and wealth, which is usually triggered by the impact of the economic superstructure. The differentiation and segregation of urban functions is an important manifestation of the quantitative growth indexes. Some quantitative indicators are more important than others. Industry and population are not necessarily indicative of modern urban civilization. Transporta-

tion links with the countryside and with other cities, on the other hand, liberate "island communities" and enable them to establish regional relationships crucial to the process of urbanization.

The qualitative measure also consists of two indicators. First, there is the organization of urban life. The quantitative aspects of growth require the evolution of an urban leadership and a communications system. Together, they must rationalize the urban economic and political system. Urban consciousness is the second indicator of qualitative growth. It is the most intangible but one of the most important of all measures. Urban consciousness is both a feeling of uniqueness and a sense of civic pride. It is not only an indicator of growth but, in a sense, marks its fulfillment.

Since George Rogers Taylor's exhaustive study of the transportation revolution in nineteenth-century America, scholars have viewed the railroad as an important catalyst in the compound of cityhood. The railroad increased the accessibility of the city to the hinterland and vice versa. In making commercial agriculture more feasible, the railroad accelerated prosperity in the countryside and ultimately in the market town. Prosperity generated capital, and capital promoted growth. The railroad was also one of the earliest forms of corporate enterprise. It thus provided entrepreneurs with corporate experience —often at the expense of public and private stockholders—which proved valuable for later corporate endeavors. Finally, the railroad helped to transform local economies into a regional and eventually a national economy. The formation of a national economy was a major theme in antebellum America.[21]

The economic superstructure led by

the railroad generated advances in population, area, and wealth. A modern, differentiated city began to emerge. The diversification of the urban economy created a labor-class consciousness. The hazy lines of distinction between employer and employee, characteristic of the colonial period, began to harden with the appearance of larger mercantile and industrial establishments. Further, residence and work became differentiated. As the city expanded spatially, the central business district evolved as just that: a business district with few residential areas. Although zoning codes did not appear in American cities until the twentieth century, segregated land use was common by the end of the antebellum era.[22]

The emergence of an identifiable, cohesive leadership to rationalize the city's quantitative growth is another indicator of cityhood. Technology and natural advantages were virtually useless without the existence of entrepreneurial skill to parlay them into effective forces for the promotion of urban growth. From the rise of the port of New York to the development of frontier settlements, the role of the civic booster was essential to success. The entrepreneur possessed not only the requisite skills and capital, but through collective leadership in most phases of urban life, he personally directed urban development. Urban leaders organized urban, and ultimately, regional growth. Voluntary associations of leaders facilitated and rationalized the process. More efficient marketing procedures, organized charity relief, and cooperative action on projects designed to improve urban life were some of the accomplishments of urban leadership.[23]

Improved communications was another qualitative index of urban growth. Besides the improvement of the mail service and the introduction of the telegraph—both of which facilitated business transactions—the development of the urban press was an important ally to city-building. The press was essential to leaders' efforts to organize the city. In antebellum America the urban press was primarily a political weapon. Toward the end of the period, however, the political press came increasingly under the influence of local leaders and began to emphasize local development. Further, nonpartisan newspapers appeared (they were called penny presses) that dedicated their columns to the promotion of their city's interests. The urban press disseminated price and market information, functioned as the city's major advertising medium, and served as both creator and defender of the city's image. The Norfolk *Southern Argus*, a leader in the new wave of urban journalism that occurred after 1847, stated an axiom of the day when it observed, "The mighty influence of this silent teacher [the press], pouring its lessons every day into the minds of men, it is impossible to estimate."[24]

The rise of local government to translate the expressions of the press and the goals of the leaders into policy was a significant development in the urbanization process. Local government was unimportant in early nineteenth-century America. Urban growth and the leaders' awareness of the efficacy of government involvement in the process of growth assured a broader role for urban government than it had ever experienced. A range of urban services from police and fire protection to street lighting and relief for the poor enabled city dwellers to cope with urbanization and, in turn, spurred further growth. Finally, the new powers of taxation—a benefit of charter amendments—imposed local government on the community as an important financial force.[25]

The development of urban consciousness was central to urban growth. Urban consciousness, or civic pride, cut across all indexes of urbanization. Demands for railroads, the differentiation of urban life, civic boosterism, the press, and the increased role of local government were all manifestations of urban consciousness. Civic pride represented a belief that the city was a distinct environment that was somehow different from the countryside and shared a commonality with cities elsewhere. Antebellum southern social critic Daniel R. Hundley observed that "nearly all classes of residents in the Southern cities differ in no essential particulars from the same classes in other cities anywhere else in the Union." Urban historian Richard C. Wade concurred with Hundley's observation in noting that urban centers were more like each other than their respective countrysides. Wade concluded that cities muted regional differences and were thus a nationalizing force.[26]

If urbanization was a nationalizing force, it contravened another major theme of nineteenth-century America: sectionalism. The apparent contradiction between the two themes as well as the reluctance of scholars to recognize southern urban growth have inhibited a study of the relationship between these two movements. In the Old South there was a connection between sectional feeling and urban growth. Articles exploiting and explaining the growing sectional crisis appeared alongside articles devoted to subjects promoting urban growth in the press and in magazines. It was not long before contributors and editors combined the two themes and championed the cause of cities as a response to sectionalism. J. D. B. DeBow related the themes of urban ascendancy and sectionalism time and again. DeBow believed that the South's port cities— Baltimore, Richmond, Charleston, Savannah, Mobile, and New Orleans— would break the stranglehold of New York on the nation's commerce and deliver the South from northern dependence. George Fitzhugh similarly urged that southern cities take up the cudgels for the South to release the region from the avaricious and threatening grasp of the North. "The South," Fitzhugh wrote earnestly, "must build up cities, towns, and villages, establish more schools and colleges, educate the poor, construct internal improvements, and carry on her own commerce." On a somewhat smaller scale, though equally urgent, the Richmond *Enquirer* claimed that developing Virginia's cities would save the South from the "indellible brand of degradation the North is trying to affix."[27]

The reasoning of these and other southern writers seemed to be that urban growth would help to strengthen the South and ameliorate sectional antagonism. The South's continued dependence invited northern economic and political aggression and depressed the section. Cities as repositories of labor, capital, expertise, railroads, industry, and mercantile establishments would enable the South to compete on a more equal basis with the North. The region's interests and institutions could thus be safeguarded. Just as New York, Boston, and Philadelphia came to characterize the economic and political leadership of the North, so the South's cities would fill a similar role for her.[28]

The example of northern cities provided southerners with awesome models for urban growth. Southern cities, of course, would possess all of the majesty and none of the social problems that beset the urban North. The dreams of majesty, though, usually overcame concern about the quality of urban life. Americans had canonized the pursuit of prosperity in the four decades preceding the Civil War, and the city seemed to be the working symbol of this American dream. The South shared the vision, and at no time was it stronger than in the 1850s. It was not surprising that the South looked to its cities for the fulfillment of that dream.

The northern urban empire had been built, to a great extent, on the trade of the West. The West held a seemingly limitless bounty, and a share of its trade was a major objective in the southern blueprint for urban growth and sectional equilibrium. Ever since John C. Calhoun and Robert Y. Hayne had successfully promoted a railroad from Charleston to up-country Hamburg, South Carolina, in 1833, southerners had cast covetous eyes upon the western trade. When a group led by Hayne secured a charter for a railroad to Cincinnati, the South Carolina senator pronounced, "The South and the West— we have published the banns—if anyone knows ought why these two should not be joined together, let him speak now, or forever after hold his peace." As for Charleston, Hayne was equally sanguine: "The far and fertile West will pour her inexhaustible treasures into our lap." The wedding announcement was premature. A decade later, under darkening clouds, J. D. B. DeBow placed the South's task in its proper economic perspective: "A contest has been going on between North and South . . . for wealth and commerce of the great valley of the Mississippi. We must meet our Northern competitors . . . with corresponding weapons."[29]

The southern city was at the point of the spear.

The contest outlined by DeBow was a difficult one for the South to undertake for at least two reasons. First, southern cities entered the contest belatedly and had to mount a massive effort in a short period of time (1847 to 1861), defying the laws of trade. The patterns of trade by the end of the Mexican War were unmistakably West to Northeast.[30] New Orleans, the urban bellwether of southern prosperity, enjoyed the return of cotton prosperity in the 1850s. Produce from the Ohio River and upper Mississippi river valleys, however, declined drastically as the railroad overshadowed the Mississippi River as a major commercial artery. Second, southerners overestimated the capacity of their cities to secure western trade in their uneven rivalry with northern urban centers. Besides railroads, financial, factoring, industrial, and direct trade linkages were essential to generate commerce. The capital, energy, and expertise that went into creating these linkages were prodigious. Moreover, these relationships could not appear spontaneously. New York, for example, had been working assiduously since the end of the War of 1812 to erect a commercial superstructure to accommodate and to attract western trade. Even by 1847 New York's economic leadership was not a monopoly.[31]

Southerners like DeBow and Fitzhugh were aware that their section and, more particularly, their cities entered the competition for commercial empire at a considerable disadvantage. It was essential, however, that the South make the challenge. They and other southerners believed that "pecuniary and commercial supremacy" were the real objectives behind the North's strident sectional and anti-slavery rhetoric.[32] If the South, through its cities, would launch a successful economic offensive, the North would respect its southern neighbors as economic equals and seek to cultivate trade, not enemies. Nothing less than the Union was at stake. "Give us [southern cities] the trade of the West," the Richmond *Enquirer* promised, "and we will pacify the nation."[33]

If some southerners linked urbanization with sectionalism, most historians have not. One persistent interpretation in the origins of the Civil War emphasizes the distinction between the agrarian, "quasi-colonial" South and the urban, industrial North and the inevitable clash of these two different "nationalities."[34] This ignores the presence of an urban South as well as a rural North, not to mention the overwhelmingly-agrarian West. In addition, the Beardian proponents and their present-day disciples assume that contemporaries perceived themselves and their section as either rural or urban and that there existed a natural animosity between the two. As I have noted earlier, Americans often blurred the differences between city and country. Their experience, in fact, confirmed the compatability between rural and urban enterprise. As the Norfolk *Southern Argus* observed, "Their [city and country] interests are often one in the same."[35]

As cities grew and prospered throughout the nation, their agricultural hinterlands developed accordingly. The agrarian South, like the agrarian West and North, moved into the orbit of its respective urban market centers. Farmers supported the efforts of their cities to extend the urban commercial network beyond sectional borders. In short, as there was a similarity between the urban South and

cities elsewhere, so there was little difference between market-oriented farms in the Old South and similar units in the North and West. Even conceding that the South was agrarian (and what section was not in 1860?), the section's agriculture was intimately bound to urban development, just as it was in the rest of the nation's farms and cities.[36] Thus, any interpretation that presumes the antagonism of urban and rural environments contradicts the experience of antebellum America.

The dominance of slavery and the slaveholder in southern society is a corollary to the agrarian thesis.[37] The argument assumes an identity between slavery and the farm. An interpretation relying on the importance of slavery in the sectional equation should include a discussion of urban slavery. The city and slavery proved congenial to each other. Increasing use of slave labor in urban pursuits sounded not the death knell for the institution but rather portended a renaissance. Urban slavery demonstrated the flexibility of the institution and the ability of the slave to learn and adapt to new techniques. In a competition against northern cities, slave labor was an important commodity. Slaves manned factories, built railroads and canals, unloaded and loaded produce, and performed other peculiarly urban tasks as southern cities utilized their section's resources to save their section and to achieve prosperity.[38] Slavery was indeed an important element in propelling the nation to civil war. It was important because the South, and southern cities in particular, viewed the demise of the institution as the end to dreams of prosperity and urban growth, and hence of achieving sectional equilibrium. Slavery thus would strengthen the commonality between the sections while its destruction would create a backward colonial, and poverty-stricken region.

Similarly, there is no denying the influence of slaveholders in determining the direction of the South to secession. Slaveholders were dominant figures in the Old South, just as property-holders were influential everywhere. Further, slaveholding was more widespread in the South than real property-holding was in the North. The portrait of a small, exclusive slaveholding aristocracy does not comport with statistics on slave ownership. About one-quarter of the adult white householders in the South owned slaves; in the cities it was usually more than one-third. Even these figures underestimate the ubiquity of the institution in the city, because numerous urban residents hired slaves. Though technically not slaveholders, these citizens were intimately bound with and dependent on the institution for their personal prosperity. Slavery and slaveholding were as characteristic of the city as it was of the countryside, and perhaps even more so. Interpretations emphasizing the rural "prebourgeois" aspects of slave and master omit a richer side of the "peculiar institution."[39]

Historians have spent careers searching for the ethereal quality that made and makes the South distinctive. These probers agree that southern experience varied sharply from the overall American experience.[40] Yet without discounting the importance of such oft-mentioned unique characteristics— dominance of agrarian society, slavery, and slaveholders' philosophy—there exists some evidence to propose a different view. These distinctions contributed to an urbanizing process that moved the Old South toward greater similarity with the North. Charles G. Sellers, Jr.,

stated the case succinctly when he observed that "the traditional emphasis on the South's differences is wrong historically." As the Civil War approached, southerners may well have been simply "other Americans."[41]

Viewing the coming of the Civil War as a conflict between sections becoming more similar to each other seems more commonsensical than to depict the decade and a half prior to Sumter as a cold war between two nationalities. It was, after all, a brothers' war. The ferocity of the war was due, in part, to the close relationship of the sections. Both sections had similar objectives as manifested in the goals of their respective cities. There could be only one victor in the economic contest, and each section saw the other as a threat to the fulfillment of a common goal.[42]

The role of the cities was crucial because it was within the urban milieu that the programs to reach sectional success were formulated and carried out. A study of the urban response to sectionalism could be fruitful on three levels. First, the absence or appearance of the indexes of urbanization in southern cities can be a convenient method for measuring not only the urban response to sectionalism in the South but also the extent and nature of urban growth compared with the North. If urbanization—a major theme of nineteenth-century American life— reputedly neutralized sectional differences, cities in both sections should share some common features. Second, the role and function of southern cities within a regional context must be discerned if the agrarian-dominated interpretations of the Old South are to be seriously challenged. Conceivably, southern cities could have been isolated way stations amid a vast sea of farms and plantations. Finally, on the national level, it would be interesting to test out an urban hypothesis on the coming of the Civil War. Most interpretations have emphasized the section's differences, and none have focused attention on the cities.

Urban Virginia is a good point of departure for such an inquiry. Virginia was not the most urbanized state in the South, nor did it contain the section's largest cities. Hence, Virginia's cities were not mutations of the larger southern environment, any more so than, say, Connecticut's cities were atypical of the northern environment. Further, Virginia was the largest slaveholding state in the nation on the eve of the Civil War. If slavery and cities were indeed compatible, and if slavery were not a significant point of distinction, Virginia would be a fair testing ground. Also, Virginia, in a sense, was both a microcosm of the Old South and of the nation as a whole. The four sections of Virginia—Tidewater, once the center of the South's greatest glory; the Piedmont, with its resurrected tobacco culture creating an agricultural pattern similar to the Deep South; the Valley, a common geographical link running from Pennsylvania through Georgia that was the heartland of southern yeomanry; and the trans-Allegheny region, Virginia's hill country that resembled eastern Tennessee and northern Alabama considerably more than neighboring parts of the Old Dominion—corresponded to the geographical division of the South as a whole. The disruption of Virginia mirrored the disintegration of the Union. Finally, if the agrarian ideal of the Old South could ever be said to have a historic lineage, its birthplace was Virginia. The study of the response of urban centers to sectionalism in a

state with such a background should prove a rigorous test for any hypothesis relating to southern urbanization and the coming of the Civil War.

NOTES

1. W. J. Cash, *The Mind of the South* (New York, 1941), vii–x; David L. Smiley, "The Quest for a Central Theme in Southern History," *South Atlantic Quarterly*, LXII (1972), 318; Eugene D. Genovese, *The World the Slaveholders Made: Two Essays in Interpretation* (New York, 1969), 123, 156; Raimondo Luraghi, "The Civil War and the Modernization of American Society," *Civil War History*, XVIII (1972), 236; see also Bayrd Still, *Urban America: A History with Documents* (Boston, 1974), 103–04.
2. Julius Rubin, "The Limits of Agricultural Progress in the Nineteenth-Century South," *Agricultural History*, XLIX (1975), 362–73.
3. Statistical references helpful to students of the urban South include the compendiums of the U.S. Census (1850 to 1870 for the antebellum era); "Progress of the Population in the United States," *Hunt's Merchants' Magazine and Commercial Review*, XXXII (1855), 191–95 (this periodical will hereafter be cited as *Hunt's*); and Donald B. Dodd and Wynelle S. Dodd, *Historical Statistics of the South, 1790–1970* (University, Ala., 1973).
4. Luraghi, "Civil War and Modernization," 237.
5. Stanley L. Engerman, "A Reconsideration of Southern Economic Growth, 1770–1860," *Agricultural History*, XLIX (1975), 343–61. See also Richard C. Wade, "An Agenda for Urban History," in George A. Billias and Gerald N. Grob (eds.), *American History: Retrospect and Prospect* (New York, 1971), 392.
6. Richmond *Daily Dispatch*, September 22, 1859; Wheeling *Argus*, quoted in Richmond *Enquirer*, September 16, 1853; Joseph C. Robert, *The Tobacco Kingdom: Plantation, Market and Factory in Virginia and North Carolina, 1800–1860* (Durham, 1938); Richard W. Griffin, "The Origins of the Industrial Revolution in Georgia: Cotton Textiles, 1810–1865," *Georgia Historical Quarterly*, XLII (1958), 355–75.
7. Clement Eaton, *The Growth of Southern Civilization, 1790–1860* (New York, 1961), 173; Randall Miller, "Daniel Pratt's Industrial Urbanism: The Cotton Mill Town in Antebellum Alabama," *Alabama Historical Quarterly*, XXXIV (1972), 5–35.
8. See Richard C. Wade, *The Urban Frontier: The Rise of Western Cities, 1790–1830* (Cambridge, Mass., 1959).
9. See Eugene D. Genovese, *The Political Economy of Slavery* (New York, 1965), 24–25, 91, 158; Still, *Urban America*, 103–104.

10. See Morton White and Lucia White, *The Intellectual versus the City: From Thomas Jefferson to Frank Lloyd Wright* (Cambridge, Mass., 1962).

11. See Genovese, *Political Economy of Slavery*, 171–73, 186, 246; and Luraghi, "Civil War and Modernization," 230–49.

12. See, for example, Jeremiah C. Harris Diary (MS in Duke University), November 28, 1859; "Inventory and Appraisement of the Estate of William Massie, 1862," (MS in William Massie Notebooks, Duke University); "Meetings of Stockholders of the Alexandria, Loudoun, and Hampshire Railroad Company," Alexandria *Gazette*, September 8, 1858; and "Annual Meeting of the Stockholders of the Orange and Alexandria Railroad," Alexandria *Gazette*, October 23, 1857. See also Fred Bateman, James Foust, and Thomas Weiss, "The Participation of Planters in Manufacturing in the Antebellum South," *Agricultural History*, XLVIII (1974), 277–97.

13. U.S. Bureau of Census, *Compendium of the Eighth Census: 1860. Mortality and Miscellaneous* (Washington, D.C., 1861), IV, 331; *Compendium of the Ninth Census: 1870* (Washington, D.C., 1871), 789–99; "Bank Capital of Cities in the United States," *Hunt's*, XVIII (1848), 326.

14. Robert W. Fogel and Stanley L. Engerman, *Time on the Cross: The Economics of American Negro Slavery* (Boston, 1974), 247–57. On the revival of southern agriculture in the 1850s see Lewis C. Gray, *History of Agriculture in the Southern United States* (2 vols.; Washington, D.C., 1933), especially vol. II; and Kathleen Bruce, "Virginia Agriculture Decline to 1860: A Fallacy," *Agricultural History*, VI (1932), 3–13.

15. See Otis C. Skipper, *J. D. B. DeBow: Magazinist of the Old South* (Athens, Ga., 1958), 123–30.

16. George Fitzhugh, *Sociology for the South; or, The Failure of Free Society* (New York, 1854), 136.

17. See, for example, Blaine A. Brownell and David R. Goldfield, *The City in Southern History: The Growth of Urban Civilization in the South* (Port Washington, N.Y., 1976); D. Clayton James, *Antebellum Natchez* (Baton Rouge, 1968); David G. McComb, *Houston: The Bayou City* (Austin, 1969); Merl E. Reed, *New Orleans and the Railroads: The Struggle for Commercial Empire* (Baton Rouge, 1966); Kenneth W. Wheeler, *To Wear a City's Crown: The Beginnings of Urban Growth in Texas* (Cambridge, Mass., 1968); Blaine A. Brownell, "Urbanization in the South: A Unique Experience?" *Mississippi Quarterly*, XXVI (1973), 105–20; Leonard P. Curry, "Urbanization and Urbanism in the Old South: A Comparative View," *Journal of Southern History*, XL (1974), 43–60; and Lyle W. Dorsett and Arthur H. Shaffer, "Was the Antebellum South Antiurban? A Suggestion," *Journal of Southern History*, XXXVIII (1972), 93–100.

18. Richard Hildreth, *Despotism in America: An Inquiry into the Nature, Results, and Legal Basis of the Slave-Holding Systems in the United States* (Boston, 1854), 139.

19. In addition to the statistical aids cited in n. 3, see Wade, "Agenda for Urban History," 391.

20. For some recent attempts at explaining urbanization see Richard D. Brown, "The Emergence of Urban Society in Rural Massachusetts, 1760–1820," *Journal of American History*, LXI (1974), 29–51; Curry, "Urbanization and Urbanism," 43–60; and Peter G. Goheen, "Industrialization and the Growth of Cities in Nineteenth-Century America," *American Studies*, XIV (1973), 49–65.

21. See George Rogers Taylor, *The Transportation Revolution, 1815–1860* (New York, 1951), Chap. 17; and see also Douglass C. North, *The Economic Growth of the United States, 1790–1860* (New York, 1961), Chap. 9, 193–94.

22. See Sam Bass Warner, Jr., *The Private City: Philadelphia in Three Periods of Its Growth* (Philadelphia, 1968).

23. On the influence of leadership on urban growth see Wade, *Urban Frontier*, 203–10.

24. Norfolk *Southern Argus*, December 29, 1853.

25. See Charles N. Glaab and A. Theodore Brown, *A History of Urban America* (New York, 1967), Chap. 7.

26. Daniel R. Hundley, *Social Relations in Our Southern States* (New York, 1860), 258; and Wade, "Agenda for Urban History," 393. See also Carl Abbott, "Civic Pride in Chicago, 1844–1860," *Journal of the Illinois State Historical Society*, LXIII (1970), 421.

27. "Commercial, Agricultural, and Intellectual Independence of the South," *DeBow's Review*, XXIX (1860), 466–88; Fitzhugh, *Sociology*, 158; Richmond *Enquirer*, February 27, 1854.

28. See George Fitzhugh, *Cannibals All! or, Slaves without Masters* (New York, 1857), 59.

29. Charleston *Courier*, August 31, 1836; "Contests for the Trade of the Mississippi Valley," *DeBow's Review*, III (1847), 98.

30. See Louis B. Schmidt, "Internal Commerce and the Development of the National Economy Before 1860," *Journal of Political Economy*, XLVII (1939), 798–822.

31. See Thomas C. Cochran, "The Business Revolution," *American Historical Review*, LXXIX (1974), 1449–66.

32. Portsmouth *Daily Pilot*, August 17, 1850. See also speech of Senator R. M. T. Hunter in U.S. Senate, quoted in Richmond *Enquirer*, April 5, 1850.

33. Richmond *Enquirer*, August 28, 1855. See also John R. Tucker to M. R. H. Garnett, January 1, 1846, in Charles F. Mercer Papers, Virginia State Library, Richmond, Va.

34. See James C. Hite and Ellen J. Hall, "The Reactionary Evolution of Economic Thought in Antebellum Virginia," *Virginia Magazine of History and Biography*, LXXX (1972), 476–88; and

Luraghi, "Civil War and Modernization," 234–36. See also Eric Foner, *Free Soil, Free Labor, Free Men: The Ideology of the Republican Party Before the Civil War* (New York, 1970).

35. Norfolk *Southern Argus*, June 16, 1854.

36. On the mutual dependence of city and hinterland, see Michael P. Conzen, *Frontier Farming in an Urban Shadow* (Madison, Wisc., 1971); Robert R. Dykstra, *The Cattle Towns* (New York, 1968); and Wheeler, *To Wear A City's Crown.*

37. See Genovese, *Political Economy of Slavery;* Eric Foner, "The Causes of the Civil War: Recent Interpretations and New Directions," *Civil War History,* XX (1974), 197–214; and Sheldon Hackney, "The South as a Counterculture," *American Scholar,* XLII (1973), 283–93.

38. See Robert S. Starobin, *Industrial Slavery in the Old South* (New York, 1969); Charles B. Dew, "Disciplining Slave Ironworkers in the Antebellum South: Coercion, Conciliation, and Accommodation," *American Historical Review,* LXXIX (1974), 393–418; and Clement Eaton,

"Slave-Hiring in the Upper South: A Step Toward Freedom," *Mississippi Valley Historical Review,* XLVI (1960), 633–78. *Cf.* Richard C. Wade, *Slavery in the Cities: The South, 1820–1860* (New York, 1964).

39. See Otto Olsen, "Historians and the Extent of Slave Ownership in the Southern United States," *Civil War History,* XVIII (1972), 101–16.

40. Some of the more recent forays into the search for southern identity are Hackney, "South as a Counterculture," 283–93; Michael C. O'Brien, "C. Vann Woodward and the Burden of Southern Liberalism," *American Historical Review,* LXXVIII (1973), 589–604; Smiley, "Quest for a Central Theme," 307–25; and George B. Tindall, "Beyond the Mainstream: The Ethnic Southerners," *Journal of Southern History,* XL (1974), 3–18.

41. Hennig Cohen, review of Grady McWhiney, *Southerners and Other Americans,* in *American Historical Review,* LXXIX (1974) 582–83.

42. See Still, *Urban America,* 114–16.

The Businessman as City Booster

DANIEL J. BOORSTIN

The American businessman—a product (and a maker) of the upstart cities of the American West between the Revolution and the Civil War—was not an American version of the enterprising European city banker or merchant or manufacturer. Not an American Fugger or Medici or Rothschild or Arkwright, he was something quite different. His career and his ideals are an allegory of an American idea of community, for he was born and bred in the dynamic American urbanism in the period of our greatest growth.

The changing meaning of his very name, "businessman," gives us a clue. In 18th-century England to say someone was a "man of business" was primarily to say he engaged in public affairs. Thus David Hume in 1752 described Pericles as "a man of business." Before the end of the 18th century the expression had begun to lose this, its once primary meaning, and instead to describe a person engaged in mercantile transactions; it became a loose synonym for "merchant." But our now common word "businessman" seems to have been American in origin. It came into use around 1830 in the very period when the new Western cities were founded and were growing most rapidly. Even a casual look at this early American businessman, who he was, what he was doing, and how he thought of his work, will show how inaccurate it would be to describe him as simply a man engaged in mercantile transactions. We might better characterize him as a peculiarly American type of community maker and community leader. His starting belief was in the interfusing of public and private prosperity. Born of a social vagueness unknown in the Old World, he was a distinctive product of the New.

The new fast-growing city, where nothing had been before, a city with no history and unbounded hopes, was the American businessman's first natural habitat. In the period when he first appeared, his primary commodity was land and his secondary commodity transportation. This transformation of land rights and transport rights from political symbols and heirlooms into mere commodities was also an American phenomenon.

The businessman's characteristics would appear in the story of any one of the thousands who made their fortunes in the early 19th century. "I was born close by a saw-mill," boasted William B. Ogden (1805-77), "was early left an orphan, was cradled in a sugar-trough, christened in a mill-pond, graduated at a log-school-house, and at fourteen fancied I could do any thing I turned my hand to, and that nothing was impossible, and ever since, madame, I have been trying to prove it, and with some success." He was destined to be an upstart businessman on a heroic scale. Born into a leading local family in a small town in the Catskills in New York, he was actively dealing in real estate before he was fifteen. Before thirty he was elected to the New York Legislature on a program to construct the New York & Erie Railroad with State aid. He was a great booster for his State, to whose growth he called the new railroad essential. "Otherwise," he argued "the sceptre will depart from Judah. The Empire State will no longer be New York. . . . Philadelphia is your great rival, and, if New York is idle, will gather in the trade of the great west."

But Ogden's enthusiasm for New York was not immovable. In 1835, the very year when the money was appropriated for the New York & Erie Railroad, he met some Eastern investors who had formed the American Land Company. They had already shown the foresight to invest heavily in Chicago real estate. One of these was Charles Butler, a politically and philanthropically minded lawyer of Albany, who married Ogden's sister. Butler himself (once a clerk in the law office of Martin Van Buren) was an energetic promoter of real estate and railroads. A man of wide public interests, he was a founder of Hobart College and of Union Theological Seminary, and an early supporter of New York University, among his other community works. He asked Ogden to go to Chicago to manage his interests. Ogden then joined in the purchase of considerable tracts there.

William B. Ogden arrived in Chicago in June, 1835. The town census showed a population of 3265, almost all of whom had come since 1832 (when the settlement had numbered under a hundred). Quickly Ogden transferred his extravagant hopes from the Empire State to the City of Chicago. In 1837, when Chicago was incorporated, Ogden was elected its first mayor, and the city census counted 4170—an increase of almost thirty per cent in two years.

"He could not forget," one of Ogden's fellow businessmen observed, "that everything which benefitted Chicago, or built up the great West, benefitted him. Why should he?" His commodity was land, whose value rose with the population. And Chicago now grew as few cities had ever grown before. The population approximately trebled, decade after decade: from 29,963 in 1850, to 109,260 in 1860, and to 298,977 in 1870. Chicago held over half a million people in 1880 and over a million by 1890, when it was already the second city on the continent. Meanwhile, real-estate values, especially in choice locations such as those Ogden was shrewd enough to buy, rose even more spectacularly. Men like Ogden proudly recorded their business success as the best evidence of their faith in their city. "In 1844," Ogden recalled, "I purchased for $8000, what 8 years thereafter, sold for 3 millions of dollars, and these cases could be extended almost indefinitely." Property he had bought in 1845 for $15,000 only twenty years later was worth ten million dollars. Successes were so common and so sudden, it was hard to know where fact ended and where fable began. Some of this purchasing was, of course, sheer speculative mania. The Chicago *American* (April 23, 1836) boasted of a piece of city property sold for $96,700 which, in romanticized arithmetic, they said had "risen in value at the rate of *one hundred per cent per* DAY, on the original cost ever since [1830], embracing a period of *five years* and a half."

Not to boost your city showed both a lack of community spirit and a lack of business sense. "Perhaps, the most striking trait of his character," a contemporary remembered of Ogden, "was his absolute faith in Chicago. He saw in 1836, not only the Chicago of today, but in the future the great City of the continent. From that early day, his faith never wavered. Come good times—come bad times—come prosperity or adversity —Chicago booming, or Chicago in ashes, its great future was to him a fixed fact." Quite naturally Ogden became a leader in community affairs, and within a few years Chicagoans called him their "representative man."

There was hardly a public improvement in which he did not play a leading role. He built the first drawbridge across the Chicago river, laid out and opened many miles of streets in the north and west parts of the city, promoted the Illinois and Michigan Canal and advocated laws for its construction and enlargement, projected and built thousands of miles of railroads serving Chicago, and did a great deal to develop Chicago's water supply, sewage system, and parks. More than a hundred miles of streets and hundreds of bridges were built at the private expense of Ogden and his real-estate clients. He helped introduce the McCormick reaping and mowing machines into the West, and helped build the first large factory for their manufacture. He was the first president of Rush Medical College (the first institution of its kind in Chicago), a charter member of the Chicago Historical Society, president of the Board of Trustees of the first "University of Chicago," and one of the first directors of the Merchants Loan and Trust Company (1857). He was elected to the Illinois Senate by the Republicans in

1860. He supported the Theological Seminary of the Northwest, the Academy of Sciences, and the Astronomical Society. The French historian Guizot only slightly exaggerated when he said Ogden had built and owned Chicago.

Characteristic also was Ogden's interest in improving transportation. An upstart community, a community of boosters measuring itself by its rate of growth, depended on transportation in a new way. Settled communities of the Old World—Bordeaux, Lyon, Manchester, or Birmingham—especially when, as in the early 19th century, they were fast becoming industrial towns, needed transportation to feed raw materials and labor to their factories and to take away finished products. But Chicago and the other upstart cities of the American West needed it for their very lifeblood. In the Old World a city might grow or decline, prosper or languish, depending on its transportation, among other facilities. But here, without transportation there was no city at all.

An American city had to "attract" people. The primary community service was to make it easier, cheaper, and pleasanter for people to join your community. In all this, too, William B. Ogden was a paragon, for he pioneered the railroads. One of the first to run out of Chicago was the Galena & Chicago Union Railroad, built to connect Chicago with the great Mississippi River traffic. Chicago businessmen bought a controlling interest in 1846, and tried to raise money from local citizens to complete the railroad. Ogden worked hard to obtain numerous individual subscriptions in small amounts. This, its first railroad, opened a new era in the life and expansion of Chicago. Citizens subscribed its stock "as a public duty, and not as an investment." "Railroads," one of Ogden's collaborators later boasted, "were built as public enterprises, and not as money-making speculations. They were regarded as great highways constructed by the people, either at the expense of the government or by means of private capital, to accommodate the public, and not for the especial benefit of the stockholders." In April, 1849, the first locomotive started west from Chicago on the Galena line.

Ogden took the lead in promoting many more railroads for Chicago. In 1853 he was a director of the Pittsburg, Ft. Wayne & Chicago Railroad; in 1857, president of the Chicago, St. Paul & Fond-du-Lac Railroad which later became part of the Chicago & Northwestern Railroad, of which he was also president (1859-68). A transcontinental railroad with Chicago as the great junction was, of course, his dream. In 1850 he presided over the National Railway Convention and, on the organization of the Union Pacific Company in 1862, its first president was William B. Ogden.

The Ogden story was re-enacted a thousand times all over America—wherever there were upstart cities. Scenes were different, stakes smaller, and dimensions less heroic, but the plot everywhere was much the same. Here was a new breed: the community builder in a mushrooming city where personal and public growth, personal and public prosperity intermingled.

Another example was Dr. Daniel Drake (1785-1852), born in New Jersey, and raised in Kentucky, whose family sent him when he was only fifteen to study in the offices of a leading physician of the small town of Ft. Washington (later called Cincinnati). Within a few years he himself became the town's most prominent practitioner. He opened a drug store where, in 1816, he pioneered in the sale of artificial mineral water; soon he was also running a general store. His *Picture of Cincinnati in 1815*, with its full statistics, and its vivid account of the archaeology, topography, climate, and promise of the city, was translated and circulated widely abroad. Drake, in his own farther way, was as much a booster as Ogden; using subtler techniques of precise and calculated understatement, he produced the first detailed account of an upstart city. Many believed him when he concluded that small towns like Cincinnati were "destined, before the termination of the present century, to attain the rank of populous and magnificent cities." Drake had established himself in the high noon of Cincinnati prosperity, before the Panic of 1819.

Drake's boosterism was as energetic as Ogden's. Hoping to make Cincinnati a great medical center in 1819, he founded the Ohio Medical College (later the Medical College of the University of Cincinnati). He did a great deal to promote all kinds of community enterprises: the Commercial Hospital and Lunatic Asylum, the eye infirmary, the circulating library, the teacher's college. He helped plan and develop canals and he promoted railroads leading toward the South, which included the successful municipal line, the Cincinnati Southern Railway.

Still another example with a more western habitat was General William Larimer (1809-75). Born and raised in Pennsylvania, he tried many different businesses around Pittsburgh: a general store, a freight service, horse trading, a coal company, a wholesale grocery, his father's hotel, railroads, and banking. When he lost everything in the depression of 1854, Larimer, quickly resolving to start afresh farther west, was in Nebraska the very next spring. There he too became the instantaneous booster of a town which did not yet exist. We have an intimate record in letters he sent east. On May 23, 1855:

I have taken two claims at La Platte, Nebraska Territory . . . and we are laying out a town. I am elected President of the Company, and secured ⅓ of the town. . . . I like this country very much indeed. . . . I think I can make a big raise here in a few years.

Already he claimed a good chance of being elected to Congress from Nebraska. Within a week his optimism had risen still higher: he planned to pay off his creditors with town lots, for he owned a thousand acres within the proposed city.

Now my plan is this: I intend to live in La Platte City. I intend to open up a large farm. I can raise hemp, corn or anything. . . . I will go on with the farm and if the land is ever wanted for a town it is ready. . . . I intend not only to farm simply but I will open a Commission House. I expect to supply the Territory with iron nails, lumber, etc., this will not only be profitable in itself but will be the great means of building up the city. If I go there I can build the city if I do not go only to sell lots as the city may never rise.

Larimer expected the transcontinental railroad to go through La Platte, but this proved a miscalculation. Then, after a heavy winter, the town suffered deep spring floods. "We were not long in coming to the conclusion that La Platte was doomed as a town site." The pattern of western hope was all-or-nothing.

From La Platte, Larimer moved on to Omaha. There he lived in a prefabricated house that had actually been framed in Pittsburgh, knocked down and shipped out in 1856. When Omaha, too, looked unpromising (as it did within less than two years) he moved to Leavenworth, Kansas. This was in 1858, just in time for him to learn of the discovery of gold at Cherry Creek by Pike's Peak. Unwilling to wait for the better traveling conditions of the following spring, Larimer and his son immediately made up a party and left that fall. After a forty-seven-day trip, the Larimers were among the first to arrive at the mouth of Cherry Creek, where they found two dozen cabins under construction.

This, the first settlement in Colorado, was named Auraria. Larimer's son recorded the events of November 17, 1858:

On our very first night here, my father, without consulting anyone outside of our own Leavenworth Party, packed his blankets and some provisions, left camp and crossed the Creek to pick out a new site. He left instructions for us to get up the oxen and join him, as he believed the east side of the Creek was much the best location for a town and no one in the country laid claim to it, or if so had abandoned it and left the country. . . . When we finally reached the eastern side of Cherry Creek, we found him near the bank with a camp fire awaiting us. He had 4 cottonwood poles crossed, which he called the foundation of his settlement and claimed the site for a town,—for *the* town which has now grown into the one of which Colorado is the proudest.

This time Larimer chose well. He had located on the site of Denver.

At first there was competition between the sites on either side of Cherry Creek. Then the stockholders combined and became a single city named Denver (in honor of the Virginian who had become Governor of the Kansas Territory) in 1860. "I am Denver City," Larimer wrote in a letter in February 1859. And his whole later career proved the extraordinary ability of the American businessmen of these upstart cities to fuse themselves and their destiny with that of their community—at least so long as the community remained prosperous or promising.

At the beginning Larimer had been put in charge of the town and made "Donating Agent," which authorized him to give two city lots to anyone who would build a cabin there measuring at least 16 by 16 feet. He promoted a good hotel and gave valuable shares to men "who were already or could be induced to become interested in the welfare of the city and might be influential in bringing a stage line into the country with Denver as its objective point." He encouraged the founding of drugstores, general stores, sawmills, and newspapers. Complaining that the town lacked the ultimate convenience, he finally helped organize a cemetery.

Examples could be multiplied. But even these three—Ogden, Drake, and Larimer—suggest the variety of opportunities, motives, and attitudes which created the new species *Businessman Americanus*. None of the characteristics of his American habitat was quite unique but their extreme American form and their American combination were.

Cities with no history. The upstart western cities were the rare examples of a dynamic urban environment where almost nothing had been pre-empted by history. Cities were proverbially the centers of institutions, where records were kept and the past was chronicled, hallowed, and enshrined. They were sites of palaces, cathedrals, libraries, archives, and great monuments of all kinds. The American upstart city, by contrast, had no past. At its beginning, it was free of vested interests, monopolies, guilds, skills, and "No Trespassing" signs. Here was the fluidity of the city —the spatial dimension of cosmopolitanism, movement, diversity, and change

—but without the historical dimension. There were no ancient walls between classes, occupations, neighborhoods, and nationalities. The American upstart cities began without inherited neighborhood loyalties, without ghettos. "Everything," recalled Larimer, "was open to us."

Quick growth and high hopes. The pace of growth of the upstart cities fired imaginations. A town where nobody was ten years ago, but which today numbered thousands, might be expected to number tens or hundreds of thousands in a few decades. Mankind had required at least a million years to produce its first urban community of a million people; Chicagoans accomplished this feat in less than a century. Within a few days' wagon ride of Drake's Cincinnati, hundreds of towns were laid out, all guaranteed to have unrivalled advantages. Precisely one week after Larimer cut his four cottonwood poles on the future site of Denver, he wrote his wife back east that "we expect a second Sacramento City, at least." In 1834, H. M. Brackenridge noted, his Pittsburgh was changing so fast that anyone returned after ten years felt himself a stranger. He confidently foresaw that the settlement which had grown from village to big city in a quarter-century would very soon reach half a million. He could not be surprised that Cincinnati had grown from a forest to a city in thirteen years. He himself had hopes "of attaining, on the Ohio or Mississippi, distinction and wealth, with the same rapidity, and on the same scale, that those vast regions were expanding into greatness." The centennial history of St. Louis in 1876 called the city's site superior to that of any other in the world, and predicted that, when its railroad network was completed, it would outstrip Chicago and the eastern metropolises. "And yet, when this has been said, we have but commenced to tell of the wonders of a city destined in the future to equal London in its population, Athens in its philosophy, art and culture, Rome in its hotels, cathedrals, churches and grandeur, and to be the central commercial metropolis of a continent."

Community before government. On this landscape too it was normal to find communities before governments. Men in sudden urban proximity, bound together by specific, concrete purposes, first felt their common needs. Afterwards they called governments into being. From force of circumstance, then, government became functional. Early Chicagoans, and their upstart counterparts elsewhere, were not confronted with the problem of evading obsolete regulations or of transmuting time-honored tyrannies. They simply combined to provide their own water, their own sewage system, their own sidewalks, streets, bridges, and parks. They founded medical schools and universities and museums. Eager for these and other services, they created municipal governments and enlisted state and federal government aid. An upstart government had neither the odor of sanctity nor the odium of tyranny. It was a tool serving personal and community prosperity at the same time.

Intense and transferable loyalties. In upstart cities the loyalties of people were in inverse ratio to the antiquity of their communities, even to the point of absurdity. Older towns could point only to the facts of limited actual accomplishment, while the uncertain future was, of course, ever more promising. Ogden removed his enthusiasm from New York to Chicago; Larimer removed

his from La Platte to Omaha to Leavenworth to Auraria to Denver. Men could do this in the twinkling of an eye, and without so much as a glance over the shoulder. Promise, not achievement, commanded loyalty and stirred the booster spirit. One was untrue to oneself and to the spirit of expanding America if one remained enslaved to a vision which had lost its promise. The ghost town and the booster spirit were opposite sides of the same coin.

Competition among communities. The circumstances of American life in the upstart cities of the West produced a lively competitive spirit. But the characteristic and most fertile competition was a competition among communities. We have been misled by slogans of individualism. Just as the competition among colonial seaboard cities helped diffuse American culture and kept it from becoming concentrated in a European-style metropolis, so the competition among western upstart cities helped create the booster spirit. Where there had been no cities before, where all were growing fast, there was no traditional rank among urban centers. If Lexington, Kentucky, could quickly arise by 1800 to be the most populous city of the West, if St. Louis and Cincinnati and Chicago had so suddenly arisen, might not some new Lexington displace them all? Many of each community's institutions had been founded to give it a competitive advantage. Dr. Drake's medical college helped Cincinnati keep ahead of Lexington, just as Ogden's streets and bridges and parks helped Chicago lead Cincinnati. Where individual and community prosperity were so intermingled, competition among individuals was also a competition among communities.

•   •   •

The emerging businessman of the upstart cities had much in common with the energetic American of an earlier generation. He was the Franklin of the West. He was the undifferentiated man of the colonial period, but in a more expansive setting. The new language of that day called him a "businessman"; the retrospective language of our century calls him the booster. He thrived on growth and expansion. His loyalties were intense, naive, optimistic, and quickly transferable.

Versatility was his hallmark. He usually had neither the advantages nor the disadvantages of specialized skills or monopolistic protection. In Dr. Drake's Cincinnati, physicians became merchants, clergymen became bankers, law-yers became manufacturers. "The young lawyer," H. M. Brackenridge shrewdly advised the Western seeker after fortune (in one of the first recorded uses of the word "businessman") "should think more of picking up his crumbs, than of flying like a balloon. He must be content to become a *business man*, and leave the rest to fortune." For success in this environment, the specialized skills—of lawyer, doctor, financier, or engineer—had a new unimportance. Rewards went to the organizer, the persuader, the discoverer of opportunities, the projector, the risk-taker, and the man able to attach himself quickly and profitably to some group until its promise was tested.

IV THE CITY IN THE AGE OF INDUSTRY

The emergence of the modern city, in the sixty years following the Civil War, parallels the unfolding of the Industrial Revolution in America. As Constance Green has written in her *Rise of Urban America*, "Which came first, the hen of mounting industrial strength or the egg of increasing urban influences, may be arguable, but the fact of profound change remains."

The question is not so much which came first but how they interacted with and buttressed each other. If railroads, heavy industries, and technological inventions helped build cities, urbanization in turn helped accelerate the hallmarks of industrialization: mass production, mass consumption, mass distribution of goods and services. If industrialization produced a more coordinated network of economic development, the network of cities became the muscles and sinews of that development—producing, selling, financing, and providing it with a market and a labor force. If industrialization meant increasing specialization, cities specialized: Cleveland with oil, Pittsburgh with steel, Milwaukee with beer, Detroit with automobiles, and Los Angeles with sunshine. If the booming factories brought affluence along with shocking working conditions, labor violence, and corruption, the booming cities dramatized the irony of the Industrial Revolution: the collision between progress and poverty—the wealth of Wall Street, State Street, Montgomery Street, and the wretched streets of Cockroach Row, Hell's Kitchen, and the Barbary Coast. Together, the massive forces of industrialization and urbanization wrought a profound change that touched every aspect of American life: the transformation of a land of farms and villages into a nation of cities and towns. The watershed, the point of no return for an old agrarian America, was here by 1920, when the census returns showed that for the first time more than half the population lived in urban areas. Americans had moved to the city.

The city came of age in this period, but it was an era of mixed blessings for the older urban giants. New York became the Empire City, the largest city in the country. It "just grew." Philadelphia and St. Louis, like New York, fed by mass migrations, foreign and domestic, continued to expand, whereas Baltimore, Boston, and New Orleans declined. It was a boom time for the "big-little city," as Kansas City, Omaha, Denver, Birmingham, and San Francisco began to take a more commanding position on the urban scene. If there was one big city that best characterized the age of industry, it was the soaring Chicago. Only the eighth largest city in 1860, devastated by fire in 1871, it rose to become second only to New York in size and power by the last decade of the century. No one has caught the flair and fixed the image of the "City of the Big Shoulders" better than Carl Sandburg:

> Hog Butcher for the World,
> Tool Maker, Stacker of Wheat,
> Player with Railroads and the Nation's
>   Freight Handler;
> Laughing the stormy, husky, brawling
> Laughter of Youth. . . .

The emergence of the industrial city represented another stage of a phenomenon, begun in the colonial period, and extremely vital to us today, one that lies at the heart of American urban history—the city as a revolution in the nature of human settlement. This theme is fundamental to each of the following essays, and its significance and complexity is shaped as each author develops it with a different emphasis.

Leon S. Marshall uses the comparative approach, enlarging our scope and decreasing our provincialism, by contrasting the American industrial city with its English counterpart. Although he points out their important similarities, he shatters any tight analogy between the two by underscoring some of their differences. He also stresses the disruptive influences of the city as an agent for the Industrial Revolution. It was not a pretty picture, as Pittsburgh ("hell with the lid off") or Manchester ("this pell-mell of society") posed new problems and enlarged old ones for the family, working conditions, the poor, crime, disease, and immorality. Bleak as life was for many of the nineteenth-century industrial cities, a more balanced view would contrast it to the farm and village of the time, which also offered its share of poverty, drudgery, disease, and immorality.[1]

Blake McKelvey raises this question: how did the basic ingredients of nineteenth- and early twentieth-century industrialization—new sources of energy and raw materials, new supplies of labor and industrial skills, new

1. See Dorothy George's provocative *England in Transition* (London: Penguin Books, 1953). For an excellent book employing the comparative approach to examine urbanization throughout the world, see Sylvia Fleis Farral (ed.), *Urbanism in World Perspective: A Reader* (New York: Thomas Y. Crowell, 1968).

machines and techniques of production—affect the emergence of the industrial city? He finds that the development was by no means uniform, in fact, there appeared a number of different *kinds* of industrial cities. One city would profit from one aspect of industrialization rather than another, some would flounder, others would blossom. Thus, some prospered as regional centers by controlling their hinterland, absorbing assessory industries, and extending urban economic services, like Pittsburgh. Others would exploit a near-by agricultural resource, as Milwaukee did with hops and beer, or Memphis in converting cotton into cottonseed oil. Many cities profited from cheap immigrant or migrant labor, such as the shoe industry in Philadelphia and New York, or the textile industries in New England and the South. Others used the specialties of skilled immigrant workers to enhance growth— witness Rochester with clothing, shoe, nursery, brewing, and woodworking industries. Still others rose to urban distinction upon the ingenious inventions of clever people—the telephone, the elevator, the trolley car, the bicycle. The classic example is the automobile and Detroit. Other cities that could not adopt new industries or save old ones, or that were plagued with absentee ownership or by-passed by the railroad, would wither away. At the close of the first decade of the twentieth century, the transition from commerce to industry as the main source of economic growth was completed. The result: urban monuments to industrial America—a leading industrial giant in its own right, now freed from dependence upon foreign factories and foreign investments.

If the foregoing essays suggest there are several ways to look at the emergence and impact of the industrial city, one enduring historical view has remained consistent from the nineteenth century to the present, embraced in varying degrees by both prourbanites and antiurbanites; namely, the direct relationship between the growth of urbanization, industrialization, and the rise of the crime rate. Many a politician has marched to high office to the tune of "crime in the streets," "safety in the streets," not to mention, "law and order." It is an old tune, only the lyrics change. City-dwellers in the nineteenth century were also terrified as newspapers, magazines, books, —and politicians—shrilly, sometimes hysterically, announced an ever increasing high tide of crime that might eventually, lacking better law and order, swamp the city. Since 1933, when criminal statistics were collected nationally for the first time, and the Federal Bureau of Investigation published its first annual statistical crime index, rhetoric has been backed by the seemingly irrefutable logic of cold hard statistical fact. Given the rise of organized crime, the turbulent decade of the 1960s with its riots, political assassinations, drug addiction, and the FBI with its "mounting crime waves," there seemed no question that rapid urbanization created a rising crime rate. One could almost expect to hear from the grave of Thomas Jefferson, an old antiurbanite, a triumphant "I-told-you-so."

But an increasing number of scholars, including Daniel Bell,[2] Robert M. Cipes,[3] and Fred P. Graham,[4] have questioned both the validity of crime waves and the statistical integrity of the FBI indexes, for any number of reasons, including the notion that "figures never lie, but figurers do." Doubt invites an historical perspective, especially of the nineteenth-century industrial city, the seedbed of modern crime. This is given us in the next essay by Roger Lane, an historian who cut his scholarly teeth on a fine study of the Boston police.[5]

Choosing the state of Massachusetts and the city of Boston, Lane picked his area well. In a time (1822–85) when reliable national statistics were difficult if not impossible to find, when city records were not conspicious for their accuracy, state and local officials in Massachusetts had an "enormous appetite" for statistical information of all kinds and kept their records well. Moreover, with one large city and several smaller cities, Massachusetts served as an excellent model of the urban industrial experience. After carefully weighing his evidence, Lane comes to several stunning conclusions: (1) there is not a necessary or inevitable connection between the rise of the city and rising crime rates; (2) from the Civil War to the end of the century, as the cities became more industrialized and more urbanized, crime actually *decreased*; (3) urbanization itself was responsible for the decrease in crime because it was a means of absorbing, adjusting, and accommodating urban dwellers to the life of the city. Urbanism, in short, was a mechanism of socialization; it demanded more cooperative habits necessary for living successfully in the city. Lane leaves us with an insight sharply relevant to our own time. Criminal activity can never be measured with any precision by the degree of public opinion. Indeed, there is a kind of irony of hysteria: the crime rate has often decreased as the public's concern about crime has mounted.[6]

If there was not an inevitable tie between the rise of the city and crime waves, there *was* one indeed between the industrial city and the rise of the American national pastime, baseball. Sometimes urban historians become so immersed with the impersonal forces of urbanization that they neglect the things of blood, flesh, and bone—city people and, as examined in the next

2. "The Myth of Crime Waves: The Actual Decline of Crime in United States," *The End of Ideology* (Glencoe: The Free Press, 1961).
3. *The Crime War* (New York: New American Library, 1968).
4. "A Contemporary History of American Crime," in Hugh Davis Graham and Ted Robert Gurr (eds.), *Violence in America*, Vol. 2 (Washington, D.C.: Superintendent of Documents, 1969). See also Fred P. Graham's *The Self-Inflicted Wound* (New York: Macmillan, 1970). Another interesting essay in Vol. 2 of the Graham-Gurr book is Sheldon Hackney's "Southern Violence."
5. *Policing the City: Boston, 1822–1885* (Cambridge: Harvard University Press, 1967).
6. For another phase of nineteenth-century crime, and one long ignored by historians, see Joseph M. Hawes, *Children in Urban Society: Juvenile Delinquency in Nineteenth-Century America* (New York: Oxford University Press, 1971).

essay, their pleasures. Gunther Barth takes us out to the ball park, "the quintessence of urban leisure: watching others do things." His purpose is to demonstrate the intimate relationship between the industrial city and its people, its impact upon urban recreational life and the changes it brought about. "Ball Park" is an example of popular cultural history at its best.

First we must say goodbye to the myths, goodbye to Abner Doubleday and Cooperstown. Baseball originated in England and not by that venerable gentleman in up-state New York. In this country it was first played not by common folk but as a genteel indulgence of the affluent, like the Knicker-bockers, elegantly dressed in white shirts, blue trousers, and, no less, straw hats. Baseball lost its aristocratic aura during the 1850s and became both an urban and national phenomenon fashioned to the goals of an industrial and capitalist economy. Communication technologies—the railroad and the tele-graph—helped it to expand nationally; the impact of corporate management, the marriage of commercialism and professionalism, epitomized by the cre-ation of the National and American Leagues, packaged it as a recreational product for the urban masses.

Internal changes in baseball are illustrated by a game in the early days when the superstars of 1869, the Cincinnati Red Stockings, won a game by 103 to 8, suggesting a certain chaos in the play. Out of chaos came order. The predecessors to baseball in spectator sports, horseracing and boxing (and gambling on both), helped prepare the way with their emphasis on speed, technique, efficiency, and excitement. The game became streamlined by systematized, uniform regulations; speed was increased by innovations like the glove and a harder, smaller ball. There were new techniques in pitching, such as the awesome curve ball; efficiency was created out of professionalism, and gambling continued. Interest in the game was accelerated by the rise of the metropolitan press, the emergence of the sports page and its creatures— a new kind of journalist and a new rhetoric, embracing all the spit and vinegar of the game of baseball. And, finally, and not the least, came the toy if not the passion of the baseball buff—the statistic, trivia enhanced into heroic proportions.

The lineage of baseball and the city brought a different type of leisure to city people, which included but went beyond the act of "watching others do things." Baseball shattered the aversions of our Puritan heritage toward leisure and recreation, and undermined the forms of recreation indigenous to an agrarian society. A new kind of leisure time emerged geared to the schedule of an urban working day and one that was oriented more to re-laxation than rest. The ball park itself was an oasis of grass and fresh air, the countryside revisited, a dramatic contrast to the brick and iron and smoulder-ing factory chimneys of the dingy city. A visit to the ball park was a tem-porary relief from a dreary job, providing not only entertainment through observation, but through the logistics of the game itself that reflected the tempo, hustle, and brisk pace of urban life. As Mark Twain once said, baseball was "the very symbol, the outward and visible expression, of the drive and push and rush and struggle of the raging, tearing, booming nineteenth century." It is one of Barth's key points that baseball educated city people to the "inner workings of new patterns of urban life." Rules, competition, a standard of excellence, speed, efficiency, and energy suggested roads of success out of the confusion and disorder of the city. Above all, the drive for winning echoed the clarion call of "making it" in nineteenth-century urban America. But as the famous poem goes, suggesting another grim reality of life, even the mighty Casey could strike out.

For the newly arrived immigrant, player and spectator alike, baseball offered a step into the Americanization process. For the gifted Irish, German, or Jewish athlete, it was a place in the sun. For the spectator, whose English might be too sketchy to enjoy a book or a play, baseball offered entertainment, excitement, and also a view into the dynamics of urban life. The game, however, ultimately transcended ethnicity. It attracted all the elements of a pluralistic urban society, a crowd of strangers, often rootless people, who, for nine glorious innings could share a common experience, binding them together and giving them a sense of community.

The English and American Industrial City of the Nineteenth Century

LEON S. MARSHALL

Cities throughout history have been the focal points of civilization; and the association of such cities as Babylon with the ancient Oriental empires, Athens with Greece, Rome with the Mediterranean empire of the Caesars and with medieval Christianity, and Venice and Florence with the Renaissance are commonplaces in history and literature. Although trite from frequent repetition, true and significant is the observation that, with all that cities have been, in no previous age has urban society had so complete domination over the life of mankind as at the present. To the student of English or American history, therefore, the rise of the industrial city of the nineteenth century is particularly important, for in that history may be found the origins of many of the critical problems troubling our own disjointed and embittered society.

The supremacy of earlier towns over their neighboring countrysides was due to the domination of commerce over industry: that is, the facilities of the city for the distribution of productions beyond the means and requirements of household and simple agrarian economy stimulated the productive energies of the surrounding population and, in consequence, the economic needs of the city set up the pattern of economic life existing around it. In the present day,

however, the economic system created by the industrial city has approached the solution of the problem of production, but has created a new set of problems arising out of that of distributing the wealth produced by this modern industrial system.

In an economic sense, an industrial city is one whose resources are almost wholly devoted or subordinated to the producing of *form* utility—the shaping of raw materials into goods for human use. London, Liverpool, and New York, where manufacturing plants are only incidental to the principal business of the city, are commercial rather than industrial cities since exchange (wholesale, retail, or financial) together with transportation is their chief activity. On the other hand, Manchester, Birmingham, and Pittsburgh, even though they are not now so predominantly characterized by factories and mills, are industrial cities because their wealth, population, and economic activities are largely devoted to the supplying of their factories and those of the surrounding communities with the essentials of industrial life, and their prosperity is dependent upon that of their leading industries.

In the first half of the nineteenth century, Manchester, Birmingham, and other towns in England developed into

From *Western Pennsylvania Historical Magazine*, Vol. 20 (September 1937), pp. 169–80. Copyright © 1937 by The Historical Society of Western Pennsylvania.

industrial cities according to a pattern which recurred in Cincinnati, Pittsburgh, and other American cities whose leading businesses were transformed by the industrial revolution. The adoption of a series of labor-saving inventions and of improved processes of manufacture led to the concentration in factories of the cotton industry around Manchester, the iron industry around Birmingham and woollen manufacture around Leeds, where facilities for labor, power, and capital were abundant. The increased prosperity and the demand for labor accompanying this concentration of industry brought in a flood of immigrants to these towns. The earlier balance in a town society composed of gentlemen, merchants, and artisans was shaken to its roots by this influx of what soon became an urban proletariat badly housed, subject to extremes of temporary affluence and poverty, and not easily adapted to the discipline of town and factory life. On the other hand, self-made capitalists accumulated fortunes by amazing combinations of luck, foresight, determination, and energy. Recognizing their importance in the community and in the nation, these frequently uncultured and ruthless factory owners seized political leadership from the older dominant interests, and ultimately forced government to protect and foster the system that had enriched them. At the same time, green spaces and quaint old buildings disappeared as land was needed for offices and warehouses, and beyond the new "business districts" grimy factories pushed rows of jerry-built dwellings past the original limits of the town. Disease, poverty, crime, industrial conflict, and social animosities broke down the traditional institutions that had controlled smaller and more orderly populations, while the bewildered and alarmed inhabitants strove to erect new political and social machinery to control and refine the social revolution that was going on around them.

Wherever this pattern of development recurred, its most striking effects appeared in the growth of urban population. By 1860 more than half the people of England lived in cities and factory towns, and by 1920 more than half the population of the United States lived in urban centers. In the first fifty years of the industrial revolution, the American, as had the English cities previously, received the greatest impact of the population movement. Paterson, New Jersey, grew from 7,500 in 1840 to 68,000 in 1890; Philadelphia from less than a hundred thousand to over a million in the same period; and Pittsburgh and Allegheny from 31,000 to a third of a million fifty years later.[1] Chicago, Cincinnati, Milwaukee, Kansas City, and scores of other cities rivaled this growth, and the rise of the automobile industry produced a recurrence of this phenomenon in the twentieth century.

The influx of population was much more rapid than the expansion of housing facilities. Congestion affected all classes, driving first the wealthy and later the middle classes to the suburbs; but for the incoming workers, too poor to afford better, the only accommodations were cheap lodging houses, and run-down tenement buildings from which absentee landlords derived as much rent with as little expense as possible while awaiting the profits of rising real-estate values. Five families living abroad and contributing little to the community in the form of taxes or improvements of their property drew most of the rentals from Pittsburgh's slums, a fact that accounts for much of the great following of Henry George's single-tax program in Pittsburgh.[2]

Until epidemics of cholera, typhoid fever, and smallpox terrified the middle classes of townspeople into attempting sanitary reforms, the disease and death lurking in the dark squalor of the slums was hardly known to the general public. Whether in England or America the discoveries made by sanitary reformers reveal a depressing similarity. Manchester with two hundred thousand inhabitants had scarcely a sewer, irregular scavengers' carts hardly touched the filth that rotted in dumps to make it more marketable as fertilizer, and until the middle of the century the town's water supply was not sufficient for more than one-third its population. Such facts as these explain why in 1841 the average expectation of life at birth in Manchester was only a few months over twenty-four years.[3] In America, a little later, few cities possessed half as many miles of sewers as of streets, and half the latter were unpaved. Fully one-third of the houses in the eighties relied upon private vaults and household utensils for the disposal of human waste. A large part of Philadelphia's million inhabitants drank water from the Delaware River into which had been emptied daily thirteen million gallons of sewage.[4] Typhus, typhoid, and scarlet fever were the natural concomitants of such sanitary inadequacies, and Pittsburgh's share in this ghastly record consisted of the highest mortality rate for typhoid in the world between 1899 and 1907, or 1.30 per thousand.[5]

Public philanthropy tried first to stem this invasion of disease and death by erecting hospitals, of which Pittsburgh added eight between 1882 and 1895.[6]

Street improvements because of the demands of traffic proceeded more rapidly than improvement in sewage, which also involved scientific knowledge as well as expense to property. Although building societies for the erection of model cottages were common in the English towns as the result of experience with congestion, only a few such attempts were made in the United States, and only where industrial corporations erected model "company houses" in the new industrial areas were these successful. Except in the new cities of the West, such as Salt Lake City, the United States lagged far behind England in city planning.

A report on a survey of Pittsburgh in 1908 pointed out as another feature of industrialism "an altogether incredible amount of overwork by everybody, reaching its extreme in the twelve-hour shift for seven days in the week in the steel mills and the railway switchyards."[7] Although the report considered the proportion of women in local industries as "menacing," Pittsburgh's mills were not so adaptable to the labor of women and children as were canning and textile factories, where light though fatiguing routine made possible their employment because of their cheapness and amenableness to discipline. In the single decade of the eighties the number of children employed increased from 1,000,000 to 1,750,000.[8] In spite of ten-hour laws the usual working day in many industries even where women and children were employed was twelve hours. Although the labor of women and children was not new, the factory and the industrial city created new problems of family disintegration, fatigue, delinquency, and industrial superannuation, and impressed the critical-ness of these problems by the vividness of the industrial scene. The public reaction to these conditions were the factory and public-health movements in England in the thirties and forties, and state agitations in America for ten-hour laws and legislation for sanitary improvements.

Legislative protection for women and children in industry in response to the demands of public opinion was achieved more rapidly in England than in America. Using as an accepted principle Sir Robert Peel's Act of 1819, which attempted to remedy abuses in the employment of children in cotton mills, societies of English humanitarians and factory workers forced Parliament to pass the Factory Act of 1834, the Mines Act of 1842, and the Ten Hours Act of 1847 in spite of the millowners' appeal to the currently accepted theory of laissez-faire in the relations between the state and industry. In America the manufacturing interests entrenched themselves in the state legislatures behind the argument that regulatory legislation would enable industries in those states not having such regulations to ruin the manufacturers of the states where the employment of women and children was limited. In spite of this opposition the National Eight-Hour League succeeded in obtaining such laws in six states. Although the effect of these laws was greatly vitiated by lax enforcement, the enlightened opinion aroused by the agitation, the example of a few states, and the constant pressure of shorter-hours advocates brought a gradual reduction of the hours of labor and an improvement in health conditions in American factories.

The increase in leisure afforded by the shorter-hours movement and the belief that the open air of the country made the agricultural population healthier than the urban produced considerable activity in the founding of parks, and in the census of 1880 the acreage and description of such places received a prominent place in the report for each town. A Boston society in 1880 provided sand gardens for children, and by 1898 thirteen other cities in the East had established children's playgrounds.[9] Philanthropic organizations such as the Women's Christian Temperance Union, the Society for the Prevention of Cruelty to Animals, the Society for the Prevention of Cruelty to Children, the State Charities Aid Association, and the Red Cross were established to deal with other problems of industrial life.

The human animal appeared to be changing his habitat and his manner of living with all the effects known to biology of such changes in animal life. The entire effect upon human physiology of the transition in dwelling place and even in diet (particularly because of the widespread use of factory-made foods) has not even yet been determined, for historians of this period have given their attention principally to the alterations of the industrial environment by which the inhabitants of the city tried to make it a more suitable place for living. That improvements were possible was due in large part to the greater productivity of the new system of manufacture and distribution.

Startling as was the growth of population in the towns of the nineteenth century, it was far exceeded by the increase in productions. In the last half of the century American textile production increased sevenfold, agricultural implements twenty-five, packing fourteen, and iron and steel, ten. In this increased productivity, laborers as well as capitalists shared. If Professor Clapham is correct, industrial wages in England advanced forty per cent and the cost of living decreased seventeen per cent in the sixty years after 1790; Miss Coman has estimated that in the United States wages increased twelve and a half per cent and prices decreased forty between 1867 and 1900;[10] thus there were approximate net gains of seventy and eighty-six per cent for the English and American workingmen, respectively, in the margin between earnings and subsistence as compared with the initial years. While capital gains from this improved position appear in the increase of savings-bank deposits and in insurance, the mass of wage earners did not invest in either of these[11] but spent the difference upon a higher standard of living which the greater variety of manufactures made possible.

From the point of view of the city, the significant fact was that this increased economic productivity and the improved economic position of the mass of its inhabitants with respect to subsistence did not bring economic security. The replacement of skilled laborers by machinery produced a series of crises in various trades. This and the constant lowering of the limit of industrial superannuation added constantly to the number of unemployed. The competition of women and children and of immigrants of low standards of living augmented suffering and discontent. Finally, incapacitation from industrial accidents and disease completed the demoralization of a large section of labor and made poverty a norm of existence even in prosperous times. Commenting on these conditions, a French visitor to Manchester in 1844 thus compared the poverty in the old with that in the new cities, "At Paris, half the population go to the hospitals and almshouses to die. At Manchester, half the births take place in the public charities."[12]

Cyclical depression, which appeared in both England and the United States almost regularly every decade after 1815, demonstrated the failure of the new system to provide economic security to the laboring population. During the depression of 1837 a charitable society in Manchester found forty thousand pawn tickets representing an indebtedness of $27,500 at sixteen per cent in four thousand working-class homes.[13] In the United States nearly half a million were thrown out of work on the railways alone by the panic of 1873, only 400 out of 666 furnaces were in operation in the following spring, bread lines were common in every large city, and wages fell on an average of ten per cent and did not reach their former level until 1890.[14] During the panic of 1907 the surveyors of Pittsburgh reported: "Low wages for the great majority of the laborers employed by the mills, not lower than in other large cities, but low compared with prices,—so low as to be inadequate to the maintenance of a normal American standard of living; wages adjusted to the single man in the lodging house, not to the responsible head of a family."[15] To Englishmen and Americans who remembered that under the domestic system the wage earner had owned a plot of ground to supply him with food in bad times and that in earlier days the West had offered homesteads to oppressed craftsmen, the pre-industrial era appeared as the golden age now replaced by suffering and chaos.

Of Manchester in 1844 Léon Faucher

said: "At the very moment when the engines are stopped . . . moral order . . . disappears in an instant. The rich man spreads his couch amidst the beauties of the surrounding country, and abandons the town to the operatives, publicans, thieves, and prostitutes, merely taking the precaution of leaving behind him a police force whose duty it is to preserve some material order in this pell-mell of society."[16] A visitor described Pittsburgh in the eighties as "hell with the lid off." Pittsburgh, Chicago, Detroit, and Cincinnati were centers of organized crime, and in the nation the homicide rate quadrupled while the population doubled.[17] The failure of the police to cope with this growing disorder was accompanied by a series of embittered industrial disputes which appeared to be the first skirmishes of a social revolt.

Between 1816 and 1850 scarcely a year passed without a great strike in either the cotton industry or the building trades in Manchester, while these conflicts were increasingly supported by unions in other cities. The panic of 1873 produced a long strike in the New England textile mills. A ten per cent cut in wages in 1877 precipitated the first nationwide railway strike marked by battles between soldiers and workmen in Baltimore, Reading, and Pittsburgh. The workers of Baltimore foreshadowed the contemporary sit-down strike when they seized the railway yards and prevented the moving of trains, and in Pittsburgh the defeat of the militia gave control of the town to a lawless mob for two days. The bloody Homestead strike of steel workers in 1892 inaugurated an almost continuous series of strikes and lockouts lasting during the remainder of the century.

To restore order to a society that appeared near self-destruction, the philanthropically-inclined wealthy and other community leaders attempted to strengthen the church, the schools, charitable institutions, and the local government. In England, the distress uncovered during the cholera epidemic led six wealthy Manchester philanthropists to found the first statistical society in the world in 1833 "to assist in promoting the social improvement of the manufacturing population" by "collecting facts concerning the inhabitants."[18] Clergymen, merchants, and manufacturers supported monitorial schools under rival organizations in the twenties; temperance societies, mechanics' institutions, and savings banks in the thirties; and associations to promote public health, factory reform, public parks, and national education in the forties. The leaders of the new British manufacturing communities neglected few opportunities to inculcate what they believed to be the virtues of urban citizenship: knowledge of the "useful arts," temperance, industry, and thrift.

So closely parallel were the problems of the cities within the industrial pattern that the counterpart of each of the foregoing activities might be found in the history of almost any American manufacturing city. Local and national scientific and social associations took up the task of fact-finding. Washington Gladden of Columbus, Ohio, and other clergymen supported the rights of labor in its battle with capital and reorganized their congregations into "institutional churches" with charitable and educational agencies.[19] American advocates of broader educational opportunities were more successful than the English in obtaining the assistance of the state to education, and illiteracy dropped from seventeen to eleven per cent in the last twenty years of the century.[20] In adult education the business genius of Redpath and Horner combined with philanthropy and local patriotism in an attempt to raise the general level of culture through the lyceum and the Chautauqua movement.

As philanthropy and mutual assistance proved at best only ameliorative, the pressure of these problems and of the interests affected by them was greatest upon government. In the 1760's the residents of Manchester had congratulated themselves on their lack of a municipal corporation, but in 1790 they began to create a series of new governmental agencies to perform tasks too complex for the traditional institutions. Beginning with watching and poor relief, the local government added before 1850 the regulation of hackney coaches (the traffic and transport problem of the day), street improvement, water supply, gas lighting, fire protection, sewage disposal, and market and public park administration. As in American municipal growth, this progress was accomplished by struggle with vested interests and against corruption: Manchester had a "boss Nadin" sixty years before New York experienced "boss Tweed."

There is not sufficient space within the limits of this article to present details illustrating the expansion of American municipal government, but the facts are sufficiently well known and depart but little from the Manchester pattern. Whether contemporary municipal government has restored the order and security demanded by its citizens is still an open question but not a new one, for the issue has been raised in each town as it has developed into an industrial city and is inherent in its life, as, indeed, are each of the problems that have been suggested as elements in the history of English and American industrial cities in the nineteenth century.

While the conception of a pattern of development is of invaluable assistance in the study of the rise of contemporary society, the student of this history must realize that four points of differentiation between the English and American industrial revolutions make parallels and analogies not only hazardous but if not carefully done very misleading. Briefly these differences are: first, the priority of the industrial revolution in England; second, the existence in England of privileged classes strongly intrenched in government and in social influence; third, the powerful influence of the agricultural West and South in America; and fourth, the enormous proportion of foreign-born population in the United States due to immigration. In these differences, however, lie additional reasons why the American social scientist should be intimately acquainted with the evolution of the English industrial city.

The first great advantage in the study of the English pattern in the nineteenth century is that in their earliest phases the basic processes of a society undergoing industrialization appear in relative simplicity, since the historian has but to consider the impact of a relatively few new developments upon a traditional background. With the passing of the West and the industrialization of the South, those purely American differentiations will be of less importance in analyzing the continuation of the processes at the present time. Finally, the influence of foreign immigration upon the United States may not have exerted so differentiating an effect as might be supposed, and because of the present immigration policy and the rapid Americanization of the descendants of the foreign-born the greater part of this difference in conditions is bound to disappear.

The industrial revolution, it has been said, has been succeeded by a scientific revolution, industrial capitalism by finance capitalism, urbanization by metropolitanization, but the process is not yet complete, and as long as remain the problems created by the industrial revolution—the control of disease, poverty, and crime by urban communities, the raising of cultural standards necessary to urban citizenship, and the removal of economic insecurity—social scientists and historians will be interested in the American and English industrial city of the nineteenth century.

NOTES

° Presented on April 10, 1937, at the eighth annual history conference sponsored by the history department and the extension division of the University of Pittsburgh. Dr. Marshall's article is based upon researches made in the preparation of his doctoral dissertation on "The Development of Public Opinion in Manchester, 1780-1820," presented to the University of Pittsburgh in January, 1937, and of a book he is writing on "The Cultural Evolution of the First Industrial City: Manchester, 1780-1850."

1. *United States Census, 1880, Social Statistics,* 18:721, 733, 773, 850.
2. Robert A. Woods, "Pittsburgh: An Interpretation of Its Growth," in *The Pittsburgh District Civic Frontage,* 17 (Paul U. Kellogg, ed., *The Pittsburgh Survey,* vol. 5—New York, 1914).
3. Great Britain, Registrar General, *Seventh Annual Report,* 338 (London, 1841).
4. Allan Nevins, *The Emergence of Modern America, 1865-1878,* 321 (*A History of American Life,* vol. 8—New York, 1927).
5. Frank E. Wing, "Thirty-five Years of Typhoid," in *The Pittsburgh District Civic Frontage,* 66.
6. Sarah H. Killikelly, *The History of Pittsburgh, Its Rise and Progress,* 393-408 (Pittsburgh, 1906).
7. Edward T. Devine, "Pittsburgh the Year of the Survey," in *The Pittsburgh Civic Frontage,* 3.
8. Arthur M. Schlesinger, *The Rise of the City, 1878-1898,* 129 (*A History of American Life,* vol. 10—New York, 1933).
9. Schlesinger, *Rise of the City,* 130.
10. John H. Clapham, *The Early Railway Age, 1820-1850,* 561, 601, 602 (*An Economic History of Modern Britain,* second edition, vol. 1—Cambridge, 1930); Katharine Coman, *The Industrial History of the United States,* 306 (revised edition, New York, 1925).
11. Clapham, *Early Railway Age,* 299, 300.
12. Léon Faucher, *Manchester in 1844: Its Present Condition and Future Prospects,* 145 (London, 1844).
13. Joseph Adshead, *Distress in Manchester,* 41 (London, 1842).
14. Nevins, *Emergence of Modern America,* 299, 300, 301.
15. Devine, in *The Pittsburgh District Civic Frontage,* 3.
16. Faucher, *Manchester in 1844,* 26, 27.
17. Schlesinger, *Rise of the City,* 114.
18. Thomas S. Ashton, *Economic and Social Investigations in Manchester, 1833-1933,* 13 (London, 1934).
19. Schlesinger, *Rise of the City,* 340.
20. Schlesinger, *Rise of the City,* 171.

The Emergence of Industrial Cities

BLAKE McKELVEY

So many ambitious towns sprang up in the early days on each frontier that many were threatened with atrophy when the railroads enabled a few to stake out broad hinterlands at the expense of their neighbors. Only through industrial enterprise could most cities hope to prosper. Some enjoyed special opportunities as a result of the timely discovery of mineral resources nearby or at points easily reached by cheap water transport. A few achieved industrial leadership through the exploitation of local water power or by the invention of machinery to process regional products more efficiently. Others escaped a way-station fate because a steady flow of immigrants spurred residents to develop new industries based in part on cheap labor and to produce for a national market. Still others prospered through the manufacture of patented or specialty articles. Several combined these tactics, and all labored to produce a marketable surplus.[1]

The rise or decline of an individual town was of major concern only to its promoters and its more settled residents; others could and did move elsewhere without loss. But the widespread survival of many threatened communities by means of industrial enterprise was of primary significance. A few such towns became the prototypes of the industrial city and endowed it with special characteristics. Several others pressed the advantages their manufacturing activities brought and did so with such vigor that they achieved metropolitan status; a few of these, notably Minneapolis, acquired regional hegemony. Moreover the emphasis they gave to industry forced their commercial rivals also to accord it increased attention. To promote these efforts, the business leaders of most communities reorganized old boards of trade or established new associations. By the turn of the century the industrial output of American cities had so outstripped that of any foreign country that the character of international trade was transformed, and with it the services performed by the great ports.

The industrialization of America is a separate story, but the impetus given to that development by the rise of the city cannot be overlooked.[2] The impetus given to industrialism by the rapid discovery and exploitation of the country's natural resources is more fully documented and understood, and so also is the effect of the great influx of immigrant workmen in this period.[3] Here, however, we are interested in the converse side of these historic movements—the contributions that new sources of energy and raw materials, new supplies of labor and industrial skills, new machines and techniques of production made to urban growth.

Because of their glamour, the successive gold rushes have long had a place in American history, yet their product never compared in value with that of the silver and copper mines and appeared insignificant when measured against the output of the iron and coal fields. Similar contrasts marked their respective towns. Gold-mining towns such as Virginia City were more pretentious than those based on silver and copper, but their permanence depended on the discovery nearby of "baser" metals. Not even the iron- and copper-mining camps became major cities (Butte, Montana, was a possible exception). Only where abundant supplies of coal or other fuels were found was manufacturing encouraged and urban growth maintained.[4]

Even in the coal fields, few mining towns became major cities. In the hard-coal region of Pennsylvania, where the ore deposits extended over several counties, numerous settlements or "patches" sprang up about many colliery shafts, creating a density of as much as 1300 persons per square mile without achieving the integration essential for urban status. By 1900 only Scranton and Wilkes-Barre had exceeded 100,000 and 50,000 respectively, and this chiefly because they were not as exclusively occupied with mining as, for example, neighboring Hazleton, which barely numbered 25,000 a decade later. In fact Scranton, at the turn of the century, had more industrial workers than either miners or tradesmen.[5]

Generally a nearby commercial or industrial city supplied the marketing, banking, and other urban services for mining districts, thus strengthening its claim to regional leadership. Sometimes a mining town developed a new in-

dustry to convert the products of neighboring collieries, as in the coke district around Uniontown and Brownville, only to see its control absorbed in time by a regional capital, in this case Pittsburgh.[6] Most mining communities, victims of absentee ownership and constricted by their specialty, failed to develop the internal leadership necessary to attract competing transport arteries or to tap new sources of credit.[7]

Other fuel strikes brought dubious benefits to communities at their sites, but presented great opportunities to the commercial marts that acquired control. The oil towns of northwestern Pennsylvania, which displayed great vitality during the seventies, were soon checked as monopoly control over refining and marketing siphoned the profits of the industry into the hands of Rockefeller and his colleagues in Cleveland and other processing centers.[8] Natural gas brought a sudden boom to several communities, notably Findlay and Toledo, Ohio, but their fortunes ebbed with the arrival of outside control.[9] Toledo, already an important railroad hub and advantageously situated for lake trade, remained primarily a regional market until civic leaders, reasserting the town's rights to its power resources, enabled industry finally to pull ahead of commerce and boost the city into the 100,000 bracket by the close of the period.[10]

Some cities prospered as processors of regional farm products. Minneapolis, a small neighbor of St. Paul in the seventies, captured leadership in the wheat belt of the Northwest during the eighties by developing mills able to produce a better flour from the spring wheat of that area than St. Louis or other rivals could mill from winter wheat. Kansas City won its independence from St. Louis and Chicago by building up its meat-packing industry. Milwaukee ventured with less success into each of these fields but achieved its greatest triumph in the brewing industry, likewise based on products of the area. Memphis competed with many other places in lumber milling but excelled in the production of cotton-seed oil. Each of these and several like them strengthened their positions by developing accessory industries and by extending urban economic services to a hinterland which they constantly endeavored to expand. All attained metropolitan status chiefly because of their manufacturing services.[11]

Many cities, even when overshadowed by near neighbors, prospered through the employment of cheap immigrant labor.[12] The shoe industry, in which the introduction of machinery after the mid-century tended to supersede old craft skills, lent itself to this use. Lynn and Haverhill had developed a reputation for shoes in earlier decades, and after the Civil War Cincinnati and Rochester, among others, began to specialize in this field. New York and Philadelphia, because of their large markets and abundant supply of newcomers, became shoe producers, although not as important as the older New England centers, where the earlier craftsmen supervised a new work force of immigrants.[13]

But cheap labor, even when supplied from abroad, did not long remain content in America, and the shoe industry produced some of the most determined union-organizing drives of these decades. Unfortunately, from the viewpoint of the cities involved, when union demands mounted in one town, many firms (except those engaged in quality production) sought new sites, such as Milwaukee, Chicago, or Manchester, New Hampshire, where the organizers had not yet penetrated. The migration of shoe companies, facilitated by the practice of leasing rather than purchasing the machinery, presented a constant threat to cities in this field. It also provided an extreme example of the industrial mobility that contributed to both the diffusion and the fluidity of America's urban development.[14]

The textile industry, too, displayed an intense interest in cheap labor, but the range of its migrations was limited. Originally established at water-power sites in New England, where textiles nurtured several of the country's first factory towns, notably Lowell and Manchester, this industry quickly replaced its early native-born labor from the first influx of Irish and other immigrant groups, thus speeding the urbanization as well as the cosmopolitan transformation of the Yankee homeland. During the post-Civil War expansion, when steam began to supplement water power, Fall River pulled into the lead among textile centers because of its easy access to water-borne coal and its cheap immigrant labor, including that of women and children.[15] Some textile towns added other specialties; Chicopee developed tool shops and began to produce bicycles; Holyoke became a paper city; Lowell ventured into woolens, carpets, knitted products, and other enterprises. Successive waves of new immigrants—Polish, French Canadian, and Portuguese—enabled management to fight off many union demands; yet pressure from the workers and the restraints of labor legislation in America's second most urbanized commonwealth presented Massachusetts textile firms with an increasing disadvantage in competition with the new cotton mills of the South.[16]

The development of the textile industry in the South had a substantial economic basis. The slow spread of cotton factories in North and South Carolina and Georgia during post-Civil War years uncovered a new supply of cheap labor in the poor whites of the Piedmont area and began in the eighties to attract northern capital, some of it from the New England firms themselves. Advances in technology—the Northrop automatic loom and the ring spindle, which eliminated the skilled mule spinners who had formed the backbone of textile unions in the North —enabled the southern mills to employ unskilled labor and to defeat the first effort at organization around 1900. Since many northern firms hesitated to make the fresh investments that new machinery required, New England textile cities saw the greater part of the expanding market after 1890 pass by by default to new towns in the South.[17]

A major reason for the embarrassment of some of the New England towns was the defection of their absentee entrepreneurs and the failure to replace their talents from among the immigrant workers.[18] On the other hand, some cities prospered because of the enterprise and skills that waves of newcomers brought. British and Dutch glassmakers strengthened the economy of Pittsburgh and Toledo and gave economic vitality to Corning, New York, La Salle, Illinois, and many other towns. German brewers helped to build up Cincinatti, St. Louis, Rochester, Chicago, and especially Milwaukee; despite some opposition from local temperance forces, they ultimately won acceptance and influence in each place.[19] Skilled mechanics and technicians from England, Germany, and elsewhere received a more immediate welcome and financial support in developing enterprises ranging in one town from buttons to optical instruments;[20] the classic example of immigrant enterprise, however, was the clothing industry, and many cities fattened upon it.

When the ready-to-wear clothing trade appeared at mid-century its most enterprising leaders were German Jews. Many who had gained a footing as tailors or peddlers or retail merchants now expanded their operations by employing some of their more recently arrived fellow countrymen. Several of these firms, which sprang up in the more populous centers and engaged the talents of vigorous salesmen, installed the newly invented sewing machines, employing women and girls to operate them. As cutting machines were perfected and the specialization of tasks increased, some of the shops blossomed into factories. Others, particularly in New York and Chicago, where the largest influx of a new wave of Eastern European Jews occurred, developed a contract system that enabled the recent comers to work under men of their own group and in neighborhood lofts where they could speak their native tongue.[21]

This activity spread widely and unobtrusively, helping to sustain sizable colonies of Eastern Jews in Boston and Baltimore, in Cleveland, Cincinnati, Rochester, and a dozen smaller places. Every member of the family lent a hand, but it soon became evident that only the contract bosses were prospering. Again a union movement developed and brought long years of bitter strife, with both the owners and the organizers seeking to gain an advantage by playing one city against another in regional lockouts and boycotts. Nevertheless the industry, responding to the rapid urban growth, continued to expand, and the companies, closely dependent on their labor supply, could not migrate freely. Wages remained low, and the wide use of sweatshops helped to foster living standards that were among the worst in America—so wretched, in fact, that the public conscience was pricked. Soon local, state, and federal investigations began to study the problem. New pressure for governmental supervision developed, and a resurgence of union effort occurred among the workers as the period closed.[22]

If the classic example of immigrant enterprise was the clothing industry, that of the native was the commercial bank, though foreign-born bankers increased in number after the seventies. Each new settlement boasted one or more of these institutions, which quickly multiplied as the towns grew. By 1880, 6532 banks with national, state, or private charters—one to every 2000 urban residents—served a variety of functions, among them the promotion of city growth. Although the accumulation and use of private savings was still a minor feature, as was investment banking, the facility these establishments brought to commercial transactions, and the concentration they effected of fluid capital in the sixteen cities designated as redemption centers under the National Banking Act of 1863-64, strengthened the leading marts within their respective regions and tied their economy to the great central reserve capital in New York.[23]

It was not the banks, however, but enterprising men who determined the direction of a city's industrial development. Sometimes an influx of newcomers with special skills transformed a town's activity. Thus at Rochester after the mid-century, when flour milling and canalling had passed their apogee, a host of immigrant craftsmen created the clothing, shoe, nursery, brewing, and woodworking industries that gave it a new burst of growth, placing it in the 100,000 bracket by 1885. The lack of convenient coal, iron, and other natural resources had threatened to blight the "Flower City's" manufacturing prospects, but the new industries depended less on raw materials than on human skills and on the excellence of their products. Such varied and specialized instruments were designed and built that they again transformed Rochester, within three decades, into a center of technical industry. A young bank clerk, George Eastman, discovered that the photographic laboratory he set up in his mother's kitchen held more fascination than a teller's cage, and the city soon shared his rewards.[24]

Enterprise in abundance characterized most cities throughout these decades. Growth itself created a rich market, not only for food and apparel and building materials but also for a variety of new articles that promised urban convenience. Ingenious men perfected the telephone, the elevator, the trolley car, the bicycle, and the automobile—to name only a few that contributed to the ease and speed of communications in cities, thus increasing the momentum of their growth. Energetic promoters extended the use of these products widely through the towns of

America and at the same time greatly benefited those where the factories were located.[25]

The widespread technological advance frequently prompted independent inventors to work on similar problems at the same time. Occasionally a city assembled so many skilled craftsmen in a particular industry that it generated innovations and attracted experts from distant places. The Edison shops at Harrison, New Jersey, the Brush Electric Company at Cleveland, and the Thomson-Houston works at Lynn drew proficient electrical workers to these centers; Eastman attracted to Rochester rival photographic and optical companies eager to share its concentration of specialized skills. Although many manufacturers, impelled to acquire patent rights that might obstruct the development of their products, hastened to absorb competitors, the formation of new firms almost in the shadow of the expanding companies often continued unabated. Some of the new concerns developed subsidiary articles which they produced for the major distributors—speed shutters for cameras in Rochester, lamp stems for incandescent globes at Harrison—thus contributing to the integration of major community industries while retaining the enterprise many restless but talented craftsmen desired.[26]

The upsurge of inventiveness flooded the patent office with the applications as the 120,000 registered before 1870 mounted by 1910 to well over a million.[27] Promoters who helped to develop the new mechanical devices generally enlisted support from local capitalists. The limited-dividend corporation, freely available under the general laws of most states, proved especially attractive, and such incorporations, almost nonexistent in manufacturing in 1860, numbered over 40,000 at the close of the century. Although they comprised barely a tenth of all establishments, they produced 60 per cent of the value, and almost completely dominated the metal and technical branches. The flexibility of these economic "persons"—their capacity for expansion or consolidation, for a shift in leadership or a change in product—fitted them admirably for growing cities faced with problems of economic integration.[28]

The most rapid increase among giant corporations occurred at the turn of the century, as they mushroomed from twelve in 1896, each valued at $10 million or more, to fifty that exceeded $50 million by 1903.[29] Even after the move for consolidation began and strong, often monopolistic groups took hold, a rapidly expanding market and more effective sales promotion frequently enabled the trust to keep all its affiliated plants in operation, at least for a time. Sometimes a new factory site was selected, as in the case of the General Electric Company, a consolidation of Edison and rival concerns, but the new beginning it made at Schenectady in 1886 could not absorb all the work in process at Harrison, Lynn, and Cleveland, among other places. Several of the old centers prospered, while Schenectady became an industrial city of high quality.[30]

Numerous towns, though not the majority, enjoyed similar benefits. The typewriter brought life to Ilion, New York, and new vigor to Syracuse; telephone factories clustered for a time at Boston and Chicago, but soon spread out; the cash register placed Dayton on the industrial map. A score of cities manufactured elevators, and many more contributed to the production of trolley cars and their equipment.[31] Bicycle companies sprang up in a host of towns during the early nineties, but shortly after 1899, when the American Bicycle Company absorbed forty-eight of them, production was centered in ten plants at Springfield, Massachusetts, and Hartford, Connecticut, each of which suffered a severe blow when the trust collapsed a few seasons later. Several former cycle factories had meanwhile shifted to the manufacture of automobiles, in which Detroit quickly took the lead. Its surplus of capital from an expiring lumber trade, together with an overabundance of skilled marine-engine mechanics, welcomed the new industry.[32]

So many cities suffered from the migration of old companies and other effects of consolidation that the antitrust forces won general approval. The long battle for the regulation of railroads had spread antimonopoly doctrines, nurturing a strong faith in competition, and prepared the way for the speedy adoption of the Sherman Anti-Trust Act in 1890. Yet its vague provisions left many issues undecided. In the courts, where the rising trusts had much more effective representation than in the legislatures, the legal curbs atrophied and almost disappeared. Protests against government interference with "free enterprise," on which the welfare, particularly of industrial cities, seemed to depend, enlisted support from most business groups and discouraged efforts to halt consolidations. Only the more flagrant invasions of local community interests aroused effective action, such as the Standard Oil Company's stranglehold over the fortunes of Toledo and other Ohio towns in the early nineties, or the Trans-Missouri Freight Association's attempt to control the traffic of the Southwest a few years later. Champions of the efficiency of large-scale enterprise multiplied, and in 1889 New Jersey provided a corporate form for the holding companies that widely superseded the old trusts.[33]

In most cities new firms quickly replaced those absorbed or otherwise lost, and many small market towns grew into promising industrial centers. The number reporting at least 10,000 factory workers increased from thirty to fifty-four during the last two decades of the century; those listing 5000 or more rose from forty-five to eighty-one. After 1900 many factories migrated to the suburbs, and this presented the parent city with new problems of economic integration. All growing towns felt an increasing need for local leadership.[34]

Boards of trade and chambers of commerce sprang up in city after city as rallying points for their businessmen. Only a few of the thirty or more such organizations formed before the Civil War had survived, notably those of Chicago, Buffalo, Pittsburgh, and New York. Now the extension of the telegraph and the laying of the Atlantic cable in 1866 opened new possibilities for long-distance trade negotiations and stimulated the formation of organizations to conduct local exchanges and disseminate trade information. Most of the new crop of business clubs were, like their predecessors, chiefly concerned with commerce, but in 1869 the Milwaukee Chamber of Commerce raised a fund of $860 "to promote the city's industrial growth." Its list of the town's advantages for trade and industry, published in 1871 and widely circulated, heralded a new, more industrial approach. A few years later, the same body initiated an industrial exposition patterned after the Centennial in Philadelphia. Its building, erected at a cost of $300,000 and opened in 1881, supplied facilities for annual exhibitions during the next two decades and inspired businessmen in St. Louis, Chicago, and Minneapolis to similar efforts.[35]

The most forthright move in this direction occurred at Philadelphia in 1894, when the city council oganized a Commercial Museum and provided it with a building and equipment to display local industrial products and to promote foreign trade. San Francisco, St. Louis, and Boston established similar museums. Not to be outdone, an Association for the Advancement of Milwaukee urged real-estate men to grant free sites or free rent to new industrial ventures and collected subscriptions from capitalists to back them. The association, which also proposed tax concessions, boasted after two years that its efforts had attracted a score of new industries to the city, helping it to reach fifteenth place by 1900.[36]

Some of the post–Civil War boards of trade declined after a few seasons, but new organizations generally appeared in response to urgent business needs. Several midwestern towns formed promotional bodies similar to Milwaukee's. In 1892 the Cleveland Board of Trade created a committee for the promotion of industry, which led in turn to the reorganization of the board as a Chamber of Commerce a year later, when a full-time secretary was engaged to handle such activities and to develop new civic and welfare functions. Other chambers, too, were seeking competent secretaries, and in 1913 as their activities became standardized the newly established Harvard Business School organized a course for them.

The effort to provide free sites or other subsidies for new industries lost favor in some chambers after concerns of questionable merit accepted such benefits only to move on when a higher bid arrived. But the promotional value of numerous trade conventions, industrial exhibitions, and publications that featured local advantages gained wide acceptance among the several hundred boards and chambers of the early 1900's. If the annual reports often sounded a bit boastful, even to local observers, such growing industrial cities as Milwaukee, Cleveland, Pittsburgh, Detroit, Buffalo, Columbus, and Rochester—not to mention several of the newer towns of the West—all gladly supported active groups.[37]

Although the basic philosophy of most of these chambers involved unfaltering support for "free enterprise," especially after events in the nineties sharpened the issue, some of their committees did try to establish voluntary standards of production and fair dealing. Their resolutions generally opposed state and federal regulations, but many were quick to appeal to the I. C. C. or to an appropriate state authority when a long-haul railroad rate schedule or some other monopoly practice seemed prejudicial to the locality. Their concern for the city's welfare often aligned them against freebooting utility combines and high-handed industrial giants. Leadership in the continuing attack on trusts and corporate monopolies generally came from other sources, but the chambers were exponents of community business interests.[38]

Most growing towns had, of course, developed a sense of the community's interest long before organizations to promote it emerged. An informal leadership, which later sociologists would call the power structure, generally directed important aspects of the development of each city. The promoters of town sites and urban subdivisions, who frequently joined the merchants to support and direct the expansive projects of the commercial centers, seldom gave effective leadership to the industrial cities. There the initiative more frequently came from ambitious craftsmen, often men with inventive talents, whose struggle to produce and market new products transformed them into captains of industry. They were the most alert developers of each town's external economy. Newcomers from abroad, and others from small towns nearby, rose in this fashion to positions of influence.

Many industrial cities developed specialties based on the skills of their workers or the inventive talents of their technicians. On the other hand the mining towns and some others largely dependent on one industry frequently lost control to absentee owners who opposed the development of independent enterprise. The widespread reaction to, or fear of, that fate strengthened the antimonopoly forces of the commercial centers, plagued by railroad pools, and hastened the triumph of the progressive movement.

The most important contribution of the industrial cities was the mounting output of their factories. Statistics show that the value added by manufacturing doubled between 1859 and 1879 and more than doubled again in the prosperous eighties, and yet again, despite two depressions, by 1909. The value added by manufacturing increased tenfold in the half-century, almost trebling the increased value of farm products.

Moreover the portion of the national income derived from manufacturing mounted from 16.6 to 20.8 per cent during the last three decades, while that derived from agriculture held steady and the contributions of both trade and transportation declined.[39]

In this period, at least, industry rather than commerce was the chief source of urban growth. Over nine-tenths of the industrial production occurred in urban factories, and as their output increased a surplus for export developed in some fields. Shipments abroad of manufactured foodstuffs and of finished industrial products mounted steadily after 1876 until, by 1898, even the latter exceeded comparable imports. As American factories progressively crowded European products out of the domestic consumer trade, the American farm was relieved of the burden of balancing foreign payments. The export of foodstuffs, both raw and manufactured, declined after the turn of the century, but the exports of other manufactured products more than took up the slack, maintaining a sufficiently favorable balance of trade to liquidate some of the foreign investments. Thus urban industrial growth freed the national economy not only from dependence on European factories, but also from reliance on foreign banks for new capital. That, however, was only a minor aspect of the industrial city's accomplishment, for the value added to its products exceeded the total value of all imports almost seven to one by 1899, as contrasted with a ratio of five to two, four decades earlier. As foreign trade diminished in relative importance, domestic trade mounted, and the industrial worker produced material goods in sufficient volume to raise the standards of consumption throughout the country.[40]

NOTES

1. Edgar M. Hoover, *The Location of Economic Activity* (New York, 1948). See Edward Ullman, "A Theory of Location for Cities," *American Journal of Sociology*, Vol. 46 (May, 1941), pp. 853-863, for a review of several theories concerning the location of cities.
2. Numerous books recognize this contribution, but few have treated it adequately. See Kirkland, *op. cit.*, pp. 237-261; Harold U. Faulkner, *The Decline of Laissez Faire: 1897-1917* (New York, 1951), pp. 92-114; Hays, *op. cit.*, pp. 48-58. For an early study of urban contributions, see Arthur Shadwell, *Industrial Efficiency* (London, 1909). For an able geographical study of urban economy, see Gunnar Alexandersson, *The Industrial Structure of American Cities* (Lincoln, Nebraska, 1956).
3. Charlotte Erickson, *American Industry and the European Immigrant: 1860-1885* (Cambridge, 1957); Eric E. Lampard in Harvey S. Perloff and associates, *Regions, Resources and Economic Growth* (Baltimore, 1960), pp. 122-221.
4. Kirkland, *op. cit.* (1961), pp. 133-142; Edmund E. Day, "An Index of the Physical Volume of Production," *Review of Economic Statistics*, II (Oct., 1920), p. 294; Ray B. West, Jr., *Rocky Mountain Cities* (New York, 1949), pp. 230-255; Paul H. Landis, *Three Iron Mining Towns* (Ann Arbor, 1938); Alexandersson, *op. cit.*, pp. 27-34. See the bibliography in Caroline Bancroft's fictionalized history of Central City, Colorado, *Gulch of Gold* (Denver, 1958), pp. 365-367.
5. T. A. Rickard, *A History of American Mining* (New York, 1932), pp. 91 and *passim;* U. S. *Census* (1900), Occupations, p. 728; Peter Roberts, *Anthracite Coal Communities* (New York, 1904); Chauncy D. Harris, "A Functional Classification of Cities in the United States." *Geographic Review*, Vol. 33 (Jan., 1930), pp. 86-96. See also Kirkland, *op. cit.* (1961), pp. 137-162.
6. Muriel E. Sheppard, *Cloud by Day* (Chapel Hill, 1947); *Cost of Living in American Towns* (Senate Doc. 22, 1911), pp. 337-339, 344-348. See also Henry L. Hunker, *Industrial Evolution of Columbus, Ohio* (Columbus, 1958), pp. 39-55, for an account of how Columbus absorbed the energies of nearby mining districts.
7. Herman F. Otte, *Industrial Opportunity in the Tennessee Valley of Northwestern Alabama* (New York, 1940), pp. 20-26; Vance and Demerath, *op. cit.*, pp. 10-12; Woodward, *op. cit.*, pp. 314-316.
8. Johnson, *op. cit., passim;* Thomas Greenwood,

A Tour of the States and Canada (London, 1883), pp. 94-100; Tarbell, *op. cit.*, pp. 74-79; Cochran and Miller, *op. cit.*, pp. 135-146. See also, John P. Herrick, *Empire Oil* (New York, 1949).
9. Chester M. Destler, *American Radicalism: 1856-1901* (New London, 1946), Chapter VII.
10. Randolph C. Downes, *Lake Port* [Lucas County History Series III] (Toledo, 1951), pp. 59-93; U. S. *Census* (1900), Occupations, p. 742; (1910), IX: 996-997.
11. Henrietta Larson, *The Wheat Market and the Farmer in Minnesota, 1858-1900* (New York, 1926); Mildred Hartsough, *The Twin Cities* (Minneapolis, 1925), pp. 36-46; Henry C. Haskell, Jr., and R. B. Fowler, *City of the Future: A Narrative History of Kansas City, 1850-1950* (Kansas City, 1950); Gerald M. Capers, *River Town, Memphis* (Chapel Hill, 1939), pp. 220-228; Alice Lantherman, "Kansas City as a Grain and Milling Center," *Missouri Historical Review*, XLII (1947), pp. 132-155; *Cost of Living in American Towns* (Senate Doc. 22, 1911), pp. 243-283; Alexandersson, *op. cit.*, pp. 34-35, 86-88.
12. Erickson, *op. cit.*, pp. 65-105; Mary R. Coolidge, *Chinese Immigration*, (New York, 1909), pp. 357-401. Boston's sudden emergence as an industrial city in the fifties has been attributed to cheap immigrant labor—see Oscar Handlin, *Boston's Immigrants: 1790-1865* (Cambridge, 1951), pp. 79-87.
13. George W. Chase, *History of Haverhill* (Haverhill, 1921), pp. 532-536; Edgar M. Hoover, *Location Theory and the Shoe and Leather Industries* (Cambridge, 1937), pp. 219-228.
14. *Ibid.*, pp. 229-255; Horace B. Davis, *Shoes, The Workers and the Industry* (New York, 1940), p. 17 and *passim;* Blake McKelvey, "A History of the Rochester Shoe Industry," *Rochester History*, Apr., 1953, pp. 6-20; U. S. Industrial Commission, *Reports*, VII: 176-180, 369-370; Alexandersson, *op. cit.*, pp. 80-82.
15. Thomas R. Smith, *The Cotton Textile Industry of Fall River, Mass.; A Study of Industrial Localization* (New York, 1944), pp. 40-99; Marcus L. Hansen, *The Immigrant in American History* (Cambridge, 1940), pp. 154-174; Arthur W. Calhoun, *A Social History of the American Family* (Cleveland, 1919), III: 67; *Cost of Living in American Towns* (Senate Doc. 22, 1911), pp. 197-203, 208-214, 231-238; Shadwell, *op. cit.*, pp. 208-230.
16. Vera Shlakman, *Economic History of a Factory Town: A Study of Chicopee, Mass.* [Smith College Studies in History, XX] (Northampton, 1935), pp. 151-225; Margaret T. Parker, *Lowell: A Study of Industrial Development* (New York, 1940), pp. 85, 118-147; Constance M. Green, *Holyoke, Mass.* (New Haven, 1930), pp. 137-251; U. S. Industrial Commission, *Re-*

port, VII (1900), pp. 68-84, 90, 219-226, 343-348; Hansen, *op. cit.,* pp. 160-174, 188-190; Alexandersson, *op. cit.,* pp. 63-70; Faulkner, *op. cit.,* pp. 142-144.
17. Anthony M. Tang, *Economic Development in the Southern Piedmont* (Chapel Hill, 1958), pp. 22-65 ff.; Smith, *op. cit.,* pp. 80-121; Herbert Lahne, *The Cotton Mill Worker* (New York, 1944), pp. 70-84, 175-195; Melvin T. Copeland, *The Cotton Manufacturing Industry of the United States* (Cambridge, 1923), pp. 27-133; F. B. Garver, F. M. Boddy and A. J. Nixon, *The Location of Manufacturers in the United States: 1899-1929* (Minneapolis, 1933), pp. 65-75; Broadus Mitchell and George S. Mitchell, *The Industrial Revolution in the South* (Baltimore, 1930), pp. 126-140; William H. Simpson, *Life in Mill Communities* (Clinton, S. C., 1943), pp. 14-25.
18. Smith, *op. cit.,* pp. 119-121; Parker, *op. cit.,* p. 210 ff. But see also Victor S. Clark, *History of Manufacturers in the United States* (New York, 1929), II. 181-198; Shlakman, *op. cit.,* pp. 196-198; Green, *American Cities,* pp. 82-90.
19. Erickson, *op. cit.,* pp. 139-147; Bayrd Still, *Milwaukee, The History of a City* (Madison, 1948), pp. 329-332 and *passim;* Pierce, *Chicago,* II: 89; Blake McKelvey, *Rochester, The Flower City: 1854-1890* (Cambridge, 1949) [cited below as *Rochester,* II], pp. 106-107, 238-240; Thomas C. Cochran, *Pabst Brewing Company: The History of an American Business* (New York, 1949); *Cost of Living in American Towns* (Senate Doc. 22, 1911), pp. 152-157, 257-265, 373-376.
20. McKelvey, *Rochester,* II: 227, 243, 322, 380; U. S. Industrial Commission *Report,* XV (1901), *passim;* Carl Wittke, *We Who Built America* (New York, 1940), pp. 392-401. See Erickson, *op. cit., passim.*
21. Jesse E. Pope, *The Clothing Industry in New York* [University of Missouri Studies, Vol. I] (St. Louis, 1905), pp. 45 ff.; U. S. Industrial Commission *Report* (1901), pp. xxiv-xxxii, xlvii, 316-384, 449-490; *Cost of Living in American Towns* (U. S. Senate Doc. 22, 1911), pp. 20-21, 23, 137-138; Edward E. Pratt, *Industrial Causes of Congestion of Population in New York City* (New York, 1911), pp. 79-86. See also Moses Rischin, *The Promised City: New York's Jews, 1870-1914* (Cambridge, 1962), pp. 51-68.
22. Mabel A. Magee, *Trends in Location of the Women's Clothing Industry* (Chicago, 1930), pp. 9-11, 133-134; Leonard A. Drake and Carrie Glasser, *Trends in the New York Clothing Industry* (New York, 1942), pp. 39-47; Louis Levine, *The Women's Garment Workers* (New York, 1924), pp. 1-195; Calhoun, *op. cit.,* III: 74-75; *Cost of Living in American Towns* (Senate Doc. 22, 1911), pp. 18-24, 75-78, 105-108, 137-141, 154-156, 162-166, 177-179, 323-324; Charles Hirschfeld, *Baltimore: 1870-1900*

[Johns Hopkins Studies in History and Political Science, Series 59, No. 2] (Baltimore, 1941), pp. 41-42, 57-63.
23. *World Almanac* (1889), p. 91; U. S. *Census* (1880), Compendium, p. 8; Cochran and Miller, *op. cit.,* pp. 135-153; Margaret G. Myers, *The New York Money Market* (New York, 1931), I: 213-233; Pierce, *Chicago,* III: 192-233; Douglas North, "Capital Accumulation in Life Insurance Between the Civil War and 1905," in William Miller, *Men of Business* (Cambridge, 1952), pp. 238-253. See also Kirkland, *op. cit.* (1961), pp. 216-236.
24. McKelvey, *Rochester,* II: 98-126, 200-256.
25. Roger Burlingame, *Engines of Democracy* (New York, 1940), pp. 95-125, *passim;* Herbert N. Casson, *The History of the Telephone* (Chicago, 1910); Hays, *op. cit.,* pp. 48-58; Kirkland, *op. cit.* (1961), pp. 163-182.
26. Harold C. Passer, *The Electrical Manufacturers, 1875-1900* (Cambridge, 1953); Blake McKelvey, *Rochester, The Quest for Quality* (Cambridge, 1956) [cited below as *Rochester,* III], pp. 256-272; Faulkner, *op. cit.,* pp. 115-134; Alexandersson, *op. cit.,* pp. 48-49, 62-63.
27. Felix Frankfurter, *The Public and Its Government* (New Haven, 1930), pp. 9-10; *Recent Social Trends in the United States* (New York, 1934), pp. 125-127; Edward W. Byrn, *The Progress of Invention in the Nineteenth Century* (New York, 1900).
28. U. S. *Census* (1900), VII: 503-509; Hirschfeld, *op. cit.,* pp. 44-46, 76-82; Kirkland, *op. cit.* (1961), pp. 196-214; Fine, *op. cit.,* pp. 146-151.
29. John Moody, *The Truth About the Trusts* (New York, 1904), pp. 453-476; William Miller, "American History and the Business Elite," *Journal of Economic History,* IX (1949), 184-208; Cochran and Miller, *op. cit.,* pp. 135-153, 181-191; Faulkner, *op. cit.,* 153-164.
30. Abbott P. Usher, *A History of Mechanical Inventions* (Cambridge, 1954), pp. 401-406; Paul W. Keating, *Lamps for a Brighter America* (New York, 1954), pp. 21 ff.; Joel H. Monroe, *Schenectady, Ancient and Modern* (Schenectady, 1914), p. 277-280; Passer, *op. cit.,* pp. 52-57, 100-104, 321-330; Kirkland, *op. cit.* (1961), pp. 195-215.
31. *MacRae's Blue Book* (New York, 1910); Byrn, *op. cit.,* pp. 76-87, 171-182, 459-460; Clark, *op. cit.,* II: 377-387; III: 165-170; Bruce Bliven, *The Wonderful Writing Machine* (New York, 1954); Lee, *op. cit.,* pp. 97-104.
32. Arthur S. Dwing, *Corporate Promotions and Reorganizations* (Cambridge, 1914), pp. 249-268; Lloyd Morris, *Not So Long Ago* (New York, 1949), pp. 229-265; Shlakman, *op. cit.,* pp. 200-205; Merrill Denison, *The Power to Go* (New York, 1956), pp. 92-180; *Cost of Living in American Towns* (Senate Doc. 22, 1911), pp. 172-175; H. H. McCarthy, *Industrial Migra-*

tion in the United States, 1914-1927 (Iowa City, Iowa, 1930), p. 10; Ralph C. Epstein, *The Automobile Industry* (New York, 1928), pp. 123, 209, 257-260, 296; Green, *op. cit.*, pp. 199-203; Alexandersson, *op. cit.*, pp. 49-54.

33. Henry R. Seager and C. A. Gulick, Jr., *Trust and Corporation Problems* (New York, 1929), pp. 48-60, 367-398; Destler, *op. cit.*, pp. 105-134; R. H. Bremner, "The Civic Revival in Ohio," *American Journal of Economics and Sociology* (1951), X: 417-429; Fine, *op. cit.*, pp. 126-164; Faulkner, *op. cit.*, pp. 175-186, 202-210.

34. U. S. *Census* (1900), VII: ccxix-ccxxiv; (1910), X: 901-975; Glenn E. McLaughlin, *Growth of American Manufacturing Areas* (Pittsburgh, 1938), pp. 127-132, 186-188.

35. Kenneth Sturges, *American Chambers of Commerce* (New York, 1915), pp. 11-43; Still, *op. cit.*, pp. 345-348.

36. Still, *op. cit.*, pp. 345-348; see also Lloyd Graham and Frank H. Severance, *The First Hundred Years of the Buffalo Chamber of Commerce* (Buffalo, 1945), p. 142 ff.; U. S.

Industrial Commission *Report*, VII (1900), pp. 16-17, 990-999; XIV: 439-460; see also Hirschfeld, *op. cit.*, pp. 36-38; Pierce, *Chicago*, III: 80, 93, 475.

37. Sturges, *op. cit.*, pp. 117-166, 231-240; William G. Rose, *Cleveland, The Making of a City* (Cleveland, 1950), pp. 537, 542; George W. Doonan, "Commercial Organizations in Southern and Western Cities," U. S. Bureau of Foreign and Domestic Commerce, *Special Agents Series*, No. 79, 1914; Hunker, *op. cit.*, pp. 53-55.

38. Sturges, *op. cit.*, *passim;* Howard L. Childs, *Labor and Capital in National Politics* (Columbus, 1930); Paul Studenski, "Chambers of Commerce," *Encyclopedia of the Social Sciences*, III: 325-329; Fine, *op. cit.*, pp. 96-125.

39. U. S. Bureau of the Census, *Historical Statistics of the United States: Colonial Times to 1957* (Washington, 1957), pp. 139-140, 283-284; Kirkland, *op. cit.* (1961), pp. 278-305, 399-409.

40. *Historical Statistics of the United States to 1957*, pp. 544-546; Faulkner, *op. cit.*, pp. 52-63.

Urbanization and Criminal Violence

ROGER LANE

America is now an urban nation, but Americans are still afraid of cities. There are many dimensions to this fear, but one of them is especially direct, and starkly physical. The current concern with "safety in the streets" echoes a belief, as old as the Republic, that the city is dangerous, the breeding ground of vice and violence. Observers of varying sophistication have pointed out that dark streets hide dark deeds, and that the anonymity and freedom of urban society, its temptations and frenzied pace, all contribute to encourage criminal behavior. From this it is easy to conclude that with metropolitan growth and the multiplication of all these conditions, the rate of violent crime is inexorably multiplied also.

But constant repetition of a myth is no substitute for proof. Under some circumstances it does in fact seem clear that migration to the metropolis has been accompanied by disruption and violence. This does not mean that there is a necessary or inevitable connection between the growth of cities and the growth of crime. In fact the existing historical evidence suggest the very reverse, that over a long-term urbanization has had a settling, literally a civilizing, effect on the population involved.

The statistical evidence for such a long-term trend is necessarily fragmentary and local. But for this purpose local studies may well be more reliable than national. Figures for the United States as a whole, compiled by the Federal Bureau of Investigation, have been available only since 1930. Based on the records of police departments with widely varying standards of accuracy, these have provided a generation of criminologists with material for argument.[1] Analyses of crime rates in individual urban areas, on the other hand, are less complicated by discrepancies in definition and in police practice. While few of these reach back to any period before the FBI's Uniform Crime Reports, these few are significant. None points to any clear proportional increase in serious crime within particular cities. And the more recent suggest, on the contrary, a sometimes striking proportional decrease.[2]

Both the decrease and some of the explanation for it may be demonstrated since it is necessary to choose a single area to represent the whole—by an examination of 19th-century Massachusetts. A stable Eastern state, with one growing metropolis and a number of thriving smaller cities, this Commonwealth had a fairly typical experience with industrial urbanization. As a result of the legislature's enormous appetite for statistical information, its official records, including all those re-

From *The Journal of Social History*, Vol. II, No. 2 (December 1968), pp. 156-63. Reprinted by permission of the publisher.

lating to criminal behavior, are probably better than any kept elsewhere.[3] And while criminal statistics are notoriously difficult to deal with, and by themselves offer no firm conclusions, the history of the Commonwealth has been abundantly studied, and may be used to help interpret the raw numerical data. Together, the statistics and the social record can illuminate several aspects of the history of criminal violence in America. These include: the changing incidence of disorder itself, the relation of this change to urban growth, the special conditions which may upset this relation, and lastly the problem of public attitudes or concern.

While all criminal statistics are subject to some doubt, the central conclusion about the figures from Massachusetts may be stated with confidence: serious crime in metropolitan Boston has declined sharply between the middle of the 19th century and the middle of the 20th. This often ragged downward trend does not, of course, apply equally to all offenses, but it does to most of the more serious common-law crimes. Three independent studies, by a lawyer, a historian, and a sociologist, confirm this basic direction.[4] While the three cover different periods, and employ somewhat different methods, they do fit together, and all are based essentially on police arrest statistics, the index most widely used by contemporary criminologists.[5] The most comprehensive, covering the years from 1849 to 1951, shows a drop of nearly two-thirds in those crimes which the FBI classifies as "major."[6]

But only half the story, at best, can be told through the figures from the metropolis alone. Our concern is with the whole society. And it has been argued that the difference in crime rates between urban and nonurban areas may be great enough so that a drop in the incidence of criminality in the cities is more than offset by the fact that a continually greater percentage of the population is living in them.[7] It is necessary, to meet this problem, to look at the statistics for Massachusetts as a whole.

For most of the 19th century, the use of police records is neither possible nor desirable on a statewide basis.[8] But other indices of real criminal activity are available. And four of them may be used to establish the changing incidence of "serious" crime, defined as that which involves real injury to persons or loss of property.[9] These four are lower court cases, jail commitments, grand jury cases, and state prison commitments, all involving the major common-law offenses against persons or property. The first date for which two of these indices were published in trustworthy form is 1834; the first year for which all four were compiled is 1860. The figures for these periods, expressed in 3-year averages, may be compared with those for the end of the century in table 1.[10]

The decline in the officially recorded crime rate is unmistakable here. And it is strongly probable that the real decline is greater than the statistics indicate. The key problem in the interpretation of criminal statistics is posed by "the dark figure," representing those illegal activities or incidents which never come to the light of official attention. But since in later years, as will be discussed below, there was both an increasing intolerance of criminal activity and a great growth in the numbers of police and investigative agents, all evidence suggests that this "dark figure" was growing propor-

Table 1
Average yearly incidence of cases per 100,000 population

	1834-36	1860-62	1899-1901
Lower Court Cases		777	707
Jail commitments		333	163
Grand jury cases	89	117	63
Imprisonments	16.8	11.9	5.9

tionately smaller as the century progressed. Thus table 1 considerably understates the real decline.

For purposes of explanation, it is almost equally important to note the pattern of this decline. The table lists offenses in the order of their severity: lower court cases generally involve the least important crimes, jailings the next, indictments next, and imprisonments the most. And with one exception—the relative rise in indictments between the 1830's and the 1860's, which will be considered later—it is especially notable that the recorded drop in the crime rate is directly pro-

tion—not only a fall over time but a fall most marked in the most serious categories.

Meanwhile, however, while the serious crime rate was falling, the total crime rate—or the officially recorded total—was actually rising. This apparent paradox results from the fact that the downward curve described above may be wholly reversed simply by adding a third official category, "Crimes Against Public Order," to the two above. When these offenses are added in—drunkenness is by far the largest of them—the results for the lower courts may be indicated as follows:[12]

Table 2
Yearly incidence of cases per 100,000 population

	1840	1860	1900
Total lower court cases	595	1,869	3,317

portional to the seriousness of the offense. This is generally true also when the four indices used are examined further and broken into subcategories. Thus for example the combined rate of commitments for homicide, rape, armed robbery, and arson in 1860-62 was 6.8 per 100,000; by 1900 it has dropped to 2.9 per 100,000.[11] Most of the other data point in the same direc-

The pattern for these minor crimes is the obverse of that for serious offenses, in that the more trivial the degree of the offense the larger its proportional increase over time. While virtually no indictments or imprisonments resulted from third-class offenses, their addition makes less difference in the case of jailings than of lower court cases:[13]

Table 3
Yearly incidence of cases per 100,000 population

	1841	1860	1900
Total jail commitments	419	548	969

This upward curve in total offenses does not have the same importance as the other, downward curve in the incidence of serious crime. The latter represents the basic statistical conclusion, in that it reflects a real situation, a real decline in the rate of criminal activity. But the former, while it is merely statistical, is nonetheless important. There is a complementary relationship between the two trends, and the nature of this relationship helps account for much that underlies the numbers.

The entire increase in the criminal statistics of Massachusetts, during the period covered, may in fact be attributed wholly to the rise in cases of drunkenness. Indeed this one offense, together with simple assault, its constant companion, may serve as a focus for much more. To understand the reasons for the rise in drunk arrests is to understand much about the social changes occurring in the 19th century, changes which affected all of its criminal patterns.

It is clear, first, that the mounting total of cases fed into the official machinery of justice does not reflect a real increase in the consumption of alcohol. The misuse of drink was throughout the 19th century a problem of enormous dimensions. The continuing debate about the nature of drunkenness, although some of it anticipated the best of current thinking, was on the whole punitive, and tended to blame the use of alcohol for virtually every individual and most social evils.[14] But even the most ardent spirits in the temperance movement did not usually suggest that there was any long-term rise in drunken behavior. They and their opponents generally united in agreeing

that the situation, in ragged fashion, was improving with time.[15] Because much of the alcohol was made and sold illegally, especially in the countryside, it is difficult to investigate this statistically. But certainly in the metropolis and probably elsewhere the evidence does suggest a decline. Early in the century even ministerial ordinations, to say nothing of less grave occasions, were frequently bibulous affairs.[16] By the 1830's a substantial portion of the middle class had renounced the use of hard liquor. The prohibition was extended later to all drinks, and its champions carried on a continuous political and educational campaign against it. In the 1830's, and again in the 1850's, law enforcement officers estimated that 1 in every 65 inhabitants of Boston—men, women, and children —were selling alcohol for a living, in the latter period in defiance of a state law which prohibited all private sales.[17] Certainly neither this proportion nor this widespread evasion of the law was matched later in the century; by about 1880 the ratio was down to 1 seller in 150 and rising fast.[18]

On one level, the rising statistics of drunk arrests simply reflect an increase in the numbers of professional police and in the penal apparatus. It was not until 1837 that Boston organized a squad of full-time professionals, and for many years these were the only ones in the Commonwealth. But by 1860 all of the larger cities had organized forces of varying sizes, and these had grown and spread to the smaller towns well before 1900.[19] The effect of this, and of a proportionate increase in the rest of the agents of justice, is easily demonstrated. In the absence of police, ordinary citizens were expected to make complaints on their own, and to call on constables only to execute warrants already sworn. But while private individuals may make the effort to initiate the processes of justice when directly injured, professionals are required to deal, in number, with those whose merely immoral or distasteful behavior hurts no one in particular. It takes real cops, in short, to make drunk arrests.

Again on this level, the relative shortage of official agents of law enforcement accounts for one of the most striking characteristics of table 12-1 above. The farther back the figures go, as noted, the higher is the relative proportion of serious crimes. The authorities, with limited resources, obviously had to deal with felony first, indictable crime next, and misdemeanor only when resources permitted.

Conversely it is notable that as time advanced and it became easier for injured citizens to complain to a policeman, the tables indicate that proportionately fewer such complaints were being made. In the city of Boston, at least, the result was a progressive decrease in the number of annual arrests made by each patrolman: in 1855, the average was 71 per man, while by 1885 this had dropped to 37.[20]

Drawn as a model, this development may explain the only apparent anomaly in table 1, already referred to. This is the fact that between the 1830's and the 1860's the figures show both a fall in prison commitments and a rise in grand jury indictments. Perhaps—the subject will be investigated further—there is no great paradox at all. District attorneys in the 1830's, faced with a high incidence of truly violent criminal behavior, may have had to concentrate on the more important prisonable offenses, to the neglect of others, even indictable ones. As their resources were increased, and as the real crime rate fell, they would be able by the 1860's to catch up on lesser indictments.

But there remains a more fundamental level of explanation. To account for the rise in lesser offenses or the drop in more serious crimes simply in terms of the expansion of police, courts, and prosecutors is to misplace the emphasis. The expansion is not cause but symptom. The machinery of justice was increased because of a felt need, a growing intolerance of behavior which had earlier been tolerated, coupled with a belief that the state and not the individual citizen was required to do the necessary job.

This process is most evident in Boston itself. Leading citizens and governmental officials were always proud of their reputation for maintaining a tidy and well-governed "order" in the city. But the definition of what constituted "order" changed considerably with time.

Josiah Quincy, one of Boston's first mayors, was also the first to boast that in no other city "of equal population, are there fewer instances of those crimes, to which all populous places are subject."[21] He had in fact assumed charge, in 1823, of a newly incorporated city of about 45,000 inhabitants, which officially issued some 697 liquor licenses and ignored the existence of a large number of illegal sellers. Relatively little attention was paid to such common offenses as simple drunkenness and assault. The night watch, largely concerned with the danger of fire or arson, was afraid to enter some of the more notorious neighborhoods.

No one patrolled anywhere in the daytime. Quincy's several terms of office were marked by frequent battles between rival gangs of firemen, whose hunger for looting threatened the whole institution of fire insurance. When, after one of the city's numerous "riots, routs, and tumultuous assemblies" had spluttered on for a full week during the long hot summer of 1825, Quincy was forced to take personal charge of a posse of citizens to put it down. This was clearly an unusual action, and the mayor refused later opportunities to risk his limbs and authority in physical combat, preferring to let mob violence burn out by itself. Nevertheless, neither he nor the voters were unduly alarmed by the prevailing level of disorder. Citizens were traditionally supposed to take care of themselves, with the help of family, friends, or servants when available. An organized professional police would certainly be expensive and might be a threat to valued freedoms. And Quincy was proud to point out, at the end of his official career, that he had not added a single constable or watchman to Boston's part-time corps of peace officers.

By the 1880's, when an aldermanic committee echoed Mayor Quincy's earlier claim that Boston was the most orderly of America's larger cities, the situation had changed considerably.[22] In 1837, after three major riots in 4 years, the city had acquired a police force.[23] Since then it had been growing steadily, at a rate faster than the population. By the Civil War, the citizens had abandoned their objection to uniforms, with their paramilitary connotations, and the patrolmen had begun to carry guns.[24] By the 1880's the force had acquired most of its familiar modern characteristics and functions.[25]

And the demand for more men continued—despite the fact that the crime rate had been dropping for some time, and with it the workload for each man on the force.

The demand for more men, then, reflected not a worsening situation but higher standards, a change in attitude. Really violent crime brought more severe retribution than formerly; the same offenses which had earned 2-year sentences in the 1830's were now punished by 3 to 4 years or more in the state penitentiary, and the average was still going up.[26] While the police stations were still being built for "defensibility," there had been—and would be —no large-scale riot for years.[27] It is impossible to imagine a late-century mayor wrestling with mobs as did Quincy in the twenties and Theodore Lyman in the thirties. All of the city had been brought under more or less effective patrol, and the voters were demanding that the streets be cleared not only of arsonists but of drunks, peddlers, and truants. Traffic problems were settled not by teamsters with their fists but by officers with whistles. The responsibility for individual safety had been decisively shifted to these agents of the law; uniformed men with revolvers were stationed not only in potentially dangerous areas but in the quiet confines of the public library.[28] And the end result, reflected in many arrests for minor breaches of conduct, was a degree of "order" which would have astonished and perhaps dismayed an earlier and rougher generation.

The progressive heightening of standards of propriety, and with it the increasing reliance on official law enforcement, were processes which, while most sharply visible in Boston, were common to the whole society. Traditionally, criminologists have interpreted the zigs and zags of recorded criminal statistics in terms of individual events or situations—war, for example, or depression. But the change in social behavior reflected in the two dominant curves of criminality in Massachusetts is so long term and so widespread as to suggest a connection with the most fundamental of contemporary social processes, that of industrial urbanization itself. The nature of that connection has never been studied in detail, but it may at least be outlined.

Massachusetts in 1835 had a population of some 660,940, 81 percent rural, overwhelmingly preindustrial and native born.[29] Its citizens were used to considerable personal freedom. Whether teamsters, farmers, or artisans, they were all accustomed to setting their own schedules, and the nature of their work made them physically independent of each other. None of the more common occupations provided any built-in checks against various kinds of personal excess. Neither fits of violence nor bouts of drunkenness disrupted any vital patterns. Individual problems, sins or even crimes, were not generally cause for wider social concern.

Under these circumstances, while scarcely a frontier, the Commonwealth could afford a fairly high degree of lawlessness. No city in the state boasted a professional police, and the machinery of justice was not equipped to handle many cases. Many of the more common forms of violence or crime were simply not reported to the agents of law, as those affected either shrugged off their injuries or struck back directly.

But the impact of the twin movements to the city and to the factory, both just gathering force in 1835, had a progressive effect on personal behavior throughout the 19th century and into the 20th. The factory demanded regularity of behavior, a life governed by obedience to the rhythms of clock and calendar, the demands of foreman and supervisor. In the city or town, the needs of living in closely packed neighborhoods inhibited many actions previously unobjectionable. Both blue- and white-collar employees in larger establishments were mutually dependent on their fellows; as one man's work fit into another's, so one man's business was no longer his own.

The results of the new organization of life and work were apparent by 1900, when some 76 percent of the 2,805,346 inhabitants of Massachusetts were classified as urbanites.[30] Much violent or irregular behavior which had been tolerable in a casual, independent society was no longer acceptable in the more formalized, cooperative atmosphere of the later period. The private, direct response to criminal injury was no longer necessary or approved. All cities and most towns had acquired police forces, constantly expanding to meet greater expectations. Throughout the state, the victims of violence and theft were conditioned to seek official help. The move to the cities had, in short, produced a more tractable, more socialized, more "civilized" generation than its predecessors.[31]

The trend in the direction of higher standards and a lower level of violence may be measured from the early 19th century through much of the 20th. But what is true in the long run is not necessarily evident in the short. While the process or urbanization has helped to raise standards of personal behavior, it may not do so by itself. And there is some indication in the history of 19th-century Massachusetts that under unfavorable conditions migration to the cities may at some times have increased the incidence of violently unsocial behavior. This may well be true, at least, of the long generation between 1835 and 1860.

The existing statistics, alone, are no sure guide to what was actually happening during these crucial early decades. The Boston arrest figures were not kept until 1849. For the state as a whole, much of the remaining evidence remains ambiguous. As explained above, the two main indices, the rate of grand jury indictments and of imprisonments for felony, point stubbornly in opposite directions. But there is good reason to suspect that the period from the mid-1830's to the Civil War illustrates at least a partial, and important, exception to the general developments previously sketched.

From the war on to the end of the century and beyond, the industrial development of Massachusetts, however painful for those involved, was at least proceeding at a pace and along lines already laid out. The era just before was the one which witnessed the turbulence of transition. No similar timespan in fact encompassed a more rapid increase in the urban population. Between 1835 and 1860, while the total population was growing from 660,940 to 1,231,066, the proportion of city dwellers leaped from 19 to 44 percent of the total.[32] At the same time, too, the major railroad lines were laid in patterns still existing. As steam began to replace waterpower as the major source of industrial energy, the factories, earlier confined to rural sites

near waterfalls, began to move into the cities.

Social dislocation, meanwhile, accompanied economic. All through the period, and especially during and after the "hungry forties," heavy Irish immigration exacerbated all of the problems of city living. By 1855, some 68,100 of the 168,031 residents of Boston were natives of Ireland.[33] Uprooted from a rural setting, wholly without skills, the newcomers experienced the kind of culture shock, prejudice, and alienation which would plague other waves of migrants later. Crowded into stinking hovels, some of them underground, their miserable conditions of living strained all of the city's institutions of charity and police. Smallpox, once virtually eliminated, became again a problem, cholera struck hard, and the death rate about the middle of the century climbed to the highest point in the city's recorded history.[34]

In terms of its effect on behavior, all of these rapid and wrenching changes promoted the worst aspects of living in the city without benefit of its compensations. It must be stressed that economic developments were not fully able to keep pace with migration. Between 1837 and 1845, it has been estimated, the amount of large-scale or factory employment did not increase at all.[35] And in the 15 years following, while the total of factory employees grew to something like 25,000 or 30,000, the number of outright paupers in the metropolitan area was increasing at an even faster rate, to reach a peak of nearly 13,000 in 1860.[36] Without the discipline imposed by regular employment, this first large-scale flow of migrants into the city was a kind of mutual disaster. The raw arrivals from the countryside, Yankees as well as Irish, had not yet learned to weave warily through crowds, with their arms held in close. Often radically insecure, in neighborhoods still unstable, they sought release in drink. But to drink with strangers requires different rules, and more restraints, than drinking in more familiar situations. In this era of swinging elbows, bewilderment, and desperate unemployment, it is hard to find evidence that the level of violence was declining.

Indeed it is easy to find the opposite. During this whole period Massachusetts was wracked by political instability, aggravated by one unpopular war and the overhanging threat of another one.[37] The 1850's, in particular, witnessed a resurgence of mob violence as Know-Nothings and Irishmen, opponents and defenders of slavery, all found occasions to take to the streets.[38] These clashes, superimposed on and partly resulting from the already unhealthy social condition of Boston, were deeply disturbing to the inhabitants. If the real incidence of criminal behavior was not actually rising at this time, then surely it was not falling at the rate apparent in the generations following the Civil War.

All evidence points to the long-term drop in criminal activity as normative, and associated with urbanization. But the process was not complete without the accompaniment of rapid industrial development also. It was this which provided the means of absorbing raw migrants, of fitting them into a "system" which socialized and accommodated them into more cooperative habits of life. Without this other process, migration to the city alone, simply by

multiplying human contacts, may very well multiply the incidence of criminally violent interaction among inhabitants unsuited to its demands.

Because of its clear connection with ethnic prejudice, and its dangerous political and social implications, the violent state of Boston during the 1850's was the source of considerable public concern. But the relation between concern about violence and violence itself is not always so uncomplicated. Both in the 19th and the 20th centuries, the attitudes of newspapers, scholars, and the public generally have been various and volatile, the product often of special interests or misinformation. This makes such attitudes difficult to measure. But they are nevertheless crucially important to the study of criminal disorder.

In the long run and in the short, popular concern has a direct effect on the shape of criminal statistics. As it was changing public standards which accounted for the rising total of arrests during the 19th century, so police departments still concentrate on those offenses of greatest current interest. Moreover, it is not simply the actual level of criminal activity, but the balance between this and social attitudes, which determines how much violence is a "problem" at any given time.

While public "attitudes" are slippery concepts to compare, it does seem that in the sense above the state of Massachusetts, and the United States in general, had a criminal problem less worrisome in the 19th century than in the 1960's. The citizens of the Commonwealth, still close to their rural antecedents, were indeed afraid of cities, which one legislative committee called "the common sewers of the state."[39] And one major source of this fear was the "poverty, vice, and crime" commonly associated with Boston, in particular.[40] But hostile critics were more interested in the first two than in the last, and reformers endlessly debated the causal relation between them. The charge that the city had lost control of its "dangerous classes" was used in several attempts to limit self-government in Boston, but mob action was the only form of violence which generally figured in these complaints, and "crime" was used typically as a synonym for "vice."[41] It is significant that the laws concerning drink, especially, were subject to constant revision, but except for a reduction in the number of cases involving the death penalty, the general criminal code was not.[42] Legislative action or inaction mirrored public concern in this case. As the sons and daughters of Massachusetts migrated to the metropolis, the image conjured by the fearful was the rake or tempter, not the robber or rapist.

Nevertheless, however overshadowed by other issues, there were periodic outbursts of concern about violence or other crime. Often these occurred in response to some new development, or threat, for which the public or authorities were unprepared. In fact, the history of these threats, and the responses to them, comprises much of the history of criminal law enforcement.[43]

Thus the multiplication of banks and bank notes, through the 1820's, provided golden opportunities for counterfeiters. The nature of the problem, in this case, required a network of private banker's agents to cooperate, across state and even national boundaries, with the appropriate public authorities. Anti-Catholic rioting, in the 1830's, was a principal spur to the development of professional police. During the 1870's, the growing sophistication of professional criminals, dramatized by a spectacular series of bank robberies, led to an overhaul of existing detective methods in many American cities. During the same period, bands of healthy native vagrants, fugitives from the new industrial age, were a subject of great concern to the readers of sensational newspapers, who feared the violent potential in these "wild-eyed" strangers. The response in this case was harsher police action, and a tightening of the rules governing charity and soup kitchens.

These concerns were at any rate real, and had often lasting effects, although they had little to do with the overall crime rate. Another and more frequent kind of scare resulted not from some genuinely new problem but from sudden attention focused on an old one. Lincoln Steffens, as a cub reporter in New York, learned how easy it was to manufacture a "crime wave," with techniques still familiar.[44] Thus a particularly brutal murder or a series of muggings could touch off a wave of arrests "on suspicion."[45] Often it was simply an investigation or expose of some endemic form of crime which generated a sudden excitement, during which the public was assured that Boston was facing a threat of unprecedented proportions.

But it is impossible, from these brief scares, to get any clear sense of direction. While the definition of the tolerable was altering with time, it was altering slowly and imperceptibly. And there is no evidence that, as the century progressed, the gap between the level of order expected and the level actually obtained was changing in any constant direction. It is true that the police often felt that they were faced with problems of unprecedented magnitude, and chiefs decades apart warned that the level of juvenile delinquency, and the general breakdown of authority, threatened the very basis of society.[46] Other observers too, perhaps beguiled by the image of a more peaceful golden age in the past, sometimes asserted that crime was growing faster than the population. But this tendency to fear was balanced throughout the century by pride in growth and progress. And the many apocalyptic statements may be countered with an equal number of others, more optimistic. Thus even in the troubled year of 1859, the State's attorney general could declare that "at no time in the history of Massachusetts have life, liberty, and property been more secure than at present."[47]

In short, while it is possible now to discover a long-term drop in the level of violence, contemporaries were simply not aware of this. The degree of public concern has never been, nor is it now, an accurate index of the degree of criminal activity. Indeed the reverse is often true. And it is doubly ironic that a drop in the actual incidence of disorder has been accompanied by—and contributed to—a heightened sensitivity to disorder. Such sensitivity, by leading to a more demanding standard of conduct, has been essential to the functioning of an interdependent urban society. But unless the process is recognized and understood, it may have unsettling effects. There are times when for various rea-

sons the level of violence overbalances current expectations. In such situations the social pressure to maintain and extend high standards, and to enforce them universally, may result in frustration. The frustration may translate into fear. And this fear, in turn, may focus on the very urban process which helped to create those standards, on the growth of cities itself.

NOTES

1. See *The Challenge of Crime in a Free Society: A Report by The President's Commission on Law Enforcement and The Administration of Justice* (Washington, 1967), p. 29.
2. Four studies are especially germane: Harold A. Phelps, "Frequency of Crime and Punishment," *Journal of the American Institute of Criminal Law and Criminology*, vol. XIX, No. 2 (Aug. 1926), p. 165-180, which covers Rhode Island between 1897 and 1927; Sam Bass Warner, *Crime and Criminal Statistics in Boston* (Boston, 1934), "Crime as a Function of Anomie," *Journal of Criminal Law, Criminology, and Police Science* (June 1966), covering Buffalo from 1854 to 1956; and Theodore Ferdinand, "The Criminal Patterns of Boston Since 1849," *The American Journal of Sociology* (July 1967), pp. 84-99, which runs to 1951. These all differ in purpose and sophistication, and none is directly concerned with the long-term decline, which helps to make their results the more striking
3. A survey of many of the official and criminal records of Boston and Massachusetts is contained in Roger Lane, *Policing the City: Boston, 1822-1885* (Cambridge, Mass.: Harvard University Press, 1967), pp. 225-229 and 239-241.
4. See the works by Ferdinand, Warner, and Lane, in footnotes 2 and 3, above. There is no attempt, in these or in this paper, to measure the extent of statutory or white-collar crime.
5. Thorsten Sellin and Marvin E. Wolfgang, *The Measurement of Delinquency* (New York, 1964), p. 31.
6. Ferdinand, "Criminal Patterns of Boston," p. 87. Together with roughly similar results in Powell's study of Buffalo, these figures suggest that the main conclusions of the present paper, which is largely confined to the 19th century, may be projected up to the founding of the Uniform Crime Reports and beyond.

7. Ferdinand, "Criminal Patterns of Boston," p. 99.

8. Statewide arrest figures were not compiled until very late in the 19th century, and comparing those for different cities involves many of the same problems as plague students of the Uniform Crime Reports.

9. In this paper except where specifically noted, no distinction is made between violent crimes—against the person—and other serious offenses. Such terms as "crime" or "disorder" are used to cover both.

10. For references in this table, see Roger Lane "Crime and Criminal Statistics in Nineteenth Century Massachusetts," *Journal of Social History* (December 1968), footnote 8.

11. For references, see *ibid.*, footnote 8.

12. For references, see *ibid.*, footnote 10. 1840 is the first year for which these figures are available.

13. For references, see *ibid.*, footnote 11. The year 1841 is the first for which these figures are available.

14. Compare *The Challenge of Crime*, p. 235, and Lane, *Policing the City, passim*, especially pp. 112-113.

15. For testimony of both reformers and conservatives, see especially Massachusetts House Document No. 415, *Reports on the Subject of a License Law . . . Together With a Stenographic Report of the Testimony* (Boston, 1867), *passim*.

16. Alice Felt Tyler, *Freedom's Ferment: Phases of American Social History to 1860* (Minneapolis, 1944), ch. 13, especially p. 311.

17. Lane, *Policing the City*, pp. 41 and 71.

18. *Ibid.*, p. 211.

19. Unfortunately, neither the federal nor the state census permits an accurate statewide count of policemen during the 19th century.

20. Lane, *Policing the City*, pp. 230-232. The trend has continued. Modern police, despite the introduction of patrol cars and call wagons, make fewer arrests, in general, than did their predecessors, especially when the whole class of minor auto violations is eliminated.

21. Quoted in *ibid.*, p. 25. For the other information in this paragraph see ch. 2 *passim*.

22. *Ibid.*, p. 204.

23. *Ibid.*, pp. 29-35.

24. *Ibid.*, pp. 104-105.

25. *Ibid.*, p. 224.

26. These are figures for the average sentences to the state penitentiary. The range of offenses listed remained about the same through the century. For references, see Lane, "Crime and Criminal Statistics," footnote 14.

27. *Annual Report of the Commissioners of Police of the City of Boston for . . . 1885* (Boston, 1885), pp. 28-30.

28. Lane, *Policing the City*, p. 173.

29. Population figures are from *The Census of Massachusetts . . . 1905* (Boston, 1909), vol. 1, p. xxxi. The urban definition is based on a population of 8,000.

30. *Ibid.*

31. It should be noted that after the 1880's, when Boston already had nearly 2 policemen per 1,000 inhabitants, which is close to the present nationwide average for major cities, it was the smaller places only where the arrest rate continued to climb dramatically. Boston, because of its very small geographical area, was ahead of most American cities in this respect. It was still possible in other places to raise the arrest figures by extending patrol and demanding higher standards in previously neglected areas, such as outlying slums. This process, and the reduction of the "dark figure" which results from better policing in general, may account for many apparent "rises" in crime rates which occur right up to the present.

32. See footnote 29.

33. Oscar Handlin, *Boston's Immigrants: A Study in Acculturation* (rev. ed., Cambridge, 1959), p. 244.

34. *Ibid.*, pp. 114-116.

35. *Ibid.*, p. 74.

36. *Ibid.*, pp. 74 and 256.

37. For political conditions in Massachusetts, see William Gleason Bean, "Party Transformation in Massachusetts, 1848-1860, with Special Reference to the Antecedents of Republicanism" (unpublished Ph.D. dissertation, Harvard University archives, 1922), *passim*.

38. Lane, *Policing the City*, pp. 72-74, 90-91, and 94-95.

39. *Ibid.*, p. 132.

40. First used by Josiah Quincy in his "remarks on some of the Provisions of the Massachusetts Affecting Poverty, Vice, and Crime" (Cambridge, 1822), these last four words became a stock phrase among the Commonwealth's reformers.

41. Lane, *Policing the City*, especially pp. 122-125, 128-134, 142-156, and 213-219.

42. *Ibid.*, passim. For the criminal code, summed up in revisions compiled in 1835, 1859, 1881, and 1900, see p. 239.

43. For references in the following paragraph, see *ibid.*, pp. 55-56, 29-35, 142-156, 157-160, and 193-195.

44. Lincoln Steffens, *Autobiography* (New York, 1931), pp. 285-291.

45. In 1865, inspired by a fear of returning veterans much like that following World War II, the police made some 2,532 such arrests. See Lane, *Policing the City*, p. 149.

46. See, e.g., *ibid.*, pp. 68, 137, and 34.

47. *Ibid.*, p. 117.

Ball Park

GUNTHER BARTH

Old men, young men, and small boys, usually "confined in offices, shops, and factories," packed the Polo Grounds on May 30, 1888, for a baseball game between New York and Pittsburgh, "and saw the popular sport to their hearts' content." The early-comers had crowded the grandstands, forcing the latecomers onto the green field, where "they formed a horseshoe around the playing lines and took a sunbath." The spectators yelled, "jumped like colts, clapped their hands, threw their hats into the air, slapped their companions on the back, winked knowingly at each other, and . . . enjoyed themselves hugely." On that afternoon, according to the account of a New York *Times* reporter, 13,333 "anxious sightseers" experienced in the ball park the quintessence of urban leisure: watching others do things.[1]

The scene, barely a few years old, seemed timeless to the spectators. Engulfed by the surging city, an urban tide flooding the land with a sea of houses, the baseball field exposed within its boundaries the remnants of a ravaged countryside in the form of scarred ravines protected by their ugliness from building construction. Here, with weathered wooden grandstands and solid clapboard fences as dikes, a lake of grass contrasted with the surrounding shades of brown. Its green faded away around the bases, where the intense play had turned the grass to dirt, a baseball diamond without a diamond's glitter. Ob-

livious of this, however, thousands of spectators looked only for the sparkle of perfection in the play on the field. To them going to the ball park meant surrender to the spell of baseball and to the motions of the players—now frozen into a stance, now sprinting with a will, throwing, batting, catching, or chasing the ball—while enjoying the suspense of America's favorite game.[2]

In addition to the excitement, a visit to the ball park provided men with a new perspective on life in the modern city. Watching a professional baseball game, as well as knowing its ins and outs, turned them into true spectators who not only saw the events on the field but also could sense their significance for everyday life. The experience made crowds of people conscious that rules regulated the happenings of their world, too, and that beyond the fences of the ball park, restraints tempered the competition to get ahead in the world.

Thousands and thousands of men, frequently mystified by the operation of the economic sphere or the actions of their fellowmen in public office, saw in the ball park how rules affected one sector of modern city life, the athletic contest. In ways they could perceive, the spectacle demonstrated the regulation of one of their elementary drives —competition. When their knowledge of the rules of baseball put them in a position to detect how at times some players tried to win by getting away with infractions, city people came to an understanding of how regulations operated in the free-for-all of the modern world. A quick assessment of the swift action on the diamond revealed that restraints curbed the struggle for success, ordinarily pursued obtrusively by reckless men or obscured by the hustle of daily life. This insight reassured the spectators that elements of order permeated the turmoil of the modern city.

The freedom to share the intense competition and the slight leisure that the modern city granted most inhabitants distinguished some of the social functions of baseball and ball park in nineteenth-century America from the roles of games and arenas in earlier societies. From its beginning, the city had fostered spectator sports, but frequently depending on a ruler's will or a priest's ritual to grant throngs of people the leisure to enjoy them. Quite early, political ambitions and religious needs nourished a popular desire for more and better diversions that only professional athletes could satisfy. Although the large numbers of spectators already suggested in antiquity the commercial potential of games, it was only the individual freedom and the economic incentive provided by the modern city that turned sports into an industry.

The practice of conducting an entire game according to established rules signaled the arrival of spectator sports as big business in the nineteenth century. Apart from their basic function of distinguishing one sport from another, rules made a game a socially acceptable outlet for emotions. By regularizing procedures, they fostered interest, shaped the sport to the liking of spectators, and provided the framework for a sequence of related events leading to a championship. The use of rules set the big-city spectacle apart from impromptu play, which is attractive because it is freely improvised, utilizes make-believe instead of rules, and provides the pleasure of assuming roles.[3] Rules also heightened enormously the popularity of a contest because they facilitated betting on the results.

The impact of rules on the outcome of a game remained doubtful until promoters dependent on paying spectators and people eager to get their money's worth ensured impartial and constant enforcement. The modern sports entrepreneur pursued a course analogous to that of a Roman emperor who in principle was supposed to decide a duel between gladiators himself according to well-defined standards but who in practice may frequently have accepted the verdict of the crowd because he had allowed the entire circus to be staged in the first place to please them.[4] The promoter altered and shaped the rules of a game until the action suited the greatest number of people and then worked to give them the impression that all went according to the regulations.

Although the fans paid admission to sports spectacles and thus influenced their development, general social and cultural trends also affected the diversions of nineteenth-century urbanites. The disintegration of traditional society that accompanied the rise of the modern city undermined forms of popular recreation that were rooted in a predominantly agrarian social system. The newly emerging leisure culture was molded according to the requirements of capitalist society and industrial production. Unlike their ancestors in preindustrial societies, relieved from incessant labor by climatic vicissitudes and rewarded for prolonged toil by seasonal feast days, in general the residents of the modern city learned to be satisfied with brief but more frequent opportunities to enjoy themselves.[5]

This formula suited their working hours, which could stretch through day and night, with some workers idle while others toiled if factory shifts required several sets of men. In consequence, the sporting events which attracted the most attention came to be reduced in length. However, the number of contests and of competitors increased and provided a steady stream of excitement that fitted most people's schedules and directed the use of leisure time toward relaxation rather than rest. In this way the spectator sports, which rose as business enterprises with the modern city, conformed to the needs of its residents.[6]

Men anxious to be distracted from their arduous daily routines provided a natural market for the product of the new industry. As soon as they had learned to live for the moment that temporarily freed them from work, they felt the urge to extend the diversion provided by spectator sports into their working hours. Presumably they had always talked on the job about athletic feats they had witnessed, but now, if they missed an event, they began looking at the columns of the metropolitan press to keep up with their pastime. They also relied on special forms of communication to bring distant contests closer.

Founded in Baltimore in 1829, the *American Turf Register*, the first sports magazine in the United States, paved the way. The New York *Spirit of the Times*, initially devoted only to racing, started covering other sports in 1831. In 1853, the New York *Clipper*, which became the major American sporting journal in the second half of the nineteenth century, began sailing the journalistic seas loaded with news about sports and the theater, underlining the bond between varieties of diversions and spectacles. These journals and newspapers and magazines steadily increased the number of sports covered, as well as the size of their audiences.

This new focus of popular attention proved irresistible to journalists. "We would rather chronicle a great boat race . . . or a cricket match . . . than all the prize poems or the orations on Lafayette that are produced in half a century," *Harper's Weekly* reported in 1857.[7] Stories about walking and running races, boxing matches, sailing regattas, and baseball games not only circulated information about athletic accomplishments but also established national standards of excellence. Reports of records established one day and broken the next diffused a historical consciousness in the modern city, among a people without a common history. They steadily expanded the vocabulary of sports writers and stimulated patterns of speaking that made sports jargon part of everyday speech.

The apostles of play expressed their insights into sports practices with a new terminology that frequently originated in London journals. Some of these phrases became so genuinely American that their English origin faded away. "A Chinaman's chance" did not originate in the California of the 1850's, as one might have suspected, but rather in the London *Weekly Dispatch* of the 1820's, which called a light-hitting boxer a "china man" because he seemed as likely to break with rough handling as porcelain. Other British terms supplanted American ones. "Fan," short for "fancy," an English expression for a devotee of dog fights and boxing matches, replaced the American term "crank" for a sports enthusiast, although in the 1890's James Cardinal Gibbons of Baltimore still explained rather apologetically to an audience that he was not a "baseball crank."[8]

Spectators sports spread almost as quickly as the sports lingo. They thrived on a network of cities connected by railroad and telegraph. The emerging sports industry soon was distributing its products to a national market. Cities furnished facilities and human resources in the form of tracks and arenas, professional athletes, and paying spectators. They provided the settings for sports activities in which both individual sportsmen and teams flourished, creating the framework for staging the selection of national champions. Above all, the intensified urbanization of the nineteenth century led to the acceptance of games and races as urban extravaganzas, because the cities attracted people with leisure in search of entertainment and sheltered others seeking escape from the doldrums of daily toil.

Most conventions rooted in the morals of seventeenth-century puritanism and the vigor of eighteenth-century industrialism, which regarded popular recreation as frivolous and unproductive and blocked the growth of spectator sports, fell by the wayside in the modern city. In the middle of the nineteenth century, ministers and physicians spearheaded a campaign against excessive labor, extolling recreation and play as remedies for the seemingly overwhelming American urge to work. Later, leaders of the Social Gospel Movement promoted industrial man's right to his recreational leisure and helped remove repressive laws that interfered with an individual's use of his free time. Baseball itself, which as *the* American sport observed Sunday laws where they were enforced until 1933, became a primary force in lifting the restrictions on play. Finally, the modern city produced self-made men who set their own leisure hours, as well as laborers who benefited from flexible working hours. Both groups turned up in sufficient numbers at the racetrack and in the ball park on weekdays, if Sunday laws prohibited sports activity, to make spectator sports profitable enterprises for entrepreneurs.[9]

The news sports spectaculars also drew into their orbits the legions of spectators urban life seemed to produce quite naturally. The modern city's ever-changing sights, the intensity of activities, and the contrast of life-styles created by the unequal distribution of wealth turned many residents into observers. The splendor of the cityscape also bred *flâneurs*, who turned observation into an art and easily became habitués of grandstand boxes and ringside seats. The flux of the modern city daily created new forms of life that encouraged the heady defiance of convention. This heightened the attraction of outlawed boxing contests and, for that matter, of all spectator sports. These novelties commanded so much attention and so disrupted what was left of the established order of things that one of the arbiters of the age disdained them as "a public nuisance."[10]

Alarmed by the impact of the crowds that spectator sports attracted, another self-appointed judge of his generation reached a similar verdict. In 1842, after a visit to a racetrack, Philip Hone felt that the "crowd and the dust and the danger and the difficulty of getting on and off the course with a carriage are scarcely compensated by any pleasure to be derived from the amusement." An accident reinforced his idea that the masses were no proper spectators. "The tens of thousands of the sovereign people who wished to see this race" had planned to take a commuter train, he related, "but the numbers were so great" that the locomotive stalled. "The mob who had provided themselves with tickets . . . became riotous, upset the cars, placed obstructions on the rails, and indulged in all sort of violence."[11]

Horse racing was the most popular spectator sport in the United States until the rise of professional baseball. Boxing was a close second. The traditional, age-old appeal of the two exerted a strong influence on the residents of the modern city. The racehorses and pugilists demonstrated feats of elementary strength, disciplined in man's favorite animal and unleashed in two fellowmen who seemed to revert, at least in the eyes of some commentators, to the level of animals. The speed of horses and the stamina of boxers increased people's fascination with sports; and exposure to track and ring prepared Americans for baseball as the great spectator sport in the closing decades of the nineteenth century.

The popular sports of mid-nineteenth-century America taught city people what to look for in a contest. In a manner of speaking, they prepared spectators for the task of watching a baseball game, expanding their horizons beyond the immediate concern with winners to discovering how victory was achieved. A swift horse sharpened their powers of observation, an agile boxer opened their eyes to finesse, and both demonstrated the efficacy of discipline and perfection, which loomed large in urban existence. The comments of sport journalists expanded these lessons, tempering impulsive enthusiasm with a shrewd reservation that grew out of knowing the ins and outs of a sport as well as the wheeling and dealing behind the scenes. The writers increased skepticism about as well as appreciation of any accomplishment and provided the rising generation of sports spectators with a frame of mind that allowed them to be both involved and detached, watching a spectacle and learning from what they saw.

Horse racing fascinated city people. They craved rural scenes, and the racetrack recaptured some of the gaiety and turmoil of a horse fair in the country. In addition the elegant side of these sights reinforced the reputation of racing as the Sport of Kings and the pastime of millionaires, and with these allusions the horse's special position in human society.

In myth, legend, and fable, the horse occupied a distinguished place because of its faithfulness and generosity, valor and speed. However, the fact that only the horse among the big domesticated animals had accompanied man into the modern city, pulling hacks, streetcars, or beer wagons and carrying policemen, may have meant more to the racetrack crowd than any memory of Pegasus speeded along by his wings or Achilles mourned by his chariot horses.

The racetrack also developed city people's fascination with swift motion and sudden action, which the ball park was to cultivate to the utmost. This growing preoccupation with speed pervaded many areas of life that were unrelated except by an infatuation with fast horses. It generated Leland Stanford's support of photographer Eadweard Muybridge's scientific study *The Horse in Motion,* published in 1878, and established the popularity of artist

Frederic Remington's horses in action. It also changed the character of horse races, revealing how people's notions of what was worth watching shaped the nature of emerging spectator sports.

After the Civil War, the standard four-mile race, which involved winning two out of three heats, disappeared, and even three-mile tests, once considered a concession to younger horses, fell by the wayside. Watching heats came to bore people chafing at the monotony of daily routines. The heats vanished entirely as a new trend developed favoring more contests per day, shorter races, and the use of younger horses. Increasingly dash racing fans became more deeply involved in the results of a race than in the event itself, because betting made the thoroughbreds a potential source of money for everyone.

Gambling on sports was widespread in the modern city just as gambling in one form or another had always permeated the life of the nation, from lotteries in England that financed the colony of the Virginia Company to lotteries during the American Revolution that provided funds to pay soldiers fighting for independence. Betting provided a way of responding to a world of change and chance. Poor men became rich overnight, and rich men poor; and between these extremes of good luck and bad lay a wide range of chances that cried out to be exploited by betting on a race or fight. Gambling appealed to some city people as a mark of gentility, or struck others as an exciting diversion from everyday problems. For some, it also affirmed a deep-seated suspicion about the inclination of heterogeneous people to transgress the morality of the lawmakers.

Betting deepened almost everyone's fascination with horse racing, beyond the rather small number of people concerned with improving the breed—one of the favorite justifications for staging races in the first place. The owners of horses had always considered wagering a part of the proceedings. Before the Civil War, auction pools in which the entries in a race were sold to the highest bidder gave spectators a chance to share what many considered the best part of racing. In the second half of the nineteenth century the spread of bookmakers further accommodated organized betting and tightened its grip on the sport. Good odds could make a betting coup more profitable than the modest purse given to the owner who had saddled a winner. Fans learned the track records and pedigrees of the horses, and this knowledge contributed to a state of mind which made them ready to question the results of any race.

The atmosphere of jockey clubs, stables, and paddocks provided grounds for speculations about imagined or real manipulations of horses by owners, grooms, and trainers to influence the outcome of races. Public indignation over actual frauds resulted in outlawing races in several states. If the desire for betting action in the poolrooms contributed to the new character of horse racing, as some people suspected, the changing atmosphere of the racetrack hardened the feeling that races were run more for betting and less for horsemanship and improving the breeds. Until the pari-mutuel system of betting, in which the winners share the total stakes less a percentage for the track management, gained acceptance in the first decade of the twentieth century, horse racing barely covered "its hideous reality" with "the mantle of social respectability" and remained under a cloud of suspicion.[12]

Boxing, the other popular spectator

sport, shared the charge tainting racing —that insiders fixed the outcomes of races in order to influence the betting on horses. It was held in special disrepute because prize fighting rarely seemed to control its brutality. In 1853, the editor of the New York *Times* found it inexplicable and humiliating that boxing bouts could take place at all, with "public sentiment opposed to animal brutality in any shape," but at the same time he made sure that his paper cashed in on the news value of the contests.[13] Although frequently outlawed, boxing held its own in the back rooms of waterfront dives and tenderloin saloons where men like "Chimmie Fadden," a hero of popular fiction at the turn of the century, took any well-to-do "student of human nature" to observe the proceedings of "de Rose Leaf Social Outin' and Life Savin' Club."[14]

Aversion to the repulsive features of prize fighting remained strong throughout the nineteenth century, but it diminished somewhat when a systematic refinement of boxing techniques led to new rules that did away with bare fists; wrestling and holding in chancery; and continuing each round until one boxer went down and the entire fight until one man, or his supporters, gave up. The 1880's, when John L. Sullivan methodically began using a right blow to his opponent's jaw to end a match quickly with a knockout, marked a new era. He demonstrated his innovation in four-round boxing exhibitions with gloves; however, in his last championship bout he still fought seventy-five rounds with bare knuckles under the old London Prize Ring rules. On that occasion, as on many others, the elementary test of strength, conducted in a narrow ring in plain view, fascinated spectators. It also commanded the attention of fans in distant cities, who crowded hotel lobbies, saloons, barbershops, and poolrooms waiting for messages from telegraph operators about the details of the endurance test.[15]

Although other spectator sports also entranced the residents of the modern city, they neither drew the number of people the racetrack attracted nor produced the excitement the boxing ring generated. With growing regularity, rowing and yachting matches followed one another year after year. Billiard exhibitions and walking races were popular attractions, while cricket and football occasionally drew large crowds. All these sports developed urban followings, but none was as distinctly urban or reflective of the lifestyle of the modern city as trotting races.

Big cities made fashionable the driving rigs used in trotting. People rode fewer and fewer horses for transportation or pleasure, but a businessman or lawyer might step from his home or office into a buggy and speed down the avenue and through the park for fresh air, exercise, and a friendly brush with other drivers. These outings regularly attracted onlookers fascinated by the speed and elegance a trotting horse could achieve if kept to the gait. However, the rapidly growing cities limited any direct role in the action to a wealthy few, so that when the straightaway turnpike receded into the country and deprived spectators of their share in the show, clubs began building tracks where they raced trotters regularly before appreciative crowds.

Trotting and other popular diversions in the second half of the nineteenth century foreshadowed the role of baseball as the big urban spectator sport. The display of the harnessed and efficient movement of a crack trotting horse or of the systematic, refined technique of a new-style boxing champion introduced into people's enjoyment of leisure an appreciation for standards of performance. The attempt to perfect these qualities in professional baseball players during a season evoked analogies to the industrial discipline of the work force in the modern city.

The fascination with controlled energy, symbolized by the central position of the Corliss steam engine in the major hall of the Philadelphia Exposition of 1876, at times reached extremes. It stimulated the enormous popularity of such seemingly inhuman endeavors as heel- and toe-walking races. The unnatural technique employed in this sport led some who tried it to conclude that they "were straining every nerve and muscle to get ahead, but had entered into an insane compact not to employ the natural and obvious means of doing so."[16]

Popular sports, connecting the urban population with a rising sports industry, shared a potential for educating as well as entertaining crowds of spectators. Among these spectacles, baseball occupied a special position as the most popular and most organized of all spectator sports in the last decades of the nineteenth century. It was the most convenient way for city people to enjoy themselves and also to demonstrate a commitment to standards of excellence in a leisure-time activity. Within a generation the game had made the transition from a pastime for gentlemen to a social institution illuminating the inner workings of new patterns of urban life.

Baseball conquered the United States in the decades between 1840 and 1870, which saw the standardization of the diamonds, the organization of teams, the refinement of rules, the establishment of game schedules, and the first grand tour by a professional baseball team. The game descended remotely from English ball games, one of them called baseball as early as 1700, and directly from the English game of rounders. In America it spread as a base-running game under various names, such as Town Ball, Round Ball, Goal Ball, or One o' Cat, according to the locality or the number of players, until the name "baseball" won out. Suffering from an attack of chauvinism at the opening of the twentieth century, baseball moguls decreed that the game had been invented by Abner Doubleday in Cooperstown, New York, in 1839, and, in their own words, "forever set at rest the question as to the Origin of Base Ball."[17] From that time on, baseball acquired an official beginning and a distinctly rural American origin, reinforced by the sandlot motif of its supposed centennial in 1939, which included a barn, house, church, and school as the appropriate background.[18]

Historical evidence links baseball, as we know it, with the modern city. In the early 1840's a group of New York gentlemen who on sunny days enjoyed playing ball games in a lot at the corner of Madison Avenue and Twenty-Seventh Street formed the first association and in 1845 adopted the first set of modern rules. These merchants, brokers, and physicians enjoyed dining and playing together. In 1846 their Knickerbocker Baseball Club played its first match against another team of gentlemen, the New York Nine, in a popular summer resort across the Hudson River. The New York *Clipper* considered that contest the beginning of baseball "as now played" in its preview of the Centennial Year season of 1876.[19] Social as well as athletic exclusiveness distinguished these early gatherings. More often than not, formal challenges initiated the contests and social events concluded them. Soon uniforms—white shirts, blue trousers, and straw hats in the case of the Knickerbockers—added another stylish note.[20]

Despite several efforts to create a uniform game, there were no generally accepted rules regulating strikes and balls until the Civil War. The time the play consumed was still of little consequence, and games often dragged on, endlessly it appeared, because the man at bat, the "striker," waited for the pitch that suited him or hoped to tire out the pitcher. Often, local circumstances dictated the number of players as well as the layout of the field, the distance between bases, the size of the diamond, and the position of the umpire.[21]

The aristocratic setting of the game vanished during the 1850's when new clubs sprang up in New York, Brooklyn, Philadelphia, Baltimore, and Boston. Fascinated with baseball, laborers, mechanics, and clerks put onto diamonds teams that rejected the assumption that the Knickerbockers arbitrated the game simply because they had organized it first. The Knickerbockers themselves never really took their obligation as arbiters seriously because they feared that an improved system of play would produce more clubs and undermine their dominant position. The competition demonstrated the mounting need for a useful structure for the sport. In 1857, many people may have agreed with the editor of the leading sports paper, the New York *Spirit of the Times,* who considered the successful organization of the German Turnverein Association and of other immigrant sports organizations a challenge to develop "some game peculiar to the citizens of the United States."[22]

The agitation for uniform baseball regulations led to the formation of scores of committees to draft guidelines and to ask the mayor of New York to allow baseball games in Central Park, a bastion of cricket. In 1858, the search for more order brought together delegates from twenty-two clubs who established the National Association of Base Ball Players. Although a far cry from a national unit, the Association placed all clubs on an equal basis by forming a rules committee, establishing procedures for new clubs to join the group, and regulating players, umpires, and scorers. Following the time-honored American practice demonstrated by churches, political parties, labor unions, and charity groups, it grew from the local level to a state, regional, and ultimately a national organization.[23]

The informality of play contributed to the rapid spread of baseball through the country before the Civil War because it allowed men to conduct the game in many ways, according to the number of available players or the condition of the field. In 1859, the game reached New Orleans, where seven teams played intraclub games abetted by strong support from the volunteer firemen. In the same year newspapers reported the operation of a baseball organization in St. Paul, which followed the lead of another Minnesota club founded two years earlier. The Eagles baseball club was organized in San Francisco in 1859.[24]

Contrary to these facts, the Civil War frequently has been credited with breaking down the geographic concentration of the game on the East Coast.[25] The military conflict, so the story goes, curtailed the games staged in the North, but players and spectators as Union soldiers or Confederate prisoners brought baseball into the South. There they knocked the ball around in bivouac during a campaign, behind the lines of siege, in a training camp, or in a stockade to relieve the monotony of the war.

Undoubtedly, the soldiers provided a captive audience, but one spectator figure from a baseball game during the Civil War borders on the incredible. On Christmas Day, 1862, a team representing a regiment of New York volunteers and a hand-picked nine from other regiments met at Hilton Head, South Carolina, before "about 40,000 soldiers."[26] That could be considered an attendance record for a sports event in nineteenth-century America; however, the report seems to have come from a player, Abraham G. Mills, who in 1907 as president of the National League also chaired the committee that created the Abner Doubleday myth.

In reality the Civil War did hasten the emergence of baseball as a game that was played everywhere in the same way. The young men liked to throw, hit, and catch, and when they met on a field as strangers they needed a standard game so that they could enjoy a contest without prolonged arguments. Whether bored by army life, ordered by officers to attend games, or fascinated by baseball, soldier spectators contributed to the emergence of a standard game because they needed to know not only what went on but also what to anticipate in order to enjoy themselves. Far from home, they watched strangers, and their interest centered more on the play as a whole than on an individual player in the field. When these captive audiences vanished with the end of the war, the systematic baseball reports in the sports press and the metropolitan newspapers sealed the uniform character of the game and contributed to the emergence of profes-

sional baseball as the great urban spectator sport.

The reports, tables, and statistics that the leading American sports journalists compiled in the 1860's and 1870's enabled thousands of spectators who flocked into the ball parks of the big cities after the Civil War to follow both teams and games methodically. An English immigrant, Henry Chadwick, saw himself in his old age as the "head gardener" who had raised the "now giant oak of the American game of baseball."[27] His didactic discourses in the New York *Clipper* expressed the fundamental rationality of the age, so often obscured by sentimentality. He considered it "important and necessary" to give "the full record of each season," and his readers' responses reinforced his view.[28] The accuracy of his scientifically oriented approach underpinned the emotional support given the game during the 1850's by William Trotter Porter in the New York *Spirit of the Times*. This editor, also credited with publishing the first box scores, had put emphasis on "inside" human interest stories and called baseball "our National Game."[29]

Chadwick's statistics became an integral part of baseball reporting, occasionally enlivened by the journalists of the metropolitan press with human interest features. In the 1870's, game statistics and baseball gossip were the mainstay of the Philadelphia *Sporting Life* and of the St. Louis *Sporting News*. However, from 1877 on, the proverbial man on the street received much of his information about the game from the New York *National Police Gazette*. This periodical, with its sweeping coverage of sensations of many varieties, reached masses of readers on a national scale. It enhanced its circulation enormously by offering reduced subscription rates to hotels, barber-shops, and saloons.[30]

The writings of Henry Chadwick and his colleagues gave baseball an identity and helped popularize game and players. They upheld faith in baseball as a noble and clean game when the fans' enthusiasm lagged in the face of reports about fixed games, gambling scandals, warring leagues, and protracted infighting between owners and players for shares in the new sports bonanza.[31] The sports writers' work also helped sell the idea of a sports page to the editors of the metropolitan press. "Regardless of what the present generation of baseball reporters is doing to promote the welfare or add to the box office receipts of the club owners," a well-known baseball writer argued in the 1920's, "the sport owes its popularity and probably its continued existence to earlier generations of scribes."[32] Their stories prepared the ground for the flowering of baseball journalism in Chicago in the 1880's which produced a new style of sports reporting by weaving wit and satire into the stories.

Before the emergence of the Chicago style of baseball reporting, accounts of games frequently read like market reports, with little of the game's excitement emerging from the sober lines. Much of the success of the first baseball writers rested on the novelty of the ball park experience, still fresh in the spectators' minds when they saw the box scores. However, after this appeal wore off, only true fans found that journalistic fare palatable. Ordinary newspaper readers not especially interested in the game initially looked for something more readable and entertaining. This apathy vanished when the language of the popular Chicago papers, unconventional and vibrant, appeared in inspired baseball stories that intrigued and informed.

In the 1880's, Chicago reporters expressing the raw energies of the wildly growing city added slang and frivolity, metaphor and simile to baseball reports and turned them into news that at times qualified as lead stories. In 1913, the Charleston *News and Courier* called the resulting style "a distinctive and peculiar tongue, . . . not English, . . . not precisely slang, . . . full of idiomatic eccentricities, rich in catch-phrases and technical terms, wonderfully expressive and in the highest degree flexible."[33] This novel approach gave such a remarkable importance to baseball that in the same year the *Nation* slyly wondered why the baseball language "should so far outdo the feats of the players whom it glorifies."[34] It also affected general reporting.

In 1896 a Chicago newspaper editor sent one of his baseball reporters to help cover the Democratic National Convention and to write a follow-up on the reception of William Jennings Bryan's "Cross of Gold" speech. The language of the sportswriter's story on the front page of the Chicago *Daily News* on July 9, 1896, documents one aspect of the impact of baseball on modern city culture. It enlivened what had been the rather staid and dull form of political reporting in an attempt to describe the "almost indescribable":

HOW BRYAN SWAYED
THE CROWD.

SCENE AFTER HIS
REMARKABLE ORATION WAS
ALMOST INDESCRIBABLE.

When Bryan's words: "You shall not crucify mankind upon the cross of gold" rang out over the throng there was a pause, a break of the smallest fraction of a second. The orator turned and made ready to leave the stand.

Then from the rearmost wall to the speaker's stand, from end to end of the gigantic hall, came like one great burst of artillery the answer of the convention: "You shall not crucify mankind upon the cross of gold." Roar upon roar, crash upon crash of fierce, delirious applause.

The people, men and women, were upon their chairs, their hats were in the air, their handkerchiefs tossing like whitecaps on the winter sea. Flags were flying, waving, streaming; the broad stripes of old glory were intermixed with the banners of states and territories and the pennons of the candidates.

Far down in the rear of the hall a woman was on her chair waving her cloak, blue with red lining, and the alternate flashes of red and blue blazed more conspicuous than any other banner in the hall.

People sprung upon Bryan as he struggled toward his chair. They leaped at him like hungry wolves and hugged him and crushed him in their strong arms. Old men, white with age and with the frenzy of the hour, tottered to him to grasp his hand.

Young men stood on the seats and strove to strike approving hands upon his shoulders as he passed by. His progress to his seat was such as never any Roman coming home to triumph had—the orator was literally whirled off his feat and borne on by the struggling masses of frantic friends.

Then some one in a western delegation uprooted the blue guidon that marked the place of his colleagues. In a second twenty other guidons were twisted from their sockets, and the men who tore them free were crowding toward the spot, where Bryan, bewildered, half frightened, panting, yet proud and satisfied was fighting off the caresses, the adoration of his myriad friends. Over the head of the Nebraska man the blue guidons were clustered. More and more the group grew in numbers every second.

As each blue guide post was added to the throng the crowd simply joined delirium to its previous frenzy. Round the hall, waving the guidons on high, marched the men of Florida, of Illinois, of Idaho.

Twenty other states followed and there would have been but one man before the public eye could a vote have been taken then. Presently, exhausted, the banner-bearers sought their places—Bryan sunk utterly wearied into his seat—the mightiest demonstration of many a convention year was over.

Most of the names of the journalists who forged the new style and formed the new order of baseball reporters are forgotten, but Peter Finley Dunne achieved an eminent place in American journalism as the creator of Mr. Dooley, the fount of big-city wisdom. By the time one writer compared the sound of a hard-hit grounder ripping toward the shortstop through the unmowed grass of the infield to "the hired man eating celery," the new trend has spread to other Midwest cities that quickly followed Chicago's lead.[35] By way of Cincinnati and St. Louis, Louisville and Pittsburgh, the Chicago style reached Boston, New York, Philadelphia, and Baltimore, where it came to be amalgamated with other journalistic innovations. Joseph Pulitzer's *World* had produced the first sports page in the 1880's, and William Randolph Hearst's interest "in stories of the great American game" led to the development of the modern sports section in his New York *Journal* in the 1890's.[36] Other journalists updated the publication time of baseball reports and made the afternoon instead of the morning paper the chief carrier of baseball news.

In general, improved reporting helped transform baseball from pastime to spectacle by making watching a spectacular victory more significant than actually playing a mediocre game. Gentlemen of leisure who had once played baseball now sought exercise and conviviality in other games. Growing numbers of spectators more than made up for the loss of this support and brought more teams that played to win onto the fields. Local rivalries intensified. When the best team from one city met its opposite from another, the match laid the groundwork for intersectional rivalries that culminated in the struggle for the national championship. They attracted a following deeply involved in the intensified drama of luck and skill, eager to see how the victor capitalized on both.

This increased exposure to spectators and to other teams raised the level of the game. As the contests produced exciting scenes and drew large crowds more regularly, the clubs caught on to the changing atmosphere of the game. They began charging admission and paying good players to devote their lives exclusively to baseball as the best way to maintain a winning team. In 1862, in Brooklyn, William H. Cammeyer built the first enclosed baseball field in the country, graded the diamond, erected a clubhouse, and charged admission. He viewed baseball as another business venture made possible by the modern city, but his dream of getting a monopoly on the game fizzled when teams built their own ball parks. It vanished totally in 1871 when New York shook off political boss William M. Tweed, whose patronage control over baseball-playing firemen had tied a New York club to Cammeyer's Brooklyn park. Cammeyer left his mark on the atmosphere of the ball park by playing at the beginning of a game a popular song, "The Star Spangled Banner," which in 1916 by presidential order became the official anthem of the United States. His practice of charging admission had been previewed four years earlier at a Long Island race course, where 1,500 spectators paid fifty cents each to see the first game of the 1858 championship series for the national baseball title.[37]

Commercialization and professionalization went hand in hand. Young men quickly spotted baseball as a new road to fortune and fame. The growing demand for good baseball put a premium on good players and induced more and more clubs to offer gifts or money to attract them. The practice violated the Association rule against paying players, so that at times clubs used unrelated salaried jobs to attract athletes who were in effect being paid for playing baseball, thus evading the regulation. Rumors about a player getting money under the table circulated as early as 1860. Albert J. Reach, soon to star as infielder for the Philadelphia Athletics, is said to have played for a straight salary in 1863. In the following year, leading New York and Brooklyn clubs began playing for shares of the gate money of a Brooklyn field that usually charged ten cents admission. With amateurism on the way out, so-called rounders or revolvers among the players deserted their teams at the first sign of better conditions elsewhere.[38]

Baseball's changing scenario led to new roles and produced new standards. The president of a club, by sheer necessity, became its business manager and the playing captain became the manager of the team. With a man's athletic abilities now clearly of greater concern than his social position in 1868, the National Association of Base Ball Players terminated its futile struggle against the monetary practices that produced professional players. The group accepted a recommendation of its rules committee to recognize two distinct classes of players, amateurs and professionals, in an attempt to straighten out the confusing variety of players.[39]

Similar considerations motivated Henry Chadwick to champion an all-professional team. The New York *Clipper* writer realized that the game could survive as a big spectator sport only if played by professionals. In his preview of the 1868 season he stressed the professional status that distinguished the Cincinnati Red Stockings from the other good teams he discussed: the New York Mutuals, the Brooklyn Athletics, the Troy Haymakers, the Chicago White Stockings, the Philadelphia Athletics, and the Baltimore Marylands. He strongly supported the Cincinnati arrangement, which had each player under contract for the entire season at a negotiated rate of pay ranging from $800 to $1,400. In the ensuing campaign for professional teams, journalist and team complemented each other well. Chadwick's articles emphasized that playing baseball was a genuine profession, which served the public with entertainment. The Red Stockings, during a spectacular tour through the centers of American baseball in 1869, demonstrated that professionals played the best baseball by completing an undefeated season. The followers of more than a thousand active baseball clubs recognized the significance of this achievement.[40]

The fabulous success of the Red Stockings quickly determined the future of the game as a spectator sport in the modern city, but it took several years to find an appropriate structure to implement the change. A score of clubs, following the new hiring practices, put together strong teams and attracted audiences without devising a stable organization appropriate for big business. Ten teams founded a professional league in 1871 but kept most of the old arrangements, changing only what mattered most to them. They added "Professional" to the title of the disintegrating amateur organization and paid their players openly. However, they restored honesty to baseball in name only, because the game became an excuse for

betting among players and spectators, and crooked play followed, as in every sport where betting took hold. "Old-time baseball men are chary, even to this day," a journalist explained in 1909, "of talking about the crooked deals which they witnessed in that time" because of "the wholesale slaughter of tainted players which occurred later."[41]

The new industry experienced dismal years, but open and definite professionalism also made the conduct of the game into something approaching a system. The momentum of money squelched the hopes of small-scale speculators who had dreamed of exploiting the new bonanza by luring players and spectators to their own teams. The big clubs built or took over ball parks and clubhouses and organized a game schedule that glorified inter-urban competition on a national basis. Carefully timed and rigorously enforced, a progression of home games against visiting teams and of road games on the home field of the opposition provided a sequence of contests between rivals strongly identified with particular cities. Methodically, all events led to determining a league champion.

General business trends indicated that gentlemen sportsmen sacrificing profits in return for public esteem were on the way out and underlined the significance of strict organization assuring a monopoly for the new economic venture. Although breach of contract and bribery, drinking and gambling tarnished the image of baseball, in Boston Harry Wright and other members of the disbanded Cincinnati superteam maintained discipline and won the Association championship for four consecutive years. In 1875, when the original clubs had shrunk to seven, the first major professional baseball league folded, but the presence of the professional players it had developed and the economic potential of professional baseball brought the National League into existence in the following year.[42]

The modern business structure of big-time American baseball grew around the organizational framework conceived in the 1870's. Attempts to break the monopoly of the National League gave rise to the American Association in 1882. Within two years the rivals were able to agree to end competition over cities and for players. The Association failed in 1890; however, ten years later, another major league formed—the American League. From 1900 on, big-time baseball operated within the context of two league championships, figuratively called the Pennants, and soon added a play-off series between the champions called the World Series.

From its start in 1876, the National League of Professional Baseball Clubs, to give it its full title, meant business. Its owners established themselves as masters of the game. William A. Hulbert, the first League president, engineered the developments. In contrast to some of the gentlemen players, political bosses, or gambling operators who had previously dabbled in managing baseball, he was a member of the Chicago Board of Trade who used his managerial experience to lay the foundation for another flourishing business. Hulbert was "a typical Chicago man" in the eyes of Albert G. Spalding, who pitched for him before becoming a successful manufacturer of sporting goods. As booster of his city, Hulbert "never spoke of what *he* would do, or what *his* club would do, but it was always what *Chicago* would do."[43] He set up an oligarchy of club owners who ran the game efficiently. With draconic measures he restored the surface honesty of the sport and the public con-

fidence in its operation that seemed so essential for good business.[44]

The governmental and economic structure of baseball became autocratic, but the atmosphere of the ball park preserved the appearance of freedom. The public, fed up with corrupt practices, largely ignored the undemocratic features of the new regime, which, in turn, struggled to square the owners' business monopoly with democracy and even make baseball its symbol. "Possibly there is no corporate body . . . with which the public comes into closer . . . contact than this association," a lawyer pointed out in 1910, "and it possibly knows less of its inner nature and working machinery than of other bodies which . . . have their being away from the limelight."[45]

The establishment of the National League offered new economic opportunities for poor men who could play baseball well; but the clubs held the power, not the players, whose contracts tied them to the organization. Strict control of city franchises, which the old Association had given away for a song, guaranteed not only the clubs' monopoly over professional baseball but also their hold on professional players, who now came to depend on the League for their livelihood. "The idea was as old as the hills," Albert G. Spalding explained in his later years, but it had never been applied to baseball before. "Like every other form of business enterprise," he argued, "Base Ball depends for results on two interdependent divisions, the one to have absolute control and direction of the system, and the other to engage—always under the executive branch—in the actual work of production."[46]

In order to assure the success of the new industry in terms of attracting paying spectators, the first systematic organization of an American spectator sport set out to refine the rules of baseball in such a way that the competition in the ball park would be of a nature to absorb the interest of large crowds. Skillful manipulation of the rules paid off. The "game has long since become an art," a Russian man of affairs living in the United States observed in 1895, "and committees meet constantly, now in one place, now in another, to adjust the details of the rules."[47]

Before these technical refinements—indeed, two decades before the last major rules changes of the 1890's—modern baseball was already drawing crowds of city dwellers because it spoke to them as a game that reflected aspects of their own lives. Thus the introduction of regulations into most phases of the contest affected not only the conduct of the game but also the atmosphere surrounding it. More and more spectators became convinced that the game fitted uniquely into their modern world. "Anything goes" was the message they eagerly distilled from the behavior on the baseball diamond because their familiarity with the rules of the game indicated to them that certain plays reflected actions they experienced daily in the modern city. The rules of the game seemed strict, but the etiquette governing the players' behavior seemed lax. The game's enormous success as the most popular spectator sport in the closing decades of the nineteenth century was based on this relationship between baseball and the larger society.

Any notion that gentlemen may once have had about the proper conduct of a ball player or the correct form of making a play vanished with the emergence of professionalism. The idea governing the related game of cricket—that some behavior on the field was "not cricket"—never took hold in pro-

fessional baseball. Its players, Bruce Catton concluded in his reflections on the game, "have borrowed nothing from the 'sportsmanship' of more sedate countries; they believe that when you get into a fight you had better win, and the method by which you win does not matter very much."[48] As soon as the skills of the professionals turned the drama of sport into an exhibition, Lewis Mumford stressed in his assessment of mass sport, the rule became "Success at Any Price" instead of "Fair Play."[49] The disappearance of a tacit understanding about the conduct of the game, as well as the necessity of basing a judgment call on an observation made in a fraction of a second, increased the interaction between player and umpire on the field.

The intense rivalry encouraged the player constantly to seek advantages by bending a rule or trying to get away with an infraction. "Boys, you've heard the new rules read," the captain of the New York Giants would say in beginning his annual talk at the opening of the season during the 1880's; "now the question is: what can we do to beat them?"[50] A generation seasoned by the Civil War began to assume that any behavior, however outrageous, was acceptable in baseball, too, and this feeling may have generated the metaphor that spoke of baseball as war. "Infractions are expected by the crowd, and hence by players, umpires and managers," explained Walter Camp, who almost singlehandedly shaped the rules of American football, in 1910. "In the long run, the people make the law," he added, unwittingly identifying the spectators' influence over the enforcement of the rules with the workings of rules committees eager to attract the largest crowds.[51]

For the people in the ball park, the

umpire represented the voice of authority. To the spectators he was a convenient target for their frequent irritations and deep-seated frustrations both within and outside the ball park. The umpire became a personification of the rulers of their lives, who in the workaday world remained hidden behind the whirl of urban life, the faceless corporate structures, the anonymity of technocracy, and the mystery of public affairs. During the strife-ridden 1880's and 1890's, in their urge to identify and challenge a villain in the drama they lived, the crowds ignored any distinction between the rules committee of the league that had made the regulations and the umpire on the field calling a play.[52]

Thus the grandstand crowds had a field day in exploiting to their hearts' content the pressure put on the umpire. Over decades of changing styles of play he was called on to decide the legality of the tricky delivery (a new overhand pitching style), unusual batting tactics, fielding aberrations, and base-running maneuvers. What mattered was that all decisions allowed the spectators to challenge vehemently and vociferously the ruler, clearly identified from the 1880's on by his dark blue coat and cap.

On the surface the umpire appeared to exercise an authority like that of some other powers that regulated life. Like constables and clerks, he also lost his standing as a gentleman. Though he had once been specifically honored because refereeing evidenced his intimate knowledge of the game, the rise of baseball as a spectator sport had made him just another member of the cast of characters in the show—at times a villainous buffoon. Before the introduction of the double umpire system at the beginning of the twentieth century,

the single man working behind either the pitcher or the catcher frequently cut a pathetic figure.

Definitely not omnipotent and hardly omnipresent, the umpire was abused or even mobbed on the field by spectators and players, and ridiculed or slandered in the sports papers as "the mortal enemy" of everyone, if "he does not especially favor the local club."[53] Among the many fatuous comments on umpire-baiting, few rivaled the explanation that rowdy fans were merely exercising their democratic right to protest tyranny. Any protection the league might have extended to the umpire, and he received none, would have interfered with his actual role. Shaping the game to maximize attendance was of utmost significance to the club owners, so that they tolerated the rowdy behavior of players, managers, and spectators as long as it enhanced the excitement of the game.[54]

This desire for an exciting spectacle eventually led to new rules speeding up the moments of spectacular action in the game and also to the introduction of protective equipment, because gloves and face masks allowed men to make without injury the rough, fast, and exciting plays of the game, in bursts of speed, that most people waited for. Speed occupied the spectators, who were constantly under pressure to match the hectic tempo of the modern city. The action in the ball park demonstrated to them that it was possible, after all, to keep up with the fleeting moment. The experience related to their world Shakespeare's line "The Spirit of the Time Shall Teach Me Speed," which the *Clipper* displayed under its title.[55]

If there had ever been a choice between cricket and baseball, the hustle and bustle of the American modern city turned the scales decisively in favor of the latter. One reminiscence about the 1850's commented, "Young America looked askance at a game that required a day and sometimes two days to play to a finish," because "such a waste of time" seemed "beyond all reason."[56] In 1854, a Scottish publisher encountered the tempo of life in the United States and concluded that "American minutes would seem almost to be worth an English day.[57] Christy Mathewson, an outstanding pitcher of the first decade of the twentieth century, expressed the logic of coupling baseball with speed when he said, "The American public wants its excitement rolled up in a package and handed out quickly."[58]

Although the players' concern for protection introduced gloves and catcher's masks into baseball, these innovations escaped being ridiculed as unmanly because the age worshipped the result they produced—memorable moments packed with action. Baseball had been played with bare hands until the glove began appearing in the early 1880's, supposedly after a shortstop had used a crude version to protect his hand. Other players followed his example when they noticed that he did not have to ease off catching the ball, could meet it solidly, and got his throw away faster than the other infielders. The spectators, who liked what they saw, supported the change, and sporting goods firms soon began furnishing gloves to professionals. A few years earlier, the first body shields had permitted the umpire to stand behind the catcher and enforce the strike and ball rules in a way that heightened the game's drama. The introduction of the mask and the fingerless glove with light padding on the palm in 1877 allowed the catcher to become the director of team action

on the field, an effective way to co-ordinate the play.[59]

In addition to the protective devices, the change from the large six-ounce elastic ball to the hard regulation ball hastened the transformation of a pastime into a spectacle. An ironic twist of circumstances accompanied these developments. While the new equipment opened up baseball to everyone it also made the professional game the exclusive domain of specialists. Hundreds of agile, hard-throwing men who had not qualified for old-time baseball because they were not born with hands and arms for barehanded fielding replaced the so-called natural players. They did not have to worry about protecting their hands while catching the ball, and their swift plays quickened the pace of the game. New waves of players, each raising the standards of performance, quickly drove each other out of big-league baseball. They constantly advanced the quality of the game, heightened the level of competition, and increased the expectations of spectators until only a handful of big-league-caliber experts could participate.

Less became more early in professional baseball, but the enthusiastic spectators caught on quickly and watched more carefully. Gloves and masks contributed to the decline of the high scores that characterized mid-nineteenth century baseball by allowing steady improvement in pitching and fielding. This intensified a trend marked by revoking the old straight-arm delivery restriction which had forced pitchers to obtain speed only by an underhand throw or a wristy jerk of the ball. In 1900, Adrian C. ("Cap") Anson, after his retirement as manager and captain of the Chicago club, called the high scores of old-time baseball "performances impossible in these days of great speed and curve pitching."[60] In 1859, in the first inter-collegiate baseball game on record, Amherst beat Williams 73 to 32. When the celebrated Cincinnati Red Stockings ruled in 1869, they trounced an opponent 103 to 8, and that was only about half the largest number of runs ever scored in an old-style game. However, at the turn of the twentieth century big-league teams rarely scored more than 10 runs per game.[61]

By that time only sandlot baseball, with the help of the mitt and, from 1896 on, such literary embellishment of baseball virtues as the feats recorded in *Frank Merriwell* by Gilbert Patten, had acquired some of the free and open features that many people identified with the sport.[62] Boys and men tried to emulate the professionals on empty streets and vacant lots, in parks and on playgrounds. In big cities amateur clubs sometimes attracted more fans than the professionals. Eighty thousand people saw the game between the Telling Strollers and the Hanna Street Cleaners for the Cleveland championship of 1914. One year later, in the same natural amphitheater, more than 100,000 cheered the victory of the Cleveland Indians over the Omaha Luxus for the world amateur championship.[63] In 1917 Frederic L. Paxson saw the rise of sports in the United States as another "safety valve" replacing Frederick Jackson Turner's frontier. Baseball "succeeded as an organized spectator sport," he observed, but it contributed something neither racing nor boxing could "in turning the city lot into a playground and the small boy into an enthusiastic player."[64]

Street baseball, which could be played in a limited space and required no expensive equipment, advanced immensely the cause of play in an urban world.[65] In 1868, *Leslie's Illustrated Newspaper* reported on "playing Baseball Under Difficulties in the Streets of New York" and emphasized that boys "will play . . . in spite of all travel and obstruction."[66] A need for removing children's games from the streets went back to the beginnings of urbanization in North America; it had been felt in Boston in 1657.[67] But at the opening of the twentieth century, street baseball increased this concern and provided a major impetus in the spread of the play movement in the urban centers of the United States. "Only in the modern city," Jane Addams emphasized in 1909, "have men concluded that it is no longer necessary for the municipalities to provide for the insatiable desire for play." Only ten cities had supervised playgrounds prior to 1900.[68] However, the pressure of children playing sandlot baseball changed all that, and on the eve of America's entry into the first World War, that number had risen to 414 cities with 3,270 play centers.[69]

While street baseball reaffirmed the social importance of play in the city, professional baseball followed "the individualistic tendencies of America" that left leisure to commerce, giving everyone who could buy a ticket the choice of watching the kind of sport he or she liked best, without making an effort to persuade a group of people to agree on playing one specific game, as an urban reformer of the age commented.[70] It ignored any urge to participate in the play and, like urban politics, followed representational lines. Professional experts took places on the field which from time to time many men in the grandstands dreamed of occupying themselves. The exclusiveness of the diamond recalled the operation of an exclusive club. In 1885, the Philadelphia *Sporting Life* compared major-league baseball clubs to closed corporations and political machines run by an "inside ring" that reaped steadily growing profits by keeping outsiders away from the inner sanctum of the enterprise.[71]

On the professional diamond itself, the physical dangers of baseball also helped keep bat and ball in the hands of a limited group of players. In 1905, an editorial in the New York *Times* stressed that "the peaceful citizen would as soon think of standing to be shot at by a small calibre rifle as by one of these new-fangled ballistas of a pitcher."[72] Almost twenty years earlier a court had declined to protect a fan from other perils of baseball when it found that even on the grandstand he must take all risk of accident. In that 1887 damage suit, a justice of the New York Supreme Court had taken the sale of a ticket as evidence of a contract signifying merely "that a seat would be provided and a game of ball played."[73]

The hazards of the game opened up baseball to gifted players from major immigrant groups. In addition to the many athletes of English and Irish ancestry who had always been present in major-league baseball, American Indians, Frenchmen, Germans, Jews, Poles, Italians, and Latin Americans entered the game. At the turn of the century some of these players had risen beyond any narrow immigrant identity to become some of the great heroes of the sport. Big Ed Delahanty, Louis Francis "Chief" Sockalexis, Napoleon "Larry" Lajoie, and John Peter "Honus" Wagner represented these giants of the game.[74] However, black players remained barred from major-league teams, perpetuating the discrimination officially introduced in 1867 when the rules of the National Association of Base Ball Players barred black players and black

clubs from membership.[75] In this respect, too, baseball mirrored life in the modern city.

Most residents ignored the gap between the harsh realities of professional baseball and the glib assertions of one of its magnates: "The genius of our institutions is democratic; Base Ball is a democratic game."[76] Their experience often contradicted the American creed, but the fans managed to live with these inconsistencies because the modern city provided a greater degree of personal freedom than most of them could have found elsewhere. They embraced the potential of American democracy for improving the quality of life, but were loath to consider the rights of others as long as many of their own expectations went unfulfilled or others seemed to be threatening their positions.

City people, at the turn of the century, considered the ball park not as a testing ground for the egalitarian promises of their society but as a source of diversion. As with their limited role in urban politics, they were satisfied with being represented on the field by their sports idols. Only a few followed the flight of fancy of a commentator who in 1914 considered baseball the only institution "that has been wholly built by our people, democratic to the last degree, and vibrant with that peculiar enthusiasm which all the world recognizes as characteristically American."[77] Most of them responded to the appeal of baseball by taking their places in the grandstand, the bleachers, or on the turf at the margin of the field.

In the ball park they watched a spectacle that responded to their concerns. The game enriched their dreary urban existence by providing a few leisure hours in the outdoors. In the warmth of the afternoon sun, the spectators transcended temporarily the physical limitations urban life imposed upon them and experienced relief from the tension of their complex surroundings. They saw plays that reduced their bewildering struggle for success to a game of one-thing-at-a-time and to the measurable progress of a successful athlete mastering one obstacle after another. They detected few gray areas in the ball park. The game presented immediate and clear-cut wins and losses and pitted good guys against bad guys.

During a few hours in the ball park, city people saw plays that they could remember afterwards because of the way specific events built up to a memorable moment—the sudden skillful triumph over an adversary. By making intense competition against an opponent its essential feature, baseball seemed to legitimize and extoll each spectator's daily struggle for success. Watching the rivalry on the diamond introduced standards of competition into the spectators' lives. The game also reduced their daily tensions because its ups and downs seemed more momentous than their own lives.

The spectators learned to appreciate baseball's demonstrations of efficiency and excellence—qualities many of them took as keys to success in industrial America. They followed the dynamic between individual competition and cooperative triumph. Their involvement in the lessons of the diamond thrived on an appreciation of a faster throw, a better catch, or a longer hit. One of the classic attempts at the close of the nineteenth century to improve the working habits of laborers and the performance of industry was also inspired by the struggle for perfection on the baseball diamond. Frederick W. Taylor, who came to personify the search for a reasonable estimate of the production capacity of man and ma-

chine, as a boy playing baseball regularly impressed his friends, one of them recalled, with the necessity "that the rectangle of our rounders' court should be scientifically accurate."[78] Ultimately the way the distances between the bases and the position of the pitcher's mound came to be arranged in the ball park reflected the triumph of the search for the balance between the possible and the impossible play.

Rounders "made scientific," the *Encyclopedia of Sport* called baseball in the 1890's, and that property fascinated enthusiasts who saw in the game a manifestation of the problems of their lives of chance in what otherwise seemed a predictable age of technology.[79] Paradoxically, the outcome of the contest on the field became more uncertain the more scientific the game itself appeared to become. A timely base hit or an untimely error could now tip the scale, while in the days of the slugging batters of old the better team, more often than not, had won on its overwhelming superiority in batting and scoring. The sophisticated nuances of play were obviously lacking when a team won by twenty, thirty or fifty runs.[80]

The fans loved the order and efficiency of professional baseball, from the meticulous arrangement of the field to the critical moments of a play when split seconds counted. Life and work in the modern city had awakened them to an appreciation for economy of motion. They marveled at the reduction of a play on the field to a few swift movements and the perfection embodied in the flawless execution that decided a contest. "In baseball," Mark Twain noted in the 1880's, "you've got to do everything just right, or you don't get there."[81]

A generation exposed to the worship

of perfection outside the ball park accepted baseball as "the most perfect thing in America." This sharing of excellence demonstrated on the field converted the enjoyment of a diversion into an education and a conditioning agent. "Even to those who simply sit on the stands and watch," a rather condescending propagandist of the sport wrote in 1911, "there comes the inspiration that follows a thing well done."[82] In the ball park, momentarily removed from their struggle for a decent existence in the modern city, fans also learned to appreciate the game's examples of fairness and decency.

The spectators recognized baseball as their game. It appealed to their highstrung, eager temperaments. "Wearisome monotony . . . is utterly unknown in Base Ball," the leading English sports journal stressed on the occasion of an American All-Star team's visit to Great Britain in 1874, "as the attention is concentrated for but a short time, and not allowed to succumb to undue pressure of prolonged suspense."[83]

Mark Twain, in a "Welcome Home" speech to a team returning from a world tour in 1889, hailed baseball as "the very symbol, the outward and visible expression, of the drive and push and rush and struggle of the raging, tearing, booming nineteenth century." He went on to use baseball as a sign to delineate the "modern world," describing the game as a new, visible equator separating the part that mattered from the remainder of the globe where men did not steal "bases on their bellies."[84] The title "world champion," given to the most successful big-league team, confirmed this new geography. It came to designate the winner of the first seven World Series, played between the champions of the National League and the Association in the 1880's. Later,

the title was awarded the victor in the annual World Series between the champions of the National League and the American League—established in the first decade of the twentieth century.

Basic to baseball's attraction was man's fascination with throwing and catching a ball. That predilection helped turn boys into enthusiastic players until they "began slowly to grasp the humiliating fact"—experienced by H. L. Mencken in the 1890's—that they were not "earmarked for a career of glory on the diamond."[85]

With the great expanse of greenery that it required, baseball also appeared to bring the countryside into the metropolis. It radiated the wholesome air of a timeless country sport which, each spring, cleansed anew the foul atmosphere of the modern city. From the 1880's on, a new feature of the baseball year strengthened the effect of conjuring up a bit of countryside. Big-league teams began to go into rural isolation, preferably a fashionable resort in the South, to get over the effects of a winter of loafing with "the hardest five weeks' grind in the world," thus seeming to extend baseball's links with country life and sunshine.[86] Big-time baseball now returned every year to the country, whence many enthusiasts assumed it had come, to recharge its energy.

Baseball's manipulation of reality extended to man-made time, too. Although its spectacular plays were the epitome of swift motion and speedy action, baseball rose above any ordinary concern for an economy of time. If the score was tied after nine innings, the game continued as long as it took to achieve victory. While mechanical time prevailed almost everywhere in the modern city, with the factory whistle and the time clock regulating laborers in factories and clerks in stores, natural time regulated baseball. Only nature itself, requiring postponement on account of rain or termination of play after sundown, could interfere with the course of play.

The game's close ties with nature were used to underscore its virtue. In order to make sure that the tangible blessings of baseball were recognized, apologists extolled those of its features that filled the needs of city people. Untouched by logic or evidence, they stressed that getting out into the fresh air of the ball park promised to open men's eyes to their "business interests" and to protect boys from "immoral association."[87] Despite news stories about dishonest games, umpire baiting, rowdy behavior on and off the field, and shady business deals, the importance of baseball as an inspiration for moral and upright behavior was rarely contested. Nothing was allowed to shatter the mystique of the popular game: upright young men fighting to excell on a green field under a clear sky in the big city. Clergymen of all denominations seemed to agree on the value of the game, and testified to their faith in baseball or used baseball as a testimony of their faith.

Cardinal Gibbons of Baltimore did the former; the Presbyterian minister William Ashley Sunday the latter. Although the Cardinal, by his own admission, knew little about baseball, in 1896 he stressed that he had never heard of baseball games being "used as vehicles for gambling," and for him that fact alone raised baseball "above the level of the average sporting event,"[88] He might have understood men's weaknesses well or the general level of sports might have been low, but during the same decade the Orioles of his Baltimore achieved notoriety for winning three consecutive pennants by getting away with "much of their brow-beating and hooliganism."[89]

Evangelist "Billy" Sunday, in 1904, began weaving into his meetings a story of how prayer saved a game when he played outfield for the Chicago White Stockings. He recalled that he had chased the crucial hit through the crowd and over the benches at the edge of the field. Praying all the way, he suddenly threw out his hand, and the ball struck and stuck in the glove. While Sunday was still reflecting on his "first great lesson in prayer," a spectator slipped him a ten-dollar bill with the words: "Buy a new hat, Bill. That catch won me $1,500."[90]

The increasing numbers of visitors to the ball park attested to the attractions of baseball. In the 1870's, with encouragement by reporters who frequently found public interest greater than they had anticipated, attendance ranged from 800 to 1,500 spectators per league game. In the following decade, the capacity of new ball parks which many owners built with the profits of the prosperous 1880's reflected the increase in spectators.

Baltimore's park, constructed in 1883, had seats for 5,000 people, as did the new, well-enclosed grandstand in Buffalo. From Chicago *Leslie's Illustrated* reported that "lovers of the sport poured in from all the adjacent cities" to see the concluding series of games between the Chicago White Stockings and the New York Giants in 1885, "and from ten to twelve thousand spectators witnessed each game."[91] Chicago had the model field of the 1880's, with space for 10,000 spectators, divided into 2,000 grandstand seats, 6,000 open seats, and standing room.

The crowds of the 1890's came close to exhausting the technical capacity of wooden stands and created a demand for bigger and more substantial grandstands that stimulated the introduction of brick-and-steel structures in the first decade of the twentieth century. Brooklyn and Chicago built ball parks in the 1890's that seated more than 10,000 people. In 1896, the new Philadelphia stadium, "the best athletic ground in the world," furnished 16,000 visitors with seats and 5,000 with standing room.[92]

Despite the setting, constantly more comfortable and lavish, the athletic contest itself remained the major attraction. The enthusiasm of the fans crowding the Boston ball park, considered the smallest of the 1890's by most observers of major-league baseball, seemed to support a lesson one of the club owners had learned from keeping both eyes on people's fascination with the game itself in order to find out how to ensure the attendance figures he wanted. His "common sense" taught him that baseball was "conducted primarily to make money," and that he could risk charging even his players' wives full admission when so many people clamored to get into the park.[93]

In 1890, the president of the Baltimore Orioles had gone one step further when he discounted any relationship between the quality of play and attendance figures. He put his team into a minor league to avoid what he thought might become a costly salary dispute with players. People will "come out to Union Park to drink beer, dance and have picnics just the same," he argued, confident that baseball and ball park had captured the loyalty of the residents of the modern city.[94] In 1908, *Spalding's Official Base Ball Guide* attested to the game's ever-broadening appeal for the steadily increasing groups of immigrants in the modern city: "The

wonderful growth of the public's interest in Base Ball during the last half decade has attracted many hundreds of thousands of people to the game to whom its history previous to the last four or five years is unknown, or at least hazy."[95]

In case enthusiasm faltered, many of the promotional stunts that big business cultivated to market its products helped to sustain the degree of loyalty that baseball magnates considered essential for financial success. Signboards, streetcar posters, handbills, balloons, and newspaper advertisements informed the fans about the game schedule for the season. Inside the park, the music of a brass band often set the tone for the afternoon's enjoyment. Bars and tables offered beer and refreshments, and in the stands vendors sold chewing gum, peanuts, tobacco, pies, sandwiches, and soda water.

Children's Day and Ladies' Day, and an Amateur Day, which admitted ballplayers free if they appeared in the uniform of their clubs, represented variations of stunts that sold baseball as a bargain. This approach triumphed in the double-headers that clubs began staging in the 1880's. Sideshows, from Buffalo Bill to bicycle races, added thrills to the spectacle of the regular game, and owners kept squeezing in so many extras that the league prohibited changing the starting time of a game by more than one hour.

In addition to the anticipation of a good game, the enjoyment of the open air, and the lure of advertising, the ball park attracted residents of the modern city who watched the game as another step in the daily process of becoming Americans. As immigrants, they surrendered to the aura of the national game, which seemed to them indeed a "true expression of the American spirit."[96] Although some of them came from countries famous for national games, the memories of this faded in the new environment as had awareness of the debt that American sports owed in particular to Great Britain.

From the beginnings of English settlement in North America, colonists had played homeland sports, and "practically every phase of sporting life in America was tinged with English influence."[97] Later on, as the industrially most advanced country in the early nineteenth century, Great Britain pioneered the organization and staging of sports spectaculars; its influence refined the play of the young nation. Ideas about sportsmanship and rules made their way across the Atlantic with English, Scottish, and Irish immigrants whose attitude toward enjoying sports and teaching games helped to reduce prejudice against organized play and spectator sports.

Many other immigrants carried with them only a rather limited sports heritage because they had never experienced the opportunity to learn or the leisure to play a sport. In the United States, work and not play was their lot, too, and they were approaching an age at which their generation thought it senseless actually to take up playing a new game. Not schooled enough in English to follow a stage play or to read a book, they were natural sports spectators, bound to the ball park by forces similar to those that drew them to the metropolitan press.

The immigrants' age and poverty marked them as the chief supporters of spectator sports. When only privileged youngsters had the time to play sandlot baseball (evoking, as a German visitor noticed, the envy of children working in mills and factories), poor men automatically belonged in the stands where they could share temporarily at least one feature of leisure in the modern city.[98] This common experience forged a bond between diverse groups of people, and watching baseball took precedence over ethnic games because rooting for a big-city team also gave rootless people a sense of belonging. It also helped them acquire a better understanding of their new world.

In the ball park, exposure to the rules of the national game educated immigrants as Americans. Familiarity with the regulations, easily acquired for a game that had eliminated the gentleman's understanding as the basis for assessing the validity of a play, bestowed a certain brand of citizenship upon the spectators. Just knowing the difference between what did happen on the field and what could have happened permitted immigrants to become involved in the American game. The ball park furnished a sphere of public life where they could avoid rejection and loss of face because of misunderstanding or ignorance. Soon their growing knowledge of the subtleties of the game made them eligible to join the turbulent democracy of protesters who noisily expressed their dissent from the umpire's decision.

The spectacle of the ball park clarified some of the newcomers' confusion about control and authority in their new world. They had left behind countries governed by explicit rules and implicit prerogatives, and now were ignorant of the underlying rationale of the precepts and restrictions which shaped the free-for-all of the modern city. As yet, they did not understand the application of the democratic maxims protecting the humanity of many people that increasingly guided behavior in the marketplace and the job market, or etiquette in the department store and on the avenue. Bewildered, they faced a maze of individual and social practices that blunted the operation of regulations and obscured the exercise of authority. As a result they saw themselves, and others, handicapped by their ignorance of the canons of conduct that governed the race for riches. When they recognized how ballplayers used rules to win and how the umpire applied the rules to keep competition within certain bounds, immigrants also began to see how webs of control affected the American modern city.

The practical lessons of the ball park spoke directly about most spectators' basic concern: getting ahead in their urban world. The exciting plays seemed to end all too soon, having barely demonstrated late-nineteenth-century morality in action, but the spectators carried home with them the message of the ball park in the form of the players' statistics. The measure of success was plain. The most runs determined the winner of a game; in the table of team standings, the number of games won and lost separated the less successful clubs from the champion of the moment. In the context of averages spanning several seasons, the achievements of players and teams created a shared historical experience among people without a common history. Such plain statistics appealed to the American passion for counting as a way of mastering reality.[99]

People eagerly absorbed game statistics and scores, conveniently reduced to a formula that fitted the routine of urban communication. Their interest gave them an excuse, particularly if the home team was on the road, to slip away from work in the late afternoon to glimpse the score in a saloon. There a telegraph operator throning on a balcony above the bar chalked the details of the innings on a blackboard. For throngs of people downtown, unable to get to the ball park or sneak into a bar, the pointers and counters of a giant scoreboard on the facade of a landmark provided contact with the progress of the innings. These special message systems in the heart of the urban world further fostered the impression that there was a relationship between competition on the diamond and in the modern city.[100]

More often than not, the immediacy of a trip to the ball park tied people, city life, and baseball together. Ball parks came to be located along the routes of streetcar lines, in easy reach of large numbers of spectators, who learned to visit them rather casually, as a matter of course. Hard-nosed speculators assessed transit franchises and real estate values, which influenced the selection of sites.[101] Eager to accommodate changing needs, they rapidly built wooden structures; at times they were also inspired by the prospect for the sale of beer. "Young man, if you can get the City Council to give you a six months' license to sell beer . . . , I will build you a ball park," one of them with obvious interests promised a manager in the 1890's.[102]

On other occasions, baseball men took over fields, such as the New York Polo Grounds, originally used for sports too exclusive for city people. They laid out the diamond, put up wooden stands, and were in business. At times the grandstands burned down as quickly as they were built. But new ones rose in a hurry, and the many projects that were built made it possible to test the usefulness of various sites until a ball park came to be fixed in the setting that offered the best location for nourishing the local roots of a "worldwide" spectacle.[103]

The characteristics of each ball park depended on many circumstances, ranging from spectators' willingness to tolerate local characters like Zane Grey's "Old Well-Well," whose roared approval identified spectacular plays and also earned him his nickname, to a given neighborhood's distinctive atmosphere.[104] In 1885, Chicago's new West Side Park featured a covered entrance for gentlemen going by carriage to the grandstand. In April 1909, in addition to the 35,000 spectators who crowded on opening day into Shibe Park in Philadelphia, the first concrete and steel ballpark, several thousand people inaugurated a special feature of the setting by buying space on the adjacent rooftops of the rowhouses of Twentieth Street that skirted the right-field wall.

The surrounding real estate occasionally determined the size of the outfield, which could differ from park to park, changing the conditions of play. Irrespective of the lay of the land, the ball parks blended into that incongruous harmony of contrasts which characterized the modern city. The street entrances of the classic parks that rose at the beginning of the twentieth such as Shibe Park and Fenway Park, Forbes Field and Ebbets Field, resembled the facades of downtown offices, department stores, or apartment houses.[105]

Despite various shapes and appearances, all ball parks conjured up ideas of leisure. "As an amusement enterprise," a ballplayer and a journalist argued in 1910, "baseball today is scarcely second to the theater," catering "to millions of spectators" and representing "an investment of perhaps

$100,000,000 in property and players."[106]

Nature itself seemed to be in league with baseball to assure a successful spectacle. The opening of the baseball season in the spring marked the return of sunny days that could be enjoyed in the open. On the field young men signaled the triumph of youth by succeeding in fierce competition. The green grass enlivened the monotony of the surrounding world of brick and stone. The carefree atmosphere, charged with the heady air of the modern city, increased the spectators' appetite for self-indulgence as they consumed beer and soda, hot dogs, peanuts, and Cracker Jacks, which had become culinary marks of mass leisure by the turn of the century. The ambience of the ball park enthralled the spectators, letting them forget everyday life forever—as suggested by one tune that became immediately popular when it was first heard in 1906—and turning the sharp edges of competition into an enjoyable spectacle.

Baseball offered a lesson in modern living in an imitation of a pastoral setting. Its features of intense rivalry as well as a limited amount of sportsmanship, general enthusiasm as well as rabid partisanship oriented crowds of people toward an acceptance of competition as a part of daily life, an awareness of a distinct urban vitality, and an appreciation for recreation. Spectators packing grandstands and bleachers intensified the pressure on factories and stores for a half-holiday once a week, lightening the routine of living and working.[107] Seeing others play ball for a living encouraged them to play sandlot baseball or to take up other sports. In the 1890's, the *Nation* called the growing interest in sports "the athletic

craze" and likened its intensity to preceding crazes involving greenbacks,
silver, and grangers.[108]

The magnetism of the ball park
pulled together crowds of strangers
who succumbed to a startlingly intense
sensation of community created by the
shared experience of watching a baseball game. One outsider, who unexpectedly came across this phenomenon
during a study of the worldwide power
of sport, saw this momentary unity as
a religious bond. Visiting Chicago in
the 1920's, this publicist of German
sports, who later did his share to make
the 1936 Berlin Olympic Games a communal spectacle serving an ideology,
detected the links forged by the ball
park even in the seventh-inning stretch:
"All the spectators rise solemnly as if in
church."[109]

The feeling of community that the
ball park could evoke among crowds of
city people struck a young Harvard
graduate writing a newspaper column
for a college pal in the late 1880's as
incongruous with the diversity of the
modern city. Ernest Lawrence Thayer
set his baseball ballad, "Casey at the
Bat," in Mudville, a rural heaven of
shared sentiments. His lines about the
luckless batter appeared in the Sunday
edition of the San Francisco Examiner,
next to the column of the avowed cynic
Ambrose Bierce.[110] Together with
"Casey's Revenge," which followed several weeks later, it might have been
lost with the weekend, had it not found
a stage larger than the ball park.

A few weeks later, a young vaudeville
performer recited the poem, fortuitously clipped by a friend, as entr'acte
in a comic opera at the baseball night
of a New York theater, when he had
to acknowledge the presence among the
spectators of members of the New York

Giants and the Chicago White Stockings. The audience "shouted its glee,"
De Wolf Hopper recalled, because it
"had expected, as any one does on hearing 'Casey' for the first time, that the
mighty batsman would slam the ball
out of the lot."[111] With "Casey," baseball reached the stage of the popular
theater that provided a setting where
people could not only laugh about their
own frustrated hopes and the shattered
illusions of others but also learn to
bridge some of the conflicts inherent in
the modern city.

NOTES

1. New York Times, May 31, 1888.
2. For general baseball history turn to Harold
Seymour, Baseball: The Early Years (New York,
1960), and Baseball: The Golden Age (New
York, 1971); David Quentin Voigt, American
Baseball: From Gentleman's Sport to the Com-
missioner System (Norman, Okla., 1966), and
American Baseball: From the Commissioners to
Continental Expansion (Norman, Okla., 1970).
3. For a theory of play and games see Roger
Caillois, Man, Play, and Games (New York,
1961), 3–10, as well as his critique of Johan
Huizinga's theory of play (in Homo Ludens [New
York, 1950], 13, 28) in his Man and the Sacred
(New York, 1959), Appendix II, "Play and the
Sacred," 152–62.
4. Roland Auguet, Cruelty and Civilization: The
Roman Games (London, 1972), 49–50, 51.
5. Keith Thomas, "Work and Leisure in Pre-
Industrial Society," Past and Present, no. 29
(December, 1964), 52.
6. For general histories of sports and spectator
sports in the United States turn to John Allan
Krout, Annals of American Sport (New York,
1929); Jennie Holliman, American Sports (1785–
1835) (Durham, N.C., 1931); John Durant and
Otto Bettmann, Pictorial History of American
Sports: From Colonial Times to the Present (New
York, 1952); John Rickards Betts, America's
Sporting Heritage: 1850–1950 (Reading, Mass.,
1974).
7. Quoted in Herbert Manchester, Four Centuries of Sport in America, 1490–1890 (New
York, 1931), 129.
8. William Henry Nugent, "The Sports Section,"
American Mercury, XVI (March, 1929), 329–
31; Albert G. Spalding, America's National
Game: Historic Facts Concerning the Beginning,

Evolution, Development and Popularity of Base Ball. With Personal Reminiscences of Its Vicissitudes, Its Victories and Its Votaries (New York, 1911), 422.

9. Robert W. Malcolmson, *Popular Recreations in English Society, 1700–1850* (Cambridge, 1973), 90–91; Daniel T. Rodgers, *The Work Ethic in Industrial America* (Chicago, 1978), 102–3; Voigt, *Baseball: From Gentleman's Sport*, 87–89; Dale A. Somers, "The Leisure Revolution: Recreation in the American City, 1820–1920," *Journal of Popular Culture*, V (Summer, 1971), 113–39.

10. Nicholas B. Wainwright, ed., *A Philadelphia Perspective: The Diary of Sidney George Fisher Covering the Years 1834–1871* (Philadelphia, 1969), 333.

11. Allan Nevins, ed., *The Diary of Philip Hone, 1828–1851*, 2 vols. (New York, 1927), II 600–1.

12. David Graham Phillips, "The Delusion of the Race-Track," *Cosmopolitan*, XXXVIII (January, 1905), 262.

13. *Times*, October 14, 1853.

14. Edward W. Townsend, "A Sporty Boston Boy," *Fadden Explains: Max Expounds* (New York, 1895), 33.

15. *Times*, July 9, 1889; New York *National Police Gazette*, July 27, 1889; Dale A. Somers, *The Rise of Sports in New Orleans, 1850–1900* (Baton Rouge, 1972), 170–73.

16. Quoted in Krout, *American Sport*, 199.

17. Robert W. Henderson, *Ball, Bat and Bishop: The Origin of Ball Games* (New York, 1947), 174.

18. *Ibid.*, 132–69; Arthur Bartlett, *Baseball and Mr. Spalding: The History and Romance of Baseball* (New York, 1951), 1–11; Seymour, *Baseball: Early Years*, 8–11. For an illuminating discussion of baseball myths see David Q. Voigt, *America Through Baseball* (Chicago, 1976).

19. "The Centennial Season's Campaign," New York *Clipper*, November 6, 1875.

20. Henderson, *Ball*, 161–65; Krout, *American Sport*, 117.

21. Carl Wittke, "Baseball in Its Adolescence," *Ohio State Archeological and Historical Quarterly*, LX (April, 1952), 120–21.

22. New York *Spirit of the Times*, January 31, 1857.

23. Seymour, *Baseball: Early Years*, 35–37.

24. Somers, *Sports in New Orleans*, 50; Cecil O. Monroe, "The Rise of Baseball in Minnesota," *Minnesota History*, XIX (June, 1938), 162; Fred W. Lange, *History of Baseball in California and Pacific Coast Leagues, 1847–1938* (Oakland, 1938), 6–7.

25. Krout, *American Sport*, 119; Frederick G. Lieb, *The Baseball Story* (New York, 1950), 34.

26. Spaulding, *America's National Game*, 95–96.

27. Henry Chadwick, "Old Time Baseball," *Outing*, XXXVIII (July, 1901), 420.

28. "The Championship Record," *Clipper*, September 11, 1875. For Chadwick's role among the emerging baseball reporters see Voigt, *Baseball: From Gentleman's Sport*, 91–96.

29. *Spirit of the Times*, November, 1856.

30. John Rickards Betts, "Sporting Journalism in Nineteenth-Century America," *American Quarterly*, V (Spring, 1973), 41, 43, 49, 50.

31. For an example see "Close of the Game. Game Riddled with Corruption," *Clipper*, November 6, 1875.

32. Hugh Fullerton, "The Fellows Who Made the Game," *Saturday Evening Post*, CC (April 21, 1928), 18.

33. "Perils of the Baseball Lingo," reprinted in *Literary Digest*, XLVII (September 6, 1913), 379–80.

34. "English and Baseball," *Nation*, XCVII (August 21, 1913), 161.

35. Fullerton, "The Fellows," *Saturday Evening Post*, CC (April 21, 1928), 19. Hugh Fullerton's article also provided the lead to the follow-up story about the "Cross of Gold" speech. For Peter Finley Dunne's baseball language turn to H. L. Mencken, *The American Language*, 3d ed., (New York, 1933), 404–5.

36. Mrs. Fremont Older, *William Randolph Hearst: American* (New York, 1936), 82; Betts "Sporting Journalism," 56.

37. Bill Shannon and George Kalinsky, *The Ballparks* (New York, 1975), 4–5.

38. Seymour, *Baseball: Early Years*, 48–48, 51–52.

39. *Ibid.*, 56.

40. Joseph S. Stern, Jr., "The Team That Couldn't Be Beat: The Red Stockings of 1869," *Cincinnati Historical Society Bulletin*, XXVII (Spring, 1969), 25–41; Robert Knight Barney, "Of Rails and Red Stockings: Episodes in the Expansion of the 'National Pastime' in the American West," *Journal of the West*, XVII (July, 1978), 61–70.

41. Will Irwin, "Baseball. IV. The Business Side of the Game," *Collier's*, XLIII (June 5, 1909), 11.

42. Robert B. Weaver, *Amusements and Sports in American Life* (Chicago, 1934), 102; David Quentin Voigt, "Baseball's Lost Centennial," *Journal of Popular Culture*, V (Summer, 1971), 60–64.

43. Spalding, *America's National Game*, 207.

44. Seymour, *Baseball: Early Years*, 76–85.

45. John W. Stayton, "Baseball Jurisprudence," *American Law Review*, XLIV (May–June, 1910), 374.

46. Quoted in Seymour, *Baseball: Early Years*, 80.

47. Peter A. Demens [Tverskoy], "Sketches of the North American United States," published in 1895: quoted in Oscar Handlin, comp., *This Was America* (Cambridge, Mass., 1949), 361.

48. Bruce Catton, "The Great American Game," *American Heritage*, X (April, 1959), 18.

49. Lewis Mumford, *Ethics and Civilization* (New York, 1963), 303.

40. Will Irwin, "Baseball. II. Working Out the Game," *Collier's* XLIII (May 15, 1909), 14.

51. Spalding, *America's National Game*, 6–8; David Lamoureaux, "Baseball in the Late Nineteenth Century: The Source of Its Appeal," *Journal of Popular Culture*, XI (Winter, 1977), 603–4; Walter Camp, "The American National Game: Professional and College Base-Ball in the Making," *Century Magazine*, LXXIX (April, 1910), 948.

52. Voigt, *Baseball: From Gentleman's Sport*, 184–85.

53. *Clipper*, November 27, 1884.

54. Voigt, *Baseball: From Gentleman's Sport*, 187–92.

55. In the early 1880's the title read: "New York *Clipper*. The Spirit of the Times Shall Teach Me Speed. *King John*, Act IV."

56. James L. Steele, "How the National Game Developed: Some Baseball Reminiscences," *Outing*, XLIV (June, 1904), 334.

57. William Chambers, *Things as They Are in America* (Philadelphia, 1854), 178.

58. Quoted in Irwin, "Baseball. II.," 14.

59. *Ibid.*, 15.

60. Adrian C. Anson, *A Ball Player's Career: Personal Experience and Reminiscences* (Chicago, 1900), 33.

61. "Amherst 73, Williams 32—Eighty Years Ago," *Amherst Graduates' Quarterly*, XXVIII (May, 1939), 219–25; Stern, "The Red Stockings of 1869," 37; Anson, *Ball Player's Career*, 36.

62. Robert H. Boyle, "The Unreal Ideal: Frank Merriwell," *Sport—Mirror of American Life* (Boston, 1963), 241–71.

63. Carl H. Scheele, "Baseball—A Shared Excitement," in Peter C. Marzio, ed., *A Nation of Nations: The People Who Came to America as Seen Through Objects and Documents Exhibited at the Smithsonian Institution* (New York, 1976), 461.

64. Frederic L. Paxson, "The Rise of Sport," *Mississippi Valley Historical Review*, IV (September, 1917), 152–53.

65. Charles Phelps Cushing, "The Baseball of the City Urchin: The Game Has Been Modified So That It May Be Played in the Streets of the City," *Collier's*, XLVII (June 10, 1911), 20, 30, and "Back-Lot Baseball: The Real Baseball, Where Grit Is Learned and Wits Are Sharpened, Is the Baseball of the Back Lots," *ibid.* (August 12, 1911), 21. For variations of the game see Stewart Culin, "Street Games of Boys in Brooklyn, N.Y.," *Journal of American Folklore*, IV (1891), 231–33.

66. *Frank Leslie's Illustrated Newspaper*, October 30, 1869.

67. Alice Earle, *Customs and Fashions in Old New England* (New York, 1909), 5.

69. Wilbur P. Bowen and Elmer D. Mitchell, *The Theory of Organized Play: Its Nature and Significance* (New York, 1928), 24–25.

70. Frederic C. Howe, *The Modern City and Its Problems* (New York, 1915), 317.

71. Philadelphia *Sporting Life*, February 4, 1885, quoted in Seymour, *Baseball: Early Years*, 190.

72. "Modern Baseball," *Times*, October 11, 1905.

73. "An Important Suit [J. E. Dolen *v.* Metropolitan Exhibition Company]," *Glipper*, March 26, 1887.

74. Scheele, "Baseball—A Shared Excitement," 462–77.

75. Seymour, *Baseball: Early Years*, 42. For "Negro baseball" turn to Robert Peterson, *Only the Ball Was White* (Englewood Cliffs, N.J., 1970).

76. Spalding, *America's National Game*, 6.

77. Edwin Davies Schoonmaker, "Baseball and the Theater," *Harper's Weekly*, LVIII (January 17, 1914), 31.

78. Frank Barkely Copley, *Frederick W. Taylor: Father of Scientific Management*, 2 vols. (New York, 1923), I, 56.

79. R. G. Knowles, "Baseball," in *Encyclopedia of Sport*, 2 vols. (London, 1897–98), I, 73. John J. Evers and Hugh S. Fullerton, *Touching Second: The Science of Baseball* (Chicago, 1910), 119–39, expounded the geometry of the game.

80. Clarence Deming, "Old Days in Baseball," *Outing*, XL (June, 1902), 360.

81. Samuel Clemens, "Welcome Home to a Baseball Team Returning from a World Tour by Way of the Sandwich Islands (1889)," *The Writings of Mark Twain. Definitive Edition*, 37 vols (New York, 1922–25), XVIII, 145.

82. M'Cready Sykes, "The Most Perfect Thing in America," *Everybody's Magazine*, XXV (October, 1911), 446.

83. London *Field*, quoted in Spalding, *America's National Game*, 186.

84. Clemens, "Welcome Home," 145, 149.

85. H. L. Mencken, *Happy Days, 1880–1892* (New York, 1940), 231.

86. Christy Mathewson, *Pitching in a Pinch: or Baseball from the Inside* (New York, 1912), 211; Seymour, *Baseball: Early Years*, 182–85.

87. Seymour, *Baseball: Early Years*, 345–49; Roger Angell, *The Summer Game* (New York, 1972), 4, 295.

88. Spalding, *America's National Game*, 442.

89. Fred Lieb, *The Baltimore Orioles* (New York, 1953), 20.

90. Spalding, *America's National Game*, 400–41.

91. *Frank Leslie's Illustrated Newspaper*, October 10, 1885; *Clipper*, September 11, 1975; Henry Hall, ed., *The Tribune Book of Open-Air Sports: Prepared by the New York Tribune with the Aid of Acknowledged Experts* (New York, 1887), iii.

92. Seymour, *Baseball: Early Years*, 194–95.

93. *Ibid.*, 193.

94. John H. Lancaster, "Baltimore, a Pioneer in Organized Baseball," *Maryland Historical Magazine*, XXXV (March, 1940), 32.

95. Quoted in Betts, *America's Sporting Heritage*, 118.

96. Allan Nevins, "Preface" to Voigt, *Baseball: From Gentleman's Sport*, vii.

97. Holliman, *American Sports*, 10.

98. Wilhelm Liebknecht, *Ein Blick in die neue Welt* (Stuttgart, 1887), 124–25.

99. Michael Novak, *The Joy of Sports: End Zones, Bases, Baskets, Balls, and the Consecration of the American Spirit* (New York, 1976), 62.

100. For an example of a downtown scoreboard see the full-page photo on the front page of the Sunday picture section, *Times*, October 20, 1912.

101. Seymour, *Baseball: Early Years*, 203.

102. Edward Grant Barrow, with James M. Kahn, *My Fifty Years in Baseball* (New York, 1951), 25.

103. Frederick S. Tyler, "Fifty-Five Years of Local Baseball, 1893–1947," *Records of the Columbia Historical Society of Washington, D.C.*, XLVIII–XLIX (1946–47), 269.

104. Zane Grey, " 'Old Well-Well'!," New York *Success Magazine*, XV (July, 1910), reprinted in *The Redheaded Outfield and Other Baseball Stories* (New York, 1920).

105. *Times*, April 13, 1909; *Harper's Weekly*, LIII (May 2, 1909), 389; Shannon and Kalinsky, *Ballparks*, 59, 90, 91, 180, 183, 197; Lawrence S. Ritter, *The Glory of Their Times: The Story of the Early Days of Baseball Told by the Men Who Played It* (New York, 1966), 104–5.

106. Johnnie Evers and Hugh S. Fullerton, *Baseball in the Big Leagues* (Chicago, 1910), 24.

107. Allen Guttmann, *From Ritual to Record: The Nature of Modern Sport* (New York, 1978), 115–16; Blake McKelvey, *The Urbanization of America: 1860–1915* (New Brunswick, N.J., 1965), 184–85.

108. "The Athletic Craze," *Nation*, LVII (December 7, 1893), 423.

109. Carl Diem, "Das Baseballspiel, *Olympische Flamme: Das Buch vom Sport*, 3 vols. (Berlin, 1942), II, 830.

110. "Casey at the Bat. A Ballad of the Republic, Sung in the Year 1888," San Francisco *Examiner*, June 3, 1888.

111. DeWolf Hopper, *Once a Clown, Always a Clown: Reminiscences* (Boston, 1927), 72, 76–77, 80–81; Tristram Potter Coffin, *The Old Ball Game: Baseball in Folklore and Fiction* (New York, 1971), 154–61.

V THE CITY IN POLITICS

Behind any topic involving the urbanization process, be it transportation, commercial developments, housing, or the immigrant, looms the omnipresent factors—politics, defined by Edward C. Banfield as "the management of conflict." And one unique phenomenon of urban politics from the Civil War to the Second World War was the rise and decline of that peculiar American urban institution, the city boss and the political machine.

Our heritage of big-city machines is as American as a black derby, a fat cigar, and a kind word at Mr. O'Higgins' wake. The city machine is an organization involved in politics as a business, the business of gaining political power by offering services to a number of diverse groups and inducements of power, prestige, and profit to its followers. In his heyday (a generation before World War I), the city boss could "deliver" the votes because the nature of American society permitted him to act as a broker in ethnic, economic, social, and political relations. But when significant social and political changes presented either obstacles or better services and inducements (e.g. the merit system, reforms in voting and registration methods, the rise of the labor union and the welfare state) the machine declined. Whereas the old-fashioned machine of a Richard Crocker in New York or a James Michael Curley in Boston became a thing of the past, some managed to survive by adapting to changing conditions, like the machine of Richard Daley's organization in Chicago and the city machine of Pittsburgh. Others managed to adapt but destroyed themselves through scandal, like the Pendergast machine of Kansas City.[1]

1. For an interesting account of how a city machine survived its nineteenth-century heritage and adapted to modern social change by creating new alliances, see Lyle W. Dorsett, *The Pendergast Machine* (New York: Oxford, 1968). Dorsett also disagrees with the long-accepted view that the New Deal destroyed the city machine, as does Bruce Martin Stave in his "The New Deal, the Last Hurrah, and the Building of an Urban Machine: Pittsburgh Committee Men, A Case Study," *Pennsylvania History* (October

In the first selection of this chapter, Robert Merton demonstrates how sociological insights can enrich the understanding of a historical problem. He asks: How do you account for the rise of the political machine? He answers: By responding to the political needs of a motley clutch of groups whose aspirations and frustrations were not satisfied by the existing agencies of society. Merton sees the machine as an alternative to formal government. Disciplined and centralized in itself, it was an alternative to the decentralized, dispersed, overlapping pattern of municipal authority, and, as such, despite its enormous waste and corruption, the city boss and his organization did serve to fulfill important social functions that society would not or could not satisfy. The machine, according to Merton, emerged because it responded especially to three groups: it humanized politics for the "deprived" classes, and through patronage, handouts, and personal relationships, it opened one of the few doors to advancement available to them; through alliances with legitimate and illegitimate business, it functioned to serve the interests of the respectable businessperson and the racketeer, both of whom wanted order created out of the chaos of unrestrained competition.

The second essay centers on a specific political organization, the Tweed Ring of New York, one of the most notorious city machines in American urban history. It is an analysis of a persistent theme in urban politics, the reformer versus the machine, in this case, the reform movement that sought to destroy Boss Tweed and his machine, and one that culminated in one of the most dramatic elections in New York City's history. The author attempts to show how the crusade against the Tweed Ring reflected the attitudes of the reformers toward reform, the machine, corruption, the poor, and urban political institutions, and how their resounding "victory" was actually an ironic defeat.[2]

Today it is almost a truism to say that urban problems are national prob-

---

1966). Stave, in fact, argues that for Pittsburgh, at least, the New Deal invigorated and strengthened the political machine.

With perception and skill, Zane L. Miller, *Boss Cox's Cincinnati* (New York: Oxford, 1968), correlates the processes of urbanization with the rise of bossism in Cincinnati. Another interesting and recent study of urban politics is that of Theodore J. Lowi, *At the Pleasure of the Mayor* (New York: The Free Press, 1964), who argues that the decline of the machine has not necessarily been beneficial for the city. For an excellent study of the changing twentieth-century urban machine that focuses on the emergence of "transitional bosses," a link between the old-fashioned and modern city boss, see Harvey Wheeler, "Yesterday's Robin Hood: The Rise and Fall of Baltimore's Trenton Democratic Club," *American Quarterly* (Winter 1955). See also Joel Arthur Tarr's insightful *A Study in Boss Politics: William Lorimer of Chicago* (Urbana: University of Illinois Press, 1971), Jerome Mushkat, *Tammany: The Evolution of a Political Machine* (Syracuse: Syracuse University Press, 1971), Bruce M. Stave (ed.), *Urban Bosses Machines, and Progressive Reformers* (Lexington: D. C. Heath, 1972). For the modern boss, see Mike Royko, *Boss: Richard J. Daley of Chicago* (New York: E. P. Dutton, 1971), David Halberstam, "Daley of Chicago," *Harper's Magazine* (August 1968), and Blanche Blank, "The New Style Boss," *The New Republic* (September 11, 1961). See also Eric L. McKittrick, "The Study of Corruption," *Political Science Quarterly* (December 1957).

2. For a brilliant interpretation of the "liberal" mind of the late nineteenth-century re-

lems. But many who make this point, especially journalists, politicians, and TV and radio commentators, tend to speak of the impact of the city upon national affairs as a recent phenomenon. Actually, it has a long history and there are innumerable examples in this book alone that show the direct and indirect influences that the city has had upon the national arena, socially, economically, and technologically. Probably the best example is the Progressive Era.

The Progressive Era provoked the first *national* reform movement that reflected the transition of an agrarian nation into an urban-industrialized giant. Of course the Populist movement of the 1890s was also a part of this transition, but its appeal was limited largely to the rural South and parts of the West and Midwest. The Progressive crusade, more than the Populist movement, was relevant to all geographic sections and all social classes, and it provoked a sharper response to the urban, industrial, and technological realities of the late nineteenth and early twentieth centuries. For some reformers it meant the redemption of democracy, for others an opportunity to resurrect an older and more virtuous America, and for still others the chance to transform innovations in business and technology into political action.

The seedtime of Progressivism was the 1890s; its heyday, the decade before the First World War; its impulse, an urban response to a new age. Although today most historians agree that the Progressive movement was largely an urban phenomenon, there is considerable disagreement about its meaning, leadership, goals, and success that his stirred up a flurry of paradoxes.[3] For the movement has been seen as liberal and conservative, a triumph and a flop, led by either the working class, the middle class, or the upper class, or a combination of politicians reflecting all classes, who either looked to the future or to the past. This debate, whose fury seems to be increasing, suggests that the Progressive movement has become a battleground for historians to argue the success or failure of the liberal tradition in the United States.

Samuel P. Hays is a good example of one who is leading a flank attack against the bastions of Progressive interpretation. An article published in 1964[4] was both a major interpretation of Progressivism and an opportunity to review other interpretations. Hays's target was a group of revisionist historians, primarily Richard Hofstadter, who sought to revise the interpretation of the Progressive historians who saw the movement as a continuation of Jeffersonian reform—a class struggle of "the people" battling acquisitive businesspersons, seeking the democratization of political institutions, fighting for an equalitarian society open to all with special privilege to none. Hof-

former, see John G. Sprout, *"The Best Men": Liberal Reformers in the Gilded Age* (New York: Oxford, 1968).

3. For an excellent bibliographical essay on the Progressive Era, see Robert Wiebe, *The Search for Order* (New York: Hill and Wang, 1967), pp. 303–24.

4. "The Politics of Reform in Municipal Government in the Progressive Era," *Pacific Northwest Quarterly* (October 1964), pp. 157–69.

stadter in his *Age of Reform* (1955) held that the movement was actually led by reasonably affluent members of the middle class who were tormented with "status anxieties" and inspired by the values of the Protestant ethic, and who sought to turn back to an older America hardly in tune with the realities of a modern urban age. Revisionism has an occupational hazard in that it often invites the criticism that can convert the victor into the victim. Hence, Hays attacks Hofstadter and the proponents of the "status revolution" theory to argue that Progressivism was in fact led by an upper-class group who, rather than alienated by society, were experts in the techniques of business management and the newer technological procedures, and who sought to introduce them into city government.[5] Hays argues that there was a striking difference between what Progressives said and what they did. They spoke as champions of the equalitarian society, enemies of special privilege, and friends of the poor. In practice, however, they destroyed a broad form of representative government, were agents of a special privileged group, and were profoundly distrustful of the lower and middle classes. These judgments come from Hays's study of the two major reforms of municipal government coming out of the Progressive period: the commission system and the city-manager plan, reforms that were in fact elitist in nature with definite anti-democratic overtones. While some historians who favor a more plural approach to Progressivism might argue there was more to the movement than this, Professor Hays does show that reform does not always advance "progressive" and "liberal" objectives. The voice of the people can also be the voice of elitism. In the next selection, Melvin G. Holli, one of the growing army of historians who have probed the motives of the liberal reformers,[6] expands some of Hays's ideas, incorporates some of his own, and broadens the panoply of reformers to include another important variety. It is an artful accomplishment in generalization.

5. For an opposing view that stresses the importance of the working class, see J. Joseph Hutchmacher, "Urban Liberalism and the Age of Reform," *Mississippi Valley Historical Review* (September 1962). See James Weinstein, *The Corporate Ideal in the Liberal State, 1900–1918* (Boston: Beacon Press, 1968), especially chapter 4, as well as the indictments of Lawrence J. R. Herson, "The Lost World of Municipal Government," *American Political Science Review* (June 1957).

6. For those historians who have made a searching and often critical analysis of the liberal reformer on various governmental levels before the Progressive period, see Geoffry Blodgett, *The Gentle Reformers: Massachusetts Democrats in the Cleveland Era* (Cambridge: Harvard University Press, 1966), Alexander B. Callow, Jr., *The Tweed Ring* (New York: Oxford University Press, 1966), Vincent P. De Santis, *Republicans Face the Southern Question: The Departure Years, 1877–1897* (Baltimore: The Johns Hopkins University Press, 1959), Ari Hoogenboom, *Outlawing the Spoils: A History of the Civil Service Reform Movement, 1865–1883* (Urbana: University of Illinois Press, 1961), James H. McPherson, *The Struggle for Equality: Abolitionists and the Negro in the Civil War and Reconstruction* (Princeton: Princeton University Press, 1964), David Montgomery, *Beyond Equality: Labor and the Radical Republicans* (New York: Knopf, 1967), Robert P. Sharkey, *Money, Class, and Party: An Economic Study of the Civil War and Reconstruction* (Baltimore: The Johns Hopkins University Press, 1959), Jack Sproat, *"The Best Men": Liberal Reformers in the Gilded Age* (New York: Oxford University

Holli examines two broad groups of reformers who differed profoundly on two of the most fundamental questions in politics: what is the proper role of government and whose interests shall it serve? The first group, by far the most numerous, he calls structural reformers, people like Grover Cleveland of Buffalo, Seth Low and John Purroy Mitchel, the "oddly puritanical Catholic," or New York, San Francisco's reform mayor, James D. Phelan, and the prototype of structural reformers, William F. Havemeyer of New York. With the battle cry of efficiency, economy, responsibility, and clean government, the structural reformers sought to return to office the "respectabilities"—the middle and patrician class—who would transform municipal government into a tight, efficient businesslike operation. It was government by businesspeople serving the interests of the business community. Reform was considered in structural terms: tinkering with city charters, hacking budgets to the bone, drastically reducing municipal services. Unless forced by scandal, little was done to interfere with vested interests. Outrageous franchise contracts, bloated gas and light rates, and services for the working and lower class all were ignored, but special tax advantages were pursued with an almost breathless zeal. Mayor Phelan, for example, suspended vital health services, allowed police to protect strikebreakers, and created such a low tax rate that the city withheld teacher's salaries. John Purroy Mitchel attacked economy with the "ledger book ethics of the corporation accountant." Clean government meant moral sanitation as well. The evils of the city were defined as the vices of the working class—drinking, gambling, and prostitution. The saloon was viewed with more moral indignation than the absence of good parks and schools.

Unlike the structural reformers, the social reformers, like "Golden Rule" Jones, Brand Whitlock, Tom Johnson, Mark Fagan, Newton D. Baker, and the prototype of the group, Hazen S. Pingree of Detroit (1890–97), felt that the business of government was not business but people. Humane and pragmatic, they dismissed legislation regulating morals as something akin to building a howitzer to kill a mouse. They felt this tactic affected only symptoms, not causes; it diverted public attention away from the real sources of corruption. As Brand Whitlock, the social reform mayor of Toledo, wrote: "The good people are always insisting upon 'moral issues,' urging us to turn aside from our large immediate purpose, and concentrate our official attention on the 'bad' people—and wreck our movement." The social reformers' immediate purpose was two-pronged. To eliminate graft, they attacked the special privileges of groups that sponsored many of the structural reformers,

Press, 1968), Irwin Unger, *The Greenback Era: A Social and Political History of American Finance* (Princeton: Princeton University Press, 1964), and Kermit Vanderbilt, *Charles Eliot Norton* (Cambridge: Belknap Press, 1959).

For a recent assessment of the Progressive reformers, see Otis A. Pease, "Urban Reformers in the Progressive Era: A Reassessment," *Pacific Northwest Quarterly*, Vol. 62 (April 1971).

such as the real estate interests, the utilities firms, the public service corporations. To redress the balance, they attempted to regulate franchises, gas,
water, and street railway rates, and equalize the tax rate. The social reformers also sought to improve the quality of urban life by promoting public
baths, schools, parks, and public welfare programs.

By the third decade of the twentieth century, it was evident that the
champions of efficiency had triumphed over the social reformers. The structural reform movement was at once radical, since it drastically changed
the government of the majority of our cities, and at the same time conservative, since it was based on the values of the business community. The structural reform movement, as they say, put it all together and reached its peak
in the city-commissioner and city-manager movements. It smacked of a
thermidor revolution. The reaction against nineteenth-century bossism made
the pendulum swing violently to the other extreme: bureaucratic elites
replaced the boss, administrative experts replaced the ward leader, "taking
politics out of politics" removed the management of conflict, and respect for
public opinion fell to a profound distrust of popular democracy. Reform government—good, clean, and decent—had won the battle, but at what price?

If Boss Tweed was an American original, a real-life figure whose craggy
hulk looked like something God hacked out with a dull axe, a man who in
the American imagination stood as the epitome of graft, the common cold of
urban politics, Frank Skeffington was not. He was a figure of the imagination
of Edwin O'Connor from whose novel, *The Last Hurrah*, the next selection
is taken. This book narrowly missed winning a Pulitzer Prize in 1956, and for
many it raises this question: is there really a better novel on urban politics in
American literature?

Frank Skeffington, however, was modeled after an historical personage,
indeed, the boss of Boston, James Michael Curley "Hisself," a charming man
of easy conscience—"I'd do it again!" (When a "natural" enemy, a Boston
Brahmin called him a thief, Curley replied, "The term 'codfish aristocracy'
is a reflection on the fish.") Like Curley, Frank Skeffington is a virtuoso in
dealing with his Irish constituency. In this selection, O'Connor examines one
specific and seemingly trivial event, Knocko Minihan's wake. Why, he asks,
all the boisterous conviviality at such a solemn occasion as a funeral? Why
wasn't the family of the deceased humiliated by all the political chatter?
Why did so many people appear when no one really liked Knocko Minihan,
a dull and sour fellow? The answer to these questions exhibits the master's
touch of Skeffington and his bond with the Boston immigrant. It also demonstrates, I think, how historical fiction can sometimes give insights and a different kind of dimension to history not seen in "straight" historical writing.

In November, 1974, a new historical publication, *Journal of Urban History*,
began its first issue with Samuel P. Hays's "The Changing Political Structure
of the City in Industrial America," the last selection in this chapter. It was an

auspicious beginning. Within the demanding restraints of the essay form, Hays measures the changing shape of the body politic in the American city from the early nineteenth century to the decade of the 1970s. To be able to interpret the ebb and flow of political, economic, social, and technological change over a period of several generations requires the gifts of a master synthesizer. It is a superb performance.

Hays argues that our vision of the city has been limited, if not distorted, by our persistence in seeing the city development in a "reform" context. Fundamentally, this is a rejection of the city; it describes the city with un-fulfilled aspirations and evaluates it in terms of what the city should be, not the way it is. We must "consider the city in its own right. . . . We must develop an approach which accepts the city as it is." Hays employs a con-ceptual framework broader in scope and less loaded with value judgments, where "urban development is considered a constant tension between forces making for decentralization and forces making for centralization in human relationships and institutions, between centrifugal and centripetal tendencies, between social differentiation and social integration."

Before industrialization, cities were "pedestrian communities," where one could easily walk from home to work or to church or the store. They were mixed communities, both physically and socially. The factory owner often lived next to his factory, across the street might be a merchant, and down a back alley, in sight of the factory, a laborer's family. Politics was dominated by the business and professional elite—bankers, merchants, lawyers.

If mixture was the theme of the pedestrian city, decentralization was the theme for the last half of the nineteenth century. Driven by the forces of industrialization, immigration and migration, and that great urban seam-buster, the trolley, the city expanded outward. Social mobility translated into geographical expansion, from downtown to suburbia. Mixed neighborhoods gave way to distinctive subcommunities, reflecting class, ethnicity, and na-tionality. Consumer-oriented enterprises flourished. Social and economic de-centralization created political decentralization, represented by the ward system and, in many cities, the city boss and his machine. The business of politics became largely concerned with building the city, from construction and streets to transportation and real estate. The old political elite of the "best men" gave way to the rise of the "middling sort," a small merchant, a real estate promoter and contractor, a skilled craftsman, a saloonkeeper, and from the ranks of the working class, a laborer.

After roughly 1900, Professor Hays charts a change in the swing of the pendulum from decentralization to integration, or centralization, especially in the city's changing downtown area. Buttressed by the technologies of structural steel, the telephone, and the elevator, a number of integrating factors centralized the central city: public office buildings, new locations for corporate management, banks, and large-scale retail enterprises. Traditional professions—doctors, lawyers, engineers, architects—and the emergence of the "empirical professions," such as health and education, all widened their horizons, cut across neighborhood boundaries, embraced and thereby integrated a citywide clientele.

A critically important integrating factor was the reemergence of the affluent into urban politics. Decentralist in residence, but centralist in economic and occupational affairs, the well-to-do, especially upper-class women, became involved in a wide variety of social welfare programs, epitomized by the settlement house movement. Supported by "good" government institutions, chamber of commerces, communication technologies, new administrative strategies, and the impact of corporate management and the professional expert "a virtual revolution" occurred highlighted by the centralization of decision-making methods in urban affairs. The casualties of change were middle- and lower-class leadership, the ward system, and much of the autonomy of the local community.

By 1929, integrative tendencies had wound down to be replaced by a tension, indeed by a tug-of-war between decentralizing and centralizing factors, that both squeezed the city inward as well as expanded it outward; and a new phase of development shaped the city for the next four decades. The automobile, the telephone, a variety of suburbias, and the relocation of various business enterprises generated expansion and decentralization. On the other hand, the continual tug toward centralization was generated by the rise of special interest groups, organized in terms of occupation, trade associations, trade unions, professional organizations, or other organizations based on ethnicity or religion. They were free from the traditional checks that might be imposed by a mayor or city council. There were not only fewer actors in the decision-making process, but decisions were made more in accordance with professional experts than from the give-and-take of open political debate. Very important, a point that Hays underscores heavily, is that decisions were made by the elite of each specialized group. For example, top union officials, with managerial skills, and not the skilled or unskilled worker, now represented the working class; blacks who served on city councils were professionals or businesspeople from the elite of the black community. The decline of community politics was complete. "Functional group politics created a new context of active urban political life limited to the upper levels of the political order, and a new balance of urban forces in which centrifugal tendencies came to be the functional groups at that level."

Professor Hays resists making value judgments about functional group politics, yet his argument does raise certain questions. Is it "good" or "bad" or a little of both? Does it reflect the realities of a modern urban world and make for a politic that is more efficient and responsive to the problems of city dwellers? Or does it bend, distort, or perhaps jeopardize the democratic process?

Latent Functions of the Machine

ROBERT K. MERTON

. . . [I]n large sectors of the American population, the political machine or the "political racket" are judged as unequivocally "bad" and "undesirable." The grounds for such moral judgment vary somewhat, but they consist substantially in pointing out that political machines violate moral codes: political patronage violates the code of selecting personnel on the basis of impersonal qualifications rather than on grounds of party loyalty or contributions to the party war-chest; bossism violates the code that votes should be based on individual appraisal of the qualifications of candidates and of political issues, and not on abiding loyalty to a feudal leader; bribery, and "honest graft" obviously offend the proprieties of property; "protection" for crime clearly violates the law and the mores; and so on.

In view of the manifold respects in which political machines, in varying degrees, run counter to the mores and at times to the law, it becomes pertinent to inquire how they manage to continue in operation. The familiar "explanations" for the continuance of the political machine are not here in point. To be sure, it may well be that if "respectable citizenry" would live up to their political obligations, if the electorate were to be alert and enlightened; if the number of elective officers were substantially reduced from the dozens, even hundreds, which the average voter is now expected to appraise in the course of town, county, state and national elections; if the electorate were activated by the "wealthy and educated classes without whose participation," as the not-always democratically oriented Bryce put it, "the best-framed government must speedily degenerate";—if these and a plethora of similar changes in political structure were introduced, perhaps the "evils" of the political machine would indeed be exorcized.[1] But it should be noted that these changes are often not introduced, that political machines have had the phoenix-like quality of arising strong and unspoiled from their ashes, that, in short, this structure has exhibited a notable vitality in many areas of American political life.

Proceeding from the functional view, therefore, that we should *ordinarily* (not invariably) expect persistent social patterns and social structures to perform positive functions *which are at the time not adequately fulfilled by other existing patterns and structures*, the thought occurs that perhaps this publicly maligned organization is, *under present conditions*, satisfying basic latent functions.[2] A brief examination of current

From *Social Theory and Social Structure*, revised and enlarged edition by Robert K. Merton, pp. 71–82. Copyright © 1949, 1957 by The Free Press, a corporation. Reprinted by permission of Macmillan Publishing, Inc.

analyses of this type of structure may also serve to illustrate additional problems of functional analysis.

SOME FUNCTIONS OF THE POLITICAL MACHINE

Without presuming to enter into the variations of detail marking different political machines—a Tweed, Vare, Crump, Flynn, Hague are by no means identical types of bosses—we can briefly examine the functions more or less common to the political machine, as a generic type of social organization. We neither attempt to itemize all the diverse functions of the political machine nor imply that all these functions are similarly fulfilled by each and every machine.

The key structural function of the Boss is to organize, centralize and maintain in good working condition "the scattered fragments of power" which are at present dispersed through our political organization. By this centralized organization of political power, the boss and his apparatus can satisfy the needs of diverse subgroups in the larger community which are not adequately satisfied by legally devised and culturally approved social structures.

To understand the role of bossism and the machine, therefore, we must look at two types of sociological variables: (1) the *structural context* which makes it difficult, if not impossible, for morally approved structures to fulfill essential social functions, thus leaving the door open for political machines (or their structural equivalents) to fulfill these functions and (2) the subgroups whose distinctive needs are left unsatisfied, except for the latent functions which the machine in fact fulfills.[3]

Structural Context: The constitutional framework of American political organization specifically precludes the legal possibility of highly centralized power and, it has been noted, thus "discourages the growth of effective and responsible leadership. The framers of the Constitution, as Woodrow Wilson observed, set up the check and balance system 'to keep government at a sort of mechanical equipoise by means of a standing amicable contest among its several organic parts.' They distrusted power as dangerous to liberty: and therefore they spread it thin and erected barriers against its concentration." This dispersion of power is found not only at the national level but in local areas as well. "As a consequence," Sait goes on to observe, "when *the people or particular groups* among them demanded positive action, no one had adequate authority to act. The machine provided an antidote."[4]

The constitutional dispersion of power not only makes for difficulty of effective decision and action but when action does occur it is defined and hemmed in by legalistic considerations. In consequence, there developed "a much *more human system* of partisan government, whose chief object soon became the circumvention of government by law. . . . The lawlessness of the extra-official democracy was merely the counterpoise of the legalism of the official democracy. The lawyer having been permitted to subordinate democracy to the Law, the Boss had to be called in to extricate the victim, which he did after a fashion and for a consideration."[5]

Officially, political power is dispersed. Various well-known expedients were devised for this manifest objective. Not only was there the familiar separation of powers among the several branches of the government but, in some measure, tenure in each office was limited, rotation in office approved. And the scope of power inherent in each office was severely circumscribed. Yet, observes Sait in rigorously functional terms, "Leadership is necessary; and *since* it does not develop readily within the constitutional framework, the Boss provides it in a crude and irresponsible form from the outside."[6]

Put in more generalized terms, *the functional deficiencies of the official structure generate an alternative (unofficial) structure to fulfill existing needs somewhat more effectively.* Whatever its specific historical origins, the political machine persists as an apparatus for satisfying otherwise unfulfilled needs of diverse groups in the population. By turning to a few of these subgroups and their characteristic needs, we shall be led at once to a range of latent functions of the political machine.

Functions of the Political Machine for Diverse Subgroups. It is well known that one source of strength of the political machine derives from its roots in the local community and the neighborhood. The political machine does not regard the electorate as an amorphous, undifferentiated mass of voters. With a keen sociological intuition, the machine recognizes that the voter is a person living in a specific neighborhood, with specific personal problems and personal wants. Public issues are abstract and remote; private problems are extremely concrete and immediate. It is not through the generalized appeal to large public concerns that the machine operates, but through the direct, quasi-feudal relationships between local representatives of the machine and voters in their neighborhood. Elections are won in the precinct.

The machine welds its links with ordinary men and women by elaborate networks of personal relations. Politics is transformed into personal ties. The precinct captain "must be a friend to every man, assuming if he does not feel sympathy with the unfortunate, and utilizing in his good works the resources which the boss puts at his disposal."[7] The precinct captain is forever a friend in need. In our prevailingly impersonal society, the machine, through its local agents, fulfills the important social *function of humanizing and personalizing all manner of assistance* to those in need. Foodbaskets and jobs, legal and extra-legal advice, setting to rights minor scrapes with the law, helping the bright poor boy to a political scholarship in a local college, looking after the bereaved —the whole range of crises when a feller needs a friend, and, above all, a friend who knows the score and who can do something about it,—all these find the ever-helpful precinct captain available in the pinch.

To assess this function of the political machine adequately, it is important to note not only that aid *is* provided but *the manner in which it is provided.* After all, other agencies do exist for dispensing such assistance. Welfare agencies, settlement houses, legal aid clinics, medical aid in free hospitals, public relief departments, immigration authorities—these and a multitude of other organizations are available to provide the most varied types of assistance. But in contrast to the professional techniques of the welfare worker which may typically represent in the mind of the recipient the cold, bureaucratic dispensa-

tion of limited aid following upon detailed investigation of *legal* claims to aid
of the "client" are the unprofessional
techniques of the precinct captain who
asks no questions, exacts no compliance
with legal rules of eligibility and does
not "snoop" into private affairs.[8]

For many, the loss of "self-respect" is
too high a price for legalized assistance.
In contrast to the gulf between the settlement house workers who so often
come from a different social class, educational background and ethnic group,
the precinct worker is "just one of us,"
who understands what it's all about.
The condescending lady bountiful can
hardly compete with the understanding
friend in need. In *this struggle between
alternative structures for fulfilling the
nominally same function* of providing
aid and support to those who need it, it
is clearly the machine politician who is
better integrated with the groups which
he serves than the impersonal, professionalized, socially distant and legally
constrained welfare worker. And since
the politician can at times influence and
manipulate the official organizations for
the dispensation of assistance, whereas
the welfare worker has practically no
influence on the political machine, this
only adds to his greater effectiveness.
More colloquially and also, perhaps,
more incisively, it was the Boston ward-
leader, Martin Lomasny, who described
this essential function to the curious
Lincoln Steffens: "I think," said Lomasny, "that there's got to be in every
ward somebody that any bloke can
come to—no matter what he's done—and
get help. *Help, you understand; none
of your law and justice, but help.*"[9]

The "deprived classes," then, constitute one subgroup for whom the political machine satisfies wants not adequately satisfied in the same fashion by
the legitimate social structure.

For a second subgroup, that of business (primarily "big" business but also
"small"), the political boss serves the
function of providing those political
privileges which entail immediate economic gains. Business corporations,
among which the public utilities (railroads, local transportation and electric
light companies, communications corporations) are simply the most conspicuous in this regard, seek special political
dispensations which will enable them to
stabilize their situation and to near their
objective of maximizing profits. Interestingly enough, corporations often want
to avoid a chaos of uncontrolled competition. They want the greater security of
an economic czar who controls, regu-
lates and organizes competition, providing that this czar is not a public official
with his decisions subject to public
scrutiny and public control. (The latter
would be "government control," and
hence taboo.) The political boss fulfills
these requirements admirably.

Examined for a moment apart from
any moral considerations, the political
apparatus operated by the Boss is effectively designed to perform these functions with a minimum of inefficiency.
Holding the strings of diverse governmental divisions, bureaus and agencies
in his competent hands, the Boss ration-
alizes the relations between public and
private business. He serves as the business community's ambassador in the
otherwise alien (and sometimes un-
friendly) realm of government. And, in
strict business-like terms, he is well-paid
for his economic services to his respectable business clients. In an article entitled, "An Apology to Graft," Lincoln
Steffens suggested that "Our economic

system, which held up riches, power and acclaim as prizes to men bold enough and able enough to buy corruptly timber, mines, oil fields and franchises and 'get away with it,' was at fault."[10] And, in a conference with a hundred or so of Los Angeles business leaders, he described a fact well known to all of them: the Boss and his machine were an *integral part* of the organization of the economy. "You cannot build or operate a railroad, or a street railway, gas, water, or power company, develop and operate a mine, or get forests and cut timber on a large scale, or run any privileged business, without corrupting or joining in the corruption of the government. You tell me privately that you must, and here I am telling you semi-publicly that you must. And that is so all over the country. And that means that we have an organization of society in which, *for some reason*, you and your kind, the ablest, most intelligent, most imaginative, daring, and resourceful leaders of society, are and must be against society and its laws and its all-around growth."[11]

Since the demand for the services of special privileges are built into the structure of the society, the Boss fulfills diverse functions for this second subgroup of business-seeking-privilege. These "needs" of business, as presently constituted, are not adequately provided for by conventional and culturally approved social structures; consequently, the extra-legal but more-or-less efficient organization of the political machine comes to provide these services. To adopt an *exclusively* moral attitude toward the "corrupt political machine" is to lose sight of the very structural conditions which generate the "evil" that is so bitterly attacked. To adopt a func-

tional outlook is to provide not an apologia for the political machine but a more solid basis for modifying or eliminating the machine, *providing* specific structural arrangements are introduced either for eliminating these effective demands of the business community or, if that is the objective, of satisfying these demands through alternative means.

A third set of distinctive functions fulfilled by the political machine for a special subgroup is that of providing alternative channels of social mobility for those otherwise excluded from the more conventional avenues for personal "advancement." Both the sources of this special "need" (for social mobility) and the respect in which the political machine comes to help satisfy this need can be understood by examining the structure of the larger culture and society. As is well known, the American culture lays enormous emphasis on money and power as a "success" goal legitimate for all members of the society. By no means alone in our inventory of cultural goals, it still remains among the most heavily endowed with positive affect and value. However, certain subgroups and certain ecological areas are notable for the relative absence of opportunity for achieving these (monetary and power) types of success. They constitute, in short, sub-populations where "the cultural emphasis upon pecuniary success has been absorbed, but where there is *little access to conventional and legitimate* means for attaining such success. The conventional occupational opportunities of persons in (such areas) are almost completely limited to manual labor. Given our cultural stigmatization of manual labor,[12] and its correlate, the prestige of white-collar work, it is clear that the result is a tendency to achieve these culturally approved objectives *through whatever means are possible*. These people are on the one hand, "asked to orient their conduct toward the prospect of accumulating wealth [and power] and, on the other, they are largely denied effective opportunities to do so institutionally."

It is within the context of social structure that the political machine fulfills the basic function of providing avenues of social mobility for the otherwise disadvantaged. Within this context, even the corrupt political machine and the racket "represent the triumph of amoral intelligence over morally prescribed 'failure' when the channels of vertical mobility are closed or narrowed *in a society which places a high premium on economic affluence, [power] and social ascent for all its members*."[13] As one sociologist has noted on the basis of several years of close observation in a slum area:

> The sociologist who dismisses racket and political organizations as deviations from desirable standards thereby neglects some of the major elements of slum life. . . . *He does not discover the functions they perform for the members* [of the groupings in the slum]. The Irish and later immigrant peoples have had the greatest difficulty in finding places for themselves in our urban social and economic structure. Does anyone believe that the immigrants and their children could have achieved their present degree of social mobility without gaining control of the political organization of some of our largest cities? The same is true of the racket organization. *Politics and the rackets have furnished an important means of social mobility for individuals, who, because of ethnic background and low class position*, are blocked from advancement in the "respectable" channels.[14]

This, then, represents a third type of function performed for a distinctive subgroup. This function, it may be noted in passing, is fulfilled by the *sheer* existence and operation of the political machine, for it is in the machine itself that these individuals and subgroups find their culturally induced needs more or less satisfied. It refers to the services which the political apparatus provides for its own personnel. But seen in the wider social context we have set forth, it no longer appears as *merely* a means of self-aggrandizement for profit-hungry and power-hungry *individuals,* but as an organized provision for *subgroups* otherwise excluded from or handicapped in the race for "getting ahead."

Just as the political machine performs services for "legitimate" business, so it operates to perform not dissimilar services for "illegitimate" business: vice, crime and rackets. Once again, the basic sociological role of the machine in this respect can be more fully appreciated only if one temporarily abandons attitudes of moral indignation, to examine in all moral innocence the actual workings of the organization. In this light, it at once appears that the subgroup of the professional criminal, racketeer or gambler has basic similarities of organization, demands and operation to the subgroup of the industrialist, man of business or speculator. If there is a Lumber King or an Oil King, there is also a Vice King or a Racket King. If expansive legitimate business organizes administrative and financial syndicates to "rationalize" and to "integrate" diverse areas of production and business enterprise, so expansive rackets and crime organize syndicates to bring order to the otherwise chaotic areas of production of illicit goods and services. If legitimate business regards the proliferation of small business enterprises as wasteful and inefficient, substituting, for example, the giant chain stores for hundreds of corner groceries, so illegitimate business adopts the same businesslike attitude and syndicates crime and vice.

Finally, and in many respects, most important, is the basic similarity, if not near-identity, of the economic role of "legitimate" business and of "illegitimate" business. *Both are in some degree concerned with the provision of goods and services for which there is an economic demand.* Morals aside, they are both business, industrial and professional enterprises, dispensing goods and services which some people want, for which there is a market in which goods and services are transformed into commodities. And, in a prevalently market society, we should expect appropriate enterprises to arise whenever there is a market demand for certain goods or services.

As is well known, vice, crime and the rackets *are* "big business." Consider only that there have been estimated to be about 500,000 professional prostitutes in the United States of 1950, and compare this with the approximately 200,000 physicians and 350,000 professional registered nurses. It is difficult to estimate which have the larger clientele: the professional men and women of medicine or the professional men and women of vice. It is, of course, difficult to estimate the economic assets, income, profits and dividends of illicit gambling in this country and to compare it with the economic assets, income, profits and dividends of, say, the shoe industry, but it is altogether possible that the two industries are about on a par. No precise figures exist on the annual expenditures on illicit narcotics, and it is probable that these are less than the expenditures on candy, but it is also probable that

they are larger than the expenditure on books.

It takes but a moment's thought to recognize that, *in strictly economic terms,* there is no relevant difference between the provision of licit and of illicit goods and services. The liquor traffic illustrates this perfectly. It would be peculiar to argue that prior to 1920 (when the 18th amendment became effective), the provision of liquor constituted an economic service, that from 1920 to 1933, its production and sale no longer constituted an economic service dispensed in a market, and that from 1934 to the present, it once again took on a serviceable aspect. Or, it would be *economically* (not morally) absurd to suggest that the sale of bootlegged liquor in the dry state of Kansas is less a response to a market demand than the sale of publicly manufactured liquor in the neighboring wet state of Missouri. Examples of this sort can of course be multiplied many times over. Can it be held that in European countries, with registered and legalized prostitution, the prostitute contributes an economic service, whereas in this country, lacking legal sanction, the prostitute provides no such service? Or that the professional abortionist is in the economic market where he is legally taboo? Or that gambling satisfies a specific demand for entertainment in Nevada, where it constitutes the largest business enterprise of the larger cities in the state, but that it differs essentially in this respect from motion pictures in the neighboring state of California?[15]

The failure to recognize that these businesses are only *morally* and not *economically* distinguishable from "legitimate" businesses has led to badly scrambled analysis. Once the economic identity of the two is recognized, we may anticipate that if the political machine performs functions for "legitimate big business" it will be all the more likely to perform not dissimilar functions for "illegitimate big business." And, of course, such is often the case.

The distinctive function of the political machine for their criminal, vice and racket clientele is to enable them to operate in satisfying the economic demands of a large market without due interference from the government. Just as big business may contribute funds to the political party war-chest to ensure a minimum of governmental interference, so with big rackets and big crime. In both instances, the political machine can, in varying degrees, provide "protection." In both instances, many features of the structural context are identical: (1) market demands for goods and services; (2) the operators' concern with maximizing gains from their enterprises; (3) the need for partial control of government which might otherwise interfere with these activities of businessmen; (4) the need for an efficient, powerful and centralized agency to provide an effective liaison of "business" with government.

Without assuming that the foregoing pages exhaust either the range of functions or the range of subgroups served by the political machine, we can at least see that *it presently fulfills some functions for these diverse subgroups which are not adequately fulfilled by culturally approved or more conventional structures.*

Several additional implications of the functional analysis of the political machine can be mentioned here only in passing, although they obviously require to be developed at length. First, the foregoing analysis has direct implications for *social engineering.* It helps explain why the periodic efforts at "political reform," "turning the rascals out" and "cleaning political house" are typically (though not necessarily) short-lived and ineffectual. It exemplifies a basic theorem: *any attempt to eliminate an existing social structure without providing adequate alternative structures for fulfilling the functions previously fulfilled by the abolished organization is doomed to failure.* (Needless to say, this theorem has much wider bearing than the one instance of the political machine.) When "political reform" confines itself to the manifest task of "turning the rascals out," it is engaging in little more than sociological magic. The reform may for a time bring new figures into the political limelight; it may serve the casual social function of re-assuring the electorate that the moral virtues remain intact and will ultimately triumph; it may actually effect a turnover in the personnel of the political machine; it may even, for a time, so curb the activities of the machine as to leave unsatisfied the many needs it has previously fulfilled. But, inevitably, unless the reform also involves a "re-forming" of the social and political structure such that the existing needs are satisfied by alternative structures or unless it involves a change which eliminates these needs altogether, the political machine will return to its integral place in the social scheme of things. *To seek social change, without due recognition of the manifest and latent functions performed by the social organization undergoing change, is to indulge in social ritual rather than social engineering.* The concepts of manifest and latent functions (or their equivalents) are indispensable elements in the theoretic repertoire of the social engineer. In this crucial sense, these concepts are not "merely" theoretical (in the abusive sense of the term), but are eminently practical. In the deliberate enactment of social change, they can be ignored only at the price of considerably heightening the risk of failure.

A second implication of this analysis of the political machine also has a bearing upon areas wider than the one we have considered. The paradox has often been noted that the supporters of the political machine include both the "respectable" business class elements who are, of course, opposed to the criminal or racketeer and the distinctly "unrespectable" elements of the underworld. And, at first appearance, this is cited as an instance of very strange bedfellows. The learned judge is not infrequently called upon to sentence the very racketeer beside whom he sat the night before at an informal dinner of the political bigwigs. The district attorney jostles the exonerated convict on his way to the back room where the Boss has called a meeting. The big business man may complain almost as bitterly as the big racketeer about the "extortionate" contributions to the party fund demanded by the Boss. Social opposites meet—in the smoke-filled room of the successful politician.

In the light of a functional analysis all this of course no longer seems paradoxical. Since the machine serves both the businessman and the criminal man, the two seemingly antipodal groups intersect. This points to a more general theorem: *the social functions of an organization help determine the structure (including the recruitment of personnel involved in the structure), just as the structure helps determine the effectiveness with which the functions are fulfilled.* In terms of social status, the business group and the criminal group are indeed poles apart. But status does not fully determine behavior and the interrelations between groups. Functions modify these relations. Given their distinctive needs, the several subgroups in the large society are "integrated," whatever their personal desires or intentions, by the centralizing structure which serves these several needs. In a phrase with many implications which require further study, *structure affects function and function affects structure.* . . .

NOTES

1. These "explanations" are "causal" in design. They profess to indicate the social conditions under which political machines come into being. In so far as they are empirically confirmed, these explanations of course add to our knowledge concerning the problem: how is it that political machines operate in certain areas and not in others? How do they manage to continue? *But these causal accounts are not sufficient.* The functional consequences of the machine, as we shall see, go far toward supplementing the causal interpretation.
2. I trust it is superfluous to add that this hypothesis is not "in support of the political machine." The question whether the dysfunctions of the machine outweigh its functions, the question whether alternative structures are not available which may fulfill its functions without necessarily entailing its social dysfunctions, still remain to be considered at an appropriate point. We are here concerned with documenting the statement that moral judgments based *entirely* on an appraisal of manifest functions of a social structure are "unrealistic" in the strict sense, *i.e.,* they do not take into account other actual consequences of that structure, consequences which may provide basic social support for the structure. As will be indicated later, "social reforms" or "social engineering" which ignore latent functions do so on pain of suffering acute disappointments and boomerang effects.
3. Again, as with preceding cases, we shall not consider the possible dysfunctions of the political machine.

4. Edward M. Sait, "Machine, Political," *Encyclopedia of the Social Sciences,* IX, 658 b [italics supplied]; *cf.* A. F. Bentley, *The Process of Government* (Chicago, 1908), Chap. 2.

5. Herbert Croly, *Progressive Democracy,* (New York, 1914), p. 254, cited by Sait, *op. cit.,* 658 b.

6. Sait, *op. cit.,* 659 a. [italics supplied].

7. *Ibid.,* 659 a.

8. Much the same contrast with official welfare policy is found in Harry Hopkins' open-handed and non-political distribution of unemployment relief in New York State under the governorship of Franklin Delano Roosevelt. As Sherwood reports: "Hopkins was harshly criticized for these irregular activities by the established welfare agencies, which claimed it was 'unprofessional conduct' to hand out work tickets without thorough investigation of each applicant, his own or his family's financial resources and probably his religious affiliations. 'Harry told the agency to go to hell,' said [Hopkins' associate, Dr. Jacob A.] Goldberg." Robert E. Sherwood, *Roosevelt and Hopkins, An Intimate History,* (New York: Harper, 1948), 30.

9. *The Autobiography of Lincoln Steffens,* (Chautauqua, New York: Chautauqua Press, 1931), 618. Deriving largely from Steffens, as he says, F. Stuart Chapin sets forth these functions of the political machine with great clarity. See his *Contemporary American Institutions* (New York: Harper, 1934), 40-54.

10. *Autobiography of Lincoln Steffens,* 570.

11. *Ibid.,* 572-3 [italics supplied]. This helps explain, as Steffens noted after Police Commissioner Theodore Roosevelt, "the prominence and respectability of the men and women who intercede for crooks" when these have been apprehended in a periodic effort to "clean up the political machine." *Cf.* Steffens, 371, and *passim.*

12. See the National Opinion Research Center survey of evaluation of occupations which firmly documents the general impression that the manual occupations rate very low indeed in the social scale of values, *even among those who are themselves engaged in manual labor.* Consider this latter point in its full implications. In effect, the cultural and social structure exacts the values of pecuniary and power success even among those who find themselves confined to the stigmatized manual occupations. Against this background, consider the powerful motivation for achieving this type of "success" by any means whatsoever. A garbage-collector who joins with other Americans in the view that the garbage-collector is "the lowest of the low" occupations can scarcely have a self-image which is pleasing to him; he is in a "pariah" occupation in the very society where he is assured that "all who have genuine merit can get ahead." Add to this, his occasional recognition that "he didn't have the same chance as others, no matter what they say," and one perceives the enormous psychological pressure upon him for "evening up the score" by finding some means, whether strictly legal or not, for moving ahead. All this provides the structural and derivatively psychological background for the "socially induced need" in *some* groups to find some accessible avenue for social mobility.

13. Merton, "Social structure and anomie," chapter IV of this volume.

14. William F. Whyte, "Social organization in the slums," *American Sociological Review,* Feb. 1943, 8, 34-39 (italics supplied). Thus, the political machine and the racket represent a special case of the type of organizational adjustment to the conditions described in chapter IV. It represents, note, an *organizational* adjustment: definite structures arise and operate to reduce somewhat the acute tensions and problems of individuals caught up in the described conflict between the "cultural accent on success-for-all" and the "socially structured fact of unequal opportunities for success." As chapter IV indicates, other types of *individual* "adjustment" are possible: lone-wolf crime, psychopathological states, rebellion, retreat by abandoning the culturally approved goals, etc. Likewise, other types of *organizational adjustment* sometimes occur; the racket or the political machine are not *alone* available as organized means for meeting this socially induced problem. Participation in revolutionary organizations, for example, can be seen within this context, as an alternative mode of organizational adjustment. All this bears theoretic notice here, since we might otherwise overlook the basic functional concepts of functional substitutes and functional equivalents, which are to be discussed at length in a subsequent publication.

15. Perhaps the most perceptive statement of this view has been made by Hawkins and Waller. "The prostitute, the pimp, the peddler of dope, the operator of the gambling hall, the vendor of obscene pictures, the bootlegger, the abortionist, all are productive, all produce services or goods which people desire and for which they are willing to pay. It happens that society has put these goods and services under the ban, but people go on producing them and people go on consuming them, and an act of the legislature does not make them any less a part of the economic system." "Critical notes on the cost of crime," *Journal of Criminal Law and Criminology,* 1936, 26, 679-94, at 684.

The Crusade Against the Tweed Ring

ALEXANDER B. CALLOW, JR.

I thank my God the sun and moon
Are both stuck up so high
That no presumptuous hand can stretch
And pluck them from the sky.
If they were not, I do believe
That some reforming ass
Would recommend to take them down
And light the world with gas.

Judge James T. Brady

For five years the Tweed Ring had led a great treasury raid. The power of the Ring, like the tentacles of an octopus, encircled city government, the courts, the police, the underworld, and the State legislature. The command centers of political power from the Governor to the Board of Aldermen were controlled by the Ring and its lieutenants. The Ring ruled over an empire of patronage with thousands of the faithful on the city payrolls. Tammany Hall had been remodeled into an awesome political machine, supported by the immigrant and the native poor, and sustained on election day by a horde of Tammany warriors, repeaters, and corrupt election officials who made a mockery out of the power of the ballot. No wonder Boss Tweed could ask the reformer, "What are you going to do about it?"

Seldom have the forces of "good" government faced such a formidable opponent as they did in July 1871. Yet five months later the Tweed Ring was destroyed. Most accounts of this campaign emphasize the Ring's sensational thefts. But few questions have been raised about the crusade itself; few attempts have been made to understand the anatomy of a reform movement on a local, grass-roots level. For example, how was the crusade conducted? What was the impact of the Tweed Ring upon the reformer's imagination and in what way did the Ring reveal his attitudes toward reform, corruption, and political institutions? If the rascals were such capital rogues, why did it take so long to destroy them?

By the fall of 1871, when damning evidence was being unearthed and New York echoed from the cries of one reform rally after another, most of the press, a multitude of reform groups, and politicians from both parties were noisily scrambling after the scalps of the Tammany Ring braves. Now that the Ring was disintegrating, all vied for the heroic role of redeemer. Samuel Tilden almost reached the Presidency on the claim that he destroyed the Ring. But Tilden was a hero of last moments. A skillful general when the enemy was in retreat, he was the soul of indecision, procrastination, and lost opportunities when the Ring was in power. In those quiet days before the great uprising, only two led the crusade against the Tweed Ring: Thomas Nast of *Harper's Weekly*, and the *New York Times*. *Harper's Weekly* began in 1868 to print Thomas Nast's brilliant political cartoons, and his talent with the poisoned-pen portrait, which could at once inspire fear and ridicule, had led many to think he was the chief wrecker of the Ring. Tweed himself thoroughly recognized Nast's artistry in making a cartoon a deadly political weapon. "I don't care a straw for your newspaper articles, my constituents don't know how to read, but they can't help seeing them damned pictures."[1]

A picture may say a thousand words, but it still took many a thousand words to excite and motivate the indignation of New Yorkers. It was the *New York Times* which published the first evidence of corruption, helped to raise the crusade to the heights of near hysteria, and therefore deserves the mantle of champion opponent of the Tweed Ring. The role played by the *Times* is a kind of case study of the enormous difficulties and stubborn persistence involved in arousing a sometimes confused and often apathetic public.

Prior to September 1870, the fight against corruption was represented by a series of angry but irregular outbursts from reform groups and newspapers. These in turn were thwarted by grand juries vulnerable to the persuasion of hard cash and lack of evidence. The Citizens' Association and the Union League, both eminent bodies of "respectabilities," had long fished in the murky waters of New York politics with only occasional luck.[2] While the reformers suspected that something was desperately wrong, the rub was in proving it. Although the Ring was organized as early as 1866, there was little awareness by reformers of either a centralized city machine or of how politics operated at the level of the ward and precinct. Instead, there was talk of a host of "rings" but uncertainty as to who were the ringleaders.

Apathy, a lack of civic conscience, and fear—which permeated every level of society—also accounted for the reformers' failure to get an audience. An absence of consensus, generated by party partisanship, divided the press and the gentry, the two groups who might have sounded the alarm and carried the fight. While the business community furnished several leaders to the reform groups, other businessmen were either afraid of the retaliatory power of Tammany Hall or they benefited from the Ring's operations, while others, too interested in making money, simply did not care.

The Tweed Ring exploited these conditions and reinforced complacency by giving something to everyone: city advertising to the press, special favors to businessmen, state aid to charitable and religious organizations, jobs and food to the poor. Tweed through his business connections and Hall through his clubs ingratiated themselves in the upper branches of society, while Sweeny and Connolly, seasoned ward leaders, were effective in the rank and file. And then there was the Astor Committee and its whitewash of the Comptroller's records, which contributed as much as any event to creating complacency.

Into this atmosphere, the champion of reform, the *New York Times,* made its "auspicious" beginning in the winter of 1870, by announcing that Messrs. Sweeny, Hall, and Hoffman were busily engaged in bringing good government to New York![3] One delicious irony was topped by another when the *Times* gave its first (and last) cheer for the Boss himself.

Senator Tweed is in a fair way to distinguish himself as a reformer. . . . From beginning to end the Tweed party has not manifested the slightest disposition to evade or prevaricate. . . . As a whole, the appointments of the heads of the various departments of the City Government . . . are far above the average in point of personal fitness, and should be satisfactory.[4]

The *Times*'s course, however, was radically altered by the summer of 1870. Ugly rumors of corruption were once again abroad, and George Jones, the *Times* publisher, apparently feeling hoodwinked and humiliated, angrily turned on the charter and its creators. An Englishman, Louis Jennings, was imported as editor. Jennings's zest for a good fight, his acerbic prose, coupled with Nast's cartoons in *Harper's Weekly,* infused the campaign with a pitch and tempo of almost evangelical fervor. For over a year, from September 20, 1870, on, there was not a day that the *Times* did not, with furious and heroic invective, assault the Tweed Ring, its organization, and allies. The *Times* begged, cajoled, scolded, and demanded that the electorate rout the rascals; nevertheless, the public, including some of the "best people," seemed to sink deeper in its apathy, and the Ring got stronger. What was wrong? Was it entirely public indifference, the usual scapegoat for corruption, or did the trouble lay partly in the nature of the crusade itself?

Two elements are necessary in any successful campaign against civic corruption: moral indignation and facts. Until July 1871, the *Times*'s attack was a grand crusade conducted without fear and without facts; it was long on denunciation, short on documentation. The slack in legal evidence was taken up in an amazing exercise of invective, the central theme of which was the wickedness of the Tweed Ring, a theme with a hundred variations on the words "thief," "rogue," and "scamp." The crusade had persistence. It had gusto. It

had all the subtlety of a sledge hammer. It was literary alchemy using the crudest of alloys. There was none of the humor or painful ridicule of a Nast cartoon, none of the dash of the *New York Herald* or the deft sarcasm of Dana's *Sun* when those two papers finally joined the bandwagon later in 1871. It was just a juggernaut of epithets, taking the edge off the crusade by dulling the reader's senses with a repetitive cry of "wolf." E. L. Godkin of *The Nation,* although admiring the newspaper's spirit, found its denunciation "tiresome."[5] Even the *Times* admitted that its readers were probably bone-tired from the constant accusations.[6] And while the *Times* spewed platitudes about political sin, the elegant Mayor of New York quipped, "Who's going to sue?"[7]

Nor was abuse heaped solely on the Ring, for the public in general, and the rich, the workingman, and the church in particular, came within the *Times*'s range as it sharpened its aim at iniquity. One major strategic device of the crusade was to arouse a feeling of guilt and shame. The public had failed its civic responsibilities. There should be a moment of self-castigation coupled with redeeming political New Year's resolutions to sweep away the apathy that allowed the monstrosities of the Tweed Ring. The rich were scorned for their complacency, hypocrisy, and lack of action.[8] They were "cowardly and effeminate," refusing to leave the comfort of their libraries for the "unpleasant smells" of the political arena.

The policy of the Ring, in fact, was to drive the honest, decent middle class out of the city and leave it to the very rich and the very poor—"the one too lazy to oppose them, and the other too ignorant."[9] If the workingman understood the elementary principles of political economy, he would not be grateful for the jobs the Ring gave him on the streets and in the parks. He should realize that the robbery of the rich was the robbery of the poor. Labor actually took the full brunt of the Ring's adventures in graft through raised rents, increased taxes, and higher priced goods.[10] As for the church, the *Times* said, at most it applauds while others fight. If only the church acted with responsibility, the public conscience would be inflamed, and the sores on the body politic would be burned out, "as if by fire."[11]

With these tactics of shock, blame, and invective, the *Times* seemed to be searching for some way to shatter the complacency of the public. An attempt was made, in a pedestrian Jeffersonian vein, to exploit the chasm between town and country, the fear—and fascination—of the city. The "hay-loft and cheesepress Democrats" were told of the moral quagmire of the Sodom-by-the-Hudson, its city-slicker politicians, its crime, its cancerous effect on the Democratic party.[12] The trouble with that approach was that upstate politicos well knew that the success of the party depended on the city Democrats' delivering a large bloc of votes, and the Tweed Ring had time and again shown it could deliver.

Perhaps an appeal to the citizens' pocketbook would help, for here lay men's hearts—"touch them there and they will wince and exhibit more sensitiveness than they will show to even the strongest appeals made to their sympathies," as the *Times* said.[13] The newspaper became choked with figures demonstrating the Ring's damage to property owners. But most of the electorate did not own real property. Columns were devoted to an awkward analysis of city finances. But the average voter would have difficulty making sense of them. As the *Times* executed its complicated sums, apathy seemed to increase.

One reason why the crusade raged on for so long amid apparent indifference from the rest of the New York press was that the Democratic press, from the *World* on down—"or rather up, for you cannot get lower than the *World*"—(as the *Times* remarked)—were infuriated over the profound Republican partisanship of Nast and the *Times*. The *Times* was fond of repeating the adage that every Democrat was not a horse-thief, but that every horse-thief was a Democrat. Moreover, according to the *Times*, "all" Democrats were corrupt; the party had "never" undertaken a "genuine" reform.[14] Righteous moral indignation was rudely compromised when the *Times* condemned city Democrats and blithely whitewashed the Grant administration.[15]

Skepticism (and perhaps jealousy) also influenced the press. The *Times* motto should read, said one newspaper, "Print everything you please, without regard to whether it is true or false, but refuse to prove anything."[16] Horace Greeley, who puffed hot and cold throughout the campaign, even suggested that the Ring sue the *Times* for libel.[17] The *New York World*, after a brief flirtation with the Young Democracy, returned to revolve around Tammany Hall; it stoutly defended the Ring, calling the crusade as "stupid and absurd as it is wicked," and designed to introduce "a reign of anarchy."[18] Moreover, both the *Herald* and the *World* liked Oakey Hall. James Gordon Bennett of the *Herald* once said approvingly of Tweed's left-hand man, "He calls a spade a spade and Horace Greeley a humbug."[19]

Thus when Tammany wildly celebrated on July 4, 1871, it seemed that Nast's cartoons and the *Times*'s river of rhetoric had produced a crusade without followers, a cause apparently lost to corruption and apathy. All had not been lost, however, for it prepared New Yorkers for what was to follow. This was made possible not by any renewed moral gusto from Tammany's "unloyal" opposition, but by a quirk of fate and an emotion common in politics—the hankering for revenge.

The first real step in the Ring's fall to disaster came on January 21, 1871, when James Watson, the trusty County Auditor and Ring bookkeeper, was killed in a sleighing accident. The Ring was to learn how indispensable he was, for the door was now open for espionage. Matthew O'Rourke was appointed County Auditor, but was not taken into the Ring's confidence. It was a fatal appointment—"a dirty traitor and a fraud," Tammany's *Leader* cried later. O'Rourke was not a happy man. He once had a claim against the city which the Ring had seen fit not to pay. A disgruntled claim-seeker could be as vicious as a woman scorned. With the patience and accuracy of a good bookkeeper, O'Rourke copied the explosive facts and figures of corruption from the Ring's account books and passed them on to the *Times*.[20]

Acting independently, Jimmy O'Brien, one of the leaders of the rebel Young Democracy, assumed the role of a political Judas. He had managed to ingratiate himself back into the good graces of the Ring, by abandoning the Young Democracy and acting as an enthusiastic trustee for the Tweed monument association. But beneath his ruddy Irish complexion, he smouldered with resentment over the Ring's refusal to pay him $300,000 in claims he collected while Sheriff. O'Brien persuaded Connolly to give one William Copeland a job in the Comptroller's office. Copeland was, in fact, O'Brien's spy, sent to obtain information to use as blackmail to get O'Brien's claims. With Watson dead, Copeland found the voucher records loosely guarded. Lush accounts, such as "County Liabilities," furnished him with a wealth of information, which he copied for O'Brien. Confronted with this political dynamite, Tweed began to pay blackmail. He paid O'Brien over $20,000 with the promise that $130,000 would be forthcoming in mortgages on prime property. O'Brien coolly pocketed the cash and turned his information over to the *Times*.[21]

The breakthrough in the crusade had come. Publisher Jones began his attack with uncommon good sense. He bought up a large block of *Times* stock, fearful the Ring might retaliate by a stock raid. And then on Saturday, July 22, 1871, the *Times* opened up with its first front-page blast: "The Secret Accounts: Proofs of Undoubted Frauds Brought to Light." Slowly and deliciously, as if opening a long-awaited Christmas package, Jones released his figures—on the armories, the courthouse, padded payrolls, judicial indiscretion—topping one horror with another.[22] On the 29th the *Times* printed a special supplement in English and German of statistics on the armory and courthouse swindles; 200,-000 copies of the first printing were quickly sold out. It was not only a sensation in New York, but it also attracted immediate national attention. For the next four months Jones never let up; front page and editorial page boiled with journalistic frenzy—and Nast drew his cartoons with even greater venom.

Now as the facts were exposed, New York stirred, rumbled, and awoke—shocked, frightened, angry. It was now time for the reformers to take more decisive action. The massive reform rally on September 4 at Cooper Union, the first of many, registered the impact of the *Times*'s exposures: the temper was explosive, the spirit was that of a back-country revival meeting. The rally was sponsored by the Committee of Seventy, whose roster bulged with some of the most distinguished names in New York, such as William F. Havemeyer, Judge James Emott, Robert Roosevelt, Charles Richard O'Conor, and Joseph H. Choate, who presented the Committee's resolutions against the Tweed Ring with the battle cry, "This is what *we* are going to do about it!"[23]

A rostrum of distinguished speakers aroused the audience to a passionate fervor: "We shall get at them. The wicked shall not always rule"; "Pitch into the boss, give it to him, he deserves it"; "There is no power like the power of the people armed, aroused, and kindled with the enthusiasm of a righteous wrath"; "What are we going to do about it?"—"Hang them," cried the voices from the audience.[24] The *Times* said afterward that if the Ring had heard the curses, hisses, and denunciations heaped on them they would have felt "too mean to live."[25]

It was evident that New York had awakened from its apathy. The Citizens' Association, the New York Council of Political Reform, and the Union League threw their weight into the crusade, and they were followed by a host of reform groups—the Young Men's Municipal Reform Association, the Apollo Hall Democracy, the Young De-

mocracy, the German Reform Organization, and the Ward Councils of Political Reform. The press joined the chorus. Prominent businessmen and attorneys like R. A. Hunter, George W. Benster, and James Whitten met and considered forming a Vigilance Committee, but cooler heads prevailed. And Samuel Tilden entered on his somewhat gray charger. It was now expedient for him to be a reformer. The crusade reached a new dimension. It was no longer the concern of two but an issue that attracted many New Yorkers.

The impact of the Tweed Ring upon the reformer's imagination once again demonstrated the American capacity to create a morality play out of politics. Here was a drama of good versus evil. The principal characters were so wonderfully wicked that little embellishment seemed necessary. But embellished they were. While the reformers' responses were varied and often contradictory, certain dominant themes emerged.

The beginning theme, which Thomas Nast did more than anyone else to fix, was the image of the city boss, a portrait of evil. Tweed was pictured as gross, vicious, lowborn, colossally corrupt. Sweeny was the man with the black brains; Connolly was dark and oily; and Nast's favorite target, Oakey Hall, was the buffoon. These "beastly rascals" were also seen not as an indigenous product of the American urban political system, but as something sinister and alien. The corruption of the Ring was compared to the treachery of a Judas Iscariot, to the cunning of a Robespierre, the slothful greed of Oriental potentates; in tyranny and insolence they "would put their Roman predecessors to the blush."[26]

But the Boss and his ministers were

only mirrors in larger size and more evil proportions of those who flocked to their support—the Irish-Catholic immigrants. One of the most significant responses to the Tweed Ring, one which rounded out the image of evil by adding fear to it, was the revival of nativism in New York. On July 12, 1871, Protestant and Catholic Irish engaged in a bloody riot which shocked New York and revived the Know-Nothing attitudes of the 1850's and nativist fears of the 1863 draft riots. The Ring was vehemently denounced for trying to prevent the annual parade for the Orangemen, which precipitated the riot, as pacifying the Catholic Irish. When the parade was allowed, the Ring was accused of protecting the Catholic rioters. No other single event so well illustrated the tie between Tammany Hall and the Irish-Catholic voter. The cry for "clean government" now emitted the voice of nativism. There was a papal conspiracy as "Irish Catholic despotism rules the City of New York, the Metropolis of free America."[27] Letters poured into the *Times* office calling for a revival of the Native American party.[28] The Citizens' Association announced that the city had become a "common sewer" for the "dregs" of Europe; an army of ignorance was being led to the polls by the Tweed Ring.[29]

Nativism, in turn, elicited another response. The reformers, for the most part of the middle and upper class—professional men, bankers, merchants, journalists, the "better" politicians—felt a distinct loss of status since their old position of leadership had been captured by the wicked and the mob. Prior to the reign of Fernando Wood, political factions were controlled by men belonging to the upper or middle class, to whom the emoluments of office,

while desirable, were not always essential. From the days of Tweed's Forty Thieves through the Civil War, a change was occurring in New York politics, gradually, not completely, not easy to recognize; like the grin of the Cheshire Cat, sometimes it was seen, sometimes it was not. The old ruling groups, even the august Albany Regency, were being slowly displaced by a group not new, but different in numbers and the ranks from which it came—the lower-middle class, and the bottom of the social heap, the immigrant and native poor. The old ruling groups had to begin to move over and make a place for a new group, the Irish. This change found its source in the city, its growth, the changing composition of its population, the nature of its government. But the old middle- and upper-class elite, especially the reformers, who largely came from these groups, never completely understood this change and felt only bitterness toward the new and not always "respectable" elite. Republican institutions under the Tweed Ring, the reformers declared, were safe only in the "rightful" hands of the educated, the wealthy, and the virtuous. Now power had shifted to those at the bottom of society, their morals decayed, their religion Romanist, their Alma Mater the corner saloon.[30] The *Times* echoed the reformer's fears: We exist over a volcano, a vast, explosive mass of the poor and ignorant—"the dangerous classes," who "care nothing for our liberty and civilization."[31] E. L. Godkin traced the phenomenon back to the excessive democratization of the 1846 New York State Constitution.[32] Others saw it compounded by another insidious development, the rise of a new political breed, the professional politician.

As New York itself grew, politics became more centralized, more disciplined, more professionalized. While the professional politician had long been on the scene in New York politics, the impact of the Tweed Ring seemed to wipe out that memory and fix the emergence and the novelty of the professional as coinciding with the Tweed era. The *Times*, in fact, wrote of the "new profession" as if it were just making its appearance.[33] The reformer gave the professional little credit for skill in handling men or for artful political techniques at the "low" level of the ward or precinct, or for his sometimes masterful sense of organization. The reformer generally was little interested in the rude day-by-day operations of politics. His middle and upper class sensibilities were congenial to ideals and principles, not to the often rough, dreary, but necessary work of the primaries. The professional, in the reformer's eyes, was not a Robin Hood to the needy, but rather a Robin the Hood to the degenerate, wasting the taxpayers' money by giving jobs to the immigrant, bailing the drunkard out of jail, and corrupting the unemployed by giving them food and cigars—a parasite undermining the Protestant ethic of civic responsibility. The New York Council of Political Reform summed it all up. It was a contest between two forces: one made up of ruffians and desperadoes, and the other of "the delicately reared, the moral, humane, and the peace loving."[34]

Thus his sense of lost status, his contempt and fear of the masses, his nativism, his reaction to the city boss as rogue and professional politician—all indicate that the reformer's response to the Tweed Ring was more than simple moralizing about political sin. But if

there was one response, a dynamic one which gave cohesion and direction to his other reactions and provided the most powerful stimulus to reform, it was the fear that civil liberties were in danger, which to a certain degree was true. This response finally gave to the crusade a sense of genuine crisis, its *raison d'être*. The capital crime, then, was not merely the plundering of the treasury, nor the danger to the taxpayer's pocketbook; it was something more sinister than that. It was that a gang of rogues and its vicious brood, an organization alien to American life, was threatening the very bases of republican institutions—the ballot box, the schools, the church, the freedom of speech and press. "This wholesale filching and slaughter of the suffrage is a deadly thrust at the very source and fountain of our liberties . . . [we must] recover our mutilated liberties and vindicate our civil rights," shouted Joseph Choate at Cooper Union.[35] The danger to civil liberties was one of the most persistent themes of the *New York Times*.[36] Judge James Emott, Henry Clinton, Henry G. Stebbins, William Evarts, and others, all repeated the same theme: the Tweed Ring had threatened "the existence of free institutions," republicanism was "poisoned," "the glories of liberty are in danger."[37] The threat was felt even outside New York. "Democratic principles can no more carry this curse of Tammany upon them than virtue can thrive in a brothel," said the *Chicago Times*.[38]

If these fears seem exaggerated, it was because the reformers of the Tweed era were faced with their first city boss and his well-organized machine. There had been corruption in the past, but no precedent of modern city bosses to temper the reformer's ideal-ism and sharpen his realism.

Although there were differences among the reformers, and their schemes often overlapped, there were broadly two schools of thought on how best to cleanse New York City. The largest school believed that the Ring was not a natural product of American municipal government but a political disease alien to New World representative democ-racy. The cure, therefore, was relatively simple. Rout the rascals, lance the boil on the body politic, and the organism would be healthy again. This prognosis reflected an implicit faith in the efficacy of American institutions. The defeat of the Tweed Ring meant the vindication of republicanism, not the questioning of it. There were, of course, minor wounds to be treated: the charter needed patching up, there were too many appointive offices, and a tight lit-tle bureaucracy should replace the Ring's bloated monster. If the Ring discredited any institution, it was the political party. Partisanship, therefore, should be replaced by efficiency, hon-esty, and the methods of business. "The government of a city," declared the Union League, "is altogether more a matter of business, than of statesman-ship." The party system led only to "lawlessness, disorganization, pillage and anarchy."[39]

For these reformers, the cause of cor-ruption could be the cure of corrup-tion. The absence of the "best people" in government had allowed the wicked to rule. Thus the call was for the return to power of men with substantial wealth, education, and virtue. "The Ring could not keep its own for a day in the teeth of a combined and vigor-ous opposition from the men of large property."[40] New York was choked with foreigners, "many of them not pos-sessed of virtue and intelligence suffi-cient for self-government."[41] Therefore, what was needed, said the New York City Council of Political Reform, under the heading of "The Effectual Remedy," was for the "right-minded" to enter "into a covenant with each other . . . and the work is done."[42] If this sounded like the voice of the happy ending, it was also the voice of elitism. By impli-cation, the "right-minded" were always the old ruling elite. It represented gov-ernment of the people, for the people, *by* the "best people."

The second group of reformers did not share the extravagant optimism of the first. Corruption had forced them to re-examine the efficacy of democratic institutions and in so doing they found them wanting. Patchwork will not an-swer, wrote James Parton. The ship of state needed an overhaul from keel to taffrail, and perhaps it was necessary to "abandon the vessel and build a new one."[43] There must be some "profound defect," said C. C. P. Clark, in the American system which produced the horrors of the Tweed Ring.[44] The de-fect these reformers saw was one of the hallowed tenets of the American dream, universal suffrage. The comments of E. L. Godkin best illustrate this posi-tion. It was nonsense to talk about the Ring as a novelty to the American scene; it was the inevitable result of a "process of evolution," and other great cities have their "mute, inglorious Tweeds" waiting for their opportunity.[45] The curse of the city, "the great city problem," *is* the "people"—or about half of them who constitute the poor, "that huge body of ignorant and corrupt voters." The poor have no conception of self-government and choose only to live off the rich. The blight of universal suffrage is the secret of the Ring's power because it gave them an army. There can be, then, only two cures: first, suffrage should be limited, because only the propertied class, those who have a stake in society, should rule, for "we must somehow put the government into the hands of men who pay taxes." And second, the municipality should be converted into a business, stripped of political influence.[46] This program did not go far enough for Francis Leiber, James Parton, and Isaac Butts. They wanted to impose a literacy test on all New York voters.[47] It was a fine irony that those who felt their civil liberties in danger should seek to curtail the liberties of others.

From whence had come these dreams for a reformed New York? Not from the reformer's own time, for which he expressed a withering indictment. The reformer turned away from his own era, which spawned chaos and upheaval, looked back over his shoulder and found his solutions in a remembrance of things past—or what he *thought* had passed. He reached back for a lost innocence, the simplicity of an older era, the chaste republican order of a golden yesteryear. When he called for the return of the "best people," he thought of past mighties—James Kent, De Witt Clinton, Edward Livingston. His plan for a small, simplified government was the vision of the clean, honest symmetry of the town meeting, which James Welsh fondly recalled as the "natural school of American statesmanship."[48] The concept of limited suffrage, that ideological dog which had had its day, was an image of Order, a responsible aristocracy balancing a rapacious

mob. The warmth of reminiscence, however, was an anesthetic to the reformer's memory. For him the Tweed era dated the decline of political virtue. Before that ranged the long years of paradise to be found again. Forgotten were the gentlemen rogues, Fernando Wood, the Forty Thieves, and Samuel Swartwout. Nostalgia even led the reformer to tidy up the Albany Regency. Now it was remembered as an organization of "culture, integrity, and character."[49] And Thurlow Weed, an able opponent of the old, honest Regency, apparently with straight face, testified that "formerly the *suspicion* of corruption in a member [of the State legislature] would have put him 'into Coventry.' "[50] As one reform pamphlet said, "Pause here, Reader, sadly to drop a tear on the grave of departed Patriotism."[51]

As the crusade accelerated and unified both reformers and the press by early fall of 1871, the Ring, realizing it was in deep trouble, fought back like a trapped tiger and made some clumsy but typical maneuvers. George Jones was offered a bribe of $500,000 to silence the *Times*. He turned it down saying, "I don't think that the devil will ever bid higher for me than that."[52] Perhaps Thomas Nast needed a rest. He was promised $500,000 if he would leave the country and study art in Europe. "Well, I don't think I'll do it," Nast said. "I made up my mind not long ago to put some of those fellows behind the bars, *and I'm going to put them there!*"[53]

For a while Tweed remained cool and calm. A reporter for the *Missouri Republican* asked him if it were true that he had stolen money. Tweed thought a while and said, "This is not a question one gentleman ought to put to another."[54] George Templeton Strong said: "Tweed's impudent serenity is sublime. Were he not a supreme scoundrel, he would be a great man."[55] Finally, on September 8 he lost his composure and declared to a *Sun* reporter:

The *Times* has been saying all the time I have no brains. Well, I'll show Jones that I have brains. . . . I tell you, sir, if this man Jones had said the things he has said about me, twenty-five years ago, he wouldn't be alive now. But, you see, when a man has a wife and children, he can't do such a thing (clenching his fists). I would have killed him.

Nor did Mayor Hall help matters. He became ensnarled in his own contradictory statements and succeeded only in deepening the Ring's guilt. At first Hall cried innocent. The disclosures of the *Times* were "a tempest of ciphers and calumny . . . a second-hand roar about the accounts of the Supervisors and the salaries of extinct sinecures." Then he admitted some frauds were committed by the "old" Supervisors, but not by the Ring. This was interesting, because Tweed was president of the old Board of Supervisors. He said he never signed the alleged fraudulent warrants, and blamed Watson. He retracted this and admitted signing them, but only as a "ministerial act." He then claimed the signatures were forged; then retracted again and said he had signed but had been "hoodwinked." He tried sonorous prose: "When at last the smoke shall clear away, it will be seen where the political sun will clearly shine, that the proudest flag of them all, waving untorn from the highest staff of the victorious army, is

that which shall never cease to be borne by Tammany Hall."[56]

And naturally Hall attempted humor. "We are likely to have what befell Adam—an early Fall."[57] In an interview with a newspaper, he showed what the *Times* called "cheek."

Reporter: "You are looking very well."
Mayor: "Oh yes, I am always cheerful. You know the true philosophy of life is to take things just as they come. How was the clever definition—let me see, I forget his name—of life? What is mind? No matter. What is matter? Never mind. That's my philosophy."[58]

Once more cupidity came to the aid of the reformers. The Committee of Seventy as well as the Citizens' Committee, composed of private citizens and Aldermen, made plans to examine Comptroller Connelly's books for further proofs of the Ring's misdeeds. On Sunday, September 10, the day before this was to happen, Connolly's office was broken into. From three small cupboards more than 3500 vouchers were stolen. It became a sensation. The Ring had panicked. The *Times* asked sarcastically why the city had spent $404,-347.72 on safes and had not given one to the Comptroller. At the same time news came from Washington that Mrs. Connolly had just put one and a half million dollars into government bonds. No longer could the *World, Sun,* and *Herald* spoof the *Times* on its crusade. Even Horace Greeley overcame his jealousy of the *Times* and admitted that a crusade was in order. The theft only intensified Tilden's efforts—he had now committed himself completely to the crusade—to find more proof, which he did when he investigated the accounts at the Ring's Broadway Bank. So careless was the Ring that duplicates of the stolen vouchers were found by Tilden at the bank.

The Ring at best had been untidy. Now all became a shambles. The pressure of the crusade was more than the Ring could endure. The thieves who had traveled so far and so long together quarrelled and split into two enemy camps. Hall and Sweeny, joining forces against Tweed and Connolly, saw a chance for survival with the voucher disaster. On September 12, 1871, Hall asked Connolly to resign. Connolly, with some logic, replied to Hall that such a step would be equal to a confession, and added: "My official acts have been supervised and approved by your superior vigilance. So far as my administration is questioned equal responsibility attaches to yourself."[59]

It was now, as George Templeton Strong put it, "skunk vs. rattlesnake." Connolly, caring little for the role of sacrificial skunk, fled to the reformers. Tilden then performed a master stroke. He persuaded Connolly to step aside for four months, naming in his place Andrew Green as Acting Comptroller. Green was a distinguished public servant, and by no coincidence, a member of the Committee of Seventy.[60] Hall had made himself ridiculous by demanding Connolly's resignation, which he had no authority to do; Connolly refused and imported some of his toughs from the lower wards to guard his office. It was now skunk vs. coiled rattlesnake. Hall asked former General George McClellan to take Connolly's post, but McClellan, cautious in peace and war, refused. The press hooted that Hall had failed. In an interview, Hall told reporters, "Gentlemen, some of you yesterday said that I had received a severe check, and in testimonium veritatis, I have, so as you see, put on a check suit."[61] Connolly did deputize Green, and so one of the principal bastions of the Ring's stronghold, the Comptroller's office, was captured.

In the meantime, treason developed on the general staff. John Foley, president of one of the ward reform clubs, applied to George Barnard for an injunction to stop the Ring from paying or raising money in any way in the name of or on the credit of the County and City. Barnard, sensing the coming debacle of the Ring, responded with all the agility of a rat leaping from a sinking ship and granted the injunction. The reformers, never expecting this boon, were elated. As Tweed explained it:

So he put the injunction upon us, and in the straitened condition of our credit, which was so extended on every side, it broke us. You see our patronage had become so enormous and so costly that the injunction, which might not have troubled us at any other time, destroyed all our power to raise money from the banks or elsewhere and left us trapped.[62]

Although the injunction was later modified, government was temporarily brought to a standstill. With the city treasury nearly empty, and no recourse to raise money, city employees went for weeks without wages. Tweed gave $50,-000 from his own pocket to help laborers and their families, and the Star, one of a few remaining journals kind to the Ring, called on the laborers to start a bread riot.[63] New Yorkers, remembering the horror of the draft riots of 1863, and the bloody Orange Parade riot of July 12, 1870, redoubled their efforts to oust the Ring.

The injunction accomplished its purpose. The main arteries of political power, money, and patronage were suddenly dried up. The thieves were fighting among themselves. With Green ruthlessly chopping off sinecure appointments, the shiny hats, stripped of place and status, were losing faith in their chiefs. With an election coming up, *Harper's* and the *Times* were joined by the rest of the New York press, and the crusade reached fever pitch. The public was daily reminded of Tweed's arrogant, "What are you going to do about it?" The Tweed Ring seemed on the threshold of disaster. But the reformers underestimated the talents of the Boss.

For the leaders of the anti-Tammany Democracy it seemed that victory was in easy grasp. All that was necessary was to control the State nominating convention at Rochester. This did not appear difficult in light of the disasters that had befallen Tweed and company. Then the reformers could elect a reform platform, reveal the further evidence compiled by the investigations of the Committee of Seventy, campaign against the horrors of the Tweed Ring, and ride to victory in the November election. Tilden made elaborate preparations to capture the convention by sending out 26,000 letters to Democratic politicos asking for support with a one-two punch: he put the name of Charles O'Conor in nomination for the attorney-generalship, and disputed the right of the regular Tammany delegates to represent the city in the convention. Thus with belated courage, Tilden arose, rallied the reformers, and denounced the Ring. He realized the Ring's only chance of survival lay in renominating its henchmen for city and state offices, and helping the election of

Republicans who had worked with it in past legislatures—but so did the Boss.

The reformers lost some of their confidence when Tweed and his entourage, gangs of New York toughs, arrived in Rochester. Threats of violence were made against anyone who should interfere with the Ring; delegates were warned that the convention would be broken up by force if anti-Tammany delegates were admitted to the floor. The reformers found themselves reliving an old story: once again they were outmaneuvered and outwitted. Crafty as usual, Tweed moved among the delegates and argued that the recent exposures were merely a local issue and that an all-out' fight in the convention would undoubtedly split the party and allow the Republicans an easy victory in November. For the sake of party unity he was willing to compromise. If the reform representatives were omitted from the roll of delegates, he would omit the Tammany representatives.

What appeared as a compromise was actually a victory. Even with the Tammany delegation missing, Tweed was able to control the convention, through lack of opposition from the reformers, and with the help of friends won by bribery. Charles O'Conor, who would never have hesitated to throw the entire machinery of the state against the Ring, was defeated for the attorney-generalship by a large majority. A state ticket bulging with names of the Ring's minions was nominated. Tweed turned against the reformers with arrogance. He called Tilden, Horatio Seymour, and Francis Kernan "three troublesome old fools."[64]

Tweed had good reason to gloat. A few days before the convention he was re-elected chairman of the Tammany

General Committee, and at the convention he was renominated for State Senator. He returned to New York in triumph. At Walton House he took the platform, removed a little Scotch tweed cap, and told a boisterous audience:

The newspapers have already indicted, tried, convicted and sentenced and sentenced (roars of laughter), but I feel perfectly free to appeal to a higher tribunal, and have no fear of the result (cheers). I do not come to you, my fellow citizens, in a circuitous way, indicative of the possession of the thought of the necessity of caution engendered by fear, but directly, openly, squarely, as a man to men, and without an appeal for your sympathy other than so far as my family have suffered from the cruel indignities that have been heaped upon them for my political actions (sensation). But asking at your hands the justice and fair play that have been denied me by bitter, unrelenting, unscrupulous, prejudiced and ambitious partisan foes (deafening shouts of approval). . . .[65]

The reformers, who had once gloated, returned to New York shaken and sober. The glitter of their confidence was dulled, but their resolution was firm—even firmer. Tweed's victory at Rochester had robbed them of a valuable tactical weapon, the opportunity to proclaim themselves the regular Democratic organization. The Ring, even though quarrelling among themselves, still commanded a powerful election-day army. But failure only reinforced the reformers' determination. What had seemed after the exposures to be an easy victory was now an uphill fight. The reformers were forced to be a rival of the regular organization, and hence a third-party group, with all the difficulties a third party faced. Many of the reformers' leaders were political prima donnas— O'Conor was known for his irascibility, Tilden could be ex-

asperatingly aloof. If thieves fell out, reformers seemed to delight in dissension and to fragment into splinter groups. If the reformers were going to battle the Tweed Ring, they needed unity, organization, and outside support. But the Republicans were notoriously weak and inept. Then, as now, thousands of eligible voters never bothered to go to the polls. There was the danger that the none-too-reputable groups, like Mozart Hall and the Young Democracy, posing as reformers now that the Ring was embarrassed, might capture leadership from the reformers.

If the odds were formidable, the reformers were driven to work together if for no other reason than the fact that election day might be the last chance to destroy the Ring. Public indignation could not be sustained at a high pitch forever. Six days before the election, the Committee of Seventy released the evidence they unearthed from the Broadway Bank accounts. Important Republicans were persuaded to unite in a common cause by voting a straight reform ticket and not to present a separate Republican ticket to complicate matters. Young Men's Reform Associations were organized. The students of New York University, to whom Hall had recently lectured with applause, tore down the Mayor's portrait from their walls. The newspapers maintained a heavy barrage, exhorting voters to register, publicizing the facts behind the Ring's schemes, and explaining all the tactics Tammany might use to defraud the public on election day. Huge express wagons, drawn by six horses, stood ready to convey a reserve police force to any scene of disorder. Plans were made to take detected repeaters to the armories for custody to avoid the sure chance of their discharge by the courts. With a burst of excitement and energy, the reformers invaded the lower wards, the central nervous system of Tammany Hall, posting signs, passing out pamphlets, haranguing the native and immigrant poor with sidewalk speeches.

The tempo increased as the clergy of New York, pounding their pulpits, spoke out against the Tweed Ring for the first time. Dr. Henry D. Northrup of the Presbyterian Church echoed a common theme: there were but two parties, he roared, God's and the devil's. Election day "is a time when every citizen should show himself to be a man and not a sneak."[66]

The reformers who now thought they could win, called several rallies to keep things at a white heat. On November 2, a rally was held to receive the report of the Committee of Seventy. The motto over the president's chair read: "What are we going to do about it?" George Templeton Strong, pessimistic as usual, did not think they were going to do anything. "The disease of this community," he wrote in his diary, "lies too deep to be cured by meetings, resolutions, and committees. We the people are a low set, without moral virility. Our rulers, Tweed and Company, are about good enough for us."[67]

But Strong's pessimism seemed to be shared by few. The cadence of protest from the reformers, the press, the clergy, was picked up in the saloons, the restaurants, the clubs. Apathy had vanished. New York was agog with one topic of conversation, not the recent Chicago fire, not the visit of the Grand Duke Alexis, but the chance—the bare chance—that the reformers might beat the Tweed Ring on November 7th. On the eve of election day, New Yorkers waited with apprehension, and prepared themselves for one of the most important and exciting elections ever held in New York City.

Much to their own astonishment, the reformers gave Tammany Hall one of the worst defeats in its history up to that time. The scandals had finally roused New Yorkers into action. There was an unusually large turn-out, and many who previously had been apathetic, went to the polls and registered their indignation with Tammany. The reformers guarded the polling places well, and were successful in protecting themselves against excessive fraud and repeating. Moreover, several of the repeater gangs sensed the fall of the Ring and withdrew their support. The reformers elected all fifteen Aldermen, thirteen Assistant Aldermen out of twenty-one, and carried fourteen of the twenty Assembly districts. Prominent among the new Assemblymen were ex-Mayor Daniel E. Tiemann and Samuel Tilden. General Franz Siegel effectively wooed the Germans and became State Register. There were impressive upstate gains. The reformers captured four out of five Senatorial seats. The one they failed to win was the sour note. O'Donovan Rossa had once led the Irish against the British but could not do the same against Tweed in New York. The people of the Seventh District stood by the man who had served them so well with patronage and charity, and Tweed won over Rossa by over 10,000 votes. The reformers' broom swept out many of the Ring's important lieutenants. Henry Woltman was defeated by Augustus Weismann, the first German-born man to be elected to the State

Senate. Timothy Campbell, Henry Genet, James Irving, and Michael Norton were all defeated. Alexander Frear and Thomas Fields were prevented from taking their seats because of election fraud. The full measure of defeat was revealed a few days later. It was announced that the annual Americus Club ball was postponed.

Once again the *Times* reported a quiet election day. It was a moot point, the newspaper said, whether this resulted from the precautions taken by the reformers or that Tammany was cowed. Of course there were some "altercations and word-combats," and "heads punched in the good old fashion so dear to the Democracy." Compared to the previous year, the reformers had won away from the regular Democrats almost 75,000 votes in the city and state, "one of the most remarkable political revolutions in the history of the country," said a contemporary, with some exaggeration.[68] The *Times* maintained that the election was won by the strong vote of the so-called neutral population, who seldom voted— "the gentlemen and quiet citizens."[69] But while there was a large registration, there were not enough neutrals to decide the election. Ironically, it was the very people the reformers despised the most, the immigrants and the native poor, who, because of their great numbers, put the reformers into office by splitting their vote between Tammany and the men running on the Democratic reform ticket.[70]

The victory over Tammany was seen as the end of a great crusade. There was much excitement. For most it meant the vindication of popular government, the triumph of the people's voice, a moral struggle where good overwhelmed evil. Under a huge headline, "New York Redeemed," the *Times* said:

The victory we have won is priceless, not only from what it gives us now, but because it will revive every man's faith in the ultimate triumph of truth and justice— because it will teach scheming politicians that the voice of the people is supreme, and that immortal principles on which this Government is founded, although they may be momentarily stifled by dishonest factions, will constantly rise triumphant, while the men who assailed them will pass away to everlasting infamy.[71]

The reformer George C. Barrett, a successful candidate, said the victory was an answer to those who had scoffed at the success of a republican form of government.[72] *Harper's Weekly* said it was one of the most significant events in the history of free governments.[73]

Only E. L. Godkin pondered whether the great "uprising" was the final and complete triumph over political corruption, whether routing the rascals was only the beginning of reform—real reform. . . .[74]

What, then, was the final reckoning of the Tweed Ring? Although Judges Barnard and McCunn were impeached, and removed from office, and Cardozo resigned but continued to practice law, none of the three were criminally prosecuted. With two exceptions, none of the Ring and its many partners in graft were ever caught or punished. Only Tweed and Ingersoll went to jail. From 1871 to 1878, Tweed spent less than half of that time in prison. Ingersoll who turned himself in, hoping for a light sentence, was sentenced to five years and seven months, but served only a few months of his term before he was pardoned by Tilden for turning

State's evidence and promising to become a witness in any forthcoming Ring trials. At the time of Tweed's death sixteen suits were pending against various members of the Tweed Ring organization.[75] None came to trial. Garvey was granted immunity to appear as a witness at the Tweed and Hall trials. Although a millionaire, he never returned any of the money he made. Woodward was granted immunity for returning $155,000, although he had stolen over a million. John Keyser had the delightful gall to claim that it was the city who owed him, and he was almost successful in being awarded a $33,000 claim based on a fraudulent contract![76] Of the twenty to two hundred million dollars estimated to have been stolen by the Ring, it cost the city $257,848.34 to recover $894,525.44, most of which came from the estates of two dead men, James Watson and James Sweeny.

The ethos of reform, however, was essentially moralistic and conservative. For some the issue was a total commitment to punishing bad men, not the examination of the institutions and conditions that made it possible for bad men to exist and thrive. To them, the cause of corruption was the work of evil men. Their optimism blinded them to the realities of a rapidly growing society, the massive growth of a great city and the effects it would have on political life. For those who questioned institutions, the answer lay not in adaptation but in a return to the good old days of rule by gentry, suffrage restrictions, tight economy, and a tiny bureaucracy. In the months, years, and decades following the Ring's fall, the reformer, imprisoned by his own social philosophy, continued to alienate the immigrant newcomer. What could have been a source of power for the reformer remained the strength of later city bosses. As the city grew and its problems multiplied, the reformer continued to turn back to that Promised Land of the good old days for his solutions to corruption, patching the charter here, passing a resolution there, always haunted by his failure to restore the profession of politics to the nobility of the Old Republic. Exposure of the Tweed Ring had given him a glimpse into the hard realities of big-city politics. But he continued to be an innocent abroad in the strange land of the professional politician and practical politics, preferring the platitude to the free cigar. He never understood the politicians who made politics their business, their appeal to the masses, their attention to the plight of the immigrant, nor, indeed, the kind of world they were living in. Thus the rascals were routed, but their supreme achievement, the city machine itself, remained essentially intact, to become a model, a legacy, to be improved upon by succeeding monarchs of New York, the Kellys, the Crokers, and the Murphys.

After all was said and done, the crusade against the Tweed Ring won the battle but lost the war. In a real sense, William Marcy Tweed had the last word, when he asked, "Well, what are you going to do about it?"

NOTES

1. Wingate, "Episode in Municipal Government," July 1875, p. 150.
2. See Citizens' Association, "An Appeal by the Citizens' Association of New York against the Abuses in the Local Government to the Legislature of the State of New York, and to the Public" (New York, 1866); "Items of Abuse in the Government of the City of New York" (New York,

1866); "Report of the Executive Council to the Honorary Council of the Citizens' Association" (New York, 1866); "Wholesale Corruption! Sale of Situations in Fourth Ward Schools" (New York, 1864); Union League Club, "Report on Cities" (New York, 1867); "The Report of the Committee on Municipal Reform" (New York, 1867).

3. Jan. 24-25, Feb. 15, 1870. The *Times* also reported on Mar. 9, 1870, that Richard Connolly was fighting the Ring.

4. Apr. 8, 13, 1870. See also Apr. 6, 12, and May 1, 1870.

5. July 13, 1871, quoted in the *Times*, July 14, 1871.

6. Apr. 3, 1872.

7. J. D. Townsend, *New York in Bondage* (1901), p. 73.

8. Nov. 3, 1870.

9. Ibid.

10. Ibid.; Sept. 16, 1871.

11. Dec. 4, 1870. When the celebrated Henry Ward Beecher said he pitied wicked men because their consciences would surely suffer, the *Times* replied in a blistering attack, saying Beecher's pity was "morbid, unwholesome, sentimental." Oct. 24, 1871.

12. Oct. 3, 1870.

13. Sept. 24, 1870.

14. Feb. 26, May 1, 1871; Oct. 3, 1870.

15. "The great strength of General Grant's Administration . . . lies in the fact that he is believed to be honest himself, and disposed to enforce honesty and fidelity in all departments of the Government under his control." *New York Times*, Sept. 21, 1871.

16. Unidentified newspaper, *Scrapbooks of Clippings Relating to the Career of A. Oakey Hall* (New York Public Library), Vol. IV, p. 113.

17. *New York Times*, Jan. 25, 1873.

18. July 28, 31, 1871. See also *New York World*, Aug. 2, 7, 10, 1871. The *New York Sun* and *New York Evening Post* also criticized the *Times*. Bowen, *The Elegant Oakey*, p. 99. Moreover, Charles Nordhoff, the managing editor of the *Evening Post*, was fired for attacking Tweed. Lynch, *Boss Tweed*, p. 355.

19. Bowen, *The Elegant Oakey*, p. 106. See also Allan Nevins and Thomas Milton Halsey, *The Diary of George Templeton Strong*, III (4 vols.), pp. 376, 383, 385-6.

20. Genung, *Frauds of New York*, pp. 9-13.

21. *Tweed Investigation*, pp. 50-55; Hirsch, "More Light on Boss Tweed," p. 272.

22. For a compilation of the *Times*'s evidence, see *New York Times*, "How New York is Governed. Frauds of the Tammany Democrats," 1871.

23. Breen, *Thirty Years of New York Politics*, p. 337.

24. *New York Times*, Sept. 5, 1871.

25. Oct. 2, 1871.

26. *New York Times*, Oct. 10, 1870; Jan. 20, Mar. 6, 1871.

27. *New York Times*, July 12, 1871.

28. Ibid. July 16, 1871.

29. "Report of the Executive Council to the Honorary Council of the Citizens' Association" (New York, 1866), p. 21. See also "Civil Rights: A History of the New York Riot of 1871" (1871), p. 20; Nevins and Halsey, *Diary of Strong*, IV, p. 352; Thomas Nast, *Miss Columbia's School, or Will It Blow Over?*, 1871, p. 71, *passim; Harper's Weekly*, July 29, 1871. For other examples of the nativist impulse, see *The Nation*, July 20, 1871, p. 36; *New York Times*, Mar. 18, Apr. 7, July 17-18, 21, 24, Aug. 17, 1871; Wingate, "Episode in Municipal Government," Oct. 1874, pp. 378-9; Townsend, *New York in Bondage*, p. 186; Nevins and Halsey, *Diary of Strong*, IV, p. 317.

While nativism was widespread in the reformers' camp, some were anti-nativist. See A. R. Lawrence, "The Government of Cities" (New York, 1868), pp. 4-5, 11.

30. *New York Times*, Sept. 17, 1869; Jan. 7, Nov. 30, 1870; Mar. 19, 26, July 16, Sept. 17, 1871. Otto Kempner, "Boss Croker's Career," p. 6.

31. July 16, 1871. See also Sept. 17, 1869; Oct. 17, 1870; Feb. 2, Mar. 19, 1871.

32. *The Nation*, Nov. 16, 1871, p. 316.

33. Jan. 25, 1871. See also *New York Times*, Jan. 24, 1870; *New York Star*, Mar. 25, 1870; Wingate, "Episode in Municipal Government," CXIX (Oct. 1874), p. 379.

34. "Statement and Plea of the New York City Council of Political Reform," p. 34.

35. *American Addresses*, pp. 61-2, 72; *New York Times*, Sept. 18, 1871; (Anon.) "Why Vote at All in '72," p. 37. Robert Roosevelt declared that the Ring "pulled away the very keystone of the arch of liberty." If the public money is stolen, wrote another reformer, "why not the public liberties too?"

36. Feb. 8, April 3, Oct. 12, 17, Nov. 3-4, 1870; Jan. 24, Feb. 24-25, Apr. 7, May 1, July 16, Sept. 5, 26-27, Oct. 27, Nov. 3, 1871.

37. Jones, *Fisk*, p. 226; *New York Times*, Sept. 4, Nov. 3, 1871. See also Abram Genung, *The Frauds of the New York City Government Exposed*, p. 41; Gustav Lening, *The Dark Side of New York*, p. 694; James Welsh, "The Root of the Municipal Evil," p. 7; Nast, *Miss Columbia's School*, pp. 39, 71; New York Council of Political Reform, "Statement and Plea," p. 40.

38. Sept. 29, 1871.

39. "Report on Municipal Reform," pp. 17-18; see also, "Why Vote at All in '72," p. 72; Welsh, "Root of the Municipal Evil," p. 5.

40. *New York Times*, Jan. 23, 1871.

41. New York City Council of Political Reform, "Report of the New York City Council of Political Reform," p. 3.

42. "Statement and Plea," p. 28. See also "Report of the New York City Council of Political Reform," pp. 4-11; The Citizens' Association, "Report of the Executive Council to the Honorary Council," p. 22; Wilson, *Memorial History*, III, p. 562; Bryce, *American Commonwealth* (1889 ed.), II, p. 353, (1895 ed.), II, pp. 391, 403.

For an interesting criticism of the "best people" theory, see *The Nation*, Aug. 24, 1871, p. 125.

43. "The Government of New York," p. 451.

44. "The Commonwealth Reconstructed," p. 26.

45. *The Nation*, Apr. 18, 1878, p. 257; Nov. 9, 1871, p. 300; Nov. 27, 1873, p. 350.

46. Ibid. Nov. 4, 1875, p. 288; Oct. 18, 1877, p. 238; Nov. 27, 1873, p. 350; Apr. 18, 1878, p. 257; Oct. 12, 1871, p. 237; Nov. 4, 1875, p. 289. See also Union League, "Report on Municipal Reform," pp. 19-20, 76-7, 88; Parton, "Government of New York," p. 463.

For an attack on this position, see Charles Nordhoff, "The Mis-Government of New York, a Remedy Suggested," *North American Review*, CCXXXIII (Oct. 1871), pp. 321-43, *passim*.

47. Francis Lieber, "Reflections on the Changes Which May Seem Necessary in the Present Constitution of the State of New York," p. 4; Parton, "Government of New York," p. 460; *Rochester Union and Advertiser*, Oct. 3, 1871.

48. "Root of Municipal Evil," p. 19.

49. *New York Times*, Sept. 11, 1869.

50. Parton, "Government of New York," p. 457.

51. (Anon.), "Why Vote at All in '72," p. 29.

52. Werner, *Tammany Hall*, p. 210.

53. Albert Paine, *Thomas Nast*, 1904, p. 182.

54. *New York Times*, Aug. 24, 1871.

55. Nevins and Halsey, *Diary of Strong*, Vol. IV, p. 394.

56. For Hall's excuses, see *New York Times*, July 12, 29, Aug. 12, Sept. 11, Oct. 10, 13; *The Leader*, Aug. 19, 1871.

57. Flick, *Tilden*, p. 213; see also *New York Times*, Aug. 29, 1871.

58. *New York Times*, Sept. 22, 1871.

59. Ibid. Sept. 17, 1871.

60. Green had served thirteen years on the Park Commission, helped to plan Central Park, suggested Riverside Drive and many of the smaller parks, established the American Scenic and Historic Preservation Society, and did much to effect the merger of the Tilden, Astor, and Lennox foundation in the New York Public Libary.

61. Wingate, "Episode in Municipal Government," Oct. 1876, p. 379.

62. Lynch, *Boss Tweed*, p. 375.

63. Sept. 27, 1871.

64. Flick, *Tilden*, p. 219.

65. *New York Times*, Nov. 5, 1871.

66. Ibid. Nov. 6, 1871.

67. Nevins and Halsey, *Diary of Strong*, Vol. IV, p. 382.

68. Wingate, "Episode in Municipal Government," Oct. 1876, p. 389.

69. Nov. 11, 1871.

70. O'Connor, *Hell's Kitchen*, p. 50; Lynch, *Boss Tweed*, pp. 383-4.

71. Nov. 8, 1871.

72. Ibid.

73. Cited with no date in *New York Times*, July 12, 1872.

74. *The Nation*, Nov. 9, 1871, p. 300.

75. *Tweed Investigation*, pp. 841-5.

76. Ibid. pp. 601-85.

Varieties of Urban Reform

MELVIN G. HOLLI

Pingree's brand of social reform—whose objectivity was to lower utility rates for the consumer and which attempted to place a larger share of the municipal tax burden on large corporations—was not the prevailing mood of urban reform in late-nineteenth and early-twentieth-century America. Far more prevalent in the programs of large-city mayors who earned the epithet "reformer" was the effort to change the structure of municipal government, to eliminate petty crime and vice, and to introduce the business system of the contemporary corporation into municipal government. Charter tinkering, elaborate audit procedures, and the drive to impose businesslike efficiency upon city government were the stock-in-trade of this type of urban executive. Mayors of this kind of reform persuasion could be found in New York, Brooklyn, Buffalo, San Francisco, and countless other cities.

Although most of these structural reformers did not articulate their positions as eloquently as Seth Low or attempt to install business methods as ruthlessly as John Purroy Mitchel, they all shared a certain style, a number of common assumptions about the cause of municipal misgovernment, and, in some instances, a conviction about which class was best fitted to rule the city. Few of them were as blatantly outspoken in their view of democracy as Samuel S. McClure, the publisher of the leading muckrake journal. He instructed Lincoln Steffens to prove that popular rule was a failure and that cities should be run by a dictatorship of wise and strong men, such as Samuel S. McClure or Judge Elbert Gary. Similarly New York's former reform mayor, Abram Hewitt asserted in 1901 that "ignorance should be excluded from control, [and] the city business should be carried on by trained experts selected upon some other principle than popular suffrage."[1]

None of the structural reformers had the unqualified faith in the ability of the masses to rule themselves intelligently that social reformers Hazen S. Pingree, Samuel "Golden Rule" Jones, or Tom L. Johnson did. "I have come to lean upon the common people as the real foundation upon which good government must rest," Pingree told the Nineteenth Century Club in 1897. In a statement that represented more than a rhetorical flourish, "Golden Rule" Jones chastised Reverend Josiah Strong for his distrust of the masses and told him that the "voice of the people is the voice of God." Tom Johnson, asserted Brand Whitlock, knew that "the cure for the ills of democracy was not less democracy, as so many people were always preaching, but more democracy." When Johnson was defeated by the Cleveland electorate at the very pinnacle of one of the most productive urban reform

From *Reform in Detroit: Hazen S. Pingree and Urban Politics* by Melvin G. Holli. Copyright © 1969 by Oxford University Press, Inc. Reprinted by permission of Oxford University Press, Inc., pp. 161–181.

careers in the nation, he told Whitlock, "The people are probably right."[2]

The structural reform movement was in sharp contrast to the democratic mood of such a statement. It represented instead the first wave of prescriptive municipal government which placed its faith in rule by educated, upper class Americans and, later, by municipal experts rather than the lower classes. The installation in office of men of character, substance, and integrity was an attempt to impose middle class and patrician ideals upon the urban masses. The movement reached its height in the second and third decades of the twentieth century with the city-manager and city-commissioner forms of government, which called for the hiring of non-partisan experts to decide questions hitherto viewed as resolvable only by the political process. Like the structural reform movement of the late-nineteenth-century, the city-manager movement reflected an implicit distrust of popular democracy.[3]

New York's Mayor William F. Havemeyer was a prototype of the twentieth-century structural reformers. Having inherited a substantial fortune, he retired from the sugar refining business at the age of forty and devoted most of his career to public service. Elected mayor in 1872 during the public exposure of the Tweed Ring, Havemeyer was a reformer who championed "clean government," "economy," and the business class point of view. Obsessed with tax cuts and retrenchment, he and his fiscal watchdog, city Treasurer Andrew H. Green, cut wages on public works and demanded elaborate procedures to account for all petty expenditures of public funds. Green's painstaking scrutiny of every claim snarled the payroll so badly that the city's laborers rioted when their pay checks got lost in an administrative tangle.[4]

To practice economy, Havemeyer sacrificed important public services and, in the process, "crippled downtown development." During a three-month period in 1874 the Mayor vetoed more than 250 bills related to street grading, paving, and widening, board of education contracts, and appropriations intended for public charities. In justifying his liquidation of work relief, Havemeyer told the Harvard Association that contributions of private individuals and Christian and charitable associations were generous enough to meet the needs of the poor. According to Seymour Mandelbaum, the lower classes and the promoters of new areas of the city suffered most from Havemeyer's policies.[5]

During his second year in office, the aging Mayor fought with the city council and accomplished nothing of lasting importance. Havemeyer and the New York Council of Political Reform were so obsessed with "honest, efficient and economical government" that they indicted every public improvement as a "job" and labeled every politician who supported such measures as an "exponent of the class against which society is organized to protect itself." The Mayor's death in 1874 mercifully ended the agony of a reform administration which was strangling the city with red tape generated by its own economy programs. Ironically, Havemeyer helped to perpetuate the widespread belief that reformers were meddling, ineffectual reactionaries, or, as George Washington Plunkitt charged, "morning glories" who wilted in the heat of urban politics.[6]

Buffalo's "fighting mayor," Grover Cleveland, 1882, was another one of the progenitors of the structural reform tradition. Preoccupied as much as Havemeyer with cutting taxes and municipal expenditures, Cleveland had no positive programs to offer, with one notable exception: he fought and won authorization for a massive interceptor sewer system to diminish the dumping of refuse into the Erie Canal. He made his mark in Buffalo by the veto of a corrupt street cleaning contract, the "most spectacular single event" of his administration in Allan Nevins's view. In addition, Cleveland fought to stop the constant proliferation of city jobs, exercised a Havemeyer type of vigilance over all claims made against the city treasury, and directed city employees to stop closing their offices at 4.00 p.m. and to perform a full day's work. His inflexible drive for economy and efficiency and his contempt for the dishonesty of city machines won him a reputation as a rugged veto and reform mayor.[7]

Seth Low, a wealthy merchant, philanthropist, and university president, was mayor of Brooklyn (1882–85) and later of New York (1902–03). Perhaps more than any other American mayor, he possessed the qualities of a high-minded, nonpartisan structural reformer who attempted to infuse a large dose of businesslike efficiency into municipal government. He was widely recognized by his generation as one of the most prominent practicing reformers on the urban scene, but he also built a considerable reputation as a scholar of municipal affairs. In countless addresses, Low argued that the answer to urban problems was charter reform to bring nonpartisanship and a centralized administration into city government. Reform of this sort would arouse a new civic consciousness and create a cohe-

sive corporate government that could be run along business lines, free from outside influences.[8]

Under the aegis of a silk-stocking Citizens' Committee, Low, with his refined eloquence and business support, had waged an effective campaign against political spoilsmanship and partisanship and won Brooklyn's mayoralty election in 1881. Low disregarded political affiliation and based his appointments on ability and merit. Although his two terms proved to be unspectacular, Low had advanced what he considered the cardinal principles of municipal reform: he had reduced the city's debt, tightened up the tax system, and conducted a vigorous campaign at Albany to stop special state legislation from interfering in Brooklyn's affairs. Such social questions as tenement house reform and aid to the aged, the poor, or workingmen were for Seth Low but special benefits which could not be considered until local partisanship had been wiped out and municipal government had been reorganized along the lines of authority and responsibility. Low's name had become synonymous with efficiency, responsibility, and clean government.[9]

After a particularly flagrant period of municipal corruption under Tammany Hall, a reform-minded Citizens' Union, which counted J. Pierpont Morgan and Elihu Root among its founders, asked Seth Low to enter the lists as an independent candidate for mayor of New York against the Tammany favorite in 1901. Low ran on a platform of home rule and nonpartisanship, avoided the social-welfare planks endorsed by the Citizens' Union, and discussed honesty, economy, and responsibility in his speeches. Low was known to the voters because he had assisted in drafting the first charter for Greater New York, which consolidated hundreds of small towns and three large cities into one unit. Low's victory in 1901 was probably less an endorsement of his brand of reform than a public reaction against the excesses of Tammany.[10]

As New York's mayor, Low brought in experts to operate the various departments, pared away Tammany's payroll padding, and set himself up as the businessman in office. He cut salaries, increased the length of the working day for municipal employees, and reduced the city's annual budget by $1,500,000. In the public transit and utility field, Low saw to it that franchises were carefully drafted to safeguard the city's interests and to provide for additional revenue. He failed to press for lower rates, to agitate for a public rate-making body, or to instruct his district attorney to investigate the corrupt alliances between private business and politicians. He balked at appointing one of the best-qualified housing reformers, Lawrence Veiller, to head the tenement house commission, apparently because Low did not wish to disturb the conservative real estate interests. Low was willing, however, to use the full force of law against Sunday drinking, petty gambling, and prostitution, which were commonly found in the immigrant and lower class sections of the city. The Bureau of Licenses also cracked down on the city's 6,000 pushcart peddlers who were operating without licenses, and the Department of Law prosecuted residents whose tax payments were delinquent. With similar zeal, the Department of Water raised nearly $1,000,000 in income from overdue water bills.[11]

Low's tinkering with the machinery of government, his charter revision and rewriting, his regularization of tax collections, his enforcement of the city statutes, his appointment of men of merit, and his reduction of city expenditures were laudable actions by almost anybody's test of good government. Unfortunately, these measures bore most severely upon the lower classes. Low's structural reforms were also very impolitic, as his defeat in the election of 1903 demonstrated. Low never seemed to realize that his municipal reform had nothing to offer the voters but sterile, mechanical changes and that fundamental social and economic conditions which pressed upon the vast urban masses of immigrants and poor could not be changed by rewriting charters or enforcing laws.[12]

San Francisco's reform mayor James D. Phelan, a wealthy banker and anti-Bryan Democrat who held office from 1897 to 1902, was also a structural reformer like his model, Seth Low, whom Phelan frequently quoted. Phelan's program for reform included the introduction of efficiency and economy to ensure "scientific, systematic and responsible government," which was also the goal of the San Francisco Merchants' Association. Franchise regulation, lower traction rates, municipal ownership, and equal taxation were not part of Phelan's design for a better San Francisco. The distinguishing mark of the Phelan administration was its sponsorship of a strong mayor, and a short ballot charter that provided rigid fiscal controls over expenditures, city-wide elections for the council, and a merit system. Known as a "watchdog of the treasury," Mayor Phelan supported a low tax rate that forced the city to withhold schoolteachers' salaries, suspend many of the essential functions of the city health department, subject patients at the city hospital to inadequate care, and turn off the street lights at midnight. Phelan crippled his administration when he permitted the president of the police commissioners (who was also president of the Chamber of Commerce) to protect strikebreakers and club pickets during a teamsters' and a dock-workers' strike against the open shop. Although the 18 unions lost their strike, they retaliated by forming their own political party and defeating the reformers in 1901. In the famous graft prosecutions after 1901, Phelan continued to act like a "member of his class" or, as Fremont Older put it, "a rich man toward a great business in which he is interested."[13] Like Low, Phelan failed to attack what social reformers recognized as the basic problems confronting the city.

Equally ineffectual in his attempt to make New York the best governed city in the nation was Mayor John Purroy Mitchel, who served from 1914 to 1917. He was an "oddly puritanical Catholic" who represented the foibles and virtues of patrician class reform. Mitchel's election in 1913 was the result of voter reaction to a decade of brazen looting by Tammany Hall. Like his reform predecessors, Mitchel was responsible for little of lasting importance and did not generate enthusiasm among the large mass of voters with his structural reforms.[14]

Mitchel's failure was due to his misconception that city government could be conducted by the "ledger book ethics of the corporation accountant." So dedicated was Mitchel to budgetary cutbacks that he adopted the Gary Plan of education, which enabled New York City to cram more children into the existing schools. He decreased appropriations for the city's night schools, thus seriously hampering the entire program; for the summer program, Mitchel asked the teachers to volunteer their services without remuneration. Mitchel also appointed cost-cutting charity agents who began either to return feeble-minded children to their parents or to threaten to charge the often hard-pressed parents if their children were kept in public supported institutions. In addition, he instituted an investigation of the city's religious child care organizations, hoping thus to cut the city subsidy; but this action brought the wrath of the Catholic church down upon him.[15] Mitchel, although well-intentioned, had a kind of King Midas touch in reverse: everything he touched seemed to turn to ashes.

Robert Moses dismissed the Mitchel administration's efficiency drives as saving rubber bands" and "using both ends of the pencil," but its flaws were much greater. The Mitchel administration and the structural reform movement were not only captives of a modern business mentality but sought to impress middle and upper class social values upon the urban community and to redistribute political power to the patrician class.[16]

Built upon a narrow middle and patrician class base and a business concept of social responsibility, the structural reform movement, with its zeal for efficiency and economy, usually lacked staying power. As George Washington Plunkitt pointed out, such crusaders were usually repudiated by lower class voters after a brief tenure in office. Unlike the social reformers, who were also interested in economy, the structural reformers had a blind spot when it came to weighing the human cost of their programs. They failed to recognize that a dose of something as astringent as wage-cutting and payroll audits had to be counterbalanced with social welfare programs if the public were to be served effectively. Too often they blamed the immigrant for the city's shortcomings or directed much of the force of their administrations to exterminating lower-class vices, which they saw as the underlying causes of municipal problems.[17]

Unlike the structural reformers, social reform mayors such as Hazen S. Pingree (1890–97), "Golden Rule" Jones (1897–1903), Tom Johnson (1901–09), Mark Fagan (1901–07), Brand Whitlock (1906–13), and Newton D. Baker (1912–16) began with a different set of assumptions about the basic causes of misgovernment in the cities. They shared the view, which Lincoln Steffens later publicized, that big business and its quest for preferential treatment and special privileges had corrupted municipal government. The public service corporations, the utilities, the real estate interests, and the large industrial concerns all had vested interests in urban America. They sought special tax advantages, franchises which eliminated competition, and other municipal concessions. They bought aldermen, councilmen, and mayors to protect these interests and, in the process, demoralized urban politics and city government. Mayor Tom Johnson's aide Frederic C. Howe was shocked when he was berated by his upper class friends for opposing a franchise steal; they explained that the public utilities have "millions of dollars invested" and had to "protect their investments." "But I do say emphatically," declared Mayor Pingree in 1895, ". . . better take [the utilities] out of private hands than allow them to stand as the greatest corruptors of public morals that ever blackened the pages of history."[18]

The programs of the social reform mayors aimed at lower gas, light, telephone, and street railway rates for the community and higher taxes for railroads and business corporations. When they were unable to obtain the regulation of public utilities, these mayors fought for municipal ownership, the only technique to redistribute economic power available to them as urban executives. Establishment of free public baths, expansion of parks, schools, and public relief were similarly attempts to distribute the amenities of middle class life to the masses. The social reformers recognized that the fight against crime in its commonly understood sense (i.e. rooting out gambling, drinking, and prostitution) was an attempt to treat the symptoms rather than the disease itself and that such campaigns would burn out the energies of a reform administration and leave the fundamental problems of the urban masses untouched. Pingree, like Jones and Johnson, believed that such binges of "Comstockery" were irrelevant to municipal reform. "The good people are always insisting upon 'moral' issues," asserted Toledo Mayor Brand Whitlock, "urging us to turn aside from our large immediate purpose, and concentrate our official attention on the 'bad' people—and wreck our movement."[19]

The saloons where drinking, gambling, and other vices flourished, Pingree, Jones, and Johnson, agreed, were but poor men's clubs and offered the workers but a few of the comforts that most rich men enjoyed. "The most dangerous enemies to good government are not the saloons, the dives, the dens of iniquity and the criminals," Pingree told the Springfield, Massachusetts, Board of Trade. "Most of our troubles can be traced to the temptations which are offered to city officials when franchises are sought by wealthy corporations, or contracts are to be let for public works." For refusing to divert public attention from the "larger and more complex immoralities" of the "privileged" interests, as Brand Whitlock put it, to the more familiar vices, the social reformers earned the bitter censure of the ministerial and "uplift" groups.[20]

The whole tone of the social reform movement was humanistic and empirical. It did not attempt to prescribe standards of personal morality nor did it attempt to draft social blueprints or city charters which had as their goals the imposition of middle class morality and patrician values upon the masses. Instead, it sought to find the basic causes of municipal misgovernment. Pingree, the first of the broad gauged social reformers, discovered the sources of municipal corruption in his day-to-day battle with the light, gas, telephone, and traction interests, the latter represented at the time by Tom Johnson. Johnson, like Mayor Newton D. Baker, knew from his own experience as a utility magnate why municipal government had been demoralized. Mayor Mark Fagan discovered that Jersey City could neither regulate nor tax the utilities and the railroads because both parties were dominated by these interests.[21]

In attempting to reform the city, Pingree, Jones, Johnson, and Whitlock lost upper class and business support and were forced to rely upon the lower classes for political power. The structural reformers, on the other hand, were frequently members of and sponsored by the very social and economic classes which most vehemently opposed social reform. "If we had to depend upon these classes for reforms," Pingree told the *Outlook* in 1897, "they could never have been brought about." "It is not so much the undercrust as

the upper crust," asserted Professor Edward Bemis, who served as a Pingree aide, "that threatens the interests of the people.[22]

The inability of the structural reformers to pursue positive programs to alter the existing social and economic order was probably a reflection of the own business and class backgrounds. Their high regard for the sacrosanct nature of private property, even if obtained illegally, limited them to treating but one aspect of the municipal malaise, and then only when corruption by urban machines reached an intolerable point. This half-way attempt at urban reform prompted Brand Whitlock to observe in 1914: "The word 'reformer' like the word 'politician' has degenerated, and, in the mind of the common man, come to connote something very disagreeable. In four terms as mayor I came to know both species pretty well, and, in the latter connotations of the term, I prefer politician. He, at least, is human."[23]

The structural reform tradition drew much of its strength from a diverse group of theorists composed of good government people, spokesmen for the business community, civic uplifters, representatives of taxpayers' associations, editors, and college professors. The most prominent and influential spokesmen of this persuasion were the Englishman James Bryce, college professors Frank J. Goodnow and William B. Munro, and the editor and scholar Albert Shaw. These theorists diagnosed problems of the city differently from the social reformers. Of fundamental importance to the models they formulated to bring about better city government was their view of the basic causes of the urban malaise. New York's problems, according to Professor Frank Goodnow, had begun in 1857, when the "middle classes, which had thus far controlled the municipal government, were displaced by an ignorant proletariat, mostly foreign born." Three decades later, James Bryce, who dealt with the problems of the city in one of the most influential books of his age, observed that the same "droves of squalid men, who looked as if they had just emerged from an emigrant ship" were herded by urban bosses before magistrates to be enrolled as voters. Such men, said Bryce, were "not fit for suffrage" and "incompetent to give an intelligent vote." Furthermore, their odious habits and demeanor had driven "cultivated" and "sensitive" men out of political life and discouraged the business classes from assuming their share of civic responsibility. One of the most able students of comparative municipal government, Albert Shaw, agreed with Bryce and Goodnow and concluded that the foreign-born had provided the opportunities for the "corruptionist and the demagogue,"[24] who had demoralized city government and lowered the tone of civic responsibility. The immigrant was central to the analyses of the theorists: although a few of them admitted other contributing factors, it is doubtful that any of them believed that the quality of civic responsibility, the level of public morality, and the honesty of urban administrations could have sunk as low had not the immigrant been present in overwhelming numbers in American cities.

Unlike the immigration restrictionists, the theorists did not distinguish between the new and old immigrants but lumped them together with the urban lower classes and attacked the political agencies that had facilitated the rise to power of these new groups. Even the newcomers from Northern Europe "know nothing of the institutions of the country, of its statesmen, of its political issues," Bryce argued. "Neither from Germany nor from Holland do they bring much knowledge of the methods of free government." Lower class representatives from the wards were not welcome in municipal circles, for presumably the district system produced "inferior men" of "narrowed horizons," or as Alfred Conkling put it, permitted the balance of power to be held by the "worst class of men." "Wards largely controlled by thieves and robbers," Cornell's Andrew D. White warned, ". . . can control the city." Harvard's Professor Munro argued that the ward system elected councils that only wasted time and money in "fruitless debate" and sent to councils men "whose standing in the community is negligible." The ward system of representation was denounced by Professors Goodnow and Munro and Delos F. Wilcox for producing the worst representatives in the city. The National Municipal League's model charter called upon municipalities to abolish local representation. In Goodnow's view there were no local interests worthy of political representation anyway.[25]

In building their case against the ability of a mass urban electorate to rule itself, the theorists also drew upon psychology and history. The "craving for excitement" and the "nervous tension" of the city had a degenerative effect, Delos F. Wilcox argued, for "urban life tends to endanger the popular fitness for political power and responsibility." City populations were "radical rather than conservative," and "impulsive rather than reflective," asserted Goodnow, and far less inclined than rural populations to have "regard for the rights of private property." This was caused in part by the fact, Goodnow continued, that urban residents, unlike rural, had "no historical associations" with the cities in which they lived and thus had a poorly developed "neighborhood feeling." The elective system that depended upon familiar relationships and a cohesive community for its success was thus a failure in the city. Goodnow was also disturbed by his study of the larger contours of Western municipal history which convinced him that when city populations had been permitted to develop free of outside control, they evinced an "almost irresistible tendency to establish oligarchical or despotic government." American cities that were under Boss rule, in his opinion, showed similar tendencies.[26]

The first solutions proposed by many spokesmen of reform were hardly original. Outright disfranchisement had been suggested frequently since the end of the Civil War. Some cities had enacted stiffer registration requirements to pare down the vote of the unwashed, and some states had followed the pattern of Michigan, which revoked the alien franchise in 1894. Just as effective, although less direct, was the 1876 recommendation of the New York commissioners for the creation of an upper house with control over money bills in New York City, which was to be elected by propertied voters.[27]

The theorists, however, appear to have been inspired by a contemporary historical event. Drawing upon the Southern experience of disfranchising the Negro, Albert Shaw and Frank Goodnow suggested that such a measure might be applied to Northern cities. The "grandfather clause" apparently convinced Goodnow that the nation was not irrevocably committed

to universal suffrage: once the people became convinced that "universal suffrage inevitably must result in inefficient and corrupt government, it will be abandoned," he predicted. The safe guards of suffrage, Fourteenth and Fifteenth Amendments, did not pose insurmountable obstacles, argued Goodnow. He dismissed the Fourteenth Amendment as merely an appeal to Congress, and he pointed out that the Fifteenth left room for educational and property qualifications.[28]

Accepting the Southern solution as reasonable, Shaw argued that the franchise in the North should be "absolutely" restricted to those who could read English, and "in the case of the foreign-born, to those showing positive fitness for participation in our political and governmental life." Furthermore Shaw argued that European immigrants should be directed southward where they would provide competition for Negroes which would result in a beneficial "survival of the fittest." In order to upgrade the quality of the urban electorate, Professor Munro recommended that the literacy test for the franchise should be extended throughout the nation. Universal suffrage was a "sacrifice of common sense to abstract principles," Bryce asserted. "Nobody pretends that such persons [immigrant voters] are fit for civic duty, or will be dangerous if kept for a time in pupilage, but neither party will incur the odium of proposing to exclude them."[29]

Although demands to purge the unfit elements from urban voting lists were often voiced during the 1890's, it became apparent that such a solution was too drastic. Few civic federations and even fewer politicians picked up the suggestion. Despite the prestige and influence of the theorists, it was evident that disfranchisement was unacceptable to the American public as a way to solve its urban problems. Clearly, less abrasive and more refined techniques would have to be found.

The theorists often spoke of installing into office the "better" classes, the "best" citizens and civic patriots. Excluded were labor, ethnic, or lower class representatives. As Goodnow put it, their choice was "men engaged in active business" or professionals, presumably associated with the business community. The theorists did not distinguish between big and small businessmen, or between enterpreneurs and financiers. What they wanted, as Conklin expressed it, was "any business or professional man . . . who has been successful in private life" and who was reasonably honest. As Richard T. Ely observed, the battle cries of the good government crowd in the 1890's had been: "Municipal government in business not politics." "Wanted, A municipal administration on purely business principles." If one accepted the premise it followed logically, as Ely noted, that businessmen were the "natural and inevitable directors of local affairs."[30]

The theorists argued that the business of city government was business and not politics. The "purely administrative functions—that is to say business functions—outweighed the political functions nine to one," declared Walter Arndt. They extensively used the modern business corporation as a model in their discussions of city government; some called the citizens "stockholders," and others referred to the council as the "board of directors" and the mayor as the "chairman of the board." They spoke of the pressing need for efficiency, the complexity of urban problems, and favored the use of experts to replace elected amateurs. Goodnow argued that a clear distinction must be drawn between legislative and administrative duties and that municipal departments must be staffed by experts. Munro warned that public opinion was the "worst" enemy of the expert and therefore should be rendered less influential in municipal decision-making. In short, the theorists were arguing that the role of public opinion and political expression should be substantially reduced in governing the modern city.[31]

In urging the reconstruction of city government, the theorists called for far-reaching changes in city charters. They advocated a strong mayor system, which accorded with what most of them knew about New York City politics: at least once during each decade since the end of the Civil War, "reformers" had been able to win the mayoralty, although they repeatedly failed to control the city council. The theorists also recommended that the mayor be given complete authority to appoint members to the various municipal boards. Board members, they argued, should serve without pay since this would remove the mercenary motive that prompted professional politicians to serve and, incidentally, would eliminate most of those without substantial wealth as well. If those who got their "living out of their salaries" could be excluded from municipal office, Goodnow argued, the way would be open for the "business and professional classes" to assume control of the city.[32] At the lower levels of municipal administration, Shaw, Goodnow, and Munro recommended a thoroughgoing application of the civil-service system, which also tended to eliminate ethnic and lower class representatives. A professional civil service at the lower grades, the theorists argued, would create a good technical and supportive staff and, as Goodnow put it, "make it possible for the business and professional classes of the community to assume the care of public business without making too great personal sacrifices."[33]

The recommendations of the theorists aimed at weakening popular control over the legislative arm of government, the city council. Goodnow was convinced that the council system, since it provided so many "incompetent if not corrupt men," should not be a powerful force in municipal government. Goodnow was more favorably impressed by municipal arrangements in Berlin, Germany, where a propertied electorate comprising less than 10 per cent of the voters elected two-thirds of the city council. "This gives to the wealthier class the directing voice in municipal affairs," commented Professor Leo S. Rowe with approval. Andrew D. White argued that men of property should be represented by a board of control, "without whose permission no franchise should be granted and no expenditure should be made." The English system which in effect disfranchised most lower class slum residents also met with Goodnow's favor. Councils elected by a nonpropertied franchise disturbed Goodnow, for such bodies often prodded cities into "undertakings which are in excess of the city's economic resources." Evidently pessimistic about changing the basis of municipal suffrage to one of property, Goodnow reversed the formula and suggested that to extend the taxpaying obligation to more citizens might produce better councils. That failing, he supported state intervention to limit taxing and spending of municipal governments. "The trouble

with leaving our cities to govern themselves, at least along purely democratic lines," argued C. E. Pickard, is "that they are utterly unworthy of trust."[34]

The theorists also argued for fewer elective offices and smaller city councils. "Men of little experience and less capacity have found it easy to get themselves elected to membership in large city councils," asserted Munro. Smaller councils would presumably concentrate responsibility and produce better men. The at-large election was a favorite device of the theorists and one of the most important structural changes they proposed. City-wide elections to the council, in their opinion, could be won only by men of commanding presence and city-wide prominence. Obviously the lower class politician or the ethnic representative who served his ward well would come out second best if pitted against a prominent businessman or professional. Not until late in the Progressive period, after the at-large system began to elect the "better classes" into office, did the theorists return to decentralizing authority and to expanding the powers of councilmen who then would be known as city commissioners. The ideas of the theorists make it difficult to quibble with Frederic C. Howe's observation: "Distrust of democracy has inspired much of the literature on the city."[35]

Agencies to regulate utility rates, to investigate tax inequities, or to foster and advance social reform were not on the drawing boards of the theorists. Few of them focused their wrath and moral indignation upon the corrupting influence of privately owned utilities and the real estate interests on city councils. They were less bothered by the businessman who bribed the city council than by the machine politician who accepted the bribe. Yerkes and Whitney seldom warranted their attention in the way that Tweed did. They chose instead to focus responsibility upon the individuals who sat on councils and the political systems that elected them rather than upon the business interests that sought favorable franchises, tax favoritism, and city services, such as paving, sewers, and water, which enhanced the value of their enterprises.

The ideas of the theorists were not lost upon the practitioners and designers of good city government. The structural reformers began to design new forms of urban organization and to codify the ideas of the theorists into new city charters. Two decades of searching and theorizing produced the city commissioner and later the city manager systems.

The theorists provided the rationale for the most radical departure the American city took in all its history. The widespread adoption of the commissioner and manager systems late in the Progressive period brought about what one scholar called a "revolution in the theory and practice of city government." Although the commissioner system had its origins in an accident of nature, it and the manager plan soon became the favored devices for achieving what the old political system could not—namely, the large scale movement of businessmen and business-minded representatives into public office. Both systems were patterned after the modern business corporation and rapidly adopted its ideals. Henry Bruère, a director of the New York Bureau of Municipal Research, boasted that commission governments were often made a "part of the progressive programs of 'boosting' commercial organizations." "Money saving and efficiency" were

pursued as key objectives under the manager plan. The "Godfather of City Managerism," Richard S. Childs, observed that the city managers at their fourth annual conference could "unblushingly point with pride" to an average savings of 10 per cent in tax levies in the cities under his brain child. The first city manager of the publicized "Dayton Plan," Henry M. Waite, admitted that the "main thing" the nation's fifty manager towns had accomplished up to 1917 was a "financial saving." "Economy, not service," James Weinstein correctly asserted, was the "basic principle" of both the commissioner and manager systems. As Harold A. Stone has suggested, and Weinstein has demonstrated, no important reform movement of the Progressive period was more peculiarly the captive of organized business than the commissioner and manager movements.[36]

Although the commissioner and manager systems achieved their greatest success in middle-sized and smaller cities, they represented the ultimate ideal of the earlier theorists (whose major concern had been large American cities). Commissioner and manager reorganization brought about in its finished form the structural arrangements that facilitated the movement into office of that class of people whom Bryce, Goodnow, Munro, and Shaw believed best fitted and qualified to rule the city. Chambers of commerce and the dominant business groups were the main force behind the movement, and, as James Weinstein and Samuel P. Hays have demonstrated, these new forms facilitated the inflow of the commercial and upper class elements into the centers of municipal power at the price of ethnic and lower class representation.[37] The business model of municipal government would eventually spread to nearly one-half of our cities, and the structural-reform persuasion would dominate the main stream of urban reform thought in the twentieth century.[38] This extension of the instruments and the ideology of the business world would help to return to power men with the temperaments of Havemeyer, Cleveland, and Low and considerably diminish the electoral prospects for men like Pingree, Jones, and Johnson—as well as like Tweed.

The conservative revolution in city government would also help to end the process whereby astute politicians and socially-conscious reformers used the political system to ease the shock of assimilation for newcomers into American life. The political machine may have been one of the most important institutions not only for acknowledging the immigrant's existence but for interpreting a new environment to him and helping him to adjust to a bewildering new society.

By concentrating on the mechanistic and bureaucratic aspects of city government and by throwing the weight of their influence behind the election of businessmen, the theorists grossly oversimplified the problems of the city. Wiping out lower class and foreign-born corruption unfortunately took precedence in their minds over the social needs of the city. The theorists confined themselves to dealing with the plumbing and hardware of city government and finally became narrow administrative reformers. In the process, they deceived themselves and helped to mislead a generation of reformers into thinking that they were dealing with the fundamental problems of the city, when in reality they were retooling the machinery of urban

government to fit the needs of the business world.

Characteristically, the manager and commissioner movement, which represented the greatest achievement of the structural-reform tradition, experienced its greatest success during the twilight of the Progressive period and during the nineteen twenties,[39] when great expectations for social reform were withering and receding. This late triumph of good government reform was not an accident of historical timing. It was not a case of cultural lag, nor can it be attributed to a late blooming of the urban Progressive spirit. If anything, new concepts and systems of organization usually appeared sooner at the urban level than at the national. The victory of the manager-commissioner system during the age of Harding and Coolidge was an historical acknowledgement of the basically conservative nature of the structural-reform tradition. The nation had finally tailored the urban political organization and molded reform thought to respond to the most powerful economic forces in the city. In this instance it was not free silver but the chamber of commerce that became the cowbird of reform. This should not be surprising, for the chamber of commerce and its affiliates had also proved to be the greatest obstacle to social reform in Pingree's Detroit.

NOTES

1. Lincoln Steffens, *The Autobiography of Lincoln Steffens* (New York, 1931), pp. 374–75; Hewitt quoted in *Pilgrim*, III (December, 1901), 4.
2. Hazen S. Pingree, "Address to the Nineteenth Century Club of New York," November 11, 1897, p. 7; S. M. Jones to Josiah Strong, November 15, 1898, Jones Papers; Brand Whitlock, *Forty Years of It* (New York, 1914), pp. 172–74.
3. Frederic C. Howe, *The City: The Hope of*

Democracy (New York, 1913), pp. 1, 2. For the elitist views of reformers who overthrew Boss Tweed, see Alexander B. Callow, Jr., *The Tweed Ring* (New York, 1966), pp. 69–71, 265–67. Charles R. Adrian, "Some General Characteristics of Nonpartisan Elections," Robert C. Wood, "Nonpartisanship in Suburbia," both in *Democracy in Urban America*, ed. Oliver P. Williams and Charles Press (Chicago, 1964), pp. 251–66. For an exposition of the views regarding municipal government of one of the most prominent twentieth-century "structural" reformers, see Richard S. Childs, "The Faith of a Civic Reformer," ibid., pp. 222–24. The "elitist commitments" of the city manager system (as prescribed in city government textbooks) can also be seen in Lawrence J. R. Herson, "The Lost World of Municipal Government," *American Political Science Review*, LI (June, 1957), 330–45.

4. Howard B. Furer, *William Frederick Havemeyer: A Political Biography* (New York, 1965), pp. 14, 144–54, 160; Seymour J. Mandelbaum, *Boss Tweed's New York* (New York, 1965), pp. 91, 97, 108, 111; Callow, *The Tweed Ring*, pp. 253–86.

5. Mandelbaum, *Boss Tweed's New York*, pp. 98–100, 111; Furer, *William F. Havemeyer*, pp. 156, 158, 160–61, 169.

6. Ibid., p. 161; Mandelbaum, *Boss Tweed's New York*, pp. 112–13; William L. Riordin, *Plunkitt of Tammany Hall* (New York, 1963), p. 17.

7. Allan Nevins, *Grover Cleveland, A Study in Courage* (New York, 1941), pp. 61–62, 83–94.

8. Harold Coffin Syrett, *The City of Brooklyn 1865–1898, A Political History* (New York, 1944), p. 134; Steven C. Swett, "The Test of a Reformer: A study of Seth Low," *New York Historical Society Quarterly*, XLIV (January, 1960), pp. 8, 9; Lincoln Steffens, *The Shame of the Cities* (New York, 1966), p. 201.

9. Syrett, *Brooklyn*, pp. 104–6, 109–19, 134; Swett, "Test of a Reformer," pp. 7–9.

10. Albert Fein, "New York City Politics From 1897–1903; A Study in Political Party Leadership" (M.A. thesis, Columbia University, 1954), pp. 19–20; Swett, "Test of a Reformer," pp. 10–14, 16–18.

11. Ibid., pp. 21–23, 26–31, 35–36; Roy Lubove, *The Progressives and the Slums, Tenement House Reform in New York City, 1890–1917* (Pittsburgh, 1962), pp. 153–54.

12. Swett, "Test of a Reformer," pp. 6, 32, 35–36, 38–41; Wallace S. Sayre and Herbert Kaufman, *Governing New York City Politics in the Metropolis* (New York, 1960), p. 695.

13. James D. Phelan, "Municipal Conditions and the New Charter," *Overland Monthly*, XXVIII (no. 163, 2nd series), pp. 104–11; Roy Swanstrom, "Reform Administration of James D. Phelan, Mayor of San Francisco, 1897–1902" (M.A. thesis, University of California-Berkeley, 1949), pp. 77–79, 80, 83, 85, 86; Walton Bean, *Boss Ruef's San Francisco: The Story of the Union Labor Party, Big Business, and the Graft Prosecution* (Berkeley, 1952), pp. 8, 9, 16, 17, 23; George E. Mowry, *The California Progressives* (Chicago, 1963), pp. 23–25; Fremont Older, *My Own Story* (San Francisco, 1919), pp. 27, 31, 65.

14. William E. Leuchtenburg, Preface to Edwin R. Lewinson, *John Purroy Mitchel: The Boy Mayor of New York* (New York, 1965), pp. 11–13; Lewinson, *Boy Mayor*, pp. 93, 95, 100, 102, 117, 124.

15. Leuchtenburg, ibid., p. 12; Lewinson, ibid., pp. 18, 151–69, 175–88.

16. Leuchtenburg, ibid., pp. 11–13; Samuel P. Hayes, "The Politics of Reform in Municipal Government," *Pacific Northwest Quarterly*, LV (October, 1964), pp. 157–69.

17. Lewinson, *Boy Mayor*, pp. 11–13, 18, 93, 95, 102; Riordin, *George Washington Plunkitt*, pp. 17–20; Swett, "Seth Low," pp. 8, 9; Allan Nevins, *Abram S. Hewitt: With Some Account of Peter Cooper* (New York, 1935), pp. 515–16, 529–30; Seth Low, "An American View of Municipal Government in the United States," in James Bryce, *The American Commonwealth* (New York, 1893), I, 651, 665.

18. Hoyt Landon Warner, *Progressivism in Ohio 1897–1917* (Columbus, 1964), pp. 32, 70–72; Whitlock, *Forty Years of It*, pp. 211, 252; Clarence H. Cramer, *Newton D. Baker: A Biography* (Cleveland, 1961), pp. 46–47; Steffens, *Autobiography of Lincoln Steffens*, pp. 477, 492–93; Frederic C. Howe, *The Confessions of a Reformer* (New York, 1925), pp. 98, 102–8; Pingree, *Facts and Opinions*, p. 196. For Mark Fagan, see Lincoln Steffens, *Upbuilders* (New York, 1909), pp. 28, 30, 33, 35, and Ransom E. Noble, Jr., *New Jersey Progressivism before Wilson* (Princeton, 1946), pp. 13–42. St. Louis Circuit Attorney Joseph W. Folk (1901–04), who began his career by investigating and prosecuting franchise "grabs," discovered that the real despoilers of municipal government were not minor city officials but promoters, bankers, and corporation directors who profited by misgovernment. After he became governor he dropped his crime-busting and supported progressive and urban reforms. Louis G. Geiger, *Joseph W. Folk of Missouri* (Columbia, 1953), pp. 32, 41, 81, 88, 93, 99–117. Robert Wiebe's assertion that the "typical business ally of the boss, moreover, was a rather marginal operator, anathema to the chamber of commerce" is at variance with what is known about the political influence wielded in Detroit by urban capitalists such as the Hendries, McMillans and Johnson or for that matter with the role played by Yerkes and Insull in Chicago, Mark Hanna in Cleveland and the Huntington interests in Los Angeles, just to cite a few examples. *The Search for Order, 1877–1920* (New York, 1967), p. 167.

19. Steffens, *Upbuilders*, pp. 3–45; Warner, *Progressivism in Ohio, 1897–1917*, pp. 71, 74; Cra-

mer, *Newton D. Baker*, pp. 50–52; Howe, *Confessions of a Reformer*, pp. 90–93, 108–9; Carl Lorenz, *Tom L. Johnson, Mayor of Cleveland* (New York, 1911), p. 152; Steffens, *Autobiography of Lincoln Steffens*, p. 480; Detroit *Free Press*, March 14, 1896, P.S.; Samuel M. Jones to Henry D. Lloyd, April 16, 1897, Lloyd Papers; Samuel M. Jones to James L. Cowes, April 27, 1897; Tom L. Johnson to S. M. Jones, May 3, 1902, Jones Papers; Harvey S. Ford, "The Life and Times of Golden Rule Jones" (Ph.D. thesis, University of Michigan, 1953), pp. 185, 284–85, 330; Whitlock, *Forty Years of It*, p. 212. William D. Miller has argued that "Boss" Edward H. Crump, who was Memphis mayor from 1910 to 1916, stands with "Golden Rule" Jones and Tom L. Johnson as a typical progressive of the period, but an examination of Miller's book raises serious doubts about that judgment. Although Crump occasionally employed reform rhetoric, established a few milk stations for the poor, and put screens on public school windows, he used most of the energy of his administration to enforce the laws and instill efficiency into the municipal government in the structural-reform tradition. Crump wiped out "policy" playing by Negroes, eliminated loafing by the garbage collectors and street pavers, forced the railroads to construct eleven underpasses, lowered city taxes, reduced waste in municipal government by extending audit procedures even to the purchase of postage stamps, and increased city income by selling empty bottles, feed sacks, and scrap. William D. Miller, *Mr. Crump of Memphis* (Baton Rouge, 1964), pp. 79–113. Brooklyn's Mayor Charles A. Schieren (1894–95), who gained some stature as a reformer by defeating a venal Democratic machine, also followed a well-trodden path of cleaning out "deceit and corruption" and installing "integrity, nonpartisanship, and routine efficiency." Like most of the reform mayors of his period, Schieren failed to advance or support social reform programs, Harold C. Syrett, *The City of Brooklyn, 1865–1898, A Political History* (New York, 1944), pp. 218–32. Geoffrey Blodgett has tried to show that Boston became for "a brief time the cutting edge of urban reform in America" under Mayor Josiah Quincy (1896–1900), who established a publicly owned printing plant and expanded the city's playgrounds. Although the Dover Street Bath House may have been a "monument to municipal socialism" as Blodgett contends, Mayor Quincy stopped his programs short of anything that would have threatened the vested interests in the traction and utility business. Geoffrey Blodgett, *The Gentle Reformers: Massachusetts Democrats in the Cleveland Era* (Cambridge, 1966), pp. 240–61. For Quincy's absurd notion that regular bathing would cause the "filthy tenement house" to disappear, crime and drunkenness to decrease and the death rate to drop, see Josiah Quincy, "Municipal Progress in Boston," *Independent*, LII (February 15, 1900), 424. Henry Demarest Lloyd was critical

of Mayor Quincy's failure to resist the traction interests and referred to the Mayor's public baths as Quincy's "little sops." H. D. Lloyd to Samuel Bowles, December 13, 1898, Lloyd Papers.
20. Ford, "Golden Rule Jones," pp. 151, 166, 339; Samuel M. Jones to Dr. [Graham] Taylor, October 5, 1897; S. M. Jones to L. L. Dagett, April 17, 1899, Jones Papers; Hazen S. Pingree address to Springfield, Massachusetts Board of Trade, March 3, 1894, Ralph Stone Scrapbook; Whitlock, *Forty Years of It*, pp. 252, 254.
21. Robert H. Bremner, "The Civic Revival in Ohio: The Fight Against Privilege in Cleveland and Toledo, 1890–1912" (Ph.D. thesis, Ohio State University, 1943), p. 25; Hazen S. Pingree, "The Problem of Municipal Reform. Contract by Referendum," *Arena*, XVII (April, 1897), 707–10; Cramer, *Newton D. Baker*, p. 46; Steffens, *Upbuilders*, pp. 28–30, 33, 35; Noble, *New Jersey Progressivism before Wilson*, pp. 25–26, 35, 38.
22. Tom L. Johnson *My Story* (New York, 1911), p. 113; Ford, "Golden Rule Jones," pp. 136–37, 70, 339; Hazen S. Pingree, "Detroit: A Municipal Study," *Outlook*, LV (February 6, 1897), 437; Bemis quoted in Detroit *Evening News:* June 21, 1899, Stone Scrapbook; Whitlock, *Forty Years of It*, p. 221.
23. Whitlock, *Forty Years of It*, p. 221.
24. Frank J. Goodnow, "The Tweed Ring in New York City," in James Bryce's *The American Commonwealth* (London, 1888), II, 335; Bryce, *ibid.*, p. 67; Bryce, *ibid.*, I, 613; Albert Shaw, *Political Problems of American Development* (New York, 1907), p. 66. According to Edwin L. Godkin, New York City's problems began with the establishment of universal suffrage in 1846 which coincided with the beginning of the great Irish migration. Edwin L. Godkin, *Problems of Modern Democracy*, ed. Morton Keller (New York, 1896, Cambridge, 1966), p. 133.
25. Bryce, *American Commonwealth*, II, 67; William B. Munro, *The Government of American Cities* (New York, 1913), pp. 308–9, 310, 312; Andrew D. White, "The Government of American Cities," *Forum*, X (December, 1890), 369; Alfred R. Conkling, *City Government in the United States* (New York, 1899), p. 49; Frank J. Goodnow, *Municipal Problems* (New York, 1897), pp. 150–53; Delos F. Wilcox, *The Study of City Government* (New York, 1897), p. 151; "Report of the Committee on Municipal Program," *Proceedings* of the Indianapolis Conference for Good City Government and Fourth Annual Meeting of the National Municipal League (Philadelphia, 1898), p. 11 (hereafter cited *Proceedings for Good City Government*).
26. Wilcox, *The Study of City Government*, pp. 237–38; Frank J. Goodnow, *Municipal Government* (New York, 1910), pp. 39, 149, 378–79; James T. Young, *Proceedings for Good City Government*, 1901, p. 230.
27. *Michigan Legislative Manual and Official Directory 1899–1900* (Lansing, 1899), p. 322; *Report of the Commission to Devise a Plan for*

the Government of Cities in the State of New York (New York, 1877), pp. 35–36.

28. Goodnow, Municipal Problems, pp. 148–49.

29. Shaw, Political Problems of American Development, pp. 65–67, 82, 125; Munro, Government of American Cities, pp. 120–21; Bryce, American Commonwealth, II, 67.

30. Goodnow, Municipal Problems, p. 278; Conkling, City Government in the United States, p. 34; Richard T. Ely, The Coming City (New York, 1902), p. 29.

31. Walter T. Arndt, The Emancipation of the American City (New York, 1917), p. 12; Frank M. Sparks, Government As a Business (Chicago, 1916), pp. 1, 7; Goodnow, Municipal Government, pp. 150, 381–82; Munro, Government of American Cities, p. 306; William H. Tolman, Municipal Reform Movements in the United States (New York, 1895), p. 34.

32. Conkling, City Government in the United States, pp. 6, 32; Goodnow, Municipal Problems, pp. 262–65.

33. Ibid., pp. 204–5, 265; Munro, Government of American Cities, pp. 241, 279–80; Albert Shaw, "Civil Service Reform and Municipal Government," in Civil Service Reform and Municipal Government (New York, 1897), pp. 3–7.

34. Goodnow, Municipal Government, pp. 142–46, 385–86, and Municipal Problems, pp. 66–67; Leo S. Rowe, "City Government As It Should Be And May Become," Proceedings for Good City Government, 1894, p. 115; White, "The Government of American Cities," p. 370; John Agar, "Shall American Cities Municipalize?" Municipal Affairs, IV (March, 1900), 14–20; C. E. Pickard, "Great Cities and Democratic Institutions," American Journal of Politics, IV (April, 1894), 385. The Boston mayor Nathan Mathews, Jr., asserted that the proposal to restrict municipal suffrage to the propertied classes was one of the most common remedies for the evils of city government of his age. Nathan Mathews, Jr., The City Government of Boston (Boston, 1895), p. 176.

35. Munro, Government of American Cities, pp. 294, 308–10; Goodnow, Municipal Problems, pp. 150–53; Leo S. Rowe, "American Political Ideas and Institutions in Their Relation to the Problem of the City," Proceedings for Good City Government, 1897, p. 77; William Dudley Foulke, ibid., 1898, p. 137; Frederic C. Howe, The City, The Hope of Democracy (New York, 1913), p. 1.

36. Henry Bruère, "Efficiency in City Government," Annals of the American Academy of Political and Social Science, XLI (May, 1912), 19; Richard S. Childs, "Now that We Have the City Manager Plan, What Are We Going to Do With It," Fourth Yearbook of the City Managers' Association (Auburn, 1918), pp. 82–83; Henry M. Waite, ibid., pp. 88–89; Harold A. Stone, Don K. Price and Kathryn H. Stone, City Manager Government in the United States (Chicago, 1940), pp. 25–27; James Weinstein, "Organized Business and the City Commissioner and Manager Movements," Journal of Southern History, XXVIII (May, 1962), 166, 179.

37. Ibid., p. 173; Samuel P. Hayes, "The Politics of Reform in Municipal Government in the Progressive Era," Pacific Northwest Quarterly, LV (October, 1964), 157–69.

38. Edward C. Banfield and James Q. Wilson, City Politics (New York, 1963), p. 148.

39. The peak period for the spread of the city commissioner and the city manager system was 1917–27. Leonard D. White, The City Manager (Chicago, 1927), p. 317; Harold Zink, Government of Cities in the United States (New York, 1939), p. 301.

Knocko Minihan's Wake

EDWIN O'CONNOR

At 7:30, Adam [Skeffington's nephew] was waiting; Skeffington, on the other hand, was not. His unpunctuality inviolable, he was fifteen minutes late, and as the long official car pulled up he said genially, "Hop in. As a taxpayer, you're entitled to. Try the comforts of the vehicle you thoughtfully provided for me."

Adam got in. Determined to remove all mystery from the outset, he said, "By the way, when we were talking this afternoon I completely forgot to ask you where we were going."

"So you did," Skeffington said. "I took it as a rare mark of confidence; now I find it was only a lapse of memory. One more illusion lost." He chuckled and said, "Actually, we're going to a wake. Knocko Minihan's wake."

"A *wake?*"

"Surprised? I had an idea you might be: there was just the possibility that you weren't in the habit of spending your free evenings in visiting deceased strangers. But I felt that tonight it might be useful for you to come along. In its way, a wake can be quite an occasion."

"You may be underestimating me," Adam said. "I've been to a few wakes. Not many, but a few."

"I don't doubt it. Probably not exactly like this one, however. Not that poor Knocko's will be unique, but it might be a little different from those you've been to." . . .

"And how did he make out after this terrible start?"

"Not too well. Save in one respect, that is. He [Knocko Minihan] married a grand woman who was a close friend of my wife's—your aunt's," he said. "In every other way he was a failure. He had a hardware store that he ran into the ground almost before the opening-day sale was over. Then he tried several other businesses, all of which petered out in no time at all. I don't know that people trusted him especially, and they certainly didn't like him. And neither," he said, rather surprisingly, "did I. However, *de mortuis* . . ."

"If nobody liked him," Adam said, "I imagine we'll run into a fairly slim attendance tonight."

"Not at all," said Skeffington. "The place'll be crowded to the doors. A wake isn't quite the same as a popularity contest. There are other factors involved. Ah, here we are." . . .

While they stood in the hall, more people came in; clearly, the wake of Knocko Minihan was expanding. As it did, Adam was struck by the altered deportment of his uncle; it was almost as if, from being one of the visiting mourners, he had suddenly become the host. He nodded and spoke briefly to all the new arrivals; without exception, all responded in identical fashion: a muttered acknowledgment of the pitiful fact of Knocko's death, followed by a perceptibly more fervent statement of good wishes. . . . "That's a role I occasionally practice: the combination physician, caterer and master of ceremonies. It's something I might have to fall back on one day when I retire from politics."

"I am impressed," Adam said truthfully. "I hadn't realized that all this was a part of your job."

"Well, this is rather a special case. The widow's an old friend, and in her present condition she's in no shape to arrange for the usual civilities. So I just had a few things sent over." It was a detail he had taken care of that afternoon; the food had come from the ample commissariat of the Wadsworth Hospital. As this was a city institution, the food had been provided for by public funds; it was, in a word, a tax-supported wake. And all for Knocko Minihan; the beneficiary, thought Skeffington, was unworthy of the occasion. He said to Adam, "I'm not so sure that all the arrangements would meet with Knocko's approval, but then of course, when you come right down to it, he's not really in much of a position to complain, is he? Come along, I want to go in here."

They entered the next door down the hall; Adam found himself in a room which compared favorably with the parlor in its size and general hideousness, but which contained many more people and a great deal more noise. It was not until he had been in this room for a moment that he realized that there was still another difference: here, the mourners were exclusively male. To his surprise, he recognized some of them as the old familiars of his uncle's outer office. They had disdained the chairs which had been set out for them in a severe row which paralleled the wall;

they preferred to stand, talking, smoking, moving, waiting. When Skeffington came in, the waiting was over. They surged around him, the noise grew, and Adam was soon separated from his uncle by a tight, struggling double ring of the self-appointed palace guard. He caught Skeffington's eye; in return he received a quick but unmistakable wink, the meaning of which was quite clear. For the moment at least, he was on his own; Skeffington had decided that it was time for his field of experience to be widened still further. . . .

Adam could not help marveling at the completeness of Knocko's failure to dominate, or even to intrude upon, his own wake. Here in the antechamber he was playing a bad second fiddle to the swapped vote and the living Skeffington; in the adjoining room, where the women were gathered before the bier, was he equally unfortunate? Presumably so: City Hall undoubtedly possessed its Ladies' Auxiliary. Yet there, perhaps the tactless presence of the casket and its contents might severely hamper political discussion; upon further consideration, however, he was inclined to doubt this. It was evident now that they had come tonight neither to bury Knocko nor to praise him; they had come to ignore him. The more one considered this neglect, Adam thought, the more callous one discovered it to be, and despite his resolutions to be prepared for all possible developments, he was somewhat shocked by this one.

Cuke and Ditto [two political small fry] had continued to talk; they were interrupted by the approach of old John Gorman. He had been standing to the left of the ring surrounding Skeffington, talking to petitioners with more modest or more localized requests. Now he came across the room, a remarkably neat, spare old man, straight as a string; when he reached them he said softly, "Ditto. Run down to the car now and tell Patsy to take you down to Ryan's for a half-dozen boxes of cigars. He'll know the kind. You'd best go along with him, Cuke. The fresh night air will do your lungs a world of good."

The two men obeyed instantly. It was, for both, an errand of pleasure, and besides, an order from Gorman was an order from Skeffington. Gorman turned to Adam, smiling faintly.

"There's no greater turn you could do Ditto," he said. "Up in the back seat of the big black car, just himself and Cuke. Almost as good as if it was just himself. Well now, did the two of them tell you all about politics?"

"Not quite," Adam said. . . . "Although the subject did manage to come up, Mr. Gorman. As a matter of fact, it was just about the only subject that did come up."

"Ah well, that's natural enough," the old man said mildly. "If you met the Pope you'd talk about religion."

Adam smiled. "I suppose so. Still, wouldn't we also talk just a bit about Knocko Minihan? Particularly if we happened to meet at his wake?"

"It would be the pious thing to do, no doubt," Gorman agreed. "But then if you both knew Knocko, you might damn well want to talk about almost anything else in a hurry. Out of respect for the dead, you might say."

"Yes, I see. But what I don't see is this: if Knocko was such a generally disliked man, why are so many people here tonight? They didn't come to gloat, obviously; they're not ghouls. But then why did they come?"

"That I'm not sure about. Still," the old man said thoughtfully, "I wouldn't think you'd be far wrong if you said

they came as you did yourself. For the very same reason, that is."

Adam stared at him. "But I came only because of my uncle."

"So you did," Gorman said. "So you did, indeed."

"Then you mean that all these other people came because of Uncle Frank, too?"

"Ah well, I wouldn't say all; that'd be a bit of an exaggeration. You had a little chat with Delia Boylan, I hear" —suddenly and irrelevantly, it occurred to Adam that there seemed to be very little that this old man did *not* hear— "and there's some that came like Delia: they just enjoy themselves going to a wake. It's like little boys and girls going to birthday parties. Then there's some that came on the widow's account: Gert's a fine woman, and she has her friends. And there may be a few no doubt came for Knocko himself; they say," he said wryly, "there's saints amongst us even today. I don't run into many myself. But most of them that are here tonight stopped by for the one reason: they knew your Uncle Frank was to come. And that's the long and the short of it." He saw no point in mentioning the delegations from the different city departments who were here in compulsory attendance; it would only complicate the issue. The boy, he reflected, was a good boy, but young; naturally, he could have no idea of the way things were done. To tell him would be to serve no purpose save perhaps an educational one, and John Gorman was really not wildly interested in telling the young the facts of life.

"And so," Adam said, "while it's Knocko's wake, it's really my uncle who's the main attraction?"

Gorman nodded. "It is."

Adam said, "And naturally business

goes on as usual; Only here instead of at the Hall?" His feeling of shock had increased; the whole business, he decided, was a really appalling mixture of hypocrisy and hardness.

"You have things a little twisty," the old man said softly, "if you don't mind me saying so." A little rap across the knuckles was in order, he decided; not a hard rap, to be sure, for he was a good lad and he was Skeffington's nephew, but a rap all the same. It was for the lad's own good; it would help to keep him from leaping about like a salmon to the wrong conclusions. He said, "You're a bit hard on your uncle, I think. The man has no need to go to wakes if he wants to collect a crowd about him; he can do that anywhere. All he has to do is stop on a street corner to light his cigar and fifty people come out of the cement to say, 'Hello Frank, and what can you do for me today?' And when he showed up here tonight is wasn't to talk politics. He can do that any minute of the day, any place he likes; he needs no dead man in the next room to help him tell Tommy Mulcahy that the polls are open from eight to eight on Election Day, and only one vote to a customer this year. What he came here for tonight is simple as simple can be: he came to bring a crowd to Knocko's wake so the widow would feel a little better. Knocko's been lying here all day yesterday, all last night, and all day today: how many people d'ye s'pose came in to see him in all that time? Maybe thirty-five, and ten of those came in to get out of the rain. Tonight there'll be hundreds here, and the widow'll think it's all Knocko's pals, waiting till the last moment to bid him good-by. But with all those people in here, and your uncle here to bring them, what in the name of Heaven are they to talk about but what

they like and what they know? God knows they can't talk about Knocko. Half of them never knew the man, and the other half that knew him didn't like him. That's not the kind of thing that makes for easy conversation. And you can't keep a roomful of men talking in soft voices about what a terrible thing death is, and will he go to Heaven, and maybe is he up there this very minute looking down on us all? Those are grand thoughts, but somehow nobody is able to keep thinking them for two hours whilst waiting for the priest to get here to say the Rosary. So they have a little food and they talk a little politics, and I don't know that they do a great amount of harm with either. And then when the priest does get in at last and they all kneel down to pray for Knocko, you might put your mind to this: there'll be ten times the people here praying for him as would be here without your uncle and all the chatter about politics. I don't s'pose they'll all be praying away as holy as St. Francis, but you never know about a thing like that; maybe some of them will mean it, and maybe it'll do Knocko a bit of good. I have the suspicion that he's in no mood at the moment to throw away any prayers from friend or foe; he's likely to be needing anything in that line that comes his way." He paused; it had been a speech of fantastic length for this ordinarily taciturn old man. Still, he reflected, sometimes a bit of gab was needed to drive a point home. He wondered: had it done the trick? He hoped so; looking at the boy, he thought so. In any case, it was all he had to say on the subject. "So that being the way it is," he concluded, his mild blue eyes resting on Adam's face, and his thin old lips twisted once more into the just perceptible smile, "don't be too hard on us, boy. I don't doubt but that it's a bit different from what you're used to here tonight, but it's no terrible thing that's being done." . . .

. . . He considered the subject for Adam's instruction now closed. With his lips slightly pursed, he began to look slowly about the room, watching for developments that might have taken place while he had been talking. One of these was in the doorway even now. He said to Adam, "Now there's your man for you, over by the door. D'ye know him?"

Adam saw a short, stout man with oddly protuberant eyes who had paused to regard the room before entering; he was middle-aged, and dressed in a rumpled gray suit; under his right arm he carried what looked to be a small shoebox. Although he stood motionless in the doorway, there was something about him which suggested perpetual and hectic movement; one felt that to see him thus at a standstill was like seeing a hummingbird forcibly immobilized: it was somehow unfair. Or at least so Adam felt; it was the first time he had set eyes on Charlie Hennessey.

Evidently Charlie had chosen Gorman and Adam as his immediate goal. He came towards them with his curious little skating steps, and was on them even before Gorman had an opportunity to identify him for Adam. In any case, such identification would have been unnecessary, for Charlie identified himself.

"Hello, my dear man," he said to Gorman. "You're looking very well, John: a nice, even, healthy color. That speaks of a good circulation. Marvelous! The blood's the thing. And this must be Frank's nephew, Adam Caulfield by name. I'm Charles Hennessey,

my dear man. I read you daily in the funny papers. Nice drawing, a good sense of humor. Marvelous! I read all the papers and everything that's in them. Well, my dear man," he said, turning again to Gorman, "I see the boss still has the touch. Oh, the grand touch! You have to hand it to the man. The most unpopular man in the ward dies and almost before he's cool there's a mob scene round the casket shouting, 'Three cheers for Skeffington for mayor!' Marvelous! Shrewd! Getting votes out of Knocko, like getting blood out of the turnip. They call it alchemy, a kind of old-time magic. And Frank's the master magician. Imagination! Foresight! The only man among us to realize that you could get a good turn out of Knocko after all: you only had to wait until the man was dead. Oh, clever! My hat's off to the man!"

Adam looked up sharply as this extraordinary man voiced what was substantially the charge he himself had made only minutes before; would he, too, suffer the Gorman rebuke? But the old man merely seemed amused; he said simply, "Ah, that's all moonshine, Charlie. All gas." To Adam he said significantly, "Charlie here is running against your uncle for mayor."

"Yes, yes, fighting tooth and nail," Charlie said briskly. "All in the interests of decent government. And of course what I'm saying is the very reverse of gas, my dear man. All truth! It's a matter of public record that Frank Skeffington has been campaigning at wakes for fifty years. Big wakes or small ones, it made no difference. If nobody died for the six months before an election he wouldn't know where to go. He's spent half a century with one eye on the coffin! A Skeffington maxim: Never neglect the relatives, friends or enemies of the deceased. I've studied the man all my life and I'm very familiar with his methods of operation, my dear man."

Gorman said, "Charlie—"

Charlie held up a warning finger, he bounced up and down for emphasis. "Which is not to say the man does no good," he said. "Far from it. Oh no no no, my dear man! In his way he does a world of good: I freely give him credit. He comes to a wake, he draws a crowd, and he keeps everybody in the house that should be crying so busy carting sandwiches they forget to cry. Occupational therapy, my dear man! The touch of a master psychologist! Another Skeffington maxim: Stampede them! Give them no time to think! And on top of that the man is charitable. A heart of gold, you can't take that away from him. If the widow here tonight should need a little cash, she'll get it without asking. If she needs a job, there'll be one waiting for her at City Hall tomorrow morning; she can sit around all day stuffing empty papers into envelopes and mailing them to herself. Nice light work and one of the best-paying jobs in the city. Marvelous! A likable trait in the man. Not good government, but likable. Generous! But by the same token, my dear man, it's not a one-way street. Oh, by no means! *Quid pro quo*, as Julius Caesar used to say. Which means, 'I'll do fine by the wake, but it'll do twice as fine by me!' Oh yes yes! Marvelous! Shrewd!"

Altogether, thought Adam, an amazing performance; however, its primary effect had been to leave him increasingly doubtful about the necessity for his own apology. Once more he looked at Gorman, anticipating some sign of rebuttal, but apparently the old man was done with argument. He said, "Charlie. Where's your cap? The one that's made out of tar or lumps of coal

or whatever it is. Did you leave it home out of respect? Could you not get a nice little one made out of black sateen you could bring to funerals and wakes?" . . .

"Oh yes! I stand on the sound truck and say, 'Dear folks, don't underestimate the mayor. Don't think he has no capacity merely because the city is going to rack and ruin around us, our fine civic buildings are all held together with Scotch tape and library paste, our nice residential streets look like back alleys in South Timbuctoo, and every man among us who owns property is taxed like the Aga Khan. But dear folks, don't condemn the mayor totally for this! Be just, dear folks! Remember that while he may be a bum administrator, we have to admit two things about him. One, he has a grand heart, and two, he's the greatest orator and crowd psychologist that this part of the world has ever produced! These are facts I'm telling you, dear folks! There's no one to touch him in that department! Oh yes,'" [Hennessey] cried, . . . weaving back and forth, his hand clutching an invisible microphone, the floor beneath his feet miraculously transformed into the platform atop his sound truck, "there's no one to touch him at all! The last surviving member of his species! Only last week I wrote letters to the sociologists down at Yale, Harvard, and Princeton, telling them to get their best men over here to watch Frank Skeffington in action before it's too late! Oh yes! Important! I told them to get them over here and watch him set the buffoons on fire, all laughing and jumping and cheering and stamping their feet, while he stands up there nodding his head and in the big air-conditioned voice telling them fifteen lies and a bedtime story to send them home happy! Marvelous! The talent is inborn, dear folks!

A terrible mayor but a great entertainer! And what's the lesson in that, dear folks? Simply this: I say to you tonight that you have to make up your minds whether or not you want an entertainer in the mayor's seat. And if you do, dear folks, if you want a good laugh while the buildings of your city are falling to the ground one by one all around you, then by all means return Frank Skeffington to office!"

This sustained performance won more laughter and applause; Skeffington had listened, greatly amused. He liked Charlie Hennessey, and while the liking was comfortably buttressed by the knowledge that, as a rival, Charlie could do him no serious damage, still, the feeling had more genuine roots. Skeffington knew that he had much common ground with this exuberant little pepperpot. They shared the same background, the same traditions, and even, to a considerable extent, the same gifts; it was just that in one of them, Skeffington reflected, somewhere along the line someone had forgotten to tighten a necessary wire, and the result was Charlie. Charlie, with all his volcanic but essentially purposeless eloquence, his thousand and one unrelated interests, his wild undisciplined quixotic pursuit of impossible ends! Looking at Charlie in full flight was for Skeffington a little like looking into a mirror in a fun house: through the lunatic distortions, he could always manage to discern just a little bit of himself. . . .

The Rosary over, it was time to go. Skeffington swiftly and efficiently made the rounds, saying the necessary goodbys; then he signaled to Adam, and uncle and nephew walked towards the front door together. They had almost reached the door when Skeffington, suddenly halting, said, "Hold on a minute. I want a word with that undertaker before we go."

They both turned and saw the head of Johnnie Degnan poking out of the kitchen at the far end of the hall; obviously he had been watching their departure. Skeffington beckoned, and he came running quietly to them.

"Ah, good evening, Governor," he said, in his swift hushed tones. "A very sad occasion. I wanted to see you before this evening, to make your acquaintance, but the pressure of my duties didn't quite allow. I'm John Degnan, Governor."

"Glad to know you, Mr. Degnan," Skeffington said. "As you say, it's a sad occasion. I'm happy to see you've done your best by it, however. I've been admiring your handiwork with the deceased."

"Thank you, Governor. Thank you very much. That's nice to hear. I did my best," the undertaker said modestly. "I don't mind telling you, Governor, that Mr. Minihan presented a very difficult case. Because of the age and the sunken cheeks and the wrinkles. I'm sure you can appreciate the difficulty of the task, Governor. Everything had to be smoothed out delicately, the youthful contours restored, and so forth."

"Yes. Now, Mr. Degnan, only one feature of your work disturbs me and that is the probable cost. You don't mind if I say that I was rather struck by the fact that the coffin, and what might be called the general deathroom décor, seem a trifle splendid for someone who was in decidedly modest circumstances?"

The undertaker smiled; it was, Adam thought, a nervous smile. "I see what you mean, Governor," he said swiftly. "I appreciate that point of view. And yet I always think the family is more satisfied if the final homage, as I like to think of it, is really nice in its every aspect. Something that the deceased would have been proud of if he could have seen it."

"Why, those are the feelings of an artist," Skeffington said. "They do you credit, Mr. Degnan. I presume, incidentally, that you've discussed all this with Mrs. Minihan?"

"Well, no. Not exactly, that is, Governor. I thought it best not to in her distraught condition. Just a few words here and there. I think you could say, more or less, that it was left to my discretion, as it so often is. I always believe in taking as many worries as possible from the shoulders of the family."

"That's very thoughtful of you. Now then, you're a young man, Mr. Degnan, but I understand you've had quite a bit of professional experience. As you might put it, you've been in charge of a good many final homages. Or as I might put it, you've buried a good many people. What would you say was the lowest price you've ever buried anyone for?"

"The lowest *price*, Governor?" The smile remained; it wavered uncertainly. "I don't quite understand. . . . What I mean to say is, Governor, I don't believe that's anything I've ever quite figured out."

"Try," Skeffington urged him. "Make a rough estimate. Would it be . . . oh, say thirty-five dollars?"

"*Thirty-five dollars!*" The gasp of astonishment and pain broke through the modulated occupational tones; the undertaker looked wildly at Skeffington and said, "You couldn't *begin* to bury anyone for that price today, Governor!"

"I'll bet you could if you really tried," Skeffington said pleasantly. "I'll bet you could both begin and end. And just to prove my confidence in your resourcefulness, Mr. Degnan, why don't you do

that very thing with Mr. Minihan? Let's give it a real try. I think you can do it. I'm sure the final bill won't read over thirty-five dollars. Matter of fact, I'll instruct the widow to that effect immediately."

"But Governor, you can't be serious!" Degnan cried. The smooth round face had become agonized; the soft hands were united in front of him in a tight, beseeching clasp. He looked as if he were about to hurl himself at his persecutor's feet, and Adam, who had not until a moment ago realized just what it was that his uncle was doing, now felt a sudden pity as well as disgust for this abject little profiteer. "The costs alone, Governor," Degnan moaned. "They're going up every day. I couldn't possibly do it. It's all *arranged*—"

"Fine," Skeffington said. "Then let it go through as arranged. But for thirty-five dollars."

"But, *Governor* . . ."

Skeffington pulled his watch from a vest pocket and examined it with apparent surprise. "It's later than I thought," he said. "Well, then, Mr. Degnan, it's all settled. I'll leave the details to you. A suitable funeral conducted for thirty-five dollars, with no cutting of corners. All the normal courtesies extended, the usual paraphernalia available. I'll have a few men on hand just to see that everything goes along well. I know you'll do a grand job. In any event, I'll be sure to hear about it: my observers will give me a full report."

The undertaker's face, which for some moments had been the color of putty, now had turned a vivid red. "But Governor! I hope you know how eager I am to co-operate in anything you suggest. How eager I *always* am. But what you're asking is *impossible*. . . ."

"Why, that's one of the words that

doesn't belong to the bright lexicon of youth," Skeffington said reprovingly. "I've always believed that nothing is impossible when one has youth and ambition. I hope you won't be the one to shake this treasured belief. Because if you do," he said, regarding Degnan with a stare which its recipient suddenly found to be as unpleasant as anything he had ever experienced, "you might shake my confidence in you. What's worse, you might even begin to shake public confidence in you. That is a bad thing to have happen to a young undertaker with dreams, Mr. Degnan. You never can tell how far it might reach. It might even reach the members of the licensing board for your profession. You never know. But we mustn't keep you from your labors any longer. I suppose you have many things to do at a time like this. Possibly even more than you'd anticipated. Good night, Mr. Degnan. Glad you introduced yourself."

They went out the door and down the steps; Degnan's anguished voice trailed them to their car. "Thirty-five dollars!" it wailed. "Governor, I *appeal* to you . . ."

Then, because there was much he was still curious about, and because a note of comradeship, almost of complicity, seemed to have been established between them on this ride home, [Adam] decided to move into more doubtful waters. He said, "Actually, he didn't talk much about himself at all. He talked mostly about you, Uncle Frank. About you and the wake."

"Reasonable enough, under the circumstances. The wake was there, and so was I."

"Yes. The thing was that he seemed to be saying that the conjunction had a rather peculiar effect on the wake,

that it changed its character pretty drastically."

Skeffington nodded. "From the funereal to the political," he said. "And what did you think of that?" Adam hesitated again, and Skeffington gave him a look of pleasant inquiry. "Go ahead," he invited. "I'll probably be able to bear it."

"Well," Adam said reluctantly, "to be honest, I had something of the same thought myself a little earlier, before Charlie arrived. I had quite a talk with Mr. Gorman about it." Now that he had gone this far, further frankness seemed unavoidable: somewhat uneasily he gave his uncle the full account of what had passed between Gorman and himself. Was it a mistake? he wondered. Probably not; it occurred to him that Gorman would himself unquestionably have mentioned it in due course.

As he talked, he kept his eyes on his uncle's face: the scrutiny proved remarkably unfruitful. The heavy features registered nothing more than a polite, unchanging interest; it was impossible for Adam to tell whether his uncle was indignant, whether he was outraged, whether he was totally unaffected. Or—in a sense, even worse —whether he was simply amused. It was most disquieting . . .

He completed his explanation. Skeffington said, "I've seldom heard of John's being so eloquent; it stands as a great tribute to your qualities as a listener. I must say he put the case for me rather well; I couldn't have done better myself. Charlie's approach, on the other hand, must have been considerably different. I imagine he probably said something to this effect." And then, while Adam stared at him, he proceeded to duplicate Charlie's speech in astonishing detail; it seemed to Adam, remembering the original, that the reproduction was virtually word for word. Finishing, Skeffington said, "Close enough?"

"Close enough," Adam agreed, bewildered. "The question is: How? You couldn't have heard it from where you were."

"Extrasensory perception," Skeffington said gravely. "A man can't go far without it today." Once again, Adam heard the familiar deep chuckle. "Of course, there is the additional fact that Charlie's principal addresses don't change very much over the years. He has the unwillingness of the artist to tamper with the perfect production. This is one of his best, a regular party piece. Or wake piece, if you prefer. I must have heard it a hundred times. It's extremely entertaining. In addition to which," he said casually, "it contains more than a little truth."

Adam looked up sharply, but his uncle seemed preoccupied in withdrawing a cigar from his vest pocket. It was long, fat, dull-greenish in color. It did not appear to be at all the same grade of cigar that had been provided in quantities for the wake.

"One over the limit," he said cheerfully, lighting it. "A happy shortcut to the Dark Encounter. Well, you see me refusing to be less than candid with you. I don't want to give you a misleading impression. I should add that while Charlie was telling the truth, up to a point, so was John Gorman. Actually, they were both right: Knocko's wake was and it wasn't a political rally. Given the circumstances, and," he added, with a faintly deprecatory wave of the cigar, "given myself, it could hardly have been anything else. You see, what you're up against here is the special local situation. To understand what happened tonight, you have to understand a little bit about that situa-

tion, and just a little bit more about my own rather peculiar position in it." . . .

"You see," he said, "my position is slightly complicated because I'm not just an elected official of the city; I'm a tribal chieftain as well. It's a necessary kind of dual officeholding, you might say; without the second, I wouldn't be the first."

"The tribe," said Adam, "being the Irish?"

"Exactly. I have heard them called by less winning names: minority pressure group (even though they've been the majority for half a century), immigrant voting bloc (even though many of the said immigrants have been over here for three generations). Still, I don't suppose it makes much difference what you call them; the net result's the same. I won't insult your intelligence by explaining that they're the people who put me in the mayor's chair and keep me there; I think you realize that the body of my support doesn't come from the American Indian. But as a member—at least by birth—of the tribe, you might give a thought to some of the tribal customs. They don't chew betel nut, and as far as I know the women don't beautify themselves by placing saucers in their lower lips. Although now that I come to think of it," he said, "that might not be a bad idea. It might reduce the potential for conversation. However, they do other things, and among them they go to wakes. And so do I."

"Which are and are not political rallies?" Adam asked. "Or was Knocko's case a special one?"

"Not at all special, except that the guest of honor was somewhat less popular than many of his predecessors. But of course when you speak about wakes as being political rallies, that's a little strong. You have to remember something about the history of the wake around here. When I was a boy in this city, a wake was a big occasion, and by no means a sad one. Unless, of course, it was a member of your own family that had died. Otherwise it was a social event. Some of my most vivid memories are of wakes. I remember my poor mother taking me to old Nappy Coughlin's wake. We went into the tenement, and there was Nappy, all laid out in a little coffin which was kept on ice. Embalming was a rather uncertain science in those days. It was a hot day in July and there were no screens on the parlor windows; there were flies in the room. I can still hear the ice dripping into the pans underneath the coffin, and I can still see Nappy. He had one of the old-fashioned shrouds on, and he lay stretched out stiff as a ramrod. And on his head he wore a greasy black cap, which his good wife had lovingly adjusted so that the peak was pulled down over one eye. It gave him a rather challenging look; you had the feeling that at any moment he might spring out of the coffin and offer to go four fast rounds with you. My mother was horrified at the sight, and I remember that she went directly over to the widow and told her she ought to be ashamed of herself, putting her husband in the coffin with his hat on. Whereupon the widow simply said that he'd never had it off; he'd worn it for thirty years, day and night, in bed and out. So naturally she left it on, not wanting to say good-by to a stranger. However, when Father Conroy came in, the hat was whisked off fast enough. I can remember—it was my first wake, by the way—going into the kitchen, where somebody gave me a glass of milk and a piece of cake. And while my mother was in the parlor talking with the other women, I was out there with the

men, just sitting around, eating cake, and listening to them talk. I hadn't the faintest notion of what they were talking about, but it didn't matter much. I was in seventh heaven. Everybody seemed to be enjoying themselves, and I knew I was. When my mother came to get me and take me home, I left with the greatest regret; I decided I'd never had a better time. Well," he said, "so much for memories of happy days. I wouldn't imagine it would sound like very much to anyone who'd been brought up today."

Adam smiled. "It sounded like a little boy having a wonderful time for himself. Although I must say that it didn't sound very much like death. Or even a political rally, for that matter."

"Matter of fact, it was the first political rally I'd ever been to," Skeffington said. "I was just too young to know it. You see, that's what all the men were talking about: politics. There was even a moment, just before I left, when Charlie McCooey himself came in: a fat man with a red face and handlebar mustache. He was the ward boss. I didn't know what that was, at the time, but I did know that the name of Charlie McCooey commanded respect and awe. I thought he must have been some kind of god. Twenty years later this childhood illusion was blasted. I gave him the beating of his life in a fight for the leadership of the ward; the vote was four to one. In the process of doing so I discovered that the god was nothing more than a dull bully-boy with no imagination and just enough intelligence to read his way through the daily adventures of Happy Hooligan. . . ."

. . . [Adam] had suddenly remembered, while Skeffington was talking, that once, years ago, and from a source he could not now place, he had heard a series of quite different stories about the old wakes; in these, the cake-and-milk had not figured largely. He said, "But I had the idea from somewhere, Uncle Frank, that many of these wakes got to be pretty violent affairs. I know there was always a certain amount of drinking, but didn't some of them actually become brawls?"

Skeffington's heavy face assumed a mildly shocked expression. "Why, I hardly know what to say," he murmured. "I have heard that drinking men occasionally forced their way into these gatherings, but I like to believe that they were instantly sobered by the sight of decent men and women shrinking from them in revulsion." He glanced at his nephew, and his lips twitched just slightly. "No," he said, "of course you're right. There was drinking and sometimes things got a little rough. You might not have enjoyed it very much. But it's all gone by the boards long ago, and it was the exception rather than the rule; while it may seem terrible enough from your point of view today, you might reflect on the fact that there just might have been some excuse for it. I think what you have to do," he said, "is to see the wakes and everything that happened to them in the light of the times. I mentioned to you the other afternoon that life wasn't exactly a picnic for our people in those days. The were a sociable people but they didn't get much chance for sociability. They were poor, they worked hard, and they didn't have much in the way of diversion. Actually, the only place people got together was at the wake. Everybody knew everybody else; when somebody died, the others went to pay their respects and also to see and talk to each other. It was all part of the pattern. They were

sorry for the family of the deceased, to be sure, but while they were being sorry they took advantage of the opportunity to have a drink and a chat with the others who were being sorry, too. It was a change, an outlet for people who led back-breaking, dreary, and monotonous lives. And if, once in a while, someone took a few too many and wanted to set fire to the widow or play steamroller in the kitchen, it was possibly deplorable but it was also slightly understandable. All in all, I've always thought the wake was a grand custom, and I still do."

"Yes," Adam said slowly. "I hadn't thought of it in that light—I mean, I hadn't thought of the wake as being a kind of *relief* from grimness. And yet I guess it must have been, all right. But what about *now*, Uncle Frank? Those same conditions don't exist, do they?"

"No," said Skeffington, "and neither does the wake. Not in the same way, that is. It's a disappearing phenomenon, like the derby hat. As the younger people grow up, the wakes are more and more changing their character: for example, they're being held now in funeral parlors rather than in the homes. The wake will still continue in some form; after all, it takes a long time to get rid of old tribal customs. And Knocko's was a bit like some of the old wakes; that's why I wanted you to see it. And as for the political discussion, that was in the grand tradition, too. By the way, did you happen to wonder why they might have been talking politics tonight?"

"Well, I naturally thought it was because you were there. But—"

"But," Skeffington said, interrupting with a look of some amusement, "was I there because they were going to talk politics? Right?" It was all too remarkably right; Adam flushed and began to

protest, but Skeffington said, "A perfectly natural question. I'd be astonished it it hadn't occurred to you. The
answer, by the way, is a little bit of
both. I suppose I went at least partly
because it was one more opportunity
to keep the ball rolling. It's almost impossible for an old campaigner to avoid
the occasions of sin. But whether I'd
been there or not, they would have
talked politics anyway. It's what interests them most. It ought to: it gave
most of them everything they have. I
mentioned to you the other day that
the main reason I went into politics
was because it was the quickest way out
of the cellar and up the ladder. A good
many others felt the same way. A lot of
the younger men wanted a nice new
dark serge suit that didn't necessarily
come equipped with a chauffeur's cap.
And the only way out was through
politics; it was only when we gained a
measure of political control that our
people were able to come up for a
little fresh air. They know that; they
think of it as the big salvation for
them; that's why they talk about it
when they all get together. It's a very
serious part of the business of living.
And when I'm around, naturally I'm
expected to talk it with them. And I
do. I may add," he said, "that I don't
find it a hardship."

Adam thought of one more question.
"And the family?" he said. "The family
of the deceased, I mean. Like Mrs.
Minihan tonight. How do they feel
while all this is going on? Don't they
sometimes mind, Uncle Frank?"

"I know what you mean," Skeffington said, "but I think you're a bit wrong
there. I don't think they mind a bit.
There is a contrary opinion, however.
Every once in a while I see where some
advanced young public servant, who
still had the ring of the pot on his seat

while all this was going on, publicly
applauds the passing of 'that cruel and
barbarous custom, the wake.' Whenever
I see that I take down my little book
and chalk up a new name in the boob
section. The man who said it obviously
hasn't the faintest notion of what he's
talking about. He hasn't the remotest
understanding of the times, the circumstances, of our people, the way they
feel and the way they regard death.
I've seen a good many people die
around here and I'll probably see a
good many more. Unless, of course,"
he added, in another of those detached
and faintly chilling parentheses which
never failed to jolt Adam, "I beat them
to it; there's always that possibility. But
I've never seen the family that thought
the wake was cruel and barbarous. They
expected it. They wanted it. More than
that, it was good for them: it was a
useful distraction, it kept them occupied, and it gave them the feeling that
they weren't alone, that they had a few
neighbors who cared enough to come
in and see them through a bad time.
And you could say, too, it was a mark
of respect for the deceased: rest assured that *he* wanted his wake. I remember what happened when the
Honorable Hugh Archer died. The
Honorable Hugh was considerably before your time; I don't imagine you'd
have heard much about him."

"No, nothing."

"He was a prominent Republican
attorney who once refused ten thousand dollars offered to him if he'd defend a notorious criminal. The noble
gesture was unprecedented in Republican circles, and immediately he became known as the Honorable. It
wasn't until much later that it was
discovered he had asked for twenty
thousand. Well, eventually he died. He
was a huge man: six foot four and

weighing nearly three hundred pounds. At that time, cremation was just coming into fashion, following closely upon Mah-jongg, and they whipped the Honorable Hugh out to the incinerator on the very day he died. Old Martin Canady went to the ceremony, out of a curiosity to see how the other half died, and when he came running back to me he was literally popeyed with shock. 'By God, Frank!' he said. 'They took the big elephant before he stopped breathin' almost and what the hell d'ye think they did with him? They put him in the oven and burned him up with the Sunday papers! When the poor man finished cookin' ye could have buried him in an ash tray! By God, Frank, I wouldn't want nothin' like that to happen to me! When I go I'm damned sure I mean to stay around the house a few days and nights so's some of the old pals can come in and have a drink and the last look! What the hell's wrong with that, now?' And," Skeffington said, "to save my soul, I couldn't think of a blessed thing wrong with it. It's the way I want to go myself. . . ."

The Changing Political Structure of the City in Industrial America

Samuel P. Hays

The rapid development of urban history in the past few years has witnessed far greater progress in the expansion of subject matter than of conceptual framework. Most urban history has been written as a narrative with a minimum of deliberately fashioned concept. As a result, the "reform" framework, inherent in the contemporary self-image of the city from year to year in the twentieth century, has become unconsciously transferred into the historical imagination to establish the prevailing pattern of writing about the city. Its sequence is simple: cities grew, they gave rise to problems, and reform forces arose to cope with those problems. The classic political contest in urban history is the struggle between those who would solve the difficulties of the city and their opponents.

The persistence of the "reform" context is surprising in view of the vast fund of information and ideas readily available for other approaches, which gives rise to concepts about patterns of human relationships in the city on a broader and less overtly normative basis. From one point of view, these concepts enable us to place the contemporary conceptions of the city's problems in context—namely, as the particular definition of problems from the particular vantage point or "image" of the city of particular groups of people. We can examine the special roots and perspectives of "reform" movements. From another point of view, they enable us to examine the entire range of human life within the city, the variety of people, the patterns they generate, and the relationships they establish among themselves, irrespective of our own normative concerns about the city. The conceptual possibilities for reconstructing the historical dimension of the city are readily available.

The "reform" context is even more unsatisfactory because it constitutes a rejection of the city, a constant unwillingness to consider the city in its own right and a constant search, through history, for something which to each writer the city instead should be. We must develop an approach which accepts the city as it is—its heterogeneity of ethnicity, religion, and race; its inequalities and the process by which vertical mobility constantly transforms one pattern of inequality into another; its tension between parochial and cosmopolitan life; its administrative and technical systems which order people as between those who manage and those who are managed. This enormous variety of human life on the part of thousands and millions of people we must appreciate and comprehend in its own right—for what it was, not for

Reprinted from *Journal of Urban History*, Vol. 1, No. 1 (November 1974) pp. 6–38 by permission of the Publisher, Sage Publications, Inc.

what it failed to be—and order into patterns so as to enhance that appreciation and comprehension.

The following essay constitutes a conceptual framework which I have found useful in comprehending the evolution of the city since the mid-nineteenth century.[1] It has been influenced heavily by works in geography and sociology. Yet by the practitioners of those arts it would be considered primitive and elementary. Here I attempt to translate simple concepts from the relatively static framework of the social sciences into a historical context so as to stress change over time. In its broadest outline, urban development is considered a constant tension between forces making for decentralization and forces making for centralization in human relationships and institutions, between centrifugal and centripetal tendencies, between social differentiation and social integration. The city holds in balance in one historical context those attempts to separate out from the wider world to establish smaller contexts of life in home, church, education, and recreation, and those attempts to discipline and link the productive and occupational activities of man into more highly organized systems. The city is an excellent context in which to examine the evolution of these tensions in modern industrial society.[2]

I

During the last half of the nineteenth century, the physical limits of cities expanded constantly. In some cases, people moved outward from the center to the periphery to establish new residential communities.[3] In others, new migrants settled in areas adjacent to but distinct from the city's older districts. These brought about a greater dispersion of urban population, a more varied and decentralized life, and the development of subcommunities. There were not similar; each had distinct ethnic, cultural, occupation, and class characteristics. The physical growth of cities, then, involved social differentiation; new subcommunities created more varied cultures and cities became more heterogeneous. This had a profound impact on the patterns of human relationships in the city so that by the end of the century it was far more decentralized than it had been seventy years before.

Prior to industrialization, cities had been relatively small, compact and integrated. They were "pedestrian communities" in that the location of activities was determined by the time it took to walk between them, between residence and occupation, church and school, store and recreation facilities. The community tended to be a face-to-face community, in which human relationships were established by personal contact over limited areas. These relationships were close. Individuals could not live free from the view of others, from their approval or disapproval. In such a social situation, those who became dominant in economic, social, and religious life established and maintained acceptable patterns for the entire community. Differences in values which might lead to differences in public demands were not readily revealed in political affairs.

Two characteristics of these relatively integrated communities stood out. One was the physical intermixture of different social groups. Although the earlier cities were relatively homogeneous ethnically and religiously, they were heterogeneous in class terms, exhibiting distinct gradations from lower to upper.[4] Different classes had long existed in the American city. But their geographical separation was not as sharp as it became in the late nineteenth century. Factory owners often built their residences next to their factories and within sight of workingmen's homes. Laborers often lived in the back alleys in blocks where the more well-to-do lived on the main street. Clear-cut expression of the particular values of a social group requires geographical separateness and distinctiveness. Since in the pedestrian community distinct social classes did not live in distinct geographical areas but were intermixed, the clarity of their political impulses was limited.

Urban political leadership reflected the integrated community. City councils were usually elected in a town meeting to represent the city as a whole. Invariably, they were composed of men dominant in the community's social and economic life—bankers, commission merchants, lawyers.[5] Rarely were those in the lower three-quarters of the vertical social order selected. In later years, when councilmen were chosen by wards, working-class wards frequently elected workingmen. Election at large gave an opportunity for those dominant in the social and economic life of the community to be dominant in its formal political life as well. This, it should be emphasized again, was not due to the lack of social differentiation. There is ample evidence to demonstrate inequalities in wealth, and there is no reason to believe that these inequalities did not lead to differences in political outlook. But the lack of geographical distinctiveness of social differentiation reduced the capacity of the middle and lower classes to develop and express effectively their political views.

This pedestrian community of the early nineteenth century changed radically by 1900. The drive toward social differentiation had proceeded apace; it found expression in a variety of urban subcommunities, each with a distinct geographical identity, residential life, cultural pattern, and representation in city government. Many of these subcommunities grew out of migration from abroad. Irish and German migration brought into almost every city newcomers who divided along both national and religious lines. German Catholics, Lutherans, and Jews settled in different areas of the city and established separate churches, schools, and social organizations. Later southern and eastern Europeans added to the variety. By seeking to live in close proximity to those of similar nativity and religion, they created distinctive ethno-religious subcultures.

Subcommunities also arose from upward social mobility which became transformed into geographical movement from the city's center to its periphery.[6] As the economy grew, opportunities at all occupational levels expanded. People moved upward in occupation and income; the drive toward social differentiation became intense. The upwardly mobile desired to establish new ways of life, to separate out from their older environments and to live in a different community, where cultural patterns were similar to their new aspirations. They sought more space for play in the form of larger yards, wished their daughters to meet more acceptable future husbands, or wanted to associate in their nonwork hours with people of their own patterns of living. Outward urban migration arose from the desire to establish new residential subcommunities with church, school, and recreational facilities in areas distinct from older subcommunities. The desire for social differentiation could be realized only through geographical differentiation.

Cheap urban transportation, the trolley and the automobile, made this process possible. Horse-drawn vehicles on rails were in operation as early as the 1850s. In the 1880s cable-cars powered by central steam plants were experimented with but soon gave way to the electric trolley. At first trolley lines radiated out from the central city to only a few areas, but by the end of the century the electric trolley had opened up almost all the surrounding territory save that which defied penetration because of natural barriers. These innovations were as profound an element of the transportation revolution as were the steamboats and the steam railroads. They generated an extensive movement of population and restructured the urban social order.

The simplest expression of this change lay in the increasing distance between place of residence and place of work. Whereas formerly one had to live within walking distance of work, now he or she could live much farther away. Professionals and business-people who worked in the central city established residential communities elsewhere. Factory owners no longer lived beside their factories. Lawyers whose work required that they be near the centralized public records and legal institutions of the city and county courts lived out in newer and economically more substantial communities. Doctors, if they were specialists such as surgeons, lived in one place and carried on their practice in another.

This distance between work and residence created more distinct geographical specialization of activities in the city. Residential communities served the family; they included home, church, school, and recreation facilities, including residential play areas—yard space —as well as country clubs and golf courses. Communities became distinctive in terms of nationality, religions, and class patterns of residential life. While residential institutions could be decentralized, work institutions could not. The individual could readily move where he lived but not where he worked. His place of work, in fact, depended upon centralizing rather than decentralizing forces, those bound up with the organization of economic life into larger systems of production, merchandising, and banking. While the desire for social differentiation enticed people into a centrifugal movement of residential dispersion, their occupations involved them in centripetal and integrative forces. During the last half of the nineteenth century, decentralizing tendencies were the dominant of the two.

The heightened geographical mobility created by the trolley greatly complicated the process of conserving residential communities. Each desired to maintain its distinctive patterns of residential life. This was extremely difficult to do, because mobility and stability were incompatible. One could not easily prevent other people of different classes, nationalities, races, or religions from moving into his community. Freedom to buy and sell property might quickly undermine established patterns. To protect themselves, communities experimented with a variety of techniques. That these were rarely successful testifies to the high degree of motion in the modern city. Upper-class communities experienced especially observable difficulties in self-maintenance.[7] During the latter half of the nineteenth century, new upper-class residential areas arose in which the wealthy, old and new, sought to disassociate themselves from the institutions and people of the older city. But, unable to control land transactions, these communities rarely lasted more than one or two generations. Real estate promoters converted their estates into smaller lots for middle- and lower-income families.

Decentralization of residential life created decentralization of related economic institutions. Community growth rapidly dispersed property ownership as larger holdings, usually in the form of estates owned by the well-to-do, were divided into smaller lots. One property owner frequently was replaced by several hundred, each one of which now had a tangible stake in community life and demanded a voice in community affairs. Since the apportionment of city council seats to various wards frequently depended upon the number of property taxpayers in the ward, expansion of property ownership directly affected municipal government. Diffusion of property ownership diffused political impulses.

New subcommunities gave rise to new consumer-oriented stores, designed to fill immediate personal and family needs. Grocery, drug, confectioner, milk, eating, and liquor stores each served a market within walking distance. Many were family-owned stores; almost all had a vital interest in the area's property conditions and its general growth and development. Ethnic communities gave rise to stores which provided the particular food, dress, and other goods distinctive to the nation-ality of the residents. Consumer-oriented small businesses expanded especially rapidly in urban immigrant settlements. The immigrant storekeeper became the backbone of the urban small-business community.

The physical development of the community generated economic enterprises which facilitated that growth—in banking, real estate, contracting, and transportation. These firms were often confined in their activities to a particular region of the city, were identified with it and had a stake in its physical growth. They catered to a wider community than did the small retailer, to a larger subsection of the city than the neighborhood best called the urban region. Real estate firms arose to change large estates owned by single individuals into innumerable small lots owned by many; banks grew up to finance these real estate transactions and the building and development that followed; contractors built the new structures, streets, and sidewalks. These men identified closely with their regions; they became recognized as leaders by the people of the region.

Urban physical expansion provided opportunities for new entrepreneurs; regional developers were very different from those who had been concerned with growth in the older section of the city.[8] Many were immigrant leaders who, while profiting from development, provided essential services for community growth and became influential community spokesmen. New real estate development provided opportunities for new entrepreneurs in the new banks, trolley lines, real estate agencies, and construction firms. The boards of directors of community banks, for example, contained far more men of recent immigrant origin and Catholics and Jews than did the older, central-city banks. The more successful immigrant businessmen often combined real estate development and rental property with banking service. They worked closely with ethnic political leaders in their projects; both rested ultimately for their influence and their leadership upon the development of urban subcommunities.

Differentiation and decentralization in social and economic life gave rise to a decentralized political system. Increasingly the ward became the focus of politics.[9] Each community demanded separate representation so that its particular needs would be dealt with. Even prior to 1850, a ward system had begun to replace citywide representation; elected by wards, councilmen now represented their communities in the council's deliberations. School government often developed in a similar manner. Each ward had its own elementary school, often a focal point for community social affairs, administered by a ward-elected school board. Ward-oriented political life took precedence over a citywide political life. Through it, the varied urban sub-communities could express their distinctive viewpoints on public affairs.

Ward representation changed the kinds of men chosen as councilmen. Whereas earlier the great majority were from upper occupational and socioeconomic classes, by the end of the century they were from the middle and lower levels. Outward migration and geographical differentiation greatly reduced the number of upper-class and increased the number of middle- and lower-class wards. Each ward tended to select as representatives people who were like the majority of its inhabitants; the character of representation

changed, as did that of the communities represented. At the same time, economic leaders of the new, decentralized communities began to play a larger role as councilmen. Identified with the real estate and business concerns of the community, they established personal ties with large numbers of residents in their business affairs. Economic and social leadership became translated into political leadership. By 1900, the typical ward-elected city councilman was a small businessman—retailer, director of a funeral home, real estate promoter and contractor, director of a community bank—a clerk, a skilled artisan, or an unskilled laborer. Professional and large business classes were greatly outnumbered.

The major concern of urban government lay with the city's physical development.[10] The overwhelming number of demands made upon city council and of city ordinances pertained to the approval of subdivisions, of streets and drainage systems, of lighting and transportation. City taxes came from property owners and city expenditures went for services to development; major council controversies came over taxation and expenditure. Considerable disagreement arose, also, over the question of private or public enterprise. Should private services be permitted without restriction, or should they be licensed and regulated? Should property owners pay for the development of adjacent streets, or should they be paid for through a general system of taxation and municipal expenditure? Whatever the answers to these questions, city government in the last half of the nineteenth century came to be a major instrument of physical growth and community development.

Because the city council consisted of

representatives of different geographical areas, controversies over taxing and expenditure for urban development became controversies between different areas of the city. This process developed in the same way as it did in the state with conflicts between different counties, or in the nation between sections. Each urban community wished assistance for development; each wanted a gas light on this or that corner. Decisions were often made by "log-rolling," in which one councilman voted for the proposals of others in exchange for their vote for his own. These controversies frequently sorted themselves out into disagreements between the city's older and newer sections. The older feared the newer. They often argued that the geographical expansion of the city was neither necessary nor desirable. Their taxes would be used to finance development in expanding areas in which they had no direct interest. They stood aghast at the willingness of the city council to incur indebtedness to finance new development. The older city usually was in the minority, for urban expansion and ward representation brought into government a large number of councilmen who reflected the views of the newly developing communities and who outvoted their opponents.

The use of city funds in community development, and the award of franchises to provide services such as transportation created opportunities for corruption. But this should not obscure the more important phenomenon of decentralized urban growth. Many controversies over physical development were, in fact, phrased in terms of the issue of corruption. The most sensational case involved the New York City "Tweed ring." That controversy was

fundamentally one between old and new New York City, a belief on the part of lower Manhattan that New York did not need to expand physically, and a demand on the part of those preoccupied with development further up the island that it did.[11] The city government threw in its lot with expansion and development and increased municipal indebtedness to help carry it out. Tweed's downfall was triggered by revelations of corruption in this venture, but the underlying opposition came from disagreement with the substance of his policies.

II

While decentralization characterized urban development in the nineteenth century, by 1900 integration, although in evidence even earlier, was emerging as a dominant force.[12] Decentralization continued, but it became overlaid with new patterns of social organization which drew people together into more closely-knit groups. As the density of population increased, the intensity of claim and counter-claim in decision-making also increased. A new political order arose to limit the variety of such claims, to channel them into fewer centers of decision-making, and to integrate more activities into a relatively small number of systems of human relationships. While the older city witnessed a process of dispersion, the new involved centralization.

Integrative tendencies in urbanization grew out of the transition from locality patterns of human relationships, which emphasized interaction among people living in the same geographical area, to functional and administrative forms of organization, which emphasized interaction among people of particular functions, no matter where they lived, and among people playing different roles in the vertical heirarchy of organized administrative systems.[13] While the locality group was inclusive, encompassing all those living in a given geographical area, functional and administrative groups were exclusive, involving only those who had a common functional interest or were within a given administrative system. Whereas in former decades the locality contest had been crucial in the effective expression of political impulses, new forms of social and political organization were more divorced from location in particular segments of the city. These new forms of organization rested on patterns of human relationships which cut across community and constituted a superstructure of contacts above and beyond it.[14]

Behind these new patterns of human relationships lay the growth of organizational technologies. Whereas production technologies, those which substituted machines for manual labor, dominated in the last half of the nineteenth century, organizational technologies came to the fore after 1875, which dramatically increased the speed and flexibility of human contacts. The telephone replaced the messenger boy, permitting contact and control—integration —in ways which had not been possible before. Organizational technologies gave rise to more precise coordination of human interaction so as to dovetail efforts efficiently. They made possible the new, more systematized, more coordinated patterns of human interaction.

The most visible expression of urban integration was the newly reorganized central city.[15] Formerly a mixture of residences, professional offices, factories, and public buildings, the central

city declined as a residential and factory area on the advent of rapid transit which stimulated movement out of the city's core to the periphery. In their place came new activities which emphasized the central city as the location of organization which reached out to gather in the entire urban area. The large office building was the most dramatic physical expression of this change. Within a few decades, these buildings replaced homes, churches, schools, the whole range of residentially related activities, in the city's center. Although innovation in structural steel and the elevator made this possible, the growth of rapid interpersonal communication reflects more precisely the state of organizational integration which lay behind it. The telephone first became a popular means of communication in the center city.

These changes can be charted also in the shifting location of private corporate management activities. In the nineteenth century, when management and coordination were relatively small compared with production, the former were carried out in the same building as the factory. As management functions grew, their physical location became more of a problem. At times, the mansions of factory owners, located near the factories, became a convenient location as the owners moved to upper-class communities. It came to be more convenient to locate near related institutions such as banks and advertising agencies, whose expertise was frequently called upon. The central office building located in the center of the city was the answer. Many of these were built either by industries for their management or by the estates of deceased entrepreneurs and then rented to the firm. In any case, the growing importance of coordination, internal and external, gave rise to a series of moves which led to the concentration of activities in the central city.

Here there grew rapidly a host of other centralizing institutions: large-scale retail establishments drawing customers from the entire city; specialized professionals, such as doctors, architects and engineers who had a citywide clientele; lawyers whose work required that they be near legal records and the courts; banks whose financial networks fanned out to link transactions throughout the city and the region; public administrative agencies in recreation, planning, health, and welfare. The larger organizational life of the city focused on the center because here a host of interrelated activities associated with coordinating human relationships took place. The reorganization of the central city was not merely a matter of physical change, but of more intense human interaction at a level high on the vertical scale of social organization.

These integrative activities found organizational, as well as locational expressions, the most important of which were the Chambers of Commerce representing the city's most powerful business men. There were several types of such bodies, distinguishable in terms of the geographical extent of their activities and clientele, on the one hand, and their role in the scale of human contacts on the other. The neighborhood boards of trade represented small, consumer-oriented businesses in the relatively small communities; the regional chambers of commerce drew in banks, real estate firms, merchants, and professionals whose activities were larger than the neighborhood but smaller than the entire city; citywide Chambers of Commerce, composed of manufacturers, downtown merchants, central-city bank-

ers, and managers of central-city property, represented the largest integrative tendencies of the city. These citywide Chambers of Commerce, rather than the smaller bodies, came to play an increasingly important role in municipal affairs. They constituted a crucial political force in the years from 1897 to 1929.[16]

The rapid rise of the empirical professions such as public health and education greatly accelerated urban integration.[17] The public health doctor was one of the most politically active professionals. The germ theory of disease not only enhanced understanding of the causes of diseases but also made abundantly clear what needed to be controlled in order to prevent them. Moreover, public health innovations could be brought about more effectively through one citywide context than many community ones. The dynamics of school politics was similar. Professional educators urged a host of innovations, such as longer school terms, more training for teachers, better facilities and equipment, teacher pensions, and new methods of capturing the interest of the pupil. But how to bring about change? Many school boards were conservative. The answer was to shift the context of school decisions from the many, local ward school boards to a central body where a more citywide perspective could be fostered and to which professionals would have direct access.

Two other professional groups, civil engineers and architects, were more concerned with urban physical organization. Civil engineers became the technical experts behind large public works such as water reservoirs, sanitary sewage systems, bridges, and paved streets. Since such matters affected the city at large, plans to facilitate them required a perspective far more extensive than that of the urban small community. And the same for that segment of architects who became interested in city planning. Often concerned with central-city office buildings, they became enamored of the possibilities of large-scale changes in the city and especially the center. This included the rearrangement of streets and buildings, the development of open spaces and parks, the extension of landscaping and beautification at the city center and elsewhere. Like the engineers, their citywide perspective prompted them to seek large- rather than small-scale physical changes.

These professional concerns were universal rather than particularist. The problems they dealt with cut across parochial community lines. The public health expert faced tuberculosis and typhoid fever not simply in Ward 6, but in the entire city; the school professional wished to educate more rather than fewer children and for longer periods of time. The civil engineer and the architect sought to rearrange diverse and far-flung sections of the city according to more universal standards of efficiency and design. Professionals were not content merely to learn more; they wished to use their knowledge to change society. The new empirical professions were not inert, but highly political. They became infused with a missionary spirit to reduce disease, to lengthen human life, to enhance the quantity and quality of education, and to redesign the physical city.

Only a few, however, shared the professional expert's values, his vision, and the urgency of his concern. He constantly had to educate others, to search for political allies, and, to overcome resistance from opponents. Since he sought to influence a wide range of people and affairs, he chose mechanisms of decision-making and action which were equally broad in scope. At the municipal level, he constructed public health departments, relatively independent of community political impulses and of the city councils which reflected those impulses, so that he could operate freely from his own professional guidelines. He supported increased executive authority in the mayor in order to protect himself from popular forces. The new empirical professions played a major role in the integration of the twentieth-century city.

The urban upper class constituted still a third force in urban integration. In its residential institutions, the urban upper class was separatist; it sought to establish homes, churches, schools, and clubs apart from other classes, and increasingly beyond the city's boundaries.[18] In this, the upper class was no different in its localistic impulses than were other classes, thereby contributing to the decentralization and fragmentation of the city. But economic concerns required that it move in the opposite direction as well and stimulate integration. The occupations of the upper class were often in the central city, the corporate systems in which it worked were headquartered there, and the property it owned often was either there physically or represented by investments in corporations based there. The urban upper class faced two ways at once; decentralist in residential institution, it was integrative in its economic and occupational life. While it sought to separate itself from the city in one way, in another it was propelled back into the center of urban affairs.

The recent history of the upper class added a special integrative factor in the early twentieth century. Many of the upper class had grown up in the center city. Faced with an infusion of new people, a rise in property values and taxes and the deterioration of their residential environment, they only recently had moved out. But many retained a strong nostalgia for the old area and could not avoid an interest in what happened there. The relocation of churches revealed this ambivalence.[19] Congregations invariably sold downtown churches for a healthy profit because of the rapid rise in land values. With the proceeds, they could build a new church in the suburbs and have funds left over. Many members, and usually those from long residence in the former location, wished these resources to be used for social welfare programs in the community where the church had been. Adding to this nostalgia was the fact that the location of the places of residence and of work of the upper class required that they pass through lower-class areas on their way between home and work, making the conditions there particularly visible to them. Such experiences as these added to the concern for welfare among the working class to limit its "disruptive" and "disintegrative" tendencies. Upward mobility reduced interclass communication drastically, but the peculiar experiences of the upper class in the early twentieth-century city gave rise to a desire on the part of some to reestablish some semblance of contact.

The urban upper class became involved in a host of social welfare programs: prohibition, control of prostitution, language instruction for immigrants, religious evangelism, public baths, playgrounds, better housing, restriction of child labor, and improvement of the working conditions of women.[20] The most visible and dramatic example of upper-class welfare was the settlement house.[21] Located in the midst of lower-class neighborhoods, the settlement house provided educational and social services for lower-income groups. Boards of directors and financing came from the upper class, who lived in outlying residential areas. They also provided the volunteer workers for settlement house activities. In this fashion, the settlement house constituted an instrument of interclass communication. The "gatekeeper" between the two classes was the settlement house director who lived and communicated within two different worlds, the world of the lower-class immigrant and the world of the affluent.

In these relationships between social classes in different sections of the city, women played an important role. Active in social welfare reforms, the members of women's organizations were drawn heavily from the upper classes who had the leisure time to give to civic affairs. "Society" clubs served as headquarters for many civic reform groups; "society" newspapers provided one of the most extensive sources of information about welfare reform; "society" women often propelled their husbands into reform activities.[22] While men became involved in urban integration through the economic system and professional life, women did so through intuitive sympathy for other women and children, their common religion and ethnicity, and their nostalgia for their childhood communities. Much of the interclass communication which lay behind this aspect of urban integration came through special lines of interaction generated by upper-class women.

Forces making for integration in economic, professional, and social life came together in a drive for integration and centralization in decision-making.[23] Reformers arose to modify the formal structure of municipal and school government and decision-making in welfare and charitable activities. They were most disturbed about the ward system of city and school affairs which gave considerable influence to the decentralizing tendencies of urban communities. This, they felt, hindered a focus on a more comprehensive view of the city —the "public interest" they called it— in order to deal with its problems. As each urban group sought to implement integrative objectives, it became dissatisfied with ward government and supported more highly centralized methods of decision-making.

One innovation was to increase the power of the mayor—for example, that he propose a budget which the council then might modify rather than vice versa. Another was the commission form of government. A third was the city manager system in which an "expert" was hired to administer the city's affairs. Almost all such plans proposed a centralization of representation, a modification or abolition of ward representation in favor of citywide representation. The most successful attempt to centralize decision-making came in school government. By the 1920s, almost every city in the nation had eliminated the ward in favor of the citywide school board. At times these were elected at large, but often they were appointed—for example, by judges of the municipal courts. Control in the school system shifted from the community to the city at large.

These drives for centralization of decision-making came primarily from the upper levels of the social order.[24] The "good government" organizations were composed of people from upper occupational groups; the candidates they preferred for public office were from the same levels.[25] Entirely missing from the reform movement were the typical ward leaders of the previous era—the small storekeeper, the white-collar clerk, the skilled artisan. Instead, it was dominated by the central-city businessman, the advanced professional, and the upper social classes. Chambers of Commerce often took the lead in reform activities: allied with them were a variety of voters leagues and civic organizations which brought in professionals and upper-class women. Their success in centralizing decision-making shifted sharply up the occupational social levels from which decision makers were drawn. Now the vast majority of council and school board members were from the upper-middle and upper classes. The greatest change came in school boards. By 1924, such boards across the country were dominated by business and professional leaders.[26] A virtual revolution had taken place, reflecting the triumph of centralizing over decentralizing forces in municipal and school affairs.

These changes in urban government marked the re-entrance into political life of members of the upper class after several decades of relative absence. Dominating urban politics in the early pedestrian community, these groups had retired from municipal government as the city expanded, as ward government generated lower- and middle-class leadership and as they were unable to exercise control in a city of varied and decentralized communities.[27] Their old methods of influence, via day-to-day contacts in the pedestrian community, no longer sufficed. By the early twentieth century, however, they had learned new methods of integrative control from their experience with corporate systems.[28] They became increasingly adept at communications technologies and the role of the professional expert in fashioning a stable and manipulable social order. Wishing to apply these techniques to public affairs and the model of the corporation to city government, they re-entered public life through reform organizations. They were not expressing just personal values; they were reshaping the political order according to the inner dynamic of the changing economic and social order. They constituted the counter-thrust toward integration within the decentralizing society of the late nineteenth century.

Tendencies toward urban integration took place at a level far above the local community. They created networks of extra-community relationships. In the face of this new social order, the local community lost much of its autonomy and its salience. Whereas in the nineteenth century is was the dominant focus of urban life, in the twentieth century it became far less viable as more of the articulate sector of the city became involved in the development of functional groups and corporate systems. Although the urban community remained as a focal point of primary group relationships for many people,[29] its significance and importance for the wider community declined as it became transformed from a creative urban force into an object of action generated elsewhere. Political institutions at the ward level declined; political involvement diminished; ward institutions became local representatives of wider systems. As innovation developed apace at the upper levels of the social order, community institutions at the lower levels atrophied and declined.

III

By 1929, these integrative tendencies had run their first course of development. During the next four decades, a new phase appeared in which both decentralizing and centralizing tendencies appeared with new vigor and a forceful interplay. The automobile and the telephone gave rise to greater mobility and flexibility in human contacts, generating a new phase of outward movement. Systematization also moved on apace, creating ever larger units of administrative action which restrained the growth of autonomous units and integrated them into more universal perspectives and more centrally directed strategies. Interaction between centripetal and centrifugal forces remained the major context of urban history.

The twentieth-century city served as a giant social escalator, involving a constant flow of individuals upward through levels of occupation, income, and standards of living and outward to newer residential areas. Children and grandchildren of post-1880 southern and eastern European immigrants moved upward rapidly after the Great Depression.[30] Whites and blacks from the rural United States moved onto and up the same escalator.[31] As occupations and income rose, so did the distance of residence from the center city; one study of the 1960 census detailed this process for blacks for whom the dynamics of upward mobility were similar to those for whites.[32] Upward mobility accelerated rapidly after the early 1950s as the mid-twentieth-century income revolution proceeded. National median family income in current dollars rose from less than $1,500 in 1939 to $3,390 in 1950 to $5,620 in 1960 and $8,632 in 1968.[33]

Technological innovations in transportation and communication—the automobile and the telephone—made possible this outward movement. By its speed and flexibility, the automobile increased the range of short-term movement between home and work or between home and shopping areas. Now one could live five, ten, or fifteen miles from work and commute. Until the early twentieth century the telephone had linked business firms almost exclusively. It soon spread to households, permitting those living in widely scattered areas to establish intensive patterns of interaction and facilitating outward movement.

These innovations generated an outward thrust of business as well, the development of manufacturing, research centers, and storage and warehouse facilities on the periphery rather than in the center of the city. The gasoline motor truck and paved streets permitted close physical contact between such businesses and their markets, their suppliers, and their administrative headquarters. The telephone permitted a constant flow of communication and enabled the firm's headquarters to exercise supervision and control over elements physically decentralized. Decentralization in the location of industry should not be taken to involve autonomy of decision-making, for such firms were integral parts of a larger system. Technology facilitated both physical decentralization and administrative control; the first depended upon the second.

This phase of suburbanization had several characteristics different from that of the nineteenth century. First, the outward spread of industry gave rise to an occupationally more varied set of suburbs; those who worked in suburban industries—blue-collar, white-collar, and professional—chose to live relatively close to them. Suburban areas did not contain middle- and upper-class groups alone, but a wide variety of classes. Second, the mere size of the suburban scene provided a far larger number of communities and of choices of residence. Since these choices were made in terms of the class level of the community with which one wished to associate, the range of suburban communities reflected a more varied and precisely defined spectrum of classes than in previous years. Third, the vast size of the suburban spectrum gave rise to lateral movement within it, increasingly becoming more important relative to the center-periphery patterns which previously dominated. A structure arose within the periphery distinguishing those who lived and worked in the same suburb, those who lived in one suburb and worked in another, and those who lived in the suburb and worked in the central city.

These outward movements took place across rather than within city legal boundaries. Because the outlying areas wished to be included in the city's services, nineteenth-century urban boundary expansion met little opposition. Much outward population flow took place within the city's legal limits. By 1930, many cities were ringed with independent towns, boroughs, and townships, each with autonomous legal power derived from the authority not of the city but of the state. Many suburbanites had moved beyond the city's borders precisely to be in a community which had such political independence. In the city, residential communities had little power to maintain their stability; they were always threatened by forces which sought to change the patterns of land use and thereby to undermine its physical base. Outside the city, in a separate corporate town or township, such control could be exercised. Here it was possible to require that house lots be of a minimum size and houses of a minimum value.[34]

Suburban political units reflected a desire to separate out one's community from the larger urban world. Nineteenth-century decentralization, within the city, did not lead to permanent political subunits. In fact, the urban community had little staying power in the face of integrative forces. Twentieth-century decentralization took place across the city's borders and enjoyed political jurisdictions separate from the city and capable of maintaining autonomous political and legal, as well as social existence. Twentieth-century decentralization had far greater staying power than did that of the nineteenth.

The process of urban integration also continued. As the city grew, so did the range of people, activities, and land use which large urban systems sought to influence. One form of this impulse was the drive for metropolitan government, to extend the city's boundaries outward to encompass growing suburban areas, often to make the city's boundaries synonymous with the county's. The drive for metropolitan government extended the former drive for centralization of city government; once the latter movement had succeeded, it began to advocate a larger metropolitan system. Such a movement developed in almost every city, some as early as the late 1920s, but succeeded only rarely.[35]

More successful was the growth of specialized public functions which extended beyond the city's boundaries. Suburbanites demanded effective transportation to their work in the city; they supported metropolitan transit authorities to develop systems of public transit which went far beyond the city's borders. Because of their wider jurisdiction, county governments usually created such authorities. Similar agencies developed for countywide trash disposal and garbage collection, sanitary sewers, water systems, and health departments. These innovations gave rise to governmental institutions as wide in scope as the metropolitan area itself, and an almost imperceptible shift in decision-making power from suburban units to the larger authority.

Metropolitan authorities were corporations established for specific purposes with general powers to achieve them. Like similar state and federal corporations, they were free from traditional restraints by council and mayor. Still further removed from the city's active political impulses than were the mayor or council elected-at-large, they could carry out their task in terms of technical standards of professional expertise at the upper levels of the political order rather than have to respond to the constant suggestions and objections of open political debate. Innovations in government in the years between 1897 and 1929 narrowed the actors in the decision-making process and the range of alternatives and debate; the authorities continued this process. Once given a grant of power, it became difficult to render the authority accountable to any other governmental body.

The urban redevelopment authority —the prime example—was not only divorced from other governmental bodies but also had the power of eminent domain. It arose to change urban patterns of land use, most frequently in the central city. What land uses should prevail? Invariably redevelopment involved a shift from buildings of lower value and tax return to those of higher. This meant the substitution of large-scale for small-scale enterprise, a perspective consistent with integrative objectives and congenial to those involved in large-scale private enterprise rather than those at the middle and lower levels of the social order. With the power of eminent domain, the authority could force property owners to sell. In this way, the expansion of the property-stake in urban affairs, which came with the decentralization of ownership in the nineteenth century, was reversed. Land used by many small property holders was transferred to a relatively few large ones through the process of urban renewal.[36]

Professional and technical experts continued to extend their manipulative ventures as the drive toward more universal contexts of action grew. So also did the gap between these and impulses of smaller scale. Public health leaders pushed such measures as fluoridation and air pollution control. Mental health programs expanded rapidly. The drive for education continued unabated, with emphasis on better facilities, more intensive instruction, influence over preschool and home environment, and junior colleges. In such programs as these, the practice of control from the top by experts grew apace. School boards, already under such a system of decision-making, concentrated on utilizing it more extensively. Public health experts were less fortunate. The fluoridation issue became especially critical. Left to community popular vote, fluoridation was rejected more often than accepted. By the 1960s, therefore, public health leaders sought to bypass the urban general suffrage, argued that public health matters were not fit subjects for democratic control, and sought

legislation to impose fluoridation on the entire state.[37]

Preference for top-level decision-making on the part of professional experts was reflected in several political tactics. One was the creation of neighborhood groups, such as parent-teacher associations and neighborhood welfare councils, which served both to convey information about potential sources of discontent to central agencies and to implement general citywide policies. Their power, however, was confined to suggestion rather than decision. Another was the heightened interest in a systematic understanding of opposition to administrative proposals, not as a means to modify objectives, but so as to implement them more effectively. They began to study the sociology of public health, of education, of mental health. They were, of course, far more interested in the sociology of those whom they confronted than of their own values and professional social systems. They simply wished a more complete understanding of their political opposition so that they could better implement their goals.

Reaction against integrative tendencies in the city took several new forms and led to new types of balance between centrifugal and centripetal forces. As centralization rose in the pre-1929 years, the community declined as a viable political force. In the depression years of the 1930s, however, a reverse trend set in momentarily. Some smaller cities abolished the city manager system; Cleveland, unique among the larger cities in adopting the plan, rejected it in the late 1920s. Other cities returned to the ward system of representation in the 1930s, and a noticeable increase took place in representation from working-class areas. In many instances, even with citywide elections, city councils contained more representatives of workingmen, but invariably these were prominent union officials who represented not geographical communities but functional organizations.[38]

Not until the political activation of urban blacks, when community became expressed through race, did community resistance against integrative tendencies revive significantly. The process was sharpened by urban redevelopment which physically destroyed urban communities, most frequently black residential areas, in sections with the lowest property values. "Urban renewal" is "Negro removal" was the cry. This threat to the black community came a a time of rising black income, education, and awareness. Moreover, concentration of blacks in limited areas of the city gave a clear spatial and community form to the expression of black political aims. In the midst of a city and school government dominated by whites, blacks frequently demanded that a ward plan of representation and government supersede citywide forms which provided minority groups little chance to express effectively their demands.

Those involved in smaller-scale economic, social, and political affairs and at the middle and lower segments of the political order found themselves cast in a defensive rather than a creative role. Initiative as to the formulation of goals for urban policy had shifted to institutions far above them. Because it focused on community change, urban redevelopment helped to reactivate these community impulses and met increasing opposition from them.[39] A variety of spokesmen arose to voice objections: homeowners, store-keepers, real estate firms, often the same types of people who once had represented the wards in city councils and school boards. Often they succeeded in changing a project, sometimes by postponing but at other times by preventing its development. To the authorities, these were major irritants; following modern views of "conflict management," they sought to overcome resistance but not always with success.

Confrontation between officials who represented dominant political institutions and those who reflected community impulses revealed the institutional strength of the former and the weakness of the latter. Officials had a myriad of institutions into which they could retreat for strength. They could parry opposition by seeking more information, by reconsidering, by shifting to a different administrative channel. The institutional routines through which they could counter-thrust, hide, escape, or protect themselves, stall and wear down opponents, seemed almost endless. Community representatives were far more exposed. Their constituencies were institutionally weak, with few information resources to provide support and backing, and few agencies to constitute a legitimate source of waiting, parrying, and regrouping. The weakness of community impulses was reflected in the weakness of institutions into which community leaders could retreat and return with new political strength.[40]

Forces from outside the community arose to aid the reconstruction of its institutions. Social workers and federal anti-poverty program employees urged residents of poor communities to organize and exercise political power, to make demands upon city government for help in improving their neighborhoods. These efforts to re-energize people at the lower levels of the political order were only sporadically successful. The apathy of residents, often highly mobile, uninvolved in their neighborhood, let alone the city, was difficult to overcome. Most frequently these efforts at community-building aroused only a small segment—one or two percent— of the inhabitants, and served to speed them up the escalator and out into the wider urban society. Their major impact was to demonstrate that the disengagement of the bottom third from the larger political order was a permanent fact of life in modern American society.[41]

The community's weakness within the city stood in stark contrast to its strength outside the city. The independent legal status of the suburban community gave it an enormous capacity for strength and persistence in the face of integrative urban impulses. It enabled them to ward off intrusions of influence from the city, such as lower income or black migrants. They could frustrate efforts at metropolitan government, either by organizing suburban units into an opposition bloc or by influencing state legislatures to stipulate electoral provisions which loaded the vote on metropolitan government in their favor. The power of the state could also be used to reduce suburban autonomy, as in school district reorganization, carried out through state legislative and administrative agencies. Against such integrative pressures from either city or state, however, the suburban·communities could throw a considerable and continual counter-force. Their capacity for resistance was far greater than was that of the urban community.

Within the city, the upper third of the social order, often similar in socioeconomic composition to the most influential suburbs, exercised far more influence than did the lower or middle third. But the form of their political involvement shifted from geographical or area organization to functional organization. Increasingly, the active elements of the city came to be organized not by locality or community, but by specialized interests or functions, some in terms of occupation, trade associations, trade unions, or professional organizations; some in terms of specialized institutions such as libraries, art galleries, colleges, and schools; still others in terms of religion or ethnicity. Active elements in each of these functional groups were not the urban masses, but those in the upper occupational and organizational levels. The setting of urban politics came to be the interplay among functional groups in the upper levels of the political order, producing a pluralist political system, but distinctively within the top segment of vertical organization.[42]

Membership in city councils and school boards reflected functional politics. Officials elected citywide were nominated by parties or, if in a nonpartisan election, by a nonpartisan group. In each case, the nominating body usually sought to "represent" all segments of the city; these "segments" in turn were thought of in functional terms. Positions were "reserved" for labor, for each of the major religious or nationality groups, for blacks, for merchants, bankers, or manufacturers. These functional representatives came from the top levels of vertical organization. The upward shift in the scale of representation and functional representation seemed to go hand in hand. Spokesmen for working-class people were no longer skilled or unskilled workmen, as in the earlier city, but top union officials who came from managerial levels of society. Ethnic and religious groups came to be represented by the very highest vertical levels of the different ethnic and religious class systems. Black members of city councils and school boards were professionals and businessmen from the upper levels of the black community.[43]

Functional group politics created a new context of active urban political life limited to the upper levels of the political order, and a new balance of urban forces in which centrifugal tendencies came to be the functional groups at that level. No longer did the centralization-decentralization balance encompass the entire social order as it had in the late nineteenth and twentieth centuries. Now it was confined, for the most part, to the active, articulate segments of the upper levels. Those seeking to integrate urban affairs more fully sought support, placated the opposition, and developed a firm political base largely within this context. Save for an occasional instance of an election, the active urban political order was limited to the upper levels of the vertical scale of society and the middle and lower levels either remained apathetic and aloof or were cast in a negative or veto role.

As American cities moved into the last half of the twentieth century, their patterns of human relationships were far different than in the mid-nineteenth century. A structure of human contacts, growing out of the greater speed and scale of communications, and the expanded range of human thought, awareness, and action had developed, far broader in scope than that of a century

before. The community of primary human relationships remained, but its influence in the entire political order had declined sharply. Above and beyond it, a network of functional and corporate institutions had developed which now constituted the context of active political life. Innovation in the political order came from this level, the "public consciousness" generated by media of mass communications was largely confined to it, and the interplay of day-to-day political differences took place within it. Over a century or more of development, the entire urban political order had expanded greatly, rearranged itself, and had undergone a sharp change in the location of political interaction and decision-making. From a previous balance which had tipped the scales of the city's active political impulses toward decentralization, they had shifted strongly toward centralization and upward in the vertical social and political order.

NOTES

1. Two general works which have contributed much to this formulation are Roland Warren, *The Community in America* (Chicago, 1963), esp. 53–94 and Scott Greer, *The Emerging City* (Glencoe, 1962), esp. 29–66.

2. Much of the original data upon which this article rests is drawn from studies of the city of Pittsburgh, most of them seminar papers and dissertations produced by graduate students in the History Department at the University of Pittsburgh. It is understood that Pittsburgh may or may not be typical and that comparative studies might modify the framework.

3. The now classic study of outward urban movement is Sam B. Warner, Jr., *Streetcar Suburbs* (Cambridge, 1962), esp. 1–66 and 153–166.

4. James Henretta, "Economic Development and Social Structure in Colonial Boston," William and Mary Quarterly, 22 (1965), 75–92 provides one example of the description of the distribution of an urban socioeconomic variable. For similar descriptions I am indebted to Robert Doherty for

data about several Massachusetts towns between 1800 and 1850 and to Walter Glazer for data about Cincinnati in the nineteenth century.

5. The Pittsburgh city council, for example, shifted from citywide to ward representation in 1834. An examination of most of the pre-1833 members revealed a predominance of representation from upper levels of the social order.

6. The first large-scale work on historical vertical mobility in the United States was Stephen Thernstrom, *Poverty and Progress* (Cambridge, 1964). Thernstrom's work is limited to a description of mobility upward from blue collar to white collar occupations. See also his later work, *The Other Bostonians* (Cambridge, 1973) and Herbert Gutman, "Class, Status and Community Power in Nineteenth-Century American Industrial Cities—Patterson, New Jersey: A Case Study," in Frederic Cople Jaher, ed., *The Age of Industrialism in America: Essays in Social Structure and Cultural Values* (New York, 1968), 263–287.

7. Several studies of Pittsburgh upper-class communities illustrate this instability: Renee Reitman, "The Elite Community in Shadyside, 1800–1920," and Thomas J. Kelso, "Allegheny Elites: 1850–1907," seminar papers, History Department, University of Pittsburgh, 1964.

8. Relevant data for Pittsburgh is in Mary Young, "The Pittsburgh Chamber of Commerce and the Allied Boards of Trade in 1910," and Frank Lukaszewicz, "Regional and Central Boards of Directors of Pittsburgh Banks in 1912," seminar papers, History Department, University of Pittsburgh, 1966.

9. This conclusion is based upon an examination of all Pittsburgh city councilmen since the establishment of the ward system in 1834, school board members at decade intervals between 1860 and 1910 for Pittsburgh, and city council members, selected at various intervals, of Cincinnati, Columbus and Cleveland, Ohio. See also John Dankosky, "Pittsburgh City Government, 1816–1850," seminar paper, History Department, University of Pittsburgh, 1971.

10. These observations are based primarily upon an examination of the proceedings of the Pittsburgh City Council between 1850 and 1910. See also Seymour Mandelbaum, *Boss Tweed's New York* (New York, 1965), for the preoccupation with physical development.

11. Some elements of this conflict are described in Mandelbaum, ibid., esp. 59–71.

12. A discussion of urban integration, as a process of organizing space, is in John Friedmann, "Cities in Social Transformation," Comparative Studies in Society and History, 4 (1961), 86–103.

13. See Scott Greer, *The Emerging City*, 37–40.

14. A more extensive elaboration of the community-society continuum, especially as it affects political life, is in Samuel P. Hays, "Political Parties and the Community-Society Continuum," in William N. Chambers and Walter Dean Burnham, *The American Party Systems* (New York, 1967), 152–181.

15. A description of the change in Pittsburgh is in Howard V. Storch, Jr., "Changing Functions of the Center-City, Pittsburgh, 1850–1912," seminar paper, History Department, University of Pittsburgh, 1965.

16. This scale has been worked out for Pittsburgh in Young, "The Pittsburgh Chamber of Commerce," and Lukaszewicz, "Regional and Central Boards of Directors." See also a similar attempt in Edward J. Davies II, "Wilkes-Barre, 1870–1920: A Study in the Evolution of Urban Leadership During Industrialization," seminar paper, History Department, University of Pittsburgh, 1972.

17. This discussion is based largely upon studies of the internal structure of several professional groups in Pittsburgh, including William H. Issel, "The Pittsburgh Teaching Profession and Its Politics, 1900–1912"; Tom Henry, "The Pittsburgh Architect—1910—and Municipal Improvement"; and Ross Messer, "The Medical Profession in Pittsburgh, 1890–1910," seminar papers, Department of History, University of Pittsburgh, 1964.

18. The most important study of the urban upper class in recent America is E. Digby Baltzell, *Philadelphia Gentlemen* (Glencoe, 1958). For some major revisions of Baltzell's argument see John N. Ingham, "Elite and Upper Class in the Iron and Steel Industry, 1874 to 1965," doctoral dissertation, University of Pittsburgh, 1973. See also Davies, "Wilkes-Barre, 1870–1920" and Burton W. Folsom II, "The Social Order of the Anthracite Region: Scranton's Economic Elite, 1850–1880," seminar paper, History Department, University of Pittsburgh, 1974.

19. The development of this process among Presbyterians in Pittsburgh is traced by Thomas Callister in "The Reaction of the Presbytery of Pittsburgh to the New Immigrants," seminar paper, History Department, University of Pittsburgh, 1963.

20. The "upper level" character of social reform is indicated by a recent study of settlement house leaders, Allen F. Davis, *Spearheads for Reform* (New York, 1967). Davis does not carry out a thorough examination of such leaders but, occasionally, describes qualitatively their origins in the upper levels of the social order. He indicates a very high level of education—more than 80% had earned a bachelor's degree or equivalent at a time when only 5% of the population age 18–21 was enrolled in all institutions of higher education. Some of the most useful newspaper sources of evidence about social welfare reform in the Progressive Era are the upper-class society newspapers, often far more valuable than the general circulation media.

21. Davis, *Spearheads for Reform*, is the most complete treatment of the settlement house to date; he does not treat it, however, as an aspect

of inter-class communication. The approach here rests upon the examination of several settlement houses in Pittsburgh. See also Elizabeth Metzger, "A Study of Social Settlement Workers in Pittsburgh, 1893 to 1927," seminar paper, History Department, University of Pittsburgh, 1973.

22. See, for example, the pages of the Pittsburgh Index and the Pittsburgh Bulletin, 1890 and following.

23. A larger statement of this view is in Samuel P. Hays, "The Politics of Reform in Municipal Government in the Progressive Era," Pacific Northwest Quarterly, 55 (1965), 157–169.

24. For Chicago see Joan S. Miller, "The Politics of Municipal Reform in Chicago during the Progressive Era: The Municipal Voters' League as a Test Case, 1896–1920," M.A. Thesis, Roosevelt University, 1966. For Philadelphia see Bonnie R. Fox, "The Philadelphia Progressives: A Test of the Hofstadter-Hays Thesis," Pennsylvania History, XXXIV (1967), 372–394, and David Amidon, "The Philadelphia Bureau of Municipal Research, 1908–1920," paper presented to the Pennsylvania Historical Association, spring meeting, 1965.

25. Distinctions between reform approved and reform opposed candidates in Chicago are developed by Miller, "The Politics of Municipal Reform in Chicago," 31–36. Reformers preferred candidates of upper occupational and educational levels and Protestant native Americans; they tended to reject those at lower levels, Catholics and immigrants.

26. George S. Counts, The Social Composition of Boards of Education: A Study in the Social Control of Public Education (Chicago, 1927).

27. Matthew Holden, "Ethnic Accommodation in a Historical Case," Comparative Studies of Society and History, VIII (1966), 168–180. Using Cleveland data on city councilmen, Holden stresses the attractiveness of corporate business activities rather than the relocation of the upper-class community as the major factor in the departure of upper-class individuals from city government.

28. The literature on the inner dynamics of systematization is extremely weak. Some suggestions as to the process are in John K. Galbraith, The New Industrial State (Boston, 1967), 11–34 and Dwight Waldo, The Administrative State (New York, 1948), 3–61.

29. The outstanding recent study of this phenomenon is Herbert J. Gans, The Urban Villagers (New York, 1962).

30. See Samuel Lubell, The Future of American Politics (New York, 1951), 61–85.

31. Black vertical mobility is indicated by the following data concerning nonwhite occupational distributions:

	1940	1950	1960	1969
White-collar	5.9%	10.2%	16.0%	26.2%
Blue-collar	16.6%	23.4%	26.0%	32.4%
Unskilled	77.5%	66.3%	58.0%	41.4%

The data is found in the annual issues of the Statistical Abstracts of the United States and the "Annual Average" reports in U.S. Department of Labor, Bureau of Labor Statistics, Employment and Earnings.

32. Leo F. Schnore, "Social Class Segregation Among Nonwhites in Metropolitan Centers," Demography, 2 (1965), 126–133. A convenient compilation of data describing Negro upward mobility is U.S. Department of Commerce, Bureau of the Census, "Social Economic Conditions of Negroes in the United States," Current Population Reports, Series P-23, No. 24 (Washington, D.C., 1967).

33. Income trends can be followed most completely in U.S. Department of Commerce, Bureau of the Census, Current Population Reports, Series P-60, or in the annual compilations by the same agency, the Statistical Abstract of the United States.

34. The recent politics of suburban areas is dealt with in Robert C. Wood, Suburbia, Its People and Their Politics (Boston, 1958).

35. An account of one case is Edward Sofen, The Miami Metropolitan Experiment (Bloomington, Indiana, 1963).

36. An account of the role of redevelopment, seen from a critical view, is Martin Anderson, The Federal Bulldozer (Cambridge, Mass., 1964).

37. For the relationship between political structure and the success or failure of drives for fluoridation see Robert L. Crain and Donald B. Rosenthal, "Structure and Value in Local Political Systems: The Case of Fluoridation Decisions," Journal of Politics, 28 (1966), 169–195. The authors argue that proponents of fluoridation come more from the upper levels of the socioeconomic order than do the opponents, and that the movement has a better chance of success in an urban government of centralized decision-making authority in which the executive is insulated from external "irregular" pressures. The strategies of fluoridation proponents, their successes and failures and referenda data can be followed most completely in anti-fluoridation literature such as National Fluoridation News (1954–present).

38. Some indication of these trends can be observed in Harold A. Stone, et al., City Manager Government in Nine Cities (Chicago, 1940); Frederick C. Mosher, et al., City Manager Government in Seven Cities (Chicago, 1940); Harold A. Stone, et al., City Manager Government in the United States (Chicago, 1940). These provide case studies of a variety of cities and carry many aspects of city manager government, including the problem of representation, down through the 1930s.

39. The opposition can be traced in Anderson, The Federal Bulldozer.

40. Lewis M. Killian, "Community Structure and the Role of the Negro Leader-Agent," Sociological Inquiry, 35 (1965), 69–79 describes these differences for the Negro confrontation with the established political system.

41. See, for example, Frank Reissman, "The Myth of Saul Alinsky," Dissent (July-August 1967), 469–478. The classic description of the new urban poor is Michael Harrington, *The Other America: Poverty in the United States* (New York, 1962).

42. The classic statement of the "pluralist" conception of community decision-making is Robert Dahl, *Who Governs* (New Haven, 1961). The limitations of the pluralist view lie in its failure to locate pluralism in the upper levels of the political order.

43. Drawn from data on Pittsburgh city councilmen, set against a study of the Pittsburgh Black upper class by Marjorie J. Allen, "The Negro Upper Class in Pittsburgh, 1910–1964," seminar paper, History Department, University of Pittsburgh, 1964.

VI THE CITY IN THE LIFE
OF THE NEWCOMER

The United States is a nation of immigrants; its cities are populated with newcomers propelled by two forces of urbanization, the waves of European immigrants and the migration of native Americans lured from the farm, the village, and the small town. Beginning with the flood of Catholic Irish and Germans in the 1840s, a major turning point in immigration history, significant changes took place in the nature and number of newcomers who came to the United States. More stayed in the cities, fewer were Protestant and middle class, more were of rural peasant stock, desperately poor and often illiterate, especially between 1880 and 1910 when eighteen million immigrants, mostly Catholics and Jews, poured in from southern and eastern Europe. By 1920, when census reports established that the United States had become an urbanized nation, more than three quarters of the urban population were people either of foreign birth or the sons and daughters of immigrants. The distribution of immigrants was uneven. The South was feeling important affects of urbanization even though it conspicuously lagged behind other regions in attracting newcomers. While cities were booming on the Pacific Slope, they could not compare to the two areas that took the greatest impact of immigration: the North Central states, and that area on the eastern seaboard from the Middle Atlantic to the New England states, which absorbed the majority of immigrants, over 70 percent of the foreign-born population.

Between 1840 and 1920 the immigrant helped to change the character of many American cities: Chicago with its Slavs, Milwaukee with its Germans, San Francisco with its Chinese, New Haven with its Italians, and New York, the most "foreign" city in the world, with its mulligan stew of nationalities. The ethnic clusters of "Little Europes" created an exciting diversity to urban living in language, customs, values, food, entertainment, and the arts. But the city also crystalized the plight of the immigrant: the pain of cutting old ties; the shock of alienation in and adjustment to a strange, new urban world; the hostility, contempt, bigotry, and fear of the "native" American.[1]

One result of this cultural collision was the emergence of what often has been called the shame of the city, the ghetto. In the first selection, David Ward asks one of the major questions in American urban history: how do you account for the origins and development of the immigrant ghetto? A large question with a thicket of thorny problems, it is subject to several approaches. One approach, often used by historians, is to stress the common hardships shared by most immigrant groups in housing, income, employment, sanitation, and the like, which helped create urban ghettos. This view highlights the similarities between various ethnic and religious groups. Ward looks at the problem with the cool and detached eye of the urban geographer, examining aspects of the ghetto not always explored by historians, such as the ecology of the inner city, differences in age, sex ratio, the spatial relationship between residences and employment, the selective influences of the central city, the death rate, business expansion, and so on. While careful to point out that he does not intend to minimize the very real difficulties faced by immigrants, he concludes nonetheless that "the internal spatial structure rather than the common deficiencies of immigrant residential districts may well be more revealing of their generic characteristics." Aside from an interpretation of the making of a ghetto, this view gives us a sense of the *differences* between various ethnic groups in the ghetto. For example: why the Irish had a higher death rate than the Russian Jew; why social organization was shattered in one ghetto and remained relatively stable in another; how the quality of sanitation varied from city to city; and how an expanding central city could have any number of effects. In Ward's view the ghetto is not fixed and rigid, but changing, in flux. It further enhances our understanding of the diversity, the rich pluralism of urban immigrant life.

Intimately related to the emergence of the ghetto in urban America, is another major theme of immigration—the difficulties of assimilation to a new culture.

In a chapter from his Pulitzer Prize winning book, *The Uprooted*, Oscar Handlin presents a poignant saga of the immigrant family and its problems of assimilation, which illuminate a larger theme of urban history: the breakdown of the traditional European communal tradition in an American urban environment. According to Handlin, the immigrant brought to the New World a highly structured concept of the family, meaningful for a village community

1. For an analysis of both immigration policy and attitudes toward the immigrant, see John Higham's brilliant *Strangers in the Land: Patterns of American Nativism, 1860–1925* (New York: Atheneum, revised ed., 1963), and Barbara Miller Solomon, "The Intellectual Background of the Immigration Restriction Movement in New England," *New England Quarterly* (March 1952).

but irrelevant to the conditions of the American city. The vital cohesion of the family, sealed by the social cement of precise authority, obligations, and responsibilities, was shattered. Poverty, the language barrier, the street gang, and American values regarding marriage and individualism dissolved old familial roles and reversed others. The family roots nourished by the village soil lay scattered on the city streets. Parental authority disintegrated and with it respect; cut by shame, misunderstanding, and the hard realities of American urban life, the European heritage was shredded. The family drifted apart, wife from husband, children from parents. Handlin sums it up when he has his immigrant mother look at her family and ask, "Would the strangeness of the setting make strangers also of these her dear ones?"

Handlin does not suggest that it happened to every family or that all immigrants were poor. But enough were poor to make it a bleak and tragic story.[2] It was not always a story, however, with a hideous ending, at least for second and third generation immigrants, many of whom in time were able to flee the ghetto into the larger life of the city. This was true for the Irish and Germans, the dominant groups of the so-called "old" immigration of the mid-nineteenth century. It is part of the interesting story, told by Thomas Kessner in the next essay, of the New York Jews and Italians, the most numerous groups of the "new" immigration from 1880 to 1915.

At the heart of the American Dream is the image of the self-made man and woman, charging up the social ladder to success. Originating in the eighteenth century and symbolized by the Statue of Liberty, it was celebrated in the nineteenth century from the pulpit, the political platform, the lecture circuit, and especially, by the novels of Horatio Alger. The theme of rags-to-riches seemed to be an enduring one until it was examined by several historians, particularly Stephan Thernstrom in the early 1960s, who declared it to be a myth. Social mobility for the native poor or the foreign newcomer was modest indeed, argued Thernstrom. Precious few made it from the basement at the bottom to the room at the top; in fact, not many made it to the ground floor. Fairly recently, a number of historians, including Thomas Kessner, have been jabbing at the myth-breakers, turning, as it were, Horatio Alger *back over* in his grave, at least part-way. Rags may not have lead to riches for all, but they were, for many, exchanged for respectability.

Kessner's thesis in his book, *The Golden Door*, is that, in so far as New York is concerned, the immigrant Jews and Italians (as well as many native

2. Does disorganization mean disaster for the family? Not necessarily, say some sociologists who argue that if the old bonds were broken, new associations arose to replace them. In effect, the family, like other institutions, responded to social change; change does not necessarily mean total disruption. See Herbert J. Gans's perceptive study of a second-generation Italian community in Boston, *The Urban Villagers* (New York: The Free Press, 1962).

poor) were able to scramble up the class ladder; their social mobility was "both rapid and widespread." But the race was not even. While Jews and Italians shared experiences, immigrating at the same time, settling in ethnic neighborhoods, facing problems in language and religion, the Jews moved upward faster. The incentives for "making it" were greater for the Jews. Urban America was the point of no return, since anti-Semitism was rising in Europe. Compared to the Italians, more Jews had urban skills. Tailoring, for example, was a happy marriage with the important garment industry in New York. Ambition, the involvement in the labor movement, the high priority on education, and ethnic self-consciousness, were some of the qualities embraced by Jews that not only established differences with the Italian experience, but also accelerated their social mobility.

Italians, on the other hand, migrated for short-term goals. Many expected to return home and many did. Many sent money home to relatives, cash that could have been "risk capital" for their own advancement here. Unlike the Jews, Italians tended to follow the occupation of the father and did not strike out on their own. If more Italians became manual laborers, they did so at a time when the city had an enormous appetite for unskilled labor because it was building and stretching outward. Within a decade, however, they were able to move up into the needles trade, for example, or into dock work, replacing the Irish and the Jews.

Nor was the ghetto for both groups such a roadblock to mobility as many historians have argued. In no way did it resemble the intense segregation of the European ghetto. And Kessner makes the interesting point that the ghetto was in fact "a mobility launcher," in the sense that it offered hospitality, jobs, political contacts, investment opportunities, and schools and settlement houses, which helped the immigrants to assimilate and acquire the necessary skills to cope with their new urban environment.

Kessner ends on a poignant note. If Jews and Italians were able to achieve mobility over time, did the materialistic rewards born of success bring happiness? In many cases it did not. "But then," as Professor Kessner reminds us, "Horatio Alger never promised happiness."

In the next selection Gilbert Osofsky charts the making of Harlem, the nation's largest ghetto, a study of internal migration and the failure of assimilation. During the First World War the travels of the black from the South to the big cities in the North constituted one of the great folk wanderings in American history. If the foreign newcomer added the spice of diversity to the American city, so did the black as he filled the bleak pockets of the ghettos of Philadelphia, New York, Chicago, Cleveland, and Washington. If the slum of the white immigrant changed during the twentieth century, allowing many to scramble upward to the more affluent ranks of middle-class America, the ghetto of the black became more and more the inner city of little or no escape, a fixed eyesore of poverty and despair, a striking contradiction to democratic aspirations.

Osofsky shows that the Manhattan ghetto of today was in fact created by the 1920s. It is the ironic tale of how one of New York's most exclusive residential areas became the city's most depressed area, where one of the main industries was the undertaking business. Of particular interest is his discussion of the split within the black community—the cultural antagonisms between the native American black and the foreign-born West Indian black, which sapped the unity that Harlem needed so desperately during the 1920s.

The Making of Immigrant Ghettoes, 1840–1920

DAVID WARD

The central concentration of urban employment after about 1850 strongly influenced the location and characteristics of the residential areas of new immigrants, most of whom sought low-cost housing close to their places of employment. People of foreign birth soon dominated the central residential quarters, and, although there was considerable mixing of ethnic groups, members of each major group usually concentrated in one area, eventually identified as a ghetto. These central concentrations of low-income groups contrasted strikingly with the peripheral location of the poor in pre-industrial cities.[1] Under the conditions of a pedestrian city, the rich lived in central areas—for convenience as well as for the prestige that came with living close to the city's political and religious institutions—and the immigrant poor tended to squat near the edge of town. Before the Industrial Revolution, the very rich often had developed small and exclusive residential sections beyond the city limits. But with the first signs of industrial and commercial development in the center, they accelerated their outward movement. The lack of transportation, however, greatly restricted suburban residence, and only after adequate systems had been developed were middle-income people able to leave central areas for peripheral cites. The vacated residences were then subdivided to provide cramped housing for new immigrants near to the growing sources of employment.

The first major influx of foreign immigrants took place before either urban employment had been centralized or local transportation had been improved; consequently, the residential pattern of the mid-nineteenth-century American city was transitional between pre-industrial and modern. Before the Civil War, Irish and German immigrants concentrated in central locations abandoned by more prosperous residents, but this source of housing served only a small part of the total influx. Others had to seek accommodation and employment in almost every section of the city, and many squatted in peripheral "shanty-towns," which were displaced only after the Civil War when streetcar systems opened new areas to middle-income development. At the same time, businesses also made claims on adjacent residential areas, and, although these areas were expanding outwards, most later immigrant arrivals were housed on the immediate edge of the central business district—by increasing the density of buildings and the number of people in each building.

Indeed, the most frequent theme of past evaluations of immigrant residential districts was the mortal and socially pathological repercussion of congested and unsanitary housing conditions.

These districts came to symbolize both material and social failure in urban America and were often erroneously identified with high rates of infant mortality, crime, prostitution, drunkenness, and various other symptoms of social ills. Thus it was assumed that the living conditions endured by immigrants undermined personal health and domestic morality. Furthermore, the tendency of immigrants of similar nationalities and religions to congregate in ghettoes was often regarded as a threat to the "Americanization" or assimilation of the newcomer. Sensitive observers argued that housing reform and the regulation of living conditions would remove the major causes of the social problems, but less optimistic observers were convinced that restricting the entry of the more recent (and apparently less desirable) immigrants would alone solve the basic causes of urban problems. The bulk of the literature on immigrant living conditions, therefore, was strongly influenced by the political polemics of housing reform or immigration restriction, and, although existing records provided detailed and often penetrating evaluations of ghettoes, they rarely isolated the generic from the purely local characteristics of their particular investigation.[2]

THE LOCATION OF IMMIGRANT
RESIDENTIAL DISTRICTS

Yet observers were generally able to agree that most immigrants congregated on the edge of the central business district, which provided the largest and most diverse source of unskilled employment. Although local transportation was improved and extended, many immigrants had jobs with long and awkward hours and preferred a short walk to work. Almost all immigrant families depended on the wages of every adult member of the family; consequently, the multiplication of low individual commuter fares inflated transportation costs beyond the means of most low-income families.[3] The tenure of most unskilled occupations was also characteristically uncertain, and daily hiring was the common procedure in general laboring. Immigrants thus faced not only constant changes in the locations of their work,[4] but also frequent spells of unemployment, and under these circumstances convenient access to the central business district was almost a necessity for workers who periodically were forced to search for substitute employment. Suburban industrial districts also attracted many immigrants, and cheap housing was built nearby, but residential areas close to the city center supported far larger numbers of immigrants because of the variety of industrial and commercial employment available there. Only in specialized manufacturing cities, where concentrations of large-scale industrial plants frequently employed more people than the central business district, were substantially fewer immigrants housed in central areas.

The first generation of immigrants to arrive in American cities in large numbers often provided almost the entire labor force in certain activities of the central business district, for the tendency of individual groups to specialize was marked. Irish immigrants found employment in the warehouses and terminal facilities they had helped to build, while German immigrants worked in the sewing machine and consumer supply trades, which were housed in the upper stories of warehouses.[5] New arrivals from Italy in part replaced the Irish as general laborers and were attracted to distributing fresh food from the central wholesale markets.[6] Jewish immigrants, equipped with long experience in the handicraft industries and the local commercial life of Eastern Europe, quickly developed many branches of merchandising at a time when the retail and wholesale segments of marketing were firmly established as distinct and specialized areas in the central business district.[7] Members of this group also rapidly took over the ready-made clothing industry, and, although they diverted production from warehouses to residential premises, the credit and informational needs of the industry still demanded locations with ready access to the central business district. Also, many of the immigrant businesses, which originally provided only for the distinctive material or dietary needs of the immigrant community, eventually expanded to serve far wider urban, regional, and national markets.

The residential fringe of the central business and manufacturing districts also indirectly provided by far the largest supply of cheap housing in most cities, for the threat of commercial and industrial expansion encouraged families whose income and working hours permitted a longer journey to work to abandon central residential areas. Before abandoned dwellings were demolished, the single-family houses were usually converted into multi-family tenements and their rear yards or surrounding grounds were filled with cheap new structures. Apartments rented at rates appropriate

to the low incomes of most immigrants, but overcrowding, dilapidated structures, and unsanitary living conditions made even low rents exorbitant. Since the rents for units providing minimum housing needs were far beyond the means of most immigrants, few satisfactory low-rent structures were built.

Yet not all centrally located residential districts were taken over by immigrants immediately after the departure of the previous residents. In particular, spacious houses once belonging to the wealthiest members of the middle class were often utilized as lodging houses for single professional and clerical workers. Generally, these houses were further removed from the edge of the central business district than were the tenement districts, and it was assumed that converting them to lodging houses would not only maintain the status of the area, but would also be less costly than conversion to multi-family units.[8] These dwellings were the only centrally located housing available to black Americans when they arrived in northern cities in large numbers after about 1900.[9] The ratio of plumbing to rooms made the houses unsuitable for multi-family occupancy, but by then all alternative central and low cost housing had been preempted by European immigrants.

Most central residential districts, however, had been vacated on the assumption that demolition and commercial redevelopment would proceed quite rapidly. Thus capital improvements to the dwellings during the period of initial immigrant occupancy were extremely limited. But, there were often unanticipated delays in the expansion of commerce or industry, and, with the continued arrival of large numbers of immigrants, dilapidated tenements were demolished or removed to the rear of the lot and new multi-story structures were built on the vacant space. In older eastern cities, and especially in New York, the complete redevelopment of an entire lot with a five- or six-story structure was common, but in newer cities the relocation of the original building and the construction of two- to six-family tenements in the remaining space was the usual course. In cities with limited amounts of older housing, low-cost dwellings were constructed on newly platted land, and frequently drainage problems and the lack of adequate utilities rather than housing density created the major difficulties. Yet it was the construction of multi-story tenements for large numbers of families that excited the greatest popular concern in the late nineteenth century, and new minimum housing standards were designed, primarily to prevent the overcrowding of lots with tall structures. Because the new standards increased construction costs, rents in the improved buildings were often too expensive for low-income immigrants, and they continued to seek accommodation in older structures.[10]

THE INTERNAL SPATIAL STRUCTURE OF IMMIGRANT DISTRICTS

Living Conditions

Although the common material deficiencies of the immigrant residential districts attracted considerable publicity and legislative activity, living conditions in those areas varied conspicuously both in quality and in the effects they had on the vital rates of the resident populations. Evaluations of conditions at the time emphasized the physically debilitating effects of overcrowded housing; nevertheless, local exceptions to the assumed relationship between mortality or morbidity and congestion aroused great curiosity. Although newly arrived immigrants tended to live in more cramped quarters than more established groups, the overall death rate of the populations of foreign birth were frequently somewhat lower than those of foreign parentage. The age structures of the newer immigrant groups, however, were dominated by vigorous young adults, whereas the earlier groups included large numbers of both very young and old people. Thus, although many earlier groups had moved into less crowded and often better housing, their more balanced age structures exposed them to the inflationary effects of higher death rates among infants and older adults.[11]

Yet age structure alone failed to explain strong contrasts in the death rates of groups with similar proportions of people of foreign birth and parentage. Russian-Jewish and Italian immigrants, for example, often lived alongside each other in extremely congested quarters, and, although the greater prevalence of family immigration among the Jews supposedly made them more vulnerable to infant mortality, such rates among the Russian-Jews were often the lowest in the city, whereas among Italians they were often nearly the highest. Most observers attributed the low death rates to the urban ancestry of Jewish people who, unlike most other immigrant groups, had made their adjustments to slum conditions long before arriving in American cities. In particular, there was an extremely low death rate among Russian Jews from pulmonary tuberculosis, one of the leading causes of death in the crowded areas; this immunity was shared by their co-religionists in European cities.[12] Some authorities attributed the extremely high death rate of Italians to dietary deficiencies and lack of familiarity with the severe American winter.[13] Even longer established immigrant groups also exhibited sharp contrasts in their mortality characteristics. People of Irish birth and parentage were afflicted with unusually high death rates throughout the nineteenth century, and tuberculosis, in particular, was more prevalent than among other immigrants who had arrived during the same period.[14] Finally, mortality rates were frequently high among people of native parentage who lived in immigrant neighborhoods because they were either the oldest or the most impoverished remaining members of the earlier resident group.

In spite of these demographic and ethnic considerations, most authorities rarely identified the spatial implications of the relationship between congested living conditions, high mortality, and large numbers of different ethnic groups and generally assumed that within the city high population density, high death rates, and high proportions of immigrants exhibited identical rather than separate distributions. On the basis of data for New York City and Brooklyn in 1890, it has been possible to demonstrate that high age-standardized death rates and a high population density per built-up acre occurred in quite separate locations which were associated with different ethnic groups.[15] For example, the population of Russian-Jewish parentage was strongly associated with high density and that of Italian parentage with high mortality, although the association was somewhat weaker. Earlier immigrant groups were not clearly connected with either high density or high mortality, and the ethnically more diverse districts occupied by long-established groups probably obscured a frequently publicized association between Irish populations and high mortality.

To summarize, a descriptive model of immigrant districts might show high mortality rates, a high population density, and proportionately large populations of immigrants as circles which occupy largely separate but occasionally overlapping locations within a large city (Fig. 1). Areas which are described by different combinations of more than one of the three most widely publicized characteristics of immigrant quarters indicated above record the effects of distinctive ethnic groups. Area A describes districts with all three characteristics and represents the worst sections of the Italian ghetto; Area B, extremely crowded districts but ones with low death rates—clearly the Russian Jewish ghetto; and Area C, less congested sections with high mortality, representing earlier and frequently Irish immigrant groups. Area D, which combines high mortality and high density, describes remnant and impoverished populations of native parentage.

Quite apart from the different adjustments of ethnic groups to their housing environment, the rapid improvements in sanitation, piped water supply, and building practices changed the quality of the urban environment. At a time when housing reformers were publicizing the mortal or morbid consequences of congestion, others were popularizing the impact of sanitary engineering on the secular decline in urban death rates.[16] The paradox of declining death rates and increasing congestion could perhaps have been resolved if declining mortality had been confined to the expanding suburban districts, but some of the most spectacular reductions in local death rates took place in overcrowded districts where sanitary conditions had improved. The material rewards of sanitary improvement, however, did not extend to all areas occupied by immigrants, for the arrangement and site conditions of the housing they inherited often defied attempts to improve the surroundings. Districts which originally had been developed as either individual dwellings set in spacious lots or as row houses with substantial front and rear grounds were swamped by cheap new structures in the form of rear tenements or of virtually inaccessible courts. Most sanitary facilities and utilities were confined to the public streets, and little attempt was made to alter this arrangement in the new buildings. The size of the original single-family residences also influenced living conditions, for large houses were frequently subdivided without the addition of new plumbing.

Local site conditions also strongly influenced sanitary improvements. For example, low-lying areas with saturated subsoil remained major centers of unsanitary living conditions. Wherever possible, shallow waterfront locations and local water bodies had been filled to create new land for both commercial and residential developments. Until about the mid-nineteenth century, there were no restrictions on the com-

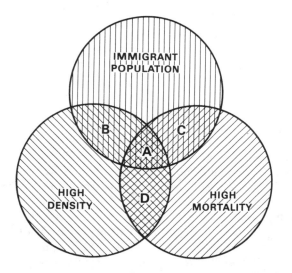

Probable Occupants: **A** Italian   **B** Russian-Jewish   **C** Irish   **D** Remnant Native

Figure 1. Model of the Internal Spatial Structure of Immigrant Residential Districts, 1890

Inter-City Contrasts in Immigrant
Housing Characteristics, 1890

*Per Cent Deviation of Each Individual City from the Mean for
All Six Cities: 1890*

Families per Dwelling:	1	2	3	4	5	6	7-9	9+
Mean Per Cent	27.2	21.9	13.9	9.3	5.5	4.7	7.0	10.4
New York	−13.8	−14.9	−6.7	−2.7	0.0	0.8	8.9	28.5
Boston	−5.8	5.3	12.1	0.5	−0.4	−0.6	−2.6	−8.4
Philadelphia	39.1	−5.8	−6.2	−4.5	−3.3	−3.3	−5.9	−10.1
Chicago	7.5	3.4	1.1	2.8	−0.2	−0.8	−4.1	−9.7
Brooklyn	−9.4	1.0	4.0	2.1	4.5	4.7	2.7	−7.7
St. Louis	4.9	16.1	−2.3	0.9	−2.2	−2.4	−4.4	−8.8

None: Statistics refer only to those wards with more than 70 per cent of their populations of foreign parentage.

position or the subsequent topography of the fill; thus buildings were often constructed on inadequate base material and were associated with threats to public health which could not be removed except by expensive redevelopments of entire localities.[17] Finally, the unsanitary practices of slaughter houses, breweries, and horse stables, which were frequently found side by side with immigrant housing, also influenced local living conditions.

For these reasons, it was possible for cities with neither extremely high-density residential districts nor extensive central concentrations of immigrants to have morbid living conditions. Even among the immigrant districts of the largest cities there was considerable variation in the proportions of high-density dwellings. For example, although more than half of the residential buildings in the immigrant districts of New York City contained more than six dwellings, more than two thirds of the residential buildings in Philadelphia were single-family dwellings. . . . In spite of these apparent advantages in housing, however, mortality rates in Philadelphia were among the highest in the nation, largely because of structural defects and the lack of adequate water supply and sewage disposal.[18] Immigrant districts in Chicago and St. Louis were characterized by large proportions of two- and three-family structures, but again structural defects and the neglect of sanitation created debilitating living conditions. Since overcrowded and ill-ventilated rooms, poor water, and lack of sewerage and street-cleaning systems were the common discomforts of most immigrant districts, the selective effects of sanitary improvements within and between cities strongly influenced the morbid effects of the urban environment.[19]

Social Characteristics

Congested living quarters were frequently regarded as a basic cause of not only high rates of sickness and death but also of social disorganization among immigrants. It was for long assumed that the behavior in many low-income immigrant neighborhoods was socially pathological and directly related to the breakdown of the traditional social organization of rural people in the impersonal and anonymous social environment of the city. Subsequent reevaluations of low-income neighborhoods have suggested that many observers failed to identify the presence of adequate and even elaborate social organization among immigrant populations largely because their behavior and priorities were different from those of suburban or native America.[20] Indeed, most newly arrived immigrants were hardly aware of the society of middle- and high-income native Americans with whom they were apparently expected to assimilate. Instead, their initial exposure was to earlier immigrant groups who had gradually gained control of segments of the political and economic life of many cities. Moreover, once a ghetto was established, it became in part a voluntary association. Most immigrants preferred to spend their early years in the city in a district where their fellow countrymen or coreligionists—often their friends and relatives—lived.[21] Under these circumstances, although few escaped the material and social discomforts of crowded living, some groups were able to avoid severe social disorganization and occasionally to attract laudatory, if often condescending, comments upon the stability and moral orthodoxy of their family and neighborhood life.[22] Although both legitimate and corrupt forms of political patronage excited popular condemnation, residential concentration provided

large immigrant groups with proportionate shares of patronage at a time when public welfare was weakly developed.[23]

These social attractions and political advantages, however, were not shared by all immigrant groups nor did they exist in all central districts. Small groups not only lacked the numbers to support their own institutions but also rarely received their share of political patronage or jobs. Young single men living in rooming houses—those who hoped eventually to return home with the profits of American employment—were particularly affected, and their social predicament was often reflected in socially pathological behavior.[24] The age structure, sex ratio, and diverse ethnic characteristics of these quarters clearly distinguish them from those more typical immigrant ghettoes in which one or two large immigrant groups composed largely of families dominated extensive residential sections.[25]

THE EFFECT OF BUSINESS EXPANSION ON IMMIGRANT CONCENTRATION

Even the largest and most stable immigrant groups were unable, however, to establish enduring ghettoes in central fringe areas threatened by the continuous invasion of business premises. Different edges of the central business district expanded at different rates at different times, and this selective expansion of commercial premises was in part responsible for the variations in the living conditions and social characteristics of the central concentrations of immigrants. Early students of urban ecology emphasized the blighting effects of the central business district on adjacent areas and, in keeping

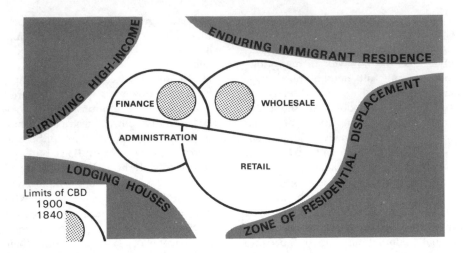

Figure 2. Diagrammatic Representation of the Relative Locations of Different Central Residential Areas

with descriptions of these locations, concentrated upon their common material and social deficiencies.[26] Nevertheless, most ecologists acknowledged that the zone of blight was occasionally interrupted by high-income residences, and, subsequently, a sector arrangement of urban residential types was suggested to accommodate substantial variations in the rent levels.[27] The survival of both high-income districts and well organized ghettoes in central locations has been related to the sentiments and values of the occupants,[28] and, although these perspectives indicate more clearly the range of living conditions and social characteristics, their relationship to the selective and sequential emergence of different segments of the central business district remains obscure.

Both the rate and the extent of the advance of the business district clearly influenced the longevity of adjacent residential quarters and therefore, the material and social conditions of immigrants who settled there.[29] From the discussion of sequential expansion in Chapter 3, it is clear that on some margins of the central business district commercial activities followed so closely after the original inhabitants had left that newcomers had neither the time nor the incentive to establish a stable community (Fig. 2). These districts were occupied most frequently by the smallest or poorest immigrant groups along with the older and often more impoverished members of earlier groups that had moved on to better locations. Manifestations of social disorganization were thus rooted in the insecurity of residential tenure, frequent population turnover, and the failure of any one immigrant group to establish the institutional fabric of the ghetto. In contrast, other margins remained remarkably stable throughout the nineteenth century. . . . Where commercial encroachment was limited, for example, immigrants were able to establish enduring ghettoes and, indeed, areas which had initially been occupied by Irish and German immigrants eventually passed to Italian, Russian Jewish, and other later arrivals toward the turn of the century.

The selective characteristics of business expansion also allowed some residents of adjacent districts to maintain their homes and, consequently, influenced the location of surviving central high-income districts. Although site or historic status were the most frequently publicized advantages of central high-income districts, most large cities had several alternative locations similarly endowed but which had capitulated to immigrant settlement and business encroachment. Yet one segment of the central business district—the financial and administrative—attracted rather than discouraged people of wealth and status . . . , and throughout the nineteenth century many families highly valued living close to the seats of financial and political power. Since this district provided decidedly limited opportunities for unskilled employment, the demand for low-rent housing was much weaker than on margins adjoining the center of unskilled employment. Ecological theory clearly recognized the spatial impact of the central business district on adjacent residential districts, but it should be noted that the impact was selective and, therefore, responsible for the impressive variations in the material and social conditions of this central residential zone.

The term "ghetto" frequently has been applied to concentrations of poverty-stricken immigrants living in congested and segregated areas. It has been suggested that the progressive enlargement and internal spatial differentiation of immigrant areas limited the generic applicability of the term to restricted parts of the city. Because of the limited supply of abandoned housing and the dispersed pattern of urban employment, the Irish and German immigrants who arrived in American cities before the Civil War found housing in almost every section of the city. The largest single immigrant concentrations were in central locations, but many also settled in "shantytowns" beyond the physical limits of the city. The expansions of streetcar systems in the 1870's and their electrification in the 1880's encouraged most middle-income people of native parentage to leave central residential locations. During the same period the concentration of employment opportunities for immigrants in the central business district encouraged a proportionately greater central concentration of new arrivals from southern and eastern Europe, and by about 1900 immigrants of diverse ethnic origins occupied extensive sections of the inner city, while many established immigrants sought new accommodations in the inner suburbs.

Immigrants and their children thus accounted for a large, if not a dominant, proportion of the total populations of many large American cities; consequently, the concentration of particular ethnic groups in well defined districts separated them from other ethnic groups housed under similar circumstances rather than from a homogenous majority group. Moreover, the boundaries of ethnic ghettoes were seldom fixed or well defined and mixed ethnic populations lived in many immigrant districts.[30] Certainly the degrees of concentration of ethnic groups

was not closely related to the quality
of their living conditions nor was
housing congestion closely related to
their vital rates. Although ghettoes
were frequently identified with the
pathological social problems of urban
society, certain advantages of residential concentration were also noted.
The variable longevity and diversity
of central immigrant concentrations,
however, depended on the timing,
scale, and direction of the expansion
of adjacent non-residential land uses
and on the appropriateness of the original housing for multi-family occupancy or a higher density of single-
families. These conclusions are not intended to depreciate the amount of
the discomfort endured by most immigrant families but rather to imply that
the internal spatial structure rather
than the common deficiencies of immigrant residential districts may well be
more revealing of their generic characteristics.

NOTES

1. G. Sjoberg, *The Pre-industrial City*, New
York, 1960, pp. 91-105.
2. E. E. Lampard, "American Historians and
the Study of Urbanization," *American Historical
Review*, 67, 1961, pp. 49-61.
3. F. H. Streightoff, *Standard of Living Among
the Industrial People of America*, Boston and
New York, 1911, pp. 22-28; United States Senate Document, No. 22, 62nd Congress, 1st Session, Serial 6082, *Cost of Living in American
Towns*, Washington, D.C., 1911, pp. iv-v; E. E.
Pratt, *Industrial Causes of Congestion of Population in New York City*, New York, 1911, pp.
116-85; H. L. Cargill, "Small Houses for Workingmen," in R. W. DeForest and L. Veiller, eds.
The Tenement House Problem, Vol. 1, New York,
1903, pp. 331-32.
4. F. W. Streightoff, *op. cit.*, pp. 30-34.
5. R. Ernst, *Immigrant Life in New York City:
1825-1863*, New York, 1949, pp. 61-77; O.
Handlin, *Boston's Immigrants*, Cambridge, 1959,
pp. 54-87.
6. R. F. Foerster, *The Italian Emigration of Our
Times*, Cambridge, 1919, pp. 332-44; E. Lord,

et al., *The Italian in America*, New York, 1905,
pp. 66-69.
7. S. Joseph, *Jewish Immigration to the United
States from 1881 to 1910*, New York, 1914, pp.
42-46; C. S. Bernheimer, ed., *The Russian Jew
in the United States*, Philadelphia, 1905, pp.
102-21.
8. A. B. Wolfe, *The Lodging House Problem in
Boston*, Cambridge, 1913, pp. 9-14, 39-50.
9. G. Osofsky, *The Making of a Ghetto*, New
York, 1967, pp. 105-49; E. F. Frazier, "Negro
Harlem: An Ecological Study," *American Journal
of Sociology*, 1937, pp. 72-88; A. H. Spear,
*Black Chicago: The Making of a Negro Ghetto,
1890-1920*, Chicago, 1967, pp. 11-27.
10. L. Veiller, "Housing Conditions and Tenement Laws in Leading American Cities," in
R. W. De Forest and L. Veiller, eds., *op. cit.*,
pp. 129-72; E. E. Wood, *The Housing of the
Unskilled Wage Earner*, New York, 1919, p.
25; C. Aronovici, "The Cost of a Decent Home,"
Forum, 58, 1914, pp. 111-12; R. Lubove, *The
Progressives and the Slums*, Pittsburgh, 1962, pp.
217-56; J. Ford, *Slums and Housing*, Cambridge,
1936, pp. 72-204.
11. W. H. Guilfoy, "The Death Rate of the City
of New York as Affected by the Cosmopolitan
Character of Its Population," *Quarterly Publications of the American Statistical Association*, 10,
1907, pp. 515-22; F. L. Hoffman, "The General
Death Rate of Large American Cities: 1871-
1904," *Quarterly Publications of the American
Statistical Association*, 10, 1906-7, pp. 1-75.
12. M. Fishberg, "Health and Sanitation of the
Immigrant Jewish Population of New York,"
The Menorah, 33, 1902, pp. 37-46, 73-82, 168-
180; L. I. Dublin, "The Mortality of Foreign
Race Stocks in Pennsylvania and New York:
1910," *Quarterly Publication of the American
Statistical Association*, 17, 1920-21, pp. 13-44.
13. Kate H. Claghorn, "Foreign Immigrants in
New York City," *Report of the Industrial Commission*, 15, 1901, pp. 449-91; R. Brindisi, "The
Italian and Public Health," *Charities*, 12, 1904,
pp. 443-504.
14. William H. Guilfoy, *op. cit.*, pp. 515-22;
Kate H. Claghorn, *op. cit.*, pp. 460-61.
15. D. Ward, "The Internal Spatial Structure
of Immigrant Residential Districts in the Late
Nineteenth Century," *Geographical Analysis*, 1,
1969, pp. 337-53.
16. F. L. Hoffman, "American Mortality Progress During the Last Half Century," in Mazyck
P. Ravenal, ed., *A Half Century of Public
Health*, New York, 1921, pp. 94-117; G. E.
Clark, "Sanitary Improvement in New York During the Last Quarter of a Century," *Popular
Science Monthly*, 39, 1891, 319-30.
17. J. S. Billings, "Municipal Sanitation: Defects
in American Cities," *Forum*, 15, 1893, pp. 304-
10.
18. C. F. Wingate, "The City's Health—Sani-

tary Construction," *Municipal Affairs*, 2, 1898, pp. 261-70.

19. United States Senate Document, No. 338, 61st Congress, 2nd Session, Serial No. 5665, *Report of the Immigration Commission*, 1911, Vol. 66, *Immigrants in Cities*, Washington, 1911, p. 5.

20. W. F. Whyte, *The Street Corner Society*, Chicago, 1943, pp. 94-104, 255-278; H. J. Gans, *The Urban Villagers*, New York, 1962, pp. 3-41.

21. R. E. Park and H. A. Miller, *Old World Traits Transplanted*, New York, 1921, pp. 60-80; C. F. Ware, *Greenwich Village, 1920-30*, Boston, 1935, pp. 3-8, 81-126; W. I. Thomas and F. Znaniecki, *Polish Peasant in Europe and America*, New York, 1927, pp. 1468-1546.

22. W. T. Elsing, "Life in New York Tenement Houses as Seen by a City Missionary," in R. A. Woods, ed., *The Poor in Great Cities*, New York, 1895, pp. 42-85; A. F. Sanborn, "The Anatomy of a Tenement Street," *Forum*, 18, 1894, pp. 554-72.

23. T. J. Lowi, *At the Pleasure of the Mayor: Power and Patronage in New York City: 1898-1958*, New York, 1964.

24. H. W. Zorbaugh, *The Gold Coast and the Slum*, Chicago, 1929, pp. 142-51; R. A. Woods, ed., *The City Wilderness*, Boston, 1898, pp. 33-57; E. Abbott, *The Tenements of Chicago: 1908-1935*, Chicago, 1936, p. 100.

25. G. C. Homans, *The Human Group*, New York, 1950, pp. 334-68; H. W. Zorbaugh, *op. cit.*, p. 129; W. I. Firey, *Land Use in Central Boston*, Cambridge, 1947, pp. 170-97, 290-313.

26. E. W. Burgess, "The Growth of the City," in R. E. Park, ed., *The City*, 1925, pp. 47-62.

27. H. Hoyt, *The Structure and the Growth of Residential Neighborhoods in American Cities*, Washington, D.C., 1939.

28. W. I. Firey, "Sentiment and Symbolism as Ecological Variables," *American Sociological Review*, 10, 1945, pp. 140-48.

29. D. Ward, "The Emergence of Central Immigrant Ghettoes in American Cities: 1840-1920," *Annals of the Association of American Geographers*, 58, 1968, pp. 343-59.

30. *Report of the Immigration Commission, op. cit.*, pp. 6-8.

Generations

Oscar Handlin

Sometimes at night she'd wake and turn to feel if he were there. She'd reach the space across to where he lay, sense the reassuring bulk of him. She'd hug the thought. *All else has passed away with our passing from that place. But this will never change. By holy matrimony he has made me wife and mother to his family. That* (fiercely) *we can hold intact.*

In morning's light the certainty was gone. Through the day the fear came that this most intimate part of life would not remain the same. At the stove later she paused while the long spoon in her hand continued its mechanical stirring; she looked in bewilderment at the gathering table. Would the strangeness of the setting make strangers also of these her dear ones? Resolve came back, but confidence not altogether. It would be a desperate battle to hold firm in these relationships, outside the context that had nurtured them.

The difficulty was that formerly the family had not been a thing in itself, but an integral element of the village community. It had been fixed in a framework of numerous links and knots that held each individual within it in his place. As the functioning unit within the economy it was the means through which bread was produced and con-sumed. No one could live except as the member of a family.

As the medium for holding and transmitting land, its stability had been vital to social order. Every change in its structure affected the whole community. On the quality of a single marriage depended the welfare of all the brothers and sisters and less directly a widening circle of other persons. The connection with the soil had also been an element in extending these affiliations beyond the single household to a broad range of other kin tied together by inheritance, of blood and of possible claims to a common patrimony.

The family had therefore never been isolated. Its concerns were those of the entire village. While each home was expected to be the source of its own discipline, the community stood ready with sanctions of its own to make sure that children were obedient, that parents were good, and that relatives were helpful to each other. The network of mutual rights and obligations had thus the support of both an inner and an outer control.

Emigration took the family out of the village. The mere going was disruptive. The struggles of departure and resettlement subjected the household to a severe strain under most trying and most unusual conditions and at the same time deprived it of the counsel and assistance upon which it had traditionally depended. When so many new decisions were to be made, they had to be made alone. That alone distinguished the new family from the old.

In America also the economic unity of the common household enterprise disappeared. The minority who found their way to the farms or who, by their labors, maintained little businesses where wife and children could work along with the father, held on to the former ways. Vestiges of the old order also remained in the sweating homework system; as the father brought back the bundles that would be sewn into shirts or twisted into artificial flowers, the gathered group in the tenement room recaptured the sense of common effort familiar in recollection from the Other Side.

These were, however, but byways in the economy. In the characteristic immigrant employment, the individual was hired as an integer. He was one line in the ledger, one pair of hands on the floor, one pay envelope at the window, with no reference to who was there at home. Ultimately this pattern supplanted all others. Would they continue to take his bidding, to toil in the dim room with him, the one to pocket all, when they could go out to be their own wage earners? There was no point to it. Of what inheritance could he deprive them?

Properly speaking the family no longer had an income; there were only the combined incomes of its members. The larger unit was now a source of weakness rather than of strength. Those who could, broke away; it was madness for a man who was capable of supporting himself to maintain the ties of uncle or cousin when those ties would only

draw off a share of his earnings. Those who remembered the old obligations, alas, were generally those more likely to consume than to produce—the aged, the weak, the ill. With these the circumstances, and with no outside force to assign the blame, the extensive family of the Old World disintegrated. *So it is now, a brother stabs his brother, a sister drowns her sister, for profit's sake.*

Steadily the relatives dropped away; the husband, wife, and children were left alone. Where need compelled additions to the income of this narrower household, it was better to take in boarders, tenants, on an impersonal, cash-down basis. The more compelling duties of the old extended family were treacherous here; it was safer by avoiding them to transform the relationship into one of mere occasional sociability.

The bonds to those left at home also disintegrated. There was a piece of land, and if he had not gone away it would have been his; but having gone away he ought not ask that it be sold and money set to him in America. Endless quarreling followed. Or the old folks, staying, bitterly resented the departed son who should have been the staff on which they might lean in age. *You went to make money and you forgot that you left parents; may God and your own children care for you as you for us.*

Is it the loss of income they minded, or the sadness of being abandoned? *We cannot know whether we shall yet speak with you, embrace you, at least once before our death.* It does not matter. The demands are too heavy on both emotions and purse. The old ties gradually are loosened. The family steadily tapers down to the conjugal unit, a father, a mother, and their immediate offspring. The New World has separated them from all the others who would have been one with them in the Old.

Perhaps for that reason she wished so intensely to hold together what was left. From mistress in an extensive household she had become mother of a more intimate group; that hard core she would labor to keep intact.

The early experiences of the new family entity fed her hopes. That they were cut off from all else that was familiar led the members to value each other the more. With whom else could they discuss the memories of the past and the problems of the present? Depending upon each other because there was no one else upon whom they could depend, they drew steadily together.

The very process of migration had been shared. Mostly they had come together, together faced the open road and the close quarters of the steerage. In the long lapse of time between departure and arrival, they were deprived of the busying occupations of the farm, of the comradeship of neighbors, and had for company only one another. The occasion was one for deeper understanding; and long after the final settlement, recollections would come back of the joys and tribulations of the way, come back to unite those who had made the journey together.

The warmth of participation in the enterprise of crossing cheered even those later immigrants who divided for the critical steps, husband first to make a start, wife and children after. Such a separation created problems of its own, but it did not of itself lessen the attachment of the partners to it. Though the ocean lay between, they were joined by the gravity of the common effort.

That is why, as the years passed and they thought back to the first exploratory days in America, it seemed to them that the family had been strongest and purest before its exposure to the new life. As strangers they had known no one. Evening brought them always back together. Excited with discoveries or downcast with disappointments, they communicated to one another the freshness of each occurrence. They knew then they were one like the meager loaf from which they would begin each to slice the sustenance of all. It was a tenement room or a sod hut. But it was home; and those who came to it worn out with wandering acquired for home an enduring devotion.

Only soon, the conditions of their being in the United States would break in upon them. The narrow family would not remain alone together. Individually, its members in going out would make each their own adjustments to the society about them, and coming back would be less alike. Man and woman, boy and girl, they would find for themselves new roles and establish for themselves new relationships. It would happen more quickly in the cities than on the farms where a rural environment extended the family's isolation. But ultimately it would happen everywhere. The woman meditating by the stove would resist it. But already as they took their places her heart chilled to the fear of failure.

Across the long table they confronted each other, the two who were now central to all. It was as if daily they felt the need of a fresh view of the familiar features in the light of the new experiences. In the anxious regards were mingled two questions. Is this the same being united to me those many years ago and now still unchanged? How adequate will this union be to the present demands upon it?

Indeed these were no longer the man and woman joined in wedlock at that distant date; they had never then imagined that such questions might ever arise. Their marriage had not been the product of an individual passion, but a social arrangement under the oversight of the community. She had accepted the obligations of her situation, to be obedient and faithful, to further his health and comfort, to be a good and kindly wife, the crown of her husband's life. He had taken on the responsibilities of the efficient provider who would safeguard her from degrading work, keep want away, and mildly satisfy her will. The union upon which fortune smiled was one blessed with the dignified respect of the partners for their rights and duties.

The day they turned their backs upon the old home, the relationship began to change. At the very outset, the course of the crossing led to troubles. In the long suspended period between departure and arrival, neither he nor she had duties or could expect fixed dues. They were then thrown more together than ever before, but as never before found it difficult to judge one another. The intimacy of shared miseries brought them together, but, as it were, only to be the more conscious of each other's deficiencies. A sorry figure he made, lounging about from day to day with nothing to do; while her derelictions of housewifely obligations were served up in the stale biscuits of every meal.

If migration involved a temporary separation as, after 1880, it often did, the results were more disruptive still.

He went away to the sound of the children's crying; and heard it echo through the months apart. In his unaccustomed singleness, he came to miss what before he had taken for granted, the warmth of the woman's presence. *As the fish thirst for water, so I long for you.*

It is hard to know what may happen across that far dividing distance. *Only I beg you write more often.* As the letters fail to appear, for she is not familiar to the pen, worries take their place, and suspicions. Resentful, he asks a friend in the village to inform him of her doings. Does she hold to the home? At the same time the fear will rise lest she be unable to manage. The stock of grain may be too small, the labor in the field too hard. Cautionary advice covers the pages he sends home.

She has the advantage of waiting in a known place in the company of the children. But her double role is burdensome; she cannot be as he was, head of the household. The boys are unruly and, though she gives them some of the broomstick, they are slow to obey. She hires a hand to help in the field, but he is negligent; he has not for her the fear as for a master. Often she thinks of her husband and what a life he must lead there among strangers, his work heavier than a stone, his strength being drained away into a foreign soil. *The day passes in labor but in the evening I long very much and at night I cannot sleep. We can be united in heart and thought but that satisfies me not. Take us or come back; let it be so or so; as it is I exist neither upon ice nor upon water.*

Sometimes the months stretch out and the separateness widens. He sets himself a goal: I will have a thousand rubles and then send for them. But the goal is never attained. Meanwhile he is hardened in his bachelor life and puts off indefinitely the day of reunion. Or she at home grows reluctant. The dread of the new place mounts up in her and feeds off the complaints in his letters. She wishes him back—enough of this America—and when the call comes, procrastinates.

Whatever division, long or short, appeared in the transplantation was not mended in the resettlement. On the farms, the man could resume his place as head of the household enterprise; but the millions who stayed in the cities found their positions drastically altered. She could not think that he was here satisfying his obligations toward the family. No longer the sole or even the main provider, he seemed to her wanting in the most critical duty of all. Why, there were times when she herself or the children earned more than he, times when he sat home idle while they went out to bring home his bread. When he was taken on, it was not at work she understood or could respect. Away at some menial task, she could not regard him as she had that husbandman who had once managed their tiny plot and had brought up her sons to follow in his steps.

Nor could he be satisfied as to her adequacy for the life of the New World. Deprived of the usual household chores of the garden, the needle, and the loom, she appeared often lethargic; the blood hardly ran in her veins. On the other hand management of the domestic economy under American conditions was frequently beyond her comprehension. When the results were unhappy—disorderly quarters, poor food—it was hard to draw the line between the effects of negligence and the effects of poverty and ignorance. The necessity that drove her to labor for others was the source of resentment, both because it reflected upon his own abilities and because it took her away from her proper job in the home.

Roles once thoroughly defined were now altogether confounded. The two got on under the continual strain of uncertainty as to their place in the family, as to their relationships to each other. And their experience, no longer one for the two, added constantly to that underlying uncertainty.

Sometimes it was he went out to the wide world, learned the language of the country, and grew sophisticated in the ways of the place, while she was confined to the flat and remained ignorant of the rudiments of English. *I at least know where there's an Eighth Street, and a One Hundred and Thirtieth Street with tin works, and an Eighty-fourth Street with a match factory. I know every block around the World Building and the place where the car line stops. But you know no more than if you had just landed.* Sometimes it was she, in service in some other's home, who earlier learned the ways— what food they ate and clothes they wore and how they sat of an evening in the polished sitting room. It was bitter hard to be the satisfying helpmate when one could hardly guess what wants the other had.

As the situation clarified, aspects at first hidden emerged with oppressive distinctness. In the Old World her status had been fixed by a variety of elements —whose daughter she was, what dowry she brought, into what family she married. Let her husband be unfortunate or unskillful or unthrifty, she had still a set place in the village. Here her fate was completely tied up in his success.

What she was or had been mattered nothing, only what he could do. Well, it was galling to see what other, lesser women had, to watch their men push their way ahead. The utter dependence on his efforts put an acrimonious tone in her greetings as he came nightly home no better than before.

Nagging demands he could not meet confirmed his own inner doubts about himself. Was not the whole migration the story of his succession of failures? He had been unable to hold on to the land, to direct the family comfortably across the ocean or to establish it securely on this side. He felt respect ebb away and carried about a gnawing shame at his own lack of capacity. Most of all, he resented his loss of authority. Indeed he became accustomed to request, not to order, but knew it was not right it should be so; and he resented his wife's growing dominance over the household. It was a poor state of affairs when the cow showed the way to the ox.

In the secret night when her stirring waked him he did not move. Fatigue pinned him down. Yet sleep would not return. Instead an angry tension crept into his heart. Her body's presence intruded on his consciousness. Limbs rigid, he pushed the thought away; to this demand too he would not respond, by so much had he now lost his manhood.

Clenched eyelids would not keep the moonlight out. Not a beam came down the narrow airshaft; still his sight tingled to the streaks reflected from a distant meadow where they had walked amidst the long grasses, and had been young, eager for the enjoyment of each other to which marriage had opened the way. There had been no strain then; what the community had to that day forbidden, it now welcomed; and these two had been carried along by confidence in the rightness of their acts, by certainty they would each be gratified.

It was coming away that had first added wormwood to the taste. They had lost the benevolent oversight of the village which by its insistence on traditional propriety had answered every how and when. Now the deed required ever a decision; it raised ever some question; and it involved ever some clash of wills, his or hers. By leaving they had created doubts they knew not how to resolve.

He remembered the darkness of successive borrowed beds. In the enforced closeness of boardinghouses and shipboard he had stifled the groping desires. Years later, the confined warmth of many bodies would come back to assault his senses, would bring the painful recollection of urges never satisfied. And in this place that was their own it was rare that wish and opportunity coincided. In the cramped quarters they had been never alone and therefore never really together. Often there was the startling chill of interruption—the uneasy stirring of a child, the banging progress of a neighbor through the ill-lit hall. Always there was the uncertainty of when and how. Even the times when, flushed with the cheap certitude of liquor or with the passing exuberance of some new job, he had asserted his passion, there had followed inevitably an aftermath of regret and doubt. What had really been given and what received in these exchanges?

Perhaps he should not have expected more. He himself knew the dull indifference that came with being often tired. He knew too her deep fear of recurrent childbirth. Not that this was a subject of conversation between them; but it took no words to convey her dismay at each discovery of her condition. But the terms must be accepted, the price paid. Worse would follow the attempt to avoid it; often enough she had heard the stories of such a one, desperate at the approach of an eighth or ninth, who had sought the relief of self-abortion and had found only the painful death of blood poisoning.

Vaguely also they suspected that there were ways of forestalling pregnancy. But the old wives' knowledge did not extend that far; in this matter the midwife was not helpful; and, as for doctors—why, if a woman had thought of them, she would have found it difficult even to frame the terms of her inquiry. The husband had once cautiously sounded out an apothecary, but got only a jocular response: *Better sleep out on the fire escape, Joe.* Besides it all smacked of the illicit and the shameful. The law frowned on it; the priest cautioned against it; and deep inner forebodings conjured up the visions of nature's reprisals for interference with her processes.

There was, therefore, not much joy to their desiring; the shadow of the reckoning was too close. There was no blame. Only, sometimes, as she nursed her discontent, the thought came to her that, if only he had managed better, all would be otherwise. And he, reading the accusations in her eyes, felt the pangs of a sudden guilt, the acknowledgment of his own inadequacies. At such times, a sullen anger entered the household, lingered unexpressed for days. The mornings when he went to work, he carried off a pained exasperation. Suspicions might come; the scandal of that other's wife, who with the

boarder shamed her home, might cross his mind. The memory galled his wounds and, returned that night, edged his answers with acerbity. Peace then departed in an exchange of taunting words, then blows, and sad conciliation.

Some men surrendered. Confronted by intolerable burdens they deserted their families, lost themselves alone somewhere and put thus an end to this striving. Then the fatherless home, adrift, was not long from its foundering.

Mostly however they held together, the man and woman. Yes, partly it was the thought of the children that kept the family whole and partly it was the consciousness that in abandoning each other they would sever every last tie with their own past, diminish thereby their own human identity. Yes, often as they lay there, longing for escape to an undefined freedom, there was no move simply because the effort seemed too great, the means far out of reach.

But it was more than that that curbed the passing wish to flee. But it was more than that that drew them at last to each other. The old fixed order of respect between husband and wife had disappeared as the obligations on which it rested became irrelevant in the New World. Without the protective cover of well-defined roles they faced each other as individuals under the most trying conditions. That was difficult. But then as he looked upon this person who shared his bed and recalled the long way she had come, the sufferings she had borne, his heart went out to her. And then as she sensed the turning of his eyes upon her and thought of the little pleasure all his efforts brought, her heart went out to him.

It was not pity that sealed them in this attachment, but the brief glimmers of comprehension that they shared a life as they shared a bed. They were individuals, separate, two, and had been so since they left the village. But they had been two together. In those moments of recognition they knew they had been partners in a common experience and were now involved in a common situation. Only in each other could these beings find the complete understanding that would alone bring what they so desperately wanted, some reaffirmation of their own human dignity. For warmth they moved toward each other, for the warmth that came from the knowledge that here was consolation. Another knew and understood. That was a precious certainty, where all else was insecure.

About the children they can feel no certainty whatever.

This country is full of children. In the morning their clatter down the staircase fills the house. In the afternoon they occupy the streets. In the evening they pour back into the waiting flat which they quickly distend with the clamor of their ceaseless activity.

The immigrants were by no means strange to the idea of full families. The little ones had always made up a sizable part of the village population. But the spot had not been so taken up with their presence. They had had each their places, where they ought to be and where they ought not to be. They had had each their functions, what they ought to do and what they ought not to do. They had not been, therefore, so prominent in the sight of their elders.

Perhaps it was because, in these matters as in so much else, the Old World community had been very specific in its definitions of proper behavior. What a parent owed his offspring was clear. The child was to be fed, clothed, and housed decently as befitted the status and the resources of his father. The boys and girls were to be properly brought up, taught the skills necessary for their own adulthood and imbued with the beliefs necessary for continued membership in the community. It was their due at maturity to receive the land or dowry that would permit them to take the rank their ancestors had held; and one was not unduly to be favored at the expense of his brothers and sisters.

The obligations of the young were equally plain. They were to obey their elders and particularly him who stood at the head of the family, him whom they were to approach always in fear and with respect as the source of all authority. They were to assist, to the extent they were able, in the labors of the common enterprise; every age had its appropriate tasks. Even those fully grown but without households of their own were still to work for their parents. The unmarried had strictly speaking no property, no possessions of their own; if they went out to toil for strangers they were expected still to hand over their earnings to the father.

The neat balance of rights and duties was enforced by the village as a whole. Parents delinquent in the support or the discipline of their progeny, children remiss in compliance, could expect the swift censure of the organized opinion of their neighbors. There was no breaking the pattern of these relationships without a complete break with the community. But conversely, separation from the community by emigration would altogether disrupt the relationships of parents and children.

They might suppose it was the same as they strolled to worship on a holiday, Papa, Mama, and the boys and girls, covering the paved walk in a pair of uneven rows. They were wrong. Even then they knew the momentary solidarity would disintegrate before the day was over. They no longer cohered as a family and, as individuals, could scarcely say how they stood to one another.

The divisions created by differences of experience were too great. The older ones, sedately in the rear, had been eight or nine or in their teens in the year of the crossing. They had vivid memories of the Old Country, of the troubles that drove them off, and of the hardships of the journey. They spoke their mother's language and their unaccustomed English bore a heavy accent that united them with their past. Trained under the discipline of the household that had been, they were still ready to accept obligations. Necessity had long since heaped responsibilities upon them; no doubt they had been wage earners since soon after their arrival.

There was impatience in their scrutiny of the younger ones. Before them were two to be watched, scrabbling along without regard for appearances. These had been infants or little more when the migration came; their early childhood had passed under the unsettled conditions of the transition. They had never learned the proper ways at home, and a brief attendance at the public school had confused them so they knew not where they stood. They were clumsy in the speech of both the old land and the new; their names came from abroad but had already been corrupted into nicknames here. They were neither one thing nor the other.

At the head of the procession toddled the citizens. These more fortunate ones had been born into their environment. They had never known the Old World; they had not shared the experience of coming. They were Americans from the start, had lisped the words in English, and often received names appropriated from the older inhabitants.

It was at such times the parents were fullest of their responsibilities. As they led the way on these occasions they became gravely conscious of a disturbing uncertainty. What if the children should cease to follow, should take it into their heads to march off in some altogether strange direction! It was difficult enough to show them the right ways around the corners of the city blocks; it was infinitely more difficult to show them the right ways around the twisting curves of the new way of life.

As they consider the heaviness of their tasks, the mother and father grow somber. They remember the failures. Their minds go to that one who came to them as if on a visit, then sickened and went away. It occurs to them that they cannot possibly meet their obligations to the children. Not only that the food will hardly go around to nurture all, not only that the mended garments pass from one to another, but that by the act of migration, they, the parents, have destroyed the birthright of their sons and daughters. These boys who should be picking berries or hunting nuts, these girls who should be approaching mastery of the stove, have all been robbed and must endure the present, enter the future without their proper due. To each other, the parents acknowledge the guilt: *Yes, dear, and therefore let us sacrifice ourselves and live only for them. If there is any hope in this world, it is not for us but for them.*

It was easier to bend the neck in readiness than to be certain that the yoke would fit. With bewilderment the immigrants learned that to be willing to sacrifice was not enough, that their children must be also willing to accept the sacrifice; and of that there could be no confidence. The initial dissimilarities of experience widened with time as youngsters ventured out from the home and subjected themselves to influences foreign to their elders. The life of school and the life of street completed the separation between the generations.

If it did nothing else to the child, the school introduced into his life a rival source of authority. The day the little boy hesitantly made his way into the classroom, the image of the teacher began to compete with that of the father. The one like the other laid down a rigid code of behavior, demanded absolute obedience, and stood ready to punish infractions with swift severity. The day the youngster came back to criticize his home (*They say in school that . . .*) his parents knew they would have to struggle for his loyalty.

That was an additional reason why the immigrants labored to create educational institutions of their own; they hoped thereby to minimize the contest. But the parochial schools were expensive and spread very slowly; they accommodated at best only a small fraction of the children. The strong-minded and well-to-do could hold out against the pleas of their offspring who wished to go where everyone else went; mostly the newcomers were compelled by circumstances and by the law to depend on public instruction.

The building itself was familiar enough; this was one of the known landmarks of the neighborhood. The idea of attendance was also familiar; this had happened already to older brothers and friends. And as the lad entered the yard, even sight of the fellows playing or waiting in line had the appearance of familiarity; he recognized some from around his own block, the others were much like himself. The public school was universal, but each nevertheless reflected the quality of the homogeneous residential district within which it was situated. In effect it was Irish or Jewish or German or Polish; the first impression it made on the new scholar was that of the altogether familiar and the altogether expected.

The ringing bell broke the continuity of his life; as he walked up the cast-iron staircase he left the narrow orbit of his home and moved into the limitless world. He stood in the stiff lines and sat motionless in the formal rows of seats. He learned silence and passivity who had never before felt restraints on his actions. He came to conform to rules: there were ways of rising and of sitting, ways to come dressed, ways to leave the room on certain occasions, and ways without words to signal the need. This order would now be his life.

Mostly the boys accede, and the girls too. At least the youngest do. There are truancies, some from their stubborn will, some from their shame at the poverty of clothing, some from necessity that keeps them home or sends them out to work. But mostly they give in and come. There is vaguely an understanding that the school will help them get on; and everyone else goes, so they go along. Besides they fear the law, want no trouble.

Only often, as they sat in the torpid classrooms, their attention wandered from the drone of recitations. Through the windows, gray filmed-over, they could see the bustle of purposeful men. By contrast, the school seemed empty of achievements, empty of the possibility of achievement. For what reason were they thus confined? What could they hope to gain from all this?

They did not ask those questions. They had long ago heard the trite answers. They came in order to grow up good and useful citizens. How would the school help them? By teaching them what was in these books.

Idly the boys fingered the battered volumes from which wisdom was to flow. There was no need to open them; the bold type of their pages was familiar enough from constant drilling. THIS IS JACK. THIS IS JACK'S HOUSE. THIS IS JACK'S DADDY. JACK GOES SHOPPING. JACK GOES TO SCHOOL. ON THE WAY HE MEETS A COW. ON THE WAY HE MEETS A SHEEP. JACK COMES HOME. JACK FALLS ASLEEP.

And surely enough, across the top from page to page the brightly colored pictures show it all. Blue-eyed and blond, Jack himself stares out over the nice white collar and the neatly buttoned jacket. Across the green lawn, from the porch of the pretty yellow house, a miraculously slim mother waves. By the side of a road that dips through the fields of corn, the animals wait, each in turn to extend its greeting. There it all is, real as life.

Except that it is all a lie. There is no Jack, no house, no brightly smiling "Mummy." In the whole room there is not a boy with such a name, with such an appearance. One can walk streets without end and there will be never a glimpse of the yellow clapboards, of the close-cropped grass. Who sleeps like Jack alone in the prim room by the window to be wakened by singing birds? *Good morning, Mr. Robin.* The whole book is false because nothing in it touches on the experience of its readers and no element in their experience creeps into its pages.

Falsity runs through all their books, which all were written to be used by other pupils in other schools; even the arithmetic sets its problems in terms of the rural countryside. Falsity runs through all their education. They learn the songs their mothers never sang. They mouth the words of precepts with no meaning: *A rolling stone gathers no moss. Make hay while the sun shines.* But what stone, what moss, what hay? The time that man appeared to speak from the platform and roused them, he shook with his talk until they cheered the thin line at Bunker Hill, at Plymouth through the snow. *Our fathers' God, to Thee. . . .* Then later they thought, *Whose fathers'?* Again a deception!

They themselves compounded the enormity of the untruth by the inability to give it the lie. From the desk the teacher looked down, a challenge they dared not meet. It was foolhardy of course to question her rightness. What an arsenal was at her command to destroy them! The steel-edged ruler across the knuckles was the least of her weapons. Casually she could twist the knife of ridicule in the soreness of their sensibilities; there was so much in their accent, appearance, and manners that was open to mockery. Without effort she could make them doubt themselves; the contrast of positions was too great. As she snapped shut the closet upon the symbols of her ladyhood within—the white gloves, the rolled-up umbrella, and the sedate hat—she indicated at once the superiority of her own status. There was visible evidence of her correctness in her speech and in her bearing, in her dress, and in the frequent intimations of the quality of her upbringing.

Perhaps a few were touched with sympathy at the condition of their charges. But what these offered was pity, nobler than contempt, but to the children no more acceptable. It was rare indeed to find the dedicated woman whose understanding of her students brought a touch of love into her work. After all, it was not of this they had dreamed in normal school when they had surrendered a part of their girlhood to acquire a profession, that they would devote the rest of their lives to the surveillance of a pack of unwashed ruffians. Mostly the teachers kept their distance, kept flickering the hope that a transfer might take them to a nicer district with nicer pupils from nicer homes. When that hope died, bitterness was born; and there was thereafter more savagery than love in their instruction. To admit the least question of the rightness of what they taught would undermine the whole structure of their self-esteem. So a boy should look and be, so a home, and so a parent. Many a woman, tired with all the years of it, looked out at her "scholars" tumbling into the street, and discovered a hidden crumb of satisfaction in the thought they were not so, nor the homes to which they'd go, nor the parents who'd greet them.

It took no uncommon sagacity to learn it was better not to question the teacher's world. The wise fellow kept his mouth shut and accepted it; he came to believe in a universe, divided as it were into two realms, one for school and one for home, and each with rules and modes of behavior of it own.

Acquiescence was no solution, however. Their lives could not be so divided. As the children of the immigrants grew up, they felt increasingly the compulsion to choose between the one way and the other. For some, the vision of the yellow house was peremptory. The kindness of a teacher, taken with the earnestness of the exceptional good student, may have opened the prospect of attaining it. Or the intense will of the ambitious youngster may have done so. Or the desperate dislike of a repressive home may have made this the only tolerable alternative. In any case, this way involved the complete identification with Jack, and that meant the total rejection of the origins and the background Jack could not have had.

Only a few, however, had the ability or the desire to make the radical break. The much greater number recognized the existence of the world they saw through school, were even willing to acknowledge its superiority, but they were not willing or, perhaps, not able to enter it themselves; their ties with their families were still binding. They developed perforce a kind of life of their own, an intermediary ground from which they could enter when necessary both the life of the school and the life of the home.

The setting generally was the street, where the young were free of oversight and masters of themselves. The boys and girls of an age who played together fell spontaneously into little coteries, for the very acts of play depended upon a sense of community and upon some degree of organization. There could be no games without rules and without subjection to the sanctions that enforced them. The interests of these groups changed as their members matured, from childhood to youth to adolescence to adulthood. But with notable persistence the members held together at least until marriage made them heads of families in their own rights or until they moved out of the neighborhood.

The structure of these organizations was simple, although they were endowed with a certain formality that mirrored the associational forms of the immigrant parents. There was a consciousness of belonging; you were in the gang and that set you off from outsiders. The sense of participation was tied to a specific place, a street or a district that was their own. Within the group each individual had a role which reflected his own capacities and qualities—the leader, the fighter, the buffoon, the clever one. And the whole was held together by a code of loyalty; they were in a common situation, understood one another and felt understood, and found strength in being together. In these matters the young folk followed the behavior and adopted the standards of their elders.

But the boys in the gang had also learned something from the school and from the world it represented. The teacher had told them, and the books, that the end was to get ahead, to make good, to strive so that success might come. They must not repeat the errors of their fathers who had not made good, had not gotten ahead. The consequences of failure were everywhere apparent about them.

They could see the point of such injunctions. Only the hoary aphorisms did not ring true. A penny saved was not in their lives a penny earned; or the best policy. They were not much in demand to fill posts as office boys, so that road to a vice presidency was closed to them; and the runaway carriage of the banker's daughter came rarely into their neighborhood. The atmosphere of the street, where so much of reality was in open view, was not congenial to the ideal of the self-made businessman.

The impulse toward success found expression in terms dictated by the nature of their own group life. In childhood they strove in the competitive play of the alley, games of pursuit and capture, of sides that struggled against each other for a goal. As the boys grew older and their gangs took form, there were fighting forays in the rivalry of block against block; or (and it was not much different), where space permitted, there were savage athletic contests for the winning's sake.

The growth of professionalism gave an enormous impetus to this interest in sports which, after 1880, persisted on through adolescence to adulthood. On the baseball diamond, in the boxing ring, a lad could win fame and fortune. In these arenas, opportunity was free and only ability counted. The tone of one's name, the manners of speech and behavior, antecedents and affiliation were matters of no consequence. The pure capacity to succeed, with no other advantages, would bring the acclaim of the newspapers and wealth beyond the reach of these boys in any other way. The outstanding athletes who actually won such prizes were, of course, few in number. But each had his tremendous following of boys and young men who gained a kind of derivative satisfaction from his achievements and who sought within their own gangs to emulate his exploits. Increasingly the thoughts of the children were preoccupied with the events of the world of sport within which were played out the vivid dramas of American success and failure.

Down by the corner where the older

fellows congregated another kind of game held out the excitement of winning and losing. Watching the parades at campaign time, the youngsters looked forward with anticipation to the age when they too might be old enough to carry a banner. Meanwhile on the outskirts of the crowd around the ladder, they heard the orators' stirring periods and yelled the slogans of their partisanship. Its members were not yet voters when the gang was pressed into service, performing the menial jobs that might nevertheless win it the boss's notice. Here too was the possibility of rewards and of public esteem; and here too they need not labor against the liability of their own background.

The pursuit of success might take still another form. On the same corner, or on another much like it, the same boys or others much like them waited to turn the fight within them to riches. The violence of their childish play would grow up into racketeering; there were opportunities in plenty for such efforts.

For some the chance came through politics itself; perhaps they gained a proper "in" through roughing-up intransigent voters near the polls. For others the knock came in connection with gambling, or boxing, or labor organization, or in illicit liquor dealing. In whatever form, the ability to amass force in the gang, the willingness to defy rules the binding quality of which they did not recognize, and the burning desire by whatever means to elevate themselves above their origins, led such young men into organized criminality.

There were still other ways of rising, the professions, for instance. But sports, of course—the church, the stage, and politics, and the rackets had a larger importance even for the passive mass of the young who never ventured to be more than followers, who married and reconciled themselves to a stolid family life without the hope for success. For in these three endeavors were the closest approximations to the American standards of achievement open to persons like themselves. In no other way could the children of newcomers readily earn the appreciation of the whole society.

In the face of this whole development the immigrants were helpless. They had neither the will nor the ability to turn their offspring into other directions. The nominal authority of the fathers was only halfheartedly used; they were cruelly torn by the conflicting wishes that their sons be like themselves and yet lead better lives than they. Sensing that the school and street would tear the next generation away, the parents knew not how to counteract those forces without injuring their own flesh and blood.

If there was a serious one favored by the teachers who came home to sneer at the family ways, it was clear enough that when he could he would break away, change names, and drop all old connections. Could or should the father therefore stand in the way of his becoming a doctor?

That the brothers ran about all day with a crowd of wild ones was also disquieting. The worried parents could see no sense in the athletics, the infantile antics of grown men playing at ball. The immigrants had a deep fear of the consequences of the use of force in the rackets and an uneasy distrust of politics. But they could not deny that these were the ways to success, that these were the means of gaining the approval of the American onlookers. Even the older folk indeed derived a kind of satisfaction from the fame of men who bore names like their own, as if John L. Sullivan or Honus Wagner or Benny Leonard, somehow, testified to their own acceptance by American society. How could they then hold the youngsters to the traditional ideals of status and propriety?

In truth, the children were more in this world than they the parents. Often it was necessary for the fathers to turn for enlightenment to their sons. *We also keep a paper, but you have read more and studied in school.* The young wore their nativity like a badge that marked their superiority over their immigrant elders. It was this superiority that gave the second generation its role as mediator between the culture of the home and the culture of the wider society in the United States.

Accepting that role, the immigrants nevertheless resented it. It reversed the proper order of things. They could remember how they themselves had feared and respected the father; and they were embittered by their own failure to evoke the same fear and respect from their children. Beyond the loose behavior at the table and in the streets, these parents sensed the tones of ridicule. In their eyes the young Americans were undisciplined and ungrateful, good only at throwing stones and snow at strangers. When the boys and girls were small, it was still possible to curb their rebelliousness; the swift punishment of the strap held them temporarily in line. But as age increased their power, they were not so amenable to authority. As they grew in knowledge and in craftiness, as their earnings rose above those of the head of the family, they ceased to bow to restraints and would no longer be ordered about.

Adolescence was therefore a time of acute crisis, and particularly for the girls. As infants they had played with their brothers, but already at seven or eight they were excluded from the society of the gang and thereafter had little to do with boys. In girlhood they stayed close to their mothers since the home was to be their place. But even they could not be shut off from the world outside. They went to school or to work, observed the American familiarity of association between men and women, and soon enough revolted against the old restrictions. They learned to dress like others, with petticoats dragging behind to shut out the air and with their waists laced up in corsets so tightly the blood could not flow; and they lost their health—or so it seemed to their elders.

The worry was that they could not be guided by the safe rules of the Old World. They knew too much, boys as well as girls. Coming down Ann Street, they could not help but notice the "jilt shops" open for the dubious satisfaction of the sailors. Sometimes they could earn pennies distributing the cards of the brothels that flourished in their neighborhoods; and it was often years before they got to understand that a hotel could be other than a house of assignation. Why, even at home, through the thin walls, through the open windows, across the narrow courts, came the revealing sights and sounds. It was all familiar enough by the time they were of an age to conduct their own exploratory operations.

Well, such a girl or boy was open to error, by betrayal or by the longing for a withheld joy. Having spent the day in the closeness of the factory, having come back to the dank room where there was no room, it was release they sought and the assertion of themselves as individuals. Everywhere crowds hemmed them in so they had never the feeling of being one, uniquely one and not one of many. And so it might happen once when the sense of inner powers would no longer tolerate constriction, and the still night offered unaccustomed privacy, and there was a yearning for identity—to be a being, to desire and be desired.

Or, it might not happen; and then only the empty wish remained, returning evening after empty evening as the moody hours went by before sleep came.

Here was the ultimate barrier between the generations: they would never understand each other's conception of marriage. Sure, the parents tried to explain the nature of this most crucial step, that this was a means of extending on in time the continuity of the family, that it involved the sacrifice of personality toward some larger end: *From a maiden you will become a married woman, from a free being a slave of your husband and fortune.* The children would not listen. For them, marriage was an act of liberation by which they cast off the family ties and expressed themselves as persons through the power to love.

Nor could the children make their parents understand the longing for individuality. To enter upon such a relationship without consultation with one's elders, to make such decisions on the basis of chance impressions, to undertake this partnership with a stranger of unknown antecedents, was a madness of the reason. To many a saddened father and mother it seemed that their sons and daughters had moved gross

passion to the center of marriage and had thereby obscured the true end of the family, perpetuation of the succession of generations.

Often enough, then, the old couple were left alone. Looking back across the years, they realized they had been incapable of controlling the course of events. Out of the village context and without the support of the community, the family as they had known it had been doomed. Though they clung to the vestige of home and urged their children to hold together, they would never recapture the essential solidarity.

Perhaps sometimes it occurred to them how much of these tribulations they would have avoided if only they had been able to find that farm and there to work united together. They need not have grieved over it. Certainly the immigrants in agriculture did not need to guard their boys and girls against the influences of the street; and there, where the father was still effective head of the household, his authority was not readily questioned. But the parents could no more keep America away in the country than in the city. As the young matured and discovered wills of their own in school and in more frequent worldly contacts, they too were rebellious and refused to be bound.

Indeed, the impact of separation, when it came, was more decisive on the farm. Lacking as rich an associational life as was possible in the urban places, the second generation had not so full a function as mediators between the cultures. The sparseness of settlement, moreover, was more likely to encourage marriage with strangers that cut the children completely off from their parents. Only here and there was an occasional township, closely knit, homogeneous, stubbornly resisting all changes in a declared antagonism to America. There the family might survive a generation in its traditional form because there the family could call on the support of communal sanctions analogous to those of the Old World. Nowhere else could it survive with its roots pulled out of the village soil.

Perhaps they never took the time to make a balance sheet of their lives, those two old ones left alone, never stopped to reckon up how much they had gained and how much lost by coming. But certainly they must occasionally have faced the wry irony of their relationships with their offspring. What hope the early seasons of their years had held was hope of efforts for their children's sake. What dreams they had had were dreams of the family transplanted, that generation after generation would bear witness to the achievement of migration.

In the end, all was tinged with vanity, with success as cruel as failure. Whatever lot their sons had drawn in this new contentious world, the family's oneness would not survive it. It was a sad satisfaction to watch the young advance, knowing that every step forward was a step away from home.

Italian and Jewish Immigrant Mobility in New York City, 1880–1915

THOMAS KESSNER

"When we possess rather detailed knowledge about . . . Newburyport, Massachusetts, in the late nineteenth century but lack comparable observations about . . . New York City, it is risky to generalize. . . ."

Stephan Thernstrom, *Reflections on the New Urban History*

Americans have long celebrated their nation as a land of unique opportunity for all men. Few other societies place such emphasis on the qualities of self-made men or the significance of social mobility. So important was this idea of a distinctive social fluidity that very early in American history it took an important place in the national ideology. Writing in 1782, the French immigrant Michel Guillaume St. Jean de Crèvecœur explained his adopted country's uniqueness by pointing to the even-handed opportunity it offered to all comers, winning them away from the Old World and its ways.

What attachment can a poor European emigrant have for a country where he had nothing? The knowledge of the language, the love of a few kindred as poor as himself, were the only cords that tied him: his country is now the country which gives him land, bread, protection, and consequences: *Ubi panis ibi patria* is the motto of all immigrants. . . .

. . . Here the rewards of his industry follow with equal steps the progress of his labor, his labor is founded on the basis of nature, *self interest;* can it want a stronger allurement? Wives and children, who before in vain demanded a morsel of bread, now, fat and frolicsome, gladly help their father to clear those fields whence exuberant crops are to arise and to feed and to clothe them all. . . . The American is a new man. . . . From involuntary idleness, servile dependence, penury, and useless labor he had passed to toils of a very different nature, rewarded by ample subsistance—This is an American. . . .
. . . After a foreigner from any part of Europe is arrived, and become a citizen; let him devoutly listen to the voice of our great parent, which says to him, "Welcome to my shores. . . . If thou wilt work I have bread for thee: If thou wilt be honest, sober, and industrious, I have greater reward to confer. . . . Go thou, and work and till; thou shalt prosper, provided thou be just, grateful and industrious.[1]

Those who accepted this bright picture have been assailed as too complacent, too willing to accept abstractions instead of spending the time and effort to investigate the issue rigorously. Thus Robert Foerster complained that Americans dismissed gritty questions on mobility by reasoning simply that "it is Eldorado that lures and is found." Concluding his own brilliant survey of Italian settlement in America, Foerster put the question directly: "Have they profited by coming? Has the game for them been worth the candle?"[2]

His response was far less sanguine than Crèvecœur's. He reported pessimistically in 1919 that Italians were scarcely better off than their predecessors had been twenty-five years earlier. Foerster dismissed such items as the $85,000,000 in savings shipped back to Italy in a single year with this basic lesson in statistics: "Wherever Croesus lives, though the mass go naked, the average wealth, strictly speaking, is high." Others may point to the Delmonicos, Gianninis, and DiGiorgios who achieved enormous success, but for the average Italian immigrant, however, "the pictures that cut across the years are somber."[3]

Recently other scholars have reopened this question that touches the core of American ideology, and have attempted to measure immigrant progress in the United States. The first iconoclastic reports concluded that mobility was mostly a myth "more conspicuous in American history books than in American history." William Miller's 1949 study of Progressive Era business elites found rich native American Protestants atop the corporate structure. Their offspring, he contended, inherited the inside track on these high positions. The sons of immigrants did not glide into corporate chairs. Not more than 3 per cent of the business leaders were drawn from either immigrant or poor farm backgrounds.[4]

Stephan Thernstrom's pioneering 1964 study of *Poverty and Progress* in Newburyport, Massachusetts, focused on mobility from the bottom up and reported that the laboring class did not experience substantial occupational mobility between 1850 and 1880. Only one in ten laborers worked himself up

the ladder to a skilled craft. Moreover, being foreign born handicapped Newburyport's Irish in the occupational competition. Based on his analysis, Thernstrom believed that "the barriers against moving more than one notch upwards were fairly high." America was better for them than Europe had been, and they did make slight progress, but this sober gradual mobility bore no relationship to the mesmerizing plots that spilled from Horatio Alger's confident imagination. "This was not the ladder to the stars that Horatio Alger portrayed and that later writers wistfully assumed to have been a reality in the day of Abraham Lincoln and Andrew Carnegie."[5]

Since 1964, a number of historians have quarreled with Thernstrom's prematurely general dismissal of American mobility. They contend that the sluggish Newburyport economy was not the proper place to test the issue. Herbert Gutman's study of thirty-odd iron, locomotive, and machine manufacturers in Paterson, New Jersey, between 1830 and 1880 convinced him that the rags-to-riches theme was appropriate. "So many successful manufacturers who had begun as workers walked the streets . . . that it is not hard to believe that others . . . could be convinced by personal knowledge that 'hard work' resulted in spectacular material and social improvement."

Clyde Griffen studied "Craft and Ethnic Differences in Poughkeepsie," and also found that social fluidity in that city was sufficient to confirm "the national faith that merit sooner or later was rewarded by success." Howard Chudacoff emphasized residential over occupational change as an indicator of social mobility in his study of Omaha, Nebraska. Nonetheless, he concluded similarly that "a large number of men improved their condition in a genuine, though limited, way."

Humbert Nelli's recent history of Chicago's Italians treats the issue of mobility in more conventional terms, eschewing the quantitative methodology employed by Griffin and Chudacoff, but he too argues that the idea of mobility was pronounced "myth" too hastily. "Whether through legitimate business activities, criminal actions or politics, Chicago's Italians made substantial headway [by 1920] in an effective economic adjustment to urban America."

Focusing on Southern cities, Richard Hopkins and Paul Worthman have detailed the same sort of steady progress. In Atlanta, Georgia, Hopkins discovered greater mobility than Thernstrom described in Newburyport and stated flatly that "the achievement of some degree of success or improvement in occupational status was fairly common [for native and immigrant] white Atlantans in the later nineteenth century." And the Worthman study of Birmingham, Alabama, which analyzed a sample of 1,500 individuals uncovered "significant rates of upward occupational mobility," and "extensive" movement from blue collar to white collar positions among whites.[6]

More recently Thernstrom has admitted that his "early work—on the laborers of Newburyport—was misleading in its emphasis on the barriers to working class occupational achievement. . . . In other communities . . . the occupational horizon was notably more open." His study of Boston produced a more conventional conclusion than his Newburyport analysis. "The American class system . . . allowed substantial privilege for the privileged

and extensive opportunity for the underprivileged." Even the oft-maligned Horatio Alger, straw man for debunking mobility studies, is resurrected as a sober social commentator. "If Horatio Alger's novels were designed to illustrate the possibility, not of rags-to-riches but of rags-to-respectability, as I [now!] take them to have been, they do not offer widely misleading estimates of the prospects open to Americans."[7]

The present study of the two largest immigrant groups in the nation's most important and most populous metropolis provides additional evidence that mobility was not restricted to a select few well-born individuals. Social mobility was both rapid and widespread even for immigrants who came from the peasant towns of southern Italy and the Russian Pale. At first they qualified only for jobs as laborers, tailors, and peddlers, but with time and effort they found in New York ample opportunities for themselves and their children.

Indeed, despite the contention by Peter Blau and Otis Duncan that "the opportunity to achieve occupational success in the course of one's career is not so good in the very large metropolis as in the city of less than one million inhabitants," New Yorkers outpaced all others in climbing the economic ladder. In fairness to these authors and their distinguished study of the *American Occupational Structure*, their conclusions are based on recent data and may well be valid for the modern period; it was not the case, however, between 1880 and 1915. The nation's major metropolis offered exceptional possibilities for progress out of the manual classes.[8]

The highest percentage of blue- to white-collar mobility in Atlanta, Omaha, or Boston for the decade between 1880 and 1890, was 22 per cent, and that was the average achievement for all citizens, natives and immigrants alike. Gotham's New Immigrants, who began the decade at the bottom of the Promised City's social order, rose out of the manual class at a rate of 37 per cent in the same decade. One might expect that New York's great flux would produce deeper valleys to match such higher peaks, but that was not the case. In Boston between 1880 and 1890, 12 per cent of the white-collar class slipped into blue-collar occupations; only 10 per cent of New York's New Immigrants suffered such a decline.[9]

For the following decade mobility statistics for Brooklyn are even more striking. Between 1892 and 1902, 57 per cent of those who could be traced graduated out of the manual division. Subsequently over the eight-year period, 1905–1913, 49 per cent made the same climb. Admittedly the directory for Brooklyn was less extensive than the one for Manhattan. But the fact that immigrant occupations (which unlike mobility were not determined from directory sources but directly from the census) were more attractive in Brooklyn suggests that the higher mobility in this borough was more than a mere artifact of the measuring device.

Manhattan data for 1905–1915 are based on stronger evidence, nonetheless the findings are not significantly different. In a comparison with other cities after 1900, New York's mobility percentage stands highest. Between 1900 and 1910, 23 per cent of Omaha's working population switched blue collars for white. The figures for such mobility in Boston, Norristown, and Los Angeles between 1910 and 1920 were 22 per cent, 16 per cent, and 8 per cent, respectively. Among Manhattan's New Immigrants, 32 per cent

managed this ascent between 1905 and 1915.[10]

Mobility was not restricted to any one group, both natives and immigrants climbed the class ladder. The amplitude and frequency of such progress were, however, functions of ethnicity. Despite the fact that Italians and Jews shared important characteristics—they came to the United States in the same years, settled in the cities in about the same proportions, formed similar ethnic enclaves in downtown Manhattan, and shared the burdens of alien language and religion—Jews from eastern Europe entered the economy at a higher level than the Italians and sustained a higher rate of cross-class movement over the entire period 1880–1915.

From 1880 on, Italian immigration was drawn primarily from the peasant towns of southern Italy, dominated by single males in their working years with few industrial skills. Almost half of these immigrants were illiterate and few brought with them significant sums of money. This made it difficult for them to qualify for anything but the lowest rung of the economy, and the transient character of the group as a whole helped keep them there.

Italians emigrated largely for short-term economic motives. As the unusually high repatriation rates demonstrate, few intended to sever ties with their mother country permanently. Even those who did not go back to Europe often failed to sink roots, flitting across the country behind the *padrone* and his promises. Consequently, ambitions were geared to the short range, foreclosing careers that were based on sustained effort and piecemeal development. Moreover, the large sums of money sent back over the ocean to Europe drained risk capital from investment and enterprise. Lacking the desperation of men without bridges behind them, Italians were often ready to return home if they gathered a sufficient bankroll or if the job market slackened.

Because the New York economy was expanding its housing, building new factories, extending its transit lines, and upgrading its port facilities, the Italian newcomer was not forced to learn a craft; he could trade on his muscles and his willingness to work hard. In short, the city did not force him to equip himself beyond his peasant origins. It stood ready to use his primitive skills as they were. Consequently three of four Italian household heads in 1880 did manual labor and more than half were unskilled.

Russian Jews took a different tack. They too included a large contingent of poor and illiterate males, but they came in family groups, brought urban skills, and settled in New York with the intention of remaining. With anti-Semitism on the rise in Europe, Jews who came to the United States did not look back so fondly at the mother country. Under such conditions they thought in terms of the long range and their settlement was more stable.

Jews in Europe had been marginal men. Precluded from owning land because of their religion and prevented from building power or prestige in the established ways, they were shunted into less desirable jobs as innkeepers, peddlers, and dealers in second-hand clothing. But this experience, so déclassé in Europe, fit the dominant needs of their New York environment. "Jews, who were commercial *faute de mieux* in manorial Europe were as peripheral as the first mammals among the dinosaurs, but fortuitously advantaged later," Miriam K. Slater has written.[11]

However much their significant concentration in tailoring may reflect previous experience, it was also directly related to the emergence of New York City as the world's center of clothing production. Their skills were very specific. Lacking American education and money, they could not compete at the white-collar level. They also would not compete for unskilled jobs. "The emigrants of other faiths coming here . . . are . . . able bodied laborers who are willing to live on almost any kind of food, and working on railroads, canals, and the like must endure considerable exposure and fatigue. To send our people to labor in that way," a representative of the Russian Relief Fund in New York explained to officials of the Alliance Israelite Universelle in 1881, "would be cruel and *futile*." For Russian Jews to succeed there had to be a clothing industry and the opportunity to peddle. Their unique good fortune in New York derived from the fact that the city provided both, permitting them to enter the economy at its middle rungs.[12]

By 1905, both groups upgraded their occupational patterns reflecting in part New York's own development, and in part their own expanded connections and control. Italians entered the needle trades and took work on the docks, displacing the Jews and the Irish. Gradually they cut their heavy reliance on unskilled labor, avoiding such stigmatized pursuits as rag picking and organ grinding. But they could not catch up to the Jews, who continued to move one step ahead. Close to 45 per cent of the Jewish immigrants claimed white-collar positions, including a good number of professionals, manufacturers, retailers, investors, and office workers.

Ethnic differences proved equally important for mobility. Both Italians and Jews found the New York economy fluid and open, but Jews moved up- wards more quickly and more often. This is apparent by comparing four separate cohorts, differentiated by length of residence in the United States. Italians and Jews showed enhanced oc- cupation profiles as the number of years spent in the country increased. Taking the longest residing cohort of significant size, those who had lived in the country between 15 and 25 years, 24 per cent of the Italians achieved white-collar status, with only 2 per cent in the upper white-collar sector. Among the Jews, 54 per cent wore white collars and a significant 15 per cent reached the upper white-collar stratum. While Italian progress proceeded along one line, shopkeeping and self-employed artisanship, the Jews took more oppor- tunities to move into both upper and lower white-collar positions.

In a second analysis of mobility, Ital- ians and Jews were traced over three separate decades. When these data are aggregated they show that 32 per cent of all Italians who started in blue-collar categories crossed to the upper class within a decade. Considering the Ital- ian reputation for sluggish mobility and Robert Foerster's gloomy conclusions about the rate of their advance, such growth is surprisingly impressive, indi- cating that almost one-third of a largely peasant group could leave manual labor behind within a decade.

The companion statistic, however, shows that fully 21 per cent of the Italian white-collar class dropped back into blue-collar categories, demonstrat- ing how tentative their ascent was. This flux helps explain Foerster's dismal con- clusions about the Italian experience in America. Looking out at the Italian- American community in 1919 he saw that they still inhabited poor houses and occupied low-paying jobs.

But he missed the interstitial changes within that community. Moreover, he was wrong to expect that a community which continued to absorb masses of incoming peasants would not show pov- erty. The proper question is, was there progress over time. And the answer is, yes. If an Italian immigrant remained in the city one decade his chance of proceeding from a blue-collar job to a white-collar position was 32 per cent— not bleak by any standard.

Russian Jews left the manual class at a rate of 41 per cent, and once they achieved the upper class they did not slip down as easily as the Italians. Only 9 per cent of the white-collar class dropped back to manual labor. If we sum the two percentages as a crude index of mobility Italians register 10.4, the Jews 31.6.

What accounted for these differ- ences? Why did the Jewish group find it easier to navigate toward the eco- nomic mainstream? Interestingly, one important explanation of differential mobility, differential fertility, favored the Italians. According to Blau and Duncan men from smaller families achieve more, and more successful men have smaller families. They quote the *capillarité sociale* theory advanced by Arsene Dumont at the turn of the cen- tury: "Just as a column of liquid has to be thin in order to rise under the force of capillarity so a family must be small in order to rise on the social scale." They further speculate that men who are more successful achieve satis- faction from their careers, while less accomplished individuals "must find other sources of social support and gratification"; hence larger families.[13]

It is suggestive to note the size of Jewish and Italian families in this sam- ple study of 16,191 New Yorkers. Ital- ians averaged 2.62 offspring per family between 1880 and 1905 while Jews averaged 3.21. Calvin Goldscheider has pointed out that the conventional picture of lower Jewish fertility was largely based on American-born Jews and that the foreign-born generation had larger families, but he assumed that as a consequence the immigrant generation was not economically mobile ("*In contrast* most second generation Jews were economically mobile"). The data indicate that the first generation not only had large families but were also quite mobile.[14]

This is not the place for a full discussion of the issue nor do the data, based only on those immigrant offspring still living at home, permit a full analysis. But within these restrictions certain observations are in order. Russian Jews had larger families living with them than did Italian Catholics. Furthermore, since Jews were unusually mobile it does not seem that family size increased as a consequence of the need to compensate for stunted progress. In view of these findings, it may well be that the inverted birth rate (higher occupation-lower family size) that researchers have found is due less to the higher mobility of smaller-sized families than to the social-psychological disposition of families, once they achieved the upper level, to have fewer children.

Other matters proved more significant, with more direct effects. Obviously the fact that Italians came in at the very bottom of the occupational hierarchy while Jews entered at step three was important. Jews were able to move into the employer class while Italians were still trying to move into skilled and semiskilled employment. This helped Jews in the blue-collar class as well, as one Italian unionist pointed out with some bitterness:

In general, . . . management was constituted of Jewish capitalists, who either because of the influence of the Rabbi of the synagogue, or because they were annoyed by the too-verbal insistence of their co-religionists, revealed themselves to be less cut-throat with the latter than they were with the Italian workers who besides not being able to express themselves in English, had a little disposition toward the niggardly characteristics of Jewish cloak-makers. And the salaries that the Italians received were very inferior to those that were realized by their fellow Jewish cloak-makers, for the latter if not inferior, at least were only equal in technical capacity to the Italians. From the wage earning viewpoint the Italian element remained several steps below the Jewish cloak-makers.[15]

Moreover, Russian Jews were driven by a demon, seeking the security that had constantly eluded them in Europe. If "ruthless underconsumption" could help one become a "sweater," a contractor, or a shopkeeper, it seemed a small price to pay for self-employment. Because of their past they did not trust outsiders, whom they considered fickle and untrustworthy. They placed great emphasis on independence, on being a *balabos far sich* (one's own boss). This ambition translated into an emphasis on professional positions, shopkeeping, and manufacturing. These had been their goals in Europe, and the fact that they were more easily achieved in New York made them no less attractive.

Persecution, marginality, and alienation from the outside Christian world in Europe made of the *shtetl* a close-knit community. Rather than the family allegiances of the Italian peasant community summed up in Edward Banfield's phrase "amoral familism," the Jews possessed an ethnic consciousness and interrelationship that provided jobs, built industries, and provided ghetto capitalists with handsome returns on investments. Isaac Rubinow long ago pointed out that "almost every newly arrived Russian Jewish laborer comes into contact with a Russian Jewish employer, almost every Russian Jewish tenement dweller must pay his exorbitant rent to a Russian Jewish landlord." Among Italians it took time to build an ethnic consciousness as an American minority group; they did not bring a wider ethnic self-image with them. As Max Ascoli noted, "They became Americans before they were ever Italians."[16]

Few southern Italians had the ambition to become big businessmen or professionals. Life in the peasant towns of the *mezzogiorno* squelched such dreams with an inescapable iron reality. No matter what one dreamed, one's lot was fixed to a life of peasant poverty. For the sake of his own equilibrium, as Herbert Gans has argued, the Italian peasant restricted his aspirations. Jews, even in the ghetto, had some mobility through commerce and education, and this kept ambitions flickering. Because Italians did not see such mobility at home, they brought to New York a truncated conception of their own possibilities; an outlook that placed self-imposed limits on ambition. "Their trip across the ocean took them from rural towns to urban villages." This peasant gestalt was kept alive in their narrowly drawn village neighborhoods. As late as 1962, Italians in Boston's West End looked upon white-collar people "as not really working."[17]

Much has been made of the different values regarding education. The specific consequences of these differences are more apparent among the second generation, but they did not fail to help first-generation Jews who were more appropriately educated for industrial America than the southern Italians. Not only were their specific skills more apt but also their exposure to a labor ideology and the inclusion of a secular intelligentsia permitted them to build a labor movement. As early as 1885 a Jewish workingman's union was formed. By 1892 the United Hebrew Trades boasted 40 affiliates. Italians did not enter the labor movement in large numbers until much later.[18]

Education in the narrower sense, literacy plus specialized knowledge, became increasingly important in the age of business bureaucracy. The expansion of corporations and the wider use of the corporate form as well as the expansion of government and municipal services demanded a larger supply of lawyers, clerks, teachers, accountants, and other educated white-collar workers. Education became an economic tool rather than merely an esthetic one. Here the Jewish respect for education gave them an economic advantage. Italians, based on their experience, considered education an irrelevant prolonging of childhood. In a perverse way this argument became self-fulfilling. Without schooling, they took blue-collar jobs. For such jobs formal education *was* irrelevant . . . and costly, by postponing entry into the job market. Only when one aspired to white-collar status could the argument be drawn that education offered pragmatic benefits.

The persistence of the Italian attitude among the offspring is evident from a number of indications: The second generation's occupational similarity with their elders, especially in the concentration of Italian sons in unskilled jobs; the persistence of Italian offspring in first-generation neighborhoods; the fact that American-born Italian offspring did not differ much from their Italian-born brothers in occupational interest; and the fact that attendance in American schools made no noticeable difference in occupational outlook.

Jewish offspring did not follow their parents so closely. They were reared to exceed their parents' achievements, and although this created tremendous tensions, as psychologists and novelists have gone to great pains to illustrate, it kept the issue before them constantly. They must succeed. They must be ambitious. They must aspire to do well. Thus by 1905 Jewish offspring were moving into white-collar positions as professionals, salespeople, clerical workers, and shopkeepers. Unlike the Italians, place of birth did make a difference. Jewish offspring born in America, open to its training and schools, did better than their European-born brethren and subsequently moved up the ladder more quickly.

Aside from fertility, ethnic background, education, and cultural differences, differential mobility has also been ascribed to the influence of the ghetto as a mobility barrier. Both groups settled tightly packed ghettos, with the Jews clustering together even more than the Italians, so that it would be difficult to show how the ghetto hindered one group more than the other. But the entire issue of the ghetto's retarding effect should be questioned. The tremendous rates of out-mobility demonstrate that New York's neighborhoods were very porous barriers. Lower Manhattan's ethnic colonies bore no resemblance to the European "ghetto." In Europe the term stood for enforced residential segregation within a regulated area of settlement, but the downtown community in Manhattan held few immigrants back

from seeking better fortune elsewhere. Between 1880 and 1890, 95 per cent of the semiskilled and unskilled Italian work force left their neighborhoods and indeed the city. The ghetto, per se, cannot be charged with restricting occupational progress.

A more compelling argument can be drawn for the ghetto as a mobility launcher. It offered the immigrant hospitality of place. It provided jobs, business, and political contacts as well as investment opportunities. The local schools and settlement houses further aided the immigrant to assimilate and to acquire essential skills. The downtown neighborhood often provided him the best base for accumulating sufficient experience and capital to move elsewhere, if he wished. Of course many moved away from the ghetto no better off than when they first settled. This was especially true of unskilled and semiskilled Italians, who often joined the "floating proletariat" to search for jobs around the country.

Persistence in the city related inversely to class. Those who did not move into higher occupational levels found it rather easy to move to other cities. Unlike the present, when geographic mobility is more common to white-collar workers, in the period 1880–1915 such movement typified the blue-collar class. At first Italians were very mobile geographically, but by 1905–1915 as they achieved better positions the number leaving the city dropped dramatically. Persistence within neighborhoods, however, was not so clearly related to class or occupation. For both job and ethnic reasons Italians tended to remain in their original neighborhoods longer.

Residential mobility, like its occupational counterpart, symbolized the broad options open before the New Immigrants. They opened new ethnic neighborhoods in Harlem, South Bronx, Williamsburgh, South Brooklyn, and Brownsville. Some of the immigrants chose to disperse among the natives, away from their own group, others moved out of the Lower East Side to fresher ghettos, but the movement itself indicated a freedom that the *paese* and *shtetl* lacked.

The relationship between occupational and residential mobility is not a direct one. As Howard Chudacoff found in Omaha, "place utility [is] multidimensional, including economic, social, psychological, ethnic and . . . other components. Residential mobility [involves] relocation of an individual to a place of higher utility. Perceptions of utility, however, are not usually optimal . . . ," nor are they restricted to the ability to pay. Gradually, however, as immigrants could afford better, the old clearing house for New Immigrants on the Lower East Side was eclipsed by newer areas.[19]

Thus American society, at least so far as New York can bear witness for the nation, afforded immigrants and their children a comfortable margin of mobility. Immigrants who carried the burdens of European poverty and persecution and settled into slums and poor jobs as aliens, were nonetheless mobile. Clearly the statue standing in New York's harbor shined her symbolic torch for the poor as well as the rich and well born. To answer a question posed by an earlier investigator of immigrant mobility: Yes, the myth of an open American society with opportunity for the common man "squared with social reality."[20]

Certain aspects of mobility are beyond the ken of studies such as this one. Daniel Bell and others have discussed the role of crime in ethnic mobility, but studies that are based on census and directory samples inevitably miss such occupations as bank robber, prostitute, or gangster. Suffice it to say that given the levels of mobility uncovered in New York, crime was not the only way up.[21]

Another point, anticlimactic as it may be, should be made. Occupational mobility helps us judge the American promise by materialist standards. In that respect Jews assimilated more quickly, and rapidly climbed the economic ladder. But this merely scratches the surface. We can move away from the issue of mobility—it existed. But did the American system provide a better quality of life? As David Levinsky asks for all who came and were successful, "Am I happy?"

There are moments when I am overwhelmed by a sense of my success and ease. I become aware that thousands of things which had formerly been forbidden fruit . . . are at my command now. . . . One day I paused in front of an old East Side restaurant that I had often passed in my days of need and despair. The feeling of desolation and envy with which I used to peek in its windows came back to me. It gave me pangs of self pity for my past and a thrilling sense of my present power. . . .

I am lonely. . . .

No I am not happy. . . .

I can never forget the days of my misery. I cannot escape from my old self. My past and present do not comport well. David, the poor lad swinging over a Talmud volume at the Preacher's synagogue, seems to have more in common with my inner identity than David Levinsky, the well known cloak manufacturer.[22]

As another immigrant son, Mario Puzo, has written,

There is a difference between having a good time in life and being happy. . . . We are all Americans now, we are all successes now. And yet the most successful Italian man I know admits that though the one human act he could never understand was suicide, he understood it when he became a[n American] success, . . . He went back to Italy and tried to live like a peasant again. But he can never again be unaware of more subtle traps than poverty and hunger.[23]

But then Horatio Alger never promised happiness.

NOTES

1. Michel Guillaume St. Jean de Crèvecœur, *Letters from an American Farmer*, in Merle Curti et al., eds., *American Issues: The Social Record* (2 vols., 1971), I, 103–10.
2. Robert Foerster, *Italian Emigration of Our Times*, 374–77.
3. Ibid.
4. William Miller, "American Historians and the Business Elite" in William Miller, ed., *Men in Business: Essays on the Historical Role of the Entrepreneur* (New York, 1962), 309–28. See also Frances W. Gregory and Irene D. Neu, "The American Industrial Elite in the 1870's: Their Social Origins," in ibid., 193–212. The less rigorously built sample of businessmen studied by C. Wright Mills and Richard Bendix with Frank Howton is discussed by Herbert G. Gutman, "The Reality of the Rags-to-Riches 'Myth': The Case of the Patterson, New Jersey Locomotive, Iron, and Machinery Manufacturers, 1830–1880," in Stephan Thernstrom and Richard Sennett, eds., *Nineteenth Century Cities*, 98–101.
5. Stephan Thernstrom, *Poverty and Progress*, 112–13, 162–65, 223.
6. Herbert Gutman, "The Reality of the Rags-to-Riches 'Myth'," 98–124; Clyde Griffin, "Workers Divided; The Effect of Craft and Ethnic Differences in Poughkeepsie, New York, 1850–1880" in Thernstrom and Sennett, eds., *Nineteenth Century Cities*, 93; Howard Chudacoff, *Mobile Americans*, 109; Humbert Nelli, *The Italians in Chicago*, 109; Richard Hopkins, "Status, Mobility and the Dimensions of Change in a Southern City: Atlanta, 1870–1890," in Kenneth Jackson and Stanley Schultz, eds., *Cities in American History* (New York, 1972), 223; Paul B. Worthman, "Working Class Mobility in Birmingham, Alabama, 1880–1914," in Tamara Hareven, ed., *Anonymous Americans: Explorations in Nine-*

teenth Century Social History (Englewood Cliffs, 1971), 193.
7. Stephan Thernstrom, "Reflections on the New Urban History," in Felix Gilbert and Stephen R. Graubard, eds., *Historical Studies Today* (New York, 1972), 329; Stephan Thernstrom, *The Other Bostonians: Poverty and Progress in the American Metropolis, 1880–1970* (Cambridge, 1973), 257–58.
8. Peter M. Blau and Otis D. Duncan, *The American Occupational Structure* (New York, 1967), 249.
9. An extremely useful summary of mobility findings is presented in Thernstrom, *Other Bostonians*, 234. The figures for upward mobility into the white-collar class between 1880 and 1890 are: Atlanta, 22 per cent; Omaha, 21 per cent; Boston 12 per cent. Corresponding downward mobility figures are: 7 per cent; 2 per cent; 12 per cent. It is true that these figures must be understood within the perspective of the methodology that produced them. Thus they may be somewhat skewed because the better situated are more easily traced, but this problem is common to all these mobility studies and therefore the figures are valid in a comparative context.
10. Ibid.
11. Miriam K. Slater, "My Son the Doctor," 369.
12. "Letter of the Russian Emigrant Relief Fund to the Alliance Israelite Universelle, 1881," Appendix B to Zosa Szajkowski, "The Attitude of American Jews to East European Jewish Immigration (1881–1883)," *Publications of the American Jewish Historical Society*, XL (Sept. 1950), 265–66. Emphasis added.
13. Blau and Duncan, *American Occupational Structure*, 295–98, 361–99, quotes are on 367 and 428.
14. Sidney Goldstein and Calvin Goldscheider, *Jewish Americans: Three Generations in a Jewish Community* (Englewood Cliffs, 1968), 116, 121, 124. Emphasis added.
15. Salvatore LaGumina and Frank J. Cavaioli, eds., *The Ethnic Dimension in American Society* (Boston, 1974), 186–87.
16. Isaac M. Rubinow, "Economic and Industrial Condition in New York," in Charles Bernheimer, ed., *The Russian Jew in the United States*, 103–4; Ascoli quoted in Eugene P. Ericksen, Richard N. Juliani, and William Yancey, "Emergent Ethnicity: A Review and Reformulation," prepared by the authors at Temple University (1974), 33.
17. Herbert Gans, *Urban Villagers*, 123–212.
18. Moses Rischin, *Promised City*, 176; Joel Seidman, *The Needle Trades*, 43, 228.
19. Chudacoff, *Mobile Americans*, 157.
20. Thernstrom, *Poverty and Progress*, 1.
21. Daniel Bell, *The End of Ideology* (New York, 1960), 115–36; Humbert Nelli, *Italians in Chicago*, places heavy emphasis on the role of crime in mobility and analyzes it functionally, 125–55. Professor Nelli is now at work on a full-scale study of Italian crime entitled *The Business of Crime* to be published in the fall of 1976. Arthur

Goren, *New York Jews and the Quest for Community: The Kehillah Experiment, 1908–1922* (New York, 1970), includes a chapter on crime in the Jewish quarter, 134–58, and Professor Goren is at work on a full study of that topic.

22. Abraham Cahan, *The Rise of David Levinsky* (New York, 1917), 525–30.

23. Mario Puzo, "Choosing a Dream," in T. C. Wheeler, ed., *The Immigrant Experience* (New York, 1971), 49.

Harlem Tragedy: An Emerging Slum

GILBERT OSOFSKY

"I sit on my stoop on Seventh Avenue and gaze at the sunkissed folks strolling up and down and think that surely Mississippi is here in New York, in Harlem, yes, right on Seventh Avenue."

The Messenger, 1923

"I have been in places where cattle and dogs sleep with masters, but never before have I been in such a filthy house."

Judge William Blau's description
of a Harlem tenement, 1922

I

The creation of a Negro community within one large and solid geographic area was unique in city history. New York had never been what realtors call an "open city"—a city in which Negroes lived wherever they chose—but the former Negro sections were traditionally only a few blocks in length, often spread across the island and generally interspersed with residences of white working-class families. Harlem, however, was a Negro world unto itself. A scattered handful of "marooned white families . . . stubbornly remained" in the Negro section, a United States census-taker recorded, but the mid-belly of Harlem was predominantly Negro by 1920.[1]

And the ghetto rapidly expanded. Between the First World War and the Great Depression, Harlem underwent radical changes. When the twenties came to an end Negroes lived as far south as One Hundred and Tenth Street—the northern boundary of Central Park; practically all the older white residents had moved away; the Russian-Jewish and Italian sections of Harlem, founded a short generation earlier, were rapidly being depopulated; and Negro Harlem, within the space of ten years, became the most "incredible slum" in the entire city. In 1920 James Weldon Johnson was able to predict a glowing future for this Negro community: "Have you ever stopped to think what the future Harlem will be?" he wrote. "It will be the greatest Negro city in the world. . . . And what a fine part of New York City [the Negro] has come into possession of!"[2] By the late 1920's and early 1930's, however, Harlem's former "high-class" homes offered, in the words of a housing expert, "the best laboratory for slum clearance . . . in the entire city." "Harlem conditions," a *New York Times* reporter concluded, are "simply deplorable."[3]

II

The Harlem slum of the twenties was the product of a few major urban developments. One of the most important was the deluge of Negro migration to New York City then. The Negro press, now largely dependent on the migrant community for support, changed its former critical attitude of migration to one openly advocating urban settlement. (The exodus was so large, a Negro minister preached, that it must have been "inspired by Almighty God.")[4] If one is looking for a dramatic turning point in the history of the urbanization of the Negro—"a race changing from farm life to city life"—it was certainly the decade of the twenties. Between 1910 and 1920 the Negro population of the city increased 66 per cent (91,709 to 152,-467); from 1920 to 1930, it expanded 115 per cent (152,467 to 327,706). In the latter year less than 25 per cent of New York City's Negro population (79,-264) was born in New York State. There were more Negroes in the city in 1930 than the combined Negro populations of Birmingham, Memphis and St. Louis. Similar population increases occurred in urban areas throughout the country.[5]

Negro migration in the twenties drew on areas of the South that had previously sent few people to New York City. The seaboard states of the Upper South —especially Virginia and the Carolinas —continued to be the main sources of New York's migrant Negro population, but people from Georgia and Florida and other Deep South states formerly under-represented also came in greater numbers: "Harlem became the symbol of liberty and the Promised Land to Negroes everywhere," the Reverend Dr. Powell wrote. "There was hardly a member of Abyssinian Church who could not count on one or more relatives among the new arrivals."[6] In 1930, some 55,000 foreign-born Negroes added to the growing diversity of the city's Negro population.

The following chart presents an exact description of the geographical origins of Negro migrants to New York City in 1930. I have selected states with 900 or more residents in the city:[7]

Negro In-Migration, New York City, 1930

Born in:	
Virginia	44,471
South Carolina	33,765
North Carolina	26,120
Georgia	19,546
Florida	8,249
Maryland	6,656
Pennsylvania	6,226
New Jersey	5,275
District of Columbia	3,358
Alabama	3,205
Massachusetts	2,329
Louisiana	2,182
Ohio	1,721
Tennessee	1,651
Texas	1,592
Kentucky	1,216
Mississippi	969
Foreign-born	54,754

The rapid settlement of a heterogeneous Negro population coincided with another population change—the migration of whites from all sections of Manhattan to other boroughs. For the first time since Dutch settlement Manhattan's population *declined* in the 1920's as first- and second-generation immigrants moved to nicer residential areas in the Bronx, Brooklyn and Queens. Many of the homes they left behind had deteriorated significantly. By 1930 a majority of New York City's foreign-born and second-generation residents lived outside Manhattan.[8] As whites moved out of Manhattan, Negroes moved in. The population of that borough declined 18 per cent in the 1920's as its Negro population increased 106 per cent. By 1930 Negroes represented 12 per cent of Manhattan's population

—although they composed only 4.7 per cent of the population of the entire city.[9]

Harlem was the New York neighborhood most radically revamped by the population movements of the 1920's, although the Lower East Side also changed rapidly. Harlem underwent a revolution—what one contemporary accurately called a "stupendous upheaval." Between 1920 and 1930, 118,792 white people left the neighborhood and 87,417 Negroes arrived.[10] Second-generation Italians and Jews were responding to the same conditions of prosperity that promoted mobility in all the immigrant neighborhoods of Manhattan—they were not *only* moving away because Negroes settled near them. Conditions of life which satisfied immigrant parents were often unacceptable to children: "The tenements which housed their parents," immigration expert Edward Corsi wrote in 1930, "are being left behind by the children. . . ." "East Harlem used to have a great deal larger population," a survey of the Mayor's Committee on City Planning during the Great Depression concluded. "Like others of the older residential districts, it has suffered by the exodus of families to newer surroundings. . . ."[11]

The city's newest migrants moved into the Harlem flats vacated by Italians and Jews. Puerto Ricans came to live in East Harlem, created community organizations, and laid the foundations for "El Barrio" of today. By 1930 some 45,000 Puerto Ricans resided in New York City and most were heavily concentrated in East Harlem.[12] Negroes moved north along St. Nicholas Avenue —"On the Heights," they called it— and south into the heart of "Little Russia," the former Jewish section. "Just Opened for Colored" signs were com-

mon in the neighborhood. Mount Olivet Baptist Church occupied, and still occupies, the once exclusive Temple Israel of Harlem. Prince Hall Masons bought a building that "was formerly a home for aged Jews." Graham Court, a magnificent block-length apartment house on One Hundred and Sixteenth Street, with eight separate elevators and apartments of seven to ten rooms, was opened to Negroes in 1928.[13] By 1930, 164,566 Negroes, about 72 per cent of Manhattan's Negro population, lived in Harlem.[14] The Negro ghetto remained and expanded as the other ethnic ghettos disintegrated. The economic and residential mobility permitted white people in the city was, and would continue to be, largely denied Negroes. Most Negroes were "jammed together" in Harlem—even those who could afford to live elsewhere—with little possibility to escape.[15] "One notable difference appears between the immigrant and Negro populations," an important federal study of Negro housing concluded. "In the case of the former, there is the possibility of escape, with improvement in economic status, in the second generation, to more desirable sections of the city. In the case of Negroes, who remain a distinguishable group, the factor of race and certain definite racial attitudes favorable to segregation, interpose difficulties to . . . breaking physical restrictions in residence areas."[16] A rather ponderous paragraph, but a significant truth.

III

The settlement of West Indian Negroes in Harlem in the 1920's added another complicating dimension to the racial problems of this community—one that fostered discord rather than harmony among the city's Negroes. There were ten times as many foreign-born Negroes in New York City as in any other American urban area. In 1930, 54,754 foreign Negroes lived in the city—39,833 of whom resided in Manhattan. Miami, the next largest American city in terms of immigrant Negroes, was settled by only 5,512 people; Boston ranked third with 3,287 West Indians. About 25 per cent of Harlem's population in the twenties was foreign-born. Harlem was America's largest Negro melting pot.[17]

In the era of immigration restriction, West Indian Negroes came to America through what a contemporary called the "side door." The immigration laws of the 1920's seriously restricted the migration of Europeans and totally excluded Orientals but had little effect on peoples of the Caribbean. At first there were no restrictions on West Indian Negroes. After 1924, they could enter the country under quotas set aside for their mother countries. Since these quotas were never filled there was, in reality, a free flow of people from the islands to the United States in the 1920's.[18]

Although American Negroes tended to lump all the migrants together in a uniform image—"There is a general assumption," one migrant wrote, "that there is everything in common among West Indians"—it is important to recognize that Harlem's Negro immigrants represented a diverse group of peoples from dozens of different islands in the Caribbean.[19] Most Negro immigrants felt a strong attachment to their homeland. They demonstrated an "exaggerated" nationalism in America—a buffer against the strangeness of the new culture and the hostility they experienced —which was typical of white immigrant groups. It was common, for example, to find former British subjects at the office of the British consul protesting some difficulty they experienced in America.[20] Nationalistic organizations kept close check on American foreign policy in the Caribbean and often gave banquets for and listened to addresses by West Indian dignitaries. West Indian Negroes from all countries had the lowest rate of naturalization of all immigrant groups. The people white Americans and American Negroes called "West Indians" were really individuals from Jamaica, Trinidad, Barbados, Martinique, St. Vincent, St. Lucia, Dominica, British Guiana, St. Kitts, Nevis, Montserrat, Antigua, Virgin Islands, Bermuda, the Bahamas, and so on. Although the majority spoke English, some considered French their first tongue; others Spanish; a few Dutch. The fraternal and benevolent associations they founded were not inclusive organizations for all Negro immigrants, but exclusive ones—landmannschaften—for people from specific islands. Danish settlers kept pictures of the King of Denmark in their homes; former British subjects held coronation pageants and balls ("Boxes, 12s. 6d.—Loges, 8s. 4d.") and flew the Union Jack in Harlem; Frenchmen had annual Bastille Day dances.[21]

Negro immigrants differed from each other in origin, yet in a broader sense they shared general experiences, desires and mores which set them apart as a group from their American brethren. Most came from societies in which class distinctions played a more important role in one's life than the color line—although the latter was certainly significant. Unaccustomed to common American racial slurs, they often refused to accept them without protest. The Pullman Company, for example, hesitated to employ West Indian Negroes, it was said, "because of their refusal to accept insults from passengers quietly."[22] Out of this heightened class consciousness came a small group of political and economic radicals in Harlem—"foreign-born agitators," local Negroes called them.[23] Many of Harlem's street-corner orators in the 1920's, though not all, were West Indian migrants. Hubert H. Harrison, a Virgin Islander, was among the most prominent. Harrison was a socialist, an expert in African history, a militant critic of American society and a proud defender of the "Negro's racial heritage." He conducted formal lectures in what he called the "Harlem School of Social Science," and others from street corners—his "outdoor university." A Harlem church, the Hubert H. Harrison Memorial Church, honors his memory. Others presented talks on "Socialism vs. Capitalism," organized tenants' leagues, published Marxist journals and tried to make Harlemites labor-conscious. Richard B. Moore, Frank R. Crosswaith and the Reverend Ethelred Brown—all Negro immigrants—were prominent local candidates for Board of Aldermen, Assembly and Congress on Socialist and Communist tickets—they usually polled an exceedingly small vote. Some organized rent strikes, "rent parades," lobbied for social legislation at City Hall and Albany and distributed radical literature in Harlem. "There is no West Indian slave, no American slave," the short-lived radical magazine *Challenge* commented. "You are all slaves, base, ignoble slaves."[24]

This concern with "class" led to the emergence of a broader tradition in America. What is striking about the Negro immigrant is the way his response to American conditions, such as his exaggerated sense of nationalism,

was similar to the typical reactions of most European immigrants. The Negro immigrant "did not suffer from the local anesthesia of custom"[25] and he tried to create a meaningful economic position for himself within American society. Menial labor was, among most first-generation Negro immigrants, considered a sign of social degradation and looked upon with "disgust." Most were forced to accept such jobs initially, but were strongly motivated by their traditions to improve themselves. As a group, West Indians became noted for their ambition, thrift and business acumen. They were called "pushy," "the Jews of the race," "crafty," "clannish."[26] Negro journalist George S. Schuyler "admired their enterprise in business, their pushfulness."[27] "The West Indians [are] legendary in Harlem for their frugalness and thrift," one student noted. When a West Indian "got ten cents above a beggar," a common local saying ran, "he opened a business." Contemporary surveys of Negro business in Harlem and Columbus Hill demonstrate that a disproportionate number of small stores—the traditional "Race Enterprise" —were owned by Negro immigrants. Dr. P. M. H. Savory, one of the leading spokesmen of New York's foreign-born Negro community from the 1920's to his death in June 1965, owned and published the *Amsterdam News*. Many others achieved success within the racial barrier.[28]

Another significant distinction between the foreign-born Negro and the American was their attitude toward family life. Slavery initially destroyed the entire concept of family for American Negroes and the slave heritage, bulwarked by economic conditions, continued into the twentieth century to make family instability a common factor in Negro life. This had not been true for most West Indians, and they arrived in America with the orthodox respect for family ties that was traditional of rural people. The West Indian family was patriarchal in structure—contrasted with the typically matriarchal American Negro home. The father, as key worker and wage earner in the islands, ruled the household with a solid hand. It was beneath his dignity to help with domestic chores. (This led American Negroes to brand West Indian men "cruel.")[29] Children were supposed to obey their parents rigidly—American Negroes considered them strait-laced; have long and formal courtships; and receive parental approval before marriage. Illicit sexual relations were considered the worst form of moral evil.[30] These traditions began to change in the second generation, but throughout the 1920's family solidarity was a pervasive force among New York's Negro immigrants.[31]

These differences in style of life were also evident in another important institution—the church. The majority of Harlemites were Baptists and Methodists; the immigrants were predominantly Episcopalian and Catholic.[32] The beautiful St. Martin's Episcopal Church was founded in Harlem in 1928 to minister to the needs of West Indian migrants. Services in immigrant churches were generally staid and quiet; Sunday a day of prayer, rest and visiting—as it had been on the islands. Observers were impressed with the differences between the emotionalism of a typical Harlem religious service and the moderation and restraint shown in churches of the foreign-born. Negro immigrants also objected to the general frivolity and "fast ways" that were part of a typical Sunday in Harlem.[33]

All these factors combined to make Harlem in the 1920's a battleground of intraracial antagonism. American Negro nativism spilled over to taint Harlemites' reactions to the West Indian. The Negro immigrant was ridiculed; his tropical clothing was mocked; children tossed stones at the people who looked so different; foreigners were taunted with such epithets as "monkey-chaser," "ring-tale," "king Mon," "cockney." "When a monkey-chaser dies/Don't need no undertaker/Just throw him in de Harlem River/He'll float back to Jamaica," was a verse from a Harlem ditty of the twenties. West Indians came to Harlem, ran another common saying, "to teach, open a church, or start trouble." "Bitter resentment grew on both sides." Each group called the other "aggressive." "We have . . . in Harlem," NAACP director Walter White wrote, "this strange mixture of reactions not only to prejudice from without but to equally potent prejudices from within." "If you West Indians don't like how we do things in this country," an American Negro said tersely, "you should go back where you came from. . . ."[34]

The obvious hostility of American Negroes forced Negro immigrants to unite in defense organizations larger than their individual national groups. The West Indian Committee on America, the Foreign-Born Citizens' Alliance and the West Indian Reform Association were founded in the twenties to soften these intraracial tensions and promote "cordial relations between West Indians and colored Americans." Radio programs were devoted to discussions of "Intra-Race Relations in Harlem," and immigrants were urged to become naturalized citizens. American Negroes, in turn, were asked to tone down their "considerable prejudice against West Indians." A semblance of co-operation was achieved as mass meetings were held in Harlem churches. The hatreds of the 1920's did not die, however, until West Indian Negroes stopped migrating to New York. During the Depression more immigrants left New York than entered and intraracial tensions slowly eased. Young Harlemites today, even third-generation descendants of Negro immigrants, are often unaware of these old divisions. The unique type of intraracial hostility so prominent in the twenties has never reappeared. While it lasted, however, it served to weaken a Negro community in great need of unity. A divided Harlem confronted major social problems that desperately called for the co-operation of all.[35]

IV

The most profound change that Harlem experienced in the 1920's was its emergence as a slum. Largely within the space of a single decade Harlem was transformed from a potentially ideal community to a neighborhood with manifold social and economic problems called "deplorable," "unspeakable," "incredible." "The State would not allow cows to live in some of these apartments used by colored people . . . in Harlem," the chairman of a city housing reform committee said in 1927. The Harlem slum of today was created in the 1920's.[36]

The most important factor which led to the rapid deterioration of Harlem housing was the high cost of living in the community. Rents, traditionally high in Harlem, reached astounding proportions in the 1920's—they skyrocketed in response to the unprecedented demand created by heavy Negro migra-

tion and settlement within a restricted geographical area. "Crowded in a black ghetto," a sociologist wrote, "the Negro tenant is forced to pay exorbitant rentals because he cannot escape." In 1919 the average Harlemite paid somewhat above $21 or $22 a month for rent; by 1927 rentals had *doubled* and the "mean average market rent for Negro tenants in a typical block" was $41.77. In 1927 Harlem Negroes paid $8 more than the typical New Yorker for three-room apartments; $10 more for four rooms; and $7 more for five rooms, an Urban League survey noted.[37] Another report concluded that the typical white working-class family in New York City in the late twenties paid $6.67 per room, per month, while Harlem Negroes were charged $9.50.[38]

Realty values which had declined significantly prior to World War I *appreciated* in Harlem in the twenties.[39] Harlem experienced a slum boom. "The volume of business done in the section . . . during the last year is . . . unprecedented," *Harlem Magazine* announced in 1920. "Renting conditions have been very satisfactory to the owners and the demand for space . . . is getting keener every year [due] to the steady increase in the Negro population," a *New York Times* reporter wrote in 1923. There was, in the language of a Harlem businessman, an "unprecedented demand for Harlem real estate."[40] For landlords—Negro and white (Negro tenants continually complained that Negro landlords fleeced them with equal facility as whites)—Harlem became a profitable slum.[41]

High rents and poor salaries necessarily led to congested and unsanitary conditions. The average Negro Harlemite in the 1920's, as in the 1890's, held some menial or unskilled position which paid low wages—work which was customarily "regarded as Negro jobs." There were generally two types of businesses in New York in terms of Negro hiring policy, E. Franklin Frazier wrote: "Those that employ Negroes in menial positions and those that employ no Negroes at all." Macy's, for example, hired Negroes as elevator operators, escalator attendants and cafeteria workers; Gimbel's used none. "We have felt it inadvisable to [hire] colored people," a Metropolitan Life Insurance Company executive explained in 1930, "not because of any prejudice on the part of the company, but because . . . there would be very serious objection on the part of our white employees. . . ."[42] Throughout the city the vast majority of Negro men worked as longshoremen, elevator operators, porters, janitors, teamsters, chauffeurs, waiters and general laborers of all kinds. Negro women continued to work as domestics ("scrub women"), although in the 1920's an increasing number were employed as factory operatives in the garment industry and in laundries. Less than 20 per cent of Harlem's businesses were owned by Negroes.[43] The average Harlem family, according to President Hoover's Conference on Home Building and Home Ownership, earned $1,300 a year in the twenties; the typical white family in the city, $1,570. A variety of social investigations noted that working-class whites expended approximately 20 per cent of their income for rent, considered the proper amount by economists; Harlemites, 33 per cent and more.[44] An Urban League study of 2,160 Harlem families demonstrated that almost half (48 per cent) spent 40 or more per cent of their earnings on rent. A 1928 sample of tenement families found that Harlemites paid 45 per cent of their wages for

housing. Similar conclusions were reached in a variety of local community studies.[45] Whatever the exact figure, few Negroes looked to the first of the month with expectancy.

Added to the combination of "high rents and low wages"[46] was the fact that Harlem's apartment houses and brownstones were originally built for people with radically different family structure from that of the new residents. Seventy-five per cent of Harlem's tenements had been constructed before 1900.[47] The Negro community of the twenties, like all working-class peoples in times of great migration, continued to be most heavily populated by young adults—men and women between the ages of 15 and 44. Family life had not yet begun for many Negro Harlemites —as it had for older Americans and earlier immigrants who lived in the community previously. In 1930, 66.5 per cent of Harlem Negroes were between the ages of 15 and 44, contrasted with 56.5 per cent for the general population of Manhattan and 54.4 per cent for New York City at large. Harlemites who were married had few children. In 1930, 17.5 per cent of Harlem's population was under 14; the corresponding figure for New York City was 24.5 per cent. The number of Harlemites under the age of 15 declined 14 per cent between 1920 and 1930, as whites left the neighborhood. There was a corresponding decrease of 19 per cent for those over 45 years of age.[48]

What all these statistics mean is simply that apartments of five, six, and seven rooms were suitable for older white residents with larger families and larger incomes—they obviously did not meet the needs of the Negro community in the 1920's. "The houses in the section of Harlem inhabited by the Negro were not only built for another race," E. Franklin Frazier noted, "but what is more important, for a group of different economic level, and consisting of families and households of an entirely different composition from those which now occupy these dwellings." "Unfortunately," Eugene Kinckle Jones of the Urban League stated, "the houses built before [the Negroes'] arrival were not designed to meet the needs . . . of Negroes." "The class of houses we are occupying today are not suited to our economic needs," John E. Nail said in 1921. Negro Harlemites desperately needed small apartments at low rentals: "One of the community's greatest needs [is] small apartments for small families with a reasonable rent limit. . . ."[49] Few realtors were philanthropic enough to invest their capital in new construction; older homes, properly subdivided, produced sufficient income. Only a handful of new houses were built in Harlem in the 1920's.[50]

A variety of makeshift solutions were found to make ends meet: "What you gonna do when the rent comes 'round," had been an old Negro song. The most common solution was to rent an apartment larger than one's needs and means and make up the difference by renting rooms to lodgers—"commercializing" one's home. In the twenties, approximately one white Manhattan family in nine (11.2 per cent) took in roomers, contrasted with one in four (26 per cent) for Negroes. Most lodgers were strangers people let into their homes because of economic necessity. It was difficult to separate "the respectable" from "the fast." "The most depraved Negroes lived side by side with those who were striving to live respectable lives," a contemporary complained. Urban reformers blamed many of Har-

lem's social problems on this "lodger evil."[51]

Every conceivable space within a home was utilized to maximum efficiency: "Sometimes even the bathtub is used to sleep on, two individuals taking turns!" Negro educator Roscoe Conkling Bruce wrote. Boardinghouses were established which rented beds by the week, day, night or hour. A large number of brownstones were converted to rooming houses: "Private residences at one time characteristic of this part of the city have been converted into tenements. . . ." One landlord transformed apartments in nine houses into one-room flats, a state commission investigating New York housing reported. Space which formerly grossed $40 a month now brought in $100 to $125. People were said to be living in "coal bins and cellars." In an extreme case, one social investigator discovered seven children sleeping on pallets on the floor of a two-room apartment. More common was the "Repeating" or "Hot Bed System"—as soon as one person awoke and left, his bed was taken over by another.[52]

An additional Harlem method devised to meet the housing crisis of the twenties was the "Rent Party." Tickets of admission were usually printed and sold for a modest price (25¢). All who wanted to come were invited to a party. Here is an example:[53]

> If you're looking for a good time,
>   don't look no more,
> Just ring my bell and I'll answer
>   the door.
> Southern Barbecue
> Given by Charley Johnson and Joe
>   Hotboy, and How hot!

Chitterlings, pigs' feet, coleslaw and potato salad were sold. Money was raised in this way to pay the rent: "The rent party," *The New York Age* editorialized in 1926, "has become a recognized means of meeting the demands of extortionate landlords. . . ." The white world saw rent parties as picturesque affairs—in reality they were a product of economic exploitation and they often degenerated into rowdy, bawdy and violent evenings.[54]

A significant part of the deterioration of the neighborhood was caused by the migrants themselves. Some needed rudimentary training in the simplest processes of good health and sanitation (Booker T. Washington, it will be remembered, preached the "gospel of the toothbrush").[55] E. Franklin Frazier called many Negro Harlemites "ignorant and unsophisticated peasant people without experience [in] urban living. . . ." They often permitted homes and buildings to remain in a state of uncleanliness and disrepair. Landlords complained that apartments were looted and fixtures stolen, that courtyards and hallways were found laden with refuse. Clothes and bedding were hung out of windows; trash sometimes thrown down air shafts; dogs walked on rooftops; profanities shouted across streets; "ragtime" played throughout the night. "Ragtime is a sufficient infliction of itself," one wag complained, "but when it keeps up all night, it becomes unbearable." "Since the so-called 'Negro invasion,'" a colored woman noted, "the streets, the property and the character of everything have undergone a change, and if you are honest, you will frankly acknowledge it has not been for the . . . improvement of the locality. . . . Are we responsible for at least some of the race prejudice which has developed since the entry of Negroes in Harlem?" Negro journals criticized "boisterous"

men who laughed "hysterically" and hung around street corners, and those who used "foul language on the streets." An editorial in the *Age*, one of many, attacked "Careless Harlem Tenants": "A great deal might be said about the necessity for training some of the tenants in the matter of common decency," it suggested. The absence of a sense of social and community responsibility, characteristic of urban life, obviously affected Negro Harlemites.[56]

All these factors combined to lead to the rapid decline of Harlem. The higher the rents, sociologists said, the greater the congestion: "Crowding is more prevalent in high-rent cities than in cities in which rent per room is more reasonable." In 1925, Manhattan's population density was 223 people per acre—in the Negro districts it was 336. Philadelphia, the second most congested Negro city in the country, had 111 Negroes to an acre of land; Chicago ranked third with 67. There were two streets in Harlem that were perhaps the most congested blocks in the entire world.[57]

People were packed together to the point of "indecency."[58] Some landlords, after opening houses to Negro tenants, lost interest in caring for their property and permitted it to run down—halls were left dark and dirty, broken pipes were permitted to rot, steam heat was cut off as heating apparatus wore out, dumb-waiters broke down and were boarded up, homes became vermin-infested. Tenants in one rat-infested building started what they called "a crusade against rats." They argued that the rats in their house were "better fed" and "better housed" than the people. Some common tenant complaints in the 1920's read: "No improvement in ten years";

"Rats, rat holes, and roaches"; "Very very cold"; "Not fit to live in"; "Air shaft smells"; "Ceilings in two rooms have fallen"; "My apartment is overrun with rats"; and so on.[59] There were more disputes between tenants and landlords in Harlem's local district court —the Seventh District Court—than in any municipal court in the five boroughs. Traditionally, municipal courts were known as "poor-men's courts"; Harlemites called the Seventh District Court the "rent court." Occasionally, socially conscious judges of this court made personal inspections of local tenements that were subjects of litigation. Without exception what they saw horrified them: "Conditions in negro tenements in Harlem are deplorable"; "Found few fit for human habitation"; "Negro tenants are being grossly imposed upon by their landlords"; "On the whole I found a need for great reformation"; were some of their comments. One municipal official accurately called the majority of Harlem's houses "diseased properties."[60]

V

And the disease did not confine itself to houses. To touch most areas of Harlem life in the 1920's is to touch tragedy. This was especially true of the health of the community. Theoretically, a section of the city inhabited by relatively young people should have ranked below the general population in mortality and sickness rates. Just the reverse was true. Undertaking was a most profitable Harlem business.[61]

From 1923 to 1927 an Atlanta University professor made an intensive study of Harlem health. His findings were shocking. During these years Harlem's death rate, for all causes, was 42 per cent in excess of that of the entire city. Twice as many Harlem mothers died in childbirth as did mothers in other districts, and almost twice as many Harlem children "passed" as did infants in the rest of New York. Infant mortality in Harlem, 1923-1927, was 111 per thousand live births; for the city, 64.5. Families wept at the proces-

Health center districts, 1930 Manhattan	Infant mortality per 1,000 live births	TB mortality per 100,000 population	Pulmonary TB new case rate per 100,000 population	Other infectious diseases, rate per 100,000 population	Venereal disease new case rate per 100,000 population	General mortality rate per 1,000 population
Central Harlem	98	251	487	987	2826	15.3
Lower East Side	62	116	302	1,160	892	14.0
Kips Bay–Lenox Hill	73	75	184	937	629	12.7
East Harlem	75	137	311	1,326	913	12.0
Lower West Side	83	156	391	1,201	1,318	16.7
Riverside	64	75	196	827	778	12.3
Washington Heights	52	72	203	937	668	10.5
Total	73	122	294	1,049	1,455	13.3

sions of "so many little white caskets." Similar statistics are recorded for deaths from tuberculosis (two and a half to three times the city rate), pneumonia, heart disease, cancer and stillbirths.[62] An astounding number of Harlemites had venereal diseases. Negro children commonly suffered from rickets—a disease of malnutrition. More women than ever reported themselves "widows" to census-takers. Negro deaths by violence increased 60 per cent between 1900 and 1925.[63] With the single exception of the Lower West Side Health District, which included the old San Juan Hill neighborhood, Harlem was the most disease-ridden community in Manhattan.[64]

Whatever the causes of Harlem's health problems—and medical investigators continue to search for all the answers—a good deal can be laid at the door of slum environment. Urban reformers consistently showed a high correlation between poverty and congestion on the one hand and disease and death on the other. Mortality rates for infants whose mothers worked away from home, for example—and twice as many Negro women as white women in the city did—was higher than for children whose mothers remained at home; working-class families in old-law tenements (pre-1901) died at a higher-rate than those in newer houses; poverty led to the consumption of the cheapest foods, and this in turn fostered diseases of poor diet; working mothers died more readily in childbirth than unemployed women; and so on.[65] Added to all these considerations, however, was a deep strain of peasant ignorance and superstition embedded in the minds of thousands of migrants—foreign-born as well as native—who settled in Harlem. Quackery abounded in the community in the 1920's.[66]

Harlem had the reputation of a "wide-open city." Whatever you wanted, and in whatever quantity, so the impression went, could be bought there. This was certainly true for the variety of "spiritualists," "herb doctors," "African medicine men," "Indian doctors," "dispensers of snake oils," "layers-on-of-hands," "faith healers," "palmists," and phrenologists who performed a twentieth-century brand of necromancy there: "Harlem sick people are flocking to all sorts of Quacksters," an *Age* reporter noted. One man, "Professor Ajapa," sold a "herb juice" guaranteed "to cure consumption, rheumatism, and other troubles that several doctors have failed in." Powders could be purchased to keep one's wife home at night, make women fertile and men sexually appealing. "Black Herman the Magician" and "Sister P. Harreld" held séances and sold "blessed handkerchiefs," "potent powders," love charms, lodestones, amulets and "piles of roots." "Ignorance, cherished superstitions and false knowledge often govern Negroes in illness and hamper recoveries," a colored physician with the Board of Health wrote in 1926. Nine wood lice gathered in a little bag and tied around a baby's neck, some believed, would end teething. An egg fried brown on both sides and placed on a woman's abdomen would hasten labor. If a mother in the course of childbirth kicked a Bible from her bed to the floor, either she or her child would die. People had faith in the medicinal qualities of dried cobwebs, rabbit brains, "dirt-dauber tea," and something called "cockroach rum." In spite of efforts of physicians, health agencies and the Negro press to bring modern-day medical information to the community, quackery "continued to thrive with impunity in Harlem." It aggravated an already tragic situation.[67]

Accompanying the proliferation of

healers, and rooted in the same rural consciousness which made quackery possible,[68] was the host of storefront churches founded in Harlem in the twenties. These were places that healed one's soul: "Jesus is the Doctor, Services on Sunday," read a sign which hung over one door. An investigator found 140 Negro churches in a 150-block area of Harlem in 1926. "Harlem is perhaps overchurched," W. E. B. DuBois said modestly. Only about a third—fifty-four —of Harlem's churches were housed in regular church buildings—and these included some of the most magnificent and costly church edifices in New York City. The rest held services in stores and homes and appealed to Harlem's least educated people. "Jack-leg preachers," "cotton-field preachers," as their critics called them, hung out their poorly printed signboards and "preached Jesus" to all who wanted to listen. One self-appointed pastor held meetings in the front room of his home and rented chairs from the local undertaker to seat his small congregation. In Harlem in the twenties one could receive the word of the Lord through such nondenominational sects as: "The Metaphysical Church of the Divine Investigation," "The Temple of the Gospel of the Kingdom," "The Church of the Temple of Love," "Holy Church of the Living God," "Temple of Luxor," "Holy Tabernacle of God," "Royal Fraternity Association," "Knights of the Rose and Cross," "Sons of God," "Sons of Christ," "Sons of Jehovah," "Sanctified Sons of the Holy Ghost," and the "Live-Ever-Die-Never" church. People not only had their worries removed in these places, a Negro clergyman wrote, but "their meager worldly goods as well."[69]

The ministers of these churches preached a fundamentalism which centered around the scheming ways of Satan, who was everywhere, and the terror and joy of divine retribution, with an emphasis on terror. One congregation expelled members who attended the theater or movies. "The devil runs every theatre," its pastor said. "He collects a tax on the souls of men and robs them of their seat in heaven." Services were fervent, loud and boisterous as members felt the spirit of the Lord and shouted and begged for His forgiveness. Tambourines sometimes kept up a rhythmic beat in the background and heightened the emotionalism to a state of frenzy. Neighbors of one storefront church sued the congregation for "conducting a public nuisance." The "weird sounds" which emanated from the building, they complained, seemed like a "jazz orchestra."[70]

Are you ready-ee? Hah!
For that great day, hah!
When the moon shall drape her face in mourning, hah!
And the sun drip down in blood, hah!
When the stars, hah!
Shall burst forth from their diamond sockets, hah!
And the mountains shall skip like lambs, hah!
Havoc will be there, my friends, hah!
With her jaws wide open, hah!
And the sinner-man, hah!
And cry, Oh rocks! Hah!
Hide me! Hah!
Hide me from the face of an angry God, hah!
Hide me, Ohhhhhh! . . .
Can't hide, sinner, you can't hide.[71]

Contemporaries were uniformly critical of these evangelists—there were many Harlem "Prophets"—and most of these preachers were probably charlatans in some form. There was at least one exception, however. A new denomination, the Church of Christ, Apostolic Faith, was founded on the streets of Harlem by the Reverend Mr. R. C. Lawson in 1919. The Reverend Mr.

Lawson, of New Iberia, Louisiana, "the only real Apostolic—Holy Ghost-Bible Preacher," presented what he called the "Full Gospel" on street corners of Harlem's worst blocks. He decried the lack of emotionalism in the more established urban churches—copying "the white man's style," he said—and offered recent migrants a touch of fire and brimstone and personal Christianity characteristic of religion in the rural South:

I have found it, I have found it, the meaning of life, life in God, life flowing through me by the Holy Spirit, life abundant, peace, joy, life in its fullness.

Lawson started preaching on One Hundred and Thirty-third Street, east of Lenox Avenue. This area "was to Harlem what the Bowery is to the lower East Side," a Negro journalist recorded. From the streets, the Reverend Mr. Lawson moved into a small building and held services for those "fast drifting to a life of eternal darkness" every day and every night of the week. His Refuge Church of Christ became the founding church of the new denomination, and the Reverend Mr. Lawson its first bishop. By 1930 the Apostolic Church had some forty branches throughout the country and ran an orphanage, elementary school and "Bible Supply House"; it continues to prosper today. Annual conventions met in Refuge Church, "the most honored in the sisterhood of the Apostolic Church," and local leaders praised and publicized its good works for Harlem Negroes: "This church has had one of the most remarkable growths of any religious organizations in the country."[72]

Harlem was also a "wide-open city" in terms of vice and gambling.[73] The annual reports of the anti-vice Committee of Fourteen, founded in 1905, showed Harlem as the leading or near-leading prostitution center of Manhattan throughout the twenties. The Committee hired a Negro doctor, Ernest R. Alexander, to do a secret study of Harlem vice in 1928. His report emphasized the "openness of vice conditions in this district." Dr. Alexander personally found sixty-one houses of prostitution in the neighborhood—more than the combined totals of four other investigators hired at the same time to survey other districts. "There is a larger amount and more open immorality in Harlem than this community has known in years," Negro alderman George W. Harris noted in 1922. "It is a house of assignation . . . this black city," Eric D. Walrond wrote bitterly in the Negro journal *The Messenger*.[74]

Her dark brown face
Is like a withered flower
On a broken stem.
Those kind come cheap in Harlem,
So they say.[75]

The Committee of Fourteen also disclosed that more than 90 per cent of these "daughters of joy" institutions were owned and managed by whites. Other evidence verifies this.[76]

Gambling also prevailed in the neighborhood: "Bootleggers, gamblers, and other panderers to vice have found it profitable to ply their vicious trades in this section." The poorest of the poor sought instant riches through the numbers racket. No sum was too small to bet—starting with pennies. "One can bet with plenty of takers on anything from a horse race to a mule race," the *Age* editorialized. Many Harlemites "would rather gamble than eat," it concluded. People selected numbers to coincide with birthdays, dreams, hymns or chapters and verses of Scripture in expectation that they would coincide with the clearing-house figures of the day. The odds were thousands to one against success, yet the smallest hope for a richer life was better than none and Negroes continued to play "policy" avidly. "The chief pastime of Harlem seems to be playing the numbers," George S. Schuyler wrote in 1925.[77]

"Buffet flats," "hooch joints," "barrel houses," and cabarets supplied Harlemites with illegal liquor, and occasionally other things, in the Prohibition era. Drugstores, cigar stores, sweetshops and delicatessens were used as "fronts" for speakeasies. "Harlem can boast of more drugstores than any similar area in the world," one Negro commented. "A plethora of delicatessen stores may be found in the Negro sections of New York, most of which are simply disguised bootlegging stores," a Harlemite concluded in 1924. "And so many confectioners! One never dreamed the Negroes were so much in need of sugar." "Speakeasies downtown are usually carefully camouflaged," a *New York Tribune* reporter noted. "In Harlem they can be spotted a hundred yards off."[78]

Poverty and family instability also led to a high incidence of juvenile delinquency. A community with fewer young teenagers should have shown a proportionally lower juvenile crime rate; as with Negro health, just the reverse was true. "The records of the Children's Court of New York for every year from 1914 to 1927 show a steady increase in the percentage of all crimes committed by Negro boys and girls," Owen R. Lovejoy of the Children's Aid Society reported. In 1914 Negro children represented 2.8 per cent of all cases before the juvenile court of New York City; in 1930 this figure rose to 11.7 per cent.[79]

Working mothers had little time to care for their children. Youngsters "with keys tied around their necks on a ribbon" wandered around the streets until families came home at night. A sub-

stantial portion were products of broken homes—families without a male head. One Harlem school principal testified that 699 of his 1,600 pupils came from families whose fathers were not living at home. Nor did the majority of Harlem schoolchildren ever have time to accustom themselves to the regularity of school life; many families were rootless. Three-fourths of all the Negro pupils registered in one Harlem school, for example, transferred to some other before the end of one school year; some schools actually experienced a 100 per cent turnover. Pupils from the South were seriously deficient in educational training: "They are at times 14 to 15 years of age and have not the schooling of boys of eight," a Harlem principal wrote. "We cannot give a boy back seven years of wasted life. . . ." The typical Harlem school of the twenties had double and sometimes triple sessions. The "usual class size" was forty to fifty and conditions were generally "immensely over-crowded": "The school plant as a whole is old, shabby, and far from modern." In some schools 25 per cent and more of the children were overage or considered retarded.

Negro children in Harlem often led disrupted and harsh lives from the earliest years of their existence: "Testimony has been given before us as to the moral conditions among children, even of tender age," a municipal agency investigating Harlem schools recorded, "which is not to be adequately described by the word 'horrifying.'" These conditions were obviously reflected in high rates of juvenile crime but more subtly, and worst of all, in a loss of respect for oneself and for life in general. Harlem youngsters developed "a sense of subordination, of insecurity, of lack of self-confidence and self-respect, the inability . . . to stand on their own feet and face the world with open eyes and feel that [they have] as good a right as anyone else."[80]

This then was the horror of slum life —the Harlem tragedy of the 1920's. "Court and police precinct records show," a municipal agency maintained, "that in arrests, convictions, misdemeanants, felons, female police problems and juvenile delinquencies, these areas are in the lead. . . ." It was no wonder that narcotics addiction became a serious problem then and that Harlem became "the center of the retail dope traffic of New York"; nor that local violence and hatred for the police were continually reported in the press.[81] The majority of Harlemites even during normal times lived "close to the subsistence level." Many were "under care" of charitable agencies in the period of relatively full employment. Those who needed money quickly and had no other recourse were forced to turn to loan sharks, Negro and white, who charged 30 to 40 per cent interest: Harlem "has been infested by a lot of loan sharks," a municipal magistrate who dealt with such cases stated. In one form or another the sorrow and economic deprivation of the Depression had come to Harlem in the twenties: "The reason why the Depression didn't have the impact on the Negroes that it had on the whites," George S. Schuyler said, "was that the Negroes had been in the Depression all the time."[82]

NOTES

1. The Mayor's Commission on Conditions in Harlem, "The Negro in Harlem: A Report on Social and Economic Conditions Responsible for the Outbreak of March 19, 1935" (unpublished manuscript in La Guardia Papers, Municipal Archives),

p. 53. This important study, prepared under the direction of E. Franklin Frazier, will hereafter be cited as "The Negro in Harlem."
2. "The Future Harlem," The New York Age, January 10, 1920.
3. John E. Nail to James Weldon Johnson, March 12, 1934, Johnson Collection, Yale University; "Harlem Conditions Called Deplorable," The New York Times, September 6, 1927.
4. "Let Them Come," "The New Exodus," The New York Age, March 3, 1923, October 16, 1920, September 14, 1929.
5. Bureau of the Census, Fifteenth Census, 1930: Population (Washington, D.C., 1933), II, 216-218; Walter Laidlaw, Population of the City of New York, 1890-1930 (New York, 1932), p. 51.
6. Reverend Dr. Adam Clayton Powell, Sr., Against the Tide: An Autobiography (New York, 1938), pp. 70-71.
7. Bureau of the Census, Fifteenth Census, 1930: Population (Washington, D.C., 1933), II, 216-218. Note the difference in Chicago's migrant population. In order of greatest numbers Chicago Negroes came from Mississippi, Tennessee, Georgia, Alabama and Louisiana.
8. James Ford, et al., Slums and Housing: With Special Reference to New York City (Cambridge, Mass., 1936), II, 311-315.
9. Ibid., p. 317; Bureau of the Census, Negroes in the United States, 1920-1932 (Washington, D.C., 1935), p. 55.
10. Winfred B. Nathan, Health Conditions in North Harlem, 1923-1927 (New York, 1932), pp. 13-14.
11. Harlem Magazine, XIX (June 1930), 8; Mayor's Commission on City Planning, East Harlem Community Study (typescript in New York Public Library, 1937), p. 16.
12. Slums and Housing, p. 370; Antonio T. Rivera to La Guardia, June 24, 1935, La Guardia Papers; "Harlem Puerto Ricans Unite to Prove Faith," The New York Times, July 2, August 9, 16, 1926; Opportunity, IV (October 1926), 330.
13. The New York Age, August 27, 1927, March 31, 1928, January 11, 1930; The New York Times, October 19, 1924.
14. Slums and Housing, p. 314.
15. The attempt of Negroes to move into Washington Heights, Yonkers and Westchester was opposed in these sections as it had been in Harlem earlier. The Neighborhood Protective Association of Washington Heights urged landlords to sign racially restrictive covenants. Mortgage pressures from financial institutions closed down a Negro housing development in Yonkers. As a result of population pressure, however, another large ghetto was created in the Bedford-Stuyvesant section of Brooklyn in the 1920's. Of the 68,921 Negroes in Brooklyn in 1930, 47,616 lived in what is now called Bedford-Stuyvesant. "Negro Community Near Yonkers Abandoned," The New York Age, July 3, 1926, March 24, August 4, 1928, April 19, 26, 1930; Slums and Housing, p. 314.

For a sketch of Brooklyn's Negro community see Ralph Foster Weld, *Brooklyn Is America* (New York, 1950), pp. 153-173.

16. The President's Conference on Home Building and Home Ownership, *Report of the Committee on Negro Housing* (Washington, D.C., 1931), p. 5.

17. Bureau of the Census, *Fifteenth Census, 1930: Population* (Washington, D.C., 1933), II, 70; Ira De Augustine Reid, *The Negro Immigrant* (New York, 1938), pp. 248-249; Barrington Dunbar, "Factors in the Cultural Background of the American Southern Negro and the British West Indian Negro that Condition their Adjustment in Harlem" (M.A. thesis, Columbia University, 1935), foreword, p. 4.

18. Reid, *The Negro Immigrant*, pp. 31-35; Reid, "Negro Immigration to the United States," *Social Forces*, XVI (March 1938), 411-417; W. A. Domingo, "Restricted West Indian Immigration and the American Negro," *Opportunity*, II (October 1924), 298-299.

19. W. A. Domingo, "Gift of the Black Tropics," in Alain Locke, ed., *The New Negro: An Interpretation* (New York, 1925), p. 343.

20. *The New York Age*, July 9, 1924, February 4, 1928; Harry Robinson, "The Negro Immigrant in New York" (WPA research paper, Schomburg Collection), p. 9.

21. Garrie Ward Moore, "A Study of a Group of West Indian Negroes in New York City" (M.A. thesis, Columbia University, 1923), pp. 19-20; Reid, *The Negro Immigrant*, pp. 126-128; *The New York Age*, February 28, 1931, July 29, 1933.

22. "The Negro in New York" (unpublished WPA manuscript, Schomburg Collection), pp. 25-27; Gardner N. Jones, "The Pilgrimage to Freedom" (WPA research paper, Schomburg Collection), p. 25.

23. Reid, *The Negro Immigrant*, p. 159.

24. *Ibid.*, p. 123; "Communists in Harlem," *The New York Age*, September 21, 1929, October 2, 9, 1926, December 24, 1927, January 21, May 12, December 8, 1928, September 21, 1929.

25. Domingo, "Gift of the Black Tropics," p. 347.

26. Robinson, "Negro Immigrant in New York," pp. 21-22; Moore, "West Indian Negroes in New York City," p. 26.

27. "The Reminiscences of George S. Schuyler" (Oral History Research Office, Columbia University, 1960), p. 73.

28. Robinson, "Negro Immigrant in New York," p. 9; "The Negro in New York," p. 25; Moore, "West Indian Negroes in New York City," p. 25; Reid, *The Negro Immigrant*, p. 133; *The Messenger*, VII (September 1925), 326, 337-338; *The New York Age*, February 22, 1930; Baltimore *Afro-American*, January 9, 1932.

29. Moore, "West Indian Negroes in New York City," p. 5.

30. Dunbar, "Negro Adjustment in Harlem," pp. 14-25.

31. Reid, *The Negro Immigrant, passim.*

32. *Ibid.*, p. 125; Greater New York Federation of Churches, *Negro Churches in Manhattan* (New York, 1930).

33. Reid, *The Negro Immigrant*, p. 174; Moore, "West Indian Negroes in New York City," pp. 20-25; Dunbar, "Negro Adjustment in Harlem," chap. IV, pp. 22-23.

34. Roi Ottley, *'New World A-Coming': Inside Black America* (New York, 1943), pp. 47-48; Gardner Jones, "The Pilgrimage to Freedom" (WPA research paper, Schomburg Collection), p. 25; Beverly Smith, "Harlem—Negro City," *New York Herald Tribune*, February 14, 1930; Reid, *The Negro Immigrant*, p. 115; *The New York Age*, July 19, 1924, March 17, 1934; Dunbar, "Negro Adjustment in Harlem," chap. III, p. 4; Walter White, "The Paradox of Color," in Alain Locke, ed., *The New Negro: An Interpretation* (New York, 1925), p. 367.

35. *The New York Age*, March 3, 24, April 21, 1928; Domingo, "The Gift of the Black Tropics," p. 344-345; Reid, *The Negro Immigrant*, p. 235.

36. "Harlem Slums," *The Crisis*, XLVIII (December 1941), 378-381; *The New York Age*, January 22, 1927.

37. New York Urban League, "Twenty-four Hundred Negro Families in Harlem: An Interpretation of the Living Conditions of Small Wage Earners" (typescript, Schomburg Collection, 1927), pp. 16-18.

38. *Report of the Committee on Negro Housing*, p. 64.

39. "Appreciation" of prices "came [when owners] remained calm. . . ." T. J. Woofter, *et al.*, *Negro Problems in Cities* (New York, 1928), p. 75. *The New York Times* printed dozens of articles on Harlem's new business prosperity.

40. "Harlem Real Estate Increasing in Value," *Harlem Magazine*, VIII (February 1920), 18b; "Unprecedented Demand for Harlem Real Estate," *ibid.*, X (November 1920), 6; "Revival of Speculative Activity on Harlem's Main Thoroughfare," *The New York Times*, January 18, 1920, July 24, 1921, June 10, 1923, February 13, 1927.

41. "Of all the gouging landlords in Harlem, the colored landlords and agents are the worst, according to the records of the Seventh District Municipal Court." "Race Landlord is Hardest on His Tenants," *The New York Age*, November 20, 1920, June 16, September 22, 1923, May 29, 1926.

42. "The Negro in Harlem," pp. 27-32; *The New York Age*, April 26, 1930.

43. Bureau of the Census, *Fourteenth Census, 1920: Population* (Washington, D.C., 1923), IV, 366-367, 1157-1179; *Fifteenth Census, 1930: Occupations* (Washington, D.C., 1933), 1130-1134; Helen B. Sayre, "Negro Women in Industry," *Opportunity*, II (August 1924), 242-244.

44. *Report of the Committee on Negro Housing*, p. 64; *Negro Problems in Cities*, p. 122.

45. "Twenty-four Hundred Negro Families in Harlem," p. 19; Sidney Axelrad, *Tenements and Tenants: A Study of 1104 Tenement Families* (New York, 1932), p. 15; New York Building

and Land Utilization Committee, *Harlem Family Income Survey* (New York, 1935), p. 3; James H. Hubert, "Harlem—Its Social Problems," *Hospital Social Service*, XXI (January 1930), 44.

46. *Report of the Committee on Negro Housing*, p. vii.

47. William Wilson to La Guardia, October 6, 1944, La Guardia Papers.

48. *Health Conditions in North Harlem*, pp. 16-17; *Fifteenth Census, 1930: Population* (Washington, D.C., 1933), II, 733-734; "The Negro in Harlem," p. 20.

49. ". . . The greatest need is the construction of model tenements. These should consist of one, two, three and four room apartments." "Modern Housing Needs," *The New York Age*, February 12, 1921, January 20, 1923, January 26, 1926, January 29, 1927; "The Negro in Harlem," p. 53; Eugene Kinckle Jones, "Negro Migration in New York State," *Opportunity*, IV (January 1926), 9.

50. Victor R. Daly, "The Housing Crisis in New York City," *The Crisis*, XXXI (December 1920), 61-62.

51. National Urban League, *Housing Conditions Among Negroes, New York City* (New York, 1915), *passim;* Ford, *et al., Slums and Housing*, p. 338.

52. "Very often it is found that there are two shifts." William Wilson to La Guardia, October 6, 1944, La Guardia Papers; *The New York Age*, March 12, 1921, February 26, 1927; "Along Rainbow Row," *The New York Times*, August 15, 1921, January 27, 1922; "Twenty-four Hundred Negro Families in Harlem," *passim;* Roscoe Conkling Bruce, "The Dunbar Apartment House: An Adventure in Community Building," *The Southern Workman*, LX (October 1931), 418.

53. *New York Herald Tribune*, February 12, 13, 1930.

54. "I promoted a weekly party, to get money to pay rent." "Boisterous rent parties, flooded with moonshine, are a quick and sure resource." "The Reminiscences of Benjamin McLaurin" (Oral History Research Office, Columbia University, 1960), p. 155; *The New York Age*, August 11, 1923, June 21, December 11, 1926; Clyde Vernon Kiser, *Sea Island to City* (New York, 1932), pp. 44-45.

55. Booker T. Washington, *Up from Slavery: An Autobiography* (New York 1959), pp. 122-123. Note the following statement of a recent study: "There are many cases in which migratory workers do not understand or properly use ordinary living facilities, such as toilets, showers, bedding, kitchen appliances, and garbage cans. The result has been unnecessary damage to property and needless expense for repairs." 87th Cong., 1st Sess., *Senate Report 1098* (1961), p. 8.

56. *The New York Age*, August 1, 1912, June 5, 1920, September 16, 1922, July 14, 1928; National Urban League, *Housing Conditions Among Negroes*, pp. 9-10; "The Negro in Harlem," p.

113; Eslanda Goode Robeson, *Paul Robeson: Negro* (London, 1930), p. 46.

57. Woofter, *et al., Negro Problems in Cities*, pp. 79, 84; "The Negro in Harlem," p. 53; Ernest W. Burgess, "Residential Segregation in American Cities," *The Annals*, CXL (November 1928), 105-115; Ford, *et al., Slums and Housing*, p. 749.

58. Owen R. Lovejoy, *The Negro Children of New York* (New York, 1932), p. 15.

59. *The New York Age*, October 28, 1922, January 17, 1925; *Housing Conditions Among Negroes, passim;* "Twenty-four Hundred Negro Families in Harlem," *passim*.

60. "I do not think I need to say that our problem of Harlem is one of the most serious we have to face." Langdon W. Post (Chairman of New York City Housing Authority) to La Guardia, April 30, 1936, La Guardia Papers. "The Negro families of the West Harlem section have undoubtedly the most serious housing problem in the City." Ford, *et al., Slums and Housing*, p. 326. *The New York Times*, September 16, 1920, October 17, 23, 1921, April 22, 1922, January 17, June 13, 1925; *The New York Age*, February 28, August 8, 1925, January 9, 1926; "Preliminary Report on the Subject of Housing (1935)," La Guardia Papers.

61. "High Cost of Dying," *The New York Age*, February 25, 1928.

62. *Health Conditions in North Harlem, passim; The Negro Children of New York*, p. 22; "Fighting the Ravages of the White Plague Among New York's Negro Population," *Opportunity*, I (January 1923), 23-24; Dr. Louis R. Wright, "Cancer as It Affects Negroes," *ibid.*, VI (June 1928), 169-170, 187; Louis I. Dublin, "The Effect of Health Education on Negro Mortality," *Proceedings of the National Conference on Social Work, 1924* (Chicago, 1924), 274-279. Hereafter cited as PNCSW.

63. ". . . Syphilitic infection is one of the most fruitful causes of stillbirths, miscarriages, and early death of infants." New York Association for Improving the Condition of the Poor, *Health Work for Mothers and Children in a Colored Community* (New York, 1924), p. 3; "The Negro's Health Progress During the Last Twenty-five Years," *Weekly Bulletin of the Department of Health*, XV (June 12, 1926); *Fifteenth Census, 1930: Population* (Washington, D.C., 1933), II, 959; E. K. Jones, "The Negro's Struggle for Health," *PNCSW, 1923* (Chicago, 1923), 68-72.

64. Adapted from Godea J. Drolet and Louis Werner, "Vital Statistics in the Development of Neighborhood Health Centers in New York City," *Journal of Preventive Medicine*, VI (January 1932), 69.

65. In 1920, 30.3 per cent of white women in the city worked, and 57.9 per cent of colored women were employed. *Fourteenth Census, 1920: Population* (Washington, D.C., 1923), IV, 367. Robert Morse Woodbury, *Causal Factors in In-*

fant Mortality (Washington, D.C., 1925); L. T. Wright, "Factors Controlling Negro Health," *The Crisis*, XLII (September 1935), 264-265, 280, 284; Mildred Jane Watson, "Infant Mortality in New York City, White and Colored, 1929-1936" (M.A. thesis, Columbia University, 1938); Charles Herbert Garvin, "White Plague and Black Folk," *Opportunity*, VIII (August 1930), 232-235.

66. For "voodoo" and "devil worship" among West Indians see Reid, *The Negro Immigrant*, pp. 48-49, 136-138.

67. ". . . Many [are] bringing with them their simple faith in roots, herbs, home remedies, [and are] imposed upon by unscrupulous vendors of worthless . . . remedies," Dr. Peter Marshall Murray, "Harlem's Health," *Hospital Social Service*, XXII (October 1930), 309-313; C. V. Roman, "The Negro's Psychology and His Health," *PNCSW, 1924* (Chicago, 1924), 270-274; *Opportunity*, IV (July 1926), 206-207; *The Crisis*, XLII (August 1935), 243; *The New York Age*, September 23, 1922, February 17, July 21, August 11, 25, 1923, January 6, April 5, 1924, February 21, March 14, 1925, January 18, July 23, 1927.

68. Note the striking similarities between the medical and healing superstitions of urban Negroes in the twentieth century and those of slaves in the early nineteenth century. The following is a description of slave superstition by an ex-slave: "There is much superstition among the slaves. Many of them believe in what they call 'conjuration,' tricking, and witchcraft; and some of them pretend to understand the art, and say that by it they can prevent their masters from exercising their will over their slaves. Such are often applied to by others, to give them power to prevent their masters from flogging them. The remedy is most generally some kind of bitter root; they are directed to chew it and spit toward their masters. . . . At other times they prepare certain kinds of powders, to sprinkle their masters' dwellings." *Narrative of the Life and Adventures of Henry Bibb, An American Slave, Written by Himself* (New York, 1849), pp. 25-31.

69. Beverly Smith, "Harlem—Negro City," *New York Herald Tribune*, February 11, 1930; Ira De Augustine Reid, "Let Us Prey!" *Opportunity* IV (September 1926), 274-278; Reverend James H. Robinson, *Road Without Turning: An Autobiography* (New York, 1950), 231.

70. *The New York Age*, February 19, 1927; *The New York Times*, September 24, 1919.

71. Zora Neale Hurston, *Dust Track on a Road* (Philadelphia, 1942), pp. 279-280.

72. *The New York Age*, January 15, 1927, February 9, 1929, August 23, 1930, August 8, September 19, 1931, July 23, 1932, August 26, 1933, September 1, 1934.

73. "A Wide Open Harlem," *ibid.*, September 2, 1922.

74. Committee of Fourteen, *Annual Reports*, 1914-1930; *The Crisis*, XXXVI (November 1929), 417-418; *The Messenger*, VI (January 1924), 14.

75. Langston Hughes, "Young Prostitute," *The Crisis*, XXVI (August 1923), 162.

76. "Gambling is popular in Harlem, but the big shots of the racket are white." Fiorello La Guardia, "Harlem: Homelike and Hopeful" (unpublished manuscript, La Guardia Papers), p. 9; "A Summary of Vice Conditions in Harlem," Committee of Fourteen, *Annual Report for 1928* (New York, 1929), 31-34; *The New York Times*, February 13, 1922; *The New York Age*, February 28, 1925, May 18, 1929. Although whites seemed to control most of Harlem vice, Virgin Islander Casper Holstein—well-known as a philanthropist and café owner—was reputed to be a head of the numbers racket.

77. "Harlem—The Bettor," *The New York Age*, March 7, 1925, November 6, 20, 1926, June 4, 1927, June 23, 1928; *The New York Times*, June 12, 1922, March 11, 1927; "New York: Utopia Deferred," *The Messenger*, VII (October, November 1925), 344-349, 370.

78. *The New York Age*, September 16, 1922, April 21, 1923; *New York Herald Tribune*, February 13, 1930; *The Messenger*, VI (August 1924) 247, 262.

79. Lovejoy, *The Negro Children of New York*, p. 37; *New York Herald Tribune*, February 12, 1930; Joint Committee on Negro Child Study in New York City, *A Study of Delinquent and Neglected Negro Children Before the New York City Children's Court* (New York, 1927).

80. Jacob Theobald, "Some Facts About P.S. 89, Manhattan," *The New York Age*, January 17, 1920; "Report of Subcommittee on Education," La Guardia Papers; "The Problem of Education and Recreation," *ibid.*; "The Negro in Harlem," p. 73; Lovejoy, *The Negro Children of New York*, p. 22; *The New York Age*, March 12, 1921.

81. "Results of the Crime and Delinquency Study," La Guardia Papers; *The New York Age*, January 6, February 17, June 23, 1923, June 12, 1926, December 3, 1927, July 28, 1928, January 4, 1930. A white Harlem policeman, at a later date, wrote the following: "Every one of [us] is made to feel like a soldier in an army of occupation. He is engulfed by an atmosphere of antagonism." *The Crisis*, LII (January 1945), 16-17.

82. Lovejoy, *The Negro Children of New York*, p. 15; "The Negro in Harlem," p. 110; *The New York Age*, February 9, 1929; "The Reminiscences of George S. Schuyler" (Oral History Research Office, Columbia University, 1960), p. 232.

VII THE CITY IN THE AMERICAN MIND

The fundamental crisis of the American city, according to one knowledgeable student of urban affairs, is an intellectual crisis involving inherited attitudes and images of the city that are either distorted or no longer applicable to the reality of an urban environment. The heart of every urban problem, be it housing, poverty, transportation, or even air pollution, evokes a judgment, an attitude toward the city itself; indeed,

the action crisis of the metropolis cannot be disengaged from the intellectual crisis, for the very definition of a metropolitan problem is dependent upon one's picture of the city and the kind of life it should contain, as the choice of action to improve or revolutionize is dependent upon one's estimate of the city as an existing entity.[1]

It has been a crisis of long standing, for the intellectual history of the American city has been a battleground of conflicting attitudes of Americans, who have argued about the value of the city and the kind of life it should contain. And for good reason. As a new form of human settlement, the city broke older village and agrarian traditions and forced new adjustments, new problems, new fears, and new hopes. As a dynamic source of social change, it was seen by some as the "Hope of Democracy," by others, many of whom measured it through the lens of agrarian or small-town America, as a corruption of democracy. Thus emerged two dominant attitudes toward the city, antiurbanism and prourbanism—the city as a House of Ill-Fame and as the House of God.

Morton and Lucia White have engagingly capsuled the raft of antiurban attitudes as:

1. Scott Greer, *The Emerging City: Myth and Reality* (New York: The Free Press, 1964), p. 21.

too big, too noisy, too dusky, too dirty, too smelly, too commercial, too crowded, too full of immigrants, too full of Jews, too full of Irishmen, Italians, Poles, too artificial, destructive of conversation, destructive of communication, too greedy, too capitalistic, too full of automobiles, too full of smog, too full of dust, too heartless, too intellectual, too scientific, insufficiently poetic, too lacking in manners, too mechanical, destructive of family, tribal and patriotic feeling.[2]

On the other side of the attitudinal fence, listen to Charles Abrams's ringing eulogy of the city:

From earliest history, the city has been linked with man's freedoms—a refuge in the days of Cain and Joshua, the hub of a vigorous political life in Greece, the impetus to law in Rome. When man's mind roamed free in Utopian dreams, it was the city that was so often closest to his conception of heaven—the "Celestial City," the "Heavenly City," the "New Jerusalem," the "Holy City," and the "City of God." Moreover, it was the city of trade, commerce, and property that helped undermine serfdom and that ushered in other freedoms in the process. . . . For despite its changes and challenges, the city still contains the raw ingredients of freedom. . . . It is still the marketplace for goods and ideas, the locus of a contractual society, the mirror for emulation, the meeting place for diversities, the center of culture.[3]

Perhaps the best examples of the ancient confrontation of antiurbanism and prourbanism are the remark made by the poet William Cowper, "God made the country, man made the town," and the spirited rejoiner of Oliver Wendell Holmes, "God made the cavern and man made the house!"

But the intellectual history of the city is not adequately depicted by the simple symmetry of pro and con. It is muddled and complex because of another dominant attitude toward the city, one of ambivalence, a mixture of attitudes reflecting a wide variety of personal, class, ethnic, and even regional differences. A Southerner, for example, might praise his own city but find New York a Sodom-on-the-Hudson.

This chapter seeks to sketch the shifting currents of thought toward the city, for what Americans *thought* was just as important as what they *did*. It is a topic vital to understanding not only the course of American urban history but also how that history reflects, at least in part, the Americans' response to their society as a whole, for the city in many ways concentrates and sharply delineates national characteristics.

Antiurbanism in all its blatant and subtle forms is the theme of the first essay in this chapter. It is concerned with the views of the most articulate and literate group of society, the philosophers, poets, and writers.

2. *The Intellectual versus the City* (Cambridge: Harvard and The M.I.T. Press, 1962), p. 222.
3. *Man's Struggle for Shelter in an Urbanizing World* (Cambridge: The M.I.T. Press, 1964), p. 10.

Morton and Lucia White argue that, with few exceptions, the intellectual has been the sharpest critic of the American city.[4] Mustering an imposing intellectual variety of some of the greatest figures in American thought, from Thomas Jefferson to John Dewey and Frank Lloyd Wright, they analyze the various patterns of urban hostility that distinguished Emerson from Thoreau, and Henry James and Henry Adams from earlier thinkers, such as Melville, Hawthorne, and Poe. The Whites conclude that although the intellectuals differed widely in their response to the city, they did share the basic disenchantment that the city subverted fundamental values prized by Americans throughout their history. The accumulated verdict, then, seems to be that the city was a failure, morally, esthetically, and physically.[5]

The Whites' essay suggest that historically the most dominant attitude toward the city was indeed antiurbanism. Perhaps it was. But the question is begged: were the attitudes of the intellectual community *typical* of the rest of society? The Whites feel they were. Yet they also suggest the intellectuals were alienated from the rest of their society. But alienated intellectuals can hardly be seen as being representative of a larger society that repels and in many ways rejects them. Thus some urban historians argue that antiurbanism has been so overstated that it has obscured other important attitudes, such as the affirmations of city-boosterism and the ambivalent attitude of both liking and distrusting the city.[6]

The next essay, in fact, points out that antiurbanism must share a place with other attitudes that make up the complex web of ideas about the city. In "Urbanism and American Democracy," Francis E. Rourke challenges the assumption of antiurbanism by showing that the city was more constructive than destructive in the unfolding of democracy. Whereas the other essay has emphasized the moral, esthetic, and physical accents of antiurban thought, Rourke, finding its origins in the Jeffersonian agrarian tradition, traces antiurbanism through American political history. He underscores an important aspect of urban thought: the skyscraper may have replaced the barn as the dominant symbol of the American landscape, but the power of agrarian thought continues through the decades of the twentieth century to our own

4. Their thesis is more fully developed in *The Intellectual versus the City: From Thomas Jefferson to Frank Lloyd Wright*.
5. See Robert Walker's excellent study, *The Poet and the Gilded Age* (Philadelphia: University of Pennsylvania Press, 1963). For an interesting account of how prose writers viewed New York City, see Eugene Arden, "The Evil City in American Fiction," *New York History* (July 1954).
6. Charles N. Glaab and A. Theodore Brown, A *History of Urban America* (New York: Macmillan, paperback edition, 1967), pp. 53–54. For a rejoinder to Glaab and Brown, see Jeffrey K. Hadden, Louis H. Masotti, and Calvin J. Larson (eds.), *Metropolis in Crisis* (Itasca, Ill.: F. E. Peacock Publishers, 1967), pp. 120–21.
For the enormous complexity of attitudes toward one city alone, see Bayrd Still's indispensable study of New York, *Mirror for Gotham* (New York: New York University Press, 1956) and his "The Personality of New York City," *New York Folklore Quarterly* (Summer 1958).

time.[7] He suggests that many Americans still feel today that the agrarian past nourished "the roots of Americanism." Some might insist that as far as urban problems are concerned, their solutions will be found not on the prairies but on the pavements.

At this point you might be tempted to tick off the virtues of the city, weigh them against the charges of the antiurbanists and try to determine your own position. You might say, however, that it is not that simple and there is more to it than that. And you would be right. Anselm Strauss in his engaging essay on the variety of American attitudes shows why.

Strauss's theme is ambivalence and ambiguity, and he develops the elaborate complexity of Americans' attitudes toward their cities. He sees the shifting images arising out of a number of clashes: the values of the city versus American values in general, regionalism versus nationalism, the old versus the new, specialization versus cosmopolitanism, and ruralism versus urbanism. If one city best attests to ambivalent, ambiguous attitudes filled with striking contradictions, it is New York. The paradoxical nature of these attitudes is fundamentally a reflection of the ambiguities and controversies about American values themselves. To add to the complexity, he demonstrates how the image of a particular city can be remarkably changed through growth and diversification. The heart of the matter is "the strain between ideal and reality, or ideal and presumed fact [which] runs like a brilliant thread through all our antithetical thinking about America and about our cities."

7. He may have overstated the agrarian dominance of the Ku Klux Klan and temperance movement. See Kenneth T. Jackson, *The Ku Klux Klan in the City, 1915–1930* (New York: Oxford, 1967), and James H. Timberlake, *Prohibition and the Progressive Movement: 1900–1920* (Cambridge: Harvard University Press, 1963).

The American Intellectual versus the American City

MORTON AND LUCIA WHITE

Although the city has become one of the most absorbing and most intensively studied social problems in America today, and although it is now fashionable for intellectuals to express an almost tender concern for its future, to hope that its decay can be arrested, and to offer plans for its revitalization, this has not always been the attitude of our greatest American thinkers. For a variety of reasons they have expressed different degrees of hostility toward urban life in America, hostility which may be partly responsible for a feeling on the part of today's city planner and urban reformer that he has no mythology or mystique on which he can rest or depend. We have no tradition of romantic attachment to the city in our highbrow literature, nothing that remotely resembles the Greek philosopher's attachment to the *polis* or the French writer's affection for Paris. And this fits very well with the frequently defended thesis that the American writer has been more than usually alienated from the society in which he lives, that he is typically in revolt against it. Throughout the nineteenth century our society was becoming more and more urbanized, but the literary tendency to denigrate the American city hardly declined in proportion. If anything, it increased in intensity.

Faced with this fact about the history of American thought, the contemporary student of the city can take one of two opposing attitudes. He, at his peril, can turn his back on the tradition of Jefferson, Emerson, Thoreau, Hawthorne, Melville, Poe, Henry Adams, Henry James, Louis Sullivan, Frank Lloyd Wright, and John Dewey. In this case he will treat some of the American city's profoundest critics as irresponsible literary men or as idle metaphysicians who fled the city rather than face its problems. Or he can regard this critical tradition as a repository of deep, though troubling, wisdom, one which raises basic questions for any urban reformer, and some of whose premonitions and fears have been more than justified by the passage of time. There is no doubt that the second is the wiser course. He who would improve the American city can only profit by an awareness of what some of our greatest minds have said, felt, and thought about one of the most conspicuous and most troubling features of our national life.

One cannot deny, of course, that there were pro-urban literary voices like Whitman's, or that there were urban sociologists like Robert Park who tried to speak up for the city. But they are voices in "the city wilderness," never comparing in volume with the anti-urban roar in the national literary pantheon. The urbanist must face the fact that the anti-urbanist does not live only in the Kentucky hills, in the Rockies, in the Ozarks, in the Cracker country, or the bayous. He lives in the mind and heart of America as conceived by the intellectual historian. The intellect, whose home is the city, according to some sociologists, has been the American city's sharpest critic. Everyone knows that Jefferson once hoped to discourage the development of the city in America, but he was only the first of a long and varied list of critics of the city.

Jefferson despised the manners and principles of the urban "mob" as he knew it in Europe and he hoped to keep it from crossing the Atlantic intact. He certainly did not think of the city as "The Hope of Democracy," as some Progressive theorists did at the turn of the twentieth century. He adopted a conciliatory tone about the city in his old age when he said in 1816 that we could not possibly depend on England for manufactures, as he had originally thought, and therefore we *needed* cities. But this does not show any *love* for the city. The country and its yeomen Jefferson loved all his life; in his old age he grudgingly accepted the manufacturing city as a necessity.

The same War of 1812 which led Jefferson to reassess his views was followed by a great expansion of the American city. It inaugurated a major phase of urban civilization between the Revolution and the Civil War. By 1860 the urban population was eleven times what it had been in 1820. The early decades of the nineteenth century saw the decline of Jefferson's empiricism among American intellectuals, and the emergence of philosophical transcendentalism, but a distaste for the city persisted among American writers.

The growth of the city in the North produced an even sharper reaction in Ralph Waldo Emerson than the European city had produced in Jefferson. Emerson's first philosophical work, *Nature*, appeared in 1836, in the middle of that interval which witnessed an eleven-fold increase in our urban population. Its very title was a protest against what he thought was happening. Partly under the influence of English romanticism, Emerson and some of his friends took to deprecating manufacture, art, and civilization, and so it was not long before they took to criticizing the city, the greatest of artifacts. The distaste for the city as an artificial creation was associated in Emerson's mind, as it was in the case of many romantic thinkers, with doubts about the value of science as an avenue to truth. And yet Emerson agreed with the scientifically minded Jefferson about the nasty manners and principles of the city. Whereas Jefferson was given to arguing the defects of the city in common-sense political terms, Emerson sought to buttress his feelings by a metaphysical theory. Hence we may label his period as the metaphysical period of anti-urbanism. To be is to be natural for Emerson. In the wilderness he said he found "something more dear and connate than in streets or villages." The life of the city was "artificial and curtailed"; it destroyed solitude, poetry, and philosophy.

One will find passages in which Emerson extolled the application of science and the virtues of civilization, the need for sociability to educate a man's sympathies, and the advantages of specialization that allow each man to develop his own talents. This suggests a more friendly view of the industrial urban society which was emerging in his own lifetime. But he always harped on the human failings of State Street and commercialism. At times Emerson could celebrate the artifice of pure technology, but he persistently attacked the debasement of moral standards by those who pursued nothing but wealth in the cities as he knew them. One is reminded of Thorstein Veblen's praise of urban industry even as he attacked its financial captains, for it was Veblen who saw the modern industrial city as the *locus classicus* of conspicuous waste.

Thoreau went even farther than Emerson in his distaste for civilization and the city, for Thoreau also attacked the village and the farm. *Walden* is a bible of anti-urbanism, in which Thoreau celebrates the life of the isolated individual, living in Nature and free of *all* social attachments. No wonder that Thoreau refused to visit the Saturday Club, which provided one of the few values of Boston in Emerson's eyes: intellectual conversation. And when Thoreau refused, Perry Miller reminds us, he put his refusal in no uncertain terms: "The only room in Boston which I visit with alacrity is the Gentlemen's Room at the Fitchburg Depot, where I wait for cars, sometimes for two hours, in order to get out of town."[1] No wonder Henry James said that Thoreau "was essentially a sylvan personage."[2]

If Jefferson attacked the city on political grounds, and if Emerson and Thoreau may be represented as criticizing it from the point of view of transcendental metaphysics, what shall we say of Poe, Hawthorne and Melville, all of whom may be added to our list of pre-Civil War critics of the city? They were far from political theorists or metaphysicians but all of them saw the city as the scene of sin and crime. Speaking of them, Harry Levin says: "For our dreamers, America was a garden, an agrarian Eden, which was losing its innocence by becoming citified. Melville had located his City of Woe in London or Liverpool; Poe had tracked down imaginary crimes in the streets of an imagined Paris; and Hawthorne had exposed sins most luridly among the ruins of Rome."[3] As in Jefferson's case, the urban models of extreme crime and sinfulness were not located in the United States by most of our pre-Civil War anti-urbanists, but they saw dark omens in the streets of American cities which made them fear that they might become like Paris, London, Liverpool or Rome.

The observant de Tocqueville expressed his worry about the American city in 1835, one year before Emerson's essay *Nature* appeared. He said that the fact that America as yet had no dominating metropolis was one of those circumstances which tended to maintain a democratic republic in the United States and to counteract that great danger to which all democracies are subject—the tyranny of the majority. But de Tocqueville thought that the "lower ranks" which inhabited Philadelphia (pop. 161,000) and New York (pop. 202,000) in the 1830's "constitute a rabble even more formidable than the populace of European towns. They consist of freed blacks . . . who are condemned by the laws and by public opinion to a hereditary state of misery and degradation. They also contain a multitude of Europeans who have been driven to the shore of the New World by their misfortunes or their misconduct; and they bring to the United States all our greatest vices, without any of those interests which counteract their baneful influence. As inhabitants of a country where they have no civil rights, they are ready to turn all the passions which agitate the community to their own advantage; thus, within the last few months, serious riots have broken out in Philadelphia and New York."[4] So seriously did de Tocqueville treat this matter that he said: "I look upon the size of certain American cities, and especially on the nature of their population, as a real danger which threatens the future security of the democratic republics of the New World; and I venture to predict that they will perish from this circumstance, unless the government succeeds in creating an armed force which, while it remains under the control of the majority of the nation, will be independent of the town population and able to repress its excesses."[5]

If this could be the conclusion of the most astute foreign observer ever to visit our shores, it is not surprising that some of our great literary figures might have developed less than an admiring view of our urban culture between the Revolution and the Civil War. Optimistic empiricists like Jefferson, optimistic transcendentalists like Emerson, pessimistic believers in original sin like Hawthorne and Melville, all forgot their philosophical differences when they looked upon the American city, even before it developed into the industrial jungle it was to become between the Civil War and the end of the nineteenth century.

Between 1860 and 1900 the urban population quadrupled while the rural population only doubled; and, what is more staggering and significant, between 1790 and 1890, while the total population of the country increased sixteen times, the urban population increased 139 times.[6] The great exodus from the countryside was in full force, and New England became the scene of deserted hill and village farms, while the city's problems became the great social problems of the nation. The city became the home of the elevated railroad, the trolley car, the cable car, the subway, the apartment house, the telephone, and the skyscraper, while it continued to en-

courage what one physician called "American nervousness."

Among the most influential and most fastidious observers of this development were Henry Adams and the younger Henry James. Both were men of literary genius, both were members of cultivated families with wealth in their backgrounds, and for both of them the American city provided a profound spiritual problem. Because Henry Adams and Henry James lived in the age of the city's supremacy, they did not speak of it, as Jefferson had, as a remote future phenomenon or as something existing in Europe alone. And, unlike Thoreau, they did not feel as though they had only the American city and the American wilderness to choose between. Adams and James were both refined, civilized, indeed urban men whose animadversions on the American city are made more significant precisely because they were not opposed to cities in principle. They demonstrate what a hard time the American city had at the hands of nineteenth-century intellectuals. For here at least were two *city* types who also found the American city sadly wanting. Their reaction to the American city is more esthetic, more literary, more psychological than that of their predecessors Jefferson and Emerson.

The two most important documents for an understanding of the views of Adams and James are the former's *Education* and the latter's *The American Scene*. It is significant that the great problem of the *Education of Henry Adams* was to steer a course between the poles of town and country, between the Boston and Quincy of his childhood. "Town," Adam tells us, "was restraint, law, unity. Country, only seven miles away, was liberty, diversity, outlawry, the endless delight of mere sense impressions given by nature for nothing, and breathed by boys without knowing it."[7] Adams also tells us that he spent his life trying to choose between the ways of life they represented, without ever making up his mind. And yet, in a sense, he did make up his mind, or the social forces of America made it up for him. He could not go back to the Quincy house of his grandfather Adams. And, being no Thoreau, he had to live in the American city if he was to live anywhere in America. But what was *the* American city in his mature years? Surely not Boston, but New York. And when Henry Adams looked at the New York of 1868, he tells us in a book which he wrote in 1905 that he felt swept aside by the forces pushing the country in a new direction. "His world," he lamented, "was dead. Not a Polish Jew fresh from Warsaw or Cracow—not a furtive Yaccob or Ysaac still reeking of the Ghetto, snarling a weird Yiddish to the officers of the customs—but had a keener instinct, and intenser energy, and a freer hand than he —American of Americans, with Heaven knew how many Puritans and Patriots behind him, and an education that had cost a civil war."[8] Adams felt like the dispossessed Indian and the buffalo in America after 1865, for it was a banker's, and neither a buffalo's nor a Bostonian's world. To Henry Adams, New York symbolized the spiritual confusion of America at the end of the nineteenth century.

Henry James, as one might expect, also complained about his birthplace, New York, after a period of flirtation with it. James attacked it most explicitly in *The American Scene,* published in 1907 as the report of an expatriate revisiting the country of his birth. He, too, spoke of the city's chaos, and even the New York skyline insulted his very ex-pressively complex sensibilities. He complained of the lack of history and of the lack of time for history in a way that reminds one of his early critical work on Nathaniel Hawthorne. The buildings, he said, "never speak to you, in the manner of the builded majesties of the world . . . towers, or temples, or fortresses or palaces with the authority of things of permanence or even of things of long duration."[9] History had given way to commerce: "The great city is projected into its future as practically, a huge continuous fifty-floored conspiracy against the very idea of the ancient graces."[10] The city lacked order, structure, dignity, history. James speaks of it as "a heaped industrial battlefield" and as a scene of "the universal will to move —to move, move, move, as an end in itself, an appetite at any price."[11] He missed what he called "organic social relations,"[12] and he felt some pleasurable relief when he visited Philadelphia, because it didn't "bristle," and because "it went back."[13] In this spirit he warned: "Let not the unwary . . . visit Ellis Island"[14] as Henry Adams might have warned in *his* snobbish way. James was upset by what he called "that loud primary stage of alienism which New York most offers to sight."[15] And he dreamed "of the luxury of some such close and sweet and *whole* national consciousness as that of the Switzer and the Scot."[16] His final head-shaking conclusion was "that there was no escape from the ubiquitous alien into the future or even into the present; there was no escape but into the past."[17]

Of course, one must not forget that Henry James was a cosmopolite, a lifelong inhabitant of cities, a man who is reputed to have dined out more than any resident of London in his day. One must be mindful of the fact that his novel *The*

Princess Casamassima represents an effort to penetrate the depths of London, as does his famous admiring essay on that city. But James viewed the *American* city in an entirely different way. After his harsh handling of the Boston reformers in *The Bostonians*, the American city did not provide him with any serious material for a full-length novel because he found neither the uptown nor the downtown of the American city sufficiently interesting, as F. O. Mathiessen has pointed out.[18] And even *The Princess Casamassima* shows a greater interest in the bizarre doings of weirdly inspired misfits and aristocrats, whose philanthropic concern with the slums James satirizes, than a sustained interest in the typical life of London. With characteristic delicacy and insight he saw the crushing, oppressive defects of the British metropolis of his day, but he could never bring himself to the same kind of sympathetic concern with the American metropolis that we find in Dreiser, Crane, or Norris.

Although we are primarily concerned with recording the theme of *anti*-urbanism in American writing and thinking, it would be absurd to argue that *every* great writer or thinker in the American pantheon was hostile to urban life. The fact is that at the end of the nineteenth century there emerged a tendency to view the American city in a more friendly manner. By contrast to his brother Henry, William James had very little desire to escape from the American city into the past. His philosophy was one of hope, of optimism, of possibility —indeed, a little bit too much so—and it was this that allowed him to view the urbanization of America in a way that might encourage Americans to do something about urban problems. Unlike Henry, he did not adore the great cities

of Western Europe. For ten days after his arrival in Florence in 1875 he "was so disgusted with the swarming and reeking blackness of the streets and the age of everything, that enjoyment took place under protest."[19] As for London, during his visit of 1889 he wrote his sister that he was "thoroughly sated" with it, and "never cared to see its yellow-brownness and stale spaciousness again."[20]

William James loved the country but his love of nature was tempered by a fondness for sociability, and therefore he was unable to subscribe either to Thoreau's primitivism or to the ultra-civilized sentiments of his brother. With Emerson he looked to the future, but unlike Emerson he did not think that the future excluded the possibility of a decent life in the cities of America. Many of William James's reactions to the buzzing confusion of New York of 1880 and 1900 had been unfavorable because of "the clangor, disorder and permanent earthquake conditions" which he experienced on his customary daylong visits. But in 1907 he spent a longer time there and as he says, "caught the pulse of the machine, took up the rhythm, and vibrated *mit*, and found it simply magnificent."[21] He spoke of it as an *"entirely* new New York, in soul as well as in body, from the old one, which looks like a village in retrospect. The courage, the heaven-scaling audacity of it all, and the *lightness* withal, as if there were nothing that was not easy, and the great pulses and bounds of progress, so many in directions all simultaneous that the coordination is indefinitely future, give a drumming background of life that I have never felt before. I'm sure that one *in* that movement, and at home, all other places would seem insipid."[22] This was written to his brother, of all people, after the appearance of the latter's *The American Scene,* but William had evidently read the manuscript, for he says: "I observe that your book—'The American Scene,'—dear H., is just out. I must get it and devour again the chapters relative to New York." William would not have liked them upon rereading them, and one can imagine how Henry must have winced when William exclaimed, "I'm surprised at you, Henry, not having been more enthusiastic, but perhaps the superbly powerful subway was not opened when you were there!"[23]

William James, like Walt Whitman, saw virtue and promise in the American city. Both William James and Whitman not only accept the city as an inescapable part of America, but they *enjoy* it, as Jefferson most certainly did not. The year of William James's discovery of what he called "the new New York" was 1907, when he delivered his most famous set of lectures, entitled *Pragmatism,* at Columbia. James thought his philosophy would mediate between the views of those whom he called "tenderfoot Bostonians" and those he labeled "Rocky Mountain toughs" in philosophy. It is not too fanciful to suppose that James identified the great future city, along with his pragmatic philosophy, as a blend of, a compromise between, the insipidity of Boston and the craggy brutality of the Rockies. A livable city on earth, one is tempted to say, is the social counterpart of James's pragmatism, and therefore he is one of the first great American writers to associate himself with the effort to accept what is good and to root out what is bad in the American city. He does not escape to the country with Emerson and Thoreau, or to the past with his brother and Henry Adams. He revives the wisdom of the older Jefferson after a century of trans-cendentalism, Brook-farming and expatriation, and adds to it a love of the city. In doing so he becomes the herald of a pragmatic phase in urban thinking.

But this pragmatic phase, in which the city was joyfully described by Frederic C. Howe in 1905 as "The Hope of Democracy," did not last very long. Indeed, Howe's book contained within itself the classical argument for the central city's impending destruction. "The open fields about the city are inviting occupancy," Howe said, "and there the homes of the future will surely be. The city proper will not remain the permanent home of the people. Population must be dispersed. The great cities of Australia are spread out into the suburbs in a splendid way. For miles about are broad roads, with small houses, gardens, and an opportunity for touch with the freer, sweeter life which the country offers."[24] Howe calls the city the hope of democracy, but he is, it would appear, a suburban booster rather than a city-lover. He shares the basic inability of greater American intellectuals to go all out in their admiration for the modern American city.

A more striking illustration of the same thing may be found in the writings of John Dewey, the disciple of William James, who sympathized with so much of James's interest in the American city. In his earlier writing Dewey expressed a typically progressive interest in the city. This was part of the political liberalism of the period, with its interest in urban planning, social work, socialism, the single tax, and muck-raking. The city was not regarded as a perfect form of life, but it was seen as having promise. And, to the extent to which it showed promise, it became the concern of all sorts of people who could criticize it in a constructive spirit quite different from that which dominated the work of militant anti-urbanists from Jefferson to Henry James. For a variety of reasons Chicago became the most conspicuous locale of this new way of looking at the city. It was the home of a great university, which had opened its doors in the 'nineties and which became a center of urban sociology and, it might be said, of urban philosophy. One can understand, therefore, why William James looked to Dewey and other Chicago intellectuals as his friends, and why they regarded him as their spiritual leader. For Chicago at the turn of the century was the home of James's pupil, Robert Park, his worshipper, Jane Addams, and his disciple, John Dewey.

As early as 1899 Dewey was urging that the congregation of men into cities was one of the most conspicuous features of the modern world and that no theory of education could possibly disregard the fact of urbanization. Indeed, *the* problem of education, as Dewey saw it in his *School and Society,* was how to adjust the child to life in the city. The earlier kind of rural environment, in which he had been raised as a boy in Vermont, had its virtues, he admitted. It encouraged habits of personal orderliness, industry, and responsibility; it led to a firsthand acquaintance with nature. But, Dewey said in 1899, "it was useless to bemoan the departure of the good old days . . . if we expect merely by bemoaning and by exhortation to bring them back."[25] The problem, as Dewey saw it, was that of retaining some advantages of the older mode of life while training the child to cope with the new urban world. The school, therefore, was to be a miniature urban community, a microcosmic duplication of macrocosmic Chicago, much as Hull House was in

Jane Addams' eyes. The essence of society, said Dewey—and in this he was joined by Robert Park and other sociologists—was communication—and therefore the school was to encourage and develop this peculiarly social phenomenon, this salient feature of the urban age. Dewey's progressivism in educational theory was defined by his broad conception of communication, his idea that it takes place while children are building blocks, dancing, and cooking, as well as on the more formal level of asserting propositions.

Soon, however, a new and more critical attitude toward the city began to enter Dewey's writing. In *The Public and Its Problems* (1927) he concluded that steam and electricity, the very forces that had created modern society, that had provided it with the means of transportation and communication that made urban concentration possible, were creating a situation in which communication at its most human level was being destroyed. The very forces which brought Bangkok and Chicago closer to each other and which brought people from isolated farms to urban centers had diminished the possibility of "face-to-face" relationships. The primary group, in the phrase of the sociologist, Charles Horton Cooley, was disappearing rapidly. And while Dewey did not use our current jargon, he said, in effect, that modern society was becoming a lonely crowd of organization men.

Dewey warned: "Unless local communal life can be restored, the public cannot adequately resolve its most urgent problem: to find and identify itself."[26] But the local communal unit of which Dewey spoke now was not the enormous city as it was coming to be known in the twentieth century. It was more like the University Elementary School at the University of Chicago, or Hull House. "Democracy must begin at home," Dewey said, "and its home is the neighborly community."[27] As a result, a curious reversal takes place in Dewey's thinking. Instead of taking the city as the model *for* the progressive school, he almost speaks as though the urban community should be modeled *on* the progressive school. Jefferson wrote at the end of his life: "As Cato concluded every speéch with the words, 'Carthago delenda est,' so do I every opinion with the injunction, 'Divide the counties into wards.'" At the end of his life Dewey seemed to conclude every speech with the words, "Divide the cities into settlement houses."

It is ironic to find the most influential philosopher of the urban age in America reverting to the localism of Jefferson, but no more ironic than the anti-urbanism of Louis Sullivan and Frank Lloyd Wright, our most distinctive architects. For functionalism, like pragmatism, is one of a complex of American ideas that could not exist in a nonurban society, and yet its greatest spokesmen seem to hate the American city. Sullivan's *Autobiography* records his distaste for Boston in his childhood, and in his *Kindergarten Chats* he fulminates against New York and Chicago. "Lieber Meister," as Wright called Sullivan, bequeathed this hostility to his disciple, and the disciple, as everyone knows, added his own powerful spice to the brew of anti-urbanism. John Dewey may have reverted to Jefferson's localism, but Wright was a little more partial to Emerson. Not only are there copious references to Emerson in Wright's books, but he adds as a red-printed appendix to *The Living City* a long excerpt from Emerson's essay, "Farming," which concludes with a typically transcendental warning: "Cities force growth and make men talkative and entertaining, but they make them artificial." And so the great American architect of the twentieth century went back spiritually to Concord, while the great American philosopher retreated to Monticello.

One moral of this tale is the city-loving urban reformers will not find much boosting or sentimental admiration of city life in the writings of those who have been canonized in our national literature and philosophy. A brief flurry of pro-urban sentiment in the late nineteenth and early twentieth century under the encouraging eye of Walt Whitman and William James was swiftly buried by the exploding megalopolis, but after it our most sensitive and gifted intellectuals went on criticizing the American city. Readers who may feel that this story is based on an excessively narrow selection of writers and thinkers should remember that other readers will find in these pages the names of our greatest political thinker, our greatest essayist, our greatest philosopher, our greatest theorist of education, our greatest novelist, our greatest autobiographer, and our greatest architect, all of them throwing up their hands about the most distinctive and most pressing features of our national life. If *their* views should not be typical of the nation's view on this topic, that in itself would be a fact that is worth recording and pondering. Moreover, it is impossible to produce a list of *pro*-urban American thinkers who remotely approach this collection in distinction and intellectual influence.

In spite of the anti-urbanism of our

literary and philosophical tradition, the city planner would make a grave mistake if he were to dismiss that tradition, if he were to treat it as a point of view from which nothing could be learned, if he were to forget it and disregard it. Those who must live in today's American city or who like to live in it can profit by taking seriously the urban criticism of our great writers, for it was deep and many-sided. It was not only esthetic but also moral in character. Henry James spoke most persuasively for those who saw the city as a scene of chaos as it presented itself to "the painter's eye." It lacked order, structure, history, and dignity in 1907, and God knows that these virtues have not been miraculously supplied in the age of urban sprawl and suburban slums. But the city, as Robert Park said, is a state of mind as well as an esthetic object, and the profoundest critics of the American city have found other faults with it.

When Jefferson warned of the dangers of what he called the city mob, when Emerson complained of the city's artificiality and conventionalism, when John Dewey lamented the decline of neighborliness, all of them thought of the city as a place in which certain basic human values were being subverted, values which are cherishable today as they were in the eighteenth century of Jefferson, the nineteenth century of Emerson, and the twentieth century of Dewey. And what are these values? Jefferson's worry about the mobs of the city arose from doubt about the American city's capacity to educate its inhabitants in a way that would preserve and extend the democratic process. And when Emerson worried about the growth of artificiality and conventionalism in the city, he was thinking, as

were his contemporaries, Kierkegaard and John Stuart Mill, about the increase in conformity, about the decline of individuality which was proportional to the increase of urbanization in America. Dewey's main concern was with the improvement of human communication within the city; and by communication he did not mean the exchange of information alone. He valued the capacity to share feelings and experiences, the capacity to discuss with, to learn from and intelligently persuade others, and to *live* with them in the profoundest sense.

Who can deny in 1960, then, that the great problem of the American city is to demonstrate at least three things: first, that it can solve the problem of education for the millions of people who are entering its gates, that it can absorb the Puerto Rican, as it has other immigrant groups, into the democratic process; second, that it can foster individuality, the capacity and the right of the human being to develop into a rounded personality who is concerned with more than merely commercial values; and third, that it can be more than a vast prison of unconnected cells in which people of different occupations, color, class, or creed fail to understand one another on the basic human issues of social life, let alone agree with one another.

The moral message of the intellectual critic of the city today is not fundamentally different from what it was in the age of Jefferson, Emerson, and Dewey. For today's serious thinker must also build upon a respect for the fundamental values of education, individuality, and easy communication among men. But, unlike his predecessors, he cannot deceive himself about the *place* in which those values must be realized to-day. The wilderness, the isolated farm, the plantation, the self-contained New England town, the detached neighborhood are things of the past. All the world's a city now and there is no escaping urbanization, not even in outer space.

NOTES

* The argument of this essay has been developed and documented more fully in Morton and Lucia White, *The Intellectual versus the City: From Thomas Jefferson to Frank Lloyd Wright* (Cambridge: Harvard University Press and The M.I.T. Press, 1962).

1. Perry Miller (editor), *Consciousness in Concord* (Boston, 1958), p. 46.
2. Henry James, *Hawthorne* (New York, 1880), p. 80.
3. Harry Levin, *The Power of Blackness* (New York, 1958), p. 234.
4. Alexis de Tocqueville, *Democracy in America* (New York, 1945), Vol. I, p. 289, note.
5. *Ibid.*
6. Arthur M. Schlesinger, *Paths to the Present* (New York, 1949), pp. 223-225.
7. Henry Adams, *The Education of Henry Adams* (Boston, 1918), pp. 7-8.
8. *Ibid.*, p. 238.
9. Henry James, *The American Scene* (reprint, New York, 1946), p. 77.
10. *Ibid.*, p. 92.
11. *Ibid.*, p. 84.
12. *Ibid.*, p. 279.
13. *Ibid.*, pp. 275, 280.
14. *Ibid.*, p. 85.
15. *Ibid.*, p. 86.
16. *Ibid.*
17. *Ibid.*, p. 115.
18. F. O. Mathiessen, *Introduction to The American Novels and Stories of Henry James* (New York, 1947), p. x.
19. Ralph Barton Perry, *The Thought and Character of William James* (Boston, 1935), Vol. I, p. 351.
20. *Ibid.*, p. 412.
21. Henry James (editor), *The Letters of William James* (Boston, 1920), Vol. II, p. 264.
22. *Ibid.*
23. *Ibid.*
24. Frederic C. Howe, *The City: The Hope of Democracy* (New York, 1905), p. 204.
25. John Dewey, *School and Society* (Chicago, 1899), p. 9.
26. Dewey, *The Public and Its Problems* (reprint edn., Chicago, 1946), p. 216.
27. *Ibid.*, p. 213.

Urbanism and American Democracy

FRANCIS E. ROURKE

"The United States," writes Richard Hofstadter in his *Age of Reform,* "was born in the country and has moved to the city. From the beginning its political values and ideas were of necessity shaped by country life." Few could disagree with this appraisal. At the time of the first census in 1790, more than nine out of ten Americans lived in rural territory, and as late as 1860 the proportion of the population living outside of cities remained well over 75 per cent. Thus, from the Revolution to the Civil War, agrarian dominance was a major fact of life in American politics. This was a time when rural ascendancy rested on the solid basis of numerical superiority rather than upon the legislative malapportionment and gerrymandering that have since served to shore up agrarian power against the steady erosion of population in rural areas.

What was most striking about this early system of domination by agrarian interests was the uncontested philosophical justification it received at the hands of Jefferson and those who followed in his wake. No such fervent ideological support was to crown the power of either of the other major groups who were in time to lay claim to supremacy in American politics—the business elite which came into prominence in the period following the Civil War, or the popular coalition which has sustained the broad outlines of the welfare state

since the presidency of Franklin Roosevelt. In the days of agrarian supremacy, political power and political ideology were linked together in a neat pattern of harmony, while since that time they have often been poles apart.

Easily the most familiar protagonist of this system of agrarian democracy was Thomas Jefferson. As Griswold points out: "No one believed so implicitly as he in a causal connection between the occupation of farming and the political system of democracy, and no one, before or since his time, has given that belief a greater impetus among his countrymen."[1] Of course the doctrine of agrarian superiority which Jefferson espoused—"those who labor in the earth are the chosen people of God" —is a very old theme in Western thought. It was widely prevalent in both Greek and Roman culture, from Hesiod to Horace, and this classical view was adopted and advanced in subsequent European literature, drawing on Christian as well as pagan sources to support the comparison it drew between the virtue and vitality of the countryside and the vices and decay of urban society.

Much of this pastoral tradition stresses the physical, economic, and moral advantages of agricultural life; but throughout it there also runs the persistent theme that farming makes for better citizens as well as healthier, no-

From *Ethics,* LXXIV (July 1964), pp. 255-68. Reprinted by permission of The University of Chicago Press.

bler, and more affluent men. Western intellectual history provided ample precedent for Jefferson's view that the farmer was not only the mainstay of the economy and the pillar of civil rectitude, but the backbone of the state as well: "The proportion which the aggregate of the other classes of citizens bears in any State to that of its husbandmen, is the proportion of its unsound to its healthy parts."

With the steady advance of urbanization in American society, the passages in Jefferson which retain the most telling impact today are those in which he takes specific note of what he considers to be the ill effects of cities upon the healthy functioning of a democratic society. For it was Jefferson who set the style for the treatment the city was to receive in subsequent political thought. Few statements in American political doctrine are as celebrated as his assertion that "the mobs of great cities add just so much to the support of pure government as sores do to the strength of the human body." But the view he put forward in a letter to Benjamin Rush was even more extreme. There he argued that a recent outbreak of yellow fever in coastal cities, however unfortunate its consequences in terms of human suffering, might at least have the advantage of discouraging the establishment of large urban centers in this country. For such cities, Jefferson declared, are more "pestilential" than yellow fever "to the morals, the health and the liberties of man."[2]

It has been suggested—most recently by Morton and Lucia White in their study of attitudes toward the city in American intellectual history—that Jefferson recanted these antiurban sentiments after he became president.[3] If

so, this retraction was a grudging one, based largely on Jefferson's belated recognition during the Napoleonic Wars that the political independence of this country might ultimately be lost if it remained completely dependent upon the industrial cities of Europe for manufactured goods. Nor was it a permanent conversion, since Jefferson returned to his agrarian outlook in the later years of his life. Certainly there is little in Jefferson's career to support the Whites' description of him as "a great intellectual defender" of the American city.

But it is interesting to note that for a time at least the harsh realities of international politics forced Jefferson to accept some measure of urbanization, even though he regarded this development as altogether undesirable for a democratic society from a purely domestic point of view. For the individual as opposed to the state, Jefferson never lost his conviction that the highest degree of political independence rested upon the economic security provided by ownership of a small farm. But as has often been true in American history, when the requirements of foreign policy required a modification of domestic political doctrine, this modification was quickly forthcoming. The needs of national security soon overcame even Jefferson's antipathy for cities. As he himself put it in a letter to DuPont: "What is practicable must often control what is pure theory."

Jefferson's views on the negative impact of urbanization were not disputed by any of the more influential of his contemporaries. James Madison, for example, faithfully echoed the same sentiment in his own writings. "The life of the husbandman is pre-eminently suited to the comfort and happiness of the individual," he wrote. "The extremes both of want and of waste have other abodes. 'Tis not the country that peoples either the Bridewells or the Bedlams. These mansions of wretchedness are tenanted from the distresses and vices of overgrown cities."

More surprising, perhaps, than the support Jefferson received from a fellow Virginian planter like Madison was the fact that there was no dissent from his adverse judgment regarding cities on the part of leading Federalists of the day. For in principle at least these Federalists were committed to a course of economic development, the encouragement of manufacturing and commerce, which would inevitably promote the growth of urban centers. Alexander Hamilton nowhere attempted to refute the Jeffersonian point of view, however much his "report on manufactures" may have contributed to urbanization, and John Adams affirmed his belief that "agriculture is the most essential interest of America."[4]

Later on, Federalists like Chancellor Kent were even to use Jefferson's attacks on cities to buttress their own aristocratic stand against eliminating suffrage restrictions. In New York, for example, the proposal to extend the franchise stirred prolonged and bitter controversy at the state constitutional convention in 1821, and on that occasion leading Federalist spokesmen sounded warnings against the city that were thoroughly Jeffersonian in tenor:

Elisha Williams, the young Van Buren's brilliant adversary in the courts of Columbia County and chief figure in the haughty Columbia Junto, explicitly dared the Democratic delegates to confront the reasoning of their great god Jefferson on the moral influence of cities. Would Jefferson's disciples spread "the contents of those [urban] sores through the whole political body" and so expose the yeoman interest to the will of "the ring streaked and speckled population of our large towns and cities, comprising people of every kindred and tongue?" "These cities," Williams warned, "are filled with men too rich, or too poor to fraternize with the yeomen of the country." With Kent, he placed the democratic menace in the city and the future.[5]

Not the least of the paradoxical aspects of Jefferson's impact on American politics is thus the fact that his prejudice against cities ultimately became a weapon in the hands of his bitterest political opponents.

THE JEFFERSONIAN HERITAGE

Since Jefferson's antiurban views were in accord with traditional political doctrine and were expressed at a time when the overwhelming majority of all Americans lived outside of cities, these sentiments certainly did not expose him to any substantial political risk. Quite to the contrary, Jefferson's agrarian posture may be said to have served him quite well from the point of view of political advantage. Much more remarkable was the way in which this Jeffersonian attitude was to persist down through American history even into the day when the great majority of Americans had come to live in an urban environment. While Jefferson's agrarian point of view was neither risky nor original, it proved to be an extraordinarily durable part of the American political tradition.

When the Jacksonian Democrats came to power, their political base rested on the support of the labor vote in the eastern cities as well as the farmers of the West. Antagonism toward the "money power" provided the bond of unity between these two divergent groups. And yet, Jefferson's dislike of cities continued to weave its spell over large sections of the Jacksonian movement, in part perhaps because the hated banking interests were themselves located in the cities. In his study of the Jackson era, Schlesinger points out that Jackson's followers were far from happy over the dependence of their party upon the votes it received in urban areas:

The situation in New York, where the country regularly voted Whig and the city Democratic, very much worried the *Democratic Review*, a fairly pious organ of Jeffersonianism. "As a general rule," the *Review* observed in some perplexity, we are free to confess that we prefer the suffrages of the country to those of the city. . . . The farmer is naturally a Democrat—the citizen may be so, but it is in spite of many obstacles.[6]

Other Jacksonian Democrats attempted to relieve their anxiety over the party's urban support by arguing that great cities need not necessarily be as "great sores" on the American body politic as Jefferson had originally believed.

In the decades immediately preceding the Civil War the Jeffersonian antagonism toward the city was clearly discernible in the arguments put forward by the southern apologists for slavery. This was one of the few occasions in which the proslavery argument had occasion to lean upon Jefferson's support, since Calhoun, Fitzhugh, and the other writers prominent in defense of the southern cause generally found it necessary to spend much of their time refuting Jeffersonian heresies, including the notion of the inherent equality of all mankind as expounded in the Declaration of Independence. But the defense of slavery was based in large measure on the proposition that the condition of the slave on a southern plantation was often a good deal better than the life

of the wage earner in northern and European cities. And in this connection southern criticism of the odious characteristics of industrial cities bore a close resemblance to Jefferson's strictures against an urban civilization. "Large cities," wrote George Fitzhugh, "are great curses, because they impoverish a world to enrich a neighborhood."[7]

Since the Civil War hostility toward the city has also found repeated expression in the various movements of political protest which have agitated rural America, from the Grangers in the 1870's to the Farmers' Holiday Association in more recent times. Much of this antiurban sentiment is implicit rather than explicit in the literature of agrarian revolt. It is reflected in the fulsome praise lavished upon the occupation of husbandry, in dogmatic assertions regarding the indispensable role which agriculture plays in the national economy, or in persistent tirades against banking and other urban commercial interests disliked by farmers. But it is praise of agriculture which is at the center of attention rather than overt attacks on the city.

William Jennings Bryan perhaps symbolized more strikingly than any other figure the spirit of agrarian protest in American politics, and Bryan's preference for the country over the city was never left in doubt. It received its most vivid expression in his Cross of Gold speech at the 1896 Democratic national convention: "The great cities rest upon our broad and fertile prairies," said Bryan in his fervent peroration. "Burn down your cities, and leave our farms, and your cities will spring up again as if by magic; but destroy our farms and the grass will grow in the streets of every city in the country." But as a presidential candidate bidding for support in urban as well as rural constituencies, Bryan could ill afford to reject the city altogether. In setting forth to begin the presidential campaign of 1896 in New York City, he spoke of his trip as one he was taking into the "enemy's country," but this was an area, he hastened to add, "we hope to be our country before this campaign is over."[8] Politicians like Bryan with ambitions which depended for their fulfilment upon urban as well as farm support were compelled to avoid the cruder kinds of assault upon the city in which a purely rural politician could indulge. Some of the lesser Populists were under no such inhibitions.

In its manifestations in the early part of this century, the antagonism toward cities was reinforced by two interdependent developments which exercised a major influence upon the course of American politics, the nativist movement and the drive for national prohibition. Early nativist sentiment was, as John Higham has shown in his *Strangers in the Land*, largely an urban rather than a rural phenomenon. The hostility toward immigrants was initially strongest in the areas where native Americans most frequently rubbed elbows with newcomers from other countries—in the great cities of the East. By the turn of the century, however, the antagonism toward the foreign-born had come to be centered in rural areas, where it blended with and helped to harden the historic agrarian prejudice against the city. The "foreign" character of American cities became one of their major liabilities in rural America—the region most aroused by the wave of nativist sentiment which swept the country in the years following World War I. Speaking of the role of the Ku Klux Klan during this period, Higham writes:

"Significantly, the Klan's home was not in the great cities. Its strength came chiefly from the towns, from the villages, and from the ordinarily tranquil countryside."

The prohibition movement was also predominantly rural in its origins, and like nativism served to sharpen hostility toward cities. The city saloon was in fact the bête noire of the temperance crusade, and the attack upon it was an effort at political as well as moral reform, since the saloon was regarded as the headquarters of, and the sustaining force behind, the system of boss rule in cities. "At the door of the saloon was laid the blame for political corruption. It was represented as the *sine qua non* of such political machines as Tammany Hall and the Cox Machine of Cincinnati, 'none of which could continue in existence for a day but for the liquor traffic.'"[9] The nativist movement likewise had the purification of city politics as a central goal in its efforts to restrict the influx of immigrants, since the support of the foreign-born was widely looked upon as a major prop upon which the power of the urban political machine rested.

The fusion between the traditional agrarian dislike of cities, nativism, and the prohibition movement came to white heat in the 1920's at both the Democratic national convention in 1924 and during the presidential campaign of 1928. In each case it was the presidential candidacy of Al Smith which triggered this reaction, since Smith was simultaneously a product of the Tammany political machine in New York City, a descendant of urban Catholic immigrants, and a "wet." It would be difficult to conceive of a less prepossessing set of qualifications from the standpoint of rural America, and the campaign against Smith became at times a crusade against the city and all that it had traditionally symbolized in American politics. Witness the viewpoint of even a liberal Republican like William Allen White: "I make no claim . . . that Smith is a Tammany plug-ugly. . . . But the Tammany system goes on to-day, as it went on 100 years ago, and, indeed, as it will go on in our American cities unless Governor Smith and the sinister forces behind him are overthrown. Tammany is indeed Tammany, and Smith is its Major Prophet."[10]

Walter Lippmann, himself a Smith supporter, explained the resistance to his candidate in these terms: "Quite apart even from the severe opposition of the prohibitionists, the objection to Tammany, the sectional objection to New York, there is an opposition to Smith which is as authentic, and, it seems to me, as poignant as his support. It is inspired by the feeling that the clamorous life of the city should not be acknowledged as the American ideal. . . . The cities exist, but they are still felt to be alien, and in this uncertainty as to what the cities might yield up, men turn to the old scenes from which the leaders they have always trusted have come."[11] And in the wake of Smith's defeat, interpretations of the 1928 election echoed the same theme. An editorial in one midwestern newspaper proclaimed that "America is not yet dominated by its great cities. Control of its destinies still remains in the smaller communities and rural regions, with their traditional conservatism and solid virtues. . . . Main Street is still the principal thoroughfare of the nation."[12]

While the agrarian prejudice against cities has thus been a continuous theme in American politics since pre-Revolutionary days, the precise nature of the danger which urbanism represents to the rural mind has varied considerably over time. During some periods it has been the propertied classes in cities—the merchants, the shippers, and the bankers—whose activities helped mold rural resentment of cities. On other occasions, and particularly in recent times, it has been the submerged proletariat which has been looked upon as the chief source of danger from urban areas—the industrial hirelings, the newly arrived immigrants, the trade union members, and, in today's metropolitan city, the non-white population.

At different times, the city has thus been regarded as a center of entrenched plutocracy and as a hotbed of radical doctrines subversive of the free-enterprise system, and it has been attacked with equal vehemence by opponents of both capitalism and socialism. Perhaps there is some reconciliation of this seeming contradiction in the fact that the farmer has, depending upon his economic circumstances, tended to regard himself both as a member of the "toiling masses" and as an entrepreneur, and these varying conceptions of the agricultural role in the economy are actually embodied in two distinct national farm organizations, the Farmer's Union and the Farm Bureau Federation.

The tendency of the city to become an odious symbol in the dialogue of American politics found its most eloquent expression in the work of Josiah Strong. Strong argued that American civilization in the closing years of the nineteenth century was confronted by a variety of perils, including immigration, Romanism, intemperance, and socialism. But it was the city which Strong identified as the focal point of all these evils. In the city, he contended, "the dangerous elements of our civilization are each multiplied and all concentered." With Strong as with other writers, the rejection of the city was—quite apart from considerations of religious and ethnic prejudice—a negative response to the industrialization which had spawned large urban centers. For it was industrialism which was regarded as the source of the worst features of urban life, especially the great extremes in wealth—"the rich are richer and the poor are poorer in the city than elsewhere"—which appeared to be so characteristic of an urban economy.[13]

THE IMPACT OF AGRARIAN THOUGHT

There is a sense in which the recurrent note of an antagonism toward the city in American political thought may be regarded as but another illustration of the lack of congruence between political doctrine and the actual course of political events. For even as the city was being treated with such persistent disdain in the formal literature of political philosophy during the nineteenth and early twentieth centuries, the general population was simultaneously voting with its feet for urban life—moving into the city in ever increasing numbers in response to economic and other incentives. The trend toward urbanization was certainly not reversed by the hostility shown the city in the American political tradition. Indeed much of this antagonism may rather be viewed as a peevish reaction against a development that could not be prevented.

And yet it cannot be assumed that the rural assault upon the city was altogether without practical effect. For while its influence cannot be precisely measured, the argument for agrarian superiority has certainly played a useful role in providing an ideological underpinning for the prevailing pattern of underrepresentation of the urban population that has characterized the legislative process in this country at both the state and national levels of government for better than half a century. The identification of farming with democracy may not have prevented the movement of population from rural areas, but it could and did provide rural politicians with a convenient line of defense against the impact this loss of population might otherwise have had upon their own power.

The extent of this urban underrepresentation has been underscored in numerous studies of state legislative apportionment in the United States. To be sure, this inequity has slowly been modified in recent years as a result of the exodus of population from city to suburb that has occurred since World War II. In many parts of the country today it is the suburbs rather than the cities which are most grossly discriminated against in terms of legislative apportionment. The movement of population thus tended to bring representation of urban centers in state legislatures into much closer accord with their proportionate share of the population even before the decision of the Supreme Court in *Baker* v. *Carr*, which provided cities with a judicial remedy against the traditional pattern of discrimination to which they have been subject. However, a statistical analysis of state legislative representation published in 1961 was still able to conclude that "as of 1960, the average value of the vote in the big city was less than half the average value of the vote in the open country, so far as electing members of the state legislature is concerned."[14]

In the debates which have taken

place across the country over the reapportionment problem, the Jeffersonian theme of urban inferiority has often been sounded by groups interested in preserving the disproportionate influence of rural areas in state legislatures. One of the oddities of this system of underrepresentation is the fact that it has very often been given impressive support by urban residents themselves. This was the case in Michigan in 1953, where urban as well as rural residents voted in favor of continuing a system of legislative apportionment highly disadvantageous to the cities. Of course the city is far from unified from a political point of view, and there are, in fact, important urban groups which have long had a vested interest in urban underrepresentation. Many of the salient economic interests centered in cities —business concerns and public utilities, for example, have strong grounds for preferring a system of legislative representation which discriminates against cities simply because the pressure for regulatory legislation adverse to their interests may reasonably be expected to originate in urban rather than rural constituencies. In many parts of the country these business interests have been as much the beneficiary of the prevailing practice of underrepresenting cities in state legislatures as the farmers themselves.

However, it is by no means inconceivable that there is an element of honest conviction as well as self-interest in the apparent willingness of urban dwellers to resign themselves to a system of legislative representation in which they are discriminated against politically. In some cases this tolerance may simply reflect the sentimental tie of many urban residents with the rural milieu in which they were raised and which they left in order to seek their fortune in the city. Hofstadter suggests that such an ambivalent orientation was characteristic of earlier periods of American history: "Throughout the nineteenth century hundreds upon hundreds of thousands of farm-born youths . . . sang the praises of agriculture but eschewed farming as a vocation and sought their careers in the towns and cities."[15]

The most confirmed of all supporters of agrarian dominance may thus be the city resident with ancestral roots in the country, just as some of the most ardent support today for the policy of preserving wilderness areas in their primitive simplicity may come from eastern urbanites, transplanted from their native habitat in the West to the alien pavements of New York. And in point of fact the agrarian vision of the city as an infamous creation has always received considerable support from the romantic fascination with nature that has been an enduring tradition in American life. The fact that the city has been so aesthetically unappealing to urban nature lovers has not been the least of the political disadvantages under which it has labored.

REFORMING THE CITY

At its root, the Jeffersonian point of view was characterized by a fundamental antipathy toward cities. If it had been possible, some of the more fervent agrarians would unquestionably have prevented the development of cities altogether, so destructive to democracy did they regard the city as a political force. And in point of fact a great deal of energy was actually expended on efforts to keep people on the farm, or to launch "back-to-the-farm" movements when periods of temporary urban distress gave such proposals hope of success. From Jefferson to Bryan, the note of overt hostility toward cities in agrarian thought is clear and unmistakable.

However, in the decades following the Civil War, a critique of the city began to emerge which was quite different in character from this Jeffersonian point of view. The source of this new criticism was the movement for urban reform which sprang up in the latter part of the nineteenth century and has remained a salient force in municipal politics down to the present time. As a group, the reformers were highly critical of the political development of cities as it was taking place in the Gilded Age. Indeed, if the movement had a text, it was Bryce's celebrated dictum in the *American Commonwealth* that the "government of cities is the one conspicuous failure of the United States." But the reformer's orientation was one of redemption rather than antagonism, the cities were to be saved, to be lifted up, and, hopefully, even to become showcases of American democracy.

The rise of the reform movement was in direct response to the widespread corruption and mismanagement which characterized municipal government in the post-Civil War period. All of Jefferson's worst forebodings regarding the evil effects which cities would eventually have upon American democracy seemed amply justified by the exposures of the Tweed Ring in New York and the other scandals which plagued municipal governments in the nineteenth and early part of the twentieth centuries. As a matter of fact it would have been much easier for Jefferson to obtain evidence to support his condemnation of cities in the decades following the Civil War than it was during his own

life time, when American cities were on the whole comparatively well governed.

The typical urban reformer did not, however, share Jefferson's pessimism regarding the city. From the reformer's point of view, there was no necessary reason why cities should have fallen to so low an estate. Frederic Howe, for example, saw cities as having great potential for improving American life. "Here life is full and eager," he wrote. "Here the industrial issues, that are fast becoming dominant in political life, will first be worked out. In the city democracy is organizing. It is becoming conscious of its powers. And as time goes on, these powers will be exercised to an increasing extent for the amelioration of those conditions that modern industrial life has created."[16] The reform creed was thus resolutely optimistic in its conviction that cities could be saved, and energetic in its pursuit of the means by which this salvation could be secured.

Within the reform movement there was widespread disagreement as to why cities had fallen upon such evil days. Some placed responsibility for municipal misgovernment upon the rapid growth of cities in the United States, and the great temptation to dishonesty that was generated by the need to develop a complex system of public works and services in urban areas within a very short space of time. Others traced the ills of urban life to the swelling tide of immigration from abroad in the decades following the Civil War and the ease with which the foreign-born population allowed itself to be exploited by corrupt political machines. And there was a strong tendency to explain the problems of cities as stemming from the failure to develop either forms of government suitable for urban areas, or a tradition of administrative expertise in the handling of municipal affairs.

But there was also a deep conviction that the corruption of urban politics reflected a very fundamental malaise in American life, the growth of a commercial spirit and a weakening in the moral fiber of the population that was endemic in society and the economy as well as government. "The boss is not a political, he is an American institution," wrote Lincoln Steffens, and this point of view was widely shared. What was needed from the reformer's perspective was a moral regeneration of American life—a "great awakening" which would cleanse and purify not only local but national politics as well, since the movement for urban reform was only part of a much larger reform effort directed at uplifting the tone of public life in every sector of the nation's business, including the practices of private institutions where they impinged on the public interest. Symbolic of this evangelical zeal for moral improvement was the fact that a number of Protestant clergymen associated themselves with the movement for municipal reform and took a prominent part in its activities. Like abolition before it, urban reform was a moral crusade.

Moreover, in its heyday, the boss system represented an effort to govern the city through the methods of politics alone. As a result, early efforts at reform tended to place almost exclusive emphasis upon the importance of competent administration to the successful functioning of city government. In reaction against the more discreditable features of machine politics, efforts were made to "depoliticize" city government and to augment the role of the impartial expert through civil service reform, the city manager plan, and other devices. Subject as it was to simultaneous influence by doctrines of moralism and scientific management, the movement for urban reform thus sought to make city government as clean as the church and as efficient as business.

At no time did reformers lose hope that substantial improvement could be effected in the government of American cities. A great deal of this optimism was based on their knowledge of the successful operation of European cities and their conviction that American municipalities could profitably be modeled after their European counterparts. *Century Magazine* stated its belief that "we can hope for no municipal reform which shall be radical and lasting till we change our leadership to the European models." "In a score of different directions," wrote Josiah Quincy while serving as mayor of Boston, "the interests of the average citizen are better and more fully cared for, his wants more fully met, in the great city of Europe than in that of America." While recognizing the difficulty of transplanting institutions from one country to another, Richard T. Ely nevertheless argued that "what is good for Berlin is likely to be good for New York, and what answers the needs of Paris will be likely to supply a want in Chicago."[17] But there was often some discomfort attached to unfavorable comparisons of American cities with Continental cities which were political subdivisions of regimes Americans looked upon as reactionary or despotic. English cities were, therefore, the object of more unqualified admiration.

Certainly there was no doubt in the reform mind regarding the urgency of doing something to elevate urban politics, lest the corrupt city eventually corrupt the nation. Elihu Root, for example, warned his Republican colleagues that the malodorous GOP organization in Philadelphia was a source of infection in their party that could not be localized. "It is my profound conviction," he declared, "that a determined effort is necessary to save national parties from the demoralization inevitably consequent upon municipal spoliation, and, as a Republican, zealous for the welfare and reputation of my party, I advocate the foundation of a non-partisan civil movement." Unless the reform of urban politics is successful, Josiah Strong asserted, "the boss will certainly rule the city when the city rules the nation," and Strong quoted Wendell Phillips as prophesying that "the time will come when our cities will strain our institutions as slavery never did."[18]

As noted earlier, the reform perspective differed sharply from the traditional agrarian outlook inasmuch as it sought to face and solve the problems presented by the city rather than turning away in a hostile rejection of the trend toward urbanization. But it should also be remembered that much of the reform argument for the city was essentially apologetic or defensive in tone. It was conceded that the city had fallen to a very low estate politically, and the claim was simply made that the spirit and practice of urban government could —with effort—be improved. Moreover, many of the reformers were gifted publicists, and their exposures of graft and corruption in urban government, while motivated by the desire to eliminate these conditions, had also the effect of reinforcing the rural image of the city as an iniquitous environment in which the ideals of American democracy were being betrayed. In essence the reform defense of cities was based on their potentialities, not their achievements.

URBANISM AND AMERICAN DEMOCRACY

Insofar as its political reputation is concerned, the city was thus only slightly better served by reformers sympathetic to it than it was by the agrarians who looked upon it as the invariable source of political corruption. And even today, the city has still to find its philosophical protagonist, at least in the area of political thought. This is true in spite of the fact that there is an impressive amount of evidence which points to the conclusion that it is with urban America that the flowering of democracy in this country can be most clearly identified. The place of the city in the American experience has in fact been much more honorific than its position in American thought.

From a historical perspective, Arthur Schlesinger points out that it was the cities of the East which led the way in the movement for national independence which culminated in the American revolution. "Throughout the decade of controversy the seaports set the pace of resistance, supplying most of the militant leaders, conducting turbulent demonstrations at every crisis, and mobilizing farmer support when possible." In a similar vein he underlies the prominent role played by the cities in the struggle to strengthen democracy once it had been established in this country: "The first great victory for freedom of press was won by a Philadelphia lawyer defending a New York editor. . . . Faced by interstate trade restrictions, stay laws and growing social turmoil, the urban business and creditor classes feared for their future welfare and the sanctity of property rights. The framing and ratification of the Constitution represented in considerable degree their triumph over the debtor groups and small farmers of the interior."[19]

Recent research in the general area of political behavior has also tended to refute the assumption that there is any necessary antipathy between the growth of cities and the vitality of the democratic process. In terms of some of the more obvious yardsticks that might be used to measure commitment to the norms of democracy, the urban citizen very often shows up much better than his rural counterpart. This is true, for example, with respect to two of the central attributes of democratic citizenship, an acceptance of the right of minorities to dissent from majority opinion, and an interest in the affairs of government as evidenced by participation in elections.

In a landmark study of civil liberties in the United States published in 1954, Samuel Stouffer found that rural residents were uniformly less tolerant of deviant minorities than urbanites. This rural attitude was partially explainable in terms of the operation of factors other than place of residence, especially the lower level of education which prevails in the countryside, but there nevertheless remained a residue of intolerance that was clearly associated with living in the country. As Stouffer put it:

Rural people in every region are less likely to be tolerant of non-conformists than city people, even when we compare urban and rural people with the same amount of schooling. There is something about life in a small community that makes it less hospitable to divergent opinions than is the case in our urban centers. In the anonymity of city life it is much easier for deviant behavior to flourish than in the goldfish bowl of a small community. In the large community there are sometimes so many goldfish that nobody bothers to look at them. In the small town a lone exotic specimen can be viewed with careful critical, and occasionally devastating attention.[20]

In support of his findings, Stouffer also cites earlier studies of the degree of tolerance which prevails in various sectors of the community, including a Gallup poll conducted in 1940 which showed rural residents as being much less willing than urban dwellers to see a Catholic elected President, and a Roper study in 1947 which revealed that urbanites were far more tolerant than their rural brethren of that most unpopular minority in recent times—members of the Communist party.

Of course the fact that city people generally exhibit so much more tolerance of nonconformity than rural residents must simultaneously be weighed against the fact that cities have been quite receptive to the appeal of totalitarian ideologies, or at least have been the areas from which Communist and Fascist political groups have traditionally recruited most of their active members in this country. If the greatest threat to civil liberties is judged to come from the small ideological groups dedicated to their destruction, then the city may well be looked upon as a greater source of peril to minority rights than the country. But if the chief danger to civil liberties is rather seen as a weakening of commitment on the part of the mass of citizens to their preservation, then it is from rural America that the right to dissent has been chiefly endangered in modern times.

As far as political participation is concerned, Robert E. Lane concluded after a comprehensive survey of the literature of political behavior that residents of large cities have a much better record in this respect than citizens living in rural areas. He finds that residents of larger cities "participate in elections more than those in smaller cities" and that inhabitants of smaller cities are "more likely to vote than residents of rural areas." According to Lane, this difference in turnout mainly reflects the heightened degree of political tension in the more densely populated parts of the country. The group conflict engendered by class and ethnic rivalries in urban centers has the effect of stimulating political activity. But a variety of other factors also plays a role here, including the greater exposure of the urban citizen to stimuli from the mass media, which helps to sharpen political awareness and a sense of civic obligation in cities.

The extent to which citizens participate in politics is also related to their sense of political efficacy—the degree to which they believe such activity will have meaningful results. In this respect also Lane finds that urban citizens show up much better than rural residents: "those living in metropolitan centers have, in general, a higher sense of political efficacy than those in rural or small town areas. Perhaps because of the greater politicalization of the urbanites, their exposure to more political news and comment, their more salient class and ethnic cleavages, and their higher educational level, they are led to make politics a more significant part of their lives."[21]

It has also been suggested that urbanization has promoted the development of a two-party system in the United States, thus invigorating political discussion and activity in all parts of the country. The growth of urban population is, for example, sometimes credited with the fact that presidential elections are now closely contested in virtually all the states. However, the actual impact of urbanization upon party competition in this country is far from clear. While some studies of state politics show a correlation between the extent of urbanization and the strength of party competition, other investigations indicate that there may well be a negative relationship between the two phenomena. Certainly, there is no disputing the fact that many of the big cities in this country have become one-party enclaves.

But if such empirical evidence as exists does not always support the conclusion that democracy is inevitably strengthened by the advent of urbanization, it certainly stands in flat contradiction to the conventional agrarian assumption that rural areas are necessarily the backbone of a democratic society. Whether this evidence will seriously undermine the Jeffersonian mystique remains, however, to be seen. The force of tradition being what it is, Americans may, in the future as in the past, continue to look for the meaning of their democratic experience in the prairies rather than on the pavements. This tendency is as pronounced in the twentieth as it was in the nineteenth century: "Somewhere in our agricultural past there lie the roots of Americanism. What we are in body and spirit is not to be discovered growing embryonically in any early city; its beginnings are to be found on the homestead or in the village, and only there."[22]

NOTES

* This study was undertaken under a grant from the Rockefeller Foundation, for which the author wishes to make grateful acknowledgment.
1. A. Whitney Griswold, *Farming and Democracy* (New York, 1948), p. 19. See also Richard Hofstadter, *The Age of Reform* (New York, 1960),

pp. 23-36, and Henry Nash Smith, *Virgin Land* (New York, 1959), pp. 138-50.

2. The quotations from Jefferson are from the *Writings of Thomas Jefferson* (Washington, D.C., 1903), II, 229-30, and X, 173.

3. Morton and Lucia White, *The Intellectual versus the City* (Cambridge, Mass., 1962), pp. 17-19.

4. Madison's comment is found in *The Writings of James Madison*, ed. Gaillard Hunt (New York, 1906), VI, 96-98, while the statement by Adams appears in *The Works of John Adams* (Boston, 1852), VII, 47.

5. See Marvin Meyers, *The Jacksonian Persuasion* (New York, 1960), p. 240.

6. Arthur M. Schlesinger, Jr., *The Age of Jackson* (Boston, 1946), p. 310, n. 11.

7. George Fitzhugh, *Sociology for the South* (Richmond, Va., 1854), p. 139. However, there were southern writers who recognized that their region was greatly weakened by its failure to develop the commercial civilization associated with cities (see H. R. Helper, *The Impending Crisis of the South* [1860], esp. pp. 331-59). And Fitzhugh himself explicitly rejected the Jeffersonian prejudice in favor of an exclusively agricultural society. "Farming is the recreation of great men, the proper pursuit of dull men," he stated. "Let the ambitious South cultivate, not spurn the mechanic arts" (*op. cit.*, pp. 156, 160).

8. See Paul W. Glad, *The Trumpet Soundeth* (Lincoln, Neb., 1960), p. 112. When the returns from the election of 1896 were in, they showed the core of Bryan's electoral strength as lying in the rural Midwest and mountain regions. However, there were some states, notably in New England, where Bryan received more support in urban than he did in rural areas (see William Diamond, "Urban and Rural Voting in 1896," *American Historical Review*, XLVI (January, 1941), 281-305.

9. Peter Odegard, *Pressure Politics: The Story of the Anti-Saloon League* (New York, 1928), p. 44.

10. As quoted in Edmund A. Moore, *A Catholic Runs for President* (New York, 1956), p. 133.

11. Walter Lippmann, *Men of Destiny* (New York, 1927), p. 8.

12. Quoted in Roy V. Peel and Thomas C. Donnelly, *The 1928 Campaign: An Analysis* (New York, 1931), p. 121.

13. See Josiah Strong, *Our Country* (New York, 1885), pp. 133, 130.

14. Paul T. David and Ralph Eisenberg, *Devaluation of the Urban and Suburban Vote* (Charlottesville, Va., 1961), p. 10.

15. Richard Hofstadter, *Age of Reform* (New York, 1960), pp. 31-32.

16. Frederick C. Howe, *The City: The Hope of Democracy* (New York, 1905), pp. 7-8.

17. "An Object Lesson in Municipal Government," *Century Magazine*, XXXIX (March, 1890), 792; Josiah Quincy, "The Development of American Cities," *Arena*, XVII (March, 1897), p. 529; and Richard T. Ely, "Model Towns," *Christian Union*, November 27, 1890.

18. See Robert Treat Paine, "The Elimination of National Party Designations from Municipal Ballots," in *Proceedings* of the Fifteenth Annual Meeting of the National Municipal League, 1909, p. 292; and Josiah Strong, *The Twentieth Century City* (New York, 1898), pp. 101-2.

19. Arthur M. Schlesinger, *Paths to the Present* (New York, 1949), pp. 213, 214, 215.

20. *Communism, Conformity, and Civil Liberties* (New York, 1955), p. 130.

21. Robert E. Lane, *Political Life* (Glencoe, Ill., 1959), pp. 265, 151-52.

22. Harry J. Carman and Rexford G. Tugwell, "The Significance of American Agricultural History," *Agricultural History*, XII (April, 1938), 100.

Some Varieties of American Urban Symbolism

ANSELM L. STRAUSS

Before we examine how particular populations have expressed themselves about American urbanization, it will be useful to scrutinize some persistent antitheses in American life. Those controversies—which amount to basic ambiguities of American values—involve the conflicts of sectionalism versus national centralization, of ruralism versus urbanism, of cosmopolitanism versus specialization, and of traditionalism versus modernism. Instead of discussing those antitheses and ambiguities abstractly, we shall relate them to the whole subject of American city symbolism. . . . By seeing first some of the larger issues of American valuation as they pertain to our cities, we shall better be able to understand the predominant urban symbolism of particular regions and populations.

A host of American cities, despite all differences in size, location, or composition, continually try to validate the claims that they are typical, authentic American communities. They balance what they are and what they feel they stand for against a tacitly accepted formula of American values and national purposes. But the facts and symbols of urban life become interchangeable in the course of argument, become confused in meeting the difficulties of expressing a city's hopes and achievements in a straightforward definitive fashion. They become confused, too,

because of certain ambiguities in what may be assumed to be *the* American way of life.

This ambiguity of American urbanity and American values is significantly reflected in a lively contention over which city best deserves the title of "most American." The admirers of Chicago, New York, Kansas City, and Detroit, at least, claim honors for the city of their choice. Such claims are not new. As far back at least at 1851, a Baltimorian reassured a local audience that Baltimore "may be said to be an epitome of the nation itself";[1] and upon occasion critics of certain American values may point to one of these cities as a repulsive exemplar of those values. But a uniform, homogeneous American culture spread evenly throughout the nation would allow no city to claim more Americanness than was possessed by other cities; nor could any then base its claim upon a different set of values.

As long ago as 1891, de Rousiers described Chicago as the most American city, remarking that "It is here, indeed, that the American 'go ahead,' the idea of always going forward . . . attains its maximum intensity."[2] Some fifty-five years later, John Gunther writes that Chicago's "impact is overwhelmingly that of the United States, and it gives above all the sense that America and the Middle West are beating upon it from all sides."[3] In other words, he is stressing less its "striving" than its central position. A thousand miles away, the admirers of New York City stress rather different values. They assert that New York represents the nation at its most civilized and most creative; that it dominates the nation in every way; and that more different kinds of Americans, drawn from more regions, live in New York than in any other metropolis.[4] The proponents of Kansas City dwell upon still different aspects of American culture; George S. Perry who described that city for the *Saturday Evening Post's* readers, saw it this way:

Kansas City is a kind of interior American crossroads and melting pot where the Southerner, the Northerner, the Easterner and the Westerner meet and become plain John American, with America unfolding . . . "in oceans of glory" in every direction. It got its start on the riches of Boston banks and Western lands and Northern furs. It is not only America's approximate geographical heart, but the center of gravity for her taste and emotion. The soap opera, movie or national magazine that doesn't "take" in Kansas City won't live long in the nation.[5]

Those who would give Detroit the honor of "most American," ignore the virtues of being of pioneer and dead-center America, and claim that Detroit best represents the spirit of modern twentieth-century America, exemplified in the city's superb system of mass production, in its drive, energy, purpose, and fusion of men and machines.[6] Pittsburgh's admirers claim similar industrial virtues for their city.[7] Indeed, a city need not even be among the largest to claim for itself, or to be proclaimed, the most typical of America. For instance:

It is a truism to say that Tulsa is the most American of American cities. All the forces that have gone into the making of a Republic have been intensified there. The successive stages through which the country as a whole has passed during three hundred years—Indian occupation, ranching, pioneering, industrial development . . . have been telescoped within the single lifetime of some of the older Tulsans. The result has been the quintessence of Americanism—its violence and strength, its buoyant optimism, its uncalculating generosity, its bumptious independence.[8]

The argument that one city best typifies America is couched in a standardized "logical" form: from a number of desirable attributes, certain ones are selected for emphasis while the remainder are ignored; and it is assumed or asserted that these selected attributes are possessed more abundantly by the admired city. In this way, many facets of American life are overlooked or given secondary status. The argument does not turn upon fact but upon value. Thus, if one values sheer quantity, then New York has most of everything; if one extolls the Midwest as the geographic heart of America and as the possessor of the most widespread and average national values, then he will deny priority to New York. In making such evaluations of their cities, Americans assess the nation's cultural assets and identify themselves with its history and destiny. When they represent a city as most American, they are conceiving it not only as unique and matchless but as the symbolic representative of esteemed national values.

Such great distinction can be claimed for few American cities; hence the citizens of the remaining urban centers must be content with a lesser assertion: namely, that their particular city represents at least one—and probably more—important aspects of American life. Thus, Iowa cities are conceived of as good places to live in because they appear to be friendly, peaceful, prosperous agricultural towns; and Fort Worth,

Texas, surrounded by cattlemen's country, epitomizes the culture of that region. Such cities are parts of many Americas. The country is vast, its aspects staggeringly varied. Cities need not compete to share the nation's glory, they have only to point to those of their features wherein they typify some aspect, or aspects, of the entire American way of life.

Yet these aspects are not entirely congruent, in fact or in value. One of the most persistent clashes of value on the American scene has long been embodied in the sentimental preference of a rural existence to a thoroughly urban one. When Jefferson spoke of the danger of an American metropolitanism fated perhaps to destroy the sturdy virtues of a predominantly agricultural society, he was but expressing a dichotomy in American thought that persists to this day. Despite the continuous trend toward urbanization, our rural heritage remains potent, entering into American thought and action in increasingly subtle ways.

Eighteenth-century seaboard agriculture was not what farming became on the prairie a century later, nor what it is today in an era of large-scale mechanization. The men who worked the American soil and the life-styles that they evolved have varied greatly in place and time. Yet an American mythology grew up by which it was maintained that agricultural pursuits necessarily bred a certain kind of man. This agrarian mythology is and was a complex set of beliefs consisting of many elements, some of which developed from the several kinds of frontier conditions and others of which evolved after the Civil War in opposition to the dreadful urban conditions. The spirit of

this agrarian ideology can be suggested by the following few sentences.

Rural life is slow and unhurried. Men lead natural, rich lives. People are friendly and their relationships are informal, yet orderly. The agricultural population is homogeneous in custom and culture, if not in racial stock. The round of existence is stable and the community is religious, moral, honest. Men are, thus, not motivated by purely individualistic impulses. If all farmers do not love one another, at least they understand each other and do not manipulate and exploit each other as do city dwellers. The very physical surroundings are healthy, home-like, restful, not dense with population. Not the least: the rural man is a sturdy democrat, his convictions nourished by his contact with nature itself and with the equalitarian discussion held around the crackerbarrel and in the meeting house.[9]

These conceptions are linked by affect rather than by logic. They evolved under considerably different historical circumstances, some during the development of the New England township, some when the prairie was settled, others while western farmers were castigating the railroad kings, and yet others at a time when rural migrants to cities became demoralized by conditions there. Although the country-city dichotomy has been with us for many generations, the content of the argument on either side has varied from decade to decade—as both cities and countrysides became transformed. Ideas die hard: in the formation of our rural mythology, old ideas accrued to new ones instead of disappearing entirely, despite their incongruence with fact and with each other. Probably no single rural community has ever stressed equally all elements of the entire ideological complex, for its very ambiguity allows its use as an effective resource. The town can use it as well as the village; and the small city can boast of home-like surroundings and friendly atmosphere, in an invidious contrast with the larger urban centers.

Sizeable cities can also be designated as outright embodiments of rural values—as when the citizens of Des Moines aver direct kinship with soil and farm; and in so doing, they may symbolically act in ways more farmlike than the equally business oriented farmer. The residents of most cities, perhaps, signify their association with sentimental rurality more obliquely, not always recognizing the nature of that feeling of kinship. Cities are referred to by their residents as "The City of Flowers," "The City of Trees," "The City of Homes." They draw upon the rich stock of rural imagery without directly stating their debt. Large cities as they grow to great size abandon such nicknames, which no longer seem to represent what the city has become, but may emphasize in curiously subtle ways that their styles of urban life also partake of America's revered earlier heritage. Chicago—once called "The City of Gardens"—still boasts that it is the city of the prairie, and lays claim to a characteristic friendliness and informality that mark it off from, say, New York or Boston. (As George Perry says, "Chicago is a thousand times more relaxed, less 'mannered' than New York.")[10]

Like the smaller towns, the larger cities may stress one or more of the varied rural themes, thereby cashing in on a much wider ideological complex. The very statement that one's city is a "city

of gardens" (albeit gardening is a far cry from farming), arouses connotations smacking of outdoor life, suggestions of qualities bred in close contact with the soil, of urbanities living a life of relaxation rather than of frantic pursuit of excessive monetary gain. The visitor to a city sometimes remarks, also, upon certain paradoxes because, while he notices that the place is marked only by a limited number of rural characteristics, he feels that these are among its important features. What he is really puzzling over is that all rural qualities are supposed to hang together; whereas in this particular city, surprisingly enough, they do not. The perception of such paradoxes is furthered by any obvious juxtaposition of rural and urban characteristics: a city nestled among beautiful mountains but marked by a high rate of crime and by horrendous slums, or a large urban center characterized by a noticeably leisured pace of life.[11] Thus about Portland, Oregon, Richard Neuberger remarks: "Torn between her peaceful past and a brawling future as the Pittsburgh of the West, Portland just can't make up her mind. . . . As a result of this strange ambivalence, Portland is a combination of the rustic and the metropolitan."[11] Similarly, Elsie Morrow writes of Springfield, Illinois, that, "At best, Springfield is a very typical American city, with a special flavor and pleasantness. At worst it is a town which has grown old without ever having grown up. It is something between a backward country settlement and a cosmopolis."[12]

The obverse of such pleasantly toned rural mythology, of course, is an affectively linked set of vices: cities are locales of demoralization, discomfort, standardization, artificiality, vulgar materialism, dishonesty, and so on through a richly invidious lexicon. But the rural-urban dichotomy allows black to be called white, and white, black. City dwellers have long characterized their cities as places of progress, opportunity, and excitement, the very image of civilization in contrast to countryside, small town, small city, in contrast, even, to those larger cities which appear provincial. Small cities and even villages have, in turn, affirmed that they participate in an urbane and urban civilization. Anyone who peruses popular urban histories will notice how very sensitive are their authors about the artistic, musical, and literary "culture" of their towns; they carefully list all "cultural" accomplishments and proclaim the progressiveness of their towns by example and assertion. A town which is not civilized, not progressive, not exciting would seem to have a narrow range of options; its citizens must balance its slight amount of urbanity with presumed rural virtues, or must assert disinterest in (un-American) urban characteristics; or, more subtly, must ignore their place in the backwash of American urbanization and remain content to be where they are.

Whatever else may be true of American cities, they are certainly a most varied lot, being neither all cosmopolitan nor all homespun. Nonetheless, particular cities become symbolized as embodiments of different facets of a cheerfully ambiguous rural-urban dichotomy. Thus, emerging styles of urban life receive relatively easy explanation or rationalization. It is as if people were to say: "We are a city like this because we grew up on the prairie, or because we are surrounded by farms, or because our main businesses were founded by farm boys, or because we have no great influx of alien peoples." Likewise, each different population within a single city can rationalize its differential mode of living by appealing to one mythology or another—or to elements of both. Moreover, a city seemingly fated by geographical position and history to be of a certain kind can be envisioned as another kind, and can be directed toward that image by strong interest groups which draw upon different sets of sustaining beliefs. Any city which unquestionably is undergoing change from a commercial to a manufacturing center, or from an agricultural town to a distributing mart, can likewise find ready interpretations to account for otherwise baffling changes in its social characteristics. All such explanations, whether vigorously contested or merely assumed, are answers to that important query: what is the meaning of this city, what kind of a place is it?

The rural-versus-urban conflict that marks American life is crosscut by another ambiguity which turns on a contrast between tradition and modernity. City adherents sometimes stress a lengthy history or a blessedly short one. Votaries of a city with a long history will tend to link its origins with those of the nation itself. Being old— the ideology runs—a long established city is less likely to be crude, vulgar, rough and ready; hence it will be more civilized, more civic-minded, more settled; its citizens will be more stable, have deeper personal and familial roots in the community; its population will be mostly native to it and its immigrants well assimilated; hence, fewer men will have been attracted there merely for opportunistic reasons. The older cities will have more cultivation of leisure, greater delicacy of human relations, and will pay more attention to matters which make for "taste" and "civilization."[13]

But the citizens of other American cities extoll the contrary virtues of youth and scant tradition. They regard their cities as relatively untrammeled by custom and convention. Just because their cities have not had time to settle down, they are supposed not to have developed rigid stances toward handling problems; they are therefore progressive and profoundly democratic, since men have fought their way to success there by their own honest efforts, benefiting neither from hereditary position nor from an elite upbringing. In these younger cities, it is believed that the lines between social classes have not yet grown into impermeable barriers; indeed, they may be denied to exist at all. A young city is conceived of as a place of freedom in still another sense. Its citizens have immigrated there of their own free will because they imagined it to be a place of considerable opportunity. Because the young community permits experimentation and the pursuit of opportunity, it is seen as an exciting place, at least more interesting than the stodgier older cities. Although the latter, by reason of their earlier origins, may perhaps rightfully claim superiority in the arts of civilization—so the argument runs—the more recently founded communities will soon overtake or surpass them; indeed the cosmopolitanism of the older cities may only, in some instances, be a form of decadence.

Ardent speakers for both younger and older cities stress only certain elements in the total available vocabularies; they glory now in a town's experimental at-titude, now in its famous traditional styles of cooking; they even combine the attributes of age and youth. Such symbolization occurs without strict regard for fact, since cities, as we have seen, may be represented as rather old when they are actually quite young, and cities of similar age may be conceived of in very different temporal terms.

Tradition and history are often given a peculiar reverse twist, so that certain eastern coastal cities are considered not to have important American qualities, while certain western centers are assigned crucial roles in the making of the nation. It is asserted or implied that there are histories and histories; but the basic history of the country concerns the clearing of the forests and settling of the frontier. The pioneer romance thus crowds out the colonial. Any city whose citizens did not participate in the pushing back of the frontier cannot, therefore, possibly possess the mystical qualities stemming from that glorious enterprise.

But the frontier is a series of conceptions, not merely a set of facts. These conceptions are linked with various rural and urban virtues, with different periods of our history, and with particular American regions as well. In those sections of the country where the frontier as a geographic reality has but recently disappeared, the frontier as a concept refers more to the mining camp and the railroad center than to pioneer agricultural settlements. The frontier was a rough and tough place, where men were men and the hardiest won out. Some of the same associations remain coupled in midwestern remembrances because of the region's boom-town tradition and because of the predominant romance of life on the open prairie. The Midwest is more than the geographic heart of the continent; many believe it to be at the core of what *is* America. Back east, the concept of the frontier has been sufficiently misted over by time so that it is referred to more obliquely ("the founders," "the settlers"), but these terms also carry a considerable charge of regional passion.

The frontier, as an idea, has also broken loose from any regional anchoring; it can be applied to endeavors in industrial, artistic, intellectual, and other non-geographic fields. Consequently, cities building upon the cumulative connotations of the frontier image can be thought of as commercial and industrial pioneers. A great metropolis like New York can strike its admirers as *the* "moving frontier" of the entire American economy and of the nation's civilization. The frontier concept allows some cities to be called currently progressive and others to be linked with the nation's slightly older history; while it may be used with relation to some cities so that it cuts both ways. An example is John Bowman's address to his fellow citizens of the Pittsburgh Chamber of Commerce, in which he reminded them of the city's great pioneer tradition:

But these qualities in men and women, you say, flared up generally among the pioneers of the time. . . . These qualities, however, did not flare up and stay flared up in any other community for so long a period nor did they reach so intense a glow as they did in Pittsburgh.

He goes on to claim that, "The significant fact now is that Pittsburgh through nearly a hundred years developed a new way of thinking, a new way of acting. These new ways became first

nature in the people." And then, by simple transmutation, he views these ways as creative acts, and Pittsburgh's creativeness "was the application of creative ability to industry." This was its great contribution to Pittsburgh. And of course, "the old creativeness, developed here through a long period, is still in Pittsburgh."[14]

But when a city settles down, this turn of events is likely to be greeted by criticism—criticism mixed, however, with expressions of nostalgia and joy over the community's improvements. The citizens may perceive that certain civic characteristics derive from the original pioneer spirit which founded and built the town, however astonished the original settlers might be if they could witness the town's transformation.[15]

When residents identify a city with different rural or urban conceptions and with different kinds of romantic histories, they may also identify it with reference to another persistent American dichotomy: regionalism versus national integration. Since our cities are so widely scattered on such different landscapes, it is difficult not to associate a city with its region. Its domestic architecture, the clothing, speech, and action of some of its residents all proclaim it— and the people themselves sometimes proclaim it with belligerence. As is usual with cultural antinomies, men find ample room for ambiguity and for subtle argument. Two cities of the same region may vie for regional supremacy on symbolic as well as economic grounds. Each will claim to represent the region better; each will stress somewhat different areal attributes. Since no region is entirely homogeneous—if only because of its competing urban centers

—there is plenty of room for dispute. In a rapidly changing region, such as the "New South," there may be even less agreement unless the resources of ambiguity are utilized in a way such that one city claims to represent the Old South, while the other is quite content to represent the New South (although a city like Charleston can claim to represent both).[16] A region is usually not exactly coterminous with a state; therefore, a city such as Biloxi, Mississippi, can affirm kinship with New Orleans and with bayou culture rather than with the rest of Mississippi.

Some cities, by virtue of the populations which founded them or immigrated to them later, are considered to be less typical of their regions than are their neighbors; these may compensate by claiming other important American values. Conversely, however, a city may receive great waves of foreign immigrants without serious impairment to its position as a regional standard bearer. A few cities are so new that they and their residents share little in common with the rest of the region, in history or in taste, and so are constrained to build some sort of urban history, however flimsy, or to engage in other ceremonial gestures to reaffirm their association with their region. An interesting case is Kingsport, Tennessee, a small city planned and founded by eastern bankers who were attracted to the site by abundant, cheap white labor. Kingsport's historian, writing when the city was only eleven years old, nevertheless argues that had the village but known it, it "was sleeping only that it might awake into a beautiful prosperous city" for "the moral and mental fibre of the sturdy, resourceful people of the Kingsport community required two cen-

turies in the making." While it "is true that the new city was incorporated and began its municipal life only eleven years ago . . . back of all this, unknown to many of the citizens themselves perhaps, is a setting which would be a pride to any of the oldest cities in the country."[17]

A few urban centers gladly spurn extensive regional affiliation. Their residents prefer to think of them as supra-national, even as "world cities," underline the city's role in the national economy, and flaunt its traits of national leadership, sophistication, cosmopolitanism, size, and other symbols of national and international placement. Some sense of the overwhelming impact of a world city is suggested by the breathless and inadequate ways its admirers attempt to sum it up. Thus, John Gunther, who first compares Chicago (the typical American city) with New York (the world city), writes that Chicago is "the greatest and most typically American of all cities. New York is bigger and more spectacular and can outmatch it in other superlatives, but it is a 'world' city, more European in some respects than American." Some pages later he writes that

now we come to New York City, the incomparable, the brilliant star city of cities, the forty-ninth state, a law unto itself, the Cyclopean paradox, the inferno with no out-of-bounds, the supreme expression of both the miseries and the splendors of contemporary civilization. . . . New York is at once the climactic synthesis of America, and yet the negation of America in that it has so many characteristics called un-American.[18]

Paul Crowell and A. H. Raskin merely say: "New York is not a city. It is a thousand cities, each with its own ninety-nine square miles."[19]

Many citizens of "world cities" make denigrating gestures toward more regionally inclined centers. They refer to those centers as less important, small-townish, hick towns, cow towns, and use other similar epithets. Consequently, these latter places may regard the more worldly centers with a suspicion that gains strength from the historic antagonism between countryside and city as well as from a regional passion against national centralization. However, no single city claims to be a national, or world, city in exactly the same way as any other does; and always regional traits are coupled with non-regional ones (even by residents of New York City).

Sectionalism is closely allied with economic specialization inasmuch as the various continental areas function differently in our national economy. Cities tend to become known for the industries, commercial enterprises, and services that are typical of the surrounding area. National cities, of course, have more varied functions; hence when New York City residents insist that it has "everything," this means more than that it performs all the important economic functions. The full significance of the claim is that all (the best—and possibly the worst) styles of life can be found in New York. But the Florida resort city, the Illinois farm city, or the New England manufacturing town can all be conceived of by their residents as simultaneously truly regional and truly American because what they manufacture or trade or service is necessary to the nation.

Some products or services which are limited to certain cities are of sufficient national importance that those cities come to represent some particular facet of America: Pittsburgh and Detroit come readily to mind. Although not all specializations are equally praiseworthy, or even savory, nevertheless observers of such cities as Reno and Calumet City can find ample justification for believing that sex, sin, and gambling are as much a part of American life as are automobiles or opera; and Pittsburgh residents could, until recently, declare that smoke-filled air and labor troubles were the inevitable accompaniment of heavy industrialization. As George S. Perry has phrased it:

Certainly Reno is an actual and highly special aspect of American life, as much as Monte Carlo is a part of European life. . . . Many Nevadans . . . referring both to the tourist business brought in and the large amount of tax load that gambling pays . . . remark simply: "You don't shoot Santa Claus." . . . For in the American mind, Reno remains to gambling and divorces what Pittsburgh means to steel and Hollywood to movies.[20]

Cities whose range of economic function is exceedingly narrow seem frequently to lack variety of social style and suffer from deficiencies in "culture" and other civic virtues esteemed in most towns. Hence residents from other cities may make them the butts of jibes and the objects of social criticism. In the main, the outsider misses the mark for, like physicians whose identities have grown up around the practice of specific medical skills or about the "ownership" of specific bodily areas, the specialized city tends to glorify its command over special skills and resources. Two spokesmen for a pair of our most specialized cities link special skills with the spirit of America. The first is Malcolm Bingay, writing in *Detroit Is My Home Town*:

This fluidity of life, this refusal to "jell" or ever to grow old helps to explain why everything that is right or wrong which happens to our nation seems to break here first. It is that very spirit which first conceived the idea of throwing away millions upon millions of dollars of machinery as obsolete to make way for better machinery and greater speed to meet competition. This horror of obsolescence is the "Americanism" which permitted us to triumph in two great wars. . . . Other countries remained static in the sense that while they understood our standardization of parts—to a degree—they never did catch the imponderable elements of mass production in which there is nothing permanent but change.[21]

The second spokesman is Carl Crow, who, in *The City of Flint*, writes:

The history of the interesting and dynamic city of Flint has been worth recording because it is more than the chronical of an individual city. It epitomizes the history of America . . . America is a story of the industrial development which has brought us such a high standard of living.[22]

Citizens who are intensely interested in the furtherance of the arts congregate in groups and associations that many other citizens believe are less central to the life of the community than other more vigorous business, social, and cultural institutions representing the interests of the town's more typical citizens. Sometimes cultural barrenness is excused in terms of the city's symbolic age. Given sufficient time, some say, the city will grow up, develop a rich cultural life, and take its place among the civilized cities of its size—and, one might add, among some cities a tithe of its size. The residents of Chicago sometimes use this strategy to console themselves or to ward off attack, and it is probably commonly used in other cities. Here is an instance from Birmingham, Alabama:

Birmingham somehow, for all her pride in the great labors which converted a cornfield into a great metropolis in little more than the span of one man's life, Birmingham is haunted by a sense of promise unfulfilled. Her more philosophic citizens are obsessed with this thought. They brood and ponder over it, and, searching their souls and the city's history, constantly seek the reason why. They come up with many answers. One is the obvious one of her youth. . . . Another answer is . . . Birmingham is a working town. . . . Painting pictures and composing music and writing books—even the widespread appreciation of those things—all rather come with time.[23]

When a specialized city becomes economically diversified, and creates or draws to it new populations with new tastes, the imagery associated with it changes radically. It remains no longer merely a steel city, a rubber town, or an agricultural community, but is represented widely as a more cosmopolitan center.

Although every city within the United States is American in a factual sense, some cities are in some other sense denied that status from time to time. Many visitors to the Southwest would agree with John Gunther that there one may feel almost as if he is leaving the United States. ("The first thing I thought was, 'Can this possibly be North America?'")[24] But that reaction is not aroused solely by regional geography or by ethnic culture, for cities may be symbolically driven off the American landscape when they offend deeply felt standards of propriety. One critic of Pittsburgh some years ago bitterly characterized it as "A city inherited from the Middle Ages," and only partly admitted that it was one of us.[25] Reno is frequently a target for obloquy: a *Reader's Digest* article titled "Reno. Parasite on Human Weakness" is representative; its author, true to his title, could not admit that Reno is genuinely American.[26] Even Los Angeles, although it shares national char-

acteristics conspicuously enough, seems
to strike many people as odd or crazy;
and, "according to its most severe critics, it is New York in purple shorts with
its brains knocked out." The phrase is
George S. Perry's; in less fanciful prose
he sums up very well the partial denial
of status to that large city when he adds
that its "civilization has been declared
to caricature, in one way or another,
that of the entire nation."[27]

The residents of certain other cities
sometimes display sensitivity to the
ways in which their cities deviate from
what they or outside critics conceive to
be the normal national or regional urban patterns. Cincinnati has never quite
recovered from Mrs. Trollope's visit nor
from its reputation as a tradition-bound
town located within a progressive, dynamic region.[28] When a city begins its
history with a great promise but then
suffers relative oblivion, it departs sufficiently from the usual regional expectations to require a set of supporting
rationalizations. Thus a loyal resident
of Marietta, Ohio, in 1903 mournfully
took stock of a century that had passed
without much progress for his town. He
remarked that

a city may open the way for progress, and
still not progress itself. . . . Evidently
other cities . . . have excelled her [Mari-
etta] in so many ways. . . . But at the beginning of the new century she stands
young, strong, and vigorous, no longer old,
except in name, with an ambition of youth
and wealth of resource. . . . While it has
thus taken a century of experience during
which time she seems to move forward so
slowly, it is well to consider that these years
were spent in laying a firm and substantial
foundation whereon to build the New
Marietta.[29]

In another passage, we can watch a citizen of Vincennes, Indiana, trying to
puzzle out why prophesies about cities

sometimes fail to materialize. Commenting on Vincennes' bustling future
after "a sort of Rip Van Winkle sleep,"
he wrote:

This bright prospect although long delayed
might have been expected from the opinions of the place and its natural advantages
expressed by the missionary fathers who
first visited it. . . . These men were far
seeing and almost with prophetic vision
foretold the future of various places they
visited. . . . In no instance have their
prophetic utterances failed of fruition unless it shall be in the solitary instance of
Vincennes.

In urging his contemporaries on to
greater civic harmony and energy, he
added, "They made the same prophetic
utterances with reference to Pittsburgh,
Cincinnati, Louisville, Detroit, Chicago,
St. Paul, St. Louis, San Francisco and
many other cities. . . . And why should
not their opinions with regard to Vincennes not be realized?"

The residents of most cities can escape feelings of non-typicality simply
by stressing other sets of American
traits, but when cities develop in astonishingly new ways, their citizens
must claim, as I have already suggested,
that clearly sanctioned American qualities (rurality, urbanity, sectionality)
are actually present or exist in new,
somewhat disguised forms.

Most curious of all is the case of New
York, a city which has been passionately
and repeatedly denied essential American status while its admirers have proclaimed it the greatest city in America.
It is one thing to feel that this great
metropolis is not the most typical of our
cities, that from it foreigners receive a
skewed and partial picture of the nation; but it is another matter to believe
that New York as partly or wholly not
American, or even "un-American." The
grounds of attack and defense bring to

sharp focus the ambiguity and clash of American values.[31]

In 1894 Theodore Roosevelt published an article titled, "What 'Americanism' Means" in which he argued:

There are two or three sides to the question of Americanism, and two or three senses in which the word "Americanism" can be used to express the antithesis of what is unwholesome and undesirable. In the first place we wish to be broadly American and national, as opposed to being local or sectional.[32]

In the second place, he reports, it is unwholesome for an American to become Europeanized, thus too cosmopolitan; and in the third place, the meaning pertains to those foreign immigrants who do not become quickly Americanized. These antitheses, which run through the arguments for and against New York City, can be found in another article titled "Is New York More Civilized Than Kansas?" which follows almost immediately after Roosevelt's in the same journal.[33] Kansas is defined as the more civilized (that is, as the more American) on a score of grounds, which include its homogeneity of ideal and tradition, its native population, its home life, its lack of class distinction, its religious and moral tone, and its optimal conditions for rearing children. New York is declared not to possess most of these qualities. The author even argues that Kansas is less isolated, in the civilizational as well as the geographic sense, because its greater number of railroads keep it in more intimate contact with all sections of the nation.

Through the years, New York has been accused of being too European, too suspiciously cosmopolitan, too aggressive and materialistic, too hurried and hectic, a city where family life and home life do not flourish but where—

it is asserted or suspected—iniquity does. New York seems to sum up all the negative balances in the rural animus against cities, in the sectional argument against centralization and cosmopolitanism, and in the frontier bias against cities which do not share the mystic pioneer experience. No other American city is the target of such great or complete antagonism.

New York's admirers, whether they are native to the city or not, counter these arguments in two ways. They can maintain that the city is not actually deficient in these various regards. For instance, the *New York Times Magazine* makes its business the occasional publication of articles about the city which tacitly or explicitly set out to prove that New York really is a friendly place having unsuspected village-like qualities, a quiet home life, plus bits of rurality and even farming tucked away here and there. They also try to show that the large numbers of immigrants and their children, are at least as American as citizens with longer native genealogies. When New Yorkers write about themselves or about their city, their affirmation of urban identity often takes that form. (Al Smith once wrote an article titled "I Have Seven Million Neighbors.")[34]

Side by side with the outright accusation that New York fails to participate in our wholesome, rural, or village heritage runs the assertion that New York is actually our most representative city because it is our greatest. "Greatness" can be attributed on quite different grounds, for each assertion rests upon certain features of American culture judged to be of the highest importance. New York is our last frontier, the place where persons of spirit are drawn as by a magnet. It is the "moving frontier" of American culture, the most important site of progress and innovation. It is the image of America, for here the melting pot is at its most intense and here the New America—racially or culturally—is being forged rather than in the most homogeneous native American centers. Although the same theme of the urban melting pot as the epitome of American civilization is applied to other ethnically diverse cities,[35] New York is a place where all narrow local sectionalism has disappeared: because it is a great world city, as is twentieth-century America—is not this the American century! Even those who hate New York may have to admit New York's typicality on the grounds that if this is the America of today, then New York certainly best represents it. Here, for instance, is Earl Sparling's anguished summation, complete with reference to the pioneer past:

I find it an appalling place, rich for making money, poor for living. . . . But all of that is one thing. It is a different thing to shrug the whole spectacle away as something completely alien and not American. America cannot be absolved that easily. Not only is New York American, but it is the mirror in which America, after half a century of confusion, suddenly sees herself for what she is. . . . New York is the soul of America. And Americans . . . see it . . . and wonder how all this happened in a free, pioneer land.[36]

Is it any wonder that there is so much ambiguity in the symbolization of this metropolis, this New York which "is at once the climactic synthesis of America, and yet the negation of America in that it has so many characteristics called un-American?"[37] The attitude—and the bewilderment—of many Americans can be summed up in the reactions of a girl from the Midwest who, visiting New York for the first time, exclaimed that it was "just a wonderfully exciting place but so unreal; it doesn't even have trees." It is summed up also in a magnificently paradoxical set of sentences written by the editors of *Fortune* magazine, as they struggled to relate New York City to the national culture:

New York may be taken as a symbol, or it may be taken as a fact. As a symbol it is a symbol of America; its noisy, exuberant, incalculable towers rise out of the water like a man's aspirations to freedom. As a symbol it is the Gateway, the promise, the materialization of the New World. . . . But taken as a fact, New York is less Dantesque. To most Americans the fact is that "New York is not America." It is un-American in lots of ways. The concentration of power that exists among those spires is itself un-American; so are the tumultuous, vowel-twisting inhabitants who throng the sidewalks.[38]

The confusion continues. Two pages later, when the editors eloquently discuss the city's role as a great melting pot, they wrote, "In that sense New York *is* America," only to blunt the force of that assertion with "more than symbolically."

The strain between ideal and reality, or ideal and presumed fact, runs like a brilliant thread through all our antithetical thinking about America and about our cities. With a fine flair for significant ambiguities, the *Saturday Evening Post* included among more than 145 cities which it surveyed after World War II an article about "a little cow town." Its author asserted that "*The Saturday Evening Post* is running a notable series of articles about American cities. All this is well enough, but . . . if we have any truly national culture, it stems from the small town and near-by farm."[39] George S. Perry, in his book, *Cities of America* could not avoid including, either, a chapter about a town of two thousand people; and, like the editors of *Fortune*, he uses those interesting terms "fact" and "symbol"—except that he applies them to a small city. "Madison, Wisconsin," he sentimentalizes,

is both a fact and a symbol that stands for many of the finest traits in the American character. It is a place where independent people get up on their hind legs and have their say. Again, it is a seat of serious learning. Moreover, it is surrounded by that basic harmony that derives from good land that has been treated intelligently and with respect. Finally, Madison's people are almost spectacularly unapathetic. They are concerned, interested, and willing to do something about almost any public question. In many ways Madison and its environs are a miniature model of the ideal America of which many of us dream.[40]

Fact and symbol, symbol and fact: it is as if the United States had developed an urbanized economy without developing a thoroughly urbanized citizen. Americans entered a great period of city building during the nineteenth century protestingly, metaphorically walking backward; and to some extent they still do, but in exceedingly subtle ways. In the various sections of the next chapter, I shall deal both with this protest against cities, and with the regional differences between American urban cultures. In the foregoing pages, we have merely scratched the surface of American urban symbolism.

NOTES

1. John P. Kennedy, "Address. Delivered before the Maryland Institute for the Promotion of the Mechanical Arts, 21st October 1851," *Occasional Addresses* (New York: Putnam & Sons, 1872), p. 244.
2. Paul de Rousiers, *American Life* (New York and Paris: Firming-Didot & Co.), p. 73.
3. John Gunther, *Inside U. S. A.* (New York: Harper & Bros., 1946), p. 369.
4. Cf. The collection of articles edited by Alexander Klein, *The Empire City, A Treasury of New York* (New York: Rinehart & Co., Inc.,

1955); or Paul Crowell and A. H. Raskin, "New York, 'Greatest City in the World,' " in Robert S. Allen (ed.), *Our Fair City* (New York: Vanguard Press, Inc., 1947), esp. pp. 37-39.
5. This article was reprinted in the collection titled *Cities of America* (New York: Whittlesey House, McGraw-Hill Book Co., 1947), p. 244; see also Henry Haskell and Richard Fowler, *City of the Future. A Narrative History of Kansas City* (Kansas City: F. Glenn Publishing Company, 1950), pp. 16-17; and Darrel Garwood, *Crossroads of America. The Story of Kansas City* (New York: W. W. Norton and Co., Inc., 1948), p. 327. The latter volume especially exemplifies the conception of "crossroads" as the basis for attributing more Americanism to Kansas City than to any other city.
6. Cf. "Midwestern Birthday," *Time*, LVIII (July 30, 1951), p. 14.
7. Frank C. Harper, *Pittsburgh: Forge of the Universe* (New York: Comet Press, 1957), p. 10; and *Pittsburgh and the Pittsburgh Spirit* (Pittsburgh: Chamber of Commerce, 1928), but especially the address by John Bowman, "Pittsburgh's Contribution to Civilization," pp. 1-10.
8. Angie Debo, *Tulsa: From Creek Town to Oil Capital* (Norman, Okla.: University of Oklahoma Press, 1945), p. vii.
9. For two excellent discussions of the agrarian myth see Richard Hofstadter, *The Age of Reform* (New York: Alfred A. Knopf, Inc., 1955), esp. Part I, "The Agrarian Myth and Commercial Realities," and Part II, "The Folklore of Populism"; and Henry Nash Smith, *Virgin Land. The American West as Symbol and Myth* (New York: Vintage Books, 1955, and Cambridge: Harvard University Press, 1950), esp. Book III, "The Garden of the World," pp. 138-305.
10. Cf. G. S. Perry, "Philadelphia," *Saturday Evening Post*, CCXVIII (Sept. 14, 1946), esp. p. 82.
11. "Portland, Oregon," *Saturday Evening Post*, CCXIX (March 1, 1947), 23.
12. "Springfield, Illinois," *ibid.* (Sept. 27, 1947), p. 28.
13. This theme can be readily recognized in such books on older eastern cities as Struthers Burt, *Philadelphia* (Garden City, New York: Doubleday, Doran & Co., 1945), and Cleveland Amory, *The Proper Bostonians* (New York: E. P. Dutton & Co., 1947).
14. John Bowman, in Harper, *Pittsburgh and the Pittsburgh Spirit, op. cit.*, pp. 5-9.
15. Dorsha Hayes, *Chicago, Crossroads of American Enterprise* (New York: Julian Messner, Inc., 1944), p. 300; and Clara de Chambrun, *Cincinnati* (New York: Charles Scribner & Sons, 1939), p. 319.
16. Cf. Robert G. Rhett, *Charleston. An Epic of Carolina* (Richmond, Va.: Garrett and Massie, 1940).
17. Howard Long, *Kingsport, A Romance of Industry* (Kingsport, Tenn.: The Sevier Press, 1928), pp. 76, 3-4.

18. *Op. cit.*, pp. 369-70, 549.
19. *Op. cit.*, p. 37.
20. "Reno," *Saturday Evening Post,* CCXXV (July 5, 1952), 70, 72.
21. (Indianapolis: Bobbs-Merrill Co., 1946), p. 19.
22. (New York: Harper & Bros., 1945), p. 205.
23. "Birmingham, Alabama," *Saturday Evening Post,* CCXX (Sept. 6, 1947), 22.
24. *Op. cit.*, pp. 886-906, esp. p. 895.
25. F. Stother, "What Kind of Pittsburgh is Detroit?" *World's Work,* LII (Oct., 1926), 633-39.
26. Anthony Abbot in *Reader's Digest,* LX (Feb., 1952), 119-22.
27. *Op. cit.*, pp. 232, 233.
28. Alvin Harlow refers to Mrs. Trollope in *The Serene Cincinnatians* (New York: Dutton and Co., 1950).
29. Thomas J. Summers, *History of Marietta* (Marietta, Ohio: Leader Publishing Company, 1903), pp. 319-20.
30. Henry Cauthorn, *A History of the City of Vincennes, Indiana* (Cleveland: Arthur H. Clark Co., 1901), p. 220.
31. For some representative statements, pro and con, see: Mark Sullivan, "Why the West Dislikes New York. The Eternal Conflict Between City and Country," *World's Work,* LXI (1926), 406-11; "New York City," *Fortune,* XX (1939), 73-75, 83-85; Charles Merz, "The Attack on New York," *Harper's,* CLXIII (1926), 81-87; Earl Sparling, "Is New York American?" *Scribner's,* LXXX (1931), 165-73; Paul Crowell and A. H. Raskin, in R. Allen (ed.), *op. cit.*, pp. 38-39; Anonymous, "What is America?" *Nation,* CXXVIII (1921), 755; and Robert Benchley, "The Typical New Yorker," in Alexander Klein (ed.), *op. cit.*, pp. 338-42.
32. *Forum,* XVII (1894), 196-200.
33. J. W. Gleed in *ibid.*, pp. 217-34.
34. *American Magazine,* CXVI (Aug., 1933), 36-38.
35. Elsie Morrow, "South Bend," *Saturday Evening Post,* CCXXIV (June 14, 1942), 87; and "Brooklyn," *ibid.*, CCXIX (Dec. 26, 1946), 14.
36. *Op. cit.*, pp. 165-73.
37. Gunther, *op. cit.*, p. 549.
38. *Op. cit.*, p. 73.
39. E. R. Jackman, "Burns, Oregon," *Saturday Evening Post,* CCXX (Jan. 31, 1948), 2.
40. *Op. cit.*, p. 221.

VIII THE CITY IN SOCIAL CONFLICT

The modern metropolis has become one of the central themes of American history in general for the twentieth century and also its number 1 domestic problem. The thread of historical continuity suggests that the city, rather than having created new problems, has highlighted and intensified very old ones. After all, racism, poverty, the traffic jam, and unimaginative city planning were not born with the metropolis. The extraordinary growth of the city has sharpened the demands for collective responsibility; and the resistance, apathy, and failure to meet these demands have led many Americans to forget the enormous creative powers of cities and see them, as Jefferson once did, as "sores on the body politic."

This chapter seeks to isolate certainly not all but several of the critical issues bedeviling Americans in the twentieth century, such as the quality of life in the metropolis, poverty, racial violence, the dilemma of the urban police, and the failure of urban renewal, and to consider what they may mean for the future of urban America.

The most confounding realities of modern urbanism are the ancient plagues of poverty and discrimination, magnified by, but not generic to, the city. The most critical problem facing the city today concerns those at the end of the line—the urban poor, especially, but not exclusively, the American black, the most urbanized element of our society and the most deprived. In his essay in Chapter VI, Gilbert Osofsky argued that the ghetto of today was created by the 1920s. Jeanne R. Lowe surveys the modern ghetto from World War II to the present and shows how the ghetto-making forces of the early part of the century have been intensified and made even more critical, particularly by the changes in technology. Like Osofsky, she asks what makes a ghetto, and, after examining housing, employment, education, the family, and class differences among blacks themselves, she shows that the answer lies in the unholy triumvirate of poverty, race discrimination, and blocked opportunity. Three parts of her interpretation need to be underscored: her criticism of urban education; the flaws in the stereotype of the black welfare recipient (which she should have developed more fully); and, a point not always grasped by Americans confused by ghetto problems, especially the *white* offspring of former immigrant families, that is, the significant differences between the black migrant and the earlier white migrant and foreign immigrant that account for the black's failure to seize a share of the American bonanza.[1]

Throughout Miss Lowe's essay there is the ring of crisis: the crisis of poverty, the crisis of racial prejudice, the crisis of housing, the crisis of education, to which Edward Banfield would probably shake his gaunt head in disbelief and mutter, "Here we go again." In 1970, coming at the end of a decade when Americans were consumed by crises, Edward Banfield published his *Unheavenly City*, one of, if not the most, controversial books on the city in the last quarter of a century. It was a godsend for conservatives for it confirmed what they felt—and then some. For those of a liberal or radical persuasion, it was an outrage. Yet in a perverse sort of way, it was a godsend to the nonconservatives because it forced them to mobilize and defend deeply held assumptions about the city. For the nonconservative, *The Unheavenly City* bristles with heresies. Banfield attacked the bastion of the Liberal Establishment with the notion that the city was not racked with a bombardment of urban crises. Indeed, if there is a crisis, Banfield argues,

1. The literature about American blacks is so enormous that no attempt will be made to cite it all here, but among some of the recent books about the urban ghetto Negro, not previously cited, the following are of interest. Peter Orleans and William Russell Ellis, Jr. (eds.), *Race, Change and Urban Society* (Beverly Hills, Calif.: Sage Publications, 1971), Warner Bloomberg, Jr., and Henry J. Schmandt (eds.), *Power, Poverty, and Urban Policy* (Beverly Hills, Calif.: Sage Publications, 1968), Daniel P. Moynihan (ed.), *On Understanding Poverty: Perspectives from the Social Sciences* (New York: Basic Books, 1969), Roland L. Warren (ed.), *Politics and the Ghettos* (New York: Atherton Press, 1969), William H. Grier and Price M. Cobbs, *Black Rage* (New York: Basic Books, 1968), Henry Etzkowitz and Gerald M. Schaflander, *Ghetto Crisis: Riots or Reconciliation?* (Boston: Little, Brown, 1969), Elliot Liebow, *Tally's Corner: A Study of Negro Streetcorner Men* (Boston: Little, Brown, 1967), Constance Green, *The Secret City: A History of Race Relations in the Nation's Capitol* (Princeton: Princeton University Press, (1967); Allan H. Speer, *Black Chicago: The Making of a Negro Ghetto, 1890–1920* (Chicago: University of Chicago Press, 1967); Lee Rainwater and William L. Yancey, *The Moynihan Report and the Politics of Controversy* (Cambridge: The M.I.T. Press, 1967); August Meier and Elliott M. Rudwick, *From Plantation to Ghetto: An Interpretative History of American Negroes* (New York: Hill and Wang, 1966); Karl E. and Alma F. Taeuber, *Negroes in Cities: Residential Segregation and Neighborhood Change* (Chicago: Aldine, 1965); Charles E. Silberman, *Crisis in Black and White* (New York: Knopf, 1964); Michael Harrington, *The Other America: Poverty in the United States* (New York: Macmillan, 1962); and Kenneth Clark, *The Black Ghetto* (New York: Harper & Row, 1965). Howard Rabinowitz, *Race Relations in the Urban South 1865–1890* (New York: Oxford University Press, 1978), Thomas Lee Philpon, *The Slum and the Ghetto: Neighborhood Deterioration and Middle Class Reform, Chicago 1880–1930* (New York: Oxford University Press, 1978); Douglas Daniels, *Pioneer Urbanities: A Social and Cultural History of Black San Francisco* (Philadelphia: Temple University Press, 1980).

it is in the mind of the beholder; it is a crisis of a distorted perception, a dilemma of misguided great expectations. According to Banfield, our tolerance for adversity is alarmingly weak. What are seen as crises—poverty, racial prejudice, housing, income, education—actually are improving, but unreasonable expectations for their solution only creates an appetite of optimism that cannot be satiated. To seek and not to find creates only frustration, anxiety, and ruin because the opposite result is often achieved. Prophecies of impending doom become self-fulling. Thus Banfield not only makes war on the War on Poverty and other programs, but attacks the very foundations of reform, the ethics of hope and charity. "If Banfield is right . . ." observes Richard Todd, "the noblest efforts of the past thirty years have been wrong, what progress has occurred has been accidental, and only a 180-degree shift in sensibility can begin to save us."[2]

The next selection is the heart of *The Unheavenly City*. It is at once an analysis of the American urban class structure and a new theory of the lower class. To Banfield the composition of the classes more than any other factor, sets the limits that prevent policy-makers from creating the "heavenly" city. Class structure is the crux of the city's existence. It determines its form, the quality of its life, and most of its problems. A change in the make-up of the classes, Banfield insists, changes just about everything else critical to the city, be it population density, income, housing, crime, the drop-out rate, urban services, or its race relations and political style. Always a sticky subject, class in America has usually been defined in terms of prestige symbols (income, education, family, housing, etc.). These symbols are *objective*, in the sense that they can be seen and measured. Banfield presents a totally different approach. He defines class in a psychologically *subjective* framework; values, not the grandeur of one's income, determine one's class. The key value is a person's orientation toward the future, and this rests on the function of two factors: the ability to imagine a future and the ability to discipline oneself to sacrifice present for future satisfactions. Thus, a wealthy man is not of the upper class if he does not have a powerful orientation toward the future. But Banfield does concede (and it is an interesting concession) that as it works out the wealthy usually do have a strong imagination and discipline for the future. Fortified with a method, he then proceeds to analyze the life-styles of the four classes: upper, middle, working, and lower.

If Thorstein Veblen highlighted the antics of the leisure class as conspicuous consumption, Edward Banfield sees the lower class as conspicuous consumers of present-oriented pleasures and immediate gratification (especially sexual and financial), unmindful of the future, except as something that cannot be controlled. Pathological, irresponsible, wallowing in squalor, relishing violence, lacking strong ties to either family, friends, or community,

2. "A Theory of the Lower Class, Edward Banfield: The Maverick of Urbanology," *The Atlantic* (September 1970), p. 52.

the members of the lower class are "unable or unwilling either to control impulses or to put forth any effort at self-improvement."

Banfield writes:

The lower-class individual lives in the slum and sees little or no reason to complain. He does not care how dirty and dilapidated his housing is either inside or out, nor does he mind the inadequacy of such public facilities as schools, parks, and libraries: indeed, where such things exist he destroys them by acts of violence if he can. Features that make the slum repellent to others actually please him. He finds it satisfying in several ways.

To such a statement, critics, as much in bewilderment as in indignation, respond in the view of Richard Sennett: "Professor Banfield seems to live in a different country because he looks at poor people as essentially a different race of beings from you and me."[3]

Critics were also led to indict Banfield for racism, since blacks make up so much of the urban poor. But as Sennett points out: "Attacks on this book as racist miss the point: it's not blacks Banfield despises, it's poor people, whether they be white, black, or brown."

It would also be a mistake to dismiss Banfield as a mindless conservative and fling his book across the room, as a student of mine did once. His book has been warmly received by a wide audience that includes government policy-makers. At best, Banfield's essay is the stuff exciting controversy is made of. Given a room filled with people committed to a variety of political styles—conservative, liberal, and radical—(hopefully oriented toward the past as well), armed with the weapons of Jeanne Lowe, Edward Banfield, and Morris Janowitz, it would be interesting to speculate the outcome, intellectual and otherwise.

The result of ghetto life—as the fiery decade of the 1960s painfully illustrate—is the violence of riots, which seem to many Americans to be one of the main themes of contemporary urban America. Historically, urban racial conflicts are nothing new. To name just a few, there were the Detroit and Harlem riots of 1943; the Tulsa riot of 1921; the Elaine, Arkansas, riot of 1919; and the particularly vicious racial explosion in Chicago in the same year. There was the East St. Louis riot of 1917, probably the worst and certainly the bloodiest in this century. There were the riots in New York, New Orleans, and Akron in 1900, and Wilmington, North Carolina in 1898, not to mention the 1863 New York draft riots, which had decided racial overtones. And one can go back further than that to the Cincinnati riots of 1841 and the Snow Hill riot in Providence, Rhode Island, in 1831. As Rap Brown says, violence is as American as "cherry pie."

3. "Survival of the Fattest," *The New York Review of Books* (August 13, 1970), p. 23.

The persistent, baffling question is what triggers riots? A blatant defiance of law and order? Lower-class young hoodlums running amuck? The inflexible fortress of white racism? The so-called "revolution of rising expectations"? The answer will seriously affect what is to be done with the ghetto and this in turn will affect the future of the American city.

In one of the most penetrating analyses to appear in years,[4] Morris Janowitz, combining history and sociology, not restricting his vision merely to the riots of the 1960s, but ranging far back into the early years of the twentieth century, sees three critical stages of urban racial violence. The first occurred during and immediately after World War I, such as the East St. Louis and Chicago riots. He labels these *communal* riots or "contested area" riots, because they involved "ecological warfare" directly between whites and blacks on the boundaries of the white and black communities. Usually triggered by whites, they represented the white fear of an expanding black community, and for the blacks, a desperate struggle for survival. The second stage, coming during World War II and reaching a peak in the years 1964–67, while incorporating some of the elements of the first stage, nonetheless takes on a different character. Rather than a confrontation between white and black on the edge of the ghetto, it was a war between blacks and the police, directly within the black community. Janowitz calls these *commodity* riots because they represented a protest against the larger society in the form of looting and destruction of property and retail stores. The third stage, coming after 1968, again incorporating some of the elements of the previous stages, took on the pattern of an "instrumental use of violence," whereby small, organized, armed groups of blacks, ideologues appealing to Black Power, employed calculated, selective acts of terrorism against the white community. These were people who believed that social change could be created only through violence.

4. The literature on urban riots is growing and will continue to grow. An important work dealing with violence in many aspects, including urban, is Hugh Davis Graham and Ted Robert Gurr, *Violence in America: Historical and Comparative Perspectives*, 2 vols. (Washington, D.C.: Superintendent of Documents, 1969). An excellent study is by Nathan S. Caplan and Jeffrey M. Paige, "A Study of Ghetto Rioters," *Scientific American* (August 1968). See also National Advisory Commission on Civil Disorders, *The Report of the National Advisory Commission on Civil Disorders* (New York: Bantam Books, 1968); two articles by Robert Fogelson: "From Contention to Confrontation: The Police, the Negroes and the Riots of the 1960's," *Political Science Quarterly* (June 1968), and "White on Black: A Critique of the McCone Commission Report on the Los Angeles Riots," *Political Science Quarterly* (September 1967); John Hersey, *The Algiers Motel Incident* (New York: Knopf, 1968); the entire issue of *American Behavioral Scientist* (March–April 1968), which is devoted to urban violence and disorder; Paul Jacobs, *Prelude to Riot: A View of Urban America from the Bottom* (New York: Random House, 1967); Jerome H. Skolnick, *Justice Without Trial: Law Enforcement in Democratic Society* (New York: John Wiley, 1966). Richard Hofstader and Michael Wallace, eds., *American Violence: A Documentary History* (New York: Vintage Books, 1971), Richard Maxwell Brown, *Strain of Violence: Historical Studies of American Violence and Vigilantism* (New York: Oxford University Press, 1975).

As causal factors linking all three stages, Janowitz goes beyond conventional explanations, such as prejudice, poverty, income, and housing, seeing these as important but only partial answers. More important, he argues, were the agencies of social change and social control, especially the police and the mass media. He analyzes both in detail and concludes that the poor performance of both account for much of the urban racial violence in the twentieth-century. But even here, Janowitz plumbs deeper. The crux to the history of race riots is more than the patterns of communal and commodity styles of violence, more than the failure of the police and the mass media. It is in part an answer to the question raised by Ralph Ellison, the black novelist, when he asked, "But can a people live and develop for over three hundred years simply by reacting?" As Janowitz says, "The Negro outbursts have been more than a reaction to police brutality and a double standard of legal justice. In a symbolic sense, they are expressions of energies to participate in and transform the larger society. In all phases of life, the Negro is not merely reacting but acting."

If the urban police have played a critical role in most of the race riots in our history,[5] scholars, from a variety of disciplines, are recognizing that the police have been a vital urban institution, a mirror reflecting the growth and evolution of the city, and importantly, society's attitudes toward law, crime, punishment, and authority.[6] It has been said that a society's attitude toward

5. See Roger Lane, Policing the City: Boston, 1822–1885 (Cambridge: Harvard University Press, 1967), and Robert Fogelson, "The Police, the Negroes and the Riots of the 1960's," Political Science Quarterly (June 1968).
6. For the decade of the 1960s, see Orlando W. Wilson, Police Administration, 2nd. ed. (New York: McGraw-Hill, 1963), Michael Banton, The Policeman and the Community (New York: Basic Books, 1965), Wayne R. LaFave, Arrest (Boston: Little, Brown, 1965), Jerome H. Skolnick, Justice Without Trial (New York: John Wiley and Sons, 1966), David J. Bordua, The Police (New York: John Wiley and Sons, 1967), Arthur Niederhoffer, Behind the Shield: The Police in Urban Society (New York: Doubleday, 1967), A Report by the President's Commission on Law Enforcement and Administration of Justice, The Challenge of Crime in a Free Society (Washington, D.C.: U.S. Government Printing Office, 1967), The President's Commission on Law Enforcement and Administration of Justice, Task Force Report: The Police (Washington, D.C.: Government Printing Office, 1967), Daniel Walker, as submitted to the National Commission on the Causes and Prevention of Violence, Rights in Conflict (New York: E. P. Dutton and Co., 1968), James Q. Wilson, Varieties of Police Behavior (Cambridge, Mass.: Harvard University Press, 1968), Gene Radano, Walking the Beat (Cleveland: World Publishing Co., 1968), William W. Turner, The Police Establishment (New York: G. P. Putnam's Sons, 1968), Paul Chevigny, Police Power: Police Abuses in New York City (New York: Pantheon Books, 1969), and "The Police and the Rest of Us," eight articles of a special supplement which appeared in The Atlantic (March 1967).
The 1970s produced a flurry of work: James F. Richardson, The New York Police: Colonial Times to 1901 (New York: Oxford University Press, 1970) and Urban Police in the United States (New York: Kennikat, 1974), James Ahern, Police in Trouble: Our Frightening Crisis in Law Enforcement (New York: Hawthorn, 1972), Gene E. and Elaine H. Carte, Police Reform in the United States: The Era of August Vollmer, 1905–1932 (Berkeley: University of California Press, 1975), Albert J. Reiss, The Police and the Public (New Haven: Yale University Press, 1971), Jonathan Rubinstein, City Police (New York: Farrar, Straus and Giroux, 1973), Mark Haller, "Historical Roots of Police

justice and the mechanism of justice is an index to a society's character. Indeed, the mere existence of the police suggests the heart of urban living— the necessity for collective responsibility.

Since the 1840s, when the first police force was established, the record of the urban police has been a checkered one for some of the following reasons. First, they have had to cope with the *difficulties* of urban life, such as the impersonality of the city, urban mobility, the problems arising from the enormous diversity of the urban population itself, diversities of culture, values, attitudes, class, religion, and racial and national backgrounds. Second, society has used the police as a kind of wastebasket for dumping its social failures. Yet the police are hardly trained or equipped to solve problems that have defeated the larger society. And, third, Americans have not been quite sure about what they want the police to police. As a result, the police have had to play a variety of roles that are both frustrating and contradictory. As one man has written, "We ask our officers to be a combination of Bat Masterson, Sherlock Holmes, Sigmund Freud, King Solomon, Hercules and Diogenes." No wonder, then, it can be said that whether you see the cops as heroes or pigs their job is one of the most difficult in urban society. The question, a perennial one, is how do we get better police?

In the next essay, James Q. Wilson, a leading authority on law enforcement, bypasses the usual answers to this question—more salary, more training, more equipment, more guns, clearer policies. Nor is better race relations, so desperately necessary, the entire answer. Wilson finds the "answer," or at least the real beginning of an answer, in the resolution of a dilemma that has plagued the police for generations. It is the question of what actually

---

Behavior: Chicago, 1890–1925," *Law and Society Review* (Winter 1976), Nicholas Alex, *New York Cops Talk Back: A Study of a Beleaguered Minority* (New York: John Wiley, 1976), Kenneth G. Alfers, *Law and Order in the Capital City: A History of the Washington Police, 1880–1886* (Washington: George Washington University, 1976), Samuel Walker, *A Critical History of Police Reform: The Emergence of Professionalism* (Lexington: Lexington Books, 1977), and *Popular Justice: A History of American Crimminal Justice* (New York: Oxford University Press, 1980), Robert Fogelson, *Big-City Police* (Cambridge: Harvard University Press, 1977), Wilbur R. Miller, *Cops and Bobbies: Police Authority in New York and London, 1830–1870* (Chicago: University of Chicago Press, 1977), Patrick V. Murphy and Thomas Plate, *Commissioner: A View from the Top of American Law Enforcement* (New York: Simon and Schuster, 1977), David H. Bayley, ed., *Police and Society* (Beverly Hills: Sage, 1977) and *Forces of Order: Police Behavior in Japan and in the United States* (Berkeley and Los Angeles: University of California Press, 1976), Herman Goldstein, *Policing a Free Society* (Cambridge: Ballinger, 1977), William Ker Muir, Jr., *Police: Streetcorner Politicians* (Chicago: University of Chicago Press, 1977), Charles E. Silberman, *Criminal Violence, Criminal Justice* (New York: Random House, 1978) and David R. Johnson, *Policing the Urban Underworld: The Impact of Crime on the Development of the American Police, 1800–1887* (Philadelphia: Temple University Press, 1979).

Two novels, written by policeman-novelist Joseph Wambaugh provide special insights into the working world of the urban police: *The New Centurions* (Boston: Little, Brown, 1970), and *The Blue Knight* (Boston: Little, Brown, 1972).

the police are supposed to do. "The history of the American municipal police," he says, "is in great part a history of struggles to define their role in our society."

After an excellent analysis of the historical development of the urban police, Wilson shows the police have become snarled in the dilemma of playing two roles which together are contradictory and self-defeating. On the one hand, there is the glamor role of "crook catching," or law enforcement. After a discussion of the nature of crime, he demonstrates how the police cannot be effective crime fighters, yet cast in that role the police face the embarrassment of *being judged by a goal they cannot attain.*" On the other hand, the bulk of policework is providing services, or maintaining order, such as dealing with quarreling families, drunks, troublesome teenagers, tavern brawls, taking the sick to a hospital, or bailing a cat out of a tree. Strengthen one role and you weaken the other. For example, the strategy for law enforcement requires centralized authority, tight surveillance of the neighborhood (with the police being seen as the adversary), precise legal codes, and clear arrest procedures. On the other hand, to maintain order and provide services requires decentralized authority, a sympathetic commitment to the neighborhood, wide discretion and tolerance, and a toning-down of arrest quotas. Wilson warns that there is no slick, magic formula to the Police Problem, but until the dilemma of role is resolved, all the money, education, and guns won't put the blue-coated Humpty-Dumpty together again.

The next selection concerns urban renewal, an issue that has stirred considerable social conflict, and one that is intimately related to both poverty and the quality of life in the city. Herbert Gans presents a critique with a question: urban renewal for whom, the slumdwellers or the affluent white middle and upper classes? His major criticism is that most urban renewal projects have used the brawn of the federal bulldozer to tear the slums down, but have not used the federal brain to properly relocate the slumdwellers they have displaced. It is a critique built around a preposterous irony: urban renewal frequently victimizes the very people it was originally intended to benefit. Slum clearance sustains the slums. By failing to follow through with rehousing the dispossessed, urban renewal forces them into other slum areas; ergo, urban renewal often becomes slum "renewal," slums are merely shifted and made worse.

Unlike some critics of public housing, Gans does not want to burn down the barn to kill the rats. He proposes several alternative solutions, most of which hinge upon more effective federal intervention. Thus, he does not find the panacea in unrestricted private enterprise, which contributed enormously to the initial creation of the slums, or in the simplistic doctrine that decent housing makes for the decent life. In Gans's view, there will be no fundamental improvement until a rehousing program is coupled with an effective attack upon poverty itself.

Race and Poverty in Cities: A Liberal View

JEANNE LOWE

Traditionally, Americans have regarded city slums as primarily a physical problem. The federal slum clearance legislation has been written in those terms. Largely because money to get rid of urban slums was available in such programs, cities tried to eliminate their slum areas by tearing down the buildings.

During the 1950's, however, while starting to use the new government instruments of urban redevelopment and renewal, local public officials began to discover that slum elimination entailed much more than the removal of deteriorated housing and hardware—or even the substitution of low-rent dwellings. Still, most failed to acknowledge the problems that cause people to live in slums.

By the early 1960's, the changing racial-social-economic composition of central cities had magnified and vastly complicated the traditional human problems of the slums, especially in the context of a generally prospering nation. A growing portion of the city population was unable to provide for itself, and the urban community was unable or unwilling to afford that portion adequate homes and jobs in the face of changing technology and racial discrimination. Depression-born welfare and housing programs were overwhelmed; cities' fiscal resources were depleted. Northern equal-rights laws, as well as

U.S. Supreme Court decisions, became empty promises as *de facto* segregation increased in core cities that were being strangled by the suburban middle-class white noose. Meanwhile, some renewal programs, caught in the crosscurrents of minority outcries of inequity and discrimination, civil rights demonstrations, the white backlash, and some apparently irreconcilable social issues, ground to a halt or radically changed direction.

The 1960 census exposed the facts about cities' changing composition. The older core cities in the North and northern central areas had lost population during the past decade, while suburbs grew. The drop varied from a little over one per cent in New York and Baltimore to 4.5 per cent in San Francisco and 10.7 per cent in Pittsburgh. The full extent of the loss was disguised, however, by the number of "new urbanites." The twelve largest cities experienced a combined net decrease in their white population of 2,000,000, but they gained 1,800,000 non-whites. Medium-size cities, too—Rochester, Fort Wayne, San Diego—which had had few Negroes before World War II, saw their Negro populations double even as their total populations dropped. Washington D.C. became the first of America's twenty-five big cities to have a Negro majority. By the 1960's, almost as many Negroes were living in northern, borderline and western cities as in the South, and 73

From Jeanne Lowe, *Cities in a Race with Time* (New York: Random House, 1967), pp. 278-310. Copyright © 1967, by Jeanne Lowe. Reprinted by permission of Random House, Inc.

per cent of all Negroes in the country lived in cities, as compared to 73 per cent on the land only half a century before.

THE WELFARE CITY

While central cities' populations fell, their budgets continued to grow, and to grow at a much faster rate than the general rise in the cost of living or the national increase in state and local spending or revenues. In the biggest cities the disproportion was worst of all.

The largest increases in expenses were for public assistance, hospitals and health services and police. More than one third of the increase in New York City's budget from $3,000,000,000 to $4,500,000,000 in the five years from 1960-61 to 1965-66 was accounted for by these three items.[1] Health and hospitals expenditures were up 72 per cent, to $337,920,221—and one third of the city's population, over 2,500,000, qualified for a projected free health-care program on the basis of their "moderate low income" in 1966. The Police Department accounted for another $364,120,276 in the 1965-66 budget, an increase of some $141,000,000 in the past five years; but it still lacked sufficient staff to deal with growing crime. The Welfare Department's requested allocation for 1966-67 was nearly two thirds of a billion dollars, $129,000,000, over that of the previous fiscal year.

These swelling costs were directly related to the changing population composition of central cities: more relatively young low-income families reproducing more rapidly than other metropolitan core residents; more elderly and disabled people; and the striking increase in non-white and other previously rural residents. But the latter group alone received welfare outlays far out of proportion to their percentage. In New York, where Negroes comprise only 14 per cent of the city, they accounted for 45 per cent of those on welfare. Puerto Ricans, forming 8 per cent of the population, represented 30 per cent of the welfare load. The same pattern was repeated in other cities in the early 1960's.

The single biggest growth item in public welfare was Aid to Dependent Children—ADC. (Of the 600,000 persons to be aided by the New York Welfare Department in 1966, well over half were children under eighteen.) Particularly striking—and headline making—was the proportion of illegitimate children receiving such public assistance. In Washington D.C., where ADC accounted for 71 per cent of the entire welfare caseload, 40 per cent of the children were born out of wedlock.

Unfortunately, such statistics on mushrooming welfare costs, when brought to public attention by the press and public officials, provoked outcries against alleged abuses, demagoguery, and pressures for residency requirements and quick cures. The city manager of Newburgh, New York became a national figure (a hero to some) in the summer of 1961 with his sweeping plan for taking "bums" and "chiselers" off relief, which accounted for 12 per cent of his city's budget. Louis J. Lefkowitz, Republican candidate for Mayor of New York City that fall, proclaimed that if elected he would remove from public welfare the "wastrels" and "chiselers." National magazines ran apparently well-researched exposés of welfare abuses. The journalistic stereotype was the shiftless mother who had child after child at the public's expense to increase her relief payments rather than go to work.

The flight to the suburbs of middle-

and upper-income taxpayers was directly attributed to their having to pay these mounting city expenses. These fleeing city dwellers did not realize that a third of welfare costs are borne by the state government and another third or more by the federal government. One can run—but not far.

GETTING DOWN TO CASES

Why the enormously disproportionate growth in welfare and aid to dependent children? The Board of Commissioners of Cook County, Illinois, which pays Chicago's welfare bills, was so alarmed by the skyrocketing of ADC costs during the 1950's—up from $1,400,000 to $4,400,000—that in 1960 it appointed a thirty-five-member committee of specialists, civic leaders, businessmen and educators to investigate. The committee, in turn, retained the New York firm of Greenleigh Associates Inc., nationally known consultants to health and welfare organizations. Their year-long study was the most extensive and thorough ever made of a local public welfare program in the United States.

It is interesting that the publication of the findings attracted so little national attention compared to the alleged welfare abuses. Perhaps the report, as its title *Facts, Fallacies and Future* suggests, challenged many of the popular and comforting notions about who is on ADC and why. Indeed, no more than 3 per cent in the sample of 1,000 interviewed fit the popular stereotype. Nor did the report offer any panaceas.

The typical ADC mother in Chicago was a native of Mississippi, a Negro, in her thirties. She had been in Chicago fifteen years and had three children under fifteen, all born in Illinois. Her husband had lost his job as an unskilled laborer and had deserted her.[2] She had had an illegitimate child since. She had waited an average of a year and four months after that before applying for ADC. Generally, she was not free to remarry, but if she was, the new husband was unable to support the child. This was her first time on ADC; she stayed on the rolls less than three years; she did not want to have more children to boost her allotment. (In fact, it only allowed twenty-one cents per meal per person.)

Most women were found to feel great guilt and resentment about having an illegitimate child, but many did not know how to prevent conception. Almost all were anxious to be self-sustaining and to return to work. However, most had no marketable skill, and many could not leave home because their children were too young to go to school.

Moreover, that illegitimacy accounted for 50 per cent of ADC was found to reflect the general growing rate of illegitimacy in Cook County. But, as the report pointed out, of the illegitimate children who were adopted—and thus who did not go on ADC—almost 98.5 per cent were white and only 1.5 per cent Negro.

In 1962 Congress amended the Social Security Act largely on the basis of some proposals in the Greenleigh Report. It provided greater federal aid for rehabilitative and preventive services for adult recipients of ADC, including financing of day-care centers for children of working mothers, more counseling and reduced workloads for caseworkers; it gave aid for an unemployed second parent to keep families together and to encourage use of parents' earnings for their children's education (books, bus fares, shoes, etc.) without cutting their relief check.

But the Social Security Act, by its nature, is supportive and could not get at the basic root of dependency found by the Greenleigh study—"the marginal level of the families" before they applied for ADC, and a history of marginal subsistence, the end product of the social and economic effects of racial discrimination.

THE GHETTO DWELLERS

No doubt the welfare programs born in the depression dramatized certain traditional predicaments of any city newcomers' situation. The period of adjustment to complex urban life is a tension-fraught, often traumatic experience for almost all migrants, white or non-white, European, Asian, Appalachian-American, Puerto Rican or Mexican. Slum living, poverty, lack of marketable skills, low-level employment and frequent unemployment, high rates of reproduction, juvenile crime, family disorganization, ghettoization (self-imposed and socially reinforced), poor housekeeping—these have generally accompanied the first stages of life in cities, especially for rural newcomers, who comprise the majority of immigrants. But in the days of the last big urban influx, our government did not assume the burden for these problems; nor had it decided that slums were opposed to the public welfare.

Furthermore, one cannot overemphasize the special situation of the newly urban American Negro—who comprises the largest group of immigrants. He brings to the city extra-heavy baggage. He has not only the "badge of color" but also the ingrained burden of generations of cultural and economic deprivation. His move to the city makes painfully and inescapably apparent the

effects of dependency and weak family organization which had their origins in slavery but were perpetuated after Reconstruction by the southern plantation system. This is the system that has shaped the mass of the "new urbanites," the people who comprise 20, 30, even 60 per cent of central cities' populations and who, during the 1970's, may be expected to increase their present number by 50 to 100 per cent.

The plantation system offered the Negro no experience with money, no incentive to save, no conception of time or progress—none of the basic experiences to prepare him for the urban money economy. Instead, it indoctrinated him to believe in his own inferiority, to be resigned, while it held him in a folk culture dominated by a spiritual, other-worldly, escapist outlook—in what sociologist E. Franklin Frazier called "the twilight of civilization."

Illegitimacy and the female-dominated household are not Negro traits. (Indeed, family instability is a characteristic by-product of male unemployment and poverty.) In the Negro's case, these traits were developed as a result of white southern culture and slavery, which deprived the Negro family of a legal base, and were perpetuated by the post-Civil War plantation system which kept the Negro male subservient, uneducated and economically insecure, usually out in the field or wandering the country looking for work, away from his family. Consequently his children were deprived of male authority and stable family life. But for the Negro man, who had almost no material possessions (he was always a tenant), his offspring were virtually the only tangible proof of his manhood, and the woman who would have him must accept this. Illegitimate children and their mothers were not rejected; instead, they were accommodated by the mothers, grandmothers and aunts who composed many lower-class southern Negro households.

But the city does not offer the mass of poor Negroes much opportunity to demonstrate the difference between what is racially and what is culturally or environmentally induced. City life tends to shatter the fragile structure of the lower-class Negro's family life and to accentuate, through differential employment opportunities, female dominance and masculine subordination. It also exposes the youngster, whose mother is probably out at work and whose father is either out of work, busy at two jobs or missing, to the worst influences of the slum.

These latest newcomers find few of the strengths of group pride in ethnic origin or the institutional supports that fortified the European immigrants. Not even the simple official process of "Americanization" which in five years is supposed to turn the foreigner into a citizen is available. The Negro's movement from one part of the country to another fails to supply that "shock of separation" which, as Oscar Handlin has written, precipitated the creation of new community organizations in cities by earlier immigrant groups. The individualized welfare services of the old city political machine have been preempted by impersonal government agencies, and the machine's municipal jobs for the faithful unskilled have been largely eliminated by civil service requirements or trade union restrictions. The politician does not even offer the traditional outings to the country; too often the Negro's political representative wants to keep his constituency as is.

The underworld, also, has a vested interest in preserving the minority ghetto and its hopelessness. To the despondent resident the criminal world offers "the poor man's democracy"— the chance of winning money in the numbers game. It also vends narcotics, an expensive, momentary retreat from despair, a lifetime hook that causes men to steal or kill for more and makes city streets unsafe.

The criminal world once afforded the uneducated youthful deviants in the ethnic slum illegitimate avenues to material success, but these paths are largely closed today. Crime has become as highly organized, remote and specialized as the rest of American life. Its numbers parlors are, as Richard Cloward and Lloyd Ohlin expressed it in *Delinquency and Opportunity*, like the local branch stores of a supermarket chain. The criminal hierarchy does not even provide the invisible discipline that used to hold many slum youths in line. Nor does it supply the cash that helped immigrants of earlier generations become entrepreneurs.

Even settlement houses commonly find themselves located in areas of lesser need today, because the residents whom they once served have moved away; or slum clearance and new development have altered the neighborhood. Meanwhile, vast new slum areas are neglected. Even so, settlement houses, like psychiatrically oriented social workers, are ineffective in trying to mitigate the society-induced traumas that infect the occupants of our cities' spreading black ghettos.

Meanwhile, a small group of "upper-class" Negroes, the supposed leaders and models, remain removed from and contemptuous of the masses (except for the many doctors, dentists, lawyers and businessmen who live in "golden ghettos" but enter the slum ghetto to make their living). And members of the growing middle class, who have worked their way out of the slum by dint of education and new job openings, are afraid of being dragged down by association with those still on the bottom. As the Greenleigh report noted, "upper-class Negroes are embarrassed and threatened by the public out-cry against ADC and low-income families."

This attitude, in turn, increases the alienation and frustration of the slum ghetto dweller. Speaking of the rioters at Watts in Los Angeles, a top-ranking Negro official of the federal Office of Economic Opportunity told an audience composed largely of middle-class Negroes, "Whitey isn't alone in being the object of their anger." Successful Negroes, he declared, should give the poor the benefit of their experience. But a highly placed Negro municipal employee in Los Angeles complained that he could not get other Negroes at City Hall to accompany him to the Watts area in order to persuade youngsters to get off the streets. "Why should I?" one rejoined. "I struggled for years to get out of there."

Why do middle- and upper-class Negroes fail to help their own? Primarily because the American reward system has failed to operate for them. Segregation and discrimination reinforce white stereotypes and have produced a Negro middle and upper class disproportionately small compared to the total number of Negroes, and poor compared to their white counterparts. Aside from the church, they lack the means to support their institutions. The Urban League, NAACP and CORE all rely heavily on white liberals' contributions.

His white peers have little opportunity through normal contacts and common interests to know a Negro as an individual. Practically his only civic association with white community leaders is on "interracial" committees concerned with integration or Negro rights. His isolation deprives him of the business and professional contacts and experience essential to advancing within the corporate and financial structure of American life. He does not have the extended clan that helped Europeans. Lacking entree into the American economic system, often denied credit, many Negro businessmen exploit the Negro mass as ruthlessly as do the whites. Like too many Negro doctors, lawyers, publishers and politicians, they have a vested interest in perpetuating the ghetto from which they make a living.

Ghettoization has consistently discouraged the development of a responsible elite. As Wilson wrote in *Negro Politics:* "Living in isolation from the city as a whole, . . . and desiring to differentiate himself from the [mass of disadvantaged Negroes], the middle- or upper-class Negro can see few rewards in civic leadership." Denied many of the rewards of upward mobility and the opportunity to play a serious role in American life, "the black bourgeoisie," as Frazier called them, escape into a "world of make believe," preoccupied with Negro "society" and conspicuous consumption (or else they try to earn still another Ph.D.). The Negro mass, though they may envy this elite, regards them not as models but as Uncle Toms, or as people who have been somehow "lucky in getting money"—as indeed most have been.

Who, then, is responsible for the newcomer, for easing his period of adjustment and helping him to advance?

During the late 1950's a new kind of municipal agency emerged in some cities. One of the first was Chicago's Committee on New Residents, appointed by Mayor Richard Daley as part of the city's Commission on Human Relations late in 1955 when the recent migrants' problems began to manifest themselves widely. The Committee published pamphlets and distributed thousands of simple illustrated brochures to acquaint the newcomers with the strange city and its facilities—its schools, parks, health clinics, adult educational opportunities, and even such rudimentary matters as how to use a telephone and shop at a supermarket. It organized housekeeping classes to show previously rural homemakers how to use gas stoves, incinerators and other urban novelties. It alerted other public and private agencies to the newcomers' special needs and set up field offices in "port of entry" neighborhoods.

The Committee's biggest job, however, was to find employment for the newcomers who supposedly had come in response to the siren call of industry in Chicago, traditionally a strong market for unskilled labor. The problem of finding work was twice as severe for non-white as for white newcomers.

But, as a top staff member of the Committee on New Residents commented in 1961, "In Chicago able-bodied men aren't allowed to go on relief. They 'assume that if you're able-bodied, you can find work. Yet there aren't jobs for the unskilled, and it's getting worse.

"In the last century, immigration was accompanied by a demand for cheap, unskilled labor. Today, you can't push a wheelbarrow or build a railroad across the country. In this highly skilled society, we can't afford to wait for the next generation. We either train them or they'll be a drag on Chicago."

One of the Committee's early acts, in 1956, had been to arrange with the city's Dunbar Vocational High School for job-training classes for newcomers. This endeavor was reported in 1959 by Ely M. Aron, chairman of the Committee, in testimony before the Board of Education calling for a larger budget.

"It seemed perfectly obvious that we only had to make known to these new residents the superb facilities . . . you had provided for trade and vocational training. Everyone—we thought—would line up to enroll in these classes, study diligently, and become a skilled worker in possibly two or three years. We sent out thousands of flyers, used every means of communication, and the result —nil.

"Now we know better. It took us a year to learn. . . . Before we can expect anyone to learn 'fine hand skills,' we must help him learn to read, understand directions, warning signals and machine dials. Today, we rejoice in the increased enrollment in the elementary school classes for adults. . . .

"It is very difficult," Aron stated, "if you're the sole head of the household, if you've moved a number of children from a rural area into a vastly complex city—it is difficult to admit that you can't read."[3]

THE BIG CHANGE

We used to have an acceptable rationalization for city slums. *Fortune* magazine, in a 1957 article on "The Enduring Slums," stated that they "are crowded because there are jobs to be had . . . sweepers at General Motors . . . scrap throwers at Inland Steel . . . handtruck pushers around New York's garment center." Slums were thus a sign of opportunity in cities, because newcomers are attracted to places of employment.

But these jobs have been disappearing. There is less and less heavy, unskilled and dirty work to be done—both in cities and on farms. During the 1950's, agricultural and fiber production increased by 27 per cent with 27 per cent fewer workers. This trend virtually forced migration to cities, especially from the newly mechanized plantation South.

It is now known that the high rate of unemployment during the late 1950's and early 1960's was caused not only by factory automation; a sluggish economy and consumer demand were also instrumental, and behind these, conservative government fiscal policies. But the fact remains, as Dorothy K. Norman wrote in the U.S. Department of Labor's *Monthly Labor Review* in 1965: "Production requirements in industry appear to have played a hoax on the Negro, by first expanding—especially during the war years of the 1940's and early 1950's—and enticing the Negroes from the farm into industrial jobs, often far from home, and then receding, as these same jobs have become increasingly vulnerable to technological and market changes.

"Industrial employment increased in a number of cities in 1964, but the totals did not rise much above 1960 levels. And in some of the largest centers—New York and Philadelphia—the downward trend persisted, the bulletin reported.

"Limited job opportunities in major centers of Negro concentration aggravate the already difficult situation in which Negroes find themselves when looking for employment. . . ."

The low-skill service jobs which untrained newcomers have traditionally filled in cities were even harder hit, relatively, by the switch to machines. For example, a great many immigrants who had never worked at any other non-farm job became elevator operators. Yet between 1957 and 1961 in New York City alone, 30,000 elevator operators' jobs were eliminated. It was anticipated that the unemployed operators could be transferred to bowling alleys. But the invention of the automatic pinsetter had eliminated thousands of these jobs as well. New mechanical cleaning processes used in many high-rise office buildings displaced still more low-skill people.

Municipal government itself, while a major growth sector for employment in recent years, has also increased use of machinery in activities that traditionally employed unskilled labor—general maintenance, street cleaning, street and road construction and administrative procedures.

The attrition in these jobs mirrors far-reaching structural shifts that have taken place in the economy since World War II. For while some jobs were disappearing, many others were being created. Between 1955 and 1965 the blue-collar work force grew only by 763,000; white-collar employment rose by 6,540,000.

Within industry itself the big shift has been from production to non-production jobs (and smaller relative pay increases for the typical factory worker). The steel industry offers an extreme but vivid picture of the shifts. Between 1950 and 1961, its blue-collar employees dropped from 503,000 to 403,000— though production rose with automated equipment, and white-collar employment in its offices and laboratories climbed from 89,000 to 117,000. In 1946 there was one white-collar worker to every nine employed in steel; there was one in four by 1963. "The time may come when it will take a ton of paper to make a ton of steel," a bulletin of the Federal Reserve Bank observed.

The many new jobs in government are also skilled or professional. This does not mean that there is not a great deal of unskilled work to be done in public service. The work merely requires public financing. The 1966 Report of the National Commission on Technology, Automation and Economic Progress enumerated six different categories of potential jobs which could produce 5,300,000 new jobs which need to be filled in order to bring public services up to levels of acceptable operation.

In manpower utilization and national wealth, the country has been moving from a goods-producing to a service economy. This fact, in combination with the exodus of manufacturing plants from the crowded old rail centers,[4] has profound implications for cities and their residents. Not only is there relatively less wealth in locally taxable property; fewer jobs are left in cities for the new population. To reach plants now relocated in the suburbs, but which were accessible by urban public transportation, the Negro or Spanish-speaking worker who is barred from suburban residence (by income if not race) must drive many miles between home and work. Often he cannot afford to do so. (Meanwhile, suburban residents commute to office and professional jobs in center city.)

Since World War II, all net growth in jobs has occurred in the service sector, a 1965 study by Victor Fuchs of the National Bureau of Economic Research revealed. Moreover, Fuchs' study points out, growth within this service sector has been in jobs that make greater use of workers with higher education and relatively less use of those with only limited schooling or with physical strength. The employment increase in the field of education alone between 1950 and 1960 was found to be greater than total employment in primary metal industries in both of those years. (Most dramatic postwar advance was made by professional, technical and kindred workers. This group doubled, and by 1964 numbered 8,500,000.)

Looking ahead to the 1970's, experts foresee a continuing decline in rural manpower needs. Only 10 per cent of the nation's population will be needed to feed the country and grow fiber for it. This means continued immigration from farms and plantations, though at a somewhat slower rate than in the recent past. But the number of Negroes, Puerto Ricans and other low-income, minority residents in central cities is expected to grow and be half again as large due to the young age and high birth rate of those already there.

The number of factory jobs nationally will increase—though probably not in the old manufacturing cities, and many traditional blue-collar production jobs will be upgraded in job requirements to a white-collar or skilled level. The manufacturers remaining in cities will have less need for additional, particularly for unskilled, workers. The big proportionate increase in skilled, white-collar and professional service jobs will continue in cities (as nationally), and cities may well benefit from this trend.

The U.S. Department of Labor warned in a publication on *Manpower Needs of the 1960's* (published in 1959) that "To fill these new requirements the youth who are entering the labor market will have to have much higher skills and education." The Department's 1965 publication on *Man-power Needs in 1975* reiterated the point. It stated that "The occupational groups requiring the least educational attainment are, in general, those which are expected to show the smallest employment growth and thus provide the fewest jobs for the growing labor force. . . . The demand of employers for better trained personnel appears to be insatiable."

EDUCATION—FOR WHAT?

Yet we have been breeding a new generation that is undereducated, unemployed or unemployable—the "dropouts" who by 1965 comprised almost one third of the nation's high-school-age students. They leave school usually by tenth grade, wander the streets, form gangs and get into trouble. When this postwar generation reaches adulthood in the early 70's, when 26,000,000 young people are expected to enter the labor market, about 7,500,000 teenagers will not have completed high school. About 2,500,000 million will have failed to reach eighth grade. According to the National Urban League, "A relatively high proportion of them will be non-white." This is particularly disturbing when it is realized that 20 percent of all the new entrants into the labor force in the late 1960's will be Negro;[5] and if present trends continue, half of them will not have had a high school education.

The prospects for these undereducated boys and girls are not bright. The recent past shows that they have three times as high an unemployment rate as graduates. They earn $27 a week less, and the disparity increases as they grow older. Their decision to quit school before graduation means a lifetime of menial jobs with meager salaries or un-employment. Indeed, many young people who dropped out of school to go to work soon found themselves out of a job and on relief. Some have recently joined the Job Corps and other new manpower training programs. Other dropouts have been adding to the urban crime wave which, during the 1960's, has seen a rise in city juvenile delinquency double the national average.

According to recent sociological studies, juvenile deviance and crime, in disproportionate amounts among the lower classes, are caused by the society that encourages certain aspirations yet withholds the possibilities of achieving these aspirations legitimately. As Cloward and Ohlin wrote in *Delinquency and Opportunity,* the cause is a discrepancy "between what lower class youth are led to want and what is actually available to them." For many young Negro males another principal cause is the early and often permanent absence of a father, as former Assistant Secretary of Labor Daniel P. Moynihan made clear in his paper on *The Negro Family.*

This combination of circumstances in ghetto areas is held to be a major cause of the recent summertime riots in Harlem, Rochester, Philadelphia, Los Angeles' Watts and other cities—circumstances to which the new government-aided anti-poverty and job training programs evidently added an extra bitter twist. The inadequately filled promise of new job opportunities and training served to exacerbate unrest in ghettos. "The Negro has gotten a much deeper sense of frustration, much deeper feelings of despair, as the gap increases between what he's actually got and what his expectations have grown to be," Dr. Philip Hauser, head of the University of Chicago's Department of Sociology, observed about the riots.

The McCone Commission, appointed by Governor Edmund Brown of California to investigate the circumstances contributing to the Watts riot, singled out inadequate schooling designed to help overcome the serious handicaps of the disadvantaged Negro child; insufficient jobs for the untrained Negro, and resentment of the police.

In a previous generation, the Italian immigrants' failure to get an education blocked their way, as they discovered too late, to economic opportunities and also led to a disproportionate rate of crime among their youth and later, among adults. For the Negro mass, moving from the twilight of civilization to cities, horizons have suddenly appeared to broaden. In cities they have achieved higher incomes and better housing conditions than in the rural South. But the newly broadened vistas of many in cities are unrealistic, considering the great obstacles.

Why should a Negro youth remain in school? Speaking primarily of the South two decades ago, ·the Swedish economist Gunnar Myrdal wrote in *An American Dilemma*: "Since Negroes are seldom in demand for jobs for which education is necessary, there is certainly nothing surprising in the conclusion that they, unlike whites, fail to improve their opportunities by staying in school longer." The scene has shifted more and more to northern and western city streets and their slums today.

The Negro may read in the papers about those who are succeeding. But the fact that success is news speaks for itself. What is new in today's city slum, Dr. James Conant observed in the early 1960's, is "the almost complete lack of . . . conviction" that they can ever work their way out of poverty on the part of Negro youth. "The unemployed floaters on the street are walking evidence to all youth that nothing can be accomplished by education." Conant placed a good part of the blame for the dropout problem on the discriminatory hiring practices of private companies.

Limited comfort might be derived by blaming the situation on the illiteracy and the consequent relative unemployability of the southern Negro migrant. Those who came to cities in the 1940's did have little schooling. During 1949-50 the highest migration to Chicago, for example, was of adults who had four years of education, and they subsequently bore the brunt of automation. But between 1955 and 1960, the great majority among the most mobile nonwhite migrants—men of twenty-five to twenty-nine years—had at least some high school training, and one fifth had a year or more of college.

Yet the percentage of unemployed Negroes during the recession of the early 1960's was two to three times as high as that of whites at *all* levels — unskilled, semiskilled and skilled. And even as the country neared "full employment" at the end of 1965, the Negro unemployment rate was still twice as high as whites, and it was even higher in the slums.[6] For Negro youth in 1966 it was 27 per cent, compared to 12 per cent for white youth. The President's Commission on Technology, Automation and Economic Progress warned in its 1966 report that "If non-whites continue to hold the same proportion of jobs in each occupation as in 1964, the non-white unemployment rate in 1975 will be more than five times that for the labor force as a whole."

The Negro has made the least advance in the growing sector of the economy—and not always for lack of education. In 1965, the Bureau of the

Census reported that "at all educational levels the Negro is less likely to be a white collar worker." According to a survey by the Census Bureau, among Negro men who had received some college training the proportion employed in lower-paid jobs was 41 per cent or twice the proportion of whites, while for male college graduates the proportion of Negroes in the lower-paid jobs was triple that of whites.

This survey stated, "Although advances have been made since 1950—the rate of progress has slowed and there remain large gaps between Negro and white achievement [even when years of schooling among Negroes are greater]. The political, economic and social issues affecting the Negro appear to arise not from lack of aspiration, but from high aspirations pressing against limited, and, in some places, declining opportunity. . . ." And fair employment laws don't help much.[7]

This highly demanding, specialized age affords the newcomer fewer of the jobs which he has traditionally filled and permits him a shorter period to become a self-sustaining member of the city economy. It also robs him of the realistic hope which served as an economic yeast for earlier generations.

The contrast is dramatized by the tale of a reunion, held in March 1962, of fifty men who had graduated half a century before from Brooklyn's now defunct Public School 43 in the "gray area" of Williamsburgh. "The gathering was a very satisfying experience," commented Nathan Smith, now a hardware merchant in Woodbridge, New Jersey, who initiated the reunion out of curiosity to learn how his classmates had turned out. "Not one of us failed to achieve at least modest success," he told a newspaper reporter who covered the

gathering. "We were mostly immigrants or children of immigrants. The only thing we had was hope and faith in the ideal of American opportunity."

The nature of that opportunity has changed. The era of the self-made, uneducated small businessman who could rise out of the slums is vanishing. He is no longer the backbone of the middle class; he is becoming part of the lower-middle class or the poor. More and more the American businessman has become an organization man; the former owner is now a manager; the clerk has been replaced by self-service. Although the current demand for new services is once again opening opportunities for small business concerns, the man who would be self-sustaining and advance on his own or in an organization must be educated.

THE PUT-OUTS

This suggests the third factor that limits the advance of the newcomers or the "culturally disadvantaged": educability. Much of this problem involves group values and cultural differences.

The lower class, whether white or non-white, differs from the middle class in its emphasis on immediate gratification and security, rather than on striving for individual status and achievement which necessitate thrift and postponement. There is practically no interest in academic education. Rather, learning is valued for immediate utility—filling out forms, applying for known civil service jobs, and so forth. Action is emphasized among the lower class; talk and reading are commonly regarded as unmasculine and are therefore eschewed.

Why should one break with one's group, become tomorrow-oriented and study hard in the expectation that doing well in school will lead to a better future? In today's slum areas, where the majority of dropouts live, many youths either see no reason to make the break or do not know how to make it.

From their earliest years, their deprived, circumscribed environment militates against the education necessary to succeed today. The family and immediate community often fail to provide the early life experiences, the sights, sounds, vocabularly and information which are necessary preschool preparations for learning; these the middle-class child receives almost automatically. Home life is crippled. The uneducated or undereducated parent speaks to the child in monosyllables and points at objects, and may even deride efforts to learn due to his own poor experience in school, or rude treatment by the child's teachers. The harassed mother shouts "Get out of my way" to too many children. There are no books, not even nursery rhymes, in the crowded noisy room or two called home. Study, even sleeping, is often impossible. The boy in the broken home (over one quarter of the Negro children live in families headed by women) is deprived of the essential male model.

Many lower-class parents are aware of the importance of education in this society. But many lack the money and time or the necessary knowledge to help their children. They may be reluctant to meet teachers because they speak poorly or dress badly; they lack the time and organizational sophistication to join PTA activities. Further, since equal opportunities and rewards are not generally available to educated Negroes, there is a tendency to protect children against rebuffs and disappointments. This is partly a defense; often it becomes a built-in lag.

Among the strongest detrimental influences on the Negro child is his negative self-image; he senses that society views him as inferior and expects inferior performance of him. This is attested by the limitations on his father and by the family's living environment, and in effect has been reinforced by the emphasis of many old-line organization Negroes on racial integration as the key to success.

This child is behind before he starts school. One out of every three children in the school systems of our fourteen biggest cities come from such "culturally deprived" backgrounds. In the 1970's, with the lower-class population explosion, there is expected to be one such child out of every two in big cities, and one out of four in many middle-size cities.

The school world has little relevance to the child's life. Its primers are illustrated with rosy-cheeked white children playing on grassy suburban lawns; his composition assignment is to describe "A Trip I Took." He may have left home without breakfast and be too hungry to concentrate. When he is confronted with a difficult problem, he abandons it quickly with a "who cares?" attitude. Teachers, unprepared for and demoralized by these students and their attitudes, spend so much time on discipline that they have little left for actual lessons.

"One of the reasons we have such a terrific discipline problem," an experienced Negro teacher in a New York "gray area" public school pointed out, "is that the children just don't care. School is a place where they are sent. Even children who are eleven and twelve years old have no ideas of their own as to what they want to get out of school." As a result, they get only one

half to one third the exposure to learning that a student usually gets. The high
residential mobility of many poor families compounds the inadequacies of the
child's education. When he reaches high
school, the situation is completely out
of hand, the street takes over, and the
gang.

The burden of blame for pupils' lower
achievement also rests on the attitudes
of teachers—on what Dr. Kenneth Clark,
in *Dark Ghetto,* called their "cultural
bias." A social worker who spent many
years in East Harlem, a vast depressed
community of 180,000 in upper Manhattan, observed: 'Teachers come in
here with stereotypes. They feel the
kids can't learn. So they don't learn."

But looking behind the statistics and
the signs of "cultural deprivation," one
discovers that the majority of the dropouts have average intelligence, and that
20 to 25 per cent even rank as culturally
superior. Recent studies indicate that
the "disadvantaged" child learns differently, more slowly, and responds to different stimuli; he apparently requires
different teaching techniques or programs than those generally available.
His disadvantage is not so much in
natural gifts as in middle-class know-
how—a lack which shows up in testing
and teaching that is oriented to the
middle-class culture.

Before many students drop out, they
have dropped backward. Their progressive retardation may go back to third-
grade level. And the boys do worse than
the girls, who are more apt to have a
suitable adult model in their mother,
and more job opportunities at the white-
collar level. Pupils who do not keep up
with their grades are promoted nonetheless. By high school, the youngsters
are so far behind in basic skills that
many teachers find them uneducable.

"The teachers call them 'drop-outs,'"
a field worker for Chicago's Committee
on New Residents commented. "We call
them 'put-outs.'"

As for the youngsters who move
ahead at grade level, guidance counselors steer them away from jobs from
which Negroes have been traditionally
barred. When they cannot read well,
they are shunted to vocational high
schools to be trained for trades that
have limited openings or are disappearing. Employers who decide to hire Negroes at higher levels or in kinds of
work previously barred are not able to
find enough who are qualified. College
scholarships for qualified Negro students at many top institutions go begging. Attending college appears so
impossible to many children from deprived communities that even preparing for it seems a fantasy. Because they
live in such a separate community, Negro youths are unlikely to hear about
the opportunities.

THE CITY SCHOOLS' PUBLIC

The changing nature of the urban population is dramatized by the two different
school systems that exist in our metropolitan areas. These differ in budget
and product as the two populations'
pocketbooks and political power differ.
The short-changing of cities by state
legislatures compounds the fiscal disparity.

During the 1950's suburban parents
put themselves and their communities
into debt to build schools, raise salaries,
expand curricula and improve teaching
methods, to give their bumper crop of
children the best education so they
could get into college. Central cities
also had an unexpectedly large number
of pupils, but they were educating a
generation of dropouts.

Dr. James Conant found that in the wealthy suburbs annual expenditures were often over $1,000 per pupil, compared to an average under $500 in slum schools; teacher pay was commensurate. (Between 1952 and 1962, nearly half the licensed teachers in New York City left the system.)

The financial issue was well put by Max Rubin, who served as chairman of the New York City Board of Education from 1961 to 1963. "Everybody wants good schools, but how far will the people go to pay for the schools?" he asked. "Politicians prefer to run on a low tax platform rather than on better schools and higher taxes. Without the priority on the part of the public, what can you expect of the school board and teachers? Until good schools become good politics, we will be struggling."

Negro organization leaders and many middle-class Negro parents have spent their energies and political leverage on integration. They have demanded that Negro children be bused into white-neighborhood schools (and the reverse), and have urged school pairing, rezoning and other expedients. They even oppose building new schools in ghettos. The Negro leaders have been reluctant to admit that the disadvantaged child (in big cities, many non-white and Spanish-speaking children test several grades below their white contemporaries) requires much more than school integration to improve his learning ability. They did not fight for the expensive special programs these children need, and they tended to ignore the uncomfortable fact that in integrated schools disadvantaged children have to attend separate classes because of their academic deficiencies.

Some significant experiments are under way on a metropolitan basis—in the Hartford, Connecticut, Boston and Los Angeles areas—to achieve greater racial balance by transferring some inner-city Negro pupils to white suburban schools. In Los Angeles the program is reported to be drawing mainly middle-class Negro children, and teachers say that poor children from Watts are upset by their exposure to Bel Air's wealth.

Perhaps the benefit of such pupil transfers is greater for the insulated suburban white children than for their Negro classmates. Associate Professor Preston Wilcox of the Columbia University School of Social Work, himself a Negro, has stated that emphasis on integration is probably harmful to the Negro child. "Psychologically, it's bad to tell a kid that he'll only make it if he sits next to a white," Wilcox comments.

In the big cities with huge and growing core ghettos, the integrationists are rapidly becoming crusaders without a feasible cause. In Philadelphia, Detroit, Chicago and New York, to cite just several big-city school systems, white pupils now form the minority, and the percentage of the white student population has been dropping a few points each year. In Washington D.C., public school enrollment in 1965 was 90 per cent Negro, compared to 85 per cent just the year before. Los Angeles was the only one of twenty-one big cities in which white enrollment did not drop that year. The trend is unlikely to level off or reverse itself, at least in the next decade.

Educational disadvantages are worsened by the unanticipated high densities in new ghetto-slum areas. Physical capacities have been overwhelmed. One old high school in East Brooklyn, built for 1,600 pupils, last year had an enrollment of 3,400, 85 per cent of them Negro and Puerto Rican. The school's wiring is so antiquated that it is not possible to use modern teaching devices to help the many students with reading problems. The need for three sessions means that some students start school by seven, eat lunch at 9:30 and are free by noon to roam the streets. Not surprisingly, the dropout rate is 40 per cent.

Middle-class Negro parents have become so dissatisfied with the quality of education in cities' public schools that a number who can afford it have also removed their children. (Unlike white families, many cannot withdraw to the suburbs.) In the District of Columbia in 1965, over 6 per cent of the Negro students were attending private or parochial schools, often at great financial sacrifice, and a surprising number were the sons and daughters of public schoolteachers.

Much of the insistence by Negroes on integration is doubtless based on a desire for quality education. (Commenting on parent attitudes, the director of an East Harlem settlement house observed, "In most neighborhoods, the teachers are cowed by the PTA. Here, the parents are cowed by the teacher.")

But a dramatic reversal seems to be coming about. In the summer of 1966, Livingston L. Wingate, director of Haryou-Act, the Harlem anti-poverty agency calling for the establishment of quality education in Negro ghettos, declared that "We must no longer pursue the myth that integrated education is equated with quality education." A poll of several ghetto areas in big cities showed that the great majority of parents are concerned with better education; only 2 per cent specifically with school integration.

A growing self-assurance and political awareness was evident among the par-

ents of children who were to enter a new $5,000,000 air-conditioned East Harlem elementary school in the fall of 1966. At first they insisted that the school not be opened unless it were integrated or they were given control. Slowly they shifted to a demand for control, with appointment of a Negro or Puerto Rican principal, and more Negro teachers.

But the problems of inadequate funds, insufficient teachers, old overcrowded schools and outmoded curriculum still remain, and in most ghetto areas the educational situation has been steadily deteriorating.

THE BUSINESSMEN AND THE EDUCATORS

Where have the big businessmen, the "civic leaders" of cities, been in the midst of the mounting school crisis? Strangely silent. The big worry of the businessman (as opposed to the father) is that spending more on schools will increase local taxes and scare away industry. His children do not use the public schools in central cities; few even live in the cities. Only rarely have top city leaders fought for central city school improvement in recent years or pressed state legislatures to revise school aid formulas and local school district taxing powers.[8]

Local business, industrial and financial leaders—the men who have been working for downtown revitalization, industrial redevelopment, freeway construction, metropolitan mass transit and a "quality" urban environment in order to stop the flight of industry, the white middle class and the tax base—show a strange lack of concern about the school crisis. If the present situation is allowed to continue, it seems obvious that their city will be less able to attract desirable business concerns, and the businessmen will be less able to get qualified workers for their own companies and attract white families to their redevelopments.

For at least six years, the U.S. Department of Labor has been putting up warnings. Perhaps the businessman does not perceive the implications of the inner-city school problems for his city's economic future, nor recognize that the undereducated central-city youths are likely to cause the urban manpower crisis of the 1970's. Perhaps it is hard for them to see the economic payoff in education; few even recognize the economic toll of discrimination practices.[9]

Yet the economists have been making a strong case for the return from investment in education, especially in post-industrial society. In 1960, University of Chicago economist Theodore W. Schultz, in his presidential address to the American Economic Association (and in a subsequent book on *The Economic Value of Education*), declared that "No small part of the low earnings of many Negroes, poor farm people and some older workers reflects the failure to have invested in their health and education. . . . We can ill afford to continue making the same mistake."

Schultz also observed that "If we were to treat education as pure investment, this result would suggest that the returns to education were relatively more attractive than those in non-human capital." Research has shown, he reported, that the impressive rise in real earnings per worker achieved in the past generation—the "unexplained increases" in the national income, came about "not as much through investment in capital goods, as generally assumed, but through greatly increased public and personal investment in human capital."

In 1965 the Committee for Economic Development, a national nonprofit organization of enlightened and industrial leaders, in effect endorsed his philosophy with a policy statement on *Raising Low Incomes Through Improved Education;* they urged that all possible resources, public and private, be brought to bear on adapting the educational system to the economic system, and vice versa. A CED member, William Benton, publisher of the Encyclopaedia Britannica, observed that "although education is our largest business, our factual information about the educational system, and about how best to achieve its goals, is astonishingly inadequate for the purposes of sensible planning and decision-making."

The Ford Foundation's Great Cities School Improvement Program, which in the early 1960's stimulated school systems in fourteen big cities to develop new methods and programs for teaching inner-city children, blamed the educators for public indifference. In 1963, a spokesman charged that the educators have failed to communicate the problems, and have been unwilling to evaluate the effectiveness of present methods.

"How can you expect the businessman to respond?" he asked. "He hears the Superintendent of Schools say everything is fine, and one morning he opens the paper and reads that half the students are illiterate.[10] He wonders what the schools have been doing with all the money they have.

"Educators have secured for themselves a unique isolation in American society. The majority of school systems have their own tax structure, are independent of City Hall and call themselves the answer to society's problems. The public goes along because Americans have an ingrained belief that education is the answer to everything. They tell the public what it should want and shortchange the process of planning with the people. But because the school systems refuse to evaluate themselves, they have not documented the case for what education can do, especially in central cities, and thus it becomes increasingly difficult to sell themselves. Further, their huge unwieldy administrative structure favors the status quo and penalizes the person who tries to innovate."

WHAT KIND OF EDUCATION IS THE ANSWER?

Not all educators remained oblivious to the special problems of educating inner-city children. Many were eagerly searching for new methods "to compensate for the deficiencies which hinder the disadvantaged child from taking full advantage of the conventional education program," as a 1963 bulletin of the National Education Association summarized the new movement.

New York City led the way in 1959 with its Demonstration Guidance Program, which was widely publicized as Higher Horizons. This approach offered culturally deprived children an enriched curriculum, including special counseling, more teacher attention and outings to sites of interest and cultural facilities in the larger community. Children in the pilot program responded well, and the program appealed to the general public. The new compensatory education approach was soon followed in other cities, while the program was expanded in New York schools.

There were stirrings and changes in many big-city schools, stimulated to a large extent by the millions in matching grants from the Ford Foundation. Extra personnel were added: guidance counselors, remedial reading teachers, assistant principals, "helping" teachers, community agents from school neighborhoods to provide a liaison with the community. Remedial programs in language skills were undertaken and class sizes were reduced; new teaching techniques were used; preschool classes prepared three- and four-year olds for learning; "alienated" parents were actively involved in school activities.

But federal money was required for a national program, and the civil rights ferment, ghetto riots and mounting concern for the urban poor pressured Congress into passing the unprecedented Elementary and Secondary Education Act of 1965. Under its Title I, over $1,-000,000,000 was made available in the first year alone for special programs for educationally deprived children in poverty areas. The recent compensatory education programs were predominant among those eligible for Title I.

This development seemed to be the most encouraging yet. Crisis had overcome local fear of federal control of education. In 1966 many cities began Higher Horizon-type programs, team teaching methods, remedial reading programs, talent development, and "preparation for work" programs. Some were also aided by the Office of Economic Opportunity. The most popular new program was for preschool children, Project Head Start, characterized as "the infant prodigy of the Great Society." President Johnson himself hailed it as "battle-tested."

In concluding this study of American cities facing their problems, it seemed necessary to document the achievements on the great new urban education frontier, and also to find out how much more federal and local money would be required to do a saturation job.

The results were disconcerting, but instructive. As of the summer of 1966, the returns from the new urban education programs generally show that "more of the same" does not have significant effect; that the "noticeable" improvements in pupils do not last under present circumstances; and that there are almost no measurable achievements to speak of.

What seemed particularly unsettling was that the U.S. Office of Education was loathe to admit to Congress or the public the ineffectiveness of most of its billion-dollar Title I program. (I later learned that the office *was* beginning to warn the educators.) HEW Secretary John W. Gardner told Congress in April that "Great educational strides can be made by specialized educational programs," and Commissioner of Education Harold Howe testified, "Our prior experience in several cities demonstrates that such special attention in and of itself will result in improved educational performance." Yet the Office of Education could not provide me with data from local schools that showed quantifiable results. It turned out that the legislative testimony was based on publications, several years old, of early efforts in the Ford Foundation Great Cities and New York's Higher Horizons.

These publications were, indeed, optimistic about the initial results. But the Ford Foundation could direct me to none of the Great Cities schools that had found significant differences between children in compensatory and conventional education programs when tested for specific achievements.[11] (Actually, these programs lacked a research component; the main concern was to get into the schools and stimulate federal action.)

Dr. Mario Fantini, formerly director of the Great Cities program in Syracuse, New York, and now a Program Associate in the Foundation's Education Program, flatly asserted that "More of the same won't have the pay-off we expect, and I doubt we'll ever have the kind of money to do the job that way. The problem with our original approach is that the schools have assumed the kids need compensation for deficiencies and that there is nothing wrong with their program. But the schools themselves are outmoded, and we have to change the process of education. There are the beginnings of a shift in this direction. But we had to start somewhere."

Pittsburgh, another of the Great Cities, has been pushing compensatory education and team teaching in slum neighborhood schools for five years and could not show measurable improvements in children's reading scores. Officials say that high pupil turnover in slum schools has made it difficult to assess the program, and the system lacks staff for more sophisticated measurements. But teachers were confident that the improved climate would eventually be reflected in achievement scores.

Coming hard on the heels of these unsettling findings, early in July a *New York Times* article reported that the city's Board of Education had quietly closed down Higher Horizons without even a press release. An independent professional evaluation of the program's first four years (grudgingly released by the Board of Education) had found virtually no measurable effect on the achievements, IQ or reading level of enrolled pupils. It was explained that budgetary limitations had made impossible the "saturation" with additional services originally envisioned. (If the original $250 per pupil had been spent on each of the 100,000 pupils involved, $250,000,000 would have been required annually; this is almost one quarter of Congress' first-year appropriation for Title I of the Education Act.) *The New York Times'* Education Editor, Fred Hechinger, called the results shown by some pupils "the triumphs of the lucky few."

But what of Head Start, the popular and battle-tested program? In most cities it had been offered only on a summertime basis, and one could not expect a great permanent effect. But New Haven, Connecticut, has had the pre-kindergarten program as part of the regular school year for the past six years, and could provide no data of measurable change. "Through kindergarten, there is enormous noticeable improvement, but by second grade it's all gone," a school official stated. "The children come up against the same large classes, no extra aides, the old program and teachers."

This situation supported the findings of Dr. Martin Deutsch, a psychologist and director of the Institute for Developmental Studies at New York University, who pioneered the pre-kindergarten program; he claimed that a constant follow-up in later grades is necessary if early gains are not to be lost. It also seemed to support warnings to Congress by Education Commissioner Howe that "initial gains evaporate if special education programs are not maintained," and, "Only a comprehensive long-term program . . . can overcome [disadvantaged children's] deficiencies."

THE FLAWS IN THE SYSTEM

We should not belittle the great side-benefits of the new concern and funds —the greater involvement of parents and other potential leaders in inner-city neighborhoods, the expanded role of schools in local community life, health benefits for the children. (In the first summer of Head Start, 70 per cent of the children had their first medical and dental examination. In Tampa, Florida, twelve cases of tuberculosis and fifty of nutritional deficiencies were found.) Many schools are also getting adequate libraries for the first time.

Moreover, the limited effect of the initial attempts may well point the way to more effective action, and even compensatory education is better than what was happening before.

The lack of research-proven premises behind this billion-dollar educational program probably reflects the government's desperate need to do "something" about ghetto children as much as educators' unwillingness to evaluate themselves. HEW Secretary Gardner makes known his concern about the lack of educational research. (One city has had three research directors and no research results to show for it. One director, who recently resigned, gave an oral report to the Board of Education, but wished to keep the findings unwritten until used for his own professional publication purposes.)

Title III of the Educational Act is promising. This relatively unpublicized provision finances local "centers for change" to stimulate schools to a more innovative approach that relates research to practice. Known as PACE—Projects to Advance Creativity in Education—Title III also encourages higher-education institutions and local cultural organizations to provide local schools with leadership, new kinds of talents and services. Another little-known program is Title IV, which encourages educational institutions and agencies on different levels to band together on a regional basis to establish "multi-institutional laboratories" for researching and developing new ideas. One recent example of university-school affiliation is New York University's "adoption" of a school in the Bedford-Stuyvesant area, assisted by Ford Foundation funds.

It is important to take note here of the three fundamental flaws in compensatory education, the "more of same" approach. These are mostly failures of society at large, not just of the educators. Indeed, much at fault is the basic American fallacy that education is a panacea. As in public housing, we have not considered all the determining variables.

The first problem is that the schools cannot remedy the deficits of home, family and slum environment. "Remember, the children only spend nine per cent of their time in school," one educator points out. A recent study by the U.S. Office of Education found that differences in the quality of a school had very little effect on the achievement scores of children who have a strong foundation for education at home. Children from disadvantaged homes benefit relatively more from a good school, but it does not fill the gap.

Secondly, much of the present school curriculum is irrelevant for inner-city children. As Dr. Conant observed in *Slums and Suburbs*, "What can words like 'freedom,' 'liberty' and 'equality of opportunity' mean to these young people? With what kind of zeal and dedication can we expect them to withstand . . . communism?" Psychologist Dr. Kenneth Clark has repeatedly pointed out that compensatory education will not work unless the content has more meaning for children from deprived

homes. A hopeful step is the publication by major publishing houses of new textbooks and readers that show Negroes, Puerto Ricans and whites as a normal part of the American scene and also include the history of the Negro in America. On the question of whether what is taught in schools is relevant, one inner-city curriculum director observes, "We're finding out how bad what we've been doing is for *both* the white and Negro child. I'd dump 90 per cent of what we teach."

Dr. Fantini asserts that "Middle class children make the schools look good. They give back what's expected of them. But what's so good about middle class know-how? We're all disadvantaged educationally. One need only examine the drop-out rate in college, the performance of most citizens in the wider social arena, the apathy towards social injustice and our inability to exercise leadership to highlight the obsolescence of current education. The deeper issue is whether the educational system is equipping people to deal with the problems of society."

Finally, there is the basic problem of motivation and discrimination. How can we persuade disadvantaged students and their parents that it is worthwhile for the youngster to remain in school and study, to defer premature employment and make the necessary personal investment of time and effort on the premise that such efforts will be rewarded? (Well over half the estimated cost of higher education in the United States comes from income deferred by students.)

As Dr. Conant concluded in *Slums and Suburbs*, "To improve the work of the slum schools requires an improvement in the lives of the families who inhabit the slums, but without a drastic change in the employment opportunities for urban Negro youth relatively little can be accomplished."

Our cities, the centers of the nation's economy, are also the end of the racial line in America. In cities we must proceed simultaneously and at full speed on two parallel fronts: improving environments *and* opportunities. There is no turning back.

NOTES

1. Making it larger than that of the State of New York.
2. As the report pointed out, ADC laws place "a premium on the absence of the father" by not giving assistance to families with employable fathers.
3. The Cook County Welfare Department established required literacy classes for such able-bodied, unemployed men.
4. Between 1960 and 1966 alone, New York City lost 80,000 manufacturing jobs; it is expected that it will lose 48,000 more by 1970, according to a study by the City Planning Commission.
5. The percentage in cities will be much higher.
6. A special Labor Department census in March 1966 of the poorest districts in the one hundred largest cities showed the overall Negro unemployment rate to be 9.4 per cent—compared to 3.8 per cent nationally. For Negro boys it was 31 per cent. Many in the prime-working-age group were not even looking for work, and thus not technically unemployed. In some "new" ghetto areas, the West Side of Chicago and Brooklyn's Bedford-Stuyvesant, unemployment ran an estimated 25 per cent in the summer of 1966, and statistics showed a sudden national increase in Negro joblessness.

7. In employment, as in housing, the effectiveness of anti-discrimination laws, including the Civil Rights Act of 1964, is hampered by inadequate enforcement powers, small budgets and weak administration, a Twentieth-Century Fund report has found. Another study reveals that extraordinary efforts, including aggressive recruiting campaigns by employers, are necessary to overcome Negroes' emotional blocks and inertia. Psychological tests have also been found to keep Negroes out of jobs.
8. One of the exceptions was Pennsylvania, led by Pittsburgh and Philadelphia and supported by Governor William Scranton. Recently, some southern states have come to spend a much higher percentage of their budgets on public education than have northern states—as part of the South's drive to attract industry from old northern cities.
9. The President's Council of Economic Advisers found that if discrimination in employment were eliminated and the Negro potential fully realized, at least $13,000,000,000 more in purchasing power would be placed in the hands of the bottom income groups, and current annual growth would double.
10. In October 1965, the New York City Board of Education released results of standardized achievement tests given to 626,148 pupils in second through tenth grade during 1964-65. These disclosed that more than half the city's pupils were behind their counterparts throughout the country in reading and arithmetic in second through eighth grade, and that sizable numbers were two, three and four years behind in reading.
11. An apparent exception has been the Banneker Schools in St. Louis, the one large-scale experiment where children are reported to be performing at grade level; but this was not one of the Ford programs and the Foundation had no evaluation of it. A part of the Banneker Schools' unusual success is believed to be the forceful personality of the principal and his use of every strategy to involve parents and students in the learning process.

Race and Class in Cities: A Conservative View

EDWARD C. BANFIELD

. . . the dominant aim of our society seems to be to middle-class-ify all of its members.

John Dollard, 1937

Much of what has happened—as well as of what is happening—in the typical city or metropolitan area can be understood in terms of three imperatives. The first is demographic: if the population of a city increases, the city must expand in one direction or another—up, down, or from the center outward. The second is technological: if it is feasible to transport large numbers of people outward (by train, bus, and automobile) but not upward or downward (by elevator), the city must expand outward. The third is economic: if the distribution of wealth and income is such that some can afford new housing and the time and money to commute considerable distances to work while others cannot, the expanding periphery of the city must be occupied by the first group (the "well-off") while the older, inner parts of the city, where most of the jobs are, must be occupied by the second group (the "not well-off").

The word "imperatives" is used to emphasize the inexorable, constraining character of the three factors that together comprise the logic of metropolitan growth. Indeed, the principal purpose of this chapter is to show that, given a rate of population growth, a transportation technology, and a distribution of income, certain consequences must inevitably follow; that the city and its hinterland must develop according to a predictable pattern and that even an all-wise and all-powerful government could not change this pattern except by first changing the logic that gives rise to it. The argument is not that nothing can be done to improve matters. Rather, it is that only those things can be done which lie within the boundaries—rather narrow ones, to be sure—fixed by the logic of the growth process. Nor is it argued that the only factors influencing metropolitan development are those that relate to population, technology, and income. Countless others also influence it. . . .

The logic of growth does not explain all that needs explaining. For one thing, it does not explain why the city expanded outward as fast as it did. When they moved, the well-off were strongly impelled by economic forces to move outward—first to the outlying neighborhoods of the central city, then to inlying suburbs, and later to outlying ones. But the well-off did not have to move as soon as they did or in such numbers. If the trolley car and then the automobile were causes of their moving, they were also effects of their desire to move. (Philadelphia was the "city of homes" long before rapid transit was invented, Adna F. Weber

From *The Unheavenly City Revisited: A Revision of The Unheavenly City* by Edward C. Banfield, pp. 25–26, 52–76. Copyright © 1968, 1970, 1974 by Edward C. Banfield. Reprinted by permission of Little, Brown and Company.

pointed out apropos of this in 1899.[1])
Also, the logic of growth does not explain why a considerable proportion of
the well-off failed to move at all. In
1960, for example, about 22 percent of
families in the central cities had incomes large enough to buy a new
house.[2] In fact, the median family income in the central cities was only 16
percent less than in the suburbs. Obviously, some families evaluate the advantages of central city versus suburban living differently than do others.
Furthermore, the logic of growth does
not explain the existence of slums. A
slum is not simply a district of low-
quality housing; rather, it is one in
which the style of life is squalid and
vicious.[3] The logic of growth *does* require that, in general, the lowest-in-
come people live in the oldest, highest-
density, most run-down housing, which
will be nearest to the factories, warehouses, stores, and offices of the inner, or downtown, part of the central
city; however, nothing in the logic of
growth says that such districts must be
squalid and vicious.

To account for these features of metropolitan development in the United
States, a second explanatory principle
must, so to speak, be placed over the
first one. This is the concept of class
culture. The purpose of this chapter
is to show how certain styles of life
that are learned in childhood and
passed on as a kind of collective heritage operate (within limits set by the
logic of growth) to give the city its
characteristic form and most of its
problems. It is one of the main conten-
tions of this book that the class cultures of the city, no less than its logic
of growth, set limits on what the
policymaker can accomplish.

American sociologists usually define
social class in terms of "prestige" or
"standing": an individual belongs to
one or another class (the number of
classes and the names they are given
differ from one writer to another) depending upon whether he is "looked up
to" or "looked down on" by the consensus of the community.[4] Frequently,
an index of easily measured attributes
—for example, income, education, occupation, and housing type—is treated as
an indicator of prestige or standing. It
generally turns out that the people
put in the same prestige class share the
same outlook and style of life, one that
is learned in childhood and that constitutes a "life style" for them. That is,
the prestige classes turn out to be cultures, or rather (since the outlook and
style of life of each class is a *variant* of
one common to all) subcultures.[5]

The class subcultures have been
described by many sociologists, although never with the rigor and completeness of an ethnographic report (a
fact that leaves some social scientists in
doubt as to whether they are really
subcultures).[6] There is general agreement as to their characteristics, and
what follows in the next few pages is
essentially a summary of what sociologists have reported about them. It differs from most other accounts, however, in that each class subculture is
characterized as having a distinctive
psychological orientation toward providing for a more or less distant future.

In the analysis to come, the individual's orientation toward the future
will be regarded as a function of two
factors: (1) ability to imagine a future,
and (2) ability to discipline oneself to
sacrifice present for future satisfaction.[7]
The more distant the future the individual can imagine and can discipline
himself to make sacrifices for, the

"higher" is his class. The criterion, it should be noted, is ability, not performance. Later on (in Chapter 10) it will be explained how a person may be psychologically capable of providing for the future and yet not do so. For the present, however, his time horizon may be thought of as a function of his class culture alone. The reason for defining class in terms of orientation toward the future is that this conception seems to lend itself better than any others to analysis of the kinds of problems that are of special interest to the policymaker.[8]

The class subcultures have numerous secondary characteristics associated with this primary one (the existence of a *pattern* of characteristics justifies the term *subculture*); most of these secondary characteristics are probably caused, directly or indirectly, by the primary one, but this is a question that need not be treated here. In any case, each subculture displays distinctive attitudes toward—for example—authority, self-improvement, risk, and violence, and distinctive forms of social organization, most notably of family organization. For the purposes of this book, however, the *defining* characteristic of a class subculture is—to repeat—the one primary factor; namely, psychological orientation toward providing for the future.

For present purposes it will suffice to describe four subcultures—those of the upper, middle, working, and lower classes—and to describe them schematically as ideal types.[9] In other words, what follows are generalized models of subcultures, which do not necessarily describe the cultural traits of *particular* individuals. The four subcultures should be thought of as bands (rather than points) on a continuous scale or

spectrum—bands that sometimes blend and overlap so that there can exist "in-between" positions equally characteristic of "adjoining" subcultures.

It must again be strongly emphasized that this use of the term *class* is different from the ordinary one.[10] As the term is used here, a person who is poor, unschooled, and of low status may be upper class; indeed he *is* upper class if he is psychologically capable of providing for a distant future. By the same token, one who is rich and a member of "the 400" may be lower class: he *is* lower class if he is incapable of conceptualizing the future or of controlling his impulses and is therefore obliged to live from moment to moment. In general, of course, there is at least a *rough* correspondence between being, for example, upper class in the present sense and upper class as ordinarily defined: this is because people who are capable of providing for a distant future tend by that very circumstance to get education (as distinct from schooling) and with it wealth, status, and power. Similarly, people incapable of looking ahead for more than a day or two or of controlling their impulses are likely to be poor, unskilled, and of low status for this very reason.

It should also be emphasized that behavior can rarely be explained solely in terms of class subculture. The individual belongs to other subcultures besides the class one—age group, occupational group, and ethnic group subcultures, for example. Moreover, culture is by no means the only determinant of his behavior; in many situations thorough knowledge of an individual's culture(s) would not help an observer make "interesting" predictions about his behavior.

Strong correlations have been shown to exist between IQ score and socio-economic status, and some investigators have claimed that these correlations are largely attributable to genetic factors.[11] These considerations suggest the possibility that one's ability to take account of the future may often depend mainly upon one's biologically inherited intelligence. The assumption being made here, however, is a contrary one—namely, that time horizon is a cultural (or subcultural) trait passed on to the individual in early childhood from his group.

THE UPPER CLASS

At the most future-oriented end of the scale, the upper-class individual expects a long life, looks forward to the future of his children, grandchildren, great-grandchildren (the family "line"), and is concerned also for the future of such abstract entities as the community, nation, or mankind. He is confident that within rather wide limits he can, if he exerts himself to do so, shape the future to accord with his purposes. He therefore has strong incentives to "invest" in the improvement of the future situation —i.e., to sacrifice some present satisfaction in the expectation of enabling someone (himself, his children, mankind, etc.) to enjoy greater satisfactions at some future time. Future-oriented culture teaches the individual that he would be cheating himself if he allowed gratification of his impulses (for example, for sex or violence) to interfere with his provision for the future.

The upper-class individual is markedly self-respecting, self-confident, and self-sufficient. He places great value on independence, curiosity, creativity, happiness, "developing one's potentialities to the full," and consideration for others. In rearing his children, he stresses these values along with the idea that one should govern one's relations with others (and, in the final analysis, with one's self) by *internal* standards rather than by conformity to an externally given code ("not because you're told to but because you take the other person into consideration").[12] The upper-class parent is not alarmed if his children remain unemployed and unmarried to the age of thirty, especially if they remain in school.[13] He does not mind being alone; indeed, he requires a good deal of privacy. He wants to express himself (he may carry self-expression to the point of eccentricity), and, in principle at least, he favors self-expression by others. He takes a tolerant, perhaps even an encouraging, view of unconventional behavior in sex, the arts, and politics. He is mindful of the rights of others and wants issues to be settled on their merits and by rational discussion. He deplores bigotry (which is not to say that he has no prejudices) and abhors violence.

It will be seen that two features of this culture—the disposition to postpone present satisfaction for the sake of improving matters in the future and the desire to "express one's personality" —are somewhat antagonistic. Upper-class (that is, future-oriented) culture permits the individual to emphasize either theme. If he thinks that his means (money, power, knowledge, and the like) are almost certainly adequate to maintain him and his "line" throughout the future he envisions, the future-oriented individual has no incentive to "invest" (that is, trade present for future satisfaction) and may therefore emphasize self-expression. If, on the other hand, he thinks that his means may *not* be adequate (he will think this, of course, no matter how large his means if his plans for the future are grand enough), he is likely to emphasize self-discipline so that he may acquire the larger stock of means that he thinks he needs. Insofar as he chooses the expressive alternative, the upper-class individual's style of life may resemble the present-oriented one of the lower class. But whereas the lower-class individual is capable *only* of present-oriented behavior, the upper-class one can choose. He may, for example, do some things that require a high degree of skill, discipline, and judgment, living the rest of the time from moment to moment. Even if he lives from moment to moment all the time, he does so by choice—it is his "thing," his mode of self-expression. By contrast, the "true" present-orientedness of the lower class is both unrelieved and involuntary.

The upper-class individual feels a strong attachment to entities (formal organizations, the neighborhood, the nation, the world) toward which he stands, or wants to stand, in a relation of fellowship. He sees the "community" (or "society") as having long-range goals and the ability to shape the future. He tends to feel that it is one's responsibility to "serve" the community by assisting in efforts for its improvement—perhaps because, his own goals being long-range ones, he has a stake in the future of the community. At any rate, he tends to be active in "public service" organizations and to feel a strong obligation (which he does not always act upon, of course) to contribute time, money, and effort to worthy causes.[14] (In the South the upper-class attitude in these matters is dif-

ferent. As W. J. Cash remarked, the aristocratic ideal of the planter became corrupted by frontier individualism, which, "while willing enough to ameliorate the specific instance, relentlessly laid down as its basic social postulate the doctrine that every man was completely and wholly responsible for himself."[15])

THE MIDDLE CLASS

The middle-class individual expects to be still in his prime at sixty or thereabouts; he plans ahead for his children and perhaps his grandchildren, but, less future-oriented than the ideal typical member of the upper class, he is not likely to think in terms of "line" or to be much concerned about "mankind" in the distant future. He, too, is confident of his ability to influence the future, but he does not expect to influence so distant a future as does the upper-class individual, nor is he as confident about the probable success of his efforts to influence it. The middle-class individual's self-feelings are a little less strong than those of the upper-class individual; he is also somewhat less desirous of privacy. Although he shows a good deal of independence and creativity and a certain taste for self-expression, these traits rarely lead to eccentricity. He is less likely than the upper-class individual to have means that he considers adequate to assure a satisfactory level of goal attainment throughout his anticipated future. Therefore, "getting ahead"—and the self-improvement and sacrifice of impulse gratification that it requires—will be more likely to take precedence with him over "the expression of one's personality." In the lower middle class, self-improvement is a principal theme of life, whereas in the upper middle class, self-expression is emphasized. Almost without exception, middle-class people want their children to go to college and to acquire the kind of formal training that will help them "get ahead." In matters of sex, the middle-class individual is (in principle, at least) "conventional," and in art and politics, too, he is more ready than the upper-class individual to accept the received opinion. He has regard for the rights of others; he deplores bigotry and abhors violence. He does not, however, hold these attitudes as strongly as do members of the upper class.

The middle-class individual does not feel as strong a sense of responsibility to the community as does the upper-class one, and he defines the community somewhat less inclusively. He wants (in principle, at least) to "belong" to a community and to be of "service" to it, and accordingly he joins organizations, including "service" ones. (In the lower middle class, the taste for public service and reform is relatively weak: the individual usually votes against public improvements that will not benefit him directly.) The middle-class individual, however, is less willing than the upper-class one to give time, money, and effort for public causes.

THE WORKING CLASS

The working-class individual does not "invest" as heavily in the future, nor in so distant a future, as does the middle-class one.[16] He expects to be an "old man" by the time he is fifty, and his time horizon is fixed accordingly. Also, he has less confidence than the middle-class individual in his ability to shape the future and has a stronger sense of being at the mercy of fate, a "power structure," and other uncontrollable forces. For this reason, perhaps, he attaches more importance to luck than does the middle-class individual. He is self-respecting and self-confident, but these feelings are less marked in him than in the middle-class individual and they extend to a somewhat narrower range of matters. As compared to the middle-class individual, he is little disposed toward either self-improvement or self-expression; "getting ahead" and "enlarging one's horizon" have relatively little attraction for him. In rearing his children, he emphasizes the virtues of neatness and cleanliness, honesty, obedience, and respect for external authority. (As David Riesman has observed, the problem in the working class is not, as in the upper middle class, to stimulate children; rather, it is to control them—"to teach them faith, respect, and obedience, rather than independence of mind and development of talents."[17]) If his children do not go to college, the working-class individual does not mind much. In his relations with others, he is often authoritarian and intolerant, and sometimes aggressive. He is not only a bigot but a self-righteous one. Violence and brutality are less shocking to him than to middle-class persons; indeed, he regards them—up to a point—as normal expressions of a masculine style. To the working class, the middle class appears somewhat lacking in masculinity, and the upper class—a male member of which may even weep under stress—appears decidedly feminine or "queer."

The working-class individual's deepest attachment is to his family (most of his visiting is with relatives, not friends). However, his relationship to his wife and children is not as stable or as close—for instance, does not involve as much companionship—as these relationships tend to be in the middle class.[18] Privacy is of little importance to him: he likes to have people around, and the noises and smells that they make seldom bother him (when he goes on vacation it is not to the country, which he finds too quiet and lonely, but to crowded resorts). The sense of sharing a purpose with others is not as important to him as it is to members of the upper classes, and when he joins an organization it is more likely to be for companionship and "fun" than for "service" or civic improvement. He may vote, especially if someone asks him to as a favor. His opinions on public matters are highly conventional (it does not seem to occur to him that he is entitled to form opinions of his own), and his participation in politics is motivated not by political principles but by ethnic and party loyalties, the appeal of personalities, or the hope of favors from the precinct captain.

THE LOWER CLASS

At the present-oriented end of the scale, the lower-class individual lives from moment to moment. If he has any awareness of a future, it is of something fixed, fated, beyond his control: things happen *to* him, he does not *make* them happen. Impulse governs his behavior, either because he cannot discipline himself to sacrifice a present for a future satisfaction or because he has no sense of the future. He is therefore radically improvident: whatever he cannot consume immediately he considers valueless. His bodily needs (especially for sex) and his taste for "action"[19] take precedence over everything

else—and certainly over any work routine. He works only as he must to stay alive, and drifts from one unskilled job to another, taking no interest in the work.

The lower-class individual has a feeble, attenuated sense of self; he suffers from feelings of self-contempt and inadequacy, and is often apathetic or dejected. (In her discussion of "very low-lower class" families, Eleanor Pavenstadt notes that "the saddest, and to us the outstanding characteristic of this group, with adults and children alike, was the self-devaluation."[20]) In his relations with others he is suspicious and hostile, aggressive yet dependent. He is unable to maintain a stable relationship with a mate; commonly he does not marry. He feels no attachment to community, neighbors, or friends (he has companions, not friends), resents all authority (for example, that of policemen, social workers, teachers, landlords, employers), and is apt to think that he has been "railroaded" and to want to "get even." He is a nonparticipant: he belongs to no voluntary organizations, has no political interests, and does not vote unless paid to do so.

The lower-class household is usually female-based. The woman who heads it is likely to have a succession of mates who contribute intermittently to its support but take little or no part in rearing the children. In managing the children, the mother (or aunt, or grandmother) is characteristically impulsive: once they have passed babyhood they are likely to be neglected or abused, and at best they never know what to expect next. A boy raised in a female-based household is likely at an early age to join a corner gang of other such boys and to learn from the gang the "tough" style of the lower-class man.[21]

The stress on "action," risk-taking, conquest, fighting, and "smartness" makes lower-class life extraordinarily violent. However, much of the violence is probably more an expression of mental illness than of class culture. The incidence of mental illness is greater in the lower class than in any of the others. Moreover, the nature of lower-class culture is such that much behavior that in another class would be considered bizarre seems routine.[22]

In its emphasis on "action" and its utter instability, lower-class culture seems to be more attractive to men than to women. Gans writes:

The woman tries to develop a stable routine in the midst of poverty and deprivation; the action-seeking man upsets it. In order to have any male relationships, however, the woman must participate to some extent in his episodic life style. On rare occasions, she may even pursue it herself. Even then, however, she will try to encourage her children to seek a routine way of life. Thus the woman is much closer to working-class culture, at least in her aspirations, although she is not often successful in achieving them.[23]

In the chapters that follow, the term *normal* will be used to refer to class culture that is not lower class. The implication that lower-class culture is pathological seems fully warranted both because of the relatively high incidence of mental illness in the lower class and also because human nature seems loath to accept a style of life that is so radically present-oriented. This is not the main reason for using the word *normal*, however. Rather, it is that *some* word is needed to designate the sector of the class-cultural continuum that is not lower class, and no other word seems preferable on the whole.

From the beginning, the cities of the United States have had upper, middle, working, and lower classes. The relative strength of the various classes has varied greatly from time to time and place to place, although the nature of the class cultures has not. At the beginning of the nineteenth century, the free population of the United States was predominantly middle class. Most were descendants of English and American yeomen, artisans, and tradesmen, a stratum of society that had long had good opportunities to better its condition and had been confident of its ability to do so.[24] The native American inherited a culture that gave prominent place to the future-oriented virtues of self-discipline and denial, industry, thrift, and respect for law and order. He was sure that these virtues would be rewarded by success; he expected to "get on" and to "improve himself" in material and other ways. The Puritans had come to America with the intention of establishing ideal communities— "a city upon a hill"—and the millennial impulse, still powerful, took many forms in the first half of the nineteenth-century. In the towns and cities, most early Americans, especially those of English origin, were skilled craftsmen or tradesmen. Of the few in New England who were day laborers, nearly all could read and write and nearly all voted.[25]

The number of working- and lower-class people was by no means insignificant, however, especially in the cities. In every sizable city there were transient laborers—and in the seaports, sailors, and in inland cities like Cincinnati and St. Louis, boatmen, wagoners, and drifters, who, like Huckleberry Finn's father, lived from hand to mouth, worked only when they had to, drank and fought prodigiously, felt no tie to the community, and left their women and children behind to fend for themselves or to be looked after at public expense once they had moved on.[26] In every city there also were unassimilated immigrants from countries—Catholic ones—whose cultures tended to be present- rather than future-oriented. It is safe to say, however, that transients and Catholic immigrants did not comprise the whole of the working- and lower-class population. In Boston, for example, which in 1817 had only about four hundred Catholics, the native American residents must have patronized the city's two thousand prostitutes (one for every six males above the age of sixteen), hundreds of liquor shops, and the gambling houses open night and day. It must also have been the native Bostonians who denied the mayor, Josiah Quincy, reelection after he waged a vigorous war on vice.[27]

Eventually, as immigration increased, the working and lower classes—especially the latter—did come to consist disproportionately of Catholic immigrants. In 1832, for example, the South Boston Almshouse held almost twice as many immigrants as natives. "To see anything like indigence or idleness," a visitor to New England from abroad wrote a few years later, "we must penetrate into the purlieus in the seaport towns, occupied by the Irish laboring population." The districts inhabited by the Irish and the Negroes formed, he said, "a painful contrast to the general air of cleanliness and comfort."[28]

After 1840 immigration increased rapidly, the immigrants coming mainly from peasant cultures—first Irish and then, after 1885, southern Italian and eastern European—that were more present-oriented than those of New England, Great Britain, and northern Europe. Coming from places where ordinary people had never had opportunities to rise by effort and enterprise, these immigrants tended to believe that the world was ruled by fate and that only a miracle or a great piece of luck could change their situation. The idea of self-improvement—and even more that of community improvement—was unfamiliar and perhaps even unintelligible to them. They were mainly concerned about survival, not progress; how to get food, drink, and shelter for the day was what preoccupied them. Their motive in coming to this country was apparently less to improve their general condition than to escape the threat of immediate starvation. "The emigrants of this year are not like those of former ones," the *Cork Examiner* noted during the peak of the Irish emigration, "they are now actually *running away* from fever and disease and hunger. . . ."[29]

Among the native Americans it was a rare day laborer who could not read, write, and cipher; among the peasant immigrants it was a rare one who could. The immigrants from present-oriented cultures were slow to see the advantages of education and of self-improvement generally. Even to some sympathetic observers it appeared that many of them would as soon live in hovels and shanties as not. Unlike the native Americans and the more future-oriented immigrants from England and northern Europe, the peasant immigrants seldom patronized the free mechanics libraries. Very few became skilled workers. In part, perhaps, this was because employers, most of whom were native, were prejudiced against them; in part also, however, it was probably because the present-oriented outlook and style did not suit the requirements of work and organization.

It was symptomatic of these different attitudes toward self-improvement and "getting on" that compulsory school attendance laws were adopted only after large-scale peasant immigration got under way. In Massachusetts, for example, the first such law was passed in 1852 and required all children between the ages of eight and fourteen to attend for twelve weeks each year. Until then it had been taken for granted that anyone able to go to school would not fail to do so.

The Jewish immigrants were very different from the peasant peoples. Like the native Americans, they were future-oriented. They believed, as had the Puritans, who were in many ways like them, that they were under a special obligation to assist in the realization of God's plan for the future. The idea of making sacrifices in the expectation of future rewards came naturally to them. Even more than the native American, the Jewish immigrant worked to acquire the capital (not only money and other material goods but also knowledge, skill, character, attachment to family and community, etc.) that would enable him to rise. Jacob A. Riis wrote:

The poorest Hebrew knows—the poorer he is, the better he knows it—that knowledge is power, and power as the means of getting on in the world that has spurned him so long, is what his soul yearns for. He lets no opportunity slip to obtain it. Day- and night-schools are crowded with his children, who learn rapidly and with ease. Every synagogue, every second rear tenement or dark backyard, has its school and its school master, with his scourge to intercept those who might otherwise escape.[30]

The future-oriented ideal diffused rapidly throughout the population. In the latter half of the nineteenth century the whole nation seemed suddenly seized with a passion for self-improvement: in every city and in thousands of towns and villages there were lyceum discusions, Chautauquas, evening lectures, and the like. Self-improvement implied community improvement, and the native American (originally Puritan) idea that it was everyone's obligation to do what he could to bring the millennial hope to fulfillment and to create "a city on a hill" became the generally accepted doctrine of "service." To immigrants like the Jews, whose native culture was future-oriented, these tendencies were highly congenial, but to others—notably the Irish—they were alien and distasteful. Eventually, however, all the immigrant groups succumbed to the native American, future-oriented ideal. Even Negroes, whose isolation as slaves and then as Southern farmhands might, one would think, have excluded them from the culture almost altogether, were drawn toward the ideal. Although they traveled at very different rates of speed, all ethnic and racial groups were headed in the same cultural direction: from less to more future-oriented.

Movement upward along the scale of class culture tended to follow increases in income and opportunity. Those people sacrificed the present for the future who had reason to think that doing so would be in some sense profitable, and the greater the prospective rewards, the more willing they were to accept the discipline and to put forth the effort required. People generally had good grounds for believing that the future-oriented virtues would pay off. To be sure, not many rose from rags to riches, as the mythology claimed, but it was very common for the son of an unskilled laborer to become a semiskilled or a skilled one and for *his* son to emerge as a manager, teacher, or professional.[31]

It is not clear, however, whether those who moved up the occupational, income, and status ladders did so because they had absorbed a more future-oriented culture. It is possible, for example, that Patrick Kennedy, who came to this country a laborer in 1848 and was still one when he died, was present-oriented and that it was because his son, Patrick Joseph, was somehow affected by the future-oriented atmosphere of Boston that he (the son) became a leading saloon-keeper and ward politician and—*mirabile dictu*—had the foresight to send *his* son, Joseph P., to the Boston Latin School and then to Harvard College. But it is also possible that the original Patrick was just as future-oriented as his son and that he remained a laborer all his life because the circumstances of his time and place made rising too difficult for him. It makes a great difference whether one supposes that (1) the American environment instilled in the immigrant a more future-oriented view; (2) it merely gave scope to those individuals whose view was such to begin with; or (3) it produced both effects.

From every ethnic group, including, of course, the native American, some individuals were born into the lower class and others dropped into it from above. The more present-oriented a group's culture was, the larger the proportion of its members who became lower class (similarly, the more future-oriented a group's culture, the higher the proportion who entered the upper classes). The Irish, for example, contributed heavily to the lower class

as compared to the Jews. From 1885 to 1890, persons born in Ireland comprised 12.6 percent of the population but accounted for 60.4 percent of the almshouse, 36.7 percent of the workhouse, and 15.5 percent of prison inmates; Jews from Russia and Austria-Hungary were 3 percent of the population but accounted for none of the almshouse, 1 percent of the workhouse, and 1 percent of the prison inmates.[32] Very likely, the present-orientedness of the Irish and the future-orientedness of the Jews had important indirect effects as well. The Anglo-Saxon Protestant elite, for example, probably discriminated against people who showed little disposition to get ahead and in favor of those who showed much.

The lower the individual was on the cultural scale, the greater the obstacles in the way of his moving up occupationally or otherwise and the less his motivation to try. At the very bottom of the scale, the desire to rise was altogether lacking—and those in the lower class rarely if ever climbed out of it. Moreover, the obstacles in the way of rising—many of which were due to the distaste future-oriented people had for the manners and morals of the extremely present-oriented—were all but insuperable. Some families doubtless remained lower class for for many generations, but most probably died out within two or three.

Each class culture implies—indeed, more or less requires—a certain sort of physical environment. It follows that a city (or district within a city) which suits one culture very well is likely to suit another very poorly or not at all.

To an upper-class individual, having a great deal of space at one's disposal is important both practically and symbolically. Being by oneself a good deal—and therefore having room enough for privacy—is essential to the development of a well-defined self; in the middle and upper classes, but not in the working class, it is thought essential that each child have a room of his or her own. The higher a family is on the class culture scale, the wider the expense of lawn (or in the case of an apartment house, the thicker the walls) that it wants between it and the neighbors. Similarly, the higher the commuter is on the scale, the more important it is to him to ride to work in solitary splendor. For the lower-middle-class person a car pool will do—it is better than the bus; the upper-middle-class person, however, finds even that distasteful.

In the middle- and upper-class cultures, one's house and grounds afford opportunities for self-improvement and self-expression.[33] To the upper-class individual, it is the latter value that is usually more important: the house is the setting for and the representation of his family line ("house"). The middle-class individual is more likely to value his house for giving scope to his impulse to improve things—not only physical things (the house and grounds) but also, and especially, his own and his family's skills, habits, feelings, and attitudes. (The do-it-yourself movement is at least in part an expression of the middle-class taste for mastering skills and "expressing one's personality.") The middle-class individual—particularly the lower-middle-class one—also regards the house as a means of improving his social status; having a "good address" helps one rise in the world.

In the upper- and middle-class cultures, the neighborhood and community are as important as the house and are hardly to be separated from it. It is essential to live where there are good schools, for otherwise the children might not get into good colleges. Other community facilities—parks, libraries, museums, and the like—are highly valued, as are opportunities to be of "service" by participating in civic organizations. The middle- or upper-class individual wants to feel that his local government is honest, impartial, and efficient. At the upper end of the scale, especially, he wants a sense of "belonging" to a "community"—that is, of standing in a fellowship relation to his neighbors (even though he may never see them) and thus of constituting with them a moral entity—not unlike the Puritan congregation of visible saints in the seventeenth century. This desire to belong to a community partly accounts for the exclusiveness of the "better" neighborhoods and suburbs. The exclusion of all who are not parties to the covenant (in the language of Puritanism) is a precondition of fellowship: a community, after all, consists of people who feel a sense of oneness. Where the principle of exclusion appears to be—and perhaps is— racial or ethnic, the neighbors are likely to see that in the pursuit of one of their values they have infringed upon another. Those who feel most strongly the obligation to be of "service" and to act "responsibly"—upper-middle and upper-class Jews, especially —often resolve the conflict by sponsoring a strenuous community effort to bring a certain number of Negroes (or whatever group is being discriminated against) into the neighborhood.[34]

To the working class, a different set of values to accord with its life style governs the choice of physical arrangements in the city. Space is less important to the working-class family than to the middle- or upper-class one. It prefers being "comfy" to having privacy; it is thought natural for children to sleep two or three to a room or perhaps even to a bed. Having neighbors —even noisy ones—down the hall or in a house that is adjoining or almost adjoining is taken for granted. The working-class individual has few deep friendships with his neighbors, but he likes knowing who they are and he likes seeing—and even hearing—their goings-on. (It was because the Italian working-class residents of Boston's West End took this interest in one another that Herbert J. Gans called his account of them *The Urban Villagers*.) From the working-class point of view, middle- and upper-class neighborhoods are dull and lonely. Riding to work by oneself is no fun either; the working-class person prefers a car pool but does not mind a bus or subway.

When he must choose between more and better community facilities on the one hand and lower taxes on the other, the working-class individual usually chooses the latter. He will be satisfied if his children graduate from high school, and any school that is not a blackboard jungle will do. Parks and libraries matter to him even less than schools. He has no desire to participate in community improvement projects and no wish to feel himself part of a community, except perhaps an ethnic one. If his neighbors are a mixed lot, some being hardly sane and others less than respectable, that does not concern him: he is likely to take the attitude that so long as they do not interfere with him, they can do or be what they please.

To this last statement an important qualification must be attached. The working-class individual is likely to become ugly and aggressive if members of an ethnic or racial group that he dislikes begin to "take over" his neigh-

borhood. He is more apt to be prejudiced than are members of the middle class and much less apt to conceal his prejudice. There is no talk in working-class neighborhoods about "responsibility for reducing racial tensions."

In some areas the movement of factories to the suburban ring has led to the building of residential suburbs that are working class. Physically, these look much like middle-class ones, but in style of life the two differ sharply. The working-class suburbanite's house is not a way station on the road to something better, as is often the case with the middle class. He is also less likely than is his middle-class counterpart to forego his favorite TV program in order to collect for the Heart Fund or "serve the community" in some other way.[35]

The lower-class individual lives in the slum and sees little or no reason to complain.[36] He does not care how dirty and dilapidated his housing is either inside or out, nor does he mind the inadequacy of such public facilities as schools, parks, and libraries: indeed, where such things exist he destroys them by acts of vandalism, if he can. Features that make the slum repellent to others actually please him. He finds it satisfying in several ways. First, it is a place of excitement—"where the action is." Nothing happens there by plan and anything may happen by accident —a game, a fight, a tense confrontation with the police; feeling that something exciting is about to happen is highly congenial to people who live for the present and for whom the present is often empty. Second, it is a place of opportunity. Just as some districts of the city are specialized as a market for, say, jewelry or antiques, so the slum is specialized as one for vice and for illicit commodities generally. Dope peddlers, prostitutes, and receivers of stolen goods are all readily available there, within easy reach of each other and of their customers and victims. For "hustlers" like Malcolm Little (later Malcolm X) and the youthful Claude Brown, the slum is the natural head-quarters. Third, it is a place of concealment. A criminal is less visible to the police in the slum than elsewhere, and the lower-class individual, who in some parts of the city would attract attention, is one among many there. In the slum one can beat one's children, lie drunk in the gutter, or go to jail without attracting any special notice; these are things that most of the neighbors themselves have done and that they consider quite normal.

Although it is the lower class that gives the slum its special character, lower-class people are by no means the only ones who live in it. Some blocks may be occupied only by the lower class, but in the district as a whole, the majority of residents may well be working-class and not a few middle-class. These are people whose incomes do not correspond to their class culture; in some cases they are the victims of bad luck—the death of a breadwinner, for example—but more often they are in the slum because racial discrimination, past or present, has deprived them of normal opportunities for education and employment.

For these working- and middle-class slum dwellers, life in the slum is a daily battle to preserve life, sanity and self-respect. They must send their children to schools where little or nothing is taught or learned and where the children are in constant physical and moral danger; they must endure garbage-filled alleys and rat-infested halls; if they shop in nearby stores, they must pay high prices for poor selections of inferior goods (the prices are often

high only for them—for the lower class, which demands credit even though its credit rating is very poor, the same prices may actually be low); they must suffer the risk of annoyance and even of serious hardship by being mistaken for members of the lower class by policemen, teachers, landlords, and others, who either cannot discern or do not trouble to look for the clues to class differences among the poor.

To the normal people who live in the slum, the worst feature of life there is fear. Many slum dwellers, Patricia Cayo Sexton writes, "live in a generalized state of fear—of being robbed, knifed, attacked, bullied, or having their children injured. This fear colors their whole lives: their ability to learn, to work, to stay sane and healthy, to venture out of their apartments or block, to live openly and freely, to be friends with their neighbors, to trust the world, outsiders, themselves."[37]

Within the limits set by the logic of growth, the mix of class cultures more than anything else determines the city's character and the nature of its problems. Almost everything about the city —population density, per capita income, the nature and quality of housing, the crime rate, the dropout rate, the level of public services, the tenor of race relations, the style of politics— depends in some way and to some extent upon the class composition of the population. When this changes, either in a neighborhood or in the city as a whole, almost everything else changes accordingly. And except as they are compatible with the realities of class culture in the city, the most carefully contrived efforts of public and private policymakers cannot succeed, for the mix of class cultures is a constraint as real as those of income, technology, or climate. It is necessary, therefore, to form the best estimate one can of the direction that change in the class system will take.

For at least a century there has been a general movement upward on the class scale from every class except possibly the lowest. A century ago the urban population was heavily working class; now it is heavily middle class. The process of "middle-class-ification," as Dollard called it, is undoubtedly continuing at an accelerating rate and will in a few decades have reduced the working class to a very small proportion of the whole population. The upper middle class has meanwhile been increasing rapidly in its relative strength, especially since the Second World War. Eventually, the distribution of population along the class scale may be decidedly bimodal, the largest concentration being in the upper middle class and the next largest (much smaller than the first) in the lower class.

No hard data bear on these predictions. Census data on education, income, and occupation cannot be made to yield more than very approximate measures of the size of classes as defined here.[38] There are, however, many indirect indicators that are to some extent relevant. One can see evidence of the process of "middle-class-ification" in changes that have occurred in the occupational structure (in 1900, 28 percent of the work force was in skilled occupations; in 1940, 43 percent; in 1964, 58 percent); in the decline of the saloon, the poolhall, and the brothel, and the rise of the family television set (the 1880 Census counted 517 brothels in Philadelphia, and Jane Addams complained at about the same time that in some wards of Chicago, there was one saloon to every twenty-eight voters);[39]

in the ever-greater sensitivity of the public to brutality such as the beating of suspects by policemen—commonplace even half a century ago—and wife and child beating ("If screams resounded through a tenement-house it was taken for granted that the child deserved all it got and more"[40]); in growing concern for civil rights (not only of Negroes but also those of women, juveniles, and persons accused of crimes); in the tendency to widen the sphere of such rights (homosexuals and hippies now receive official protection in some cities as a matter of right); in increased public support for plans to eliminate inequalities of income and opportunity (the "war on poverty" is supposed to benefit not only the poor but the old, the young, the physically disabled, the "culturally deprived," and in general the "powerless"); in the decline of the political machine and the rise of a politics of principle and ideology (in the eyes of the New Left any politics that does not allow full self-expression by all is defective); and in the growth of a mass audience for serious literature, music, and art (readers, listeners, and viewers are counted now by the millions, whereas a generation or two ago they were counted by the thousands).

The mass movement from the working into the middle class and from the lower middle into the upper middle class accounts as much as anything for the general elevation of standards that . . . makes most urban problems appear to be getting worse even when, *measured by a fixed standard*, they are getting better. The new standards are those of a higher class. It is because the process of "middle-class-ification" has given great numbers of people higher perspectives and standards that dissatisfaction with the city is so widespread. The city that was thought pleasant when most people were working class is thought repellent now that most are middle class, and it will be thought abhorrent when, before long, most are upper middle class.

The ascendancy of the middle and upper middle classes has increased feelings of guilt at "social failures" (that is, discrepancies between actual performance and what by the rising class standards is deemed adequate) and given rise to public rhetoric about "accepting responsibility" for ills that in some cases could not have been prevented and cannot be cured. The dropout, for example, in turning his back on education "is telling us that we never really connected with him, that in our preoccupation with others we never gave him enough time or attention."[41] This is typical. In the upper-middle-class view it is always society that is to blame. Society, according to this view, could solve all problems if it only tried hard enough; that a problem continues to exist is therefore proof positive of its guilt.

In this tendency to find society responsible for all ills, including those that are a function of rising standards, two dangers appear. One is that the allegation of social guilt may lead the individual to believe that he can do nothing to help himself. The dropout, for example, may feel himself excused from all effort once it has been established that he was never given enough time or attention, just as the juvenile delinquent may excuse himself when it has been established that he is the product of wrong social conditions. The other danger is that many people will take the talk of social guilt seriously and conclude that the society is one for which they can have no respect and in which they can place

no trust. Such condemnation is mainly to be expected in those sections of society—the upper classes, especially their youth—that are most alive to moral issues, and in those other sectors —notably the poor and the minority groups—that have obvious grounds for thinking themselves victims of social injustice. To the rhetoricians, the guilty society will be "not worth saving." To those who have known all along that it is society's fault that they are at the bottom of the heap, the case will be that much clearer and their righteous anger that much hotter.[42]

NOTES

The quotation at the head of the chapter is from John Dollard, *Caste and Class in a Southern Town* (Garden City, N.Y.: Anchor Books, 1957), p. 433. The original edition was published in 1937.

Richard F. Muth, *Cities and Housing, The Spatial Pattern of Urban Residential Land Use* (Chicago: The University of Chicago Press, 1969), a technical treatise in economics, makes an important contribution to the subjects discussed in this chapter. Unfortunately, it was received too late to be mentioned in the text.

1. Adna F. Weber, *The Growth of Cities in the Nineteenth Century* (New York: Macmillan, 1899), p. 469.

2. This estimate assumes that to buy a house costing $12,500 without spending more than 20 percent of income one must have an income of at least $9,000.

3. The *Oxford English Dictionary* defines a slum as "a thickly populated neighborhood or district where the houses and conditions of life are of a squalid and wretched character." Squalor is defined as "a combination of misery and dirt." In *The Urban Villagers* (New York: The Free Press, 1962), p. 309, Herbert J. Gans says that slums are residential districts that "have been proven to be physically, socially, or emotionally *harmful* to their residents or the larger community" (italics in the original). Robert Hunter, in *Poverty* (New York: Harper Torchbooks, 1965), p. 108, considers it a "great injustice" to use the word to refer "to working-class districts or to poverty-stricken districts relatively free from vice."

4. See the discussion of class in Gans, *The Ur-*

ban Villagers, chs. 2 and 11. See also Joseph A. Kahl, *American Class Structure* (Holt, Rinehart & Winston, 1959), especially ch. 7.

5. In many (but not all) particulars the account of class culture that follows depends heavily upon the work of Herbert J. Gans and Walter B. Miller. See especially *The Urban Villagers,* ch. 11, and Miller's articles, "Implications of Urban Lower-Class Culture for Social Work," *Social Service Review,* Vol. 33 (September 1959), and "Lower Class Culture as a Generating Milieu of Gang Delinquency," *Journal of Social Issues,* Vol. 14 (1958). See also A. B. Hollingshead, *Elmtown's Youth* (New York: Wiley, 1949); Allison Davis, "The Motivation of the Underprivileged Worker," in William Foote Whyte, ed., *Industry and Society* (New York: McGraw-Hill, 1946); William Foote Whyte, *Street Corner Society,* 2nd ed. (Chicago: University of Chicago Press, 1955); Mirra Komarovsky, *Blue-Collar Marriage* (New York: Vintage Books, 1967); A. B. Shostak and W. Gomberg, *Blue-Collar World: Studies of the American Worker* (Englewood Cliffs, N.J.: Prentice-Hall, 1965); D. G. McKinley, *Social Class and Family Life* (New York: The Free Press, 1964); Lee Rainwater, "The Lower Class: Health, Illness, and Medical Institutions" in Irwin Deutscher and Elizabeth J. Thompson, eds., *Among the People: Encounters With the Poor* (New York: Basic Books, 1968), and St. Clair Drake and Horace R. Cayton, *Black Metropolis* (New York: Harper & Row, 1945), in addition to the works cited below.

6. See Charles A. Valentine, *Culture and Poverty: Critique and Counter-Proposals* (Chicago: University of Chicago Press, 1968). Valentine complains of the use that writers on poverty make of the concept of culture; their conceptions, he says, prejudge empirical questions in the direction of policies he deplores.

Gans reassesses his views as presented in *The Urban Villagers* in *People and Plans: Essays on Urban Problems and Solutions* (New York: Basic Books, 1968), ch. 22.

7. For a critique of the claim that lower-class people cannot control their impulses ("probably the most frequently used element in discussion of lower class life") see S. M. Miller, Frank Riessman, and Arthur A. Seagull, "Poverty and Self-Indulgence: A Critique of the Non-Deferred Gratification Pattern," in Louis A. Ferman et al., *Poverty in America: A Book of Readings* (Ann Arbor: University of Michigan Press, 1965), pp. 285-302. Here, too, the argument turns largely on the implications of the concept for the content of policy. It should be noted in passing that the question of whether or not lower-class people are aware of the future is largely and perhaps wholly independent of the question of whether or not they can (or do) control their impulses. One may conceptualize the future and yet (for one reason or another) *not* be able to control an impulse.

8. Most of the statements about time horizons in what follows are empirical: they employ a somewhat special terminology to report facts that have been observed by social scientists and others. The main proposition, namely, that individuals and cultures have differing orientations toward the future, is of this character; so are many subsidiary propositions, such as that present-oriented persons tend to be in constant search of sensual gratifications. Some propositions, however, are *implications* of the main proposition; they are themselves deductive but they have been arrived at from premises that have been inductively established. No "data" support the statement that present-oriented persons are unconcerned about the welfare of their grandchildren yet unborn; such a statement follows from the *meaning* of present-orientedness.

9. An ideal type "is a freely created mental construct . . . by means of which an attempt is made to 'order' reality by isolating, accentuating, and articulating the elements of a recurrent social phenomenon . . . into an internally consistent system of relationships." Julius Gould and William L. Kolb, eds., *UNESCO Dictionary of the Social Sciences* (New York: The Free Press, 1964), p. 312.

10. The difference is greatest with respect to the class here called upper. In ordinary usage this class would probably be called upper-middle. It is not called that here because it seemed that a scale of classes running from lower to upper-middle (there being no upper class that could be placed on the same scale as the others) would be even more likely than the present terminology to cause confusion.

11. C. Burt, "Intelligence and Social Mobility," *British Journal of Statistical Psychology,* 14 (1961): 3-24. The case for the relative importance of genetic factors is argued by Arthur R. Jensen in "How Much Can We Boost IQ and Scholastic Achievement?" *Harvard Educational Review,* 39 (Winter 1969): 1-123. Rejoinders by several other educational psychologists and by Jensen appeared in the next two issues of the *Review* (Spring and Summer 1969).

12. Melvin L. Kohn, "Social Class and Parental Values," *American Journal of Sociology,* 64 (January 1959): 340, 344, 350. See also his "Social Class and Parent-Child Relationships: An Interpretation," *American Journal of Sociology,* 68 (January 1963): 475.

13. Kenneth Keniston, *The Young Radicals* (New York: Harcourt, Brace and World, 1968), p. 265. Keniston's observation was made with respect to the upper-middle class.

14. For data on the voting behavior of various classes on local public expenditure issues, see J. Q. Wilson and E. C. Banfield, "Public-Regardingness as a Value Premise in Voting Behavior," *American Political Science Review,* 58 (December 1964): 876-887. For data on participation in organizations, see Murray Hausknecht, *The Joiners: A Sociological Description*

of *Voluntary Association Membership* (Totowa, N.J.: Bedminster Press, 1962).

15. W. J. Cash, *The Mind of the South* (New York: Knopf, Vintage Books, 1941), p. 80.

16. Cf. Basil Bernstein's description of the British working class, "Some Sociological Determinants of Perception," *British Journal of Sociology,* Vol. 9 (1958):

> The specific character of long-term goals tends to be replaced by more general notions of the future, in which chance, a friend or a relative plays a greater part than the rigorous working out of connections. Thus present, or near present, activities have greater value than the relation of the present activity to the attainment of a distant goal. The system of expectancies, or the time-span of anticipation, is shortened and this creates different sets of preferences, goals and dissatisfactions. This environment limits the perception of the developing child of and in time. Present gratifications or present deprivations become absolute gratifications or absolute deprivations for there exists no developed time continuum upon which present activity can be ranged. Relative to the middle-classes, the postponement of present pleasure for future gratifications will be found difficult. By implication a more volatile patterning of affectual and expressive behaviour will be found in the working-classes.

17. David Riesman (in collaboration with Nathan Glazer), *Faces in the Crowd,* abr. ed. (New Haven: Yale University Press, 1965), p. 254.

18. According to Lee Rainwater, in *Family Design: Marital Sexuality, Family Size, and Contraception* (Chicago: Aldine, 1965), p. 55, in the "upper-lower class" (the working class as defined here):

> Though husband and wife may not go their separate ways as much as in the lower-lower class, they tend to adhere to a sharper division of labor than is true in the lower-middle class, and though they may participate together in many family activities, this seems to be more the result of default (they are thrown together in the same small home) or of a desire to keep away from unwelcome involvements outside the home than to be dictated by the values of equality and togetherness that dominate the thinking of lower-middle class men and women.

19. Erving Goffman, in "Where the Action Is" (*International Ritual* [Garden City, N.Y.: Anchor Books, 1967], p. 268), says:

> Looking for where the action is, one arrives at a romatic division of the world. On the one side are the safe and silent places, the home, the well-regulated role in business, industry, and the professions; on the other are all those activities that generate expression, requiring the individual to lay himself on the line and place himself in jeopardy during a passing moment. It is from this contrast that we fashion nearly all our commercial fantasies. It is from this contrast that delinquents, criminals, hustlers, and sportsmen draw their self-respect. . . .

20. Eleanor Pavenstedt, "A Comparison of the Child Rearing Environment of Upper Lower and Very Low-Lower Class Families," *American Journal of Orthopsychiatry,* 35 (1965): 89-98.

21. On this and on the "foci" of lower-class culture, see the articles by Walter B. Miller cited earlier.

22. Jerome K. Myers and B. H. Roberts, *Family and Class Dynamics in Mental Illness* (New York: Wiley, 1959), p. 174. See also Hollingshead and Redlich, *Social Class and Mental Illness,* p. 175, and S. Minuchin et al., *Families of the Slums* (New York: Basic Books, 1968), p. 34.

23. Gans, *The Urban Villagers,* p. 246.

24. Ralph Barton Perry in *Puritanism and Democracy* (New York: Vanguard, 1944), p. 298, remarks of the English and colonial American yeomen, artisans, and tradesmen: "They were neither so unfortunate as to be imbued with a sense of helplessness, nor so privileged as to be satisfied with their present status. They possessed just enough to whet their appetites for more and to feel confident of their power to attain it."

25. Theodore Sedgwick, *Public and Private Economy* (New York: Harper and Brothers, 1836), part 1, p. 8. See also T. C. Grattan, *Civilized America* (London, Bradbury and Evans, 1859), 2: 376.

26. Cf. Richard C. Wade, *The Urban Frontier* (Chicago: University of Chicago Press, Phoenix Books, 1964), pp. 217-220.

27. J. Leslie Dunstan, *A Light to the City* (Boston: Beacon Press, 1966), pp. 41-43.

28. Grattan, *Civilized America,* 1: 98-99.

29. Quoted by Oscar Handlin in *Boston's Immigrants* (Cambridge, Mass.: Harvard University Press, 1959), p. 51. (Italics in the original.)

30. In Robert A. Woods et al., *The Poor in Great Cities* (New York: Scribner's, 1895), pp. 102-103.

31. Stephan Thernstrom, *Poverty and Progress; Social Mobility in a Nineteenth Century City* (Cambridge, Mass.: Harvard University Press, 1964), pp. 103, 107.

32. *Reports of the Industrial Commission Immigration,* Vol. XV (Washington, D.C.: U.S. Government Printing Office, 1901), p. 480. On ethnic differences relating to mobility, see Bernard C. Rosen, "Race, Ethnicity, and the Achievement Syndrome," *American Sociological Review,* 24 (1959): 47-60.

33. James Q. Wilson, in "A Guide to Reagan Country," *Commentary,* May 1967, pp. 40-41, has described vividly the care that his generation of Los Angeles boys lavished on their cars. "After marriage," he continues, "devoting energy to the improvement of a house was simply a grown-up extension of what, as a juvenile, one had done with cars."

34. Opinion polls have shown that the higher a person's socioeconomic status is, the more likely

he is to favor integration of housing, transportation, and schools, as well as other forms of integration. See Paul B. Sheatsley, "White Attitudes Toward the Negro," in Talcott Parsons and Kenneth B. Clark, eds., *The Negro American* (Boston: Houghton Mifflin, 1966), p. 315.

A study of social class and voting behavior in Little Rock found: "The higher the social class, the stronger was support for desegregation. Conversely, the lower the social class, the greater was support for segregation." Harlan Hahn, L. Michael Ross, and Thomas F. Pettigrew, unpublished paper, 1966.

35. Cf. Bennett M. Berger, *Working-Class Suburb: A Study of Auto Workers in Suburbia* (Berkeley: University of California Press, 1960), ch. 5.

36. Cf. John R. Seeley, "The Slum: Its Nature, Use and Users," *Journal of the American Institute of Planners*, 25 (February 1959): 10-13. 1965), p. 116.

37. Patricia Cayo Sexton, *Spanish Harlem; Anatomy of Poverty* (New York: Harper & Row, 1965) p. 116.

38. The problem of estimating the size of the classes from these and other data is discussed in the Appendix.

39. Blake McKelvey, *The Urbanization of America* (New Brunswick, N.J.: Rutgers University Press, 1963), p. 94; Jane Addams, "An Effort Toward Social Democracy," *The Forum*, October 1892, p. 228.

40. Mrs. Helen Campbell, *Darkness and Daylight; or, Lights and Shadows of New York Life* (Hartford, Conn.: Hartford Publishing Co., 1896), p. 170. On brutality in general, see Richard O'Connor, *Hell's Kitchen* (Philadelphia: Lippincott, 1958).

41. Patricia Cayo Sexton, *Education and Income* (New York: Viking, 1961), p. 200.

42. Consider, for example, the probable meaning to all concerned of the announcement (*New York Times*, July 13, 1966) by New York City's chief health officer, Dr. Howard J. Brown, that thousands of wooden benches would be burnt in "a public declaration of conscience" as symbols of dehumanized medical services in the city's clinics. That the service provided by the city to its poor was remarkably good by any standard except that of the more affluent middle class ("No hospital in the world has better professional talent," Dr. Brown admitted) was a fact obscured by the announcement ("disgraceful . . . patients . . . have to barter their dignity for their health"). That people sat on benches rather than in chairs and waited without appointments until a doctor could see them was not, until the rise of new class standards made it so, an affront; it is therefore factually incorrect to use the benches as symbols of mistreatment *in the past*. The effect of the announcement, however, must have been to make upper-middle- and upper-class people ashamed of a city which has long treated its poor so shabbily and also to tell the poor that if by any chance they thought they were fortunate in being cared for by professionals as good as any in the world they were being outrageously put upon and that they should be aggrieved and angry at not always having been given the deference and amenities that the middle class now gives to itself.

Patterns of Collective Racial Violence

MORRIS JANOWITZ

Race riots are the dramatic hallmark of the injustices of race relations in the United States. They have an explosive, destructive, and amorphous character which makes generalization very difficult. As a form of "collective behavior," their natural history is not easily recorded or analyzed. Students of race relations believe that one of the most adequate and comprehensive studies of a particular race riot still remains that prepared by the Chicago Commission on Race Relations on the Chicago rioting of 1919—the result of the careful work of the late Charles S. Johnson, which was done under the supervision of Robert E. Park of the University of Chicago.[1] Nevertheless, it is the purpose of this paper to present a sociological interpretation of changed patterns of collective racial violence in the United States over the last century. The history of race riots reflects not only the expanded aspirations of the Negro but also the techniques that have been used to maintain his inferior social position. The history of race relations in the United States has been grounded in a system of law enforcement that has denied to Negroes due process and equal protection, and that therefore has weakened the legitimacy of the agents of law enforcement, especially in the lowest Negro income areas.

The purpose of this paper is to trace the transformation in the patterns of collective racial violence in urban areas over the last 50 years through three different phases. First, the typical race riot of the period of World War I and thereafter, the communal riot, was an interracial clash, an ecologically based struggle at the boundaries of the expanding black neighborhoods. Second, during World War II, communal riots began to give way to large-scale outbursts within the black community. These riots represented a form of collective behavior against the agents and symbols of the larger society. They can be described as commodity riots because of the extensive looting that gives symbolic meaning to these outbursts. Third, the commodity-type riots that reached a high point during the period of 1964-67 have shown signs of being replaced by a new form of racial violence, a more selective, terroristic use of force with political overtones, again mainly against whites, by small organized groups of blacks.

The form and extent of collective racial violence, it is assumed, are expressions of the social structure and the agencies of social change and social control. Therefore, in particular, the role of the police and law enforcement agencies and of the mass media in fashioning patterns of collective urban violence will be explored.

A central "sociological assumption" supplies a point of departure. There

From Hugh Davis Graham and Ted Robert Gurr (eds.), *Violence in America*, Vol. 2 (Washington, D.C.: U.S. Government Printing Office, 1969). Reprinted by permission of the author.

is a considerable body of evidence to support this assumption, but it is best to consider it as an assumption. Social tensions generated by discrimination, prejudice, and poverty offer essential but only partial explanations of Negro mass rioting in the urban centers of the United States. Social conditions conducive for collective violence have been much more widespread than the actual selective outbursts. Allen Grimshaw, one of the most careful students of race riots, concluded in 1962 that "there is no direct relation between the level of social tension and the eruption of social violence."[2]

It is not necessary to accept all that this proposition implies because the evidence is not that solid, and more important, because significant "indirect relations" may well have operated. It is enough to reemphasize the obvious fact that, in the United States, social tensions exist where riots break out, and to accept his alternative formulation that "in every case where major rioting has occurred, the social structure of the community has been characterized by weak patterns of external control."[3] Because of the widespread potentials for racial violence, in the language of sociology, the agencies of social change and social control are crucial in accounting for actual urban racial outbreaks. Moreover, the manner in which outbursts are handled and controlled deeply influences race relations and subsequent patterns of violence. It is well to keep in mind that the supporting evidence for this basic assumption rests on the events before the mid-1960's, when a new and intensified wave of urban racial violence broke out in the United States.

On the whole, statistical studies designated to account for which cities have been struck by riots have not been highly rewarding. However, one carefully matched comparison of riot and nonriot cities by Stanley Lieberson and Arnold R. Silverman of 76 race riots between 1913 and 1963 confirms and amplifies this perspective.[4] For the period before the new wave of riots of the mid-1960's, they found (a) no support for the contention that rapid population change accompanies riots; (b) no confirmation for the hypothesis that unemployment level is a direct factor, but rather that encroachment of Negroes on the white occupational world evidently tends to increase chances of riots; and (c) no support for the notion that race riots are a consequence either of low Negro income or relatively large Negro-white discrepancies in income. Nor, for that matter, does poor Negro housing serve to distinguish riot cities from nonriot cities.

However, their evidence supports "the proposition that the functioning of local government is important in determining whether a riot will follow a precipitating incident." Thus, (a) cities with more racially integrated police forces had fewer riots; (b) cities which had more representative forms of local government (e.g., citywide election of councilmen versus district elections) had fewer riots; and (c) cities were less riot prone that had a large percentage of Negroes who were self-employed in retail trade, such as store, restaurant, or tavern owners—that is, cities that had stronger independent middle-class business groups. In short, these measures were indicators of the articulation of the Negro into the social and political fabric of the metropolitan community, reflecting stronger and more viable patterns of social control.

In addition, if one is interested in the institutional aspects of race riots, it is necessary to focus attention on (a) the professional and organizational limitations of law enforcement agencies, and (b) the impact of the mass media. The record of law enforcement agencies over the last half century has been one of inadequate equal protection for minorities and limited capacity for dealing with urban disorders, with noteworthy exceptions and with slowly and definitely increasing levels of professionalization. Likewise, the growth of the mass media, especially television, has not been accompanied by increased standards of performance. The impact of the mass media, in its lack of a constructive role in describing problems of social change, plus its imagery of violence and its treatment of riots and law enforcement agencies, has made a positive contribution to violence.

FROM "COMMUNAL" TO "COMMODITY" RIOTS

Racial violence has a history as old as the nation itself. The institution of slavery was rooted in ready resort to violence. After the Civil War, the political control of the freed Negro was enmeshed in a variety of illegal forms of resort to violence. For the purposes of this analysis, however, the particularly devastating and explosive outbreak of collective mass racial riots can be thought of as a distinct phenomenon, although any effort at categorization is a tricky and elusive intellectual effort. The draft riots of the Civil War had clear racial overtones. But "modern" riots can be traced to the racial outbreaks that were generated during the period of World War I and again during World War II. There were, of course, riots during the interwar period, but the heaviest concentration was during wartime years. The riots of

this historical era need to be distinguished from the outbursts that took place during the 1960's.

During World War I and its aftermath, the modern form of the race riot developed in Northern and border cities where the Negro was attempting to alter his position of subordination. These outbreaks had two predisposing elements. First, relatively large numbers of new migrants—both Negro and white—were living in segregated enclaves in urban centers under conditions in which older patterns of accommodation were not effective. The riots were linked to a phase in the growth and transformation of American cities. Second, the police and law enforcement agencies had a limited capacity for dealing with the outbreak of mass violence and often conspired with the white rioters against the Negro population. The historical record indicates that they did not anticipate such happenings.

The riots of this period could be called "communal" riots or "contested area" riots. They involved ecological warfare, because they were a direct struggle between the residents of white and Negro areas. The precipitating incidents would come after a period of increasing tension and minor but persistent outbursts of violence. For example, the Chicago riot of 1919 was preceded by 2 years of residential violence in which more than 27 Negro dwellings were bombed. Typically, the precipitating incident would be a small-scale struggle between white and Negro civilians—often in a public place such as a beach or in an area of unclear racial domain. In the major riots of the large cities, tension and violence would spread quickly throughout various parts of the larger community. Thus, deaths and injuries were the result of direct confrontation and fighting between whites and Negroes.

Within a few hours the riot was in full swing, and continued intermittently with decreasing intensity for a number of days. Whites invaded Negro areas and very often the riot spread to the central business district where the white population outnumbered the Negroes. Much of the violence took place on main thoroughfares and transfer points as Negroes sought to return to their homes or sought some sort of refuge. Symbolically, the riot was an expression of elements of the white community's impulse to "kick the Negro back into his place."

Despite the wide areas that were engulfed and the number of casualties inflicted, the whites involved were limited to very small groups or nuclei of activists, often encouraged by vocal bystanders to take the initiative. White youth gangs and their leaders were in the forefront in a number of cities. The Negroes fought back in time, but they seldom invaded white areas. According to available documentation, the whites were mainly armed with bricks and blunt sticks, and they fought with their fists. There were a limited number of handguns (pistols) and rifles. On occasion, Negroes were better armed because they had more of these weapons and knives as well. These riots had many incidents of direct, personal, and brutal struggle between the contestants. The personalized aspect of the violence can be inferred from reports such as that of the Chicago Commission report, which stated that "Without the spectators, mob violence would probably have stopped short of murder in many cases."[5]

Gunshots were directed at specific and visible targets, often where one side had the overwhelming superiority.

Nevertheless, deaths by beating and mauling greatly outnumber those from gunshots. Newspaper reports of snipers were exaggerated. In the East Chicago riots of 1917, there was only one case of repeated gunfire, and in Chicago in 1919, the Commission found one such serious incident and a number of more scattered occurrences, as Negroes sought to retaliate against white marauders passing by in automobiles. In fact, instead of the term "sniper" fire, the reports of the period around World War I speak of occasional "volley firing."

During these riots, rumors about specific incidents of racial strife were spread by word of mouth. Newspapers contributed to racial tension by frequently and repeatedly publishing inflammatory reports such as one that Negroes slaughtered a defenseless white child. Since the riots often lasted for several days, news reports served to recruit white activists from other parts of the city and even from out of town. Editorial efforts to calm public opinion and to demand effective law enforcement developed slowly and hardly balanced the presentation in news columns.

The restoration of civil order required the police to separate the two groups and to protect the enclaves of Negroes from whites. Frequently the police were very deficient in their duties and occasionally assisted the white rioters. In any case they were not prepared for such outbreaks. The state militia or federal troops were used repeatedly and generally displayed a higher level of professional standards. Without overlooking the casualties that were caused by the police themselves, the fundamental anatomy of these riots was a communal clash between Negroes and whites.

During World War II, the pattern of rioting underwent a transformation which took full form with outbreaks in Harlem and Brooklyn in 1964, in Watts in 1965, and in Newark and Detroit in 1967. For lack of a better term, there has been a metamorphosis from "communal" riots to "commodity" riots.[6] The Detroit riot of 1943 conformed to the communal or contested area pattern. It involved concentrations of recently arrived Negro migrants, and the precipitating incident occurred in a contested area, Belle Isle. The violence spread rapidly and produced clashes between Negroes and whites. However, the Harlem riots of 1943 contained features of the new type of rioting. The Negro population was composed of a higher concentration of long-term residents in the community. Most important, it was a riot that started within the Negro community, not at the periphery. It did not involve a confrontation between white and Negro civilians. It was an outburst against property and retail establishments, plus looting—therefore the notion of the commodity riot in the Negro community. These establishments were mainly owned by outside white proprietors. The deaths and casualties resulted mainly from the use of force against the Negro population by police and National Guard units. Some direct and active participation by white civilians may take place in such a riot, as was the case in Detroit in 1967, but this is a minor element.

THE NATURAL HISTORY OF COMMODITY RIOTS

There have been repeated efforts to describe the various stages in the natural history of race riots, especially the commodity-type riots.[7] Two considerations need to be held in mind in pursuing this goal. The style of intervention by the law enforcement officers has deeply influenced the anatomy of race riots in the United States. During the period of the initial communal riots, the effectiveness of local police forces varied greatly, reflecting their high degree of decentralization. The increased ability of local police to seal off contested areas reduced the prospect of communal riots. Since the riots of World War I, there has been a gradual growth in the capacity of local police to prevent riots at the periphery of the Negro community, but not without conspicuous exceptions. The use of radio communications and motorized local police forces have been the essential ingredients of control. Most Northern cities have witnessed a steady and gradual expansion of the Negro residential areas, accompanied by bitter resentment and continuous minor outbreaks of violence, including bombings. But the police almost daily contain these tensions, which could explode into communal riots if there were defects in their performance. But the capacity of local enforcement agencies to deal with "border" incidents has not been matched with a capacity for controlling the resort to violence within the Negro community. The outbreak of commodity riots produced very different police responses in various communities, ranging from highly effective and professional behavior to weak and irresponsible action that exacerbated rioting and prolonged tension. Thus, the stages of a riot are not predetermined but reflect the pattern of intervention of law enforcement agencies.

Second, it is, of course, very difficult

to assemble accurate documentation in order to describe the natural history of a riot and especially the behavior of rioters in a commodity riot. The riots of the 1960's have produced a number of official inquiries and a variety of private studies, but there are few adequate analyses in depth.[8]

The President's Advisory Commission on Civil Disorders (Kerner Commission) sponsored a variety of social research studies that focused mainly on the attitudes of the public and the rioters. The methodology of the sample survey was emphasized, which does not make possible a full analysis of the dynamics of the "collective behavior" of a racial riot. While teams of investigators are required to collect basic documentation, the natural history and anatomy of a riot is still best assessed by a single person who is concerned with cross-checking sources. Brig. Gen. S. L. A. Marshall has demonstrated how a single investigator can reconstruct a complex and fluid battle by after-action group interviews. This procedure has not generally been applied to race riots. Perhaps the most analytic account of a commodity riot was presented by Anthony Oberschall, a Yale University sociologist.[9]

From all sources, one conclusion emerges, namely the absence of organized conspiracy in commodity riots. However, the absence of organized conspiracy does not mean the absence of a pattern of events. Thus, Jules J. Wanderer's analysis of 75 riots during the period 1965-67 demonstrates the pattern of events in these outbursts. By means of the Guttman scale techniques, he demonstrated the consistent cumulation of a very similar configuration of violence from low to high intensity.[10] The difference from one outburst to another involved the extent to which each one proceeded through the various stages of increased and intensified collective behavior.

The motivation of contemporary commodity riots is clearly not desperation generated by the anticipation of starvation, such as in food riots in India during famine times. One is struck by the repeated reports of the carnival and happy-day spirit that pervades the early stages of a commodity riot. The new type of rioting is most likely to be set off by an incident involving the police in the ghetto where some actual or believed violation of accepted police practice has taken place. The very first phase is generally nasty and brutish: the police are stoned, crowds collect, and tension mounts. The second stage is reached with the breaking of windows. Local social control breaks down and the population recognizes that a temporary opportunity for looting is available. The atmosphere changes quickly, and this is when positive enthusiasm is released. But all too briefly. If the crowds are not dispersed and order restored, the third stage of the riot is the transformation wrought by arson, firebombs, and sniper fire and the countermeasures taken by police and uniformed soldiers.

There can be no doubt that the countermeasures employed deeply influence the course of rioting—even in some cases prolonging the period of reestablishing order. One is, of course, struck by the great variation in local response to escalated rioting and in the skill and professionalism of the forces in their counterefforts. Differences in police strategy have been partly accidental and partly the result of conscious policy, because law enforcement officials have a past record to draw on, and are continuously alerted to the possibility of riots. Thus, for example, there were wide differences in response patterns to early manifestations of disorder by local police in the 1960's. In Detroit, Ray Girardin, a former police reporter who became police commissioner, explicitly acknowledged that he followed a loose policy in the early phase of the Detroit rioting, assuming that local civilian Negro leadership would contain the disorder. He cited his previous experience in which this approach worked effectively. In his theories of riot behavior, he made frequest recourse to "sociological" terms.

By contrast, the operational code of the police in New York City under Commissioner Howard Leary and in Chicago has been to intervene with that amount of force judged to be appropriate for early stages of the confrontation. The objective was to prevent the spread of contagion. Special steps were taken to prevent routine police performance from developing into incidents which might provoke tension. However, if an incident became the focal point for tension and the collection of a crowd, the police responded early and in depth in order to prevent the second stage from actually expanding. Numerous police were sent to the scene or kept in reserve nearby. The police sought to operate by their sheer presence, not to provoke further counteraction. They sought to prevent the breaking of windows and the starting of looting that would set the stage for an escalated riot. If actual rioting threatened, one response was the early mobilization of local National Guard units and their ready reserve deployment in inner city garrisons. In part, this was designed to reduce the time required for their deployment on city streets and in part it was policy that enabled the local police to commit their reserves with the surety of having a supporting force available.

Whereas the communal riot involved a confrontation between the white and the black community, the commodity riot, especially as it entered into the third and destructive phase, represents a confrontation between the black community and law enforcement officials of the larger society. The question of the extent of the exchange of gunfire emerged as one of the most problematic dimensions. The reports in the mass media of the use of weapons during and immediately after the riots by the rioters were exaggerated, according to the investigations of the Kerner Commission.[11] In fact, the deaths inflicted by sniper fire were few. For example, it is reported that 5 of 43 deaths during the Detroit disorder were linked to sniper fire, and in Newark, 2 of 26 deaths.[12] These observations did not involve comparisons with earlier riots or an assessment that the gunfire contributed to conditions in which extensive arson developed. In fact, direct comparisons with the communal type riots underline the greater dispersal of firearms and the much more intense use of firepower. They are escalated riots because of the more extensive but still scattered use of weaponry.

A distinguishing characteristic of commodity riots is not only the widespread dispersal of small arms and rifles among the rioters, and correspondingly, the increased capacity of the local police to concentrate armed personnel in a given area. There are no adequate statistics on the distribution of weapons in the hands of participants before any particular riot started. However, there is clear evidence that, over the years, the sale and home storage of firearms has continually increased, made possible by affluence, the absence of adequate gun control legislation, and stimulated by fears of racial violence. These trends have taken place both in the white and in the Negro community. As Zimring has demonstrated in the case of personal violence, the sheer availability of weapons has tended to escalate racial conflict.[13] In addition to the already available arms, a significant stock of weapons appears to have been accumulated during the actual rioting in particular areas. Important sources of supply have been looted including sporting goods stores, general merchandise establishments, and pawnshops.

Available documentation indicates that during the third phase of the commodity riots, when sniper fire developed, it usually involved single individuals, occasionally groups of two or three persons. There is little evidence of forethought by rioters in the deployment of weapons for effectiveness or mutual fire support. Supporting fire by such snipers could render them much more destructive. In isolated cases, there is evidence of limited coordination and planning of firepower. But these cases are of minor importance in accounting for the firepower involved or its destructiveness. The crucial impact of the sniper fire derived from its interplay with arson activities. Sniper fire immobilized firefighting equipment, which permitted widespread destruction by fire, which in turn contributed to more rioting and sniper fire. In this sense, the commodity riots were escalated in intensity and sheer destruction as compared with the communal outbreaks. They were esca-

lated also in the sense that the mass media rapidly disseminates the image and reality of mass fires and widespread looting on a scale not found in the earlier ones. The spread of fire was frequently facilitated by various incendiary bombs of a homemade nature. These firebombs have been used as antivehicle bombs, but generally with little effectiveness.

The phase of scattered sniper fire is, in some respects, a type of quasimilitary situation, but the notion of an insurrection has little meaning, for snipers had no intention or capability for holding territory, nor were they part of a scheme to do so even temporarily. Frequently the sniper fire exposed police officers and National Guard units without experience to dangers with which they were not accustomed. Personal risk was clearly present. The scattered source of fire often enveloped the law enforcement units. It was this envelopment fire, especially from behind, which has led to the use of the term "guerrilla tactics," but the guerrilla concept is also not relevant since guerrillas are part of an organization, proceed with a plan, prepare paths of withdrawal, and develop sanctuaries.

Overresponse and excessive use of firepower by police and National Guard units in turn contributed to the escalation of the rioting.[14] The police were at times surrounded and, in the absence of effective command and control, were exposed to an environment that most had not previously experienced. Their behavior was conditioned by the sheer feeling of the unreality of the rioting situation and the physical disruption that takes place. They often responded with indiscriminate and uncontrolled fire. The immediate result was that they exposed numerous civilians to danger. Such fire does not suppress snipers, who can only be eliminated by carefully directed fire and counter-sniper procedures. In fact, the initial counterfire actually mobilized new rioters.

The summers of 1964 through 1967 demonstrated wide variations in the capacity of National Guard units to respond to and assist local police. On the whole, National Guard units had received little specific training in riot control and the content of any such training did not appear to have been particularly germane to actual problems. The level of National Guard effectiveness derived from their military preparedness in general. The performance of National Guard units in Newark and in Detroit has been judged by expert observers to be deficient. By contrast, the behavior of the National Guard units in Maryland and in Wisconsin (Milwaukee) has been reported to be much more in accordance with the requirements of the constabulary function; namely, the minimum use of force to restore civil law and due process. The basic question is fire control and an effective communications network. By contrast, federal troops used in Detroit were highly professional units with extensive training, who clearly displayed a higher degree of unit control and were less prone to employ unnecessary fire. The superiority of the federal troops reflects past experience and indicates that more effective military training per se (even without additional civil disorder training), and more effective officers, produces more appropriate responses.

There is some evidence that one index to National Guard effectiveness is the extent of integration of units. Be-cause of its fraternal spirit, most National Guard units have been able to resist Federal directives and Negroes accounted for less than 2 percent of its personnel in 1967. In those cases where integration took place, it meant that the units were seen as more legitimate by the local population. Moreover, units that were forced to integrate were more likely to be concerned with problems of conflict in the unit and developed an officer corps concerned with these issues. For example, units in Detroit and Newark were not integrated while Chicago-based units that were employed during the summer disturbances of 1965 were integrated and had Negro officers.

PARTICIPATION IN COMMODITY RIOTS

The extent of participation and the social characteristics of the riots are revealing indices of underlying factors in the social structure that condition these collective outbursts. There is every reason to believe that in the commodity riots of the 1960's, a larger number of Negroes and a greater percentage of the population of riot-torn communities actively participated in the outbursts than was the case during the older, communal-type confrontations. The commodity-type riots take place within the confines of the black ghettos, which have grown greatly in size and population since World War I. Within these massive ghettos during the hours of the most intensive outbursts, it appears as if social controls were momentarily suspended. The sheer size of the ghettos and the greater remoteness of the outer community contribute to this breakdown and to the "mobilization" of numbers.

It is understandable that in the second phase of milling and looting, many residents were swept up by the sheer contagion of events, especially where law officers stood by passively while stores and shops were being entered.

It is also necessary to emphasize that the societal context had radically changed during the period of transition to commodity riots. Through the mass media, the demands of the Negro population had received widespread and favorable publicity and there was considerable sympathy in the nation for their plight. The civil-rights movements had achieved strong legitimacy. Within the black community there was strongly increased sensitivity about minority status. All these factors contributed to the intensity and participation during actual rioting.

The size of the groups rioting and their percentage of the available population, as well as their social characteristics, became matters of public debate. The Kerner Commission devoted efforts to probing these questions and refuting the claim that only a very tiny percentage—for example, less than 1 percent—of the Negro population was involved in riot-torn communities.[15] The Commission argued that the riots included a much larger active group who were generally representative of lower class slum dwellers and therefore could not be characterized as a tiny criminal element. The size of the rioting group could be estimated from direct observation, a most hazardous approach; from extrapolations from arrest data—a technique that probably underestimated the number of the activists; or from self-reports gathered by sample surveys after the riots—an approach that grossly overstated the case. On the basis of different sources, it was estimated that between 10 to 20 percent of the potential population was involved in the riots of 1967. The lower figure of 10 percent appears to be more accurate, although even this estimate is open to serious question. Aside from the reliability of the data, the question hinges on the differing definitions of participation. To speak of even 10 percent participation is to include those persons who were caught up in the collective processes of the riot as the contagion spread.

Although there are numerous statistical and methodological weaknesses in the various analyses of the arrest data and sample surveys, the findings are relevant for describing the social characteristics of the rioters. All sources agree that women were a significant minority of the activists in the commodity riots, reflecting a broadening of the base of involvement as contrasted with the communal riots, which were mainly a men's affair. Interestingly enough, the police tended to arrest few women, either because their infractions of the law were minor or because they believed that women were not at the core of the riot.

As expected, the bulk of the rioters were young males between the ages of 15 and 34 whose skill levels were low. In a social profile of the 496 Negro males arrested in Detroit, the typical participant has been characterized as "a blue collar worker in a manufacturing plant where he earned about $120.00 a week. Although currently employed, he had experienced more than 5 weeks of unemployment in the past year. He had not participated in a government training or poverty program." In some groups of arrested Negro youths, the unemployment level reached almost 40 percent.[16] In addition, among samples of those caught up in the riots and arrested in 1967, previous arrest records comparable to the equivalent age groups in the black population at large were found. The explanation for this finding is that it is very common for young Negro males to have an arrest record—in some categories, a majority.

Clearly, these data indicate that the activists were not a tiny minority of chronic law offenders nor highly unrepresentative in terms of selected social background characteristics. The full personal and social dynamics will probably never be adequately described, for involvement relates not merely to the demographic and social characteristics but to the patterns of primary and informal group structures of the ghetto community, as well as social personality and attitude. Some clues can be drawn from the observation of various surveys that the participants over-represented single men, who frequently lived outside of family units. These were persons who were less subject to the informal group structure linked to family life and more to informal street and community life. Anthony Oberschaal is one of the few analysts who sought to probe the role of youth gangs in riots, in his case, Watts:

Another informant who has been close to some of the gangs in South Los Angeles reported, however, that gang members, in an effort to prove their claims upon leadership in a certain territory and in competition with each other, were vying for leadership over the crowds during the riots, and this meant among other things actively participating in the skirmishes against the police, breaking into the stores and setting them on fire.[17]

In other cities, especially in Chicago in 1968, gang leaders were active in seeking to dampen tensions and violent outbursts. Fogelson reports on the social difference between those arrested as disorderly persons—who tended to be younger, unemployed, and native born in the locality—and the looters, who tended to be older, less unemployed, and Southern born.[18] In other words, the looters, who joined the riots after they were under way, were more integrated into the adult occupational world.

In contrast to the criminal interpretation, the alternative formulation of the commodity riots as a form of political insurrection appears equally inadequate, if by insurrection is meant an armed social movement with an explicit set of goals. The very absence of evidence of prior planning—either rightist or leftist—would weaken such an interpretation. In 23 disorders studies by the Kerner Commission, none were "caused by, nor were they the consequence of any plan or conspiracy."[19] But more important, it is striking that during the riots of 1964 to 1967, there was a remarkable absence of visible leadership—either existing or emergent—that sought to press for collective demands. It is, of course, clear that the leadership and support of the civil-rights movement were not centrally involved in the riots. The emphasis of the civil-rights leaders on issues such as school integration, access to public accommodation, and voting rights were less directly relevant to the immediate lives of slum dwellers, who were mainly concerned with the welfare system and with immediate employment opportunities. The impact of the riots of 1967 on the civil-rights movement was drastic in that it made the movement's demands more militant. But clearly the leaders of the civil-rights movement were not activists in these outbursts. If anything, they occurred because of the inability of the civil-rights movement to accomplish sufficient social change in the slums, although the movement made a decisive contribution in intensifying aspirations and group consciousness.

Many participants, after the riots, could consciously verbalize their social and economic dilemmas and link their situation to their behavior. In interviews, they had a tendency to highlight "police brutality" as the underlying cause. Of course, many who participated merely took the events as a given fact of life and offered little explanation for their involvement.

In contrast to the communal riots, where the Negro response was a direct and primitive struggle for survival, the commodity riots had overtones which might be called parapolitical, in the sense that group consciousness pervaded this particular form of collective behavior. In balance it can be said that the commodity riot by 1967 was a form of collective action, which on occasion was large scale and included a broadly representative segment of the lower socioeconomic class of the urban community. Regardless of the amount of sympathetic interest they mobilized among middle-class Negroes, the commodity riots were a "violent lower class outburst."[20]

A final aspect of participation has been the active involvement of those in the Negro community who sought to dampen or inhibit the spread of the riot. In official reports, they have come to be described by the awkward and unfortunate term, "counterrioters." In the communal riot, such a role was not possible and, paradoxically, such behavior by Negroes during a riot was a consequence of an increase in integration of the Negro into the larger social structure as compared with the period of communal rioting. Already in the Harlem riot of 1943, more than 300 Negroes were given Civilian Defense insignias and armbands, and used as deputies. For the summer of 1967, the Kerner Commission reported that in all but 6 of 24 disorders they investigated, Negroes were actively on the streets attempting to control rioters.[21]

In some cities, political and community leaders sought to address gathering crowds. On other occasions, religious leaders and community workers walked the streets urging persons to disperse, while still other local residents assisted police and firemen in their tasks. Some of these activities were officially recognized and even sanctioned by the local authorities, but the bulk of the efforts seem to have been without official sponsorship. It is very difficult to evaluate the effectiveness of these efforts, especially in communities where extensive rioting broke out. However, it does appear that such activities had the greatest effect in communities which were on the verge of rioting and in which rioting was avoided.

SUMMER RIOTS OF 1968

It will remain for future historians to assess whether the summer of 1968 was in fact a turning point in the era of communal riots. The trend in racial conflict from 1964 to 1967 was one of continued, and even expanded, outbreaks that appeared to reach one high point with the massive destruction of Newark and Detroit.

In the winter and spring months of 1968, the outlook for the summer of that year was bleak. Racial tensions remained high. Extremist and even moderate leaders anticipated even higher levels of violence, and a variety of analysts were thinking in the same direction. One of the writers for the Kerner Commission, assessing public opinion polls, stated "on the eve of the summer of 1968, these responses are anything but reassuring."[22] The tensions of the Vietnam crisis continued. There was no new massive national response to the social and economic needs of the black community, except in the important employment sector where industrial corporations started to abandon rigid recruitment and training procedures and to engage an increasing number of inner city personnel who would develop their qualifications on the job. Community relations were made more difficult by extremist statements by some individual police officers, who spoke of the necessity of a "tough" policy and of their plans to use heavier hardware for control purposes. The tragic assassination of Dr. Martin Luther King, Jr., served as a final element in the prelude to the summer of 1968.

However, race relations during the summer had a different character from these anticipations. In October 1968, the Department of Justice released a report by Attorney General Ramsey Clark which revealed a decline in the scope and intensity of racial riots. Quantitative measures of riots are difficult to construct, but these appear to be of relatively high validity. The definitions were carefully worked out and the same data collection procedures used to compare the months of June, July, and August, 1967, with the same months of 1968. The results showed a decline in "major" disturbances from 11 to 7, and of "serious" ones from 35

to 18, while minor outbursts increased slightly from 92 to 95. The most dramatic indicator of the decline was the drop in deaths from 87 to 19. To some degree, these data understate the full decline from 1967 to 1968, since the category "major" riots included all riots which lasted longer than 12 hours and included more than 300 persons. The very large-scale riots such as Newark and Detroit were absent in 1968. This is reflected in part in the marked decline in estimated property damage, from $56 million in 1967 for three riots in Cincinnati, Newark, and Detroit to $4 million for all damage during June, July, and August of 1968. It is, of course, very possible that no new long-term trend was at work. One hypothesis to account for the short-term and immediate pattern was the development of new tactics and new organizations that permit more effective expression of black interests and black solidarity. Another hypothesis is that improved police-community relations and higher levels of police professionalism contributed to the decline. These data seem to indicate that, while minor outbreaks continued, interaction between the police and the black community was able to reduce and contain larger and more widespread riots.

Under pressure of political and community leadership, many police took initial steps to improve communications with the Negro community through devices such as special conferences, the assigning of special officers of community relations, and improved police training. The criticism of the police in some communities and the relative success in other areas led to more professional behavior. The advocates of deescalation had more and more influence; the slogan became "manpower and not firepower." Older doctrines of riot control, which emphasized weaponry and technical characteristics, gave way to new and more flexible approaches. Police departments sought to improve their internal communications and their ability to mobilize manpower. They sought to strengthen supervision and control in the field and emphasized the need for restraint. There was a much more professional response to the problem of sniper fire, in that police were instructed not to respond with indiscriminate firepower. There was some progress toward deescalation of police response to more appropriate levels. Despite the publicity given to those few police officers who spoke about the need for tanks and Mace, the major trend in local police work was in the opposite direction.

National Guard and federal troops were deeply involved in the events of the summer of 1968. The lack of professional competence on the part of the local police to deal with problems of urban racial violence in part reflects the particular system of law enforcement that developed in the United States. Deeply influenced by British institutions, the nation did not develop a national police force that had responsibility for the control of civil disorder, in contrast to France for example. However, the United States has had extensive civil disorders throughout its history and the country found its equivalent to a gendarmerie in the state militia and later in the National Guard. The National Guard especially was organized and trained for national defense purposes, so that it seldom developed professional standards for local police support. The result has been that in both labor disputes and in race riots, federal troops have performed with high levels of effectiveness, not because of their specialized training for the task but because of generally higher organizational effectiveness.

But the division of responsibility between local, state, and federal agencies greatly complicates the conditions under which federal troops will intervene in a riot. In the Detroit riots of July 1967, federal troops were not deployed on the basis of the request of State and local authorities, but only after the Presidential representative, former Assistant Secretary of Defense Cyrus Vance, had personally inspected the city and certified the need for federal troops. There was local criticism that this procedure unduly delayed the dispatch of necessary troops. The office of the President has had to struggle to avoid premature commitment of federal troops whenever local authorities feel under pressure, but at the same time maintain the credibility of swift federal intervention if required. As a result, the Department of the Army established a Directorate for Civil Disturbance Policy and Operations to oversee such involvements. Greater use was made of federal troops in 1968 than in 1967. These troops underwent specialized training, but it was their general organizational effectiveness and command structure that enabled them to operate with the greatest restraint. They very seldom made use of their weapons; their sheer presence was mainly responsible for limiting riot behavior. (For example, in the Washington, D.C., operation, at most 15 bullets were fired.) In fact, there were numerous occasions in which the local population welcomed the arrival of federal troops, with the clear implication that they preferred not to be policed by local personnel.

With reliance placed on the National Guard, it became abundantly clear during the summer of 1967 that racial integration in these units had to be pressed with much greater vigor. It had been federal policy to encourage such integration, and in fact all Negro units were disbanded, but the recruitment of Negroes into the National Guard lagged. Where integration of the Negro into the National Guard had taken place, it was the result of state and local political leadership. Therefore, on August 10, 1967, the President's Commission on Civil Disorders unanimously issued a set of recommendations to produce short-term improvements in riot control. These recommendations called for increased recruitment of Negro personnel into the National Guard, the establishment of standards for eliminating inferior officers, and greater reliance on specialized training. During the next year, these federal policies began to have an effect, especially in the area of improved training.

NEXT STAGE: POLITICAL VIOLENCE

Each stage in the transformation of racial violence already carries with it the elements of the next stage. In the midst of the mass rioting of 1967, there was anticipated marked decline in such outbursts and an emergence of a more selective, more delimited form of violence.[23]

The social position of the Negro in American society was changing, with an effect on patterns of racial tension. In our open society, it is necessary to underline that the commodity rioting of 1964-67 bears a parallel to one explanation of the outbursts of militancy in the trade union movement in the 1930's. The unions displayed their vigor not during the depth of the depression but during 1936 and 1937, a period of halting but increasing prosperity. It may well be that the ghetto

outbursts, especially of 1965-67, were linked to the first stages—slow and incomplete—in new levels of opportunity and achievement for the Negro community. If social and economic progress were to continue, the conditions conducive to tension would then start to decline.

Although the topic is outside the scope of this paper, continued improvement of the relative socioeconomic position of the Negro in American society depends on a variety of elements of social change. Much social learning has taken place since the initial phase of the "war against poverty." The main lines of effective innovation are beginning to emerge: federal assistance in family planning, radical modification of the present welfare system including a negative income tax, special youth work training enterprises, and decentralization, plus improved quality of public education. Of special importance are the efforts to locate employment opportunities in depressed areas. Experience to date indicates that such industrial esablishments become training stations that serve to incorporate youngsters into the labor market for the first time and that, after a period of work experience, they develop incentives to seek additional training or better employment in the wider labor market. No doubt, regardless of their limited immediate impact, some of the community organizations being developed in Negro areas with foundation, trade union, and federal funds serve as a learning experience for training new leadership.

Any anticipation of a continued decline of commodity riots is also based on the assumption that a more professional police force would both extend more equal protection and would be more effective and more humane in avoiding collective outbursts. Likewise there would be a more equitable judicial system that would accord more due process to the Negro community. Thus the likelihood of destruction on the level of Newark and Detroit declines, although the escalated riot remains a possibility in any area of heavy Negro population concentration. Likewise, as Negro enclaves develop in suburban areas, forms of communal riots between Negroes and whites become a reality in these areas.

However, the essential trend was that escalated rioting and the rioting of commodity looting appeared in 1967 to be giving way to more specific, more premeditated, and more regularized uses of force. It was as if the rioters learned the lesson emphasized in the mass media, that mass destruction achieves too few tangible benefits. New outbursts appeared to be more goal directed—a diffuse goal at times, at other times a very specific one. It is almost appropriate to describe these outbursts as political violence or political terror, or even conspiratorial violence. It is not inaccurate to describe this shift as one from expressive outburst to a more instrumental use of violence. Those involved were persons who came to believe that white society cannot be changed except with violence.

The participants were likely to be persons who have taken part in previous outbursts. There was an element of organization, at least to the extent that activists are concerned with personal survival and avoidance of the police. There was an element of organization to the extent that the target seems to be selected, and the patterns repeated for a specific purpose. The local school was a particular target. The form of violence can be the harassment of a group of white schoolteach-

ers active in union work, an assault on teacher picket lines during a strike, or a small-scale outburst at the neighborhood schoolyard and on occasion sniper fire against the police. Housing projects, especially integrated housing projects, were repeatedly subject to rifle fire and fire bombing. These incidents are created for the purpose of developing solidarity in local gangs and in paramilitary groups. The United Automobile Workers Union reported the use of terror tactics, including knifings and physical assault, against both white and black workers in the Detroit area. The union identified a group, League of Revolutionary Black Workers, in its documentation.[24]

The object seems to be to establish a vague political presence. Conspiratorial overtones are involved and the assaults spill over against social agencies and local political leaders. The line between random outbursts and these forms of political violence or political terror is difficult to draw. However, these outbursts often take place with the explicit appeal of Black Power. Traditional youth gang activities tend to resist political orientations, but signs of conscious political orientation become more visible.

Dramatic manifestations of the third phase of political violence, or conspiratorial violence, were the shootouts which occurred with police personnel during the summer of 1968 in New York City, Cleveland, Pittsburgh, Oakland, Los Angeles, and elsewhere. The amount of prior planning is difficult to ascertain, but focused selection of police personnel as specific and delimited targets is obvious. In some cases the action appears to have been a response to presumed harassment by the police. In other cases the police were responding to a call for help. In still other cases police cars were attacked without warning. For example, on September 29, 1968, a man wearing a "black cape lined with orange walked up to a police car in Harlem early yesterday and without provocation, opened fire on two patrolmen, wounding them both. . . ."[25] Other incidents developed around a police action such as the removal of a disabled vehicle. Generally these incidents seem to involve loosely and informally organized groups. It is much rarer but perhaps indicative of emerging trends that a formal organization such as the Black Panthers finds itself in repeated gun battles with the Oakland police. The shootout in Cleveland on July 26, 1968, created such community tension that Mayor Carl B. Stokes responded by the unprecedented withdrawal of white police officers and deployment of Negro officers and 500 black community leaders to maintain peace. This procedure was rapidly terminated.[26]

Such activities appear to be a new form of "defiance" politics. In the past, organized racketeers, including groups which penetrated political party organizations, made use of violence to extract a financial toll from slum communities. These traditional groups confined violent outbursts to the maintenance of their economic privilege. Practitioners of political violence and political terror are now more open in advocating violence and opposition to the larger society. They represent an effort to achieve goals much broader and vaguer than those of the racketeer. There are crude ideological overtones and especially a desire to carry violence into the white community.[27]

It is very difficult to contain terroristic eruptions of political violence. The toll is small at a given point and therefore does not produce a violent public reaction. The tactics and organizational plans are more secret and only official surveillance and covert penetration supplies an effective technique of management. The forms of organization are those of a combination of a conspiratorial and predatory gang and a paramilitary unit with overtones of a "liberation" outlook. The more secret and cohesive the group, the greater the problems of surveillance. Even though many of these paramilitary groups will break into factions, the task of control will become extremely difficult. It bodes ill when it is necessary to rely on covert operators. The control of secret operations is at best difficult; in the United States, it is very difficult.[28] The task becomes even more complex and troublesome when these surveillance agencies develop the conception, as they often do, that to collect information is not enough. They begin to believe that they must act as active agents of control, particularly in spreading distrust within these organizations. The task becomes endless and dangerous if the operators play a game without an end or develop an interest in maintaining the groups whom they are supposed to be monitoring.

The failure of the larger society to meet the needs of the black community would contribute to an environment in which conspiratorial violence will continue to flourish. However, such violence has a life of its own. Small groups of terrorists have on historical occasion been able to achieve important goals and political objectives. It is hazardous to even speculate about the conditions under which they are able to succeed. In the past, they appear to have succeeded when they were struggling against a political elite that ruled by terror and without a broad base of support. They have also succeeded when terror is merely an opening step in a broad political campaign. Neither of these conditions seems applicable. Instead it may well be the case that political violence will have counterproductive features. Only limited amounts of political violence can be employed before a point of diminishing return is reached for both the user and the social order in which it is applied.[29]

THE IMPACT OF THE MASS MEDIA

Another important institution of social control that has special relevance for collective racial violence is the mass media. A debate on this issue has raged among social scientists since the early 1930's when the Payne Foundation underwrote a group of University of Chicago social scientists in the first large-scale study of the impact of the mass-media, in this case, the consequences of movies for young people.[30]

The mass media both reflect the values of the larger society and at the same time are agents of change and devices for molding tastes and values. It is a complex task to discern their impact because they are at the same time both cause and effect. Controversies about the mass media focus particularly on the issue of their contribution to crime and delinquency and to an atmosphere of lawlessness. Among social scientists, it is generally agreed that consequences of the mass media are secondary as compared with the influence of family, technology, and the organization of modern society. But differences in the meaning and importance attributed to this "secondary factor" among social scientists are great. "Secondary" can mean still important enough to require constructive social policy, or "secondary" can mean that a factor is trivial and unimportant.

Two separate but closely linked issues require attention. First, what are the consequences of the mass media, with its high component of violence, on popular attitudes toward authority and on conditioning and acceptance of violence in social relations? Second, what have been the specific consequences of the manner in which the mass media have handled escalated rioting since the period of Watts? The managers of the mass media run their enterprises on a profit basis and one result has been that the content of channels of communication, especially television, in the United States have a distinct "violence flavor" as contrasted with other nations. This content emphasis continued to persist as of the end of 1968 despite all the public discussion about this standard of the mass media.[31] In this respect, self-regulation of the mass media has not been effective except to some extent in the comic book industry.

In my judgment, the cumulative evidence collected by social scientists over the last 30 years has pointed to a discernible, but limited, negative impact of the media on social values and on personal controls required to inhibit individual disposition into aggressive actions. Other students of the same data have concluded that their impact is so small as not to constitute a social problem.

Many studies on media impact are based on limited amounts of exposure, as contrasted to the continuous expose of real life. Other studies made use of ex post facto sample surveys that are too superficial to probe the psychological depths of these issues. More recent research employing rigorous experimental methods has strengthened the conclusion that high exposure to violence content in the mass media weakens personal and social controls.[32]

These new findings are based on probing fantasy and psychological responses of young people after exposure to violence content. They have special importance for lower class groups because of the high exposure of these groups to television. These lower class groups have less involvement in printed media, which has less violence material.

The issue runs deeper than the concentration of materials on violence in the mass media. It involves as assessment of the mass media's performance in disseminating a portrayal of the Negro and social change in depth. It also involves the access that the mass media extends to the creative talent of the Negro community. The Kerner Commission emphasized the lack of effective coverage of the problems of minority groups by the mass media and the absence of minority group members, especially Negroes, in operating and supervisory positions in these enterprises. The events of the riots and the recommendations of the Kerner Commission on this aspect of the mass media produced "crash" programs to recruit and train minority group personnel. The contents of the media have become more integrated, including advertising, and a long-run impact on public opinion is likely to be felt, especially in younger persons.

It is also necessary to assess the coverage of the riots themselves by television and the impact of this coverage on social control. For example, the National Advisory Commission on Civil Disorders sought to probe the immediate impact of the mass media coverage of the riots of the summer of 1967 both on the Negro community and on the nation as a whole. They commissioned a systematic content analysis study which, despite its quantitative approach, did not effectively penetrate the issue or even satisfy the Commission itself. The content study sought to determine if "the media had sensationalized the disturbances, consistently overplaying violence and giving disproportionate amounts of time to emotional events and militant leaders."[33] The conclusion was negative because of findings that, of 837 television sequences of riot and racial news examined, 494 were classified as calm, 262 as emotional, and 81 as normal. "Only a small proportion of all scenes analyzed showed actual mob action, people looting, sniping, setting fires or being killed or injured." In addition, moderate Negro leaders were shown on television more frequently than were militant leaders. Equivalent findings were reported for the printed media.

But such a statistical balance is no indicator of the impact of the presentation. Even calm and moral presentations of the riots could have had effect on both black and white communities; more certainly, persistent presentation of "hot" messages, even though they constitute only a part of the coverage, would have an impact. Therefore, the Commission modified and in effect rejected its own statistical findings and more appropriately concluded that (1) "there were instances of gross flaws in presenting news of the 1967 riots"; and (2) the cumulative effect was important in that it "heightened reaction." "What the public saw and read last summer thus produced emotional reactions and left vivid impressions not wholly attributable to the material itself." The Commission concluded that "the main failure of the media last summer was that the totality of its coverage was not as representative as it should have been to be accurate."

The national crisis produced by escalated riots warranted massive coverage according to existing standards of mass media performance. The coverage was so extensive that there was an imbalance in presentation of the total scene in the United States, and in particular, a failure to cover successful accomplishments by community leaders and law enforcement agencies. In fact, there were overtones in the coverage of racial violence which conformed to the "crime wave" pattern of news. The result was to bring into the scope of coverage violent events that would not have been reported under "normal" circumstances.

Television has served as the main instrument for impressing the grim realities of the riots onto the mass consciousness of the nation. On-the-spot reportage of the details of the minor riots and their aftermath was extensive and was buttressed by elaborate commentaries. If the fullest coverage of these events is deemed to be necessary as a basis for developing constructive social policy, the costs of such media coverage should not be overlooked. It is impossible to rule out the strong contention that detailed coverage of riots has had an effect on potential rioters. Such a contention does not rest on the occasional instance in which the television camera focused on the riot scene and led either rioters or police to play to the television audience. Of greater importance is the impact of pictures of the rioting on a wider audience. Again we are dealing with a process of social learning, especially for potential participants. Rioting is based on contagion, the process by which the mood and attitudes of those who are actually caught up in the riot are disseminated to a larger audience on the basis of direct contact. Television images serve to spread the contagion pattern throughout urban areas and the nation. Large audiences see the details of riots, the manner in which people participate in them, and especially the ferment associated with looting and obtaining commodities which was so much at the heart of riot behavior. Television presents detailed information about the tactics of participation and the gratifications that were derived.

A direct and realistic account of the tactical role of the mass media, in particular television, can be seen from specific case studies, such as reported in depth by Anthony Oberschall on the Watts riot. He writes:

The success of the store breakers, arsonists, and looters in eluding the police can in part be put down to the role of the mass media during the riot week. The Los Angeles riot was the first one in which rioters were able to watch their actions on television. The concentration and movements of the police in the area were well reported on the air, better than that of the rioters themselves. By listening to the continuous radio and TV coverage, it was possible to deduce that the police were moving toward or away from a particular neighborhood. Those who were active in raiding stores could choose when and where to strike, and still have ample time for retreat. The entire curfew area is a very extended one.[34]

The media disseminate the rationalizations and symbols of identification used by the rioters. The mass media serve to reenforce and spread a feeling of consciousness among those who participate or sympathize with extremist actions, regardless of the actions' origins. In particular, television offers them a mass audience far beyond their most optimistic aspirations. Knowledge of the riot would spread in any case, but immediate extensive and detailed coverage both speeds up the process and gives it a special reality. On balance, I would argue that these images serve to reenforce predispositions to participate and even to legitimate participation. To be able to generate mass media coverage, especially television coverage, becomes an element in the motivation of the rioters. The sheer ability of the rioters to command mass media attention is an ingredient in developing legitimacy. In selected high-brow intellectual circles in the United States, a language of rationalization of violence has developed. The mass media serve to disseminate a popular version of such justification. The commentaries on television were filled with pseudo-sociological interpretations and the rioters themselves given ample opportunity to offer a set of suitable rationalizations.

In the past, when rioting was of the contested area variety, the newspapers were the major mass media. In many areas they developed an operational code, informally and formally, to deal with news about rioting. The practice was to apply an embargo on news about a riot during the actual period of the riot. After the event, it would be covered. The goal was to prevent the newspapers from serving as a means for mobilizing rioters, as was the case in the riots of Chicago in 1919. With the growth of television and an intensification of competition between the press and television, this practice broke down.

It is difficult to estimate the short- and long-term effects of the mass media portrayal of riots on white and Negro opinions. However, the riots projected a new element in the mass media imagery of the Negro, if only for a limited period of time. In the past, the mass media served to reenforce the system of segregation by casting the Negro exclusively in a minority position as well as by describing and characteriz-

ing him as weak. The portrait of the Negro as weak in the mass media served to mobilize and reenforce aggressive sentiments and emotions against these groups. The extremely prejudiced person is more disposed to release his aggression if he believes that the object of his aggression is too weak to respond to his hostile feelings and emotions.[35]

Since the end of World War II, the mass media have been helping to modify the imagery of the Negro and thereby to weaken the prejudiced symbolism. The advances of the Negro in economic, social, and political life have supplied a basis by which the mass media could project a more realistic and more favorable picture of the Negro. The reasoned and moral arguments in defense of racial equality by black and white leaders provide the subject for extensive editorial commentary in the mass media. Mass media images of the Negro were enhanced by the role of Negro troops in the Korean conflict and by the increasing presentation of the Negro as policemen. Regardless of Negro leadership opinion on the war in South Vietnam, the Negro soldier's role has served to modify in a positive direction the image of the Negro in both white and Negro communities. The early phase of the civil-rights movement, with its emphasis on orderly and controlled demonstrations, served also to altar the symbolism of the Negro from that of a weak, powerless figure. The climax of this phase of change, as presented by the mass media, was the dramatic March on Washington led by the late Dr. Martin Luther King, Jr. As an event in the mass media, it was unique. The national media were focused on a predominantly black assemblage moving in an orderly and powerful fashion.

In a real sense, it was a symbolic incorporation of the Negro into American society, because of the heavy emphasis on religion and the setting in the nation's capital.

In the elimination of prejudiced imagery, the Negro in the United States obviously has had to face much greater psychological barriers than any other minority group. Hostility and prejudice formed on the axis of color runs deep. Nevertheless, the secular trend in negative stereotypes toward the Negro from 1945 to 1965 has showed a dramatic decline, and the mass media have had an effect in this trend.

Even in the absence of adequate psychological studies in depth, some speculation is possible about the image projected by the riots. The view of Negroes as a group growing in strength and direction was for the moment shattered. Instead, a partial image of explosive irrationality has been dramatized. The use of sheer strength for destructive purposes rather than to achieve a goal that the white population could define as reasonable and worthwhile has served only to mobilize counter hostility and counteraggression. No doubt these images fade away as the mass media focus on reporting in depth the realities of the black community and the processes of social change that are at work.

Thus, in conclusion, the history of the race riot is more than an account of the change from communal to commodity type conflict. It is more than the history of the gross inadequacies of the system of law enforcement and the limitations in the performance of the mass media. It is in part an answer to the question posed by Ralph Ellison, the Negro novelist, "But can a people live and develop for over three hundred years simply by reacting?"[36] The Negro outbursts have been more than a reaction to police brutality and a double standard of legal justice. In a symbolic sense, they are expressions of energies to participate in and transform the larger society. In all phases of life, the Negro is not merely reacting but acting.

NOTES

1. Chicago Commission on Race Relations, *The Negro in Chicago: A Study of Race Relations and a Race Riot* (Chicago: The University of Chicago; 1922). For another riot that has been documented in depth, see Elliott M. Rudwick, *Race Riot at East St. Louis* (Carbandale: Southern Illinois University Press, 1964).

2. Allen D. Grimshaw, "Factors Contributing to Color Violence in the United States and Great Britain," *Race*, May 1962, p. 18. See also Robin M. Williams, "Social Change and Social Conflict: Race Relations in the United States, 1944-1964," *Social Inquiry*, Apr. 1965, pp. 8-25.

3. Allen D. Grimshaw, "Actions of Police and Military in American Race Riots," *Phylon*, Fall 1963, p. 288.

4. Stanley Lieberson and Arnold R. Silverman, "Precipitants and Conditions of Race Riots," *American Sociological Review*, Dec. 1965, pp. 887-898.

5. The Chicago Commission on Race Relations, *op. cit.*, p. 23.

6. See also Allen D. Grimshaw, "Lawlessness and Violence in the United States and their Special Manifestations in Changing Negro-White Relationships." *Journal of Negro History*, Jan. 1957, pp. 52-72.

7. See for example, Hans Mattick, "The Form and Content of Recent Riots," *Midway*, Summer 1968, pp. 3-32.

8. See Allen A. Silver, "Official Interpretations of Racial Riots," *Urban Riots: Violence and Social Change, Proceedings of the Academy of Political Science*, vol. XXIX, No. 1, July 1968, pp. 146-158.

9. Anthony Oberschall, "The Los Angeles Riot of August 1965," *Social Problems*, pp. 322-334.

10. Jules J. Wanderer, "1967 Riots: A Test of the Congruity of Events," *Social Problems*, Fall 1968, pp. 193-198.

11. National Advisory Commission on Civil Disorders, *op. cit.*, p. 180.

12. Arnold Katz, "Firearms, Violence and Civil Disorders," Stanford Research Institute, July 1968, p. 10.

13. Frank Zimring, "Is Gun Control Likely to Reduce Violent Killings?" *The University of Chicago Law Review,* Summer 1968, pp. 721-737.
14. Louis C. Goldberg, "Ghetto Riots and Others: The Faces of Civil Disorder in 1967," *Journal of Peace Research,* p. 120.
15. Robert M. Fogelson and Robert B. Hill, "Who Riots? A Study of Participation in the 1967 Riots," *Supplemental Studies for the National Advisory Commission on Civil Disorders,* July 1968, pp. 221-248.
16. *The Detroit Riot: A Profile of 500 Prisoners,* Department of Labor, Mar. 1968, 28 pp.
17. Anthony Oberschall, *op. cit.,* p. 335.
18. National Advisory Commission on Civil Disorders, *Supplemental Studies,* p. 239.
19. *Ibid.,* p. 89.
20. Anthony Oberschall, *op. cit.,* p. 329.
21. The National Advisory Commission on Civil Disorders, p. 73.
22. *Ibid.,* p. 243.
23. Morris Janowitz, *The Social Control of Escalated Riots* (Chicago: The University of Chicago Press, 1967).
24. *New York Times,* Mar. 13, 1969, p. 22.
25. *New York Times,* Sept. 29, 1968.
26. For a list and analysis of 25 reported sniping incidents in July and August 1968, see *Riot Data Review* (Lemberg Center for the Study of Violence), No. 3 (Feb. 1969), pp. 1-38.
27. See Harold Cruse, *The Crisis of the Negro Intellectual* (New York: William Morrow, 1967), pp. 347-401, for an analysis of the ideologies of violence in the black community.
28. Paul Blackstock, *The Strategy of Subversion* (Chicago: Quadrangle Books, 1964).
29. Paul Blackstock, "Anarchism, Manipulated Violence and Civil Disorder," unpublished manuscript, 1968.
30. See W. W. Charter, *Motion Pictures and Youth* (New York: Macmillan, 1933).
31. See *Christian Science Monitor,* Oct. 4, 1968 for details of a survey conducted by that newspaper's staff.
32. Leonard Berkowitz, Ronald Corwin, and Mark Heironimus, "Film Violence and Subsequent Aggressive Tendencies," *Public Opinion Quarterly,* vol. XXVII (Summer 1963), pp. 217-229.
33. National Advisory Commission on Civil Disorders, p. 202.
34. Oberschall, *op. cit.,* pp. 335-336.
35. For a discussion of this psychological mechanism, see Bruno Bettelheim and Morris Janowitz, *Social Change and Prejudice* (New York: The Free Press, 1964).
36. Ralph Ellison, *Shadow and Act* (New York: Random House, 1964), p. 315.

The Dilemma of the Urban Police

JAMES Q. WILSON

Current discussions of the problems of the American police seem fraught with paradox. While everyone seems to agree about remedies, criticisms of the police arise out of radically different conceptions of the police function. Some people see the police as the chief means of ending or reducing "crime in the streets"; others see them as an agency by which white society confines and suppresses black ghettos; still others view them as an organization caught on the grinding edge of a class conflict among competing standards of order and propriety. Yes despite these utterly disparate diagnoses, the prescribed treatment tends to be quite conventional and generally endorsed—higher salaries, better training, clearer policies, more modern equipment. And a further paradox: despite this apparent agreement on what should be done, little, in fact, happens. In some places, voters and politicians appear to be universally sympathetic to the needs of the police, but they are unwilling to appropriate more money to meet those needs. In other places, the extra funds have been spent but the criticisms remain—little, apparently, has changed.

One reason for this confusion or inaction lies, I believe, in the fact that the police perform a number of quite different functions. The controversies in which the police are embroiled reveal this as various disputants empha-size crime prevention, or law enforcement, or the maintenance of order, or political power. Liberty, order, legitimacy—important and fundamental values are in conflict. The adherents of various points of view take refuge in a common (and perhaps peculiarly American) set of proposals: spend money, hire better men, buy more things. I suspect that spending more money and hiring better men *are* essential to police improvement, but I also suspect that one reason so little extra money is spent and so few men are hired is that beneath our agreement on means, we remain in deep disagreement on ends. Spend the money on *what*, and *why?* What *is* a "better" policeman, anyway?

This is not a new issue. The history of the American municipal police is in great part a history of struggles to define their role in our society. What makes the controversy so intense today is only partly that it is linked to the question of race; indeed, in the past the police have repeatedly been in conflict with new urban migrants of whatever color. The reason for the heat generated by the police question is probably the same as the reason for the emotions aroused by the crime issue: we compare present circumstances with an earlier period when we thought we had solved the problem. Police behavior, like crime, was not a major issue

From *The Atlantic*, Vol. 223, No. 3 (March 1969), pp. 129-35. Reprinted by permission of the publisher.

in the 1940s and 1950s. When the police did become an issue, it was usually because a department was found to be corrupt, and that discovery produced a standard response—bring in a reform chief, reorganize the force, and get back to work.

CROOK CATCHERS

That work was law enforcement, or so it was thought. The job of the police was to prevent crime and catch crooks. Corruption was a serious problem because it seemed to mean that crime was not being prevented and crooks were not being caught. Organized criminals were buying protection, or petty thieves were putting in a "fix," or the police themselves were stealing on the side. Reforming a department not only meant ending corruption and alliances with criminals; it also meant improving training and developing new methods—more courses on crime detection, tighter departmental discipline to prevent misconduct, better equipment to facilitate getting to the scene of a crime and analyzing clues. When the public was invited to inspect a refurbished department, it was shown the new patrol cars, the new crime laboratory, the new communications center, and perhaps the new pistol range. The policeman was portrayed as a "crime fighter," and to an important degree, of course, he was.

But that was not all or even the most important thing he was. Given the nature of the crime problem, it was impossible for him to be simply a crime fighter. Most crime is not prevented and most criminals are not caught, even in the best-run, best-manned departments. Murder, for example, is a "private" crime, occurring chiefly off the streets and among "friends" or relatives. No police methods can prevent it, and only general domestic disarmament, an unlikely event, might reduce it. Many, if not most, assaults are similarly immune from police deterrence. Most crimes against property—burglary, auto theft, larceny—are also crimes of stealth, and though the police might, by various means, cut the rate somewhat, they cannot cut it greatly because they cannot be everywhere at once. Street crimes—robberies, muggings, purse snatches—are more susceptible to police deterrence than any other kind, though so far few, if any, departments have had the resources or the community support to carry out a really significant strategy to prevent street crime.

The result of this state of affairs is that though some police departments are regarded as "backward" and others as "modern" and "professional," neither kind seems able to bring about a substantial, enduring reduction of the crime rate. If this is true, then the characterization of the police as primarily crime fighters places them in a potentially embarrassing position, that of *being judged by a goal they cannot attain.* In the 1950s, when crime rates were either stabilized or ignored, this awkward situation and the police response to it were not apparent.

What most policemen were doing even when they were being thought of as crime fighters was not so much enforcing the law as maintaining order. In a recent study, I have tried to show what makes up the routine workload of patrolmen, the police rank which has the largest number of men. The vast majority of police actions taken in response to citizen calls involve either providing a service (getting a cat out of a tree or taking a person to a hospital) or managing real or alleged conditions of disorder (quarreling families, public drunks, bothersome teenagers, noisy cars, and tavern fights). Only a small fraction of these calls involve matters of law enforcement, such as checking on a prowler, catching a burglar in the act, or preventing a street robbery. The disorders to which the police routinely respond are not large-scale. Riots and civil commotions are, in any given city, rare occurrences, and when they happen, the police act en masse, under central leadership. Rather, the maintenance of order involves handling disputes in which only two or three people participate and which arise out of personal misconduct, not racial or class grievances.

The difference between order maintenance and law enforcement is not simply the difference between "little stuff" and "real crime" or between misdemeanors and felonies. The distinction is fundamental to the police role, for the two functions involve quite dissimilar police actions and judgments. Order maintenance arises out of a dispute among citizens who accuse each other of being at fault; law enforcement arises out of the victimization of an innocent party by a person whose guilt must be proved. Handling a disorderly situation requires the officer to make a judgment about what constitutes an appropriate standard of behavior; law enforcement requires him only to compare a person's behavior with a clear legal standard. Murder or theft is defined, unambiguously, by statutes; public peace is not. Order maintenance rarely leads to an arrest;

law enforcement (if the suspect can be found) typically does. Citizens quarreling usually want the officer to "do something," but they rarely want him to make an arrest (after all, the disputants are usually known or related to each other). Furthermore, whatever law is broken in a quarrel is usually a misdemeanor, and in most states, an officer cannot make a misdemeanor arrest unless he saw the infraction (which is rare) or unless one party or the other will swear out a formal complaint (which is even rarer).

Because an arrest cannot be made in most disorderly cases, the officer is expected to handle the situation by other means and on the spot, but the law gives him almost no guidance on how he is to do this; indeed, the law often denies him the right to do anything at all *other* than make an arrest. No judge will ever see the case, and thus no judge can decide the case for the officer. Alone, unsupervised, with no policies to guide him and little sympathy from onlookers to support him, the officer must "administer justice" on the curbstone.

EARLY PATTERNS

In the nineteenth century, it was widely recognized that the maintenance of order was the chief function of the police. Roger Lane's informative history, *Policing the City: Boston, 1822-1885* (Cambridge: Harvard University Press, 1967), recounts how that department, the oldest in the United States, was first organized as a night watch to keep the peace in the streets. Beginning in 1834, men drafted from the citizenry were required to take their turns in seeing (as the governing statute required) "that all disturbances and disorders in the night shall be prevented and suppressed." Wild creatures, human and animal alike, were to be kept off the street, and a hue and cry was to be set up should fire or riot threaten.

The job of law enforcement—that is, of apprehending criminals who had robbed or burgled the citizenry—was not among the duties of the watchmen; indeed, it was not even among the duties of the government. A victim was obliged to find the guilty party himself. Once a suspect was found, the citizen could, for a fee, hire a constable who, acting on a warrant, would take the suspect into custody. Even after detectives—that is, men charged with law enforcement rather than the maintenance of order—were added to the force in the nineteenth century, they continued to serve essentially private interests. The chief concern of the victim was restitution, and to that end, the detectives would seek to recover loot in exchange for a percentage of the take. Detectives functioned then as personal-injury lawyers operate today, on a contingency basis, hoping to get a large part, perhaps half, of the proceeds.

Since in those days there was no law against compounding a felony, the detectives were free to employ any methods they wanted to recover stolen property. And with this as their mission, it is not surprising, as Lane notes, that the best detectives were those who by background and experience were most familiar with the haunts and methods of thieves.

The emergence of a municipal police force out of its watchmen antecedents was not so much the result of mounting crime rates as of growing levels of civil disorder. In time, and with the growth of the cities to a size and heterogeneity too great to permit the operation of informal social controls, the problem of order maintenance became too severe to make reliance on part-time or volunteer watchmen feasible. The Boston Police Department was created to deal with riots, as was the Department in Philadelphia. The Boston police first acquired firearms in the aftermath of the Draft Riot of 1863, though they were not fully armed at public expense until 1884.

The Philadelphia case is illustrative of many. Like Boston, that city relied on watchmen rather than an organized, quasimilitary constabulary. But a series of riots among youthful gangs (the Rats, the Bouncers, the Schuylkill Rangers, and the Blood Tubs, among several) persuaded the city fathers that stronger measures were necessary. To a degree, the riots were under semi-official auspices, thus magnifying the embarrassment the politicians faced. It seems that volunteer fire companies were organized to handle conflagrations. The young toughs who sat about waiting for fires to happen found this boring and, worse, unrewarding, whereupon some hit upon the idea of starting a fire and racing other companies to the scene to see who could put the blaze out more quickly, and just as important, who could pick up the most loot from the building. Though this competitive zeal may have been a commendable aid to training, it led to frequent collisions between companies speeding to the same fire, with the encounter often leading to a riot. It is only a slight exaggeration to say that the Philadelphia policemen were created in part to control the Philadelphia firemen.

SOMETIMES ON SUNDAY

The growth and formal organization of the police department did not, in themselves, lead to changes in function. The maintenance of order was still the principal objective. What did lead to a change was twofold: the bureaucratization of the detectives (putting them on salary and ending the fee system), and the use of the police to enforce unpopular laws governing the sale and use of liquor. The former change led to the beginning of the popular confusion as to what the police do. The detective became the hero of the dime novel and the cynosure of the public's romantic imagination; he, and not his patrolman colleague, was the "real" police officer doing "real" police work. Enforcing liquor laws caused the police to initiate prosecutions on their own authority rather than on citizen complaint, particularly in cases where the public was deeply divided regarding the wisdom of the law. In Philadelphia, enforcing the Sunday closing laws, especially with regard to saloons, was widely resented, and when the mayor ordered the police to do it, he was, according to a contemporary account, "caricatured, ridiculed, and denounced." In Boston Mayor Jonathan Chapman was led to remark that police enforcement of temperance laws had created a situation in which "the passions of men are aroused and the community is kept in a constant state of ferment."

What kept the police from being utterly destroyed by the liquor controversy was their determination to do no more than was absolutely necessary, given whatever regime was in power. Edward Savage, the able chief of the Boston force in the 1870s and 1880s, was a man of modest but much exercised literary talents, and in one of his better-known essays, entitled "Advice to a Young Policeman," he set forth the essential rule of good police work: "In ordinary cases, if you find yourself in a position of not knowing exactly what to do, better to do too little than too much; it is easier to excuse a moderate course than an overt act."

In addition, the police provided on a large scale a number of services to citizens, especially to those who, because of drink, indolence, or circumstance, were likely to become sources of public disorder. Roger Lane calculates that in 1856 the Boston police provided "lodgings" to over nine thousand persons, not including those who had been arrested for drunkenness. By 1860 the total exceeded seventeen thousand. Perhaps because the police were the principal city agency to witness the lot of the poor, perhaps because one of the original collateral duties of the police chief was superintendent of public health, the officers provided a wide range of services in addition to lodgings—coal for needy families, soup kitchens for the hungry, and jobs as domestics for girls they thought could be lured away from a life of prostitution.

In time, this service policy, which probably did much to mitigate the hostility between police and public occasioned by the enforcement of liquor laws, was curtailed on the complaint of the leaders of the organized charities who objected, apparently, to unfair competition. The advocates of "scientific charity," it seems, did not believe the police were competent to distinguish between the deserving and the undeserving poor.

The relations between police and public even during the period of free soup were not consistently amicable. One issue was the appointment of Irish police officers. For political purposes, the Boston Whigs demanded that, as we would say today, "representatives of indigenous and culturally-deprived groups" be added to the force. Then as now, the "culturally deprived" were responsible for a disproportionate share of those arrested for crimes. Then as now, the police objected to the appointment of an Irishman on the grounds that the man selected by the politicians was not qualified and had himself been arrested for a crime a few years earlier—it seems he had participated in a riot. The police, of course, denied that they were prejudiced but claimed that appointing a person on grounds of ethnicity would be destructive of morale on the force. The mayor insisted that the appointment take place. On November 3, 1851, the new man reported for work, announcing himself loudly and proudly as "Barney McGinniskin, fresh from the bogs of Ireland!"

THE CHIEF EVIL

By the end of the nineteenth century, the groundwork had been laid for the modern municipal police force, and for the modern problems of the police. The bureaucratization of the detectives and the police enforcement of liquor laws had not as yet overshadowed the order-maintenance function of the police, but two events of the twentieth century ensured that they would—Prohibition and the Depression. The former required the police everywhere to choose between being corrupted and making a nuisance of themselves; the latter focused public attention on the escapades of bank robbers and other desperadoes such as John Dillinger, Baby Face Nelson, and Bonnie and Clyde. Police venality and rising crime rates coincided in the public mind, though in fact they had somewhat different causes. The watchman function of the police was lost sight of; their law enforcement function, and their apparent failure to exercise it, were emphasized.

President Herbert Hoover did what most Presidents do when faced with a major political issue for which the solution is neither obvious nor popular—he appointed a commission. In 1931 the National Commission on Law Observance and Law Enforcement—generally known, after its chairman, as the Wickersham Commission—made its report in a series of volumes prepared by some of the ablest academic and police experts of the day. Though many subjects were covered (especially the question of whether immigrants were more criminal than native-born Americans), the volume on the police was of special importance. On page one, the first paragraph stated a twentieth-century conception of the police function and a new standard by which policemen were to be judged:

The general failure of the police to detect and arrest criminals guilty of the many murders, spectacular bank, payroll, and other hold-ups, and sensational robberies with guns, frequently resulting in the death of the robbed victim, has caused a loss of public confidence in the police of our country. For a condition so general there must be some universal underlying causes to account for it.

Now, of course there may have been some "universal underlying causes," but the ones that come readily to mind— Prohibition, post-war readjustment, and the economic cycle—were not ones about which a presidential commission could at that time speak very candidly. Besides, it was far from clear what could be done about at least the second and third of these causes. What was necessary was to find a "universal cause" about which something could be done. Needless to say, two groups on whom we have long felt free to cast blame for everything from slums to hoof-and-mouth disease—the police and the politicians—seemed appropriate targets. Accordingly, the Commission wrote:

The chief evil, in our opinion, lies in the insecure, short term of service of the chief or executive head of the police force and in his being subject while in office to the control of politicians in the discharge of his duties.

SOME PROPOSALS

Following on this analysis, the Commission detailed a number of specific proposals—putting the police on civil service, buying modern equipment ("the wireless"), and of course, hiring better men and giving them better training. In truth, there probably was a need for some police reforms; many departments had become dumping grounds for the fat relatives of second-rate politicians, and modern bank robbers were in many cases more mobile

and efficient than the police chasing them. But the "professional" view of the police went further than merely proposing changes in equipment and manpower; it argued in addition that since the police *can* prevent crime, if the crime rate gets out of hand, it is in good measure because the police are incompetent as a result of political influence.

Now, some members of the Commission were no doubt perfectly aware that the police do not cause crime, but, like many commissions anxious to make a strong public impression and generate support for desirable changes, they inevitably overstated the case in their report. A report that said that many improvements in police practice were necessary but that these improvements, if adopted, would have only a slight effect on the crime rate would not generate many headlines. (Thirty-seven years later, the Kerner Commission had not forgotten this lesson; what made the newspapers was not its proposals for action but its charge of "white racism.")

The consequences of assigning to the police a law-enforcement, crime-prevention function to the exclusion of anything else were profound. If the job of the police is to catch crooks, then the police have a technical, ministerial responsibility in which discretion plays little part. Since no one is likely to disagree on the value of the objective, then there is little reason to expose the police to the decision-making processes of city government. *Ergo,* take the police "out of politics." So powerful (or so useful) did this slogan become that within a few decades whenever a big-city mayor tried to pick his own police chief or take charge of his department for the purpose of giving it a new direction, *the police themselves* objected on the grounds that this was an effort to exercise "political influence" over the force.

Furthermore, if the technical objective of law enforcement was primary, then non-law-enforcement duties should be taken away from the police: no more soup kitchens; no more giving lodging to drunks; no more ambulance driving. These things are not "real police work." Let the police see the public only in their role as law enforcers. Let the public, alas, see the police only as adversaries. Of course, these changes were more in the public's mind than in everyday reality. If politics was taken out of the police, the police were not taken out of politics. They continued—in fact, with the decline of party machines, they increased —their involvement in electoral politics, city hall intrigue, and legislative lobbying. And whatever professional police leadership may have said, the patrolman on the beat knew that his job was not primarily law enforcement—he was still handling as many family fights and rowdy teen-agers as ever. But lacking support in the performance of these duties, he came also to believe that his job "wasn't real police work," and accordingly that it was peripheral, if not demeaning.

But perhaps the most important consequence was the police response to the public expectation that they could prevent crime. Their response was perfectly rational and to be encountered in any organization that is judged by a standard it cannot meet— they lied. If police activity (given the level of resources and public support available) could not produce a signifi-

cant decline in crime rates, police record-keeping would be "adjusted" to keep the rates in line. Departments judged by professional standards but not controlled by professional leaders were at pains to show progress by either understating the number of crimes or overstating the number of crimes "cleared" by arrest. Often this was not the policy of the chief, but the result of judging officers by crime and arrest records.

In the public's eye, the "hero cop" was the man who made the "good pinch." For a while (until the mass media abandoned the standards of the middle-aged and the conservative in favor of the standards of the young and the radical), the ideal cop was the "G Man." FBI agents, of course, are different from municipal police forces precisely because their task *is* law enforcement, and often enforcing important laws against quite serious criminals. Few special agents need to wade into a skid-row brawl. But within city departments, the emphasis on the "good pinch" grew. This was only partly because the newspapers, and thus the public, rewarded such accomplishments; it was also because the departments rewarded it. The patrolman could look forward, in the typical case, to remaining a patrolman all his life *unless* he could get promoted or be made a detective. Promotion increasingly came to require the passing of a written examination in which college men would usually do better than less articulate but perhaps more competent "street men." Appointment as a detective, however, was in many departments available to men with a good arrest record (or a strategically placed friend in headquarters). If you want to get away from drunks, kids, and shrews, then make a pinch that will put you in line for becoming a dick. Though there is in principle nothing wrong with rewarding men for having a good arrest record, one frequent result of this system has been to take the best patrolmen off the street and put them into a headquarters unit.

POLICE REFORM: THE CHOICES AHEAD

Today, the conception of the police role underlying the foregoing arrangements is being questioned. Perhaps the landmark event was the 1967 report of the President's Commission on Law Enforcement and Administration of Justice, the executive director of which was James Vorenberg of the Harvard Law School. Unlike the Wickersham or Kerner Commission reports, this document made relatively few headlines, and the reason, I think, was that it did not provide the reporters with a catchy slogan. The nine volumes of the Vorenberg report insisted that the problems of crime and police work are complicated matters for which few, if any, easy solutions are available. There were no dramatic scandals to uncover; the police "third degree" (on which the Wickersham Commission, in the report drafted by Zechariah Chafee, lavished much attention) had declined in occurrence and significance. Most police departments had been taken out of the control of party machines (in some cases, it would appear, only to be placed under the influence of organized crime). Instead, the Commission devoted considerable attention to the order-maintenance function of the police:

A great majority of the situations in which policemen intervene are not, or are not interpreted by the police to be, criminal situations in the sense that they call for arrest. . . . A common kind of situation . . . is the matrimonial dispute, which police experts estimate consumes as much time as any other single kind of situation.

The riots in Watts and elsewhere had, by the time the report appeared, already called the attention of the public to the importance (and fragility) of public order. The rise of demands for "community control" of various public services, including the police and the schools, has placed the problem of order on the political agenda. Whether the problems of managing disorder can best be handled by turning city government over to neighborhood groups is a complicated question. (Provisionally, I would argue that war becomes more, not less, likely when a political system is balkanized.) In any case, we have come full circle in our thinking about the function of the police.

Or almost full circle. The current anxiety about crime in the streets continues to lead some to define the police task as wholly or chiefly one of crime deterrence, and thus any discussion of redefining the police role or reorganizing police departments to facilitate performing their other functions tends to get lost in the din of charges and countercharges about whether or not the police have been "hand-cuffed." This is unfortunate, not because crime in the streets is a false issue (the rates of street crime, I am convinced, *are* increasing in an alarming manner), but because handling this problem cannot be left solely or even primarily to the police; acting as if it could raises false hopes among the citizens and places unfair and distorting demands on the police. At least as much attention to the courts and correctional systems will be necessary if much progress is to be shown in reducing street crime.

The simultaneous emergence of a popular concern for both crime and order does put in focus the choices that will have to be made in the next generation of police reforms. In effect, municipal police departments are two organizations in one serving two related but not identical functions. The strategy appropriate for strengthening their ability to serve one role tends to weaken their ability to serve the other. Crime deterrence and law enforcement require, or are facilitated by, specialization, strong hierarchical authority, improved mobility and communications, clarity in legal codes and arrest procedures, close surveillance of the community, high standards of integrity, and the avoidance of entangling alliances with politicians. The maintenance of order, on the other hand, is aided by departmental procedures that include decentralization, neighborhood involvement, foot patrol, wide discretion, the provision of services, an absence of arrest quotas, and some tolerance for minor forms of favoritism and even corruption.

There is no magic formula—no pre-packaged "reform"—that can tell a community or a police chief how to organize a force to serve, with appropriate balance, these competing objectives. Just as slogans demanding "taking the police out of politics" or "putting the police in cars" have proved inadequate guides to action in the past, so also slogans demanding "foot patrolmen" or "community control" are likely to prove inadequate in the future. One would like to think that since both points of view now have ardent advocates, the debate has at last been joined. But I suspect that the two sides are talking at, or past, each other, and not *to* each other, and thus the issue, from being joined, is still lost in rhetoric.

The Failure of Urban Renewal

Herbert J. Gans

Suppose that the government decided that jalopies were a menace to public safety and a blight on the beauty of our highways, and therefore took them away from their drivers. Suppose, then, that to replenish the supply of automobiles, it gave these drivers a hundred dollars each to buy a good used car and also made special grants to General Motors, Ford, and Chrysler to lower the cost—although not necessarily the price—of Cadillacs, Lincolns, and Imperials by a few hundred dollars. Absurd as this may sound, change the jalopies to slum housing, and I have described, with only slight poetic license, the first fifteen years of a federal program called urban renewal.

Since 1949, this program has provided local renewal agencies with federal funds and the power of eminent domain to condemn slum neighborhoods, tear down the buildings, and resell the cleared land to private developers at a reduced price. In addition to relocating the slum dwellers in "decent, safe, and sanitary" housing, the program was intended to stimulate large-scale private rebuilding, add new tax revenues to the dwindling coffers of the cities, revitalize their downtown areas, and halt the exodus of middle-class whites to the suburbs.

For some time now, a few city planners and housing experts have been pointing out that urban renewal was not achieving its general aims, and social scientists have produced a number of critical studies of individual renewal projects. These critiques, however, have mostly appeared in academic books and journals; otherwise there has been remarkably little public discussion of the federal program. Slum-dwellers whose homes were to be torn down have indeed protested bitterly, but their outcries have been limited to particular projects; and because such outcries have rarely been supported by the local press, they have been easily brushed aside by the political power of the supporters of the projects in question. In the last few years, the civil rights movement has backed protesting slum-dwellers, though again only at the local level, while rightists have opposed the use of eminent domain to take private property from one owner in order to give it to another (especially when the new one is likely to be from out-of-town and financed by New York capital).

Slum clearance has also come under fire from several prominent architectural and social critics, led by Jane Jacobs, who have been struggling to preserve neighborhoods like Greenwich Village, with their brownstones, lofts, and small apartment houses, against the encroachment of the large high-rise projects built for luxury market and the poor alike. But these efforts have been directed mainly at private clearance outside the

From *Commentary* (April 1965), pp. 29-37. Copyright © 1965 by the American Jewish Committee. Reprinted by permission of the publisher.

federal program, and their intent has been to save the city for people (intellectuals and artists, for example) who, like tourists, want jumbled diversity, antique "charm," and narrow streets for visual adventure and aesthetic pleasure. (Norman Mailer carried such thinking to its farthest point in his recent attack in the *New York Times Magazine* on the physical and social sterility of high-rise housing; Mailer's attack was also accompanied by an entirely reasonable suggestion—in fact the only viable one that could be made in this context—that the advantages of brownstone living be incorporated into skyscraper projects.)

But if criticism of the urban renewal program has in the past been spotty and sporadic, there are signs that the program as a whole is now beginning to be seriously and tellingly evaluated. At least two comprehensive studies, by Charles Abrams and Scott Greer, are nearing publication, and one highly negative analysis—by an ultra-conservative economist and often irresponsible polemicist—has already appeared: Martin Anderson's *The Federal Bulldozer*.[1] Ironically enough, Anderson's data are based largely on statistics collected by the Urban Renewal Administration. What, according to these and other data, has the program accomplished? It has cleared slums to make room for many luxury-housing and a few middle-income projects, and it has also provided inexpensive land for the expansion of colleges, hospitals, libraries, shopping areas, and other such institutions located in slum areas. As of March 1961, 126,000 dwelling units had been demolished and about 28,000 new ones built. The median monthly rental of all those erected during 1960 came to $158, and in 1962, to $192—a staggering figure for any area outside of Manhattan.

Needless to say, none of the slum-dwellers who were dispossessed in the process could afford to move into these new apartments. Local renewal agencies were supposed to relocate the dispossessed tenants in "standard" housing within their means before demolition began, but such vacant housing is scarce in most cities, and altogether unavailable in some. And since the agencies were under strong pressure to clear the land and get renewal projects going, the relocation of the tenants was impatiently, if not ruthlessly, handled. Thus, a 1961 study of renewal projects in 41 cities showed that 60 per cent of the dispossessed tenants were merely relocated in other slums; and in big cities, the proportion was even higher (over 70 per cent in Philadelphia, according to a 1958 study). Renewal sometimes even created new slums by pushing relocatees into areas and buildings which then became overcrowded and deteriorated rapidly. This has principally been the case with Negroes who, both for economic and racial reasons, have been forced to double up in other ghettos. Indeed, because almost two-thirds of the cleared slum units have been occupied by Negroes, the urban renewal program has often been characterized as Negro clearance, and in too many cities, this has been its intent.

Moreover, those dispossessed tenants who found better housing usually had to pay more rent than they could afford. In his careful study of relocation in Boston's heavily Italian West End,[2] Chester Hartman shows that 41 per cent of the West Enders lived in good housing in this so-called slum (thus suggesting that much of it should not have been torn down) and that 73 per cent were relocated in good housing—thanks in part to the fact that the West Enders were white. This improvement was achieved at a heavy price, however, for median rents rose from $41 to $71 per month after the move.

According to renewal officials, 80 per cent of all persons relocated now live in good housing, and rent increases were justified because many had been paying unduly low rent before. Hartman's study was the first to compare these official statistics with housing realities, and his figure of 73 per cent challenges the official claim that 97 per cent of the Boston West Enders were properly re-housed. This discrepancy may arise from the fact that renewal officials collected their data after the poorest of the uprooted tenants had fled in panic to other slums, and that officials also tended toward a rather lenient evaluation of the relocation housing of those actually studied in order to make a good record for their agency. (On the other hand, when they were certifying areas for clearance, these officials often exaggerated the degree of "blight" in order to prove their case.)

As for the substandard rents paid by slum-dwellers, this is true in only a small proportion of cases, and then mostly among whites. Real-estate economists argue that families should pay at least 20 per cent of their income for housing, but what is manageable for middle-income people is a burden to those with low incomes who pay a higher share of their earnings for food and other necessities. Yet even so, Negroes generally have to devote about 30 per cent of their income to housing, and a Chicago study cited by Hartman reports that among non-white families earning less than $3,000 a year, median rent rose from 35 per cent of income before relocation to 46 per cent afterward.

To compound the failure of urban renewal to help the poor, many clearance areas (Boston's West End is an example) were chosen, as Anderson points out, not because they had the worst slums, but because they offered the best sites for luxury housing—housing which would have been built whether the urban renewal program existed or not. Since public funds were used to clear the slums and to make the land available to private builders at reduced costs, the low-income population was in effect subsidizing its own removal for the benefit of the wealthy. What was done for the slum-dwellers in return is starkly suggested by the following statistic: *only one-half of one per cent* of all federal expenditures for urban renewal between 1949 and 1964 was spent on relocation of families and individuals; and 2 per cent if payments are included.

Finally, because the policy has been to clear a district of all slums at once in order to assemble large sites to attract private developers, entire neighborhoods have frequently been destroyed, uprooting people who had lived there for decades, closing down their institutions, ruining small businesses by the hundreds, and scattering families and friends all over the city. By removing the structure of social and emotional support provided by the neighborhood, and by forcing people to rebuild their lives separately and amid strangers elsewhere, slum clearance has often come at a serious psychological as well as financial cost to its supposed beneficiaries. Marc Fried, a clinical psychologist who studied the West Enders after relocation, reported that 46 per cent of the women and 38 per cent of the men "give evidence of a fairly severe grief reaction or worse" in response to questions about leaving their tight-knit community. Far from "adjusting" eventually to this trauma, 26 per cent of the women remained sad or depressed even two years after they had been pushed out of the West End.[3]

People like the Italians or the Puerto Ricans who live in an intensely group-centered way among three-generation "extended families" and ethnic peers have naturally suffered greatly from the clearance of entire neighborhoods. It may well be, however, that slum clearance has inflicted yet graver emotional burdens on Negroes, despite the fact that they generally live in less cohesive and often disorganized neighborhoods. In fact, I suspect that Negroes who lack a stable family life and have trouble finding neighbors, shopkeepers, and institutions they can trust may have been hurt even more by forcible removal to new areas. This suspicion is supported by another of Fried's findings—that the socially marginal West Enders were more injured by relocation than those who had been integral members of the old neighborhood. Admittedly, some Negroes move very often on their own, but then they at least do so voluntarily, and not in consequence of a public policy which is supposed to help them in the first place. Admittedly also, relocation has made it possible for social workers to help slum-dwellers whom they could not reach until renewal brought them out in the open, so to speak. But then only a few cities have so far used social workers to make relocation a more humane process.

These high financial, social, and emotional costs paid by the slum-dwellers have generally been written off as an unavoidable by-product of "progress," the price of helping cities to collect more taxes, bring back the middle class, make better use of downtown land, stimulate private investment, and restore civic pride. But as Anderson shows, urban renewal has hardly justified these claims either. For one thing, urban renewal is a slow process the average project has taken twelve years to complete. Moreover, while the few areas suitable for luxury housing were quickly rebuilt, less desirable cleared land might lie vacant for many years because developers were—and are—unwilling to risk putting up high- and middle-income housing in areas still surrounded by slums. Frequently, they can be attracted only by promises of tax write-offs, which absorb the increased revenues that renewal is supposed to create for the city. Anderson reports that, instead of the anticipated four dollars for every public dollar, private investments have only just matched the public subsidies, and even the money for luxury housing has come forth largely because of federal subsidies. Thus, all too few of the new projects have produced tax gains and returned suburbanites, or generated the magic rebuilding boom.

Anderson goes on to argue that during the fifteen years of the federal urban renewal program, the private housing market has achieved what urban renewal has failed to do. Between 1950 and 1960, twelve million new dwelling units were built, and fully six million substandard ones disappeared—all without government action. The proportion of substandard housing in the total housing supply was reduced from 37 to 19 per cent, and even among the dwelling units occupied by non-whites, the proportion of substandard units has dropped from 72 to 44 per cent. This comparison leads Anderson to the conclusion that the private market is much more effective than government action in removing slums and supplying new housing, and that the urban renewal program ought to be repealed.

It would appear that Anderson's findings and those of the other studies I have cited make an excellent case for doing so. However, a less biased analysis of the figures and a less tendentious mode of evaluating them than Anderson's leads to a different conclusion. To begin with, Anderson's use of nation-wide statistics misses the few good renewal projects, those which have helped both the slum-dwellers and the cities, or those which brought in enough new taxes to finance other city services for the poor. Such projects can be found in small cities and especially in those where high vacancy rates assured sufficent relocation housing of standard quality. More important, all the studies I have mentioned deal with projects carried out during the 1950's, and fail to take account of the improvements in urban renewal practice under the Kennedy and Johnson administrations. Although Anderson's study supposedly covers the period up to 1963, much of his data go no further than 1960. Since then, the federal bulldozer has moved into fewer neighborhoods, and the concept of rehabilitating rather than clearing blighted neighborhoods is more and more being underwritten by subsidized loans. A new housing subsidy program —known as 221(d) (3)— for families above the income ceiling for public housing has also been launched, and in 1964, Congress passed legislation for

assistance to relocatees who cannot afford their new rents.

None of this is to say that Anderson would have had to revise his findings drastically if he had taken the pains to update them. These recent innovations have so far been small in scope—only 13,000 units were financed under 211-(d)(3) in the first two years—and they still do not provide subsidies sufficient to bring better housing within the price range of the slum residents. In addition, rehabilitation unaccompanied by new construction is nearly useless because it does not eliminate overcrowding. And finally, some cities are still scheduling projects to clear away the non-white poor who stand in the path of the progress of private enterprise. Unfortunately, many cities pay little attention to federal pleas to improve the program, using the local initiative granted them by urban renewal legislation to perpetuate the practices of the 1950's. Yet even with the legislation of the 1960's, the basic error in the original design of urban renewal remains: it is still a method for eliminating the slums in order to "renew" the city, rather than a program for properly rehousing slum-dwellers.

Before going into this crucial distinction, we first need to be clear that private housing is not going to solve our slum problems. In the first place, Anderson conveniently ignores the fact that if urban renewal has benefited anyone, it is private enterprise. Bending to the pressure of the real-estate lobby, the legislation that launched urban renewal in effect required that private developers do the rebuilding, and most projects could therefore get off the drawing board only if they appeared to be financially attractive to a developer. Thus, his choice of a site and his rebuilding plans inevitably took priority over the needs of the slum-dwellers.

It is true that Anderson is not defending private enterprise *per se* but the free market, although he forgets that it only exists today as a concept in reactionary minds and dated economics texts. The costs of land, capital, and construction have long since made it impossible for private developers to build for anyone but the rich, and some form of subsidy is needed to house everyone else. The building boom of the 1950's which Anderson credits to the free market was subsidized by income-tax deductions to homeowners and by F.H.A. 2nd V.A. mortgage insurance, not to mention the federal highway programs that have made the suburbs possible.

To be sure, these supports enabled private builders to put up a great deal of housing for middle-class whites. This in turn permitted well-employed workers, including some non-whites, to improve their own situation by moving into the vacated neighborhoods. Anderson is quite right in arguing that if people earn good wages, they can obtain better housing more easily and cheaply in the not-quite-private market than through urban renewal. But this market is of little help to those employed at low or even factory wages, or the unemployed, or most Negroes who, whatever their earnings, cannot live in the suburbs. In consequence, 44 per cent of all housing occupied by non-whites in 1960 was still substandard, and even with present subsidies, private enterprise can do nothing for these people. As for laissez faire, it played a major role in creating the slums in the first place.

The solution, then, is not to repeal urban renewal, but to transform it from a program of slum clearance and reha-

bilitation into a program of urban rehousing. This means, first, building low- and moderate-cost housing on vacant land in cities, suburbs, and new towns beyond the suburbs, and also helping slum-dwellers to move into existing housing outside the slums; and then, *after* a portion of the urban low-income population has left the slums, clearing and rehabilitating them through urban renewal. This approach is commonplace in many European countries, which have long since realized that private enterprise can no more house the population and eliminate slums than it can run the post office.

Of course, governments in Europe have a much easier task than ours in developing decent low-income projects. Because they take it for granted that housing is a national rather than a local responsibility, the government agencies are not hampered by the kind of real-estate and construction lobbies which can defeat or subvert American programs by charges of socialism. Moreover, their municipalities own a great deal of the vacant land, and have greater control over the use of private land than do American cities. But perhaps their main advantage is the lack of popular opposition to moving the poor out of the slums and into the midst of the more affluent residents. Not only is housing desperately short for all income groups, but the European class structure, even in Western socialist countries, is still rigid enough so that low- and middle-income groups can live near each other if not next to each other, and still "know their place."

In America, on the other hand, one's house and address are major signs of social status, and no one who has any say in the matter wants people of lower income or status in his neighborhood.

Middle-class homeowners use zoning as a way of keeping out cheaper or less prestigious housing, while working-class communities employ less subtle forms of exclusion. Consequently, low-income groups, whatever their creed or color, have been forced to live in slums or near-slums, and to wait until they could acquire the means to move as a group, taking over better neighborhoods when the older occupants were ready to move on themselves.

For many years now, the only source of new housing for such people, and their only hope of escaping the worst slums, has been public housing. But this is no longer a practical alternative. Initiated during the Depression, public housing has always been a politically embattled program; its opponents, among whom the real-estate lobby looms large, first saddled it with restrictions and then effectively crippled it. Congress now permits only 35,000 units a year to be built in the entire country.

The irony is that public housing has declined because, intended only for the poor, it faithfully carried out its mandate. Originally, sites were obtained by slum clearance; after the war, however, in order to increase the supply of low-cost housing, cities sought to build public housing on vacant land. But limited as it was to low-income tenants and thus labeled and stigmatized as an institution of the dependent poor, public housing was kept out of vacant land in the better neighborhoods. This, plus the high cost of land and construction, left housing officials with no other choice but to build high-rise projects on whatever vacant land they could obtain, often next to factories or along railroad yards. Because tenants of public housing are ruled by a set of strict regula-

tions—sometimes necessary, sometimes politically inspired, but always degrading—anyone who could afford housing in the private market shunned the public projects. During the early years of the program, when fewer citizens had that choice, public housing became respectable shelter for the working class and even for the unemployed middle class. After the war, federal officials decided, and rightly so, that public housing ought to be reserved for those who had no other alternative, and therefore set income limits that admitted only the really poor. Today, public housing is home for the underclass—families who earn less than $3000-$4000 annually, many with unstable jobs or none at all, and most of them non-white.

Meanwhile the enthusiasm for public housing has been steadily dwindling and with it, badly needed political support. Newspaper reports reinforce the popular image of public-housing projects as huge nests of crime and delinquency—despite clear evidence to the contrary—and as the domicile of unregenerate and undeserving families whose children urinate only in the elevators. The position of public housing, particularly among liberal intellectuals, has also been weakened by the slurs of the social and architectural aesthetes who condemn the projects' poor exterior designs as "sterile," "monotonous," and "dehumanizing," often in ignorance of the fact that the tightly restricted funds have been allocated mainly to make the apartments themselves as spacious and livable as possible, and that the waiting lists among slum-dwellers who want these apartments remain long. Be that as it may, suburban communities and urban neighborhoods with vacant land are as hostile to public housing as ever, and their opposition is partly responsible for the program's having been cut down to its present minuscule size.

The net result is that low-income people today cannot get out of the slums, either because they cannot afford the subsidized private market, or because the project they could afford cannot be built on vacant land. There is only one way to break through this impasse, and that is to permit them equal access to new subsidized, privately built housing by adding another subsidy to make up the difference between the actual rent and what they can reasonably be expected to pay. Such a plan, giving them a chance to choose housing like all other citizens, would help to remove the stigma of poverty and inferiority placed on them by public housing. Many forms of rent subsidy have been proposed, but the best one, now being tried in New York, is to put low- and middle-income people in the same middle-income project with the former getting the same apartments at smaller rentals.

Admittedly, this approach assumes that the poor can live with the middle class and that their presence and behavior will not threaten their neighbors' security or status. No one knows whether this is really possible, but experiments in education, job training, and social-welfare programs do show that many low-income people, when once offered *genuine* opportunities to improve their lives and given help in making use of them, are able to shake off the hold of the culture of poverty. Despite the popular stereotype, the proportion of those whom Hylan Lewis calls the clinical poor, too ravaged emotionally by poverty and deprivation to adapt to new opportunities, seems to be small. As for the rest, they only reject

programs offering spurious opportunities, like job-training schemes for nonexistent jobs. Further, anyone who has lived in a slum neighborhood can testify that whatever the condition of the building, most women keep their apartments clean by expenditures of time and effort inconceivable to the middle-class housewife. Moving to a better apartment would require little basic cultural change from these women, and rehousing is thus a type of new opportunity that stands a better chance of succeeding than, say, a program to inculcate new child-rearing techniques.

We have no way of telling how many slum-dwellers would be willing to participate in such a plan. However poor the condition of the flat, the slum is home, and for many it provides the support of neighboring relatives and friends, and a cultural milieu in which everyone has the same problems and is therefore willing to overlook occasional disreputable behavior. A middle-income project cannot help but have a middle-class ethos, and some lower-class people may be fearful of risking what little stability they have achieved where they are now in exchange for something new, strange, demanding, and potentially hostile. It would be hard to imagine an unwed Negro mother moving her household to a middle-income project full of married couples and far removed from the mother, sisters, and aunts who play such an important role in the female-centered life of lower-class Negroes. However, there are today a large number of stable two-parent families who live in the slums only because income and race exclude them from the better housing that is available. Families like these would surely be only too willing to leave the Harlems and Black Belts.

They would have to be helped with loans to make the move, and perhaps even with grants to buy new furniture so as not to feel ashamed in their new surroundings. They might be further encouraged by being offered income-tax relief for giving up the slums, just as we now offer such relief to people who give up being renters to become homeowners.

Undoubtedly there would be friction between the classes, and the more affluent residents would likely want to segregate themselves and their children from neighbors who did not toe the middle-class line, especially with respect to child-rearing. The new housing would therefore have to be planned to allow some voluntary social segregation for both groups, if only to make sure that enough middle-income families would move in (especially in cities where there was no shortage of housing for them). The proportion of middle- and low-income tenants would have to be regulated not only to minimize the status fears of the former, but also to give the latter enough peers to keep them from feeling socially isolated and without emotional support when problems arise. Fortunately, non-profit and limited dividend institutions, which do not have to worry about showing an immediate profit, are now being encouraged to build moderate-income housing; they can do a more careful job of planning the physical and social details of this approach than speculative private builders.

If the slums are really to be emptied and their residents properly housed elsewhere, the rehousing program will have to be extended beyond the city limits, for the simple reason that that is where most of the vacant land is located. This means admitting the low-income population to the suburbs; it also means creating new towns—self-contained communities with their own industry which would not, like the suburbs, be dependent on the city for employment opportunities, and could therefore be situated in presently rural areas. Federal support for the construction of new towns was requested as part of the 1964 Housing Act, and although Congress refused to pass it, the legislation will come up again in 1965.[4]

To be sure, white middle-class suburbanites and rural residents are not likely to welcome non-white low-income people into their communities even if the latter are no longer clearly labeled as poor. The opposition to be expected in city neighborhoods chosen for mixed-income projects would be multiplied a hundredfold in outlying areas. Being politically autonomous, and having constituencies who are not about to support measures that will threaten their security or status in the slightest, the suburbs possess the political power to keep the rehousing program out of their own vacant lots, even if they cannot stop the federal legislation that would initiate it. On the other hand, experience with the federal highway program and with urban renewal itself has demonstrated that few communities can afford to turn down large amounts of federal money. For instance, New York City is likely to build a Lower Manhattan Expressway in the teeth of considerable local opposition, if only because the federal government will pay 90 per cent of the cost and thus bring a huge sum into the city coffers. If the rehousing program were sufficiently large to put a sizable mixed-income project in every community, and if the federal government were to pick up at least 90 per cent of the tab, while also strengthening the appeal of the program by helping to solve present transportation, school, and tax problems in the suburbs, enough political support might be generated to overcome the objections of segregationist and class-conscious whites.

Yet even if the outlying areas could be persuaded to cooperate, it is not at all certain that slum-dwellers would leave the city. Urban renewal experience has shown that for many slum-dwellers, there are more urgent needs than good housing. One is employment, and most of the opportunities for unskilled or semi-skilled work are in the city. Another is money, and some New York City slum residents recently refused to let the government inspect—much less repair—their buildings because they would lose the rent reductions they had received previously. If leaving the city meant higher rents, more limited access to job possibilities, and also separation from people and institutions which give them stability, some slum residents might very well choose overcrowding and dilapidation as the lesser of two evils.

These problems would have to be considered in planning a rehousing program beyond the city limits. The current exodus of industry from the city would of course make jobs available to the new suburbanites. The trouble is that the industries now going into the suburbs, or those that would probably be attracted to the new towns, are often precisely the ones which use the most modern machinery and the fewest unskilled workers. Thus, our rehousing plan comes up against the same obstacle—the shortage of jobs—that has frustrated other programs to help the low-income population and that will surely defeat the War on Poverty in its present form. Like so many other programs, rehousing is finally seen to depend on a step that American society is as yet unwilling to take: the deliberate creation of new jobs by government action. The building of new towns especially would have to be coordinated with measures aimed at attracting private industry to employ the prospective residents, at creating other job opportunities, and at offering intensive training for the, unskilled after they have been hired. If they are not sure of a job before they leave the city, they simply will not leave.

The same social and cultural inhibitions that make slum residents hesitant to move into a mixed-income project in the city would, of course, be even stronger when it came to moving out of the city. These inhibitions might be relaxed by moving small groups of slum residents en masse, or by getting those who move first to encourage their neighbors to follow. In any case, new social institutions and community facilities would have to be developed to help the erstwhile slum-dweller feel comfortable in his new community, yet without labeling him as poor.

Despite its many virtues, a rehousing program based on the use of vacant land on either side of the city limits would not immediately clear the slums. Given suburban opposition and the occupational and social restraints on the slum-dwellers themselves, it can be predicted that if such a program were set into motion it would be small in size, and that it would pull out only the upwardly mobile—particularly the young people with stable families and incomes —who are at best a sizable minority among the poor. What can be done now to help the rest leave the slums?

The best solution is a public effort to

encourage their moving into existing neighborhoods within the city and in older suburbs just beyond the city limits. Indeed, a direct rent subsidy like that now given to relocatees could enable people to obtain decent housing in these areas. This approach has several advantages. It would allow low-income people to be close to jobs and to move in groups, and it would probably attract the unwed mother who wanted to give her children a better chance in life. It would also be cheaper than building new housing, although the subsidies would have to be large enough to discourage low-income families from overcrowding—and thus deteriorating—the units in order to save on rent.

There are, however, some obvious disadvantages as well. For one thing, because non-white low-income people would be moving into presently white or partially integrated areas, the government would in effect be encouraging racial invasion. This approach would thus have the effect of pushing the white and middle-income people further toward the outer edge of the city or into suburbs. Although some whites might decide to stay, many would surely want to move, and not all would be able to afford to do so. It would be necessary to help them with rent subsidies as well; indeed, they might become prospective middle-income tenants for rehousing projects on vacant land.

Undoubtedly, all this would bring us closer to the all-black city that has already been predicted. For this reason alone, a scheme that pushes the whites further out can only be justified when combined with a rehousing program on vacant land that would begin to integrate the suburbs. But even that could not prevent a further racial imbalance between cities and suburbs.

Yet would the predominantly non-white city really be so bad? It might be for the middle class which needs the jobs, shops, and culture that the city provides. Of course, the greater the suburban exodus, the more likely it would become that middle-class culture would also move to the suburbs. This is already happening in most American cities—obvious testimony to the fact that culture (at least of the middlebrow kind represented by tent theaters and art movie-houses) does not need the city in order to flourish; and the artists who create high culture seem not to mind living among the poor even now.

Non-white low-income people might feel more positive about a city in which they were the majority, for if they had the votes, municipal services would be more attuned to their priorities than is now the case. To be sure, if poor people (of any color) were to dominate the city, its tax revenues would decrease even further, and cities would be less able than ever to supply the high quality public services that the low-income population needs so much more urgently than the middle class. Consequently, new sources of municipal income not dependent on the property tax would have to be found; federal and state grants to cities (like those already paying half the public-school costs in several states) would probably be the principal form. Even under present conditions, in fact, new sources of municipal income must soon be located if the cities are not to collapse financially.

If non-whites were to leave the slums en masse, new ghettos would eventually form in the areas to which they would move. Although this is undesirable by conventional liberal standards, the fact is that many low-income Negroes are not yet very enthusiastic about living among white neighbors. They do not favor segregation, of course; what they want is a free choice and then the ability to select predominantly non-white areas that are in better shape than the ones they live in now. If the suburbs were opened to non-whites—to the upwardly mobile ones who want integration now—free choice would become available. If the new ghettos were decent neighborhoods with good schools, and if their occupants had jobs and other opportunities to bring stability into their lives, they would be training their children to want integration a generation hence.

In short, then, a workable rehousing scheme must provide new housing on both sides of the city limits for the upwardly mobile minority, and encouragement to move into older areas for the remainder. If, in these ways, enough slum-dwellers could be enabled and induced to leave the slums, it would then be possible to clear or rehabilitate the remaining slums. Once slum areas were less crowded, and empty apartments were going begging, their profitability and market value would be reduced, and urban renewal could take place far more cheaply, and far more quickly. Relocation would be less of a problem, and with land values down, rebuilding and rehabilitation could be carried out to fit the resources of the low-income people who needed or wanted to remain in the city. A semi-suburban style of living that would be attractive to the upper-middle class could also be provided.

At this point, it would be possible to begin to remake the inner city into what it must eventually become—the hub of a vast metropolitan complex of urban neighborhoods, suburbs, and new towns, in which those institutions and functions that have to be at the center—the specialized business districts, the civil and cultural facilities, and the great hospital complexes and university campuses—would be located.

Even in such a city, there would be slums—for people who wanted to live in them, for the clinical poor who would be unable to make it elsewhere, and for rural newcomers who would become urbanized in them before moving on. But it might also be possible to relocate many of these in a new kind of public housing in which quasi-communities would be established to help those whose problems were soluble and to provide at least decent shelter for those who cannot be helped except by letting them live without harassment until we learn how to cure mental illness, addiction, and other forms of self-destructive behavior.

This massive program has much to recommend it, but we must clearly understand that moving the low-income population out of the slums would not eliminate poverty or the other problems that stem from it. A standard dwelling unit can make life more comfortable, and a decent neighborhood can discourage some anti-social behavior, but by themselves, neither can effect radical transformations. What poor people need most are decent incomes, proper jobs, better schools, and freedom from racial and class discrimination. Indeed, if the choice were between a program solely dedicated to rehousing, and a program that kept the low-income population in the city slums for another generation but provided for these needs, the latter would be preferable, for it would produce people who were able to leave the slums under their own steam. Obviously, the ideal approach is one that coordinates the elimination of slums with the reduction of poverty.

As I have been indicating, an adequate rehousing program would be extremely costly and very difficult to carry out. Both its complexity and expense can be justified, however, on several grounds. Morally, it can be argued that no one in the Great Society should have to live in a slum, at least not involuntarily.

From a political point of view, it is urgently necessary to begin integrating the suburbs and to improve housing conditions in the city before the latter becomes an ominous ghetto of poor and increasingly angry Negroes and Puerto Ricans, and the suburbs become enclaves of affluent whites who commute fearfully to a downtown bastion of stores and offices. If the visible group tensions of recent years are allowed to expand and sharpen, another decade may very well see the beginning of open and often violent class and race warfare.

But the most persuasive argument for a rehousing program is economic. Between 50 and 60 per cent of building costs go into wages and create work for the unskilled who are now increasingly unemployable elsewhere. A dwelling unit that costs $15,000 would thus provide as much as $9000 in wages— one-and-a-half years of respectably paid employment for a single worker. Adding four-and-a-half million new low-cost housing units to rehouse half of those in substandard units in 1960 would provide almost seven million man-years of work, and the subsequent renewal of these and other substandard units yet more. Many additional jobs would also be created by the construction and operation of new shopping centers, schools, and other community facilities,

as well as the highways and public transit systems that would be needed to serve the new suburbs and towns. If precedent must be cited for using a housing program to create jobs, it should be recalled that public housing was started in the Depression for precisely this reason.

The residential building industry (and the real-estate lobby) would have to be persuaded to give up their stubborn resistance to government housing programs, but the danger of future underemployment, and the opportunity of participating profitably in the rehousing scheme, should either convert present builders or attract new ones into the industry. As for the building trades unions, they have always supported government housing programs, but they have been unwilling to admit nonwhites to membership. If, however, the rehousing effort were sizable enough to require many more workers than are now in the unions, the sheer demand for labor—and the enforcement of federal non-discriminatory hiring policies for public works—would probably break down the color barriers without much difficulty.

While the federal government is tooling up to change the urban renewal program into a rehousing scheme, it should also make immediate changes in current renewal practices to remove their economic and social cost from the shoulders of the slum-dwellers. Future projects should be directed at the clearance of *really harmful* slums, instead of taking units that are *run down but not demonstrably harmful* out of the supply of low-cost housing, especially for downtown revitalization and other less pressing community improvement schemes. Occupants of harmful slums, moreover, ought to be rehoused in decent units they can afford. For this purpose, more public housing and 221 (d) (3) projects must be built, and relocation and rent assistance payments should be increased to eliminate the expense of moving for the slum-dweller. Indeed, the simplest way out of the relocation impasse is to give every relocatee a sizable grant, like the five-hundred dollars to one thousand dollars paid by private builders in New York City to get tenants out of existing structures quickly and painlessly. Such a grant is not only a real incentive to relocate but a means of reducing opposition to urban renewal. By itself, however, it cannot reduce the shortage of relocation housing. Where such housing now exists in plentiful supply, renewal ought to move ahead more quickly, but where there is a shortage that cannot be appreciably reduced, it would be wise to eliminate or postpone clearance and rehabilitation projects that require a large amount of relocation.

Nothing is easier than to suggest radical new programs to the overworked and relatively powerless officials of federal and local renewal agencies who must carry out the present law, badly written or not, and who are constantly pressured by influential private interests to make decisions in their favor. Many of these officials are as unhappy with what urban renewal has wrought as their armchair critics and would change the program if they could—that is, if they received encouragement from the White House, effective support in getting new legislation through Congress, and, equally important, political help at city halls to incorporate these innovations into local programs. But it should be noted that little of what I have suggested is very radical, for none of the proposals involves conflict with the entrenched American practice of subsidizing private enterprise to carry out public works at a reasonable profit. The proposals are radical only in demanding an end to our no less entrenched practice of punishing the poor. Yet they also make sure that middle-class communities are rewarded financially for whatever discomfort they may have to endure.

Nor are these suggestions very new. Indeed, only last month President Johnson sent a housing message to Congress which proposes the payment of rent subsidies as the principal method for improving housing conditions. It also requests federal financing of municipal services for tax-starved communities, and aid toward the building of new towns. These represent bold and desirable steps toward the evolution of a federal rehousing program. Unfortunately, however, the message offers little help to those who need it most. Slum-dwellers may be pleased that there will be no increase in urban renewal activity, and that relocation housing subsidies and other grants are being stepped up. But no expansion of public housing is being requested, and to make matters worse, the new rent subsidies will be available only to households above the income limits for public housing. Thus, the President's message offers no escape for the mass of the non-white low-income population from the ghetto slums; in fact it threatens to widen the gap between such people and the lower-middle-income population which will be eligible for rent subsidies.

On the other hand, as in the case of the War on Poverty, a new principle of government responsibility in housing is being established, and evidently the President's strategy is to obtain legislative approval for the principle by combining it with a minimal and a minimally controversial program for the first year. Once the principle has been accepted, however, the program must change quickly. It may have taken fifteen years for urban renewal even to begin providing some relief to the mass of slum-dwellers, but it cannot take that long again to become a rehousing scheme that will give them significant help. The evolution of federal policies can no longer proceed in the leisurely fashion to which politicians, bureaucrats, and middle-class voters have become accustomed, for unemployment, racial discrimination, and the condition of our cities are becoming ever more critical problems, and those who suffer from them are now considerably less patient than they have been in the past.

NOTES

1. M.I.T. Press, 272 pp., $5.95.
2. See the November 1964 issue of the *Journal of the American Institute of Planners.* The article also reviews all other relocation research and is a more reliable study of the consequences of renewal than Anderson's.
3. See "Grieving for a Lost Home," in *The Urban Condition,* edited by Leonard Duhl.
4. Meanwhile, several private developers are planning new towns (for example, James Rouse who is building Columbia near Baltimore, and Robert Simon who has already begun Reston, outside Washington) in which they propose to house some low-income people.

IX THE CITY IN POSTINDUSTRIAL SOCIETY

The city in post-industrial society is that giant complex, the metropolis, swallowing the hinterland with its clusters of suburban communities and satellite cities. One of the chief characteristics of the metropolis is decentralization. Accelerated by the automobile, the growth of the suburbs, and the relocation of industry and manufacturing, decentralization has boomed in the twentieth century to produce the metropolis, the super-city, which in itself represents a new phase of urban growth. Between 1900 and 1950, cities with a population of one hundred thousand or more increased from 52 to 147 percent, which meant an increase in the total U.S. population of 32 to 56 percent. Thus, Charles Glaab and A. Theodore Brown can conclude that "the growth of the metropolis constitutes the central theme of twentieth-century American urban history."[1]

Hans blumenfeld begins this chapter with an ambitious, sweeping essay. He sees the evolution of the city in terms of what went before and what may come after. By combining the approaches of an historian, an economist, an ecologist, and a city-planner, he examines three stages of "the emergence of a basically new form of human settlement," the preindustrial city, the nineteenth-century industrial city, and the modern, sprawling metropolis of today. He attempts to answer the difficult question of what were the main forces that transformed the preindustrial city into a modern metropolis (an urban area that "derives its identity from a single center"). To do this, he first discusses a number of crucial differences between the preindustrial city and the metropolis and then delineates what he feels to be the major features of the metropolis—the central business area, manufacturing and related industries, housing and services, and open land—and the plans by which it may be manipulated into the city of the future.

Although he discusses the strengths and weaknesses of several schemes for

1. *A History of Urban America*, p. 270.

the future metropolis, such as the so-called constellation, linear, and stellar metropolises, and the requirements for rational planning, he does not see the oft-accepted notion that the megalopolis is the destiny of American cities. "Megalopolis"[2]—a huge urbanized area made up of several metropolises that have expanded and grown together, such as the cities of the Ruhr in Germany or the urban strip running from Boston to Washington in the United States— is not a concept that can be applied with precision to the American scene, Blumenfeld argues, because as much as it is possible that American cities will further spill by rapid growth into one another, they will still maintain their separate identities, and, therefore, remain metropolises.

Is this too optimistic? Unlike other commentators on urban affairs, Blumenfeld is not a prophet of doom. Will the metropolis, for all its problems, be able to solve them as he suggests? Can the American city really withstand the glut of megalopolis? Can rational planning triumph over the ancient protagonists of urban sprawl—the special and vested interests of speculators, landowners, municipalities, and the free-wheeling forces of the market place?

One aspect that is fundamental to the nature of modern urban life is the suburb, which, like the central city, evokes ambivalent and contradictory attitudes. As Humphrey Carver sums them up:

Everyone likes to live in the suburbs. Everyone pokes fun at the suburbs. That's fair enough. Everyone respects those who made the suburbs. Everyone despises the suburbs. Everyone's friends live in the suburbs. Everyone hates the kind of people who live in the suburbs. Everyone wants bigger and better suburbs. Everyone thinks there is just too much suburbs. You and I live in the suburbs—it's lovely to have a nice home in the suburbs. The whole idea of the suburbs fills us with dismay, alarm and frustration. Almost everyone's business is dedicated to making life in the suburbs more and more and more enjoyable. The suburbs are a crashing bore and desolating disappointment. The suburbs are exactly what we asked for. The suburbs are exactly what we've got.[3]

Herbert Gans, a sociologist, has done much to cut through the ambivalence and seeming paradoxical qualities of suburbia. In a seminal essay he attacks the "folklore" of the intellectuals and especially the theorists of the mass-society concept that have stereotyped the suburb as the faceless, numbing, debilitating refugee of conformity and homogeneity, so well characterized by Gertrude Stein's crack, "There is no there there."[4] He destroys the notion that the move from city to suburb has caused major behavior and personality

2. See Jean Gottman, *Megalopolis* (New York: Twentieth Century Fund, 1961).
3. *Cities in the Suburbs* (Toronto: University of Toronto Press, 1962), p. 3.
4. "Urbanism and Suburbanism as Ways of Life: A Re-evaluation of Definitions," from Arnold Rose (ed.), *Human Behavior and Social Process* (Boston: Houghton Mifflin, 1962), pp. 625–48.

changes. Above all, he shows that despite physical and demographic differences, there are more similarities than differences between the suburb and the city, especially between the suburban and the outer city.

According to Gans, the suburb *is* the city. Part of the folklore of the suburb is that it is a recent phenomenon, beginning particularly at the end of World War II, with the boom of low-cost housing, the subsidies of the Federal Housing Administration, and the soaring exodus from the central city. Urban historians have long argued that the suburb emerged well over a hundred years ago and was a part of such urbanization processes as transportation, economic developments, and population migrations.[5] As the most "modern" outer ring of the city, the suburb is an integral part of the metropolitan decentralization so characteristic of the modern super-city. Thus, to set up separate monolithic entities, such as "city" and suburb" is only in Gans's view to confound the realities of modern urbanism.

With these notions in mind, the question is begged: how do you account for the historical development of the suburbs? In the next essay in this chapter, Joel Schwartz, an historian, examines the historical evolution of the suburbs in urban America.

While historians might quarrel about when suburbs took form, Professor Schwartz sees the first "recognizable outward movement" occurring during the social changes in the Jacksonian era. Prior to that time, American cities looked much like the "preindustrial" cities described by Gideon Sjoberg in the first chapter of this book; that is, the outer edge of the city was the balliwick of the poor, while the middle-class and the affluent were located in the inner city, the locus of wealth, power, and prestige. From the Jacksonian period on, industrialization, immigration, and a transit revolution— the horsecar, steam railroads, and especially the electric trolley cars—"turned the city inside out," with the poor being drawn into the inner city and the middle-class and upper classes into the suburbs. During the latter part of the nineteenth century, urban imperialism, or what Schwartz calls "the metropolitan outreach," expanded and devoured via annexation communities in the immediate hinterland. For example, Boston annexed Roxbury, Dorchester, Brighton, and West Roxbury; and Chicago in 1889, in probably the largest gulp of all, swallowed Hyde Park township, increasing the city's land area four times. Individuals seeking a better place to live, or the business community seeking relief from taxes, labor trouble, and corrupt municipal politics, created a variety of suburbs: factory towns like Pullman, and university suburbs, like Evanston and Northwestern University, and communities promoted by downtown entrepreneurs as bucolic outposts, close to nature,

5. See Sam Bass Warner, *Streetcar Suburbs: The Process of Growth in Boston* (Cambridge: M.I.T. and Harvard University Press, 1962), a first-rate scholarly performance, as is also Robert C. Wood, *Suburbia: Its People and Their Politics* (Boston: Houghton Mifflin, 1959).

just a wee bit short of Paradise. Suburbia was seen as the escape from the social, political, and economic troubles of the city.

At the turn of the century, suburbia ironically was caught up in a Catch 22: the social distance between the "man with the checkbook" and the "man with the dinner pail" was shortened; the nickle trolley that allowed the "better" people to ride from the suburban homes to work and back, also carried "undesirables" from the city—"foreigners," saloons, and multiple dwellings. The "integrity" of the suburb was seen as threatened. Suburban consciousness increased, and suburbanites seized on several Progressive administrative and corporate reforms, such as regional planning commissions, and gas, water, sewage, and park "authorities" (each with its own tax base and administrative apparatus), to block metropolitan expansion and increase autonomy as an alternative to annexation. Zoning, however, was the premier device to control the anarchy of urban sprawl. Adopted in New York in 1916, comprehensive zoning embraced much of the "scientific management" and "business efficiency" notions of Progressive reform. Zoning was based on the view that each city had "natural" areas for the exclusive use of industrial, commercial, or residential functions. The job was to identify and "protect" these distinctive areas by restrictions on building height, bulk, and very importantly, use. Thus the "wholesome" village center could be saved from ticky-tacky commercial developments, the single-dwelling home with its precious garden could be protected from its "mortal enemy," the apartment house. Many communities also found that zoning could "protect" whites from blacks by tucking them away in segregated and often sterile multiple-housing units.

But the automobile was not a respecter of suburban virtue. The advent of the automobile age, another wheel in the revolution of rapid transit, fueled the further decentralization of the metropolis and the proliferation of the suburbs. While the impact of the automobile is critical to the growth of suburbia, it has been overestimated. For example, it was not as decisive a factor in those cities that already had well-established rapid transit systems. The automobile, Schwartz warns, should not obscure the fact that other forces, which had suburbanized a seventh of the population for a hundred years prior to 1930, continued to operate. Thus the automobile by 1930, *as well as* the modernization of other types of transit, the decentralization of industry, the outward movement of retail business beyond the central business district, the burgeoning housing market, and the individualism that influenced the home buying decisions of suburbanites, "laid down the infrastructure to handle much future growth."

The fragmented city and the sprawling suburbs suggest a necessity always implicit in American urban history but particularly crucial in the complexities of the postindustrial city: the need for effective city planning. John L.

Hancock examines the historical evolution of city planning in America from 1900 to 1940. He traces its origins as a professional art and science, its fits and starts, its emerging theoretical maturity—and its frustrations, which defined the requirements for a city planner as "the wisdom of Solomon, the heart of a prophet, the patience of Job, and the hide of a rhinoceros."

Hancock's central theme is the discrepancy between the planner's goals and their fulfillment. On the one hand, the profession evolved in the Progressive Era from a motley crew ranging from landscape artists to lawyers, long on hope, short on theory. Increasing their skills, specializing their abilities, widening their vision from statistical projects and majestic but inadequate historic models, to the fusion of scientific and humanistic methods into generalized theories incorporating urban into regional planning, the planners built a profession. The consultant became the professional. On the other hand, public apathy, and special interest groups demanding the expediency of short-term "practical" goals, undermined attempts for meaningful city planning. Of the multitude of projects, few were completed. City planning became "city-mending"; patchwork replaced comprehensive planning. Thus city planning has bobbed and weaved between two legacies from the past: the goals of the Progressives of placing the group above the individual in planning for the general welfare, and the heritage of laissez-faire, which sacrifices over-all planning to the individual interests of commercial groups. Despite the profession's increasing sense of comprehensive planning and social responsibility, "most physical change in today's booming cities is conducted by private interests under public auspices for speculative purposes." Hancock makes it clear that the future of the American city and the quality of its life will be decided by which legacy ultimately triumphs.[6]

6. In the massive literature on this subject, see Mel Scott, *American City Planning: Since 1890* (Berkeley: University of California Press, 1969), Ernest Erber (ed.), *Urban Planning in Transition* (New York: Grossman Publishers, 1970), Ian L. McHarg, *Design with Nature* (Garden City, N.Y.: The Natural History Press, 1969), Victor Gruen, *The Heart of Our Cities* (New York: Simon and Schuster, 1964), Jack Tager and Park Dixon Goist (eds.), *The Urban Vision* (Homewood, Ill.: The Dorsey Press, 1970), Henry S. Churchill, *The City Is the People* (New York: W. W. Norton, 1962), John Burchard and Albert Bush-Brown, *The Architecture of America: A Social and Cultural History*, (Little, Brown, 1966), Scott Greer, *Urban Renewal and American Cities* (New York: Bobbs-Merrill, 1966), Charles Abrams, *The City Is the Frontier* (New York: Harper & Row, 1965), and Jane Jacobs, *The Death and Life of Great American Cities* (New York: Knopf, 1961). For an excellent critical review of Ms. Jacobs's books, see Hans Blumenfeld, *The Modern Metropolis: Its Origins, Growth, Characteristics, and Planning* (Cambridge: The M.I.T. Press, 1967), pp. 180–89. In a class all its own is John W. Reps's magnificent *The Making of Urban America; A History of City Planning in the United States* (Princeton: Princeton University Press, 1965). See also John W. Reps, *Town Planning in Frontier America* (Princeton: Princeton University Press, 1969), and *Monumental Washington: The Planning and Development of the Capital Center* (Princeton: Princeton University Press, 1967).

There are two first-rate readers that present a comprehensive view of urban renewal:

In the minds of many who have observed the growth of the American city, the phrase "urban crisis" is as firmly planted in the rhetoric as was the phrase "the American way" accepted by those who celebrated agrarian life in the eighteenth and nineteenth centuries. Urban crisis has the ring of disaster, indeed one can almost hear the hoofbeats of the Four Horsemen of the Apocalypse as they thunder down the streets of the American city. It is not to belittle the importance of this notion to suggest that one can hardly talk or write about the city without raising the specter of an urban crisis. In the last two essays of this book, two writers, each with a different background and perspective, T. D. Allman, a journalist, and Richard Wade, an urban historian, comment on this phenomenon: Allman reviewing the period from the Second World War within the context of the interplay between the federal government and the city, Wade casting an historical eye over the past hundred years.

Allman presents us with a stunning array of contradictions, paradoxes, and ironies incorporated in the seemingly improbable title of, "The Urban Crisis Leaves Town." Since the war, the sense of crisis has accelerated with the failure of urban renewal in the 1950s, the ugly twins of race riots and poverty during the 1960s, and the apparently insurmountable fiscal troubles of the 1970s, which were epitomized in 1977, the year of the doomsayers. The cities of the Northeast and Midwest seemed to be on the edge of disaster: Manhattan, the Bronx, Brooklyn, Baltimore, Detroit, Cleveland, St. Louis, to mention a few, seemed doomed. President Carter, promising to fulfill a campaign promise, outlined an urban program that would "revitalize" the cities. A year later Carter's urban policy proved totally inadequate, and yet there was no catastrophe. There were no ghost towns, grass did not grow in Wall Street, and even Cleveland was still with us. Cities, in fact, were booming with money and energy. What on earth happened to the urban crisis? According to Allman, it was incorrectly perceived by policy makers in the Johnson, Nixon, Ford, and Carter administrations. As the economist Roger Vaughan explained, "There always is a gap of at least several years between the problem, and our political perception of it. . . . We should be worrying about what we're not worrying about." Allman carries it further. "It involves the gap between what the government is doing, whether it knows it or not, and those immense social, demographic, economic, and technological forces that exceed the capacity of the federal government to control them." Further-

---

Jewel Bellush and Murray Hausknecht (eds.), *Urban Renewal: People, Politics, and Planning* (Garden City: Anchor Books, 1967), and James Q. Wilson (ed.), *Urban Renewal: The Record and the Controversy* (Cambridge: The M.I.T. Press, 1967).

Although not in the "recent" category, Martin Meyerson and Edward C. Banfield, *Politics, Planning, and the Public Interest* (New York: The Free Press, 1955), is indispensable.

more, cities were renewed by an influx of money, foreign and domestic, and the reentry of the middle class; as the crisis of race and poverty increased, the urban crisis left town and moved to the suburbs.

What actually happened, then, was that the profoundly prourban policies of Lyndon Johnson, ironically, sucked money out of the cities, creating an outflow of capital, jobs, and people, destroying neighborhoods and crippling industrial economics already having trouble. His policies encouraged the poor to remain in northern cities at the time that viable opportunities were appearing in the suburbs and the South. Such were the tortuous turns of good intentions that they helped to set the stage for a later urban crisis. The anti-urban Republicans (except where the Republican suburbs were concerned) vowed a limit on federal largesse. President Nixon made it *very clear* "you can't solve problems by throwing money at them," and Gerald Ford, displaying a certain insensitivity to the fiscal plight of New York, adopted policies creating an astonishing influx of federal money back into the cities. What was a trickle of federal money into city treasuries during Johnson's reign became a flood under the Republicans. Under Carter, or rather through programs already started, it became a monetary hailstorm, so much so that analysts who once felt lack of money would starve the cities now feared that "cities might become sick with surfeit." Allman notes wryly: "It seems that at least some problems in cities begin to be solved, if you throw enough money at them." The subtitle to this saga could well be "Alice in an urban wonderland."

The second chapter of the story involves an "odd" urban renaissance where the cities were deluged with Third World money; odd, in the sense that, as the old song goes, "in the meantime and in between time, the rich get richer and the poor get poorer." Using the research of Franz Schurmann at Berkeley, Allman suggests the cities could "turn themselves inside out again" as did the preindustrial city, with the palaces of trade and culture glittering in the central city, surrounded by the hovels of the poor.

And, finally, the urban crisis moved to the suburbs, "slumming the suburbs." Before 1975, the suburbs were the showplaces of housing, opportunities, and jobs. After this date, the suburbs dramatically declined and the inner cities outpaced them in creating jobs, and, not the least, cheaper housing. Ironically, the reversal of roles occurred at the time blacks were leaving the city in unprecedented numbers for the suburbs.

The epilogue, of course, lies in the future. Allman suggests that perhaps the real issue behind the dissidence of the urban crisis was raised by Nicholas Carbone, of the Hartford City Council, who anticipated urban recovery. "There is no doubt cities will be saved," he said during the heyday of the doomsayers. "The real question is who cities will be saved for: the big corporations and the returning middle class, or for the poor, the jobless, the people who always seem to be shortchanged by our society? Are cities collections of skyscrapers, or groups of human beings? Who will cities be saved for?"

It is fitting that Richard Wade's essay should end this book because it is an overview, among other things, of many topics discussed in this volume and will give the reader an orderly, historical perspective of the past. The title, however, "America's Cities Are (Mostly) Better Than Ever," might provoke a debate of some sound and fury. The stench of a Harlem tenement, the mindless crush of a Los Angeles freeway, the hideous urban sprawl that characterizes many American cities, or, above all, the violence of the race riots of the 1960s, might suggest to many a title that is, well, more appropriate. But give Professor Wade his day in court. He is certainly aware of these calamities, but as an historian he is also aware of how a narrow, present-minded orientation to the recent past can warp the meaning of these events. Americans often have a withering indictment of the present while, at the same time, consumed with nostalgia, they look back at the good old days when things were done the American way.[7] Nostalgia can distort the past and demean the present. As an antidote for reality, an historical perspective that measures past and present is not only "educational," it can also provide guidelines for policy-makers of the future.

Richard Wade argues that an almost infinite variety of urban crises have long plagued the American city. At the turn of the century, tenements were overcrowded and unsanitary. Smoke from chimneys and debris from stockyards polluted the air, and sewage polluted the streets. While there is no statistical data measuring the amount of crime in the cities of 1900, it is likely that urban crime was as much a problem then as it is today. Police were often the political footballs of politicians, and police collusion with criminals was common. Municipal government in many cities was a shambles, riddled by corruption, and devoured by special interests. Indeed, as Wade observes, "the present city, for all its problems, is cleaner, less crowded, safer, and more livable than its turn-of-the-century counterpart. Its people are more prosperous, better educated, and healthier than they were seventy years ago."

Cities improved from 1900 on because of qualities always inherent in the city—its capacity to lure those of talent and wealth—as well as the impact of several historical conditions particular to the twentieth century, such as improvements in medical science, new technologies of domestic comforts and conveniences, governmental changes, educational advances, and the democratization of entertainment, to mention a few.

However, after the Second World War, two divisive confrontations—the suburb versus the city and blacks versus whites—battered the metropolis,

---

7. See Otto L. Bettmann, *The Good Old Days—They Were Terrible!* (New York: Random House, 1974).

"destroying its economic and governmental unity and profoundly altering its social structure." As we have seen in the previous essays of Schwartz and Allman, the city brought its problems to the suburbs and the suburbs were in trouble. But Wade sees hope here, in the sense that the suburbs, no longer self-sufficient, may end the hostility against the city with a new attempt to create cooperation and unity with the metropolis. The racial problem is another matter. While Wade asserts that racism is by no means an American but is in fact an international problem, it does threaten to create a permanent, institutionalized underclass in American urban life, threatening the aspirations of a democratic society. Even here Wade finds some hope. The decade of the 1970s witnessed demographic changes that eased racial relations, the black birth rate dropped, the great folk wandering from the South ran its course, and blacks were able to achieve political power. Some readers may find Wade too optimistic; others may not.

The fact remains, however, the concept of urban crisis still remains viable particularly if race and poverty remain disruptive forces in metropolitan and national life. Together they sour everything they touch; together they infect the quality of urban life. Can we cope with them as we have other urban crises? Considering the political and social climate of the 1980s, do we have the patience or even the desire to realistically attack these two abcesses in the American experience? Time will tell. But is time running out? What do you think?

The Modern Metropolis

HANS BLUMENFELD

. . . We [are going to] speak of the product of . . . [the] evolution [of cities] not as the modern city" but as "the modern metropolis." The change of name reflects the fact that from its long, slow evolution the city has emerged into a revolutionary stage. It has undergone a qualitative change, so that it is no longer merely a larger version of the traditional city but a new and different form of human settlement.

There is some argument about the term. Lewis Mumford objects to "metropolis" (from the Greek words for "mother" and "city"), which historically had a very different meaning; he prefers the term "conurbation," coined by Patrick Geddes, the Scottish biologist who was a pioneer in city planning. This word, however, implies formation by the fusion of several preexisting cities; most metropolises did not originate in that way. The term "megalopolis," coined by the French geographer Jean Gottmann, is generally applied to an urbanized region that contains several metropolitan areas, such as the region extending from Boston to Washington. On the whole it seems best to retain the term "metropolis," now commonly adopted in many languages as the name for a major city center and its environs.

"Metropolitan area" can be defined in various ways; the U.S. Bureau of the Census, for instance, defines it as any area containing a nuclear city of at least 50,000 population. The new phenomenon we are considering, however, is a much bigger entity with a certain minimum critical size. In agreement with the German scholar Gerhard Isenberg, I shall define a metropolis as a concentration of at least 500,000 people living within an area in which the traveling time from the outskirts to the center is no more than about 40 minutes. Isenberg and I have both derived this definition from observations of the transformation of cities into metropolises during the first half of the 20th century. At the present time—at least in North America—the critical mass that distinguishes a metropolis from the traditional city can be considerably larger—perhaps nearing one million population.

The emergence of a basically new form of human settlement is an extremely rare event in the history of mankind. For at least 5,000 years all civilizations have been characterized predominantly by just two well-marked types of settlement: the farm village and the city. Until recently the vast majority of the population lived in villages. They produced not only their own raw materials—food, fuel and fiber —but also the manufactured goods and services they required. The cities were inhabited by only a small minority of the total population, generally less than 20 percent. These people were the ruling elite—the religious, political, military and commercial leaders—and the retinue of laborers, craftsmen and professionals who served them. The elite drew their subsistence and power from the work of the villagers by collecting tithes, taxes or rent. This system prevailed until the end of the 18th century, and its philosophy was well expressed by physiocrats of that time on both sides of the Atlantic, including Thomas Jefferson.

The industrial revolution dramatically reversed the distribution of population between village and city. A German contemporary of Jefferson's, Justus Moeser, foresaw at the very beginning of the revolution what was to come; he observed that "specialized division of labor forces workers to live in big cities." With increasing specialization there had to be increased cooperation of labor, both within and between establishments. The division of labor and increased productivity made concentration in cities possible, and the required cooperation of labor made it necessary, because the new system called for bringing together workers of many skills and diverse establishments that had to interchange goods and services.

The process fed on itself, growth inducing further growth. Many economists have noted that the rapid rise of productivity has been largely instrumental in bringing about a progressive shift of the main part of the labor force from the primary industry of raw-material production to the secondary industry of material processing and finally to the tertiary industry of services. Less attention has been paid to a related, equally important factor behind this shift, namely the "specializing out" of functions. The farmer's original functions of producing his own motive power (work animals), fuel (hay and oats), tools, building materials and consumer goods have been specialized out to secondary industries that supply him with tractors, gasoline and his other necessities. Today, in the tertiary stage, much of the work connected with secondary industry is being specialized out to purveyors of business services (accounting, control, selling, distribution). Even the functions of the household itself (personal services, housekeeping, repairs, shopping, recreation, education) are taken over by consumer-service industries.

The dual spur of specialization and cooperation of labor started a great wave of migration from country to city all over the globe. In the advanced countries the 19th-century development of long-distance transportation by steamship and railroad and of communication by the electric telegraph made it possible for cities to draw on large regions and grow to populations of millions. For a time their growth was limited by internal restrictions. Travel within the city still had to be by foot or by hoof. A New York businessman could communicate quickly with his partners in Shanghai by cablegram, but to deliver an order to an office a few blocks away he had to send a messenger. This situation limited cities to a radius of only about three miles from the center. In the absence of elevators the city was also limited in vertical expansion. The only possible growth was interstitial, by covering every square inch of available space. Residences, factories, shops and offices all crowded close together around the center. The result was a fantastic rise in the price of city land compared with the cost of the structures that could be built on it.

This was only a transitory phase in the growth of the city, but its heritage is still with us, in structures, street patterns, institutions and concepts. We still think and talk and act in terms of "city and country" and "city and suburb," although these concepts have lost meaning in the modern metropolis and its region. The transformation was set in motion toward the end of the 19th century and early in the 20th with the invention of the telephone, the electric streetcar, the subway and the powered elevator. Even more far-reaching was the impact on the city of the automobile and the truck. With the acquisition of these aids to communication and mobility the city burst its eggshell and emerged as a metropolis. (It is worth noting that the telephone and the automobile had equally profound effects on rural life, fragmenting the old farm village and giving rise to huge, scattered farms.)

The centripetal migration from the country to the city continues unabated, but now there is an equally powerful centrifugal wave of migration from the city to the suburbs. Although on a national scale more and more of the population is becoming urban, within the urban areas there is increasing decentralization. The interaction of these two trends has produced the new form of settlement we call the metropolis. It is no longer a "city" as that institution has been understood in the past, but on the other hand it is certainly not "country" either. The fact that it is neither one nor the other has aroused nostalgic critics, who appeal for a return to "true urbanity" and to a "real countryside." But in view of the inexorable technological and economic trends that have created the metropolis these terms also require a new and different interpretation.

It has become fashionable to describe the transformation of the city into the metropolis as an "explosion." The term is misleading on two counts. The change is not destroying the city, as "explosion" implies, nor is it a sudden, unheralded event. The movement of population from the center of the city outward to an ever expanding periphery has been going on for at least a century. In the metropolitan region of New York, New Jersey and Connecticut, where the average density of population within the cities and towns of the area increased steadily up to 1860, it began to drop after that date. The outward spread of the city was nearly as strong between 1860 and 1900 as it has been since 1900. In Philadelphia the population movement away from the center of the city was actually proportionately greater in the half century between 1860 and 1910 than in the period 1900 to 1950.

Analysis of the population density in the metropolitan area of Philadelphia and that of other cities shows that the centrifugal wave of movement to the suburbs has proceeded with amazing regularity. From the center of the city out to the periphery at any one time there is a consistent decline in residential density from one zone to the next. As time has passed, the curve representing this decline has become less steep; that is, the center has lost or stood still in density while the outer areas have gained, so that the difference between them is less. Interestingly, the density gradient from the center to the periphery has also become smoother (that is, less lumped around outer towns), which seems to indicate that the center is actually strengthening its influence over the outer areas. In each zone the rise in density with time eventually flattens out, as if the density has reached a "saturation" level for that zone; this level is lower for each successive zone out to the periphery. With the passage of time the crest of the wave (the zone of fastest growth) moves outward in a regular fashion. The innermost zone at the center of the city seems to show an anomaly, in that its population density is lower than that of the surrounding area, but this merely reflects the fact that the center is occupied predominantly by stores and offices. If its daytime working population were included in the census, it would have a far higher density.

One can outline a "natural history" of the modern metropolis. The metropolis is characterized first of all by a certain measure of mutual accessibility among its various parts, which determines its total size. As I have mentioned, in most cases the area embraced by the metropolis has a radius represented by a traveling time of about 40 minutes in the principal vehicle of transportation (train or auto), or about 45 minutes from door to door. With improvement in the speed of transportation the extent of the metropolis in miles can, of course, expand. In most metropolitan areas the average travel time to work for the working population as a whole is about half an hour. No more than 15 percent of the workers spend more than 45 minutes in the daily journey to work.

This may sound surprising in view of the frequent complaints of commuters about the length of their journey. The complaints are not new. A century ago a German observer declared that the distance people on the outskirts of cities had to travel to work had reached the limit of what was bearable. Probably the range of travel times to work then was wider than it is in the metropolis today. There are strong indications, however, that the half-hour average has been more or less standard. In most American small towns, although a majority of the workers are employed within the town, a sizable minority do travel long distances to work in other communities, usually because they cannot find a job in the hometown and must seek work elsewhere but do not wish to change their home.

It is one of the great advantages of the metropolis that people can change jobs without moving their homes. Breadth of choice—for workers, for employers and for consumers—is the essence of the metropolis. The worker has a choice of employers; the employer can find workers of a wide variety of skills, including professional and managerial. Even more important is the accessibility of a variety of goods and services on which any business enterprise depends. Only a metropolis can support the large inventories, transportation facilities and specialized services —particularly those of a financial, legal, technical and promotional nature—that are essential to modern business. Such services constitute the main source of economic strength of the metropolis—its true economic base. They are especially important to small, new and experimental enterprises. The metropolis, in particular its central area, therefore serves as an incubator for such enterprises. Contrary to a common impression, the big city is most suitably a home for small industries rather than large industrial complexes. The big plant, being more nearly self-sufficient, may often be as well off in a small town. This fact is reflected in the statistics of employment: in most metropolises the number of people that are employed in manufacturing is decreasing, relatively and sometimes absolutely, while the number that are employed in services is increasing rapidly.

What is true of business services is also true of consumer services: the metropolis attracts the consumer because it offers a wide freedom of choice. Only the large population of a metropolis can support the great proliferation of special services found in the big city: large department stores, many specialty shops, opera houses, art galleries, theaters, sports stadia, special schools, large and well-equipped institutions for medical care and adult education and a host of other necessities for the full life.

To sum up, the modern metropolis differs from the traditional city in several crucial respects: (1) it combines the function of central leadership with the functions of providing the main bulk of material production and services; (2) its population is up to 10 times larger than that of the biggest preindustrial city; (3) with modern fast transportation, which has increased its commuting radius about tenfold, it is up to 100 times larger in area than the biggest city of former times; (4) it is neither city nor country but a complex of urban districts and open areas; (5) its residential and work areas are no longer combined in one place but are located in separate districts; (6) its workers have high mobility in the choice of jobs and occupations.

The feedback cycle of metropolitan growth enlarging freedom of choice and freedom of choice in turn attracting further growth has given the metropolis amazing vitality and staying power. In the premetropolis era cities laid low by war, pestilence or loss of prestige were often abandoned or reduced to weak shadows of their former glory. Even Rome became little more than a village after it lost its empire. In contrast, all the big cities destroyed in World War II have been rebuilt, most of them to beyond their prewar size. Particularly significant is the experience of Leningrad. During the Russian Revolution and again in World War II it lost about half of its population. Moreover, the revolution ended its former role as the center of government and finance and deprived it of most of its markets and sources of supply. Yet the population of Leningrad is now four million—four times what it was in 1921. This growth is especially remarkable in view of the Soviet government's policy of restricting the growth of the major cities, a policy based on Karl Marx's condemnation of big cities because of their pollution of air, water and soil. As a metropolis Leningrad is an outstanding testament to the viability of the species.

Attempts to halt the growth of the big city have been made ever since the phenomenon first appeared on the human scene. They have been singularly unsuccessful. Elizabeth I of England and after her Oliver Cromwell tried to limit the growth of London by circling it with an enforced greenbelt, but this method failed. In any case such a device, applied to a growing city, can only lead to overcrowding. To avoid big-city problems nearly all countries today have embarked on programs of industrial decentralization, often with unsatisfactory results. In the Western nations the most far-reaching attempt at decentralization is Great Britain's "new towns" plan. This program has been eminently successful in creating new centers of industry as "growth points," but it has not availed to stop the growth of London or to limit other cities, new or old, to their planned size. Significantly, all but one of the 17 new towns built in Britain since the war are satellite towns within previously existing metropolitan regions.

The U.S.S.R., by virtue of centralized planning and ownership, has been able to carry out decentralization on a continental scale. Its program has been remarkably effective in slowing the growth of Moscow and promoting that of smaller cities. Between 1939 and 1959 the towns in the U.S.S.R. with populations of less than 200,000 grew by 84 percent; those in the 200,000-to-500,000 class grew 63 percent; those in the 500,000-to-one-million class grew 48 percent, and Moscow itself increased only 20 percent in population. Moscow has, however, gone well beyond the limit of five million that the government planned: it is now at six million, nearly four times the city's population in 1921.

In the U.S., where the forces of the market rather than central planning determine industrial locations, the growth rates in the decade 1950-1960 were 27 percent in metropolitan areas of 50,000 to 500,000 population and 35 percent in those of 500,000 to two million population. In the metropolises with a population of more than two million the average growth rate was smaller: 23 percent. This average, however, was heavily weighted by the comparatively slow-growing centers of the Northeastern sector of the nation; in Los Angeles and San Francisco, the only two metropolises of this class outside the Northeast, the growth was far above the national average for all metropolitan areas.

There is no denying that the growth of the huge metropolises has brought serious problems, chief among which are traffic congestion and the pollution of air and water by smoke, household wastes, detergents and gasoline fumes. Many cities also object that the metropolis can exist only by draining the countryside of its economic, demographic and social strength. These problems are

not essentially unsolvable, however. Effective methods for control of pollution exist; they need to be applied. The economic and social complaints about the metropolis seem to have little substance today. The city now repays the country in full in economic terms, as we have noted, and with the improvement in sanitation and lowering of the high 19th-century urban death rate it contributes its share of the natural population increase.

The most persistent accusation against the metropolis is that it has dissolved the family and neighborhood ties that existed in the small town and has produced anomie: the absence of any values or standards of behavior. This is questionable. A number of sociological studies in metropolises of North America and western Europe have shown that family ties remain very much alive and that a considerable amount of informal community organization can be found even in their slums.

In considering the future of the metropolis the central question is that of crowding. How much bigger can the metropolis grow? Will it eventually be "choked to death" by its own growth? Data are available for examining these questions.

It is widely believed that in a big metropolis there can only be a choice between crowding together at high densities or spending an excessive amount of time traveling to work. Actually a reasonable travel radius from a central point takes in an amazing amount of territory. At an overall travel rate of 20 miles per hour, typical for present rush-hour trips from the center to the periphery in the largest American metropolitan areas, a radius of one hour's travel describes a circle with a total area of about 1,250 square miles. No more than

312 square miles would be required to house 10 million people if they lived in single-family houses on 30-by-100-foot lots. Including streets, schools and other neighborhood facilities, the total area needed for residential use would amount to about 500 square miles. Commercial, industrial and other non-residential facilities could be accommodated amply on 150 square miles. There would be left, then, some 600 square miles, almost half of the total area within an hour's distance from the center, for parks, golf courses, forests, farms and lakes.

If the travel speed were increased to 30 miles per hour, quite feasible for both private and public transportation, the area within an hour's distance from the center could accommodate 15 million people in single-family houses on 60-by-100-foot lots, take care of all business uses and leave 1,000 square miles of open land. It may be objected that an hour is an excessive time to spend in travel to work. In practice, however, the radius from the center to the periphery would not represent the traveling distance for most workers. Relatively few would live close to the periphery, and most of these would be working at places near home rather than in the center of the city. In a metropolis of such dimensions only a small minority would have to travel more than 45 minutes to their jobs.

Evidently, then, the modern metropolis does not inherently necessitate either very high residential densities or excessively long journeys to work. The problem in planning it therefore lies in achieving a rational distribution of its components and a suitable organization of transportation facilities to connect the components.

What are the major components of the metropolis? Basically there are four: (1) the central business complex, (2) manufacturing and its allied industries, (3) housing with the attendant services and (4) open land. Let us examine each in turn.

The central area epitomizes the essence of the metropolis: mutual accessibility. It attracts particularly those functions that serve the metropolis as a whole and those that require a considerable amount of close interpersonal contact. The most conspicuous occupant of the center is diversified retail business: large department stores and specialty shops. It is surpassed in importance, however, by the closely interrelated complex of business services that occupy the giant office buildings characteristic of the central area of a metropolis: the headquarters of corporations, financial institutions and public administration and the professionals who serve them, such as lawyers, accountants and organizations engaged in promotion and public relations. Also grouped in the central area with these two categories of services are various supporting establishments, including eating and drinking places, hotels, job printers and many others.

Surprisingly, surveys show that, in spite of the recent proliferation of new office skyscrapers in the center of cities, the size of the working population in the central areas of the largest American metropolises has not actually increased over the past 30 years. Toronto, a smaller and newer metropolis, shows the same constancy in the number of central workers during the past 13 years. The explanation lies simply in the fierce competition for and the rising cost of the limited space in the center; it has caused an outward movement of those functions that can conveniently relocate farther out. Housing in the main moved out long ago; manufacturing and warehousing have tended to follow suit; so has a considerable part of the retail trade, and some of the routine business services that do not require continuous contact with their clients have also moved to less expensive locations away from the center. Modern means of communication have made this spatial separation possible. Moreover, the growth of population and purchasing power in the peripheral areas has provided bases of support there for large shopping centers, including department stores, and for many business and consumer services.

All of this indicates that the central area is undergoing a qualitative change in the direction of concentration on "higher-order" functions and at the same time is maintaining stability in quantitative terms. The forces of the market act to control overcrowding of the center. There is not much basis for the widespread fear that the metropolis will choke itself to death by uncontrolled growth.

As for manufacturing and its satellite activities, the increasing volume of production and changing technology, with a consequent requirement for more space, have made their move out to the periphery of the metropolis imperative. This is true of factories, warehouses, railroad yards, truck terminals, airports, harbor facilities and many other establishments. Three technical factors are at work: the increasing mechanization and automation of production, which calls for more floor area per worker; a switch from the traditional multistory loft building to the one-story plant, which demands more ground area; the new practice of providing open land around the plant for parking, landscap-

ing and plant expansion. The combined effect of these three factors has been to raise the amount of land per worker in the modern factory as much as 100 times over that occupied by the old loft building.

The next major category of land use in the metropolis—housing—accounts for the largest amount of occupied land. It also presents the greatest ills of the metropolis: slums and segregation of people by income and race.

In all metropolises the low-income families tend to be segregated in the older, high-density areas toward the center of the city. This is not by choice but because they cannot afford the prices or rents of the more spacious new homes in the outer areas. The alarming result of the centrifugal movement of new residences toward the periphery is an increasing segregation of the population by income, which in the U.S. is compounded (and partly obscured) by segregation by race. The situation is more disquieting in the metropolis than it was in the smaller city or town. There, although the poor lived in older, shabbier houses, they at least shared the schools and other public facilities with the higher-income groups. In the metropolis the people living in low-income districts, particularly the housewives and children, never even meet or come to know the rest of their fellow citizens.

Poor families are effectively prevented from moving to new housing in the suburbs not only by economic inability but also by deliberate policies of the suburban governments. Squeezed between rising expenses and inadequate tax resources, these governments have quite understandably used their power of zoning and other controls to keep out housing that does not pay its way in tax revenue. More recently the central cities have adopted policies that have much the same effect. Their programs of slum clearance and redevelopment, financed in the U.S. by the National Housing Act, have failed to replace the housing they have destroyed with sufficient new housing at rents the displaced families can afford [see "The Renewal of Cities," by Nathan Glazer, in *Cities*, Editors of *Scientific American*, eds.]. It should be obvious that housing conditions cannot be improved by decreasing the supply. Half a century ago Geddes observed: "The policy of sweeping clearance should be recognized for what I believe it is: one of the most disastrous and pernicious blunders . . . the large populations thus expelled would be . . . driven into creating worse congestion in other quarters."

Obviously the blight of slums and class segregation can be overcome only by enabling the lower-income groups to live in decent houses in desirable locations, primarily in the expanding peripheral areas, along with the middle and upper classes. The annual cost of such a program in the U.S. has been estimated at $2 billion—a modest sum compared with the amounts alloted to less constructive purposes in the national budget.

The fourth major category of metropolitan land use—open land—consists in North America at present mainly of large tracts held privately for future development. With increasing leisure there is a growing need to turn some of this land to recreational uses. In this connection we should also look at the "metropolitan region," which takes in considerably more area than the metropolis itself.

Donald J. Bogue of the University of Michigan, examining 67 metropolitan centers in the U.S., has shown that the sphere of influence of a large metropolis usually extends out to about 60 to 100 miles from the center. Typically the metropolitan region includes a number of industrial satellite towns that draw on the resources of the metropolis. The metropolis in turn looks outward to the region for various facilities, particularly recreational resorts such as large parks, lakes, summer cottages, camps, motels and lodges. In Sweden, C. F. Ahlberg, head of the Stockholm Regional Plan, has emphasized this role of the region around the capital city by naming it the "Summer Stockholm"—the widened horizon that opens up for Stockholmers when the snows have gone. Metropolises do, of course, have their winter horizons as well, typified by the ski resorts that flourish as satellites within driving distance of many an American city.

Increasingly the outer-fringe metropolitan region is becoming a popular place for retirement for people on pensions or other modest incomes who can live inexpensively in the country without being too far from the amenities of the city. This is an intriguing reversal of the ancient pattern in which the countryside was the locus of productive work and the city was the Mecca for the enjoyment of leisure.

While we are on the subject of the metropolitan region, I should like to clarify the distinction between such a region and a "conurbation" or "megalopolis." The predominant form of the metropolis is mononuclear: it derives its identity from a single center. This is the way metropolitan areas are generally organized in the U.S. and it is the only form they take in a new young settlement such as Australia, where the population is concentrated mainly in five large metropolitan areas, each centered on a single city. In the older countries of Europe, on the other hand, conurbations—metropolitan regions formed by the gradual growing together of neighboring cities—are fairly common. The outstanding examples are the cities of the Ruhr in Germany and the circle of cities that form what is known as "Randstad Holland" (including Amsterdam, Haarlem, Leiden, The Hague, Rotterdam and Utrecht). The Ruhr conurbation grew up around the coal mines. Along the French-Italian Riviera a conurbation now seems to be developing around seashore play.

There seems to be a general disposition to assume that the Boston-to-Washington axis is destined soon to become a new conurbation on a vastly larger scale than any heretofore. The available evidence does not support such a view. Each of the metropolitan areas along the seaboard remains strongly oriented to its own center. The several metropolitan regions are separated by large areas of sparse development. Conurbation can occur only when the crests of the waves of two expanding centers overlap, and except perhaps between Washington and Baltimore that is not likely to happen anywhere in North America during this century.

To get back to the problems of planning for the metropolis: How should the four main components—central business, production, residence and open land—be organized spatially? The aims here can be expressed most clearly in the form of pairs of seemingly contradictory requirements.

First, it is desirable to minimize the need for commuting to work and at the same time maximize the ability to do so.

Obviously most people would like to live close to their place of work, but to seek such an arrangement as a general proposition would be unrealistic and too restrictive. It is estimated that half of all metropolitan households contain more than one gainfully employed person, and they are not likely to be employed in the same place. Furthermore, the preferred locations for residence and work do not necessarily match up. The situation in Hudson County, N.J., across the river from Manhattan, offers a striking illustration. In 1960 the county contained 244,000 jobs and 233,000 employed residents—apparently a neat balance. On analysis, however, it turns out that 35 percent of the jobs in the county were held by people who commuted from homes elsewhere, and 32 percent of the workers who lived in the county commuted out to work. Freedom of choice, both of the place to live and of the place to work, will always depend on opportunity to travel from one place to the other.

A second ideal of planning is to provide quick access to the center of the city and also quick access to the open country. Most people have tried to achieve a compromise by moving to the suburbs. The resulting pattern of urban sprawl, however, has made this move self-defeating. The more people move out to the suburbs, the farther they have to move from the city and the farther the country moves away from them.

Third, the functions of the metropolis must be integrated, yet there are also strong reasons to separate them—for example, to separate residences from factories or offices. Isolation of the functions by rigid zoning, however, threatens to break up the metropolis into barren and monotonous precincts. Evidently there is no pat answer to this problem. The optimal grain of mixture will vary with conditions.

Fourth, the social health of the metropolis requires that its people identify themselves both with their own neighborhood or group and with the metropolis as a whole. Since identification with an ingroup often leads to hostility toward outgroups, great emphasis is needed on measures that create interest and pride in the metropolis.

Fifth, the metropolis must strike a balance between continuity and receptiveness to change, between the traditions that give it identity and the flexibility necessary for growth and adaptation to new conditions.

Most of the schemes that have been proposed for shaping the future growth of the metropolis are tacitly based on these criteria, although the requirements have not generally been spelled out in precisely this form. The plans are designed to decentralize the metropolis in some way, with the dual aim of minimizing traffic congestion at the center and bringing the city closer to the countryside.

One proposal is the satellite plan I have already mentioned. In that arrangement each of the satellite towns outside the center is largely self-sufficient and more or less like the others. Another scheme somewhat similar to this is called the "constellation" plan; it would set up several widely separated units each of which would specialize in one function, such as finance, administration, cultural institutions and so on. Still another plan is the "linear" metropolis, several variants of which have been proposed. It would not be oriented to-

ward a single center but would contain a series of them strung in a line. The advocates of this plan are attracted primarily by the possibilities it offers for easy access to open land and for unlimited expansion. Decentralization was pushed to its ultimate conclusion in the "Broadacre City" plan suggested by Frank Lloyd Wright. He proposed to disperse the activities of the city more or less evenly over the whole metropolitan region. Such a plan would be practicable only if the time and cost of travel were reduced essentially to zero. They may approach but certainly will never reach that condition.

Probably the most realistic of the many proposals is the plan called the "stellar" or "finger" metropolis. It fingers in all directions. Each finger would retain the center and thrust out would be composed of a string of towns and would be comparable to a linear city. The towns in the string would be connected to one another and to the metropolitan center by a rapid-transit line. Between the fingers would be large wedges of open country, which would thus be easily accessible both to the fingers and to the main center. The metropolis would grow by extending the fingers. This outline is the basis of current plans for the future development of Copenhagen and Stockholm and of the "Year 2000" plan for Washington, D.C.

Any plan that seeks to control the growth of the metropolis rather than leaving it to the play of market forces will require the setting up of new forms of control. Because it inevitably entails transfers of value from one piece of land to another, planning of any sort is bound to come into conflict with the existing vested interests of landowners and municipalities. It is obvious, therefore, that the implementation of rational planning would call for: (1) the creation of an overall metropolitan government for the metropolis, (2) public ownership of all or most of the land that is to be developed, (3) tax revenues sufficient to enable the metropolitan government to acquire the land and carry out the public works required for its development, (4) a national housing policy that would eliminate segregation by providing people at all income levels with freedom of choice in the location of their dwellings.

In terms of current American political folklore these are radical measures. Each of them, however, has been carried out in varying forms and to a varying degree by more than one European nation within the framework of democratic capitalism.

In the long run the development of the metropolis is likely to be influenced most powerfully by improvements in transportation and communication and by the increase in leisure time. The first may lead to an expansion of the metropolis that will embrace a whole region. The second, depending on future developments in mankind's social structure and culture, may lead to *panem et circenses* ("bread and circuses") or to *otium cum dignitate* ("leisure with dignity"). Both are possible in the metropolis.

Evolution of the Suburbs

JOEL SCHWARTZ

Suburbs present a special challenge to the American historian. The remarkable metropolitan growth of the last quarter century climaxed by the startling 1970 census which declared America a suburban nation makes urgent an understanding of the origins and parameters of this development. Regrettably, historians have not easily related to this field. Scholars accustomed to the slow accretion of institutional artifacts find "suburbia" an overnight wonder on a thousand housing tracts, bulldozed of all "history" save the crabbed antiquarian who recalls established families overrun by "the newcomers." Yet the history of suburban America reaches back one hundred and thirty years. For at least that long, urban dwellers have tried to escape the city's grime, immigrants, and disorder and searched for outlying retreats with institutional structures to protect their preserves when distance alone did not suffice. The first recognizable outward movement occurred during the social upheaval of the age of Jackson. Before World War I a distinct suburban consciousness emerged which, building upon a tradition of insular politics, utilized the latest techniques of regional planning and zoning. "Ticky-tacky" houses, shopping centers, and even auto expressways, all synonymous with mass suburbia of the late 1940s, made their impact on the metropolitan landscape before the 1929 crash. But at the most intimate level,

records of countless communities reveal the extent to which the euphemism "metropolitan growth" has obscured those class and ethnic conflicts deflected to the city's periphery. The American metropolis has been a seamless web of migratory peoples and institutions, with suburbs sharing more than they have cared to admit of the ways of life of the inner city.

Traditionally, "suburbs" have been the haunts of the poor on land not yet taken up by the rich. In "preindustrial" cities across the globe, established caste groups clung to the civic centers where palace, cathedral, and guild hall dispensed wealth and prestige. The less affluent found lodging where they might, while the poor and outcast huddled beyond the walls, whether London's Cheapside or Paris' swamp, the Marais. American communities up to the 1850s took much the same form. Wealthy merchants built town houses on expensive real estate around the central commons, leaving the poor, free blacks, and a growing number of Irish to crowd in jerry-built shelters on cheaper outlying lots. Had the nation possessed a different social ethic which emphasized rigid corporate structures, its cities might have preserved this traditionalism, much like the staunch caste lines, bolstered by a *conquistador* mentality, which still keep Indians, mixbloods, and Bantus beyond the pale in Mexico City and Johannesburg. But in America, urban wealth and privilege has proved vulnerable to a commercial utilitarianism which reckoned everything by an impersonal calculus. Attempts at social control, whether a Puritan sense of commonweal, the voluntary night watch, or walled private blocks, were overwhelmed by the upheaval of the nineteenth century.

As a conseqeunce, suburban communities formed from a largely middle-class migration reflected a peculiar ambivalence toward downtown. While they bought homes on the fringe to escape factories, immigrants, and Negroes, the middle class remained tied to umbilical commuter routes, habituated to urban consumer standards and to a thousand delights which only downtown could provide. The suburbanite sought a pastorial retreat which was paved, electrified, and serviced by trained professionals. He dreamed of a private garden spot, but one never far removed from the easy camaraderie enjoyed back in the city. The homeowner sought to preserve his beloved ground by sheer distance and a welter of restrictive covenants, but found that community solidarity crumbled when offered tempting real estate profits. Because of this vulnerability, the suburbanization of America has meant more than physical removal beyond the built-up portions of the city; it has also included a pervasive yearning, often frustrated by an individualistic ethos, for some sense of attachment to a covenanted community.

SUBURBAN ORIGINS:
THE PROTESTANT CITY
IN TRANSITION

In colonial America, urban elites, repelled by the growing disorder of their seaports yet drawn by their commercial vigor, found it difficult to leave their cities completely. Boston's merchants who moved to Dorchester Neck and Roxbury in the 1720s and Manhattan aristocrats who built mansions in Harlem village before the Revolution sought seasonal escape from dreaded yellow fever while enjoying the villa existence of the semiretired. As long as the primitive division of labor required personal supervision of industry, active merchants maintained in-town residences and usually lived above their workshops. Street life and pageantry also exerted an undeniable pull. The ambitious, personable man of "affairs," like Benjamin Franklin, found much to engage his interest: church vestries, fire companies, militia troops, Fourth of July parades, Bunker Hill celebrations, and civic festivals of all kinds.

The first large-scale suburban migration coincided with the industrialization and immigration which transformed city life before the Civil War. Steam hammers drowned out church bells, railroad viaducts tore through established neighborhoods, and coal soot drifted down everywhere. After the 1837 panic, hard times aggravated the shift from handicraft to factory employment. German and Irish immigrants swamped the cities in the 1840s. Their Popish rites offended staid Protestants and their fire "laddies" collided with Protestant associations in the streets. Ethnic tensions coupled with sharper job competition set off nativist riots that scarred the next decade. While ministers exhorted a return to Sunday pieties, commercial elites invigorated police forces, militia commands, and lockups. The rich began to seek asylum in Beacon Hill or Girard Row, exclusive neighborhoods with restrictive covenants and a social hauteur that kept out interlopers. Few of these enclaves went as far as the private "places" of St. Louis' West Side, controlled by property-owners' associations, surrounded by gates, and patrolled by hired guards. For the time being, stout granite walls along with platooned police served to keep the city's chaos at a distance.

The intellectual spirit of the Jacksonian age, however, was convinced that only total removal to the countryside would suffice. Sharing Jefferson's suspicion of cities, inspired by European Romantic musings, and, above all, unnerved by the preternatural growth of New York and Boston, a generation of writers from Thoreau to William Cullen Bryant searched for God's immanent presence in the country. Ante-bellum reformers also believed that urban poverty and vice could be eliminated by egalitarian and harmonious villages built afresh outside the cities. Fourierites like Parke Godwin urged the planting of factories in the fields and encouraged working-men's advocates to include "land reform" among their legislative proposals. To uplift the harried urban gentry, landscape architects Andrew Jackson Downing and Calvert Vaux designed Greek Revival cottages in leafy groves, which also proved ideal backdrops for the sentimental novelists determined to place Woman on her pedestal. Horace Greeley, Manhattan's rural cultivator, temperance advocate, and dabbler in Utopian socialism and a hundred other nostrums, summed up the era's faith in the country:

Secure to the family the inducements of a home, surrounded by fruits and flowers, rational village movements and sports, the means of education and independence. Get them out of the cities and would-be cities into scenes like those, and the work is done.

Dreams turned to reality when a fundamentalist revolution in urban transportation made a long-distance commute feasible for thousands. By the 1820s, paddle steamers churned along the East River, transforming village Brooklyn into Manhattan's bedroom suburb, while Hoboken, Jersey City, and Staten Island swelled with waterborne commuters. The year of Andrew Jackson's inauguration saw the start of hack service between downtown Boston and Dorchester Neck. By the 1850s, "White Line" omnibuses offered six-cent trips between this South Boston suburb and "The Hub" every five minutes. Expensive fares still limited travel to merchants and professionals. But when the omnibus switched to rails, enabling horse teams to drag much longer coach bodies, the resulting economies ushered in an era of relative "mass" transit. Horsecars received franchises in the eastern cities by the early 1850s. During 1860, Boston's horse railways moved 13 million passengers, while Manhattan's carried a phenomenal 45 million. Now a broader sector of the community, including middle-class clerks and skilled artisans as well as bankers, could think about settling uptown. Real "rapid" transit came with steam railroads which by mid-century radiated from Boston across the Charles River and from Manhattan north across the Harlem into Westchester. The new service was not an unmitigated boon, however. For the privilege of living at greater distances from the city, these pioneer commuters paid higher fares and often endured reckless engineers, open platforms exposed to the elements, and unannounced changes in schedule. In 1859, one such "old trick" on the New York and Harlem line left a "large number of 'eight o'clockers' to make their way to the city as best they could." Dismayed, but nonetheless convinced that suburban ambience made it all worthwhile, many merchants partook of the haggard life.

The transit revolution had an immense impact on the social geography of the developing metropolis. Twenty- to fifty-cents-per-day commuting acted as a selective filter on class movement. Proprietors, master artisans, and the growing white-collar sector could afford the new technology and escape from downtown. But not so the urban masses who barely earned a dollar a day. Gradually, the horsecars and steam railroads "turned the city inside out," transforming the preindustrial landscape with its poor hoveled on the outskirts, into the modern American metropolis, with its upper-income neighborhoods segregated on the periphery. But the process seemed painfully slow to many contemporary suburbanites disconcerted by the noisome institutions which continued to exist on the urban fringe. In 1847, South Boston property owners bitterly complained that the Common Council viewed their locality as the "Botany Bay of the City, into which could be thrust those establishments which the City Fathers would consider nuisances in the neighborhood of their own private dwellings, such as Alms Houses, Prisons, and Small-pox Hospitals." The outskirts also contained powderworks, slaughterhouses, glue factories, and other pariahs barred from the central area by primitive building codes. A suburban rambler might easily stumble on one of the "model villages" over which lorded an ironmaker, piano manufacturer, or brewer inspired by some ethnic reclusiveness or Fourier whim to gather his workers around.

Unsurveyed land was often dotted by the rude hovels of the immigrant poor. Irish and Germans settled "down Neck" in Newark's "Hamburg Place" at the same time a large jerry-built village of free Negroes and slaves grew on Charleston's "Neck." Through these districts ran Post Roads, plank roads, and turnpikes, often lined with saloons or more sedate wayside inns, which catered to itinerant peddlers, weary Irish dayworkers, or occasional militia companies out for a Sunday target shoot. These acres long remained the haven of gamblers, prizefighters, race touts (whether at Democratic boss John McKane's ground in Coney Island or the Chicago machine's more elegant Washington Park), camp meetings, circuses, and baseball players.

The suburban hinterland was broken up not in montonous middle-class subdivisions, but in a kaleidoscope of settlements which reflected the full spectrum of Jacksonian community aspirations. Lowlands and highlands harbored the social extremes. By the turnpikes, behind the saloons, on the banks of streams that meandered into malarial "sloughs" squatted Irish or Negroes, trying to make a seasonal income as day laborers in nearby fields. On the hilltops lived the wealthy in pseudo-Norman castles, Italianate chateaux, or carpenter Alhambras. Cincinnati's Avondale and East Walnut Hills, Wilton in Westchester County, and West Orange outside Newark all had baronial establishments, complete with cavernous libraries, independent gas facilities, racing stables, and all else that satisfied a gentleman's taste for solitary grandeur. Far below, the industrial villages, with their planned Fourier grids, became the nucleus for German or other ethnic enclaves. Nearby, usually taking advantage of cheap horse or steam cars in the turnpike district, the moral reform societies of the 1850s, applying Greeley's advice, laid out tracts, like Pittsburgh's Temperanceville on the south side of the Monongahela, Cincinnati's Glendale, and the Westchester villages of Bronxville and Morrisania, which featured small house lots, liquor restrictions in the deeds, and specially arranged "workmen's commutation." Gradually as these subdivisions meshed together, they formed virtual extensions of the city. South Boston, Morrisania in Westchester County, and Cincinnati's Mount Auburn all were macadamized, flagged, and sidewalked, gaslit, served by horsecars, and eager for other improvements which downtown had to offer after the Civil War.

THE METROPOLITAN OUTREACH

By the second half of the nineteenth century, this disarrayed suburban patchwork sharply contrasted with the systematic expansion of the central city. The disparity fed the pervasive sense of metropolitan "manifest destiny," a conviction held by downtowners and suburbanites alike, that money, technology, and professional resources could steamroll over any difficulty. While the city reached imperialistically into its hinterland, many outlying communities proved eager to be absorbed by the new order.

Residents of the turnpike districts, painfully aware of the discrepancies between suburban shortcomings and downtown accomplishments, usually instigated the township debates for annexation to the metropolis. Aloof hilltop barons blasé about trunk sewers or macadam and local squires aghast at the thought of higher city assessments cried out against the passing of the

"old-fashioned, pure democracies" which they dominated. But more middle-class voters, starved for urban amenities, determinedly carried through the referenda. Philadelphia's Northern Liberties, Spring Garden, and Kensington found by 1854 that only a metropolitan police force, free to range across municipal boundaries, could suppress street gangs which "infested" these inner suburbs. Envious of Manhattan's Croton water system and her professional police and fire departments, Morrisania and West Farms voted overwhelmingly to join New York City in 1873. Between 1867 and 1873, Boston successively annexed Roxbury, Dorchester, Brighton, and West Roxbury, suburbs that suffered lower water tables and choked on their own sewage dumped into tidal estuaries. The most startling envelopment came in 1889, when Chicago swallowed up Hyde Park township, quadrupling the city's land area and raising its population to nearly one million.

While many suburbs were a topographical chaos, garbage strewn, prey to "agues," dependent on well water and rowdy amateurs for fire protection, central cities supplied pure drinking water, "professional" police and fire departments coordinated by telegraph, and expert sanitary inspection. Between Appomattox and the 1873 depression, cities vastly increased their capital debts to splurge on spectacular improvements. At the same time, Republican party strategists had erected metropolitan districts to regulate everything from saloons and sanitation in the New York-Brooklyn area to police in Hudson County, New Jersey, to "Copperheads" in the District of Columbia. These frankly political structures, often run by city businessmen who kept metropolitan patronage in partisan hands, gave many boulevard engineers, park builders, and water-supply experts their first view of regional needs. Union Army generals, their military projects behind them, carved the outskirts into drainage districts, laid new aqueducts, and ran broad boulevards leading to park systems like Boston's Fenway and Van Courtlandt in the Bronx. More than just the source for capital improvements, the central city from 1865 to the 1890s beckoned the material well-being, professionalism, and efficiency connoted by "metropolitan" activity.

More and more this expansive spirit was epitomized by the industrial corporation whose enlarged operations built cities upward and out. During the prosperous 1880s, magnates began the search for economies of scale on the metropolitan periphery. Some sought to avoid labor radicalism, taxes, and inefficient, corrupt municipal services by building new factory towns on the cities' edges. The most celebrated of these "satellites" was Pullman, on Chicago's far South Side, where "palace" car shops sprawled with the demands of railroad logistics. The company's feudal paternalism provided workers' tenements and a central shopping arcade, but strictly barred saloons, brothels, and other unbusinesslike diversions. After the 1894 Pullman strike, however, businessmen plunged their money into factory layouts, with less concern about "amenities." The narrower outlook resulted in new communities like Gary, Indiana, which embodied "the spirit of the Corporation—efficiency." On Indiana lake-front dunes, twenty-five miles southeast of Chicago's Loop, United States Steel sited a blast-furnace complex according to the latest scientific principles. A residential quarter was platted on a strict checkerboard with back alleys reserved for utility lines, while in front the gridirons quickly filled with crowded tenements. Although Cincinnati's Oakley and Norwood contained planned industrial parks and the best railroad sites, only well-paid foremen could afford the company-built housing. Eventually, many of these working-class satellites, like Pullman, lost their "model" features and housed the saloons, commercial strips, and servant population upon which higher-class suburbs depended but preferred not to see in their midst.

In their leisure some industrialists turned to another community form equally important to the development of the metropolitan periphery, the suburban university. Although imported graduate studies may have shaped the intellectual side, higher education's physical plant often resulted from the largesse of traction owners and real estate boosters who counted on pseudo-Gothic quadrangles to lend prestige to neighboring subdivisions. The master of the Manhattan Elevated, Jay Gould, helped underwrite New York University's move to its Bronx "Heights" quarters, a site which lay astride the new steam railroad he was building into Westchester. In the 1890s, the horsecar promoters who boosted Westminster, seven miles outside Denver, aspired to make their Bible college another Northwestern, their straggling village another Evanston. Edgar G. Lewis, the erratic publisher, shrewdly concocted his "University City" between the Washington University campus and the St. Louis World's Fair grounds in Forest Park. If only his credit had lasted, Lewis could have prospered as the city grew into these western suburbs. As late as 1925, UCLA's benefactors hoped the school would anchor posh Bel Air and Westwood in western Los Angeles.

The business decisions which had the greatest impact on suburban development, however, were those which underwrote the trolley revolution. Soon after Frank J. Sprague mated electric power with the Union Passenger horsecars of Richmond, Virginia, in 1887, promoters found that electricity slashed operating costs and could move vehicles ten miles per hour in open country. By 1891, "electrics" captured 40 per cent of all traction mileage, while the imminent conversion of anachronistic cable roads and horsecars attracted the attention of large-scale financiers. The Consolidated Traction Company of New Jersey, behind which stood Prudential Insurance and United States Senator John F. Dryden, laced together the Oranges, Bloomfield, and Montclair across Essex County. Reflecting the vast resources of Thomas Fortune Ryan and William C. Whitney and their ties with Tammany boss Richard Croker, the Union Railway replaced the decrepit "bobtail" cars in the Bronx and Westchester and reached White Plains and Scarsdale with electrics by 1895. Henry M. Whitney's West End Street Railway brought high-class suburbs like Somerville, Brookline, and Cambridge within minutes of Boston's "Hub." By 1902, twenty-five giants out of 817 companies controlled more than one fifth of street railway mileage in the country. The largest operators also plunged ahead with high-speed electrics that ran on standard-gauge track. Detroit's "interurbans" provided downtown service to Palmer Park and Royal Oak. After twenty years of construction, Henry E. Huntington's Pacific Electric cars ran from the San Bernadino Valley in the east to Santa Monica's beaches, from San Fernando in the north to the oilfields at San Pedro—an empire that crisscrossed 1,164 miles around the old Los Angeles core.

Ironically, the electrics' phenomenal success brought on grave transit crises, as central business districts choked under new waves of suburban traffic. "Look at the city of Detroit," lamented a University of Michigan engineer in 1915. "You couldn't get any more [street] cars there. It is nothing but a moving platform now. If they expect to have more cars, they will have to build elevateds or subways." In city after city business leaders and politicians, anxious about trolley-clogged downtowns, struggled to separate suburban passenger service from local street traffic. In the 1890s, William Vanderbilt sunk the New York Central's tracks below Manhattan's street level, providing the Hudson, Harlem, and New Haven Divisions for the first time with transit routes without grade crossings down to Grand Central Station. The Pennsylvania Railroad spent $112 million tunneling under the Hudson and East Rivers, blasting under Manhattan's schist to give electric-train passengers, from New Jersey and Long Island, direct access to magnificent Penn Station at Thirty-fourth Street. Viaduct or subway "loops" down Chicago's State Street, under Philadelphia's Market Street, and under Boston's State Street testified to the determination of downtown elites and their "Tammany" allies to maintain the vitality of the central district. The fear of commercial extinction was no less acute in Los Angeles, where lines of streetcars jammed the old *pueblo* core. But the city's political and business leaders failed in 1906, 1917, and 1926 at attempts for authority to construct a downtown Pacific Electric underground or viaduct. The city's weak Democratic machine, backed by the relatively small immigrant population, vitiated by "progressivism" at the turn of the century, could hardly ram through a downtown bond issue over the vetoes of the Americanized suburbs.

By the turn of the century, metropolitan expansion also rested upon those downtown salesmen who packaged suburbia for varied classes in the city. From Manhattan offices, fugitive southern and rural publicists like Walter Hines Page and Liberty Hyde Bailey led the siren call "back to nature." Their slickly edited, brightly illustrated *Suburban Life, Countryside, Outing*, and similar magazines shrewdly played on the anxieties of the urban elite. Articles urged the removal of stunted tenement children to "fresh air" camps or advised how bucolic surroundings could restore a businessman's frazzled nerves. Advertising quickly took on the new suburban idiom. Gibson girls with Palmolive-pure complexions sunned on country club verandahs, while golfers eyed Cadillacs parked in the driveways —such were the images that tantalized the wealthy. Much suburban encomiums came from trolley executives, most notably from Henry M. Whitney, promoter of Boston's giant West End Street Railway. Whitney tirelessly harangued metropolitan audiences, churned out editorials, and provided colorful copy for his view that trolleys and suburban cottages would eradicate social unrest. Other streetcar managers dressed up the outskirts in gaudy colors for the masses. The Census Bureau reported in 1902 that one third of the nation's transit roads had built, owned, or leased parks, lager gardens, and country resorts. While some were dignified groves, like Cincinnati's Ludlow Lagoon, operated in the Kentucky country-

side by the Covington interurban, others were honky-tonks, like Chicago's "Sans Souci," between Washington Park and Race Track, which offered a Japanese pagoda, electric fountain, a Temple of Palmistry, and shooting galleries. Thanks to the trolley corporations' aggressive promotional campaigns, millions glimpsed suburbia in "Coney Island style" fairgrounds or in more sedate, contemplative retreats in the country.

THE STRUGGLE FOR THE CORRIDORS

Although trolleys, interurbans, and steam railroads distended the shape of the city, the nickel ride, in particular, foreshortened the social distance between classes which suburbanites had come to accept by the 1890s. Built-up areas of many cities, the census reported in 1902, "consist of long fingers or tentacles reaching out from the more solid centers, each owing its growth to a radiating street railway." Whether along Bloomfield Avenue connecting Newark with the Oranges, or Vincennes Avenue from Chicago's Loop down to Blue Island, or Commonwealth Avenue which brought Boston commuters back home to Brighton and Brookline, the electrics greatly increased contact between income levels hitherto separated by more inefficient and expensive transit. To the consternation of the wealthy "man with the checkbook," trolleys seemed to serve as a magnet for multiple dwellings, saloons, and the "man with the dinner pail."

Beginning in the 1890s, many suburbs underwent what sociologist Herbert Gans has called "definitional struggles" to determine whether working- or middle-class culture would prevail along transit corridors. The running battle which the Montclair Citizens Committee of 100 had fought since the mid-1880s to limit saloons along Bloomfield Avenue boiled over in 1894 when North Jersey Street Railway sought a franchise for its "electrics." The hilltoppers who could afford carriages to the Delaware and Lackawanna train station thought the trolley's moral incursions outweighed its boon to speculative real estate. "By so much as Montclair is brought nearer to Newark," a Protestant minister pointed out, "by so much is Newark brought nearer to Montclair, and the character of the town would be changed." Many antifranchisers also doubled as supporters of the "Cambridge Plan," after these Montclair residents learned how the Boston suburb had used its YMCA and "union" church meetings to evangelize against the saloon. In 1894, the upland Protestants voted changes in local town government to limit Irish-Democratic strength to just one ward straddling the thoroughfare. The new majority easily imposed high licenses on saloonkeepers and stymied for several years North Jersey's franchise efforts.

The traction lobby eventually won its fight, however, and the new century saw increased fears of newcomers and property deterioration. "Montclair is a town without a slum," boasted a 1907 account, admitting, "to be sure . . . poorer quarters along the railroad tracks, and off the business streets . . . [where] may be found the few, the very few saloons." This complacency ended with the opening of the McAdoo tubes under the Hudson River and census estimates of a startling influx of Italian and Negro residents. In 1908 the Montclair Civic Association held a planning conference and called in landscape architect John Nolen to suggest improvements. Nolen urged beautification of

the Lackawanna railway station, development of a town hall–civic center–school complex, regulated cornice heights and Georgian brick or Tudor half-timber for commercial structures along Bloomfield Avenue. Taxpayers balked at such costly social cohesion and eventually chose cheaper, simpler restrictions. By the First World War, the suburb had adopted prohibition by local option, centralized planning, and established a commission government to contain the spread of downtown "blight."

The Montclair experience typified confrontations along many corridors opened up by the nickel trolley. Struggles usually were waged by local "town improvement" clubs, formed in the 1880s to "cultivate public spirit and foster town pride, quicken intellectual life, promote good fellowship, and uplift the sagging New England village." Now this civic gospel focused on breaches in the metropolitan line, whether Flushing's Good Citizenship League which in 1894 rallied against a trolley and a Manhattan-run race track or the Scarsdale "Town Club" founded in 1904 to watch encroachments by both New York City and White Plains. "Let the suburbs shame the city," urged the American Civic Association, "with clean and sightly homes on model streets, with public utilities held subject to public use and public beauty, and the city will profit." The trolley zone's ugliness particularly offended suburban civic pride. The billboard which "follows the railroads, trolley lines, and boulevards out into the suburbs," met organized opponents in East Walpole, Milton, and Wellesley. These societies in metropolitan Boston launched the Massachusetts Civic League to coordinate the attack against the "tramp menace" and the multiple dwelling and endorsed the "Direct or Crowbar Approach" against outdoor advertising. Improvers in Brookline, disturbed by trolley unsightliness, transformed Beacon Street from a fifty-foot roadway into a "splendid parkway" with a central streetcar "reservation" screened by shrubbery. Other groups emerged as protectors of shade trees "menaced by corridor gas mains, utility poles, and wires." The East Orange Shade Tree Commission borrowed the New Jersey Republicans' "New Idea" rhetoric to attack power companies who "ruthlessly mutilated and destroyed trees along highways for the passage of overhead wires." Transit corridors also harbored "dust evils," tuberculosis, and other insidious germs from the horse droppings scattered by speeding vehicles. Dust-suppression campaigns went on with particular vigor in Brookline and Arlington, Massachusetts; Tuxedo Park, Garden City, and Mount Vernon, New York, and other high-class areas. Pasadena typified many communities when it went to extra expense to make Marengo Avenue a beautiful "oiled road."

Faced also with the spread of downtown saloons, suburbs launched local-option and high-license campaigns to contain Demon Rum. In Westchester County, communities which straddled busy travel routes took the earliest action. Scarsdale went "dry" in 1899, soon after trolley service improved on the White Plains Road; White Plains followed in 1905. Temperance reformers were well aware that votes to close down localities often depended upon the existence of convenient nearby saloon strips, "safety valves" for the suburbanite to drink or buy packaged spirits. By 1900, Cambridge, the largest liquor-free suburb in the country, was followed by dry Somerville, Chelsea,

Malden, Newton, Everett, Medford, Melrose, Brookline, and Reading. The Massachusetts Total Abstinence Society acknowledged, however, that these contained residents who "could get all the liquor they required" in the Hub, but who "preferred to keep the saloon away from their homes." This attitude was apparent in an 1899 referendum, when teetotal Cambridge voted against statewide prohibition, no doubt, to keep packaged liquor available in neighboring communities. By 1916, from Winnetka to Oak Park and Riverside to Berwyn, a broad saloonless belt had formed around Chicago. Here, too, drinks could be bought in Blue Island, Cicero, and other nearby working-class sections. In 1913 communities like Hawthorne, Lyndhurst, and Ridgefield Park had taken up provisions in New Jersey's Walsh Act to institute a local prohibition option as well as commission government. When the legislature enacted state-wide local option in 1917, the suburbs that took the pledge included most of those west of Newark: East and South Orange, Montclair, Rutherford, North and South Caldwell. In the meantime, many Garden State towns made do with selective enforcement, like Englewood, which initiated a "dry Sunday" campaign in 1906 and clamped down on saloons along Palisades Avenue, but allowed the Town and Golf clubs to operate on Bergen County licenses.

Suburbs, served by commuter railroads and farther away from the trolley's incursions, could resort to less urgent devices to maintain a homogeneous environment. Ornamental arches were the rage in Southern California, where realtors felt they lent entire tracts "that air of exclusiveness and privacy which characterizes the private villa." Other planners urged beautification of train stations and commuter plazas. The Boston and Albany's efforts to clothe its terminals with tailored shrubbery won the laurel "Garden Railroad" from appreciative commuters. After the founding of Brookline's Clyde Park Country Club in the mid-1880s and the golf craze at the turn of the century, the private sports club often served as the nucleus around which local government developed. With property owners empowered to vote and make policy, the "incorporated club" controlled garbage pickups, police patrols, road repair, and street lighting from the Heathcote Colony in Scarsdale to the "Homes Association" of Palos Verdes on the Pacific. *American City*, an ardent champion of "progressivism," found the "Civic League" of Roland Park, Maryland, to be the exemplary commission government, where trustees who managed the interests of property owners literally applied the ideal of "business principles" to politics.

Areas faced with direct urban encroachment, however, required more systematic controls. "Slum germs are at work," warned the Massachusetts Civil League in 1911. "Foreigners are coming in increasing numbers, and with them are also coming the shack, the converted house . . . the familiar frame tenement, and the wooden 'three decker'." The last, a League spokesman claimed, had spread throughout eastern New England "like the cholera or yellow fever." Winthrop, a short trolley ride east of the Hub, had enough triple deckers to give it an undesired "Dorchestry" look. The Brookline planning board complained that "stores of unattractive type" had encroached upon property lines and spoiled Beacon Street's "generous, dignified appearance." Struggling against the multiple dwelling, the Civic League lobbied a tenement-house bill for small towns through the State Legislature in 1912. The law which went into effect by local town referendum, limited building height, bulk, yard space, and prohibited certain wooden-frame tenements. Armed with their trusty stereopticons and exhibit booths, Bay Staters barraged their communities with housing publicity. Within three years, twenty-three towns had implemented the act, nearly all in the suburban belts around Boston, Quincy, and Lynn.

Philadelphia's Main Line suburbs, finding themselves in the "danger zone" of the city's westward expansion, counterattacked in 1911 with sophisticated social surveys conducted by professional charity workers. They uncovered delapidated rowhouses, rear tenements, and backed-up privies along the Lancaster Turnpike in Haverford; jerry-built hovels near the Rosemont trolley; and "squalid" multiple dwellings on Highland Avenue in Wayne. An alarmed coalition which called itself the Main Line Housing Association pressed suburban health boards for strict local inspections. Civic leaders denied, however, that this effort to upgrade housing would price apartment rentals on the Main Line much beyond what the working class could afford.

THE EMERGENCE OF SUBURBAN REGIONALISM

Gradually, after the turn of the century, isolated community struggles to contain the corridors developed into a regional suburban consciousness. In part, this wider viewpoint resulted from encroachments by the trolley-borne city. Stimulus came from suburban magazines, "progressive" planning ideas, and the city beautiful movement, which had flourished after the 1893 Chicago

World's Fair. Individual communities had also gotten together to settle specific problems as well as relationships with downtown. By World War I a co-ordinated response had evolved to oppose metropolitan expansion.

Suburbs first began serious mutual discussions within the framework of "special improvements districts" which had sprung up to handle the growing burden of sewage disposal, water supply, and road repair. These were not mere patronage districts erected by the GOP during the Civil War, but service bureaucracies, paid for by suburban tax levies, and using electricity, telephones, cheap asphalt, and other new inventions that signaled suburban independence from downtown technology. Many traction experts, utilities engineers, and corporate lawyers had now moved out from the city, bringing their regional viewpoints and political connections to suburb-wide coalitions. In 1898, a pollution crisis in New Jersey's Passaic River Valley coincided with downtown boasts about a "greater Newark" absorbing her hapless suburbs in the valley. The Oranges, Irvington, and Vailsburg sent plenopotentiaries to parley with Newark about extending her sewer lines throughout the region. Protracted negotiations, however, did not result in annexation to Newark but rather in the legislature's creation of the Passaic Valley Sewer District, supported with assessments from enrolled communities, which provided access to a large outfall sewer in Newark Bay. Annexations beyond the Boston peninsula in the 1860s and 1870s were now replaced by successive layers of special districts: Metropolitan Sewage District, formed in 1889; Parks, 1893; Water, 1895; Water and Sewage, 1901; combined Metropolitan, 1919; Planning, 1923; Transit, 1929. Each "authority" had its own tax base and

bureaucratic superstructure. Through them the suburbs gained the technology and political leverage that offered an alternative to annexation.

Suburban opinion inevitably drifted from talk of districts to anticipated regional growth. Westchester County planning originated in anxieties about the deteriorated spine of settlement along the Bronx River north of the New York City line. "Where the riverbed was wide enough to justify a settlement," an expert recalled, "population came and of a class which could not improve, and must perforce, defile the surroundings." In 1907, Scarsdale Republicans convinced the State Legislature to create a special corridor in Westchester and Bronx Counties under the aegis of a Bronx River Parkway Commission. But while this body labored against "centers of disorder and disease," deterioration had extended far beyond its jurisdiction. Between 1900 and 1910, Westchester grew at an uprecedented rate. New York Central and New Haven steam depots had become crowded with "ramshackle" buildings, lumberyards, light industry, and multiple dwellings. Urged by realtors and the Chamber of Commerce, County Supervisors in 1914 appointed a Planning Commission to advise on "the best land to be selected for residence districts, with the class of residents which naturally, because of topographical and commercial surroundings, would occupy such land." Mandated to inventory overall county needs, planners actually focused on worrisome eyesores: a "Coney Island" trolley park razed at Rye Beach, overhead streetcar wires screened at White Plains' Broadway Park, and civic plazas in place of congested flathouses along the corridors in New Rochelle and White Plains.

A similar understanding of planning

emerged from conferences, starting in 1913, between metropolitan Boston and vocal suburban representatives on Massachusetts planning boards and the State Homestead Commission. Downtown spokesmen, including Mayor James Michael Curley, dwelled on the tenement-house congestion, city fire and police efficiency, and plans to upgrade health care. In contrast, suburban delegates, distressed by a "general lack of harmony" in their localities, saw planning as largely an aesthetic venture in

towns [that] are more or less nondescript character, with narrow streets and congested traffic; elaborate buildings surrounded by cheap, tumbledown structures, and with no approaches in keeping with the character of the building; fine residential districts with cheap and unsanitary tenement properties adjoining them.

Here the litmus test was suburban reaction to the Homestead Commission's proposals to take the pressure off crowded Boston by relocating working-class homes on the metropolitan outskirts. To the suburban-dominated planning boards, city deconcentration meant the location of "model tenements," not in low-density suburbs, but in the immigrant wards of peripheral cities like Lynn.

Suburbs in Delaware and Montgomery counties, finding themselves in the "danger zone" of South Philadelphia's westward expansion, appropriated regional planning as a sophisticated defense. While the Main Line Housing Association stoically acknowledged that "Wherever communities are built, the poor, the day laborer, and the mechanic are needed," its members strenuously policed substandard housing largely inhabited by Negroes, Italians, and other "foreigners." Campaigning for restrictive sanitary inspections, importing

downtown social workers, and seeking the Massachusetts precedent of a tenement law for small towns, the Association exhausted the usual "progressive" techniques for housing uplift. Looking for greater political leverage, Main Line leaders in 1912 sponsored a series of conferences of all local improvement groups within a twenty-five-mile radius of Philadelphia's City Hall. At one session John Nolen, Frederic C. Howe, and experts from New York's Bureau of Municipal Research described the latest advances in the civic revival. At the Ardmore YMCA delegates heard Philadelphia's chief of public works herald Mayor Rudolph Blakenburg's "great reconstruction work" which welcomed the "participation" of the outlying communities. But the suburban leaders had already begun to think beyond downtown initiatives. Some urged suburbs pool resources to overcome the "absence of radial and circumferencial thoroughfares" which prevented intersuburban contact, while an Ardmore representative argued that with community cooperation, "a united front could be presented before the legislature." In November, 1912, enthusiasts launched a Suburban Co-Operative Planning Association, which organized housing lectures and exhibits, sponsored contests for the design of "model tenements," and cajoled more "progressive" builders to improve working-class dwellings. When the Association sought official sanction from the Pennsylvania legislature in 1913, they strenuously lobbied for absolute local control over all development decisions. The legislature obliged with a Metropolitan Planning District, a harmless advisory board on which twelve suburban delegates could readily veto proposals made by three from Philadelphia. Whether in Westchester County, greater Boston, or metropolitan Philadelphia, suburbanites fluently spoke the argot of progressive regionalism, but never relinquished a localism that remained staunchly aloof from downtown.

SEMIDETACHED AMBIENCE; SUBURBS FOR THE MASSES IN THE TWENTIES

During the 1920s, the spectacular growth of upper-income suburbs borne by the auto obscured those fundamental trends that continued methodically to expand the metropolitan hinterland. During the decade, Glendale, California, grew by 3,000 per cent; Beverly Hills by nearly 2,500 per cent; and Shaker Heights, Ohio by 1,000 per cent. Car registration spiraled upward, prompting social theorists to envision new unbounded communities, "radial frontiers" pioneered by motorists. Census figures soberly confirmed what sociologist Harlan Paul Douglass called the "suburban trend." In 1920, the Bureau counted over 11,000,000 people living beyond city boundaries in sixty-two metropolitan areas. By 1930, population of the outer rings had expanded at twice the rate of their core cities and contained more than 17,000,000—perhaps one in every seven Americans. Still, much of this growth represented the intensification of earlier patterns: the decentralization of industry, the movement of retail stores beyond the central business district, and the modernization of commuter transit. Although the auto's impact was undeniable, it proved hardly decisive in those large cities with established transit networks. Millions rode crowded "Els," subways, and streetcars (supplemented by bus service) out to garden apartments, duplex bungalows, or semidetached houses. For just $600 down

and $48 per month, second-generation Americans emerging from inner-city tenements could share a patch of grass and some sunlight in the city limits.

Thousands of manufacturers, encouraged by outlying belt-line railroads, long-distance electric transmission, and telephone exchanges, sought industrial space on the metropolitan periphery. The 1910 census found that in the previous decade an increase in the number of suburban factory jobs far outpaced the central cities'. Once Boston's "streetcar suburb," Cambridge now had one fifth of Boston's industrial output and was soon to become the fourth largest industrial city in New England. Paterson's famed silk and worsted mills, along with their "operatives," had spilled into Garfield and the "Botany" section of Clifton. Metalworks, printing lofts, and food processors had drifted from Manhattan into the deepened tidal streams of Greater New York. The shift came most dramatically where heavy industry required sprawling acreage. As early as the 1890s, Chicago realtors had packaged special "industrial districts," with railroad sidings and utility conduits, far from the Loop. The most famous was Calumet Harbor, recovered from lake dunes, and lined by 1910 with vast steelworks and chemical plants. Industrial satellites ringed Chicago on the south and west: Cicero (the home of Western Electric's giant Hawthorne plant), Harvey, Blue Island, Chicago Heights, Hammond, Indiana, and the huge U. S. Steelworks in Gary. Henry Ford's "on line" assembly factories changed the social landscape of greater Detroit. He located thousands of jobs beyond the city line—at Highland Park, Northville, Flat Rock, and, of course, River Rouge.

By the 1920s, not only did more urbanites work on the metropolitan

periphery, but more shopped and enjoyed their entertainment there as well.
New commercial subcenters sprouted at
transit intersections, where homebound
commuters switched from trains to
streetcars. National chains gravitated to
these high-volume locations; United
Cigar Stores, Walgreen's, and Wool-
worth's attracted customers who preferred "neighborhood" convenience. As
early as 1910, Chicago had six distinct
subcenters, including Sixty-third and
Halsted on the southwest side, the
second largest shopping district outside
the Loop; and 111th and South Michigan Avenue, which served Pullman and
Blue Island. Life in New York's "outer
boroughs" pulsed around the 149th
Street "Hub" in the Bronx and "downtown" Flushing and Jamaica in Queens.
The streetcar concentration at the Market Street "El" and 69th Street made
Upper Darby the major shopping center
for both West Philadelphia and nearby
suburbs. After dark, these areas glittered
with neon-trimmed movie "palaces"
built by theater chains that met the
outlying audiences' demand for the
latest "Broadway" movies. By 1924
Balaban and Katz and lesser-known
chains had constructed theaters in all
of Chicago's subcenters and had bought
out vaudeville theaters in Aurora, Elgin,
Des Plaines, and other communities.
That same year, Loew's entered the suburban New York market, taking over a
"first run" house in White Plains. Department stores, which had extended
telephone order and delivery service,
grudgingly began to trek after their
affluent customers. Upstart competitors
generally led the exodus, like Wie-
boldt's, which in 1910 became the first
Chicago department store to branch
beyond the Loop. Sears, Roebuck, wary
of downtown competition and closely
attuned to motorists' buying habits, be-

gan a concerted subcenter strategy for
its housewares and auto-supply stores
in 1926. By contrast, Marshall Field's
waited until 1929 to open specialty
branches in upper-income Evanston,
Oak Park, and Lake Forest.

While the motorist monopolized
newspaper space and advertising copy,
the straphanger, whether in a railroad
train, streetcar or motor coach, carried
the burden of suburban commuting.
The auto made considerable strides in
smaller metropolises like Kansas City,
Missouri, where 41 per cent drove into
the business district in the mid-twenties;
or Washington, D.C., with 55 per cent.
But in Boston only one in four drove;
Chicago one in five; and Detroit, the
"Motor City," counted just 18 per cent
in 1927. The spectacular growth of
Long Island and Westchester County
depended less upon the automobile
than upon the enormous expansion of
the Long Island and New York Central
rail service. Suburban Nassau County's
population nearly quadrupled between
1910 and 1930, but the Long Island's
commuter haul, thanks to its huge
Sunnyside yards (completed in 1910)
and overhead electrification that went
into effect in 1924, expanded ten times.
Roads linking suburbs to central cities,
long under the thumb of county politics
and debt ceilings, looked archaic, in
contrast.

Highway engineers less responsible to
suburban commuters than truck farmers
took a dim view toward "speedways"
for the wealthy that would, as a Wayne
County, Michigan, engineer remarked
in 1915, "array one class against another." Well into the twenties, traffic
experts, co-ordinated by the nation's
chief engineer, Secretary of Commerce
Herbert Hoover, reflected this conservatism. Instead of new roads, the professionals urged widened lanes, grade

separations, bans on "promiscuous access and parking," and traffic lights synchronized to "platoon" cars as acceptable expedients. An alternative had existed, of course, in the aesthetic drives that for decades had graced metropolitan park systems. In the wake of the city beautiful movement, landscape architects urged that these "limited access" parkways should "skirt" around outlying town centers rather than funnel bumper-to-bumper cars on main streets. Not until the Bronx Park commissioners built the Bronx River Parkway (opened in 1925) and public works czar Robert Moses let the dirt fly on the Long Island highway system in the 1930s, did motorists benefit from high-speed traffic arteries that bypassed commercial intersections.

For millions of urban dwellers the better life amounted to an affordable, compromised suburbia within walking distance or motor-coach fare of the "Els" in the "outer wards." Suburban Westchester and Nassau counties soared spectacularly during the twenties, adding 350,000 residents, yet this was less than half those who found semisuburban neighborhoods *within* New York City, like Flushing and Jamaica, Queens; Pelham Bay in the Bronx; and Midwood or Flatbush in Brooklyn. This nether world between old tenement ghettos and isolated suburban freeholds existed around garden apartments, rowhouses, or semidetached duplexes (mortgaged to a building and loan association) on a "block" whose tone, at least, was determined by the settlement of "coreligionists." For middle-class Jews in South Philadelphia, upward mobility meant moving west to "Strawberry Mansion" and joining B'nai Jeshurun Synagogue. Later in the twenties, this migration extended beyond Fairmount Park to Wynnfield, with the

aid of Jewish builders who subcontracted carpentry, masonry, and brickwork within the ethnic community. Eastern Queens and South Brooklyn were patchworks of Irish, Germans, Jews, and Italians lured by the mass transit lines from Manhattan and downtown Brooklyn. Large-scale developers like Bryan L. Kennelly in Woodhaven, E. O. Jahrsdorfer in Ridgewood, and Lewis H. May, Andrew N. Miller, and the Morgenthau organization in Jackson Heights and Richmond Hill reached the Irish, German, and Jewish communities through ethnic media such as the *Yiddisher Morgen Journal* which boasted that its real estate ads reached "the investing class of Jews." On a finer scale, relying on a Catholic church or synagogue as ethnic compass points, Italian contractors erected rows of one-family stuccoes on East Thirty-seventh Street, Flatbush; Irish developers projected two-family brick houses in Ridgewood; Jewish realtors handled the subdivision of Edgemere.

These ethnic concentrations in the outer wards met suburbia largely on their own terms. Many could not have moved without the two-family houses, bought with a down payment borrowed from parents or in-laws, which perpetuated (through the upstairs apartment) close family relations that had existed in the tenements. Families and friends settled in tandem, honeycombing the streets with relationships dominated by family ties rather than "neighborliness." For the well-off middle class, Wednesday afternoon Mah-Jongg or Friday night pinochle brought city acquaintances together. But for most in the lower-middle and working class, leisure meant six o'clock suppers, radios on in the "living room," or "stoop" lounging until mosquitoes forced them indoors. Despite the 25' x 100' lots, families cultivated a new privacy, broken down only by their children, who played basketball or stickball in the driveways and loitered under streetlights or outside corner candy stores. Catholic churches and Jewish synagogues held greater importance in defining the neighborhood's ethnic identity than in providing a fulcrum for associational activities. They became secular "centers" for the community's intense worship of organized recreation, for its homeowners' association, and political life. Generally, however, those families that had predominated religious life in the old neighborhoods simply continued in the new, leading the men's clubs, sodalities, and sisterhoods. For middle-class breadwinners, haggard from a trip on the subway, the six-room boxes offered a new privacy, which they jealously guarded.

STANDARDS AND STANDARDIZATION

By the middle 1920s, realtors had reached a consensus on how to settle the new suburbanite in regions outside city limits. "The good subdivider," "a creator, a man of vision and achievement," worked best on a generous scale, preferably three hundred acres or more, on a site where natural or man-made boundaries limited an otherwise "endless spread of urban expansion." He preferred 40′ x 100′ lots, reserving side alleys for underground utility conduits and auto "strips." Unsightly over head utility lines and back alleys had become "a thing of the past." Proper deed restrictions assured home buyers about "the cost of buildings, build-back, race, etc." Developers emphasized careful deed exclusions, where practical, against Negroes and other minorities who might drag down values. Experts, like the improvers of Shaker Heights, Ohio, ad-

vised a careful separation between modes of transit access: "It is a mistake to put high-grade, refined residents on a car line which is used largely by a foreign population or a low class of laborers." Others relied on the golf craze to sell home lots. "The American businessman wants his golf," insisted Hugh E. Prather, who successfully incorporated the game into his Highland Park subdivision outside of Dallas. One landscaper alone, Tom Bendelow, laid out seven hundred courses throughout the nation and Canada during the decade.

Many of the newest developments, whether aimed at a working- or high-class market, employed several or all of these design techniques. The Van Sweringen brothers, who moved from Cleveland traction to real estate, controlled trolley approaches as well as the overall design of their Shaker Square. While architects fashioned a traction depot and commercial center into a pseudonineteenth-century village, elaborate deed restrictions prohibited multiple dwellings, saloons, and discordant home designs. At Los Angeles' Palos Verdes Estates, whose rambling hillsides offered spectacular views of the Pacific, the Olmsted Brothers' surveyors followed natural contours, laying a central streetcar thoroughfare and subsidiary motor drives. Lots varied from 60′ x 125′ to an acre, but all home designs had to meet specifications of a paid "art jury." Six business centers provided community focal points, around which grouped a limited number of multiple dwellings and less expensive bungalow courts, which the Olmsteds screened from lower-density acreage through the use of school parks and golf courses. Even Torrance, another Los Angeles project designed to attract workers in the San Pedro industrial district, reflected aesthetic rudiments. Here again, the Olmsteds designed a broad avenue separating residential districts from a special industrial preserve. While forbidding tenements and boardinghouses as well as saloons, the land company sold frame and concrete bungalows "on easy terms" to "mechanics." For more recent arrivals, it reserved "a special section . . . as a foreign quarter, unlike in every respect the usual Ghetto and Latin quarter."

Suburban retailing proved even more difficult to contain with the onset of the automobile. Small business extensions alongside trolley routes looked tidy when compared to the rank commercial growth stimulated by this new mobility. The car encouraged roadside stands, "gasoline fill-ups," and stores, creating miles of ugly "string streets" which distressed aesthetes, "quality" realtors, and downtown merchants alike. A few subdividers experimented with regulated business arcades and commercial blocks integrated into their design. Both Roland Park, outside Baltimore, and the Van Sweringens' Shaker Heights clustered retail stores otherwise prohibited from residential streets. But merchandisers, convinced that sales meant window displays close to the stream of traffic, even if double or triple parked, remained conservative. In the early twenties, however, developers showed how retailers could break away from the linear street arrangement to one which profitably met the demands of the outlying motorist. J. C. Nichols' Country Club Plaza in Kansas City, Missouri, and Hugh Prather's River Oaks Shopping Center both employed unified "business" architecture, landscaping, and off-street parking. Later, in 1931, at Highland Park outside Dallas, Prather turned his stores away from the main thoroughfare and surrounded them with customers' parking lots. The wisdom of locating retail trade where suburbanites already lived particularly made sense to new retail chains, anxious to avoid direct competition with the established department stores in the central business district. By the late 1920s, Sears, Roebuck, followed by Montgomery Ward, carefully picked sites at the confluence of highways. Large, reinforced-concrete, windowless structures, surrounded by a hundred parking slots and dominated by the bold Sears logo, became a familiar sight on outlying crossroads. Led by Nichols, who was emphatic that "neighborhood" groceries, meat markets, and drugstores need be clustered at no less than half-mile intervals, landscape architects casually integrated the park-and-shop arrangement in planned subdivisions. Located on the "homegoing side" of an arterial boulevard, on the tract's periphery, the shopping center became an anchorage for low-income housing and multiple dwellings as well as a focal point for large acreages of detached homes.

To preserve these inchoate patterns amidst the motorcar's anarchy, suburban developers resorted to zoning. In 1916 Manhattanites had used zoning to prevent the spillover of immigrant garment loft "operatives" into fashionable Fifth Avenue and imposed a "comprehensive" zoning ordinance, the nation's first, on all of New York City. The device epitomized much of the "scientific" rationalism and "business efficiency" of progressive reform. Adherents explained that every metropolis contained areas "naturally" meant for exclusive industrial, commercial, or residential functions. Once these "zones" were identified, overall restrictions on building height, bulk, and use would protect and enhance their "natural" development. The idea's chief apostle, Flatbush lawyer Edward M. Bassett, advised local enthusiasts across the country, compiled digests of legal decisions, and publicized model zoning codes. He resolved to protect the wholesome, "old-fashioned village center" against the onslaught of the autoborne metropolis and its "garages and filling stations," and championed the single, detached home on a generous garden plot against its mortal enemy, "the out-of-place apartment house." His convictions had legions of supporters. "A single-house region," observed George C. Whipple, in a typical pamphlet, *Zoning and Health*, sponsored by the Massachusetts Federation of Planning Boards, "once infected with an apartment house tends to accumulate other apartments, and the neighborhood tends to change from a stable, home-owning population to a shifting, renting class, a class lacking in neighborliness and civic pride and leading an impoverished family life." If they belonged anywhere in the suburbs, apartment houses had to be relegated to major traffic arteries or next to industrial plants to enable factory workers to walk to their jobs. Zoning in many new suburbs gave legal sanction to realtors already inclined to prohibit prewar places of idle amusement from residential streets. Away went barber-shops, luncheonettes, candy stores, garages, poolrooms, and cheap movie houses—banished to thoroughfares zoned "commercial" on the edges of subdivisions. Here, as well, Bassett argued against casual business clutter. A "freeway" he defined as a "strip of land dedicated to *movement* over which the abutting owner has no right of light, air, or access," a concept vital to the emerging view of the "bypass highway."

Prohibition campaigns, housing reforms, and planning, all were absorbed by the new interest in zoning, the most ingenious guarantor of the new segregated life-style. Only thirty-five American municipalities adopted comprehensive zoning ordinances up to 1920, while 438 joined the trend in the next five years. Scarsdale enacted New York State's first suburban law in 1922. Three years later, when builders applied to the Town Zoning Board for a "variance" to erect multiple dwellings with stores near the railroad station, the Scarsdale Board, with Bassett's help, denied the move and successfully fought the encroachment in the courts. New Jersey communities such as Englewood, Hackensack, and Montclair used zoning to keep large Negro populations in well-defined multiple-dwelling reserves. In Nutley, a suburban village up the Passaic between Paterson and Newark, an ordinance contested a Greek immigrant's opening of a fruit stand in a "residential" section. While the Nutley code stumbled in the State Supreme Court, the New Jersey League of Municipalities carried on the struggle and put a state-wide enabling ordinance on the ballot, a referendum which the voters approved in 1927. By the late twenties, cities, already well girdled by low-density communities, were ringed as well by suburban zoning laws and new ·ad hoc suburban interest groups. Organizations surrounding New York City included: the Fairfield County Planning Association, the Westchester County Planning Federation, the Passaic Planning Association, the Essex County Zoning Conference, and the Bergen County League of Municipalities. They eschewed any earlier sentimentalism about regional interdependence and working-class "model tenements" in favor of hard-nosed lobbying and legal fights to uphold the zoning settlement.

The Commerce Department's Division of Building and Housing, joining forces with local groups, emerged as the chief co-ordinator of the movement toward subdivision control. The Division distributed proven house designs and model structural specifications to modernize builders' practices. With Secretary Herbert Hoover's enthusiastic approval, it supported "Better Homes for America," a nationwide federation of five thousand neighborhood improvement clubs aimed at upgrading the suburban enviornment and encouraging the building of "sound, beautiful, single-family houses." Zoners recognized the Division as their "official headquarters," from which flowed a raft of model ordinances and pamphlets, as well as Bassett's legal digests. Its surveys of local zoning and planning codes accurately charted their national spread. The fitting climax to these efforts to control and plan for the new automobile communities was President Hoover's Conference on Home Building and Home Ownership in 1931. By then, however, the Wall Street collapse had frozen further residential construction. Metropolitan Cleveland found itself with 375,000 lots, 45 per cent of them empty. Overzealous real estate activity had given Detroit 1,250,000 lots, enough for the population of three Motor Cities. Within several spring seasons, depression weeds had grown tall enough to cover stakes pounded in with such hope months before.

The outward rush after World War II has largely obscured the slow incremental process which suburbanized a seventh of the population during the century before 1930. To some the whole process seemed a formless chaos; a "wilderness of suburbs" was Lewis Mumford's plaintive critique in 1921. For all the apparent formlessness, the chaotic free market in housing, the in-dividualism which dictated home buyers' decisions, the suburbs have long shown a surprising degree of communal control and forethought. By the late twenties, at the crest of this first great advance, suburban America had laid down the infrastructure to handle much future growth. Communities had added tangibles like water and sanitary districts, protean shopping centers, and a start at peripheral highways. They had joined to a precocious development of suburban vested interest, a deft use of zoning laws and regional planning conferences. In 1928, one of their own even made it to the White House. Herbert Hoover, staunch champion of the suburban way of life, defeated Al Smith, the Irish-Catholic hope from the expanding metropolis.

BIBLIOGRAPHY

Suburban historiography owes a great debt to the sociologists, particularly Harlan Paul Douglass' *The Suburban Trend* (New York, 1925), which recognized early the heterogeneous nature of suburban communities. The impact of social class behavior is explored in Herbert J. Gans, "Urbanism and Suburbanism as a Way of Life: A Re-evaluation of Definitions," in Arnold Rose, ed., *Human Behavior and Social Processes* (Boston, 1962) and his definitive *The Levittowners: Ways of Life and Politics in a New Suburban Community* (New York, 1967). The crucial "sector" theory of metropolitan expansion is delineated in Homer Hoyt's *The Structure and Growth of Residential Neighborhoods in American Cities* (Washington, 1939). Historians have just recently laid the groundwork for their own suburban analysis. Sam Bass Warner, Jr., *Streetcar Suburbs: The Process of Growth in Boston, 1870–1900* (Cambridge, 1969) brings a startling order to the laissez-faire "wilderness" of expanding Boston. Kenneth T. Jackson has written a perceptive pioneering survey, "The Crabgrass Frontier: 150 Years of Suburban Growth in America," in Raymond A. Mohl and James F. Richardson, eds., *The Urban Experience: Themes in American History* (Belmont, California, 1973). There are some excellent regional histories, including Robert M. Fogelson's institutional study, *The Fragmented Metropolis, Los Angeles, 1850–1930* (Cambridge, 1967); and Richard C. Wade and Harold M. Mayer's indispensable *Chicago* (Chicago, 1969).

No shortage exists, however, of histories of the naive genre, some bittersweet reflections on the passing years and local "worthies," some multitomed "county" histories written for subscription, which poured from the Lewis Historical Publishing Company and similar presses before the First World War. Among the more interesting of the former are: Thomas C. Simonds, *History of South Boston, formerly Dorchester Neck, now Ward XII of the City of Boston* (Boston, 1857); Sidney D. Maxwell, *The Suburbs of Cincinnati, Sketches Historical and Descriptive* (Cincinnati, 1870); S. C. G. Watkins, *Reminiscences of Montclair* (New York, 1929); and Harry Hansen's serene view of one of the most posh communities, *Scarsdale* (New York, 1954). *The Autobiography of Edward M. Bassett* (New York, 1939) gives a mellow glimpse of suburban Brooklyn by the pioneer zoner. To these should be added a growing list of doctoral studies: Arthur E. LeGacy, "Improvers and Preservers: A History of Oak Park, Illinois, 1833–1940" (unpublished Ph.D. dissertation, University of Chicago, 1968); Harry A. A. Jebsen, "Blue Island, Illinois; The History of a Work-

ing-Class Suburb" (University of Cincinnati, 1971); and Joel Schwartz, "Community Building on the Bronx Frontier; Morrisania, 1848–1875" (University of Chicago, 1972). The evolving suburban scene can also be glimpsed in the pages of contemporary professional and special-interest magazines: *Country-Side Magazine and Suburban Life, Country Life in America, Landscape Architecture, American City,* and two that closely monitored the switch in transportation developments, *Street Railway Journal* and *Public Roads.*

On changing transit forms, see Glen E. Holt's wry survey, "The Changing Perception of Urban Pathology: An Essay on the Development of Mass Transit in the United States" in Kenneth T. Jackson and Stanley K. Schultz, eds., *Cities in American History* (New York, 1972); George Rogers Taylor's analysis of antebellum innovations, "The Beginnings of Mass Transportation in Urban America," *Smithsonian Journal of History,* I (1966). U. S. Bureau of the Census, *Special Reports on Street and Electric Railways* (Washington, 1902) provides a wealth of statistics and commentary on the streetcar revolution. The forces behind highway development in the twentieth century are outlined in American Association of State Highway Officials, *A Story of the Beginning, Purposes, Growth, Activities and Achievements of the AASHO* (Washington, 1964). The highway builders' maturing philosophy is well discussed in W. Brewster Snow, ed., *The Highway and the Landscape* (New Brunswick, 1959).

Several books survey varied motives which pushed the urban-industrial order into the countryside at the end of the nineteenth century. Graham R. Taylor's *Satellite Cities: A Study of Industrial Suburbs* (New York, 1915) is a balanced account of synthetic factory towns, while Stanley Buder has detailed a remorseless paternalism in *Pullman: an Experiment in Industrial Order and Community Planning, 1880–1930* (New York, 1967). Peter Schmitt, *Back to Nature: The Arcadian Myth in Urban America* (New York, 1969) illuminates the intense media campaign to market "the country" for city appetites.

For material on metropolitan government and the annexation movement, see Kenneth T. Jackson's discussion which strikes the right balance between the motives of planners and politicians, "Metropolitan Government Versus Political Autonomy: Politics on the Crabgrass Frontier," in Jackson and Schultz, *Cities in American History*. For Boston, see James A. Merino, "A Great City and Its Suburbs: Attempts to Integrate Metropolitan Boston, 1865–1920" (unpublished Ph.D. dissertation, University of Texas, 1968); for Northern New Jersey: Stuart Galishoff, "The Passaic Valley Trunk Sewer," *New Jersey History*, LXXXVIII (Winter, 1970); and for Los Angeles: Winston W. Crouch and Beatrice Dinerman, *Southern California Metropolis* (Berkeley, 1963), which all stress more the rationalism than the political implications of metropolitan structures. One should not overlook two pioneering surveys of metropolitonism in the twenties: Paul Studenski, *The Government of Metropolitan Areas in the United States* (New York, 1930), and R. D. McKenzie, "The Rise of Metropolitan Communities" in *Recent Social Trends; Report of the President's Research Committee on Social Trends* (New York, 1933).

The suburbanization of the twenties is best seen in the McKenzie article, Douglass' *Suburban Trend*, and the handy statistical compendium, U. S. Bureau of the Census, Fifteenth Census, *Growth of Metropolitan Areas* (Washington, 1932). "Progressive" building and subdividing practices are described in the National Association of Real Estate Boards, *Home Building & Subdividing*, III (Chicago, 1925); President's Conference on Home Building and Home Ownership, *Reports* (Washington, 1931); and Better Homes in America, *Guidebook for Better Homes Campaign* (Washington, 1929). The spread of Los Angeles before and after the automobile age is well documented in Fogelson's *Fragmented Metropolis*. The automobile's impact on retailing is ominously surveyed in U. S. Department of Commerce, *Vehicular Traffic Congestion and Retail Business* (Washington, 1926). For the background of decentralized shopping, see J. C. Nichols, "Mistakes We Have Made in Developing Shopping Centers," Urban Land Institute, *Technical Bulletin No. 4* (August, 1945), and Boris Emmet and John E. Jeuck, *Catalogues and Counters: a History of Sears, Roebuck and Company* (Chicago, 1950).

Two histories of zoning which stress its social-control implications are Stanislaw J. Makielski, *The Politics of Zoning: The New York Experience* (New York, 1960) and Seymour I. Toll, *Zoned American* (New York, 1969). The zoning gospel can best be sampled in Edward M. Bassett, *Buildings: Their Uses and the Spaces About Them* (New York, 1931).

Finally, we should keep in mind that the suburbs are really extensions of downtown forms. Perhaps the best glimpse of the traditional "preindustrial" American town is Benjamin Franklin's *Autobiography*. The elite preserves of eastern cities are discussed in Edward Pessen, *Riches, Class, and Power before the Civil War* (Lexington, Mass., 1973), and of St. Louis, in Scott Mc-

Conachie, "Public Problems and Private Places" (A revised paper first delivered at the Missouri Conference on History, May, 1970). Such fixity should be compared with the extreme geographical mobility discerned by Peter R. Knights, *The Plain People of Boston, 1830–1860: A Study in City Growth* (New York, 1971). Two fascinating discussions of metropolitan expansion divide the nineteenth-century urban world between them: Sam Bass Warner, Jr., *The Private City, Philadelphia in Three Periods of Growth* (Philadelphia, 1968), and Seymour J. Mandelbaum, *Boss Tweed's New York* (New York, 1965).

Planners in the Changing American City, 1900-1940

JOHN L. HANCOCK

THE MODERN CHALLENGE

If *planning* in the broadest sense is man's attempt not to displace reality but to clarify it and bring all of its elements into harmony with human purpose,[1] then the urban planner's task has changed enormously in the past few hundred years. Cities have been uniquely unequal, functional concentrations of such reality since late neolithic times—the nexus of what we call "civilization." But the reality of man's traditional societies is fast disappearing as he learns nature is not just "out there" but is everywhere a constantly modifying state he can partially manipulate to free himself of life chiefly dependent upon human and animal labor. In the emerging transitional societies where growth and change are the normal condition, modern reality finds not just a small percentage of mankind urbanized but a world urbanizing so rapidly that most of the population will be drawn into its orbit in this century. This means great change: not discovery of preconditions for group life, but sustained mechanization, surplus economic growth, and social investment already bringing undreamed material comfort, intensive specialization, fragmentation and "leisure" for a third of the world; not hierarchial social division in segmented if similar containers but egalitarian, pragmatically interwoven diversity; not fatalistic acceptance of one's lot but "rising

expectations."[2] It means demand for new balances of community, wealth, health, beauty, privacy, identity and so on, promoting not only cultural survival, adaptability and modification, but also human enrichment. In such fluid times a "plan" is tyranny and no planning is madness. Planning becomes an agent *for enhancing life* in an ever-changing but massing world—or it is nothing.

In this context, planning's alignment with American urban policy appropriately began with AIP's charter members in the reform decade before World War I, when the nation first confronted its "new" converging culture. The city, they said, was physically urbanized but not democratically organized. "There seems to be a sort of fatalism in American cities which compels them to follow mechanically a system once inaugurated no matter what it may be," an uncontrolled spread of cities "unusually inconvenient, insanitary, wasteful, ugly, degrading, inefficient."[3] They were not the first to say so; but in adopting reformer views of cities as dynamic *human* systems whose welfare could be partially guided and enhanced by willful public action, they were the first to propose that the means include "the new social ideal of unified and comprehensive city planning."[4] Reinforced by events to 1940, the pioneer planners were instrumental in making their ambitious proposal the very essence of modern American urban policy—in theory. In fact, however, while they had

From *Journal of the American Institute of Planners*, Vol. XXXIII, No. 5 (September 1967), pp. 290-304. Reprinted by permission of the publisher.

found the proper focus for our times, their record in developing it through several decades of reform and change exposes still unreconciled social aims and cultural practices in urban America.

THE AMERICAN CITY
SURFACE, 1800-1940

Historic American civilization is a classic example of continuing surface change. Following the initial breakdown of traditional western society, the United States prospered in material growth and suffered much societal displacement in the 15 generations separating colonial clearings from the cities of 1900. As compared to 1790, the nation was 19 times more populous, had 72 times as many urban places (doubling per decade in the period 1840-70 when manufacturing's value began exceeding agriculture's in the gross national product), covered a domain three times as large crossed in 102 hours by train or minutes by wire. It had attained the world's highest mean (not minimum) living standard, the highest population growth rate (1800-1910) and perhaps the most blurred socially mobile society.

In the profession's early years to 1940, the GNP would quadruple again; urban places and wages double; the average work week reduce a full day; cross-country travel time reduce to a day; public works spending would extend from transportation and communication to utilities, reclamation-conservation, streets-highways, and housing-community development. Urban space needs would more than double and keep changing in character as innovations like the automobile (the largest industry by 1929) helped stimulate the construction industry (next largest), and altered town form and the whole technological net.[5]

Yet amid bountiful natural, technological, and human resources, the American *manner* of settlement and the values associated with it were profoundly disruptive, especially before the 1900's. Under pragmatically developing Crown and federal encouragement of towns "Fittest for such as can trade into England" and "for a rising nation, spread over a wide and fruitful land, traversing all the seas with the rich productions of her industry . . . advancing rapidly to destinies beyond the mortal eye," urban policy was merely commercial-expansionist, permitting any local standards and practices not in conflict with mercantile contracts or democratic constitutions from which the towns derived their charters. Thus, all cities were political wards of Crown and then states, which were loathe to broaden local powers but encouraged *de facto* sources of growth. The cities all flourished according to their ability to secure external power, market, and supply. All were dominated by profit-minded oligarchies following "settle and sell, settle and sell" boom-bust practices in pursuing growth at whatever social costs. In Andrew Carnegie's words, "The American . . . need not fear the unhealthy or abnormal growth of cities. . . . The free play of economic laws is keeping all quite right. . . . Oh, these grand, immutable, all-wise laws of natural forces, how perfectly they work if human legislators would only let them alone."[6] Most did, while pursuing happiness by a reversed golden rule.

In this narrow milieu, environmental needs—civic, health, family, personal, and so forth—were subordinated to developmental ones, usually economic, in the carrying through of "city plans" too. The fact that Savannah's plan was so rigidly maintained by her philanthropist sponsors in England despite resident demands for change (they were forbidden to sell or even to profit from the land, for example) suggests in part why she was the least prosperous, least populous colonial city by the Revolution. In contrast, Philadelphia, desiccating her "greene countrie towne" plan, became the largest, most influential commercial city in the colonies and early Republic. Similarly, planning in the best of several hundred proprietor towns built between 1775 and 1906 fell apart in a generation by inability or unwillingness of the sponsors to control peripheral or later internal growth as at Lowell, whereas those paternalists who maintained planning control but failed to anticipate or permit resident desires to flourish economically and politically suffered a similar fate in town development. (As Richard Ely said of Pullman, "It is a benevolent, all-wishing feudalism which desires the happiness of the people in such a way as shall please the authorities.") Thus American developers characteristically rejected comprehensive plans altogether and used an exploitable grid core of streets and plats—in all 50 of the SMA's of 1900 and 95 per cent of today's metro cores. The common pattern in some 200 such cities by 1900 was of identical lots, 20 to 40 per cent substandard housing with dense tenantry near the center, long before the elevator and steel frame made it so dramatic. There were few permanent open spaces or neighborhood foci. There was grade-level high speed movement on main streets well before rapid transit and cars quadrupled urban travel (1890-1920), preferential location for high-paying commercial-industrial functions, permissive public controls (little municipal land ownership), sprawling peripheral growth—these were

all superimposed on unaesthetic "once-for-all" plans without adequate provision for systematic revision or extension in advance of settlement.[7] Simple to lay out, describe, convert to many uses, and extend, the stark grid of public-private origins unquestionably was yesterday's most adaptable American plan—a meritorious one for limited purposes.

Thus, the booming city did not arise from the culture floor while our backs were turned and we were tending our gardens. As an emergent development *process*, however, it bespoke the futility of rigid *a priori* and *laissez-faire* approaches or the abnegation of direction for fluid situations—and the difficulty of trying anything else.

PRESSURE FOR REORGANIZATION AND REFORM

The haphazard physical growth and social disorder accompanying American urban development, however, stimulated increasing demands for amenity, systematic physical reorganization and social reform which preceded and helped shape the modern planning movement. Physical design by the nineteenth century's new architects and landscape architects, for example, gradually assumed "comprehensive dimension, moving beyond the context of *unit* into that of *system*." Public gardens appeared about the time that Timothy Dwight urged places where "inhabitants might always find sweet air, charming walks, fountains refreshing the atmosphere, trees encircling the sun . . . objects 'found' in the country" (1821); naturalistic suburbs and *cul-de-sac* streets by the 1830's; in-city parks by the 1850's; boulevards and garden towns, idyllic leisure-class resorts and planned industrial communities by the 1870's; metropolitan park systems by the 1890's and civic centers by the 1900's. The "utopian" Mormons put 49 agricultural-industrial satellite communities around Salt Lake City using cooperative public-private methods to establish their broad streets, superblocks focused on major cultural buildings, and reclamation of a theocratic region covering the most desolate third of the nation before federal intervention. Indeed, Robert Gourlay even recommended that the Boston "district" adopt a "science of city planning" implemented by existing public powers for large-scale land reclamation, separation of major localities by green areas, and rail ties to the hub. This was a generation before Horace Bushnell (1864), urging a "new city planning profession" of specially trained men to devise "breathing spaces" without inhibiting future needs, asked why the city should "be left to the misbegotten planning of some operator totally disqualified? . . . Nothing is to be more regretted . . . than that our American nation, having a new world to make, and a clean map on which to place it, should be sacrificing our advantage so cheaply. . . ."

More characteristic of the mainstream was designer-booster collaboration on the "city beautiful" at the Chicago world's fair (1893) whose neoclassical plan, reflecting pools, greenstrips, statuary, massive buildings, macadem roads, electrification, and hidden utilities well illustrated coordinator Daniel Burnham's remark that "Beauty has always paid better than any other commodity." Convinced that physical order equalled social order, viewers went home to plan more fairs and to plant, paint, clean, and partially rebuild their cities. The

first was Washington itself which, under the McMillan Commission, secured a Park Commission (1895); District Highway Plan (1896); the first enforceable (but not enforced) building heights and zoning laws (1899); a Planning Committee under Burnham, Frederick Law Olmsted, Sr., and others (1901); and "mapped streets" (1900-06).[8] There were just a few such works before 1900, however, most of them backed by wealthy private sponsors rarely able to continue such revitalization by themselves.

The social reformers' broader search was similar in its increasing comprehensiveness and expertise. Theodore Parker advocated planned "industrial democracy" featuring low-rent housing, and improved work and health standards in the 1830's, a generation before organized civic interest in tenement reform, public health, and migrant population control (encouraging "normal distribution in town and country," reduction of urban densities, and so on—a kind of stay-on-the-land movement in contrast to the unsuccessful "back-to-the-land" resettlement efforts of the 1900-1940 period). After the Civil War a rising chorus of voices rose with those of Henry George and Edward Bellamy to promote an "economizing of social forces"; with "Golden Rule" Jones, other reform mayors and the National Municipal League (1894) to obtain more democratic local government; and with those of Richard Ely, Simon Patten, Albion Small, and others in a few universities to secure serious urban study and research on the "new America." On the grand scale perhaps, Henry D. Lloyd (lawyer, social critic, administrator, and teacher) put many of these ideas together in his proposal to raze and transform central Chicago into a permanent cultural park focus for a regional "No Mean City" of self-contained urban-rural towns built on the latest garden city, cooperative, condemnation, and electrification methods in 1899.[9]

The merger of these interests with the more prosaic, somewhat remedial, but decidedly militant national reforms of the next generation signaled the real beginning of responsible social change in modern America. The period's very name—the *progressive era*, 1906-16 (variously dated 1900-19)—indicated the demand for orderly forward transition to a world of "social justice," "social welfare," and, as John Dewey said of the era's greatest challenge, "the possibility of constructive social engineering." It demanded that these assume primacy in the quest for human progress. The ideological response to the popular demands was a clear YES.[10] The measureable results were basic change in mood and a small but crucial reorganization of mixed-enterprise democracy, which has since broadened in scale if not purpose.

THE PROFESSION EMERGES, 1907-19

The mood and means were of vital significance to the planning profession. Progressive Republicans, reform Democrats, Socialists, and nonpartisans who had led in securing state-legislated local government changes, such as home rule, new charters, reapportionment, and so forth, also brought in the first "expert planning advisors" to lecture, show slides of work elsewhere, and in several hundred cases to survey and/or replan their cities—to show people how to rebuild cities. Given the city's increasing predominance, a *laissez-faire* past more blundering than purposeful in human

terms, and faith that man must plan (though no one really knew how) in times changing more rapidly than anyone comprehended, the era's mandate for renewal fairly cried for a new profession of urban specialists. Was the mandate important? In Franklin D. Roosevelt's words on first hearing of planning (1909), "I think from that moment on I have been interested in not the mere planning of a single city but in the larger aspects of planning. It is the way of the future."[11]

Aside from a few inspiring piecemeal reports prior to 1906, there were no surveys, general planning, or professional planners as such, and as John Nolen later recalled, "no knowledge of, no interest in city planning among the people generally." Between 1907 and 1917 over 100 towns undertook "comprehensive planning"—half the 50 largest cities, 13 per cent of all with populations over 10,000. Ninety-seven municipal planning commissions and two dozen zoning codes were enabled in a few urban states. By 1917 there were dozens of municipal information clearing houses, a shelf of technical literature, and three planning-oriented magazines "to record knowledge of intelligently and earnestly and systematically planned cities" and "the history of municipal science in the making." Eleven universities offered 23 courses on planning "principles" (subordinated to other curricula); two others gave courses on the "Economics of City Planning" and "Urban Sociology." There were four annual urban conferences (one devoted specifically to planning) plus an international meeting, planning divisions in the other design professions, and an American City Planning Institute. By the war's end practically every urban interest group in the country called for an urban cabinet post or a "Federal Bureau of Municipal Information" collating and distributing "all urban information . . . instead of confining it solely to planning."[12] The art and science of planning as a force in urban reform policies was clearly underway, then, in the progressive era.

The pivotal inaugural year was 1909 when the first National Conference on City Planning and the Problems of Congestion convened at Washington with representatives from health, housing, law, social work, engineering, gardening, real estate, government, philanthrophy, conservation, architecture, landscape architecture, and so on, all calling for reform. Supported thereafter by the Russell Sage Foundation, NCCP (last part of title having been dropped in 1910) became the chief forum for bringing the movement's emergent elements together and broadcasting them in its publications (for example, City Plan, 1915). It met in different cities each year (in Washington once during each new administration). Most importantly for the new profession, NCCP's executive and program committees were dominated by planners who used this forum to fashion their common social commitments and systematic technical approaches into a viable pattern for urban redevelopment. "What is needed in city planning?" asked Nolen, the 1909 keynoter:

Everything . . . a wiser husbanding of our aesthetic and human as well as natural resources . . . legislation that meets more meaningfully the needs of twentieth century life . . . using to our advantage science, art, skill and experience. . . . [but above all] We should no longer be content with mere increases in population and wealth. We should insist upon asking, "How do the people live, where do they work, what do they play?"

In 1910 NCCP president Frederick Law Olmsted, Jr., called this approach "the new social ideal of unified and comprehensive city planning":

City planning, applied with common sense and with due regard for human limitations of time and place, has a breadth and ramification at once inspiring and appalling. Any mind with sufficient imagination to grasp it must be stimulated by this conception of the city as one great social organism whose welfare is in part determined by the action of the people who compose the organism today, and therefore by the collective intelligence and good will that control those actions.

By 1911 president Charles Mulford Robinson called it the "science of city planning"—a decided shift from his earlier views (see Modern Civic Art, 1903). Beautification was not discussed as a major NCCP topic between 1910-20 but "planning" (rather than "plan" or "plan-making"), "system," "efficient and intelligent public controls," the "ordinary citizen," and the "common welfare" became commonplace in the idiom. Remarkably free of dogma, the planners were chiefly interested in "comprehensive planning." They discussed it as a major topic in seven of the meetings between 1910-20 along with continuing discussion of its "elements": financing and administration, zoning-planning law, and official commission practices; streets, transportation, industrial, recreation and land planning; "limited dividend" (4 per cent) low-cost housing (public-private); minimum standards (some via "model" studies); the merits of particular plans and useful European practices.[13] Finally, as the war began, they created the American City Planning Institute, a professional division within NCCP whose object "shall be to study the science and advance the art of city planning." ACPI gave full membership to trained professionals and to "others who shall have special attainments in city planning," associate membership with voting privileges to related non-professionals (no more than four of whom could sit on the 21-man Board of Governors) and a few (rare) honorary memberships.[14]

The systematization of these elements was a gradual process, of course. James Sturgis Pray introduced his seminal "Principles of City Planning" class into the landscape curriculum at Harvard in 1909, the year that Patrick Abercrombie opened the School of Civic Design at Liverpool. Benjamin Marsh's textbook *Introduction to City Planning* the same year urged government responsibility ("the most important element") for the common health and welfare, stressed housing, and termed planning "the most efficient method of projecting municipal efficiency." The planners got a most vital new perspective and preplanning tool from Shelby Harrison and Paul Kellogg's *Pittsburgh Survey* (1907-09, published 1914), whiched mapped data on population, traffic, health, housing, building (location-condition-use), property values, assessments, areas served by schools, and so on. It also appended legal-fiscal suggestions for public planning from such data. On the other hand, the most famous planning report of 1909 was Daniel Burnham and Edward Bennett's magnificently rendered, vaguely regional *Plan of Chicago*, which "quite frankly takes into consideration the fact that the American city, and Chicago preeminently, is a center of industry and traffic." It merely saluted housing needs, termed planning inexpensive (not requiring large public expenditure, taxation, or public control) but stressed

(and proved) that "aroused public sentiment; and practical men of affairs" could secure new traffic, park, and building programs giving "unity and dignity" to the city.[15]

Most comprehensive reports and several texts incorporated all these elements into the planning process by 1916. The reports, for example, generally had three major parts—preplanning surveys (mapping of physical, economic, and social data), a "General Plan" with detailed parts, and appended methods of implementation. Sometimes the latter were put into the main text for emphasis. Some surveys included evidence of the city's historic "individuality" (its achievements and deficiencies in land use, for example) so that planner and public alike might "frame a concept, an ideal of what we wish the city to be" and make it a controlling factor in the plan's development. Most specific suggestions for implementation urged better employment of existing law, more home rule and degrees of municipal authority approaching those in Europe. Few suggested planning was inexpensive or short term. ("At bottom the question is whether real values are to be had from this sort of city planning, and whether the community can provide the ways and means necessary to purchase these values.") Most spoke of spending efficiently and the major reports encouraged "equitable distribution of current taxes," increased borrowing capacity, extended bonded periods, municipal condemnation "with a much larger share for the community in increasing land values," and special tax and land incentives to encourage large-scale, low-cost housing development. No two plans were alike but the basic idea was to modernize and broaden public uses by opening up and decentralizing the city where possible so as to promote environments "having a more sensitive regard for the common welfare . . . past, present and future."

Recommendations thus included differentiated building zones and street flow, overall circulatory flow, landscaped "gateways" (such as waterfronts) for public uses, park systems covering "at least 10 per cent of the city area," rerouting or elimination of grade-level transit traffic (transit systems were encouraged in larger cities), economic "zones" (blocks) but mixed income neighborhoods (new ones grouped in park-like settings around shops or schools on the city's edges to further break the grid and reduce unplanned encroachment), downtown core of facilities, and rather formal civic groupings from which major streets radiated to the various sub-centers.[16] In a more abstract, technical manner, Robinson's *City Planning* detailed thoroughfare and residential platting standards in advance of settlement; Nelson Lewis' *Planning the Modern City* concentrated on traffic circulation and control standards, drawing heavily from his experience with New York's influential "building districts" (zoning) report; NML's *Town Planning for Small Cities* by Charles Bird (manufacturer and major Progressive Party figure in Massachusetts) recommended the reorganization of several towns of 30,000 people or less into regional districts by garden city planning principles; and NML's *City Planning* (1917) by 18 authors under Nolen, brought all such "Essential Elements of a City Plan" into one text spelling out "lines of investigation, planning and control which have been found most sound in theory and most successful in practice." These texts emphasized planning's flexibility and al-

ternatives, suggesting minimums for local work but discouraging universal, textbook solutions. They simultaneously looked toward "scientific exactness." As George Ford said in his essay on the socioeconomic factors in planning:

Satisfactory methods can be arrived at only by applying modern scientific methods. It is now realized that the city is a complex organism, so complex that no doctor is safe in prescribing for it unless he has made a thorough-going and impartial diagnosis of everything that may have even the remotest bearing on the case.[17]

If there was a definite system in this work by 1917, however, there was as yet more hope than adequate empirical data for making meaningful generalizations for this inexact science.

Who were the collaborators? All were originally trained in other fields; some formed temporary teams or permanent offices for major projects (like Ford and E. P. Goodrich's Technical Advisory Corporation). Several were Europeans working extensively in North America (like Edward Bennett, Thomas Adams, and Werner Hegemann). The 18 NML authors, for example, were almost all urban-born, lectured in the universities, wrote extensively, traveled abroad regularly, and half had worked or studied (half having at least one degree from Harvard or MIT) under men whose work was largely done before ACPI was formed. By training, their breakdown into two architects, four lawyers, five landscape architects, six engineers, a realtor, a civic reform leader, and a professor of social ethics (housing specialist) parallels that of ACPI's original 75-man roster in the first two membership categories—10 architects, 12 lawyers, 18 landscape architects, 23 engineers, 6 realtors and 7 others—with leadership unevenly divided. (Beginning with Olmsted, Sr., most ACPI presidents through 1942 were originally trained in landscape architecture or engineering.) While questions of training, ethics and leadership were frequent, however, all agreed that a "planner" was defined by his experience and focus, not by special training.[18]

In 1917 when the mood was much greater than the means for planning, actual practices were very primitive, even those that were official. Judging from 250 accounts, the work usually began with a lecture or preplanning survey of needs and opportunities in which the planner sought local support —public or private (usually a civic or commercial group, occasionally a wealthy patron). If mutually agreeable, a contract was signed making the planner responsible for all plan preparations and the sponsor responsible for eventual adoption and enforcement. This step often involved forming a larger "amalgamated" citizen group to clarify goals, assist the technical staff, review detail proposals, secure an official commission with "advisory powers," and push for planning throughout the city. During the next two to three years, field representatives collected data, encouraged the movement, reported back on its pulse, and sometimes lived in the area. The home office made all basic decisions, did the final drafting, and then presented the general program for local acceptance after an appropriate publicity program. If the plan was adopted, the planner also encouraged implementation, periodic review and cooperation with other communities (particularly contiguous ones) in the urban region. His firm often performed partial services as well—having contracts for park systems, subdivisions, campuses, industrial districts, housing programs, addi-

tional surveys not followed up and so on. The Nolen office (the largest firm between 1915 and 1925), for example, had contracts in 200 cities of which 10 were for new towns and 29 for comprehensive replanning rather evenly distributed in five basic groupings from towns of 10,000 or less to metropolitan areas of 1.5 million people or more. Less than half of the plans were implemented, a third of these with any degree of fullness—a fair average in the whole period to 1940.[19]

The climax of these early activities was the federal "emergency" wartime housing-town planning program, finally combining the expertise, standards, aims, large resources *and* public powers necessary for realization. Planner-directed teams collaborated on 67 projects averaging 25 acres in size, abandoned the grid and alleys where possible, introduced the latest technical standards, sought harmonious variety (house styles and groupings, plantings, street patterns, and so forth), preserved natural features, developed the land in large pieces to avoid economic waste and to increase pedestrian convenience, and grouped major buildings to give "definite center and point to the whole design." They did such an excellent job from the resident's point of view that there was a waiting line for purchase or occupancy up to World War II, while Congress and realtors called them "too costly" for war workers and disbanded the incompleted experiment with alacrity at the war's end. As Olmsted, Jr., saw "the very valuable lesson":

We have been convinced not only theoretically but by practical experience, that the cooperation of all those who have special knowledge in the arrangement, construction and running of towns is essential to any real "town planning" and that it is perfectly possible to bring about the cooperation and to apply it efficiently in actual work.

For many of the younger collaborators too, this experience provided "a tremendous enthusiasm to build a new and better world," as Clarence Stein said of himself and Henry Wright.[20]

Thus, the profession had taken some long first steps by 1919, even if they were steps that needed more complete public authorization and more versatile and imaginative planner conceptualization by today's standards. There were definite physical changes too,—a park system, a low-cost housing program, better circulation, an active public agency, occasionally all of these in one city—but, most importantly, there was a new intent behind this work, a new standard of measurement. As Harland Bartholomew put it in 1917, "The welfare of the group is . . . now generally considered to supercede the *rights of the individual* when questions of health, safety and general welfare arise."[21]

FLUX AND FLOW, 1920-40
But moods change, as was indicated in the sharp tensions distinguishing urbanization's spread in the period 1920-40. Bracketed by wars, the opening years assumed "prosperity" and "normalcy" obtained with minimal public direction, while the latter ones affirmed—perhaps conclusively—the lie in merely voluntary subscription to modern social responsibilities and again advanced broadly empowered public-private unions to enhance, if not insure, them. Influenced by both attitudes, the profession's markedly improved technical, legislative, and conceptual approaches to urban, regional, and national problems were more theoretical than tested until the mid-1930's.

Cities which had begun planning earlier were quickest to resume and expand. Major reports now commonly included more sophisticated handling of social data, zoning and land use maps (late 1930's), capital improvement budgets (late 1920's), and detail and alternate plan proposals within the "Master Plan"—the new name for general or comprehensive plans. They were increasingly supported by empirical research in the profession (see for example the *Harvard City Planning Series*, 1931 ff.), the social sciences and federal reports making possible more exacting scientific generalizations. *But the record and manner of public acceptance in the 1920's was no better or essentially different, however "official."* Approximately one-fifth of the thousand city planning, zoning and housing reports made in this decade—three times as many as in the preceding one—were actually followed through to any degree; over 95 per cent of the general plans made were by private firms, though now generally under city contract. Most firms were larger. They periodically revised survey and planning data, sometimes left a field man as local commission head, dropped mixed transportation recommendation (for example, rapid transit) in favor of automated traffic planning almost exclusively, and perhaps under pressure to be "practical" said less about the common welfare in adjusting to what clients would accept. Typical of the general case, according to several studies, the largest firm (Bartholomew Associates, after 1925) dropped housing altogether (1923-36), obscured the priority of community over private rights, emphasized physical elements alone, and fitted local situations to general standards (for example, population, density, traffic projection) which were sometimes not flexible enough to suit rapid modern changes, although its chief remained critical of these trends (except the last) "outside the confines of his business contracts."[22]

An era affects its planners then, as everyone else. (Even Walter Lippmann wrote in 1927 that "the more or less unconscious and unplanned activities of businessmen are for once more novel, more daring and in general more revolutionary than the theories of the progressives." *Men of Destiny*. New York: Macmillan, 1927.) Consider the permissively drawn and coordinated legislative "progress." By 1935 every state had planning, zoning, plat control, or all of these written into its organic law. Public planning commissions rose from 297 in 1919 to be included in all but two of the larger cities (over 100,000 people) plus hundreds of others by 1934—95 per cent of them official, the reverse of 1919. But only a fifth had comprehensive plans, few were applying them, most were powerless advisory bodies composed of citizens often serving without pay or understanding. Massachusetts, the first state to require planning commissions (1913) had 97 by 1929, but 80 cities, including Boston, still lacked plans. Before the court approved Euclid Village's comprehensive zoning code (building and land use, height-bulk-density in "reasonable" and "substantial" relation to community safety, health, welfare, and "morals") in 1926, only 76 cities had zoning ordinances. By 1936, 1,322 or 85 per cent of the cities had them, but less than half were comprehensive, and the cities (not compelled to zone) often used them to perpetuate *status quo* discrimination and whim. Extra-territorial plat control (up to five miles, based on ACPI guidelines) permitted planning along topographical as well as jurisdictional lines in half the states by 1929,

but only a few cities adopted it, almost none in conformance with master plans. Planners approved the potential significance of these legal developments but protested their loose application and the tendency to adopt zoning *in lieu of* planning. Realtors, however, were enthusiastic after some initial doubts and real estate actually emerged as "the last great individualistic American enterprise" long after industry and finance had become large-scale, mixed corporate operations. Indeed into the early depression, national administrations urged Americans to "lay plans for making plans," provided occasional models and left everything else to local good will because "at present . . . this phrase represents a social need rather than a social capacity." Thus implementation and coordination were difficult at best, apathy was common, and expediency certain. The result, in Thomas Adams' phrase, was "city-mending."[23]

Partly because of such frustrations amid growing needs, the profession did sharpen its training, roles, and theories. With programs still subordinated to other curricula in the 80 schools (1925) offering or requiring planning courses, Harvard initiated a master's degree in Landscape Architecture in City Planning, published *City Planning Quarterly* (forerunner of the *Journal*) in 1925, and, with a Rockefeller Foundation grant, inaugurated a full three-year School of City Planning under Henry Hubbard in 1929. Columbia, Cornell, and MIT also granted the MCP degree by 1940. In courses the planner's "role" was now described as analyst, creative artist, critic, and coordinator having

above all . . . the social and civic welfare point of view, for the motive back of all city and regional planning is to improve the daily life and working conditions—to develop the "good life" . . . a difficult and elaborate process . . . [requiring] the wisdom of Solomon, the heart of a prophet, the patience of Job, and the hide of a rhinoceros.

In the new civil service category of "city planner" (created for the National Capitol Park and Planning Commission with ACPI help in 1926), the role demanded a man or woman (age 25-55) university graduate in landscape architecture with "at least five years of responsible and successful experience" or equivalent scholarship to head a staff preparing plans, recommendations, and regulations for an awesome number of physical "and other proper elements of city and regional planning." (Charles Eliot II received the first appointment.) The profession's growing belief that this was an increasingly specialized task may be seen in its exclusion of the new profession of public administrators from ACPI membership in 1924 and, as the renamed American Institute of Planners, its total separation from NCCP in 1934. NCCP (also keeping administrators off its executive board) then merged with ACA to become the American Planning and Civic Association, and the administrators formed under Walter Blucher (1935) into the American Society of Planning Officials. Thus, a mixed urban alliance divided into four rather specialized policy groups (including NML), with planners the only group eligible for all four memberships.[24]

The profession's most notable innovations in this period, however, had to do with broadening the concept of man's environment, its future and its planning. Adding psycho-biological to the earlier socioeconomic considerations of well-being, the enlarged views held that the search for and growth of individuality and diversity were as vital to existence in massing society as commonality of rights and opportunities. Refusing to plan from statistical projections or the noblest historic examples alone, the planners became less harsh in their blending of scientific and humanistic wisdom, perhaps less certain about future needs but certainly much concerned with the importance of the immediate, of what happens today, in getting there. Thus, Lewis Mumford urged NCCP in 1927 to develop "new social instruments and policies on a regional rather than an urban scale" which did not lead merely to more mechanized or congested cities. The planner's idiom increasingly contained such metaphors as "symbiosis," "human-scale," and "flow" (Mumford); the natural region," and "living" rather than "making a living" (Benton MacKaye); "excessive concentration [not as synonymous with congestion but] . . . as a psychological as well as economic and physical problem," and having "a more natural biological life under pleasanter and more natural conditions . . . to enjoy life itself." (Nolen)[25]

Several dozen elaborate experimental studies and abbreviated works resulted from these emphases. For example, Arthur Comey proposed "city-state" planning for three major cities joined by "interstate" freeways and arterial routes to surrounding towns, all separated by greenbelts, with population growth "automatically controlled" along the freeways until the region's "natural" limits had been reached. MacKaye preferred a smaller optimum-size (50,000 people each), "regional" city exercising conservation (natural, technical, human) and "commodity-flow" control in concert with requirements of other area foci. Several thick-volumed metropolitan, state, and regional studies by large staffs of planners, social scientists and officials defined joint public-private means for removing destructive socio-physical agents. They laid down advance guidelines according to natural or actual settlement instead of by arbitrary politics or economic expediency, clarified project priorities and area relationships, and prepared master plans as guides to the area's overall needs not as substitutes for local planning and development. All believed regions were the logical modern contexts for coordinating local and national priorities, although of course these reports lacked official sanction or enablement, as they generally still do. Similar principles were employed in the development of new towns and housing projects, notably those by the City Housing Corporation and Regional Planning Association of America (Stein, Wright, Mumford, MacKaye, Fritz Malcher, and others), whose superblocks, "steady-flow" traffic, greenbelts, and grouped housing arrangements sought stability, sociability, diversity, and (with proper enforcement and subsidized building methods) blight prevention. Failing to attract industry, technological interest in mass-housing, or private investors able to sustain the large initial costs and low unit profits, however, none of the period's 63 new towns (36 in the 1920's) was finished as planned. "Farm-city" and other rural resettlement proposals of the 1920's were not even constructed until the New Deal (and not really successfully then). And almost all of these "new towns" in city or country became half-finished upper-income suburbs little different in effect (not design) from ordinary ones[26]— going to people who already had more blessings, sunshine, and cultural insularity than anyone else.

The depression, however, made planning not only fashionable again but also imperative under the New Deal.

Whereas Hoover pursued *recovery* using government's "reserve powers" to protect citizens against "forces beyond their control," Roosevelt also undertook programs for permanent *reform* on the broadest possible front, using these powers very pragmatically in the search for ways to renovate the whole cultural fabric. To guide them, he said in a popular explanation, "The time called for and still calls for planning." Indeed, as he told Congress that same year (1934):

I look forward to the time in the not too distant future, when annual appropriations, wholly covered by current revenue, will enable the work to proceed with a national *plan*. Such a plan will, in a generation or two, return many times the money spent on it; more important it will eliminate the use of inefficient tools, conserve and increase national resources, prevent waste, and enable millions of our people to take better advantage of the opportunities which God has given our country.[27]

Roosevelt (whose uncle Frederick Delano was a charter NCCP member) got many, if not most, such ideas directly from the profession. For example, upon entering office he canvassed a National Land Use Planning Committee (including ACPI members Alfred Bettman, Jacob Crane, Nolen, and Eliot II) "with reference to the technique of making planning effective." From their recommendations for a federal agency for national planning policy, research, and administration came the short-lived Civil Works Administration (1933-34), whose 10,000 employees made state and local surveys and plan studies, among other things. Another result was the seminal, *ex-officio* National Planning Board (renamed the National Resources Board in 1934, the National Resources Committee in 1935-36, and the National Resources Planning Board until Congress disbanded it in 1943). It unofficially reviewed all public policy on natural, industrial and human resources, served as a "permanent long-range commission" for research, planning, and co-ordinating of related private-public development; gathered the most complete data on American resources assembled through 1943; and lent professional talent and planning advice to whoever wanted it—41 states, 70 counties and regions, 400 towns and cities before 1940.[28]

The New Deal's pragmatic approach did not sweep away the *laissez-faire* past, but its massive planning began early, spanned the period, and seems to have made the difference between national chaos and general crisis—the century's continuing condition. Most development programs came out of the First Hundred Days legislation: NRPB, TVA (to 1937 it included town planning under Earle Draper and Tracy Augur), conservation and public works (CWA, Public Works Administration, and so forth), home financing and improvement (partly inspired by Hoover's Home Loan Bank), housing and slum clearance (PWA's Housing Division under Robert Kohn, Federal Housing Authority 1936, U.S. Housing Authority absorbing all town planning in 1937), and urban-rural resettlement (Subsistence Homesteads and the Greenbelt programs). Four of these programs originated in omnibus bills of 1933. Only NRPB and resettlement—perhaps the most revolutionary programs—failed to be made continuing works. All utilized professional services extensively as many of today's senior planners will attest. All were supported by enormous expenditures as compared to the World War I period (247 millions spent on renewal in 1940, a third of it federal as opposed to one million spent by the federal government in 1917-18), and

all emphasized planning for permanent social improvement this time not omitting that "one-third of a nation ill-housed, ill-clad, and ill-fed." As the Urbanism Committee described the "new" emphasis:

The prosperity and happiness of the teeming millions who dwell there are closely bound up with that of America, for if the city fails, America fails. The Nation cannot flourish without its urban-industrial centers, or without its countryside; or without a sound balance between them. City planning, county planning, rural planning, state planning, regional planning must be linked together in the higher strategy of American national policy, to the end that our national and local resources may best be conserved and developed for our human use.[29]

The nearly continuing state of war which has consumed so much of the nation's resources and attention since 1939 has perhaps unduly clouded our application of this comprehensive view of domestic development policy. But with its formal acceptance as the very center of such policy up through the national level, planners ceased to be merely semiofficial consultants and two generations of professional growth came to a close—in theory if not always in practice.

RETROSPECT: THE PAST AS INDEX OF PLANNING'S PLACE IN FUTURE POLICY

The contributions of any one group to the endless reorganization of American cities are both small and inseparably bound with the events to which they responded. Nevertheless, while contemporaries must draw their own conclusions knowing today's planning needs are more complex and the procedures more sophisticated and potent, one judges historical significance according to how well a people approach the fundamental problems of their own time, not necessarily by how well they also anticipate ours. But by either definition, certainly by the first, the profession's development of basic premises and relationships through 1940 seems critical to the organization of life-giving reality in this century. These might be summarized as follows:

1. In a massing democracy, communities built for social and personal well-being take precedence over mere economic-technological-physical growth.

2. The city's reorganization in these terms can be partially guided, unified, and enhanced by comprehensive planning which informs but does not inhibit the future.

3. Planning, the art and science of environmental development, is a process in which democratic choice can become meaningful, and capability can approach desire by identifying needs, amenities, minimum standards and so on and by implementing them in numerous designs for new communities in town and countryside which preserve and extend the most desirable features of each as appropriate to time and place.

4. Such planning requires collaboration of means, continuing reallocation of resources, full public empowerment and intelligent human subscription—a slow and gradual process whose success depends largely upon education to its human purposes—for layman and planner alike. The planner's role herein is as analyst, creative designer, critic, and coordinator, at the very least.

5. Planning of the "natural region" not the urban one alone seems the ideal democratic context for coordinating the flow of national and local priorities, resources, and initiative, because cities overlap in needs but are deficient in means as presently constituted.

Of course, the discovery and elaboration of these ideas was more pronounced than their implementation in the period. Hence, a good part of their significance lies in prospects for the growth of such *ideas* as a departure from the past rather than in any dramatically evident humanization of the spreading cities— which was far less than one would have hoped.

How pertinent are such views in our time? Practically every close observer since reformer Frederick Howe in 1906 finds them indispensable to a world with centers but vanishing bounds, with as much disruption as convergence, with continuing economic-technological fascinations that make any planning for liveable cities difficult to obtain, although man's psychosocial needs for contact, love, privacy, beauty, greenspace and so on are "not frills or luxuries but real biological necessities," as René Dubos says.[30] Contemporary planners can point to thousands of operative public agencies; more scientific land use, economic and demographic base studies; integration of training and research with the social, behavioral, and natural sciences; and more widespread public support. But as Melvin Webber says in his AIP policy paper on "Comprehensive Planning and Social Responsibility," none of these insures our ability "to induce those patterns that will effectively increase accessibility to the diverse opportunities for productive social intercourse that are latent in an advanced civilization." Rather "Improving capacity for rationality must be joined with improving wisdom—there is no other name. It is *here* that the road forks, the one route leading to technocratic control by elites, the other to guided expansion of individual freedom." Moreover, the early planners' legacy to the present—"an egalitarian ethic and a pragmatic orientation to betterment" which Webber states and history affirms—also implies working with the events, techniques, and potentials of one's own time in pursuing and expanding the environmental vision,[31] *without* becoming mesmerized by any of them.

Who can tell what lies ahead? Obviously the city continues its rapid surface growth while its development remains sublimated to pressures unalterable even by the best planning alone. Most physical change in today's booming cities is conducted by private interests under public auspices for speculative purposes—rebuilding business centers, transport lines and suburbs where they hope the markets are; exploiting human weaknesses and upping pressures to conform—or deceive; and relocating as fast and as far from the centers for "making a living" as incomes permit. They are not villains, but our historic attachment to *a priori* decisions covering all human possibilities in yesterday's universe and to quantitative empirical standards as the only valid proof of anything combines to fill space with cheap structures, more controlling agencies than control, and a general meanness which cuts us off from one another at home and abroad. No thriving Hometown, USA, claims to be a fast-growing democracy; it invariably claims to be the fast*est* growing population or market area in its region. Unfortunately the penalties attached to such behavior include bland acceptance of affluence by most of us, alienation or intransigence by those who cannot or will not, probably growing public wariness, loneliness and helplessness generally. Few of us escape. All these signs of imbalance on scales unknown to traditional societies indicate our need for more mix, for new definitions of *man, living,* and *community* rather than for more distinct socioeconomic categories in a

free society. If our present use-and-throw away culture is weirdly appealing, it also is a commentary, then, on our unwillingness to seek and hence our inability to begin creating handsome, balanced, *many-sided* lifeways.

So planning's future in urban policy is hardly assured despite three generations of planner pressure. Thus one comes back to the millions of individual decision-makers, perhaps most of us now indifferent, who will affect any such policy; one comes back to our mutual *desire* for life lived as freely, fully, openly, and peacefully as possible. However absurd the desire, however needing restatement today—and both are considerable—it is the profession's good fortune to have been closely identified with it since near the century's turn.

NOTES

1. Lewis Mumford, *The Culture of Cities* (New York: Harcourt, Brace, 1938), pp. 374-87, 376.
2. Ernest Weissman, "The Urban Crisis in the World," *Urban Affairs Quarterly*, I (September, 1965), pp. 65-82; V. Gordon Childe, *Man Makes Himself* (New York: Mentor Books, 1951), pp. 180-88; Gideon Sjoberg, *The Preindustrial City: Past and Present* (Glencoe: Free Press, 1960), pp. 321-44; and Walter W. Rostow, *The Stages of Economic Growth* (London: Cambridge University Press, 1960), pp. 4-11.
3. John Nolen, *Replanning Reading* (Boston: G. H. Ellis, 1910), p. 3; and "Planning Problems of Industrial Cities—Niagara Falls as an Illustration," *Proceedings of the Eleventh National Conference on City Planning* (New York: NCCP, 1919), p. 23.
4. Frederick Law Olmsted, Jr., "Basic Principles of City Planning," *Proceedings . . . Second NCCP* (Boston: NCCP, 1910), pp. 3-4.
5. Donald J. Bogue, *The Population of the United States* (Glencoe: The Free Press, 1959), pp. 4-40, 126-27, 138-39; *Historical Statistics of the United States* (Washington: Government Printing Office, 1960), *passim;* Simon Kuznets and Dorthy S. Thomas, eds., *Population Distribution and Economic Growth*, 3 vols. (Philadelphia: American Philosophical Society, 1957-63) I, pp. 2-3; II, pp. 32-38, 53, 182-83, 205-71.
6. Quoted in Walter M. Whitehill, *Boston: A Topographical History* (Cambridge: Harvard Uni-

versity Press, 1959), p. 1; "Thomas Jefferson, 1st Inaugural Address" (1801), Inaugural Addresses of the Presidents of the United States (Washington, D.C.: Government Printing Office, 1952), pp. 11-13; Thomas Cochran and William Miller, The Age of Enterprise (New York: Macmillan, 1942), pp. 3-51, 252-53, 354-58, quoted 39; Andrew Carnegie, Triumphant Democracy (New York: Charles Scribner's Sons, 1886), pp. 47-48.
7. Richard Ely, "Pullman: A Social Study," Harpers Magazine, LXX (February, 1885), pp. 405-06; Daniel J. Boorstin, The Americans: The Colonial Experience (New York: Random House, 1958), pp. 33-96; figures from Bogue, Population Growth in Standard Metropolitan Areas, 1900-50 (Washington D.C.: Government Printing Office, December, 1953), pp. 10-11, checked against George Ford, ed., City Planning Progress in the United Sates, 1917 (Washington D.C.: American Institute of Architects, 1916), pp. 5-193; Richard M. Hurd, Principles of City Land Values (New York: The Record and Guide, 1903), pp. 1-74, 142; Homer Hoyt, The Structure and Growth of Residential Neighborhoods in American Cities (Washington, D.C.: Government Printing Office, 1939), pp. 101-04, 9-122; Nolen, New Ideals in the Planning of Cities, Towns, and Villages (New York: American City Bureau, 1919), pp. 1-19, quoted 27; John Reps, The Making of Urban America (Princeton: Princeton University Press, 1965), pp. 294-438.
8. Norman J. Johnston, "A Preface to the Institute," Journal of the American Institute of Planners, XXXI (August, 1965), pp. 198-209, quoted 201; Timothy Dwight, Travels in New England and New York, 4 vols. (New Haven: np, 1821-22), I, pp. 490-91: Reps, Making of Urban America, pp. 263-514; Leonard J. Arrington, Great Basin Kingdom (Cambridge: Harvard University Press, 1958), pp. 161-94, 235-414; Gourley, Plans for Beautifying New York and Improving the City of Boston (Boston: Saxton Pierce, 1844), pp. 1-38; Bushnell, "City Plans," Work and Play (New York: Charles Scribner, 1864), p. 376. (My thanks to Prof. Joseph Smeall, UND, for this source.) Ford, ed., City Planning Progress, pp. 183-86. There were world's fairs in Atlanta 1895, Omaha 1898, Buffalo 1901, St. Louis 1904, Seattle 1909, and San Diego-San Francisco 1914-15.
9. Quoting Parker and Lloyd in Daniel Aaron, Men of Good Hope (New York: Oxford University Press, 1951), pp. 45-66, 155-56, passim; Roy Lubove, The Progressive and the Slums (Pittsburgh: University of Pittsburgh Press, 1962), pp. 1-48, 217-56; B. O. Flower, Progressive Men, Women and the Movements of the Past Twenty-Five Years (Boston: New Arena, 1914), passim.
10. Dewey, Characters and Events, in J. Ratner ed., (New York: Henry Holt, 1929), p. 830; Woodrow Wilson, The New Freedom (New York: Doubleday, 1913), quoted pp. 283, 294; George Mowrey, The Era of Theodore Roosevelt and the

Birth of Modern America, 1900-1912 (New York: Harper & Brothers, 1958), pp. 16-84, 250-95; John Ihlder, "The New Civic Spirit," American City, IV (March, 1911), pp. 123-27.
11. "Growing Up By Plan," Survey, LXVII (February, 1932), p. 506.
12. Nolen, "Twenty Years of Planning Progress in the United States, 1907-27," Proceedings . . . Nineteenth NCCP (Boston: NCCP, 1927), pp. 1-44 quoted; editorials, American City, I (September, 1909), p. 3, VIII (January, 1913), p. 95, and XX (February, 1919), pp. 127-29 quoted; Robinson, "College and University Instruction in City Planning," City Plan, II (April, 1916), pp. 21-23; Albion W. Small, "Fifty Years of Sociology in the United States," American Journal of Sociology, XXI (May, 1916), pp. 734-68; Ford, ed., City Planning Progress, pp. 194-99; Harlan James, "Service–the Keynote of a New Cabinet Department," Review of Reviews, LIX (February, 1919), pp. 187-90.
13. U.S. Congress, "Hearing . . . on the Subject of City Planning," 61st Congress, 2nd Sess., 422 Senate Documents, LIX (1910), pp. 57-105; Flavel Shurtleff, Minutes of the Conference, the General and Executive Committees, and Correspondence, NCCP, 1910-17, and "Six Years of City Planning in the United States," Proceedings . . . Seventh NCCP (1915) pp. 33-41; cf. General Index of the Proceedings of the NCCP (Boston: University Press, 1928); Nolen, "What Is Needed in City Planning?," Hearing, pp. 74-75; Olmsted, Jr., "Basic Principles in City Planning," Proceedings . . . Second NCCP (1910), pp. 3-4; Robinson, "Problems in City Planning," Proceedings . . . Third NCCP (1911), pp. 217-18.
14. Pamphlet, "Constitution and By-Laws of the American City Planning Institute," 1917, quoting Article II; "Resolution Adopted by the Ninth NCCP . . . on May 9, 1917," NCCP Executive Minutes.
15. Frederick J. Adams and Gerald Hodge, "City Planning Instruction in the United States: The Pioneering Days, 1900-1930," Journal of the American Institute of Planners, XXXI (February, 1965), pp. 43-51; Marsh, An Introduction to City Planning with a technical chapter by George Ford (New York: np, 1909), pp. 1-2; Kellog, ed., The Pittsburgh Survey (New York: Survey Associates, 1914); Richard S. Childs, "What Ails Pittsburgh? A Diagnosis and Prescription," American City, III (July, 1910), pp. 9-12; Charles Moore, ed., Plan of Chicago . . . (Chicago: Commercial Club, 1909), pp. 1-4.
16. Ford, ed., City Planning Progress, pp. 5-193; W. S. Morgan and H. M. Pollack, Modern Cities (New York: Harper and Brothers, 1913), passim; Nolen, Replanning Small Cities (Boston: B. W. Huebsh, 1912), quoted pp. 5, 28, 58-60, 155-62, passim; NCCP, "Model Plan Study," special supplement in Landscape Architecture, III (April, 1913), and comment by Olmsted, Jr., "A City Planning Program," Proceedings . . . Fifth NCCP

(1913), pp. 1-16 (see winning design by F. H. Bourse, A. C. Comey, B. A. Holdemann, and J. Nolen).

17. Robinson, *City Planning* (New York: G. P. Putnam, 1916); Lewis, *Planning the Modern City* (New York: John Wiley and Sons, 1916); Bird, *Town Planning for Small Cities,* and Nolen, ed., *City Planning,* both (New York: D. Appleton for the NML, 1917, 1916), quoting p. 353.

18. Nolen, ed., *City Planning,* pp. xiii-xxiv; "Recommended for Membership, ACPI," ACPI *Minutes,* October 25, 1917, and January 23, 1918.

19. Ford, ed., *City Planning Progress,* quoted pp. 3-4; Norman J. Johnston, "Harland Bartholomew: His Comprehensive Plans and Science of Planning," and Hancock, "John Nolen and the American City Planning Movement: A History of Culture, Change and Community Response, 1900-1940," both unpub. Ph.D. dissertations, University of Pennsylvania, 1964, pp. 1-29, 87-133, and 231-349, respectively.

20. U.S. Bureau of Industrial Housing and Transportation, *Report of the United States Housing Corporation,* James Ford and Henry Hubbard, eds., 2 vols. (Washington, D.C.: Government Printing Office, 1919-20), quoting Hubbard I, pp. 70, 77, and Olmsted, Jr., II, p. 186; U.S. Shipping Board, *Housing the Shipbuilders,* in Frederick L. Ackerman, ed. (Philadelphia: np, 1920), pp. 1-24; E. D. Litchfield, "Yorkship Village in 1917 and 1939," *American City,* LIX (November, 1939), pp. 42-43; Roy Lubove, "Homes and 'A Few Well Placed Fruit Trees': An Object Lesson in Federal Housing," *Social Research,* MV (Winter, 1960), pp. 469-74; "Town Planning Lessons to be Learned from Government Housing Operations," *Minutes* of the Third ACPI Meeting, Philadelphia, January 26-27, 1919; Stein to author, June 14, 1961.

21. *Problems of St. Louis* (St. Louis: City Plan Commission, 1917), p. xxii (Bartholomew's italics).

22. Henry and Theodora Hubbard, *Our Cities Today and Tomorrow* (Cambridge: Harvard University Press, 1929), Appendix II: Thomas Adams, *Outline of Town and City Planning* (New York: Russell Sage Foundation, 1935), pp. 5-29, *passim;* Robert Walker, *The Planning Function in Urban Government* (Chicago: University of Chicago Press, 1941), pp. 23-26, 106-220; Hancock, "Nolen," pp. 350-607; Johnston, "Bartholomew," pp. 1-29, 134-242, quoted 183.

23. Adams, *Outline,* pp. 208-309, quoted 213; Hubbards, *Our Cities,* pp. 46-76, 142-61; Massachusetts Federation of Planning Boards, "Planning Progress in Massachusetts," *Bulletin 20* (1929), pp. 1-5; Edward M. Bassett, *Zoning* (New York: Russell Sage Foundation, 1936), pp. 13-222; Euclid Village, Ohio, *v.* Ambler Realty Co., 272 *U.S.* 265 and 47 *Sp.Ct.* 114 (1926), quoted; Charles Abrams, "Economic Changes in Real Estate," *New Architecture and City Planning,* in Paul Zucker, ed. (New York: Philosophical Li-

brary, 1944), quoted p. 272; President's Commission, *Recent Social Trends,* in Wesley Mitchell, Charles Merriam *et al.,* eds., 2 vols. (New York: Macmillan, 1933), I, quoted p. xxxi.

24. Adams and Hodge, "City Planning Instruction," pp. 43-51; John Gaus, *The Graduate School of Design and the Education of Planners* (Cambridge: Harvard, 1943), pp. 3-50; "Report of a Conference on a Project for Research and Instruction in City and Regional Planning," Columbia University, May 3, 1918, mimeographed; and Nolen, "Professions Concerned in City Planning," September 29, 1933, both in Nolen Papers (Harvard folders), quoting last 2-4; U.S. Civil Service, "Planner Requirements," 1926, quoted; NCCP and ACPI *Minutes* and member correspondence, "Report of the Committee on Reorganization of the NCCP," March 2, 1934; ACPI to members, March 19, and November 7, 1924; ACPCA, memorandum, "To the Board of Directors," May 29, 1935; American Society of Planning Officials, *Newsletter* (1935), p. i. Note: the *Quarterly* became the *Planners Journal* in 1934 and the *Journal of the American Institute of Planners* in 1944.

25. Mumford, "The Next Twenty Years in City Planning," *Proceedings . . . Seventeenth NCCP* (1927), pp. 45-58, quoted 56, *passim;* MacKaye, *The New Exploration* (New York: Harcourt, Brace, 1928), *passim;* Nolen, "Random Notes and Reactions," 1914-20, *passim;* letter to Olmsted, Jr., October 31, 1923, and to New York *Times,* November 25, 1931, all in Nolen Papers (New York Regional Plan file); *cf.* Regional issue of *Survey,* LIV (May 1, 1925).

26. Comey, "An Answer to the Garden City Challenge," *American City,* XXIX (July, 1923), pp. 36-38; MacKaye, *New Exploration,* pp. 24-30, 56-75, quoted 26, 30; Nolen, *New Towns for Old* (Boston: Marshall Jones, 1927), pp. 133-57, *passim;* and "Regional Planning," *Encyclopedia of the Social Sciences,* XIII (1934), pp. 205-08; Russell V. Black, "County Planning Proves Its Value," *American City,* XLIV (May, 1931), pp. 116-18; National Resources Committee, *State Planning* (Washington, D.C.: Government Printing Office, 1935, 1940), and Urbanism Committee of the NRC, *Urban Planning and Land Policies* and Supplementary Report, both (Washington, D.C.: Government Printing Office, 1939), pp. 45-117, and 3-161; Roy Lubove, *Community Planning in the 1920's* (Pittsburgh: University of Pittsburgh Press, 1963), pp. 107-27; *Radburn Garden Homes* (New York: City Housing Corporation, September, 1930), brochure; *The Farm Cities Corporation* (Washington: The Corporation, nd-1923) booklet; Malcher, *The Steadyflow Traffic System* (Cambridge: Harvard University Press, 1935); Stein, *Toward New Towns for America* (New York: Rheinhold, 1957).

27. Herbert Hoover, *The Memoirs of . . . ,* 3 vols. (New York: Macmillan, 1951-52), II, p. 78; Roosevelt, *On Our Way* (New York: John Day, 1934), p. xii; and *Public Papers and Messages,* in

S. I. Roseman, ed., 13 vols. (New York: Random House, 1938-45), III, p. ii.

28. Crane to Nolen and L. C. Gray, April 27, 1933, quoted ("Memorandum on the Relation of Emergency Relief Work to Planning"; "Report of the National Land Use Planning Committee," February 15-18, 1932, both Nolen Papers (NRPB folder); First Annual Report: Conference on Rural Land Utilization and Planning (Washington: USDA, July, 1933), pp. 5-16; Federal Emergency Relief Administration, Bulletin WD-3, March 2, 1934; National Resources Committee, PWA, First Through Thirteenth Circular Letters, 1933-34; and "A Plan for Planning," Report, December 1, 1934.

29. NRPB, Our Cities: Their Role in the Growth of the Nation (Washington, D.C.: Government Printing Office, 1937), quoted p. xiii; and Urban Planning and Land Policies, pp. 73-309, passim; Francis Perkins et al., The Federal Government Today (New York: American Council on Public Affairs, 1938), see individual reports; Paul Conkin, Tomorrow A New World (Ithaca: Cornell University Press for the American Historical Association, 1959), pp. 93-233, 326-31.

30. Howe, The City: The Hope of Democracy (New York: Charles Scribner's Sons, 1906), pp. 300-13; Charles Beard, "Conflicts in City Planning," Yale Review XVII (October, 1927), pp. 65-77; David Reisman et al., The Lonely Crowd (New York: Doubleday Anchor Books, 1955), p. 348, passim; John K. Galbraith, Five Speeches (Washington: Urban America, 1966), pp. 1-6; Dubos, "Man's Unchanging Biology and Evolving Psyche," Center for the Study of Democratic Institutions, Center Diary: 17 (March-April, 1967), pp. 38-44, quoted 41.

31. Webber, "Comprehensive Planning and Social Responsibility: Towards an AIP Consensus on the Profession's Roles and Purposes," Journal of the American Institute of Planners, XXIX (November, 1963), pp. 232-41, quoted 234, 236.

The Urban Crisis Leaves Town

T. D. ALLMAN

Whatever happened to the urban crisis?

Last year, the cities of the Northeast and Midwest seemed less in the midst of municipal difficulties than in the path of the Four Horsemen of the Apocalypse. The Bronx was in flames and Buffalo was buried in snow. The "underclass," perhaps the most subtle epithet ever directed against nonwhite Americans in need of a job, was looting Brooklyn, and taking over Washington east of Rock Creek Park. In Hartford the civic center had fallen down. All the statistics and all the media images testified to the same melancholy truth: Jobs were still disappearing from cities, and so were taxpayers. While the welfare class dismantled the temples of urban America stone by stone, selfish people in the suburbs refused to share their wealth, and smug people in the southern climates lounged beside their swimming pools. The federal system was robbing the poor to give to the rich; America's cities were writhing in poverty, arson, and decay. At stake, as a group of big-city mayors pointed out, was not just "the survival of our cities" but the "survival of the American way of life as we have known it." "While every American city is not tottering on the brink of disaster," they said, "all are moving toward it."

The press, politicians, and urbanologists all agreed on one thing. With cities and their people, as a Presidential policy group put it, in distress, the only hope left was for a national urban policy, the kind of "massive effort to achieve the revitalization of our cities" that Jimmy Carter had promised in the 1976 election. So through the summer of 1977 and the cold and bitter winter that led into 1978, the northern cities waited, as the idiom current at that time put it, to be "saved." Finally the President spoke.

"I am convinced that it is in our national interest," Jimmy Carter announced last March, "to save our cities. The deterioration of urban life in the United States is one of the most complex and deeply rooted problems we face. The federal government has the clear duty to lead the effort to reverse that deterioration. I intend to provide the leadership." He then announced a series of programs "designed to marshal the immense resources of America in a long-term commitment to pursue that goal." Had not our cities become disintegrating warrens of poverty and despair? The President promised a labor-intensive public-works program to put the chronically unemployed back to work rebuilding decaying business districts. Had not private corporate capital callously abandoned its social obligations in the very cities that had generated its enormous profits? The Carter national urban policy promised a National Development Bank to provide venture capital for inner-city economic revival. Had not the suburbs, like shortsighted parasites, selfishly shirked their metropolitan responsibilities, refusing to share revenues and closing their borders to the urban unemployed? The White House would create federal incentives to make the states part of the urban solution. Had not Southern Shift, and Washington's own irrational proclivity for pouring federal money into Atlanta and Phoenix at the expense of Cleveland and Baltimore sentenced the northern cities to fiscal doom? Under Jimmy Carter, the Treasury would provide direct federal budgetary assistance to help impoverished inner-city governments stand on their own two feet again.

"Let there be no doubt," the President concluded, "that today marks a turning point."

THE HORSEMEN PASS BY

These days, to look at what has happened to cities since the President made his pledge is to look in the face of a paradox. Big-city politicians, bureaucrats in Washington, urbanologists around the country agree on two things that, at first glance, seem contradictory. The first is that Jimmy Carter's urban programs are inadequate—and abysmally inadequate—either to save cities, or to confront the urban crisis that so recently was considered this nation's most troublesome domestic problem. The second thing on which they agree is that the catastrophe has not taken place. In spite of the dire consequences predicted for the nation if Washington did not come to the rescue, 1978 was not the year the sky fell on St. Louis, the skyscrapers were abandoned on Wall Street, or Detroit burned to the

ground. It was the year the northern cities confounded the prophets of inner-city doom. Once dismissed as anachronisms of the presuburban past, cities like Boston and Baltimore proved themselves to be vital human centers with futures far more promising than either their detractors or their beleaguered proponents imagined possible.

In the months following his announcement of the national urban policy, Jimmy Carter's grandiose promise to rebuild the South Bronx "brick by brick and block by block" never went beyond tokenism. But the World Trade Center, once dismissed as a white elephant, achieved a 90 percent occupancy rate, and the Citicorp Tower, the eighth highest skyscraper in the world, opened in midtown Manhattan. The Administration's commitment to revive decaying inner-city neighborhoods never was translated from the drawing boards to the tenements of Bushwick and Dorchester. But from Boerum Hill in Brooklyn to Capitol Hill in Washington the fastest growing social problem was not the departure of the white middle class; it was the displacement of the poor and nonwhite, as affluent, taxpaying professionals bid up the prices on brownstone houses and cooperative apartments in what once were dismissed as unsightly slums. Urban specialists now refer to this process as inner-city "gentrification."

Today the National Development Bank, like the incentives for state aid, remains no more than a proposal on a piece of paper, marked over by Congress, and seemingly forgotten in the White House. But without waiting for Washington to show them how, small businessmen competed avidly for rental space in downtown Boston's Quincy Market and a major utility expanded its operations in Newark. The Urban Land Institute estimates that 70 percent of all sizable American cities today are experiencing a significant revival in what once were called "deteriorated" areas. According to a study for the Pacific News Service City Project by Thomas Brom, corporate investment is flooding American cities, and the influx of American capital into downtown areas is being matched by funds coming from Europe, the Mideast, Japan, as well as from other areas that were once supposed to offer investment opportunities far better than devastated Detroit or run-down old New York. While automobile money flowed into Renaissance Center in downtown Detroit, Olympia and York Developers of Toronto began sinking $350 million into a real estate package of seven office buildings in New York. Money Market Directories estimates that over the next few years America's 300 largest corporate funds will invest more than $6 billion in real estate, and for many foreigners, American cities seem to be the most alluring investment opportunity. Nowhere else can Europeans invest money and have some assurance that it will still remain their property ten years later.

But wasn't New York destined to become a ghost town unless President Carter provided money and jobs? The President's labor-intensive public-works bill was never passed, yet over the past two years, in spite of the fiscal crisis and the layoffs at City Hall, New York has added more than 100,000 jobs—nearly half the workforce of Atlanta—to its payrolls. Today the unemployment rate in Cleveland, erstwhile ruin beside Lake Erie, is 6.8 percent. In Atlanta, workshop of the New South, it is 7 percent. Miami has more of its workers unem-

ployed than Boston. Baltimore, Detroit, and St. Louis all have lower unemployment rates than El Paso. Houston and Dallas are still booming, but Chicago, with its run-down ethnic neighborhoods, has a lower unemployment rate than Los Angeles. (See Table 1.)

But aren't America's cities going broke? What happened to the municipal bonds no one would buy? What was the fate of the teachers and policemen whom northern cities couldn't pay unless heroic action was taken in Washington? NEW FISCAL PROBLEM: TOO MUCH MONEY; FEARS OF DEFICIT CRISIS VANISH AS CITIES, STATES FACE PROBLEM OF RISING SURPLUSES, read one headline during 1978. The Carter proposal for direct budgetary assistance for cities still has not been enacted either. Yet the prophecies of urban fiscal disaster, serious as the economic condition for many cities remains, have been disproved by an astonishing fact: in calendar 1977 the aggregate state and local government budget surplus reached the remarkable level of $29 billion, the highest in history. Instead of being "black, brown, and broke," cities are attracting affluent people from all over the world, and in some fortunate cases at least, finding themselves with more revenues than they know how to spend. For all the diagnoses of senility, and all the prognoses of imminent death, it is increasingly difficult to deny that the northern cities have turned out to be remarkably durable—holding their own economically and fiscally, in spite of the people and jobs they lost from the end of World War II through the early 1970s, while reasserting their traditional social and cultural preeminence at the very moment it was supposed to be gone forever.

Since the beginning of the year the

Table 1

Northern Cities Narrow the Unemployment Gap
Comparison of unemployment rates in select cities for 1976 and 1978

	1976			1978		
Northern Cities	Employed	Unemployed	Unemployment Rate (%)	Employed	Unemployed	Unemployment Rate (%)
St. Louis	210,629	19,852	8.6	226,972	10,144	6.6
New York	2,730,000	344,000	11.2	2,838,270	279,000	8.8
Cleveland	287,744	32,892	10.3	297,731	21,818	6.8
Baltimore	379,815	40,133	9.6	385,781	26,799	6.5
Boston	272,246	34,074	11.1	299,368	23,979	7.4
Detroit	600,183	75,085	11.1	631,805	62,009	8.9
Southern Cities						
Denver	222,429	16,873	7.1	240,774	15,960	6.2
Los Angeles	1,221,611	134,526	9.9	1,273,114	114,779	8.3
Dallas	428,876	25,408	5.6	478,094	22,473	4.5
Houston	709,008	36,192	4.9	816,233	40,333	4.7
Phoenix	313,017	33,939	9.8	353,725	19,645	5.3
Atlanta	244,376	31,676	11.5	216,225	16,319	7.0

SOURCE: U.S. Department of Labor, Bureau of Labor Statistics.

whole tenor of urban discourse has changed, with visions of inner-city renaissance prevailing over the old prophecies of doom. In August I asked several members of the House and Senate, and a number of urbanologists and staff members in Congress, the Department of Housing and Urban Development, and in the White House—all grappling with urban problems—how they thought America's "dying inner cities" would be faring five or fifteen years hence. Without exception they believed the cities would be much better off than they are now. Where policy makers once were so pessimistic, they now seemed to foresee a future for cities that the so-called Sunbelt and suburbs might envy. "For the next twenty years," Kenneth McLean, staff director of the Senate Committee on Banking, Housing and Urban Affairs, told me, "the good life in America will be urban." "I'm optimistic," added Rep. William Moorhead of Pittsburgh, who is chairman of the similar committee in the House. "There has been a fundamental shift. People are rediscovering, in a massive way, the advantages of city life." Moorhead—who lobbied diligently to win Congressional support for fiscal aid to New York—has never been one to pretend that urban problems don't exist. But he doesn't see cities as needy relics of the Industrial Revolution any more, but rather as pacesetters of the post-industrial age. "We won't get back the old manufacturing jobs," he points out, "but cities will benefit greatly from the explosion in the service sector. Today in Pittsburgh, the biggest single employer isn't U.S. Steel or the government bureaucracy. It's the University of Pittsburgh."

Pittsburgh, of course, cleaned up pollution years ago. It has one of the most homogeneous populations of any big American city—and the incredible wealth of the Mellon family on its side. Surely spokesmen for cities that are less fortunate don't buy all the new talk of urban revival.

"I made a mistake when I propounded the abandonment theory," Rep. Parren Mitchell of Baltimore, the chairman of the Congressional Black Caucus, told me when we sat down to talk in the ornate cloakroom of the House of Representatives. "I did not reckon with the fact that white capital would not let its urban investment go down the drain." Mitchell, who represents a predominantly black district, thinks his city, and others, have turned the corner. The 1980 census, he concedes, will reflect the population losses many older cities suffered in the early 1970s. But he points out that while city populations may decline more, the per capita wealth of those who remain seems bound to increase. Mitchell believes long-term events will show that the last few years were not the nadir of the urban crisis, but the period when the American city turned around. "When I moved deeper into the ghetto a few years ago," the Congressman said, "even my black friends said I was crazy. Today the next street over is predominantly white middle class, and on my own block, black professionals are buying up houses and renovating them.

"In fifteen or twenty years," Mitchell concluded, "America's worst national problems won't all be concentrated in-

side cities as they are now. Cities at the worst will be doing fairly well."

CATCHING UP WITH REALITY

What is going on when a national crisis seems to abate, without the President of the United States having vindicated the great-man theory of history, without Congress having passed a single piece of major national urban legislation? Elinor Bachrach, who, in her work for the Senate Banking Committee, has been intensively involved in urban fiscal problems for years, suggested that it might be a matter of fashion. "Washington is a town of fads," she said. "I can remember when 'environment' was the buzz word. Then we got all excited about the energy crisis. The city craze," she elaborates, "has now been killed off by the Prop 13 fashion." Politicians last year were saying only new programs could bail cities out; this year they are cutting every tax they can find. With so many swings in the Washington tiller, why has the national ship not run aground long ago? "It is fortunate," Ms. Bachrach said, "that beyond the limits of the District of Columbia there exists a real world, with real forces that manage to operate without an Act of Congress."

While that sentiment is little shared on the banks of the Potomac, Roger Vaughan, an economist who has made many studies of urban problems for the Rand Corporation, has a theory even more disconcerting for those who imagine that by debating policy they determine events. As one of the authors of a study on the urban impact of federal policies sponsored by both private funds and the federal government, Vaughan has said, "There always is a gap of at least several years between the problem, and our political perception of it." After years of gathering and analyzing thousands of statistics, Vaughan works on the assumption that if a problem provokes the greatest possible public concern, it already is being solved. He remembers how environmental pollution became the raging public concern at the precise moment when the flight of industry was dissipating city smog; that the energy crisis came to obsess political discourse in the midst of the greatest oil glut in history. "It was the same way with the urban crisis," Vaughan told me. "By the time we became aware of Southern Shift, it already was beginning to ebb. We were too busy suddenly discovering what harm we had done to cities in the 1950s and 1960s to notice that, in the 1970s, events had started to favor cities again." Vaughan does not suggest that there is never anything to worry about, just that Presidents, Congressmen, and journalists tend to run around worrying about the wrong things. He suggests that "we should be worrying about what we're not worrying about."

So while tax surpluses increase, a President tells us about "the distress of the most fiscally strained communities" —and when word of the taxpayers' revolt reaches the capital a few months later, the political elite reacts with astonishment and alarm. Prestigious newspapers print editorials about the crisis of urban disinvestment while the Arabs put up a skyscraper next door. In the halls of Congress, Senators and Representatives make speeches about the advancing blight in our cities while outside their office windows, on Capitol Hill, seedy sandwich shops are being metamorphosed into pretentious French restaurants, and rundown, $15,000 welfare rooming houses are being subdivided into apartments costing $85,000 apiece. The divergence between policy and reality—most graphically illustrated in the happy divergence between the fate of Jimmy Carter's urban programs and the fate of America's cities—in fact operates on two separate levels. The first concerns the federal government itself, and involves the gap between "news" and what really is happening even when no one notices it; between "debate" and what already has been decided by events even when the crisis managers go home at five; and between "policy" and what the federal government, with its immense weight on affairs, effects even when there is no policy at all. The second level concerns a national and international reality larger than the federal government. It involves the gap between what the government is doing, whether it knows it or not, and those immense social, demographic, economic, and technological forces that exceed the capacity of the federal government to control them.

On the first level—that of the effect of the federal government on events— it is now clear that the concentration in the press, in Congress, and in the White House on specific urban programs frequently has blinded almost everyone to the effects on cities of unprogrammatic federal spending, whatever its intention. This was true in the 1960s when, under the rubric of the War on Poverty, ostensible policy and programs were as pro-city as they ever have been, but the aggregate of federal spending nonetheless was accelerating the outflow of capital, jobs, and people from inner cities at a rate no amount of Great Society programs could reverse. Today it is the continuing tendency to confuse *programs* (that is, what the President, Congress, and the federal bureaucracy say, and sometimes even believe, they are doing) with what the federal government is actually doing, and an almost complaisant lack of attention to *spending* (that is, to what the government is really doing, whether it wants to do it, or even knows it is doing it) that continues to becloud understanding of the impact of the federal government on cities.

Lyndon Johnson said he was trying to help cities; Lyndon Johnson believed he was helping cities, with "urban renewal" programs that destroyed neighborhoods, and with "equal opportunity" programs that gave the jobless and poor incentives to stay in northern cities at the very moment opportunity was shifting to the suburbs and the South. So the conventional wisdom grew up that Lyndon Johnson poured so much money into so many cities to so little effect that he proved "you can't solve problems by throwing money at them." Richard Nixon, in his turn, made it very clear that it was not his policy to throw money at problems. So it became the conventional wisdom that cities got into trouble because of Nixon's stinginess. Later, as city problems got worse, Gerald Ford demonstrated his insensitivity to New York City. Such, even after Watergate, was the implacable faith of Americans in their supreme magistrate that it was widely assumed a metropolis of more than 7 million people might expire before our very eyes, because a President of the United States had indicated it was fine by him if it did. Finally Jimmy Carter promised his national urban policy; again it was believed a fundamental change in direction would occur, because the man in the White House had said so. The statistics (which, like policy, al-

ways lag behind events) are now available. They make short work of all those conventional wisdoms.

It now is clear that, whatever his intentions, Lyndon Johnson's Great Society programs bore no more relationship to the real problems of America's cities than the Domino Theory did to the security of Connecticut. Far from throwing money at urban problems (and much future grief might have been avoided if he had), President Johnson presided over a federal money machine that as late as 1968 still was constantly sucking wealth out of northern cities, and enfeebling urban industrial economies that already were in trouble. While LBJ paid ghetto dwellers to stay put in Harlem and Roxbury studying obsolete trades, he used New York and Massachusetts tax dollars to build the manned space center in Texas. The Great Society was not misplaced largesse; it helped set up cities for the crisis that broke a few years later. Nixon and Ford, for their part, may not have intended to throw money at problems, but throw money they did, or rather the federal bureaucracy and Congress, sometimes in spite of Presidential vetoes, did. To the extent American cities faced a major crisis during the Nixon-Ford years, the cause lay as much in the federally encouraged outflow of urban assets that had occurred under the Democrats as in the anti-city policies of their Republican successors. (Of course, Nixon's partisan use of revenue sharing to help Republican suburbs hurt cities, and above all Republican mismanagement of the economy, resulting in two major recessions in the early 1970s, greatly intensified the problems cities already faced.)

Nonetheless a truly remarkable influx—not outflow—of federal moneys into cities had occurred by the end of the Nixon-Ford Administration. The transfer of federal wealth to cities that occurred under two Republican Presidents has played the same causal role in helping cities now that the outflow of money under Johnson earlier played in creating the urban crisis of the Nixon-Ford years. Under Jimmy Carter the direction of federal spending in cities has not changed at all, even though the direction of policy ostensibly has. It has only accelerated. What was the merest trickle of federal funds into municipal coffers in Johnson's day had become a flood by the time Ford left office. Today it is a deluge, so that urban analysts who once feared that cities would expire for lack of outside money now fear that cities might become sick with surfeit. As data assembled by the Advisory Commission on Intergovernmental Relations indicate, a fundamental change has occurred in the financing of city budgets over the last twenty years, largely independent of the specific policy of the specific President in the White House. And when these figures are linked with the other indications of urban revival we now have, they would tend to debunk that most hardy perennial of all policy myths: It seems that at least some problems in cities begin to be solved, if you throw enough money at them.

As Table 2 indicates, so far as cities were concerned the transition from

Table 2

Accelerating Federal Aid to Cities
Direct federal aid as a percent of city's general revenue, selected cities
and fiscal years 1957–1978

City	Fiscal Years				Per capita federal aid based on 1975 population	
	1957	1967	1976	1978 (est.)	1976	1978 (est.)
St. Louis	0.6	1.0	23.6	54.7	$86	$223
Newark	0.2	1.7	11.4	55.2	47	251
Buffalo	1.3	2.1	55.6	69.2	163	218
Cleveland	2.0	8.3	22.8	68.8	65	217
Boston	°	10.0	31.5	28.0	204	203
Baltimore	1.7	3.8	38.9	53.3	167	258
Philadelphia	0.4	8.8	37.7	51.8	129	196
Detroit	1.3	13.1	50.2	69.6	161	248
Atlanta	4.3	2.0	15.1	36.0	52	150
Denver	0.6	1.2	21.2	24.2	98	140
Los Angeles	0.7	0.7	19.3	35.7	54	120
Dallas	0	°	20.0	17.8	51	54
Houston	0.2	3.1	19.4	22.7	44	68
Phoenix	1.1	10.6	35.0	58.3	57	116

° Less than .05 percent.
SOURCE: Advisory Commission on Intergovernmental Relations staff computations based on U.S. Bureau of the Census data.

Eisenhower, with his fear of deficit spending, to the Administrations of Kennedy and Johnson and all their Keynesian advisers, made little difference at all. Under Lyndon Johnson, direct federal aid amounted to only 1 percent in St. Louis, only 1.7 percent in Newark, and only 2.1 percent in Buffalo of the general revenues those cities raised themselves, from their own local property, sales, and other taxes. These sums were too small even to compensate for the competitive advantage other federal programs—notably FHA mortgages and the Interstate Highway System—then were lavishing on the suburbs and the South and West, let alone to help solve social problems. Meanwhile Phoenix—in the heart of the so-called Sunbelt[1]—was getting 10.6 percent from Lyndon Johnson. By the end of the Nixon-Ford years, direct federal aid to many cities had skyrocketed—to 23.6 percent of the revenues St. Louis raised, 11.4 percent in Newark, and no less than 55.6 in Buffalo. Of course Nixon and Ford—as their liberal critics often pointed out—also rained money down on affluent suburbs and the southern areas when the money was more needed elsewhere. Phoenix by the end of the Nixon-Ford years was getting direct federal aid amounting to 35 percent of its own burgeoning revenues, while direct federal aid to expanding cities like Denver, Los Angeles, and Houston—where the problem wasn't urban decay at all, but uncontrolled growth—had risen from almost nothing to a full fifth of those cities' own revenues.

Under Jimmy Carter, or much more accurately speaking, under the tendency of federal programs, once started, steadily to gain in both mass and velocity, the federal manna falling on cities has become a blizzard. St. Louis, which was getting less than $3 in annual per capita direct federal aid during the War on Poverty, was getting $86 by the time President Ford turned his back on the cities. Today St. Louis receives $223 in direct federal aid for every man, woman, and child within the city limits. It would be astonishing under such circumstances if economic conditions did not improve. Over the past two years, St. Louis has gained more than 16,000 new jobs, and the number of unemployed has been cut almost in half—from 19,852 then to 10,144 this year. Since 1976 per capita aid to Newark has risen from $47 to $251, and now amounts to 55.2 percent of all locally raised revenues. In Buffalo, the current figures, respectively, have risen to 69.2 percent and $218; in Baltimore, to 53.3 and $258; and in Phoenix, the ever fortunate, to 58.3 and $116. Since the *end* of the War on Poverty, some $400 billion has been spent in direct federal aid for cities and the people who live there. On an annual, virtually self-renewing basis, without any additional new programs, some $80 billion in federal money now goes specifically for urban aid programs, and for social programs aiding people who live in cities. These figures do not include other federal spending in cities, for example salaries for federal employees, or the share of this year's mammoth $117 billion military budget that will be spent in urban areas in spite of the continuing southern and suburban bias of most defense spending.

ELUSIVE CRISES

How can such a stupendous, in many instances desirable, transfer of wealth into cities not merely have been ignored so totally in analyses of the urban "crisis," but the policy debate on cities have been premised so universally, and for such a long time, on the completely opposite assumption—the assumption, as Senator Moynihan, for example, never ceases to iterate, that the real reason for urban problems is that the federal government keeps taking much more out of cities than it puts back? A major reason, it needs to be reemphasized, is the perpetual tendency of the press, Congress, even the policy makers themselves to confuse policy with what really is going on. A year ago, inner-city spokesmen were calling for a "Marshall Plan" for cities. When Jimmy Carter finally announced his urban policy, it contained specific new program proposals that would have added $4.4 billion in direct new federal spending for cities. The conventional wisdom at the time was that Carter was "the most fiscally conservative Democratic President since Grover Cleveland," that he had decided to make cities eat crumbs, and give them no cake.

But alarming as the thought to policy makers may be, policy is not where the action is. Sen. William Proxmire of Wisconsin no doubt is right when he points out that to give American cities today what Europe got under the Marshall Plan would be to inflict mass cutbacks in urban spending that not even the lunatic fringe of the Proposition 13 crowd would espouse. The Marshall Plan provided $13 billion over five years—or $2.6 billion a year—to seventeen countries with a population larger than the whole of the United States. Today cities are getting $2.4 billion each year in mass transit funds alone, and $4.5 billion annually from the Environmental Protection Agency. "The federal government spends twenty-three times per year the amount we spent per year under the Marshall Plan," Proxmire points out. "Even when we allow for inflation, we now put about ten times more into our cities each year than we put into Europe under the Marshall Plan."

Proxmire—like others who no longer support the urban catastrophe scenario —is no enemy of cities; he is not trying to invent excuses to stop spending money where it is needed. But he is appalled to see federal funds shoring up affluent neighborhoods while garbage goes uncollected in marginal areas; to watch Community Development grants pouring into the richest census tracts, while poor neighborhoods collapse further into ruin. Proxmire wonders why so little of the federal money goes to Harlem, or to give tax breaks to struggling factories providing jobs in Queens, why the only significant piece of urban legislation Congress passed in 1978 was a $1.6 billion loan guarantee for the big Wall Street banks. "Providing credit for New York City, the credit capital of the world," he suggests, "was like shipping dairy cows to Wisconsin."

Without a doubt much of what Proxmire says is correct; a large portion of this influx of federal money into cities is utterly wasted, so far as solving inner-city social, economic, and fiscal problems is concerned. As much as $20 billion of the $80 billion given to cities each year leaks into the suburbs. An enormous amount of it goes to people and neighborhoods that don't need help at all. Meanwhile much of the money that actually reaches inner cities and people in distress serves to create a permanent dependent population, rather than new jobs; it does absolutely nothing to revive inner-city school systems, or to preserve municipal capital, ranging from bridges to sewers, which is deteriorating at an alarming rate. To the extent that cities suffered in the past from the unprogrammatic impact of federal spending, whatever the policy of the moment happened to be, for the foreseeable future they will benefit to a similar extent from the reverse phenomenon. But the inflow of federal money into cities certainly until now has not had, and may never have, whatever the rhetoric current in Washington, that surgical precision that the advocates of "targeting"—the great new urban policy buzz word—talk about. Instead, the federal funds being spent in cities should be regarded more as an act of nature, like a change in climate, than as an act of conscious policy implementation. And one should be just as wary of the "countercyclical" claims made for federal spending. In both cases the theory is straightforward. When the economy goes down, the conventional doctrine holds, federal spending should go up; this is the theory of countercyclical programs. The theory behind targeting is that, whatever the overall state of the national economy, federal money should be spent on the areas, and people, that need help the most.

These theories are attractive, not merely because we should minimize the human costs of a cyclical economy, or because we should help people who need help even when the economic indicators are going up, whether they live in East Orange or south Texas— these theories are attractive because they foster the illusion that the federal government is more a policy instrument, and less an act of political nature. Alas, our whole experience with trying to use big government to solve big social problems over the past few decades shows not, as the conservatives pretend, that it can't, but simply, as liberals won't accept, that we really don't have all that much control over whether it does or not. It is one thing to rain down money on the South for twenty years, and then move the rainmaking machine to the cities. But there are several problems with trying to do much else.

The first problem is political. It is far easier to get the 535 members of the House and Senate to approve legislation that helps all their constituents than it is to get them to vote funds that help only a few districts and states, however deserving they may be. In a political system in which it is also much easier to extend old programs than to initiate new ones, "countercyclical" money tends to go on being spent, even when the economy enters a new cycle, just as "targeting" tends to broaden out into pork barrel legislation that helps Riverdale as much as it does the South Bronx. We have seen this tendency operating with particular force during the current session of Congress. The problem is not that the legislators have failed to help people and cities in distress, but that, jumping on the Proposition 13 bandwagon, they have cut taxes for everyone. The President started out by asking Congress for some labor-intensive public works to help chronic unemployment; he may wind up having to veto legislation that would give every corporate vice-persident's son a summer job.

The second problem is far more serious; it might be termed cultural. It quite simply is that, in American society, programs once in effect, whatever their initial intent and specific provisions, invariably help the rich more than the poor, the white more than the black, the educated more than the functionally illiterate, and those who have something more than those who have nothing at all. In the 1960s, Project Head Start was metamorphosed quickly from a program for underprivileged ghetto youth into an amenity for the preschool children of the affluent. CETA jobs help those who already know the ropes in City Hall more than they help the chronically unemployed. Today anti-redlining legislation, currently a great reformist cause, is the most conspicuous example of this tendency. In the long run it probably will hurt the very people it is supposed to help, by encouraging white middle-class families to buy up inner-city houses, and displace the poor blacks and browns who live there now. Even among the disadvantaged this tendency operates: It takes a high level of literacy, considerable industry, and a keen sense of how bureaucracies work to be a successful welfare chiseler. One of society's real victims is unlikely even to know how to get food stamps.

These warps in causality between what we achieve and what we have set out to achieve are not, as those who mistake making policy for manipulating reality like to think, indications that what is needed is just a little more fine tuning. Like the distortion in an amplifier, like the errors of margin in the weapons we used in Indochina, they are inherent parts of the process. And finally, because of the inevitable lag between crises and the political perception of them, to say nothing of the chronic delays in appropriating money and then spending it, one must count in the tendency of the federal government to throw money at the places where

problems once were, not at the places where they are now.

Today the perception lag remains, and all the other limitations of what we try to do with policy, too. Does this worry Jimmy Carter? The surprising thing is that this advocate for Zero-Base Budgeting, with his dream of an end to deficit spending, appears far more aware of what really is going on, and far less troubled by it, than those who spend their time picking over his proposals for a National Development Bank. Last March, for example, when the President announced his national urban policy, he divided it into three parts, in descending order of significance. Carter first pointed to "the very substantial increases" he already had made in the volume of federal moneys flowing into cities, and correctly pointed out that "total assistance to state and local governments already had been increased by 25 percent," from $68 billion to $85 billion, even before he announced the policy. The second major element in his urban policy, the President said, was "the reorientation of federal activities to make certain that they support our urban goals." Only third and last did the President mention the "new initiatives"—the programs that offered so little new money, and that Congress has not enacted anyway—that left so many urban advocates disappointed. Two other sentences from the President's speech are worth quoting. "The Defense Department," he said, "will set up a new program to increase procurement in urban areas." "And the General Services Administration will retain facilities in urban areas and will put new ones there." He later followed these promises up with executive orders.

Thus—as with the New South and

the suburbs before—the money seems likely to keep pouring in, whether it goes where it is needed or not, and whether we know it or not. Jimmy Carter in fact has put himself in the business, whether he fully realizes it or not, of taking back with the right hand what Lyndon Johnson once gave —while giving back with the left hand what LBJ took away. The reverse symmetry hardly could be more exact. The War on Poverty was a *policy* that purported to cure America's gravest social ills; but while Johnson was raising millennial expectations, federal *spending* patterns in fact were making inner-city problems worse. Jimmy Carter's policy didn't offer very much, beneath the rhetoric, in new programs; and what he offered has not become law. But the new federal spending patterns that Carter did not originate, but which he is certainly helping to accelerate, are offering cities something all the liberal rhetoric of the Great Society never could: money, which is like manure. Spread enough of it around, no matter how indiscriminately, and something is bound to spring up. If the urban crisis has not turned out to be the gaping wound in society it once seemed, neither has the balm spread upon it.

The easiest way to dispose of old myths is to create new ones. Cities were believed to be dying only a short time ago, asphyxiating for lack of money. Nothing would be easier now than to suggest that cities are in the midst of an amazing renaissance that has solved all their problems. The truth is that many double-edged forces, cutting into the lives of millions of people in complex ways, are at work in cities, and on the whole country. If there never was an "urban crisis," at least not in the terms assumed by those

who make policy and report it, the lesson to be drawn is not that the opposite conventional wisdom is true. It is that we should stop bounding every few years from one inadequate metaphor for the situation we face to another.

The energy crisis; the population crisis; the pollution crisis; the crisis of crime in the streets and the crisis created by the revolution of rising expectations. The crisis of the falling dominoes, and the missile gap crisis. The whole history of policy discourse over the past twenty years often has been no more than a pantomime in which vast amounts of money and officials, technology and newsprint have been marshalled to fight crises that, it eventually was discovered, weren't really crises at all. We have tended to confuse unstoppable evolutions with sudden breaks in the dike. We have assumed that events which threatened our preconceptions were "problems"— and conversely, we have imagined that when the problems turned out to be not what they had seemed to be, we had nothing to worry about at all. We shall hear less and less about the "urban crisis" in the future; new buzz words are already taking its place.

AN ODD RENAISSANCE

For two years, Prof. Franz Schurmann, an expert in international relations at the University of California at Berkeley, has been studying the problems of America's cities. Starting on the outside and working in, concentrating on the world-wide forces affecting Anacostia or the Upper West Side, he has come to the same conclusion that many urbanologists have reached, beginning with tenements and tax receipts—that

American cities face a dynamic future, not slow death as relics of an outmoded past. Rather than trying to sort out the "crises" and break them down into "problems" that can be solved, he and other members of his Third Century America Project, working with a grant from the Ford Foundation, have tried to understand the whole: to discover how situations like the declining rate of return on European capital investment or the growth of agribusiness in Mexico relate to the Manhattan condominium market, or the dynamics of the illegal labor market in Chicago.

By forgetting about the crises for a little while, and the "policy implications" of his research, too, Schurmann has discovered that what we face is less an urban crisis, and much more a national transformation. He sees the influx either of poor Third World peoples or of foreign capital into our cities not as problems to be solved, but simply new facts of life we must begin to understand. With Manila and São Paulo looking more and more like Manhattan, he wonders, is it so surprising to see New York and Los Angeles looking more and more like Third World cities? American cities, he points out, are getting richer and poorer at the same time. The problem is not merely that any one conventional wisdom is wrong, but that when put together, so many of them are true: He sees an urban crisis and an urban renaissance going on at the same time. What he considers most important is not that affluent whites are rediscovering the urban life-style at the same time Third World migrants are filling our cities, or that petrodollars are flooding New York while industry continues to leave. What he considers important is the convergence of all these events. Efforts to turn back the clock—whether

New Left attempts to save archaic steel mills, Nixon's stab at "Project Independence," or Carter's own efforts to reduce dependency on foreign oil—only create the illusion, he warns, that scatter-shot policies can be a substitute for taking advantage of fundamental new changes that we cannot reverse. "What the economic realities say," according to Schurmann, "is that our dependence on the world economy is not due to oil. By the middle of this year, oil had slipped to third place on the list of U.S. imports; machinery and transport equipment headed the list, followed by manufactured goods. The U.S., which a century ago became the world's leading industrial nation, is now rapidly becoming primarily a trading nation."

And far from being bypassed by events—whether we consider those events good or bad—cities instead are becoming, as Professor Schurmann puts it, "the nodal points in a great transition not just of American society but of the whole world economy."

After trying to piece all the "crises" together, Schurmann has worked out his own scenario of what is happening to American cities. It falls into three parts, and bears little resemblance either to the old prophecies of urban doom, or to the new talk of a happy urban ending. First, he believes, "downtown centers of U.S. cities will continue to boom, with office buildings like the new Citicorp Tower going up, and areas of gentrified living like [New York's] SoHo continuing to expand." Barring a major change in the world economy, he has concluded that American cities will continue to benefit from the worldwide transition into a new "post-industrial era involving compact high technology, a huge service sector encompassing everyone from million-aire real estate analysts to Spanish-speaking housemaids earning less than the minimum wage, as well as sizable culture and leisure sectors. Cities," he emphasizes, "are central to the new era."

But what will happen, as this meta-morphosis goes on, to the people who already are in cities? "Second," he ob-serves, "as downtown and gentrified areas expand, the poor and jobless are being crowded into the outer cities, and beyond." As Schurmann and mem-bers of his project see it, the fact that cities will become richer doesn't mean that problems like poverty will go away. Far from it. "The difference," he points out, "the characteristic of this new ur-ban era, is that this time it is the rich who are coming in and pushing the poor out." Our cities will become more and more like the European cities American urbanologists often have en-vied—but in ways they have not antici-pated. "The likelihood," Schurmann comments, "is not just that downtown America will become more like the smaller charming European towns—high-finance and high-culture centers with lots of palaces, theaters, and res-taurants—but that the revived centers of cities like Boston and Baltimore, like the bombed-out European centers that were rebuilt following World War II, will be ringed by dingy working-class suburbs or, as one now frequently sees in Europe, 'bidonvilles,' tin-can and clapboard shacks housing Europe's mi-grant workers, the counterparts of our own illegal aliens." As American cities become increasingly internationalized, he has concluded, the American econ-omy will not just more and more re-semble foreign ones, but American society will change, too. In the third phase of Schurmann's scenario, "strati-fication will turn more and more into class, as the lines between different kinds of people no longer are sociologi-cal abstractions, but become visible traits" under these new urban circum-stances. He foresees many more white affluent city neighborhoods, many more expanding slums in which English is hardly spoken, money being poured into new skyscrapers and elegant restora-tions, while elsewhere the deterioration has only begun.

If these kinds of changes amount to a solution of an urban crisis, it is an odd sort of renaissance, in which urban problems are not so much solved as switched around within metropolitan regions; in which problems once con-sidered the exclusive bane of northern cities increasingly afflict the suburbs and the South, too, while the inequal-ities in our society are not diminished by a period of great social ferment and economic transformation, only made more intense. Not even the most opti-mistic forecasts of inner-city revival see the big-city ghettos disappearing. But are there Sowetos in our future too?

"Slumming of the suburbs is already evident in many American metropolitan regions," Schurmann comments. "It is especially evident in many close-in sub-urban centers." "The suburban crisis is no longer on the horizon." Roger Vaughan adds. "In the older and inner suburban cities it is already here." Re-search by the Rand Corporation (see Table 3), conducted for the Economic Development Administration, compares how fast cities were generating new jobs with how fast their suburban counterparts were generating them dur-ing the period when perceptions of the urban crisis were most intense, and fears

Table 3

City–Suburban Gap Narrows
In the 1960s, suburban economies were growing faster than cities, but in the 1970s
the gap began to close°

	Old Manufacturing Belt		Sunbelt		Mountain and West		National Average
	Central Cities	Suburban Centers	Central Cities	Suburban Centers	Central Cities	Suburban Centers	
1960–1970							
Employment growth	4.2%	18.0%	28.2%	58.9%	25.1%	53.1%	19.4%
Population growth	5.8%	17.1%	34.6%	72.2%	22.7%	99.7%	13.3%
1970–1975							
Employment growth	4.2%	5.4%	21.7%	18.2%	25.8%	14.9%	7.9%
Population growth	−3.5%	0.4%	13.3%	9.2%	11.0%	10.9%	4.2%

° Analysis compared 388 central and suburban cities of populations exceeding 50,000.
SOURCE: Rand Corporation analysis of Bureau of Labor Statistics data for Economic Development Administration.

for the economic future of cities were greatest. Covering the years from 1970 to 1975, these data indicate that even back when the alarums about the urban crisis were shrillest, it already was time to disabuse ourselves of another policy myth—the conventional wisdom that downtown business districts were turning into deserts of joblessness, while the suburban shopping mall was the scene of a perpetual economic miracle. Instead, all across the country, inner suburban growth rates were slowing down, while the rate at which cities were generating new jobs was catching up. Though the pattern was the same everywhere, it was particularly instructive in the old manufacturing-belt metropolitan regions, where the flight of jobs to the suburbs was supposed to be most serious.

The data show that during the 1960s,

the suburban centers indeed were outperforming the downtown economies at an extraordinary rate. In the Northeast and Midwest, suburban centers like Cherry Hill in suburban Philadelphia and Nassau County in suburban New York were generating new jobs more than four times faster than their respective city centers. In the South and West, this was the period when Orange County began to outperform Los Angeles, and San Jose to overtake San Francisco in job growth. There, suburbs were generating new employment twice as fast as the inner cities.

But by 1975—the very year the fiscal crisis broke and urban economic decline became a major national issue—the situation had changed dramatically. In the South and West, the ratio had reversed itself. Cities were now generating new jobs twice as fast as the nearer suburban centers. And in the Northeast and Midwest, cities were outperforming suburban centers, if one takes into account the fact that while the growth of new jobs in cities continued, their populations were declining —that the new jobs cities were creating had to be shared out among fewer and fewer people.[2]

All this hardly means that Harlem is becoming the showplace of the American economy, and that Scarsdale soon will have to go on the dole. But it does show that inner-city economies were stronger, even in the depths of the recessions of the early 1970s, than seemed possible. In fact, since 1975, as the employment statistics for cities like St. Louis and Cleveland show, cities have accelerated the rate at which they have generated new jobs. Outlying exurban areas and the newer suburban districts are still growing fast, but what can be said is that factors once actively biased against cities now are increasingly favorable toward them. It seems likely that both the Southern Shift and the great migrations to the suburbs have largely run their course. Many inner cities already have passed through the social trauma associated with deindustrialization; it is now Westchester and North Carolina that must worry about losing jobs—to Taiwan and Korea. The suburbs also face structural limitations on growth that cities do not. Cities expand vertically, suburbs laterally, and there is not much horizontal space left for new growth in many suburban areas, as one discovers when one seeks cheap, large tracts of developable land these days in either Nassau or Los Angeles County. The result is that while cities today are generating new employment opportunities sometimes faster than, or at least as fast as, many sub-

urban areas, the suburbs themselves are falling prey to social problems once confined within city limits. Interstate highways, on which the suburbs heavily depend, have begun to deteriorate, as have stocks of suburban housing, hastily built with FHA mortgages in the 1950s. New York's Suffolk County has one of the fastest growing dependent populations in the country. It would be as simplistic to herald doom for suburbia now as it once was to regard skyscrapers as tombstones. But it hardly seems too early to point out that the controversy over "suburban exclusion" —like the one over redlining—has come too late, and is an example of yet another lag in perception between the social problem and the political debate. There is no doubt now that increasing numbers of the poor and of racial minorities finally are getting their chance to move to suburbia. But barriers preventing the poor, jobless, and nonwhite from getting a house with a picket fence around it are beginning to tumble precisely at the moment when suburban opportunities are beginning to ebb—and the affluent are beginning to discover not just the charms of urban life, but the high cost of suburban mortgages and commuting.

Like most urban "solutions," the changing composition of inner-city populations creates as many problems as it solves; not the least of these is the danger that what political influence black Americans have been able to gain as a result of their long march from the rural South into the slums of urban America now will be eroded as the forces of gentrification gather momentum. Urban policy debate still tends to focus on the immense losses in white middle-class populations that cities suffered from the end of World War II into the middle 1970s. We take far less note of the fact that poor and non-white populations are leaving their ghettos today almost as dramatically as ethnic whites deserted the old neighborhoods in the 1950s. According to U.S. Census Bureau data, of the fifty Congressional districts that have lost 5 percent or more of their population since the 1970 census, forty-six of them have a majority of their populations in urban areas—and almost all of these districts have populations that are largely nonwhite or poor or both. Fourteen of fifteen Congressional districts represented by blacks have lost population since 1970, and the nation's only predominantly Puerto Rican district, New York's 21st, has lost nearly a third of its total population in less than eight years. Where are these people going— or being pushed? Many are simply being transferred to otherer areas within the same city, but black migration to the suburbs is now a significant demographic pattern, and for the first time since the inauguration of the Underground Railroad, more blacks are emigrating to the South than are leaving it. (See Table 4.)

The conclusion is an obvious, and in many ways unflattering, one about the way our society works. So long as suburban land was cheap, and the South booming, we could afford to cede our downtown areas to dependent populations, and abandon their stagnant economies to the "underclass." But now that the scent for an urban revival is in the air, cities increasingly look like those reservations we ceded so solemnly to the Indians—until we noticed they had uranium underneath. While sociologists detect changing cultural attitudes toward city life, it is probably best to seek the reason for what is

happening in market forces. The truth —whatever cultural enlightenment may be involved—is that the cost of a suburban split-level has only to soar so high, and the price of an inner-city brownstone to plummet so low, before people in Westchester start finding even certain neighborhoods in The Bronx colorful and cultivated places to live. As with the bombed-out cities of Europe thirty years ago, one of the northern cities' greatest present assets is their past misfortune. For thirty years the cost of inner-city land, real estate, and labor has been declining, and the cost of those commodities in the suburbs rising, in relationship to each other. Whether the arsonists of the South Bronx have created a graveyard of urban civilization, or the biggest bonanza for the smart money developers yet, depends on the eye of the beholder. But even if one does consider Walter Wriston a philanthropist for building Citicorp Tower, or Henry Ford's investment in Renaissance Plaza a selfless gesture of noblesse oblige, it does no harm to keep in mind the comment of one big-time realtor: "Any corporation today that decided to sell in Baltimore and buy in L.A.," he said, "would be acting irrationally in terms of the market. Everything would cost more in California, and they would be putting 3,000 miles between themselves and what is still the richest, biggest market in the world, the Northeast megalopolis."

PROBLEMS MOVE OUT

What will be the long-term effects on cities of the sudden rediscovery that they not only can be pleasant places to live, but profitable places to buy land? Even while working hard to attract

Table 4

Black Flight

In the 1950s and 1960s the influx of poor, nonwhite populations created social and fiscal problems for cities. Today the problem is reversed. Nonwhite political gains are threatened by ghetto flight. Every one of the sixteen urban Congressional districts with either black or Puerto Rican majorities has suffered major population losses in the 1970s. The result: Nonwhites may lose political representation after the 1980 census, in spite of urban "revival." (N.B.: Two black members of Congress, Ronald Dellums and Yvonne Brathwaite Burke, both of California, represent districts that do not have a black majority.)

Majority Nonwhite Congressional Districts

District	City	Representative		Per Cent Population Loss, 1970–1976
California 29	Los Angeles	Hawkins	(*)	—6
Illinois 1	Chicago	Metcalfe	(*)†	—15
Illinois 7	Chicago	Collins	(*)	—12
Maryland 7	Baltimore	Mitchell	(*)	—9
Michigan 1	Detroit	Conyers	(*)	—11
Michigan 13	Detroit	Diggs	(*)	—19
Missouri 1	St. Louis	Clay	(*)	—20
New Jersey 10	Newark	Rodino		—9
New York 12	Brooklyn	Chisholm	(*)	—15
New York 14	Brooklyn	Richmond		—11
New York 19	Manhattan	Rangel	(*)	—14
New York 21	Bronx	Garcia		—29
Ohio 21	Cleveland	Stokes	(*)	—21
Pennsylvania 2	Philadelphia	Dix	(*)	—7
Tennessee 8	Memphis	Ford	(*)	—9
Texas 18	Houston	Jordan	(*)	—6

(*) = Member of Congressional Black Caucus.
† Rep. Ralph H. Metcalfe died in October.
SOURCES: The Almanac of American Politics 1978; Congressional Quarterly; U.S. Census Bureau.

private investment, many city officials have mixed emotions about the strategy. Officials in Hartford recently mounted a major campaign to persuade an airline to open a headquarters downtown. The effort was a success, but virtually all the new jobs created are held by commuters, not the inner-city unemployed. Officials in Boston point out that the revival of Quincy Market and the surrounding area, impressive as it has been, has saddled the business district with tax-exempt government offices, and that most of the revenues the new restaurants and boutiques bring go into the state treasury. Meanwhile, more than one thousand small-scale loft industries, employing mostly low-wage workers who are now on the unemployment rolls, were destroyed by the redevelopment process.

It is already clear that many problems once considered exclusively "urban" now seem less troublesome for cities not because they are being solved, but simply because they are being pushed beyond the city limits. Meanwhile even more serious city problems are not even being displaced. They are only being masked by current political, economic, and social trends. Inner-city education, for example, is in appalling shape. But we are hearing less and less about the blackboard jungle for two reasons, both of which have nothing to do with the fact that we seem to have lost the knack for teaching people how to read and write. The first reason is that more and more Americans, including non-white Americans, are having fewer and fewer children. The second is that the kind of people who can command attention in Congress and in the press now increasingly send their children to private schools, especially when they live in cities. Nineteen-seventy-eight was the year it became fashionable for cultivated people with high incomes to extol the charms of city life, to confess they had found life in the suburbs just a little dowdy. But it was also the year that Congressmen and state legislators fell all over each other in a mad scramble to give tax credits to those who take their children out of public schools. New York, having earlier abolished free tuition at City University in the name of fiscal solvency, this year enacted generous tax credits for parents who send their children to private universities. So while the tax revolt spreads, and there is less and less money for P.S. 10 or the Bronx High School of Science, the academies of the new urban gentry enjoy important new indirect subsidies. This is hardly a prescription for solving inner-city social problems, let alone restoring American cities to their former roles as the Great Integrators of American life. Education in most American cities today is not only separate and unequal, but scandalously so. The real question is not whether the deterioration of most big-city school systems can be stopped, but how to begin constructing new ones. The issue is hardly even raised.

We also should take less comfort than we do from the declining crime rates in cities. They bespeak no particular victory for either law or order, let alone any success in making our courts more just or converting our prisons into institutions of rehabilitation. It is just that violent crime is essentially teenage crime, and with Americans showing less and less of an interest in reproducing themselves, teenagers of all races form a rapidly dwindling proportion of most inner-city populations. We have demography— not any new wisdom in transmitting civility and skills to city youth—to thank if there is less terror in the subways, fewer assaults on city streets. (See Table 5.) Indeed, if the death of the American city has proved to be an illusion, part of the reason is that the death of the American family is becoming a fact. As Dr. Thomas Muller of the Urban Institute points out, families are still fleeing big cities; one must go to much smaller cities in upstate New York and Pennsylvania to find any real renaissance in traditional neighborhood life. Instead the new gentrified neighborhoods are filled with trendy restaurants, not family markets; and big old houses are broken up into one-room studios, for that majority of our adult population that now either divorces or never marries at all. Commuting becomes intolerable, a place in town suddenly becomes attractive, when both spouses work. But it would be quite wrong to suggest that urban areas suddenly are becoming more congenial to

Table 5

The Declining Significance of Crime*

The larger the city, the faster crime has been declining

Cities by Population	Number of Cities	Percent Change in Crime Rate 1977–78
more than 1 million	6	−4
250,000–1 million	49	−2
50,000–250,000	371	−1

Crime is decreasing fastest in the Northeast and in the Midwest

Crime index trends by geographic region

Region	Percent Change in Crime Rate 1977–78
Nationwide	−2
Northeast	−6
Midwest	−5
South	−1
West	+2

Number of crimes are decreasing in Northeastern and Midwestern cities, while they are still growing in Southern and Western cities

Increase or decline in numbers of offenses known to police

Northeastern and Midwestern Cities	Changes in Number of Crimes 1977–1978	Southern and Western Cities	Changes in Number of Crimes 1977–1978
New York	−26,505	Los Angeles	+7,025
Chicago	−7,892	Houston	+4,103
Boston	−2,201	Phoenix	+3,050
Baltimore	−929	Atlanta	+2,988
St. Louis	−2,066	Miami	−326
Detroit	−6,527	Dallas	−1,433

* Statistics compare change from 1977 to 1978 during the period January–June.
SOURCE: Federal Bureau of Investigation Uniform Crime Reports, September, 1978.

the nurturing of our national future. In many ways it is just the other way around.

Another looming problem for the northern cities and the whole country is the massive deterioration of our public capital stock, which no amount of private restoration or speculation in real estate can reverse. As much as a third of the drinking water piped into New York City is lost through seepage before it reaches the city limits. Arson, abandonment, and other forms of disinvestment continue to extort an enormous public cost even when property values rise. And to the potholed streets and seeping tunnels of the North, the collapsing freeways and disintegrating sewer systems of the suburbs and South will be added sooner than we imagine. Probably the most serious mistake in urban policy always has been the tendency to confuse the fiscal solvency of cities with their physical health. If a city's budget is in the black, it is always assumed, then it is somehow a successful human society; if a city is going bankrupt, it must bespeak some terrible crisis of urban civilization.

The truth is that there tends to be little difference in the black teenage unemployment rate in solvent cities like Houston and fiscally troubled cities like New York. States like Connecticut, New Jersey, and New Hampshire for years escaped financial trauma by keeping taxes low. But this did not turn Newark into the Dallas of the North, or make the little mill towns of New England, with their vanishing industries, better places to look for a job than Manhattan or Boston. It is very instructive, as one looks back at what has happened to cities over the last few years, to note how successfully our political and economic system has dealt with the money problems, while scarcely addressing the human ones at all. For all the scare headlines and Congressional questioning, the bank guarantees for New York came through. Indeed all the members of what President Carter calls his "new urban partnership"—federal officials, state officials, city officials, Congressional officials, corporate officials—did not so much bail out the city as themselves from the financial and economic complications default would have entailed.

But one can hardly say the same things about New York's—or most other cities'—underlying problems. What is the value of a balanced budget if it means a continual deterioration in city services? What is the benefit of a deluge of federal spending if it means a widening, not narrowing, gap in incomes between the very rich and the very poor? What will have been accomplished, even if cities enjoy a real renaissance—if all the problems we formerly kept locked in the ghetto are just sent off to roost someplace else?

There was a fiscal crisis in American cities three years ago, one which was mistaken for an urban crisis that never existed in the terms that were assumed. Today the fiscal surplus in some American cities—the cities with the worst problems are still very short of cash—risks being interpreted in a way that bears no more relationship to the complex problems of city life than the old scare-talk did. What is especially troubling is not that some local governments had so little money three years ago, and that they have so much of it now. It is that the financial response of our system remains so unpredictable and volatile, and so unrelated to the chronic problems we face. For decades cities and their budgets have tended to be both more vulnerable to recession and more responsive in times of recovery than the nation as a whole. While default has been avoided, cities still face the unsolved fiscal problem that they are given the least money when they need it most, and have to carry burdens that other levels of government can shirk as they please, while remaining so vulnerable to the irrationalities of both our cyclical economy and the flow of federal dollars. What will happen if there is another big recession by 1980, and in the interim the taxpayers' revolt means that the federal Treasury is no longer throwing money at problems? The gnawing doubt behind all the rosy urban forecasts now is that the favorable indicators we see reflect only the general, and relatively modest, recovery of the national economy since 1975. It will be interesting to see how all the new theories stand up, which way all the straws of urban revival will blow, when they are exposed to an unfavorable wind.

Oddly enough, one of the first times I heard the urban catastrophe thesis disputed, and a much more positive future for American cities predicted, was at a time when inner-city unemployment rates were still at Depression levels, and the municipal deficits had not yet begun to turn into surplus. I did not hear it from an investment banker or academic or a politician in Washington, but from Mayor Kenneth Gibson of Newark, the city Americans still somehow consider to exist outside the framework of our national possibilities. For years Gibson has had a quite opposite view. He has called Newark "the city of the future"—the place where the hardest problems hit first, but also where the outlines of the future might first become visible. "Watch where Newark is now," Gibson said for years, "and you will see where your own city will be five or fifteen years from now." It always seemed like a prophecy of doom. But more than a year ago, Gibson was saying that the urban crisis had bottomed out, that cities were on the way up again. "Newark is a city with a future," he told me back in those days when that seemed difficult to believe. "The energy crisis has guaranteed the future of the American city."

Even earlier, about the time of the New York City blackout and riots in the summer of 1977, Nicholas Carbone, head of the Hartford city council, was predicting urban recovery too, and appending to his prediction a question. "There is no doubt cities will be saved," Carbone was saying at a time when so many cities seemed doomed. "The real question is who cities will be saved for:

the big corporations and the returning middle class, or for the poor, the jobless, the people who always seem to be shortchanged by our society? Are cities collections of skyscrapers, or groups of human beings? Who will cities be saved for?"

Perhaps that was the real question underlying the great urban debate, and today we have the answer. It is visible in the newly gentrified neighborhoods with their marble fireplaces and parquet floors, in the ticky-tacky little suburbs where the blight has already begun; in the soaring new palaces downtown, and in those downtrodden parts of rural south Texas where, for all the talk of Southern Shift, the glitter of Houston has never reached. As always we face a maddening inability to grasp the conditions that plague us, a truly American genius for casting them into brilliant new forms.

NOTES

1. Like most conventional wisdoms, the arbitrary antithesis between "Sunbelt" and "Frostbelt" is a crutch that has crippled understanding of cities and their problems, and should be eschewed. In some of the frostiest of the "Frostbelt" cities—notably St. Paul, Minneapolis, Milwaukee, and Chicago—urban problems have been far less severe than in cities like St. Louis, Baltimore, and Oakland, where the snow falls less often or not at all. The distinction also ignores the problems of growth in cities like Houston and Los Angeles, even though these are often as severe for human beings as the problems of stagnation and decay.
2. Cities probably have performed better in generating new employment than these data indicate, because the official statistics by definition disregard the "subterranean" economies flourishing in most U.S. cities. One whole stratum of urban America—illegal aliens—and the work they do is almost entirely left out because of the way we collate numbers. Another group, U.S. blacks, also is significantly disfranchised from the statistical life of the nation because of the inherent bias in how we count urban population and assess economic activities in cities. Does a houseful of

Caribbeans in The Bronx not exist because our census takers do not speak Spanish? Do the profits and losses of a drug dealer have any less effect on a city than those of a corner grocery? Most inner cities have not lost nearly as many people or jobs as official statistics indicate, and as anyone who has ever lived in a ghetto—or experienced poverty—knows, life on the other side of the tracks is an existence not of indolence, but of constant hustle. We should not imagine "they don't want to work" or are not even there, just because their livelihoods and lives fall outside the purview of what is considered legitimate economic and social activity.

America's Cities Are (Mostly) Better Than Ever

Richard Wade

More than a decade ago the phrase "urban crisis" crept into our public conversation. Since then it has become a cliché, connoting a wide range of persistent and dangerous problems confronting our cities. Moreover, the phrase, like "missile crisis" or "energy crisis," suggests both newness and immediate danger. The rioting, arson, and looting that erupted in the 1960's fortified this general impression. Presumably something unprecedented had happened. Urban life had become unmanageable; in the professional and popular view, cities were "ungovernable."

Something new, indeed, had happened. It was not that American cities had not known violence and race conflict before. They ran like thick red lines through the history of many cities. But the scale and ubiquity of the modern outbreaks had no earlier analogue. Large and small cities, both north and south, witnessed almost simultaneous explosions; the number of dead and injured and the amount of property damage easily exceeded those of anything previous. Few people predicted the rioting, hence most sought for an explanation in very recent developments —black migrations, the slow pace of desegregation, unemployment, broken families, and the Vietnam War.

Yet the fires of the 1960's were not the arson of a single decade or generation. Urban society had been accumulating combustibles for well over a century. The seventies have simply tamped down the flames while the ashes still smolder and, unless the historical sources of the present crisis are better understood and public policy changed, a recurrence, next time probably worse, is almost inevitable. New York City's experience during the 1977 black-out ought to have served as the first alarm for the nation.

What baffled most commentators in the sixties was that the convulsions came at a time when urban experts confidently had asserted that the nation's cities were overcoming their afflictions. There had been, for example, a marked decline in the percentage of substandard housing; there were relatively fewer urban poor than ever before; hospital beds had caught up with need; federal programs were bringing health care to an unprecedented number of people; schools had reduced class size; new skylines attested to renewed downtown vitality; municipal government, though scarred by occasional scandals, was demonstrably more competent than it once had been.

To the historian the argument had a superficial validity. One only had to compare the city of 1970 with the city of 1900 to measure municipal progress. At the turn of the century every city had its concentrations of wretched

From *American Heritage* (February/March 1979), pp. 6–13. Reprinted by permission of the author.

neighborhoods where poor people huddled in run-down or jerry-built houses and in tenements lacking even toilets or running water. Primitive coal stoves provided the heat; kerosene lamps the light. Family cohesiveness, always fragile, often cracked under the weight of these oppressive circumstances. Nor were these conditions exceptional. Jacob Riis's *How the Other Half Lives* described the festering slums on New York's Lower East Side in 1890; but as the title suggests, he was also discussing the predicament of over 50 per cent of the city's population. Indeed, a congressional inquiry into urban housing at about the same time demonstrated that every metropolis matched New York's dilapidated, unsanitary, and dangerous dwellings.

Nor was there much in the neighborhood to compensate for the miseries of home life. The droppings of thousands of horses made even crossing the street hazardous. Garbage clogged thoroughfares; sanitation carts picked their way through congested avenues and alleys once a week at best. Cheap shops and uninspected markets lined the sidewalks. No traffic regulations prevented horse-drawn trucks and carts, electric trolleys, and private hacks from creating a continual cacophony, day and night. And dense smoke from coal-burning factories and office buildings rolled darkly through downtown. Worse still, crime and violence were constant companions of slum dwellers.

Three institutions attenuated the misery of the slum—the church, the school, and the saloon. And they were attractive precisely because they provided what the tenement and neighborhood lacked. The church was clean and uncongested; its friendly priest, minister, or rabbi cared about the parishioners and their families. Even

the most primitive schools took the children out of the tenement and into rooms that were at least heated in the winter. The saloon was bright and congenial, and the husband could meet with friends and neighbors away from the oppressive crowding of the apartment. Yet these oases could not conceal—indeed they only magnified—the grinding deprivation of the lives of these people. Later commentators would invest the "good old neighborhood" with charm, conviviality, and livability; but to most of its residents, life was a losing struggle against filth, noise, and disorder.

The whole family was drawn into the contest. Jobs for anyone were scarce and irregular. Good, steady work that permitted the father to feed, clothe, and shelter his family on his own was very rare. The wife and children usually had to enter the already overcrowded job market. Mothers and daughters sewed, packaged nuts, made artificial flowers. Young boys sold newspapers, picked coal, collected rags, ran errands. Frequent depressions did away with even these menial tasks.

Schooling was brief. Children dropped out, not at fourteen or fifteen, but at eight or nine. Even so, education was often inadequate: classrooms were crowded, teachers poorly trained and politically selected. No audiovisual aids or paraprofessional help assisted the beleaguered instructor; the truant officer became a familiar figure in the neighborhood. Reformers sought vainly to get class sizes down to fifty and replace patronage appointments with professionals.

Conditions in the area were tolerable only because those who lived there considered them temporary. Residential turnover was high; one of every five families had a different address each year. Most, of course, moved only a short distance and often because they could not pay the rent. But a significant number found housing in more pleasant communities away from the old slum. Scholars later argued over the percentage who "made it" out; yet every resident knew someone who did; a relative, perhaps, or someone on the block or in the parish. But the possibility of escape was as much a part of the experience as confinement.

The change over the subsequent three-quarters of a century was dramatic. In 1902 Robert Hunter estimated that over half the urban population lived beneath the poverty line. By 1970 that figure had fallen to less than 20 per cent, even though the definition of poverty had been raised substantially. Density in the inner city dropped drastically; Jacob Riis found over 300,000 people per square mile living in New York's tenth ward; today, any concentration over 75,000 a square mile is considered intolerable. Public policy and private development removed the most visible downtown slums, though cancerous nodes remained behind. Public housing, with all its problems, replaced the most depressed and dilapidated areas. New building in the outer city and suburbs provided modern accommodations for an exploding urban population. In the sixties, experts argued over whether "substandard" housing composed 15 or 18 per cent of the total stock; judged by the same standards seventy years earlier, it would have composed more than half.

Even the crime rate was probably higher in 1900, though there is no way to prove it. Police organization was primitive, and systematic reporting of crime was still decades away. Politicians hired and fired the force; collusion between criminals and police was common. Constant gang warfare jeopardized the peace of nearly every downtown area. Political reformers always promised the "restoration of law and order."

Municipal governments were too weak to control matters. State governments granted cities only modest powers, and then only grudgingly. Corruption riddled most city halls and municipalities. Political bosses and special interests united to plunder the public till. Lincoln Steffens made a national reputation with the book entitled *The Shame of the Cities*, which chronicled the boodle, bribery, and chicanery that he contended characterized nearly every American city. Good government forces occasionally broke the unseemly ring, but usually not for long.

In short, the present city, for all its problems, is cleaner, less crowded, safer, and more livable than its turn-of-the-century counterpart. Its people are more prosperous, better educated, and healthier than they were seventy years ago.

The slow but steady improvement in municipal affairs was the result of both particular historical conditions of the twentieth century and the efforts of many generations of urban dwellers. American cities enjoyed continued growth and expansion for most of the period. They were also the vital centers of a surging national economy. As the country became increasingly urban, the best talent and greatest wealth gravitated to the metropolis, where a huge pool of skilled and unskilled labor could be easily tapped. This combination made it possible for the United States to become the most powerful industrial nation in the world.

Technological changes, themselves largely products of the urban explosion, permitted new advances in municipal management. Subways, elevateds, and automobiles facilitated the movement of people throughout the expanding metropolis, retiring horses to the country. Modern medicine increased the effectiveness of public health measures. Electricity and central heating improved the comfort of new housing, and the long-term mortgage made home ownership easier to manage. Movies, radio, and television democratized entertainment, if they did not always elevate it. New laws forced more children into schools and kept them there longer.

Though progress was often sporadic, city government widened its competence and improved its performance. Tensions between reformers and urban machines resulted in permanent gains, for after each revolt was beaten back, some improvements were always retained. Civil service slowly produced a bureaucracy that, for all its clumsiness, was distinctly superior to the earlier rampant patronage system. Zoning put a measure of predictability, if not control, into land use. And nearly everywhere the quality of urban leadership was noticeably better than before. A few old-time bosses persisted, but they were viewed as quaint anachronisms rather than as the logical expressions of city politics.

This considerable achievement rested on two historical conditions—the general prosperity of the period and the ample municipal limits which permitted expanding economic activity to take place within a single political jurisdiction. Except for the Great Depression and occasional sharp dips in the business index, American cities generally witnessed sustained growth. Even wartime did not interrupt the expan-

sion; indeed, immense military spending acted as a swift stimulus to urban economies. Municipal progress cost money—a lot of it—and American cities generally had it to spend. And when they did not, they borrowed, confident that the future would be even more prosperous.

This was, moreover, the age of the self-sufficient city. Municipal boundaries were wide and continually enlarging. In 1876 St. Louis reached out into neighboring farm land and incorporated all the area now within its city limits. In one swift move in 1889 Chicago added over 125 square miles to its territory. And in 1898 New York absorbed the four surrounding counties —including Brooklyn, the nation's fourth largest city—making it the world's Empire City.

In 1900 municipal boundaries were generous, almost always including unsettled and undeveloped land. As populations grew, there were always fresh areas to build up. This meant that all the wealth, all the commerce, all the industry, and all the talent lay within the city. When serious problems arose, all the resources of the metropolis could be brought to bear to solve them. More prosperous than either the state or federal governments, the cities needed no outside help; indeed they met any interference with the demand for home rule.

For as long as these historical conditions prevailed, American cities could make incremental progress in attacking even the most vexing problems. But after the Second World War, two divisive elements entered the metropolis, destroying its economic and governmental unity and profoundly altering its social structure. The first division was between suburb and city; the second between black and white. Actually, these fissures always had been present, but not on the same scale or with the same intensity, and certainly not with the same significance.

Suburbanization is almost as old as urbanization. American cities always have grown from the inside out; as population increased, it spilled outside municipal limits. Initially these suburbs were not the exclusive resort of the wealthy; many poor lived there to avoid city taxes and regulations. But railroad development in the mid-nineteenth century produced modern commuting suburbs: Chicago had fifty-two of them by 1874. Though suburbs grew rapidly, their numbers were always relatively small and their locations governed by rail lines. By the 1920's the automobile spawned a second generation of suburbs, filling in the areas between the older ones and setting off an unprecedented building boom beyond the municipal limits.

The crash of 1929 put an end to suburban expansion for fifteen years. During the Depression, people could not afford new housing, and when war came, the military consumed all available construction material. But the pent-up demand broke loose with the coming of peace. By 1970 the census reported that more people in the metropolitan regions lived outside the municipal boundaries than within. All cities, even smaller ones, were surrounded by numerous small jurisdictions, self-governing, self-taxing—and growing.

The historical remedy to this problem—annexation of surrounding areas —was no longer available. In most states the process required a majority of the voters in both the cities and the suburbs to support consolidation, and after 1920 the outlying areas were in-creasingly against incorporation. The cities, now with fixed boundaries, gradually lost population, while the suburbs experienced steady growth.

Moreover, this demographic change profoundly altered the social structure of the metropolis. The middle class rapidly evacuated the old city in favor of the suburbs. In turn, they were replaced by migrants from the South and from Latin America. The newcomers were mostly poor and racially distinct. With little education or skills, they were tax consumers rather than tax producers. They needed help on a large scale. Most of all they needed jobs. But industry and commerce had followed the outward movement of people. At just the time municipal government faced additional responsibilities, it saw its revenue base shrinking. Inevitably, various groups fell to quarreling over these limited resources, producing new tensions and anxieties.

The rioting of the 1960's revealed another fissure in the metropolis—the division between black and white. Some blacks always had lived in cities, even under slavery. But the "peculiar institution" had confined most to the Southern countryside. After the Civil War, former slaves without land or urban skills drifted into Southern cities, where they quickly composed a large portion of the population. The urban South accommodated the newcomers within an elaborate system of segregation. The separation of the races was accomplished both by custom and, after 1896, under Jim Crow statutes.

The massive Northern migration of rural Southern blacks in this century, however, slowly altered the racial composition of nearly every city across the country. Municipal governments adopted no new policies to deal with the influx. Indeed, they assumed that the same process that had incorporated millions of immigrants into the metropolitan mainstream would also be available to blacks. That is, the newcomers initially would congregate at the heart of town, increase their numbers, get an economic foothold, and then gradually disperse into more pleasant residential neighborhoods away from the congested center. This process, though often cruel and painful, had served the immigrants, the city, and the country well.

But the blacks' experience was fundamentally different. They did, indeed, gather at the center, and there they found what immigrants always had found: wretched housing, overcrowded neighborhoods, high unemployment, inadequate schools, littered streets, garbage-strewn alleys, rampant crime, and endemic disorder. However, the new ghetto, unlike the old, did not loosen and disperse. Rather it simply spread block by block, oozing out over adjacent communities. White residents retreated while blacks moved into new areas beyond downtown. Later a generation would grow up that knew only the ghetto and its debilitating life.

The immigrant ghetto had been tolerable because it was thought to be temporary, a rough staging ground for upward and outward mobility. Blacks increasingly perceived the ghetto to be their permanent home. And each federal census fortified this apprehension as the index of racial segregation moved steadily upward. There was, of course, some modest leakage here and there, but the barriers to escape remained formidable.

This confinement had two consequences that were different from those of the old ghetto. The first was the alienation of its black middle class. They, after all, had done what they were supposed to do: stayed in school, kept out of serious trouble, got higher education, and made good money. But they were still denied, by the color of their skin alone, that most important symbol of success in America—the right to live in a neighborhood of their own choosing with schools appropriate to their ambitions for their children.

The size of this black middle class is large; indeed, no other group has had a success story quite equal to it. In 1950 the federal census listed about 10 per cent of American blacks as "middle class"; by 1960 that figure had climbed to nearly 18 per cent; by 1970 it had jumped above one-third. To be sure, it often required two breadwinners in the family to achieve this status; that, plus ambition and hard work. For these people, continued *de facto* residential segregation was especially cruel. Even in fashionable black neighborhoods, hope turned into resentful bitterness.

For the less successful, the situation was much worse. The black ghetto contained the city's worst housing, schools, and community institutions. It generated few jobs and experienced soaring unemployment. Crime rates were high, gang warfare common, and vice rampant. All this contributed to the breakdown of family life and the encouragement of dependency. Newcomers always had found it difficult to adjust to the ghetto; race compounded the problem. In the sixties, daily frustrations spilled over into violence. The young struck out against the symbols of their oppression that were closest at hand, reducing large ghetto areas to ashes.

Race, then, greatly widened the already yawning gap between city and suburb. Every important issue that arose within the metropolis reflected this division. School busing became the symbolic question: without residential segregation, no busing would be necessary. "Affirmative action" became a euphemism for introducing minorities into employment areas previously monopolized by whites. The collapse of mass transit left blacks riding in the front of the bus but with diminishing numbers of white companions. While crime rates rose in the suburbs, popular stereotypes still associated violence with inner-city minorities. In short, uniting the metropolis would have been difficult enough; the addition of race introduced an enormously complicating factor.

In the seventies the inner cities quieted down. But the new tranquillity came from black resignation rather than from a larger measure of justice. The unemployment figures contained the warning: 10 per cent in older cities; 20 per cent in the ghettos; 40 per cent among minority youth. In addition, middle-class blacks ran into all kinds of obstacles when trying to escape to the suburbs. The courts were ambivalent about legal restrictions, especially zoning, which had the effect of exclusion. And social pressures in the suburbs were often not very subtle. As a result, the ghetto still festered; indeed, its boundaries expanded each week.

Yet certain factors hold out some hope for the future. For example, suburbs are finding that they are no more self-sufficient than the cities. The same forces that led to urban decay earlier are now spreading into the surrounding communities. This is particularly true of those suburbs adjacent to the city limits. Indeed, the phrase "inner suburbs" surely will join "inner city" as shorthand for the long list of urban ills in the eighties. And for much the same reasons. They are the oldest part of suburban America. In order to keep taxes down, they allowed most of their land to be developed. Now there is no room for expansion. The new suburbanites go farther out; new industrial and commercial installations also bypass the closer-in suburbs. Large numbers of older residents, their children now gone, head for retirement areas or back to the city. Newer shopping centers in outlying suburbs skim off dollars from local merchants. Worse still, crime rates grow faster in these communities than in any other part of the metropolis.

In addition, suburban government is the weakest link in our governmental system. Until recently, residential participation in local affairs was low; most communities hired professional managers to make budgets and administer day-to-day affairs. Voting was light for local offices, and though suburbanites vote heavily Republican in national elections, suburban politics remain consciously nonpartisan. Hence, when the crisis moved in, most suburbs lacked the tradition or tools to grapple with it. By the 1970's new suburban newspapers began to reveal the often scandalous relations between some developers and many town halls. Voters increasingly turned down bond issues, even for schools. The inner suburbs' one trump card is that they still control the suburban lobby in most states. They played that card to get some relief for all local governments, hence they became the major beneficiaries. Yet neither this nor federal revenue-sharing programs could do more than postpone the inevitable fiscal impasse. When New York City slid toward bankruptcy, Yonkers, located in one of the nation's richest suburban counties, was placed in receivership.

The extension of city problems into the suburbs poked large holes in the crabgrass curtain that previously had separated the two parts of the metropolis. Now their common predicament created the possibility of a new co-operation to replace the hostility that historically had divided city and suburb. The inner suburbs were reluctant to recognize their own decline, but by the seventies they recognized that they had to trade part of their independence for outside help.

For the first time, a substantial suburban population has a stake in a united metropolis. The inner ring is no longer self-sufficient. It relies increasingly on state and federal aid rather than on its indigenous tax base. Hence, its most serious problems cannot be solved without cooperation with the city as well as with neighboring suburbs. In the 1950's the movement for metropolitan government was essentially a big-city strategy; now that concept has natural allies. To be sure, the notion of a single governmental jurisdiction is politically impossible except in a few places.

A consolidation of effort by function, however, is already imperative. In housing, education, transportation, water, pollution, and police, control depends on devising programs that employ a concentrated, cooperative regional approach. Even this requires a change in state and federal policies, which presently funnel funds into old governmental units rather than into intergovernmental ones. But the crisis of the inner suburbs has produced the necessary condition for a fundamental shift in public policy based on metropolitan realities rather than on anachronistic political jurisdictions.

New demographic changes also brought some easing of racial tensions. The massive movement of blacks from the South to Northern cities virtually has stopped; indeed, some experts detect a slight reverse of the flow. The breaking of segregation and the availability of jobs in Southern cities made them at least as attractive as Northern ones. Moreover, urban black birth rates dropped rapidly. This reduced ghetto tensions somewhat but not ghetto conditions. In addition, the election of black mayors in many parts of the country lessened the feeling of isolation and powerlessness of urban blacks. The relative quiet of the ghetto in the seventies was somewhat deceptive but did provide some breathing space for the nation if the nation had the ingenuity and will to seize it.

But time is running out and we have not used it wisely to heal racial divisions or reduce urban-suburban tensions. Federal policy has neglected cities in favor of surrounding communities. Revenue-sharing formulas were based largely on population rather than on need; government installations usually were placed in outlying areas; special programs for the inner cities were either reduced or dismantled. Worse still, urban economies, historically the nation's most resilient, recovered more slowly from recurring recessions than the suburbs with their newer facilities. And the outward flow of jobs and middle-class city dwellers continued unabated. The problem is more severe in the older areas of the Northeast and Midwest. Yet the "Sunbelt" cities show the same symptoms. The acids of urban decay do not recognize the Mason-Dixon line.

The persistence of the urban crisis has led many Americans to look elsewhere for solutions. But a look outward indicates that what some thought was a peculiarly American question is, in fact, an international urban crisis. Rome's fiscal management makes New York's look frugal; the inadequacy of London's inner-city schools is more than a match for their American counterparts; Frankfurt's pollution experts travel to Pittsburgh for advice; few American housing commissioners would trade jobs with their opposite numbers in Sydney. Russian urban experts see their limited growth policies overwhelmed by illegal migration; the smog in Sarajevo would frighten even an Angelino; Rumania's ambitious satellite city plan has not inhibited the growth of Bucharest or produced any "new towns"; more than three decades after World War II, no major city in Eastern Europe has dented its housing shortage.

The record of foreign cities on race is no more instructive. British urban centers are producing their own "New Commonwealth" ghettos; not a single black sits in Parliament. Amsterdam cannot handle its old colonists of different color. Paris and Marseilles have been unable to assimilate their French Algerians. Moscow couldn't manage even a small number of African students; in Bucharest, urban renewal is gypsy removal. In Sydney and Auckland, the aborigines, though small in number, face the usual range of discrimination. Indeed, the immigration policies of Canada and Australia are designed to avoid the issue.

The fact is that no society has learned to manage a large metropolis, nor has any society succeeded in solving the question of race. If these problems are to be solved, it will be done here in the United States. Perhaps that is the way it should be. Our national history has been almost conterminous with the rise of the modern city; racial diversity always has been a part of the American experience. We have managed in the past to take millions of people with different backgrounds, languages, and religions and incorporate them into the metropolitan mainstream.

In facing the present urban crisis, we only need draw upon our best traditions. But if we do not begin to unite the metropolis and to disperse the ghetto in the next few years, the eighties will be a decade of renewed tension and turmoil and will bear out Wendell Phillips' grim prophecy of a hundred years ago: "The time will come when our cities will strain our institutions as slavery never did."